The Practice of Public Relations

ninth edition

Fraser P. Seitel

Managing Partner, Emerald Partners
Senior Counselor, Burson-Marsteller

Upper Saddle River, New Jersey 07458

Library of Congress Cataloging-in-Publication Data
Seitel, Fraser P.
    The practice of public relations / Fraser P. Seitel.—9th ed.
      p. cm.
     Includes bibiographical references and index.
     ISBN 0-13-102025-0
      1. Public Relations—United States. I. Title
   HM1221.S45 2003
   659.2—dc21

Senior Editor: Bruce Kaplan
Editor-in-Chief: Jeff Shelstad
Assistant Editor: Melissa Pellerano
Editorial Assistant: Danielle Rose Serra
Media Project Manager: Anthony Palmiotto
Executive Marketing Manager: Michele O'Brien
Marketing Assistant: Amanda Fisher
Senior Managing Editor (Production): Judy Leale
Production Editor: Blake Cooper
Production Assistant: Joe DeProspero
Permissions Supervisor: Suzanne Grappi
Associate Director, Manufacturing: Vincent Scelta
Production Manager: Arnold Vila
Design Manager: Maria Lange
Designer: Steve Frim
Interior Design: Judy Allan
Cover Design: Steve Frim
Manager, Print Production: Christy Mahon
Composition/Full-Service Project Management: Carlisle Communications
Printer/Binder: RRDonnelley

Credits and acknowledgments borrowed from other sources and reproduced, with permission, in this textbook appear on appropriate page within text (or on page 555–556).

Pearson Education LTD.
Pearson Education Singapore, Pte. Ltd
Pearson Education, Canada, Ltd
Pearson Education–Japan

Pearson Education Australia PTY, Limited
Pearson Education North Asia Ltd
Pearson Educación de Mexico, S.A. de C.V.
Pearson Education Malaysia, Pte. Ltd

10 9 8 7 6 5 4 3 2 1
ISBN 0-13-102025-0

Dedicated to the memory of my friend Professor Bill Adams

brief contents

brief contents

Part I ▪ Evolution

Part II ▪ Preparation/Process

Part III ▪ The Publics

Part IV ▪ Execution

Part V ▪ Future

contents

Part II ■ Preparation/Process

Part III ■ The Publics

Part IV ■ Execution

Foreword

The corporate scandals of 2002, in which Enron and other companies were looted by their own executives, focused fresh attention on the theory and practice of many aspects of business including public relations.

Indeed, businesses large and small are looking increasingly to public relations to help restore the public confidence that is such an indispensable element of their success.

As Fraser Seitel points out in this ninth edition of his text, the well-being of stock-holders, customers, employers, and employees is tied to principled policies disseminated by communications professionals who understand that basic integrity must take priority over rosy quarterly reports.

In the classroom, I have found that students are all in favor of integrity but are often confused by the theoretical aspects of public relations, on the one hand, and their practical applications on the other. They read about concepts such as attitudes, ethics, public opinion, persuasion, and social responsibility but have difficulty fitting them into discussions about organizing a PR department or agency, preparing PR campaigns, dealing with the media and the Internet, managing a crisis, and measuring results.

The Seitel text makes a special effort to bridge this gap between theory and practice and succeeds admirably in doing so. Through cogent explanations and the use of features such as sidebars, case studies, interviews, news photos, and other techniques, the text makes current issues come vividly alive. This latest edition includes timely interviews with and cases about newsmakers like Jesse Ventura, Rudy Giuliani, Jack Welch, Gary Condit, Trent Lott, Martha Stewart, and others, focusing on their encounters with the media.

In the wake of recent disclosures, CEOs are relying on their PR counselors more than ever in matters of strategy and policy as well as communications. As keepers of the corporate reputation, PR people must build trust by sending truthful and credible messages out to the public. The ninth edition of *The Practice of Public Relations* emphasizes this more strongly than ever and illustrates how it can be done most effectively.

Joseph T. Nolan

In a communications career spanning half a century, Joseph T. Nolan, Ph.D., has worked for the *New York Times*, RCA, Monsanto, and Chase Manhattan Bank, where he was senior vice president in charge of public and government relations and advertising. He has taught at the University of South Carolina, University of Florida, University of North Florida, and Flagler College in St. Augustine, where he makes his home. A Fellow of the Public Relations Society of America, Dr. Nolan was saluted at PRSA's 2001 Legends Luncheon, honoring those who have helped define the profession, and was cited by *Business Week* magazine as one of the "Top Ten Executives in Corporate Public Relations."

$\left(\text{Preface}\right)$

The initial years of the 21st century have shown graphically how critical the practice of public relations is to society.

The tragic terror attacks on America and around the world; the consequent hostilities and ill will provoked by intolerance, jealousy and hatred; the shameful corporate scandals and unscrupulous business executives in the United States casting a pall over the entire free enterprise system—all have underscored the necessity and importance of two-way communications to knock down barriers and build bridges to understanding and mutual respect among people and institutions.

That, in essence, is what the practice of public relations is all about—building relationships.

Public relations remains at base a personal, relationship-oriented practice, demanding experienced judgment and finely honed interpersonal communications skills. And so, this ninth edition of *The Practice of Public Relations* has been recast to place its emphasis on the principles, processes, and practices that lead to building positive relationships.

The book's "relationship-building makeover" is manifest in refinements in theory, organization, and application.

New Theoretical Focus

This edition offers a sharpened focus on the theoretical underpinnings of effective communications.

The process of communication to achieve specific goals—informing, motivating, persuading, building mutual understanding—is explored more broadly and emphasized more specifically.

Accordingly, the book's introductory chapters place greater attention on how communications theory and public opinion understanding can be applied to strategic public relations planning and creation of believeable and persuasive messages.

New Organizational Structure

The bolstered theoretical framework serves as a natural departure point for a more logical chapter structure, from evolution and process through publics and applications toward building relationships.

Specifically, this edition is divided into five discrete parts:

- *Part I, "Evolution,"* looks at the field's antecedents and pioneers and what defines it.

- *Part II, "Preparation/Process,"* deals with the key conceptual framework areas that underpin the field—communication, management, public opinion, ethics, law, and research.

- *Part III, "The Publics,"* discusses the field's most important constituencies, from employees and the media to consumers and the government to investors, international publics, and communities of diversity.

- *Part IV, "Execution,"* reviews the primary technical skills that public relations professionals must possess—from writing for the eye and ear and working online to integrated marketing communications and crisis management.

- *Part V, "The Future,"* discusses the challenges and opportunities presented to public relations in its "golden age" in the 21st century.

New Applications

The strength of this book is in its application of theory to real-life practice. This aspect, too, has been fortified in this edition.

- *First,* the importance of building relationships across national borders has been captured in a new chapter devoted to "International Relations."
- *Second,* the disconcerting dismantling of trust with investors and stockholders is confronted in a new chapter devoted to "Investor Relations."
- *Third,* greater attention has been placed on the multicultural diversity of public relations work, particularly through interviews with leading minority practitioners.

- *Finally,* for the first time, a sampling of "hypothetical student cases"—on such issues as sex discrimination, Internet sabotage and surveillance, and organizational positioning— have been added to complement the book's traditional exploration of front- page public relations cases.

Unique Elements

At the heart of public relations practice are the real-life contemporary experiences—cases—that alter the communications landscape and redefine how we assess and handle communications challenges, among them:

- New York City Mayor Rudy Giuliani's handling of the September 11, 2001 horror
- President Bush's campaign to "sell the war effort" overseas
- The violations of trust by the nation's wealthiest executives and biggest companies, from Enron to WorldCom to Tyco
- The self immolation of domestic diva Martha Stewart, Senator Trent Lott, and Congressman Gary Condit
- The Catholic Church's confrontation with the worst crisis in its history
- The unlikely emergence of Donald Rumsfeld as a public relations superstar

Most of these cases involve issues of ethics and propriety. All play a part in public relations lore and learning. And they're all here.

Beyond this, a number of unique elements set this book apart:

CASE STUDY

They're Heeere!

Suppose you gave a party and *60 Minutes* showed up at the door. Would you let them in? Would you evict them? Would you commit hara-kiri?

Those were the choices that confronted the Chase Bank at the American Bankers Association convention, when *60 Minutes* came to Honolulu to "get the bankers."

The banking industry was taking its lumps. Profits were lagging. Loans to foreign governments weren't being repaid. Financings to bankrupt corporations were being questioned. And it was getting difficult for poor people to open bank accounts.

Understandably, few bankers at the Honolulu convention cared to share their thoughts on camera with *60 Minutes*. Some headed for cover when the cameras approached. Others barred the unwanted visitors from their receptions. In at least one case, a *60 Minutes* cameraman was physically removed from the hall. By the convention's third day, the *60 Minutes* team was decrying its treatment at the hands of the bankers as the "most vicious" it had ever been accorded.

By the third night, correspondent Morley Safer and his *60 Minutes* crew were steaming and itching for a confrontation.

That's when *60 Minutes* showed up at our party.

For 10 years, with your intrepid author as its public affairs director, Chase Manhattan had sponsored a private convention reception for the media. It combined an informal cocktail party, where journalists and bankers could chat and munch h d'oeuvres, with a more formal, 30-minute press conference with the bank's presi The press conference was on the record, no-holds-barred, and frequentl news coverage by the wire services, newspa and magazines th

A QUESTION OF ETHICS

One of a Kind

With all the abuse heaped (properly) on CEOs in the first years of the 21st century, the story of Malden Mills CEO Aaron Feuerstein stands out as a tribute to doing what's right—even at great personal cost.

On the night of December 11, 1995, a fire engulfed much of the Malden Mills Industries complex in Lawrence, Massachusetts.

Twenty-four people were injured, and the company's manufacturing facilities were substantially affected. It was one of the largest factory fires in New England history. The next day, as the embers still smoldered, CEO Feuerstein vowed, "The tragedy will not derail Malden Mills' leadership position in either the local community or the world textile market."

Most people probably took the CEO's vow with a grain of salt. At 70 years old and his factory fully insured, the Malden Mills chief could have been excused for taking the insurance money, retiring to a warmer climate, and leaving his 2,400 workers to fend for themselves.

But CEO Feuerstein was built better than that. He and his family kicked in $15 million to keep paying wages and benefits for the full three months it

took to get the factory back to speed. When the employees returned, their productivity skyrocketed, and union workers rose to support the executive who had stood up for them.

Alas, by late 2001, the company again faced a crisis, this time because of skyrocketing debts, and was forced into filing for bankruptcy protection. Once more, CEO Feuerstein vowed, "This company will survive."

And once again, less than a year later, Malden Mills emerged from bankruptcy. Said the chairman:

Today there's some kind of crazy belief that if you discard the responsibility to your country, to your city, to your community, to your workers, and think only of the immediate profit, that somehow not only your company will prosper but the entire economy will prosper as a result.
I think it's dead wrong.*

*For further information, see Lynnley Browning, "Fire Could Not Stop a Mill, but Debts May," *New York Times* (November 28, 2001): C1-5; "Malden Mills to File Plan to Emerge from Bankruptcy," *New York Times* (August 6, 2002): C4; Jeffrey L. Seglin, "A Boss Saved Them. Should They Save Him?" *New York Times on the Web* (January 20, 2002).

▶ The prominence of ethics in the practice of public relations is highlighted with "A Question of Ethics" box feature in every chapter.

SIDEBAR

Test Your Workplace Ethics

So you want to enter the workplace? The question of ethics looms larger today than at any previous time, especially with the advent of technology and the potential abuses it brings.

To test how you might measure up as an ethical worker, answer the following questions. And don't cheat!

1. Is it wrong to use company e-mail for personal reasons?
2. Is it wrong to use office equipment to help your family and friends with homework?
3. Is it wrong to play computer games on office equipment during the workday?
4. Is it wrong to use office equipment to do Internet shopping?
5. Is it unethical to visit pornographic Web sites using office equipment?
6. What's the value at which a gift from a supplier or client becomes troubling?
7. Is a $50 gift to a boss unacceptable?
8. Is it okay to take a pair of $200 football tickets as a gift from a supplier?
9. Is it okay to take a $120 pair of theater tickets?
10. Is it okay to take a $100 holiday fruit basket?
11. Is it okay to take a $25 gift certificate?
12. Is it okay to accept a $75 prize won at a raffle at a supplier's conference?

Answers from a cross section of workers at nationwide companies were compiled by the Ethics Officer Association, Belmont, Massachusetts, and the Ethical Leadership Group, Wilmette, Illinois.

1. 34% said personal e-mail on company computers is wrong.
2. 37% said using office equipment for schoolwork is wrong.
3. 49% said playing computer games at work is wrong.
4. 54% said Internet shopping at work is wrong.
5. 87% said it is unethical to visit pornographic sites at work.
6. 33% said $25 is the amount at which a gift from a supplier or client becomes troubling. Another 33 percent said $50. Another 33 percent said $100.
7. 35% said a $50 gift to the boss is unacceptable.
8. 70% said it is unacceptable to take $200 football tickets.
9. 70% said it is unacceptable to take $120 theater tickets.
10. 35% said it is unacceptable to take a $100 fruit basket.
11. 45% said it is unacceptable to take a $25 gift certificate.
12. 40% said it is unacceptable to take the $75 raffle prize.

◀ "Sidebar" features complement the text with provocative examples of what's right, what's wrong, and what's wacky about public relations practice today.

LAST WORD

Research is a means of both defining problems and evaluating solutions. Even though intuitive judgment remains a coveted and important skill, management must see measurable results.

Nonetheless, informed managements recognize that public relations may never reach point at which its results can be fully quantified. Management confidence is still a prerequisite for active and unencumbered programs. Indeed, the best measurement of public relations value is a strong and unequivocal endorsement from management that it supports the public relations effort. However, such confidence can only be enhanced as actitioners become more adept in using research.

Frankly, practitioners don't have a choice. With efficiency driving today's bottom line d with communications about organizations percolating at a 24/7 clip around the world rough a variety of media, organizations must always know where they stand. It is the job public relations to keep track, record, and research changing attitudes and opinions out the organizations for which they work. Therefore, it will become increasingly incument on public relations people to reinforce the value of what they do and what they d for through constantly measuring their contribution to their organization's

◀ Chapter Summaries and Discussion Starter Questions highlight the key messages delivered in each chapter.

Discussion Starters

1. Why is research important in public relations work?
2. What are the differences between primary and secondary research?
3. What are the four elements of a survey?
4. What is the difference between random and stratified sampling?
5. What are the keys to designing an effective questionnaire?
   t is a communication audit?
   ls are used to measure public relations outcomes?
   ent in public relations research?
   nent in evaluating a Web site?

TOP OF THE SHELF

Internet Search Engines

The Internet and the continuous proliferation of Web sites have revolutionized every aspect of research, including the typical research tasks faced by public relations practitioners. Businesses and organization can even keep tabs on their competitors and opponents. Enormous databases—including those of hundreds of government agencies—are easily accessible, often for free. Most standard directories are also available online, and for obvious reasons they are more up-to-date than their print versions.

A selection of some of the Web sites commonly used by public relations researchers is included in Suggested Readings. Most of them also provide numerous links to related Web sites.

Search engines are the researcher's Holy Grail. Search engines allow you to search the contents of the World Wide Web, usenet groups, and other Internet data. Once you keyboard in a search term, you receive a list of items that match your query. Here are the leading search engines:

- AltaVista. www.altavista.digital.com. (Digital Equipment Corp.)
- HotBot. www.hotbot.com. The favorite search engine of Shel Holtz, author of *Public Relations on the Net* (see Chapter 10).
- InfoSeek. www.infoseek.com. A combination index and engine.
- Lycos. www.lycos.com. A combination index and engine.
- Search.Com. www.search.com. An index of search engines and indexes.
- Yahoo! www.yahoo.com. Considered by many the best of the search indexes, including other elements such as news, weather, and maps.
- Google. www.google.com. Like Yahoo!, Google is a comprehensive and immensely helpful search engine—at times overwhelming unl you know how to refine your search crit

Suggested Readings

Barzun, Jacques, and Henry F. Graff. *The Modern Researcher*, 6th ed. Ft. Worth, TX: HB College Publications, 2002.

Bell, Quentin. "Beware of Sailing into the Shallow Sea of Research," *Marketing* (February 19, 1998): 7. Discusses the superficiality behind surveys and public relations research

Berger, Arthur Asa. *Media Research Techniques*, 2nd ed. Thousand Oaks, CA: Sage Publications, 1998.

Boyatis, Richard E. *Transforming Qualitative Information*. Thousand Oaks, CA: Sage Publications, 1998.

Broom, Glen M., and David M. Dozier. *Using Research in Public Relations: Application to Program Management*. Upper Saddle River, NJ: Prentice Hall, 1996.

www.businesswire.com. Business Wire, "The International Media Relations Wire Service," offers news releases on major U.S. corporations, including a majority of For tune 500 and NASDAQ companies.

kson, Robert, and Kent L. Tedin, *American Public Opinion, Its Origin, Contents and pact*, 6th ed. New York, NY: Longman, 2000.

▶ Updated Suggested Readings, nourishing Appendices, and "Top of the Shelf" book reviews supplement the text with the field's most current literature.

TIPS FROM THE TOP

Two Perspectives on Diversity and Community Relations

Pat Tobin

I. The African American: An Interview with Pat Tobin
Pat Tobin is cofounder and president of the National Black Public Relations Society. When she founded Tobin & Associates, few in the industry had ever heard of an African American–owned, woman-operated, public relations firm. In the year 2000, she celebrated her 18th year in business, and Tobin & Associates has become one of the most prominent African American–owned public relations firms in the nation. In addition to assisting major corporations in communications work, she is a member of the board of directors of Women in Film (WIF) and serves on the Planning Committee for the Children's Defense Fund.

What is the state of community relations in American industry today?
Community relations should be a way of life for everyone. You must ensure that you are involved in your community and that you're "giving back" to it, no matter who you are. And I think people are giving back more today. After Sept. 11, people are more aware of their community and their neighbors.

come more and more involved with an entire diversity program. This effort includes minority participation from procurement to advertising to employment to retail initiatives. It is very comprehensive. They sponsor Hispanic conferences and scholarships. They're active in the United Negro College Fund, the Urban League, the NAACP. That's what I'm talking about.

How important is the African American market today?
African American spend $600 billion a year in this economy. That's $600 billion with a "b." We are a market to be reckoned with, not to be taken for granted. If we'[re] buying your product, then you have to give back to ou[r] community. Smart companies are getting that message

How did you get started?
Twenty years ago, I left the CBS media department, and I became an entrepreneur. I opened an agency to reach the minority community. I told people, "Look, I'm black. I've been black all my life. You can't tell me about reaching blacks." So I worked with people like Spike Lee to promote his movies and kept going. We've always tried to exceed our client's expectations. I sa[y] "I don't like excuses. I like results." That's how [we've] been successful.

What is the stat

◄ "Tips from the Top" interviews air the views of the field's most prominent professionals—from President Bush's first White House Press Secretary Ari Fleischer to United Nations public relations chief Shashi Tharoor to the leaders of the field's most prominent trade associations—as well as the CEO newsmakers who presided over the field's most striking moments, from Minnesota Governor Jesse Ventura to ValuJet CEO Lewis Jordan to PepsiCo CEO Craig Weatherup to Dow Corning CEO Richard Hazelton to the eminent management guru Dr. Peter Drucker.

All of these elements add to the excitement of this book. So, too, does the full-color format that underscores the liveliness, vitality, and relevance of the field.

Supplements

▶ **Instructor's Manual**

Prepared by the author himself, this resource contains support material to guide the instructor in preparing a class lecture. Discussion starters, suggested approaches in solving the case studies in the text, plus potential answers to the case questions are provided. Features also include review quizzes and section examinations.

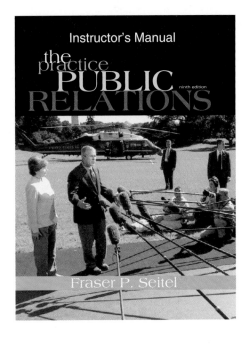

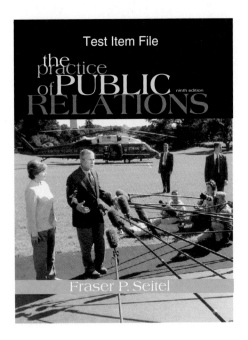

◀ **Test Item File**

Extensively revised for the ninth edition, the Test Item File contains more than 900 items, including multiple-choice, true-false, and essay questions that are graded for difficulty and page-referenced to the text. Also available is the new TestGen-EQ test generation software, a computerized package that allows instructors to custom design, save, and generate classroom tests. The test program permits instructors to edit, add, or delete questions from the test bank; analyze test results; and organize a database of tests and student results. The new software allows for greater flexibility and ease of use. It provides many options for organizing and displaying tests, along with a search and sort feature.

▶ **PowerPoint Presentation**

A PowerPoint set containing more than 400 electronic slides covers key concepts and includes complete lecture notes with key figures and ads from the text. These files are available on the Instructor's Resource CD-ROM and may also be downloaded from the text's Web Site.

Markers of Public Relations Growth

United States growth:

- 200,000 U.S. public relations professionals

- Employment growth increasing faster than average through the year 2010

- The amount of respect and public relations spending are correlated among Fortune 500 companies

1-3

▶ **Instructor's Resource CD-ROM**
One source for all your supplement needs. This CD contains the Instructor's Manual, Test Item File, and PowerPoint Presentation on a single CD-ROM. Enjoy the freedom to transport the supplements package from office, to home, to classroom. The Instructor's Resource CD-ROM enables you to customize any of the ancillaries, print only the chapters or materials you wish to use, or access any item from the package within the classroom.

▶ **Case Video**
Video segments are provided that bring to life specific cases in the text. Included are new segments (Danny's and Taco Bell, among others) that will facilitate the learning experience, plus some classic segments (Pepsi and GM) that also provide reinforcement of material covered in class.

▶ **Web Site**
A Web site to accompany the text may be found at www.prenhall.com/seitel. Students can review chapter key points and take various types of self-tests. Instructors can download the PowerPoint files, among other faculty resources.

Unique Perspective

The *Practice of Public Relations, Ninth Edition,* is, in short, different from other introductory texts in the field. Its premise is that public relations is a thoroughly engaging and constantly changing field. Although other texts may steer clear of the up-to-date cases, the ethical challenges, the "how to" counsel, and the public relations conundrums that force students to think, this book confronts them all.

It is, if you'll forgive the vernacular, an in-your-face textbook for an in-your-face profession.

Most important, *The Practice of Public Relations, Ninth Edition,* is built around the technical knowledge of process and practice, judgmental skills, and personal relationships that underlie public relations practice and will be so essential in building back the trust and respect of diverse communities in the 21st century.

Fraser P. Seitel

ACKNOWLEDGEMENTS

The ninth edition of *The Practice of Public Relations* emphasizes the relationship nature of public relations that will never be replaced by a computer.

Obviously, the practice of public relations, like every other pursuit, has been impacted mightily by email, the Internet and instant communication. But at its base, the practice of public relations still depends on personal relationships. This public relations book therefore still depends for its relevance and inspiration on people.

Among them, I am grateful to the top executives who sat with me for interviews. The CEOs of PepsiCo, Dow Corning, ValuJet, Governor Jesse Ventura, management legend Peter Drucker, and the others originally were interviewed for *Public Relations Strategist* magazine, from which these conversations were excerpted. If public relations is to be accepted as a "management function," then public relations people must hear the views of top managers.

I am indebted also to the public relations leaders who were most kind to participate in this project. Among them were Ari Fleischer, President George W. Bush's first press secretary; Sunny Mindell, press secretary to Mayor Rudy Giuliani; Shashi Tharoor, United Nations Secretary General Kofi Anan's public relations chief; Joann Kileen, former president of the Public Relations Society of America; Pat Tobin, president of the Black Public Relations Association; Executive Recruiter par excellence Bill Heyman; and a host of multi-talented others.

As in past editions, I relied on the expertise of friends Paul Swift, who kindly prepared the bibliographic material and "Top of the Shelf" box features and even sat for an interview; Laurie Gannon at Taco Bell and Karen Randall at Advantica Corp., two of the field's most outstanding professionals.

I am also delighted that we were able to coax this field's most outstanding professional, Dr. Joseph T. Nolan, out of retirement to pen the most thoughtful Foreword in the history of public relations texts.

On the other end of the project, of course, is the proud and talented team at Prentice Hall, led by our captain, Senior Editor Bruce Kaplan. He runs a tight ship and is supported by publishing's best; most particularly the ever-capable Danielle Serra, supplements editor Melissa Pellerano, production editor par excellence Blake Cooper, and permissions editor Suzanne Grappi.

And of course, there are the other distinguished public relations professors, whose contributions and insightful suggestions aided this ninth edition. Among them, Shaunee Lenise Wallace kindly submitted to a delightful interview; Bonnie Grossman charitably offered the research expertise of her students in Charleston; Keith Sheldon was similarly generous with his Chico crew; and Long Island communications entrepreneur extraordinaire Jack Mandel was helpful as well. Thank you all most sincerely.

In addition, the very kind professors who critiqued this edition were :

Carolina Acosta-Alzuru, University of Georgia

Bill Brewer, Miami University

Meta G. Carstarphen, University of North Texas

Jerry M. Engel, Ithaca College

Lisa Ferree, Eastern Kentucky University

Susan Gonders, Southeast Missouri State University

Carole Gorney, Lehigh University

Kirk Hallahan, Colorado State University

Christine R. Helsel, Eastern Illinois University

Liese L. Hutchison, Saint Louis University

Ken McMillen, University of Oklahoma

Robert J. O'Gara, Point Park College

E. Jerald Ogg, The University of Tennessee at Martin

Michael G. Parkinson, Texas Tech University

Betty J. Pritchard, Grand Valley State University

Robert S. Pritchard, Ball State University

William E. Sledzik, Kent Sttae University

Don W. Stacks, University of Miami

Thomas Bivins at the University of Oregon, Charles Lubbers at Kansas State University, and Nancy Wolfe at Elon College all were quite helpful. They join in the Hall of Thanks those other distinguished professors who have reviewed past editions: Nickieann Fleener, Department of Communication, University of Utah; Mort Kaplan, Department of Marketing Communication, Columbia College (Chicago); Jack Mauch, Department of Communication, University of Idaho; Donnalyn Pompper, Department of Communication, Cabrini College; Cornelius B. Pratt, Department of Communications, Michigan State University; J. D. Rayburn II, Department of Communication, Florida State University; Nancy Roth, Department of Communication, Rutgers, The State University (New Jersey); William C. Adams, School of Journalism and Mass Communications, Florida International University; John Q. Butler; Rachel L. Holloway, Department of Communications Studies, Virginia Tech; Diana Harney, Department of Communication and Theater, Pacific Lutheran University; Cornelius Pratt, Department of Advertising, Communications, and Public Relations, Michigan State University; Robert Cole, Pace University; Janice Sherline Jenny, College of Business, Herkimer County Community College; Craig Kelly, School of Business, California State University, Sacramento; Lyle J. Barker, Ohio State University; William G. Briggs, San Jose State University; E. Brody, Memphis State University; John S. Detweiler, University of Florida; Jim Eiseman, University of Louisville; Sandy Grossbart, University of Nebraska; Marjorie Nadler, Miami University; Sharon Smith, Middle Tennessee State University; Robert Wilson, Franklin University; Jack Mandel, Nassau Community College; Carol L. Hills, Boston University; George Laposky, Miami-Dade Community College; Mack Palmer, University of Oklahoma; Judy VanSlyke Turk, Louisiana State University; Roger B. Wadsworth, Miami-Dade Community College; James E. Grunig, University of Maryland; Robert T. Reilly, University of Nebraska at Omaha; Kenneth Rowe, Arizona State University; Dennis L. Wilcox, San Jose State University; Albert Walker, Northern Illinois University; Stanley E. Smith, Arizona State University; Jan Quarles, University of Georgia; Pamela J. Creedon, Ohio State University; Joel P. Bowman, Western Michigan University; Thomas H. Bivins, University of Oregon; Joseph T. Nolan, University of North Florida; Frankie A. Hammond, University of Florida; Bruce Joffe, George Mason University; Larissa Grunig, University of Maryland; Maria P. Russell, Syracuse University; and Melvin L. Sharpe, Ball State University.

Finally, the top management team of Chief Executive Officer Rosemary Seitel, Chief Operating Officers Raina and Adam Gittlin, and Treasurer David Seitel merit special consideration. As do office managers, Coco Seitel and Theo Gitlin.

I thank you, one and all.

—Fraser P. Seitel

About the Author

Fraser P. Seitel is a veteran of more than three decades in the practice of public relations. In 2000, *PR Week* magazine named Mr. Seitel one of the "100 Most Distinguished Public Relations Professionals of the 20th Century."

In 1992, after serving for a decade as senior vice president and director of public affairs for Chase Manhattan Bank, Mr. Seitel formed Emerald Partners, a management and communications consultancy, and also became senior counselor at the world's largest public affairs firm, Burson-Marsteller.

Mr. Seitel is a frequent contributor to cable television. Among other programs, he has appeared on Fox News Channel's *The O'Reilly Factor, Fox and Friends, Rivera Live, Fox Weekend,* and *On the Record with Greta Van Susteren;* MSNBC's *The News with Brian Williams and Nachman;* CNBC's *Wall Street Journal Report;* and CNN's *Connie Chung Tonight, Inside Politics,* and *Larry King Live.*

Mr. Seitel has counseled hundreds of corporations, nonprofits, associations, and individuals in the area for which he had responsibility at Chase—media relations, speech writing, consumer relations, employee communications, financial communications, philanthropic activities, and strategic management consulting.

Mr. Seitel is an Internet columnist at odwyerpr.com and a frequent lecturer and seminar leader on communications topics. Over the course of his career, Mr. Seitel has taught thousands of public relations professionals and students.

After studying and examining many texts in public relations, he concluded that none of them "was exactly right." Therefore, in 1980, he wrote the first edition of *The Practice of Public Relations* "to give students a feel for how exciting this field really is." In more than two decades of use at hundreds of colleges and universities, Mr. Seitel's book has introduced generations of students to the excitement, challenge, and uniqueness of the practice of public relations.

PART I Evolution

Chapter 1

Defining Public Relations

On September 11, 2001, after planes piloted by terrorists slammed into the World Trade Center, the Pentagon, and crashed in western Pennsylvania, the first administration official dispatched to reassure a shaken nation was President George W. Bush's public relations counselor, Karen Hughes (Figure 1-1).

"As you know," Ms. Hughes calmly reported from a makeshift crisis center at the FBI headquarters in Washington, "President Bush was in Sarasota, Florida, when the first attack occurred this morning. Air Force One has now landed at Offut Air Force Base in Omaha, Nebraska, and the president is in a secure location.

"Our fellow citizens and our freedom came under attack today. And no one should doubt America's resolve. President Bush and all our country's leaders thank the many Americans who are helping with rescue and relief efforts. We ask our fellow Americans for your prayers for the victims, for their families, for the rescue workers, and for our country."

The fact that the nation's number-one public relations officer would be called on to deliver the administration's first pronouncement after the most tragic domestic attack in American history underscores the growing importance of the practice of public relations in modern society.

Ten months later in July 2002, when Ms. Hughes resigned as counselor to the president, she was hailed as "the most powerful woman ever to serve in a White House. Her influence on Bush and his policies has been virtually limitless."[1]

One and one half years later, in the spring of 2003, another public relations counselor, Victoria Clarke, stood at center stage as the United States, Britain, and other allied nations went to war with Iraq.

Ms. Clarke, assistant secretary of defense for public affairs, won great credit for encouraging Defense Secretary Donald Rumsfeld and his top generals to hold daily press briefings in Washington and the field. Even more consequential, it was Ms. Clarke who presided over the Pentagon's decision—for the first time in history—to "embed" more than 500 reporters to work alongside the troops as they went to war.

Karen Hughes and Torrie Clarke epitomized the expanding role of the public relations professional as counselor, communicator, strategist, orchestrator, director,

1

FIGURE 1-1 **Public relations counselor extraordinaire.** Karen Hughes with President George W. Bush.

producer, writer, stage manager, and all-around confidante to organizations of every size and variety and the individuals who run them.

In the 21st century, the power, value, and influence of the practice of public relations have never been greater.

Prominence of Public Relations

Public relations as a field has grown immeasurably both in numbers and in respect over the last three decades and today is clearly a growth industry.

- In the United States alone, public relations is a multibillion-dollar business practiced by more than 200,000 professionals, according to the U.S. Bureau of Labor Statistics. Furthermore, the bureau says public relations "employment is projected to increase rapidly—much faster than the average for all occupations through 2010. The need for good public relations in an increasingly competitive business environment should spur demand for public relations specialists in organizations of all sizes."[2]
- Around the world, the practice of public relations has grown enormously. The International Public Relations Association boasts a strong membership, and the practice flourishes from Latin America to Africa and from Europe to China.
- In a 1999 study of the Council of Public Relations Firms to assess the corporate communications spending patterns of Fortune 500 firms, a direct correlation was found between how much a company spends on public relations and how much it is respected.[3]
- Approximately 250 colleges and universities in the United States and many more overseas offer a public relations sequence or degree program. Many more offer public relations courses. In the vast majority of college journalism programs, public relations sequences rank first or second in enrollment.

- The U.S. government has thousands of communications professionals—although none, as we will learn, are labeled "public relations specialists." The Department of Defense alone has 7,000 professional communicators spread out among the Army, Navy, and Air Force.
- The 20 largest public relations agencies generate in excess of $2 billion in revenues annually, and the rest of the industry generates another $1 billion each year.[4]
- The field's primary trade associations have strong membership, with the Public Relations Society of America encompassing nearly 20,000 members in 117 chapters and the International Association of Business Communicators including 13,500 members in more than 58 countries.

In the 21st century, as all elements of society—companies, nonprofits, government, religion, sports, the arts, and all others—wrestle with constant shifts in economic conditions and competition, security concerns, and popular opinion, the public relations profession is expected to thrive, with more and more organizations interested in communicating their story.

Perhaps the most flattering aspect of the field's heightened stature is that competition from other fields has become more intense. Today the profession finds itself vulnerable to encroachment by people with non–public relations backgrounds, such as lawyers, marketers, and general managers of every type, all eager to gain the management access and persuasive clout of the public relations professional.

The field's strength stems from its roots: "a democratic society where people have freedom to debate and to make decisions—in the community, the marketplace, the home, the workplace, and the voting booth. Private and public organizations depend on good relations with groups and individuals whose opinions, decisions, and actions affect their vitality and survival."[5]

What Is Public Relations?

Public relations is a planned process to influence public opinion, through sound character and proper performance, based on mutually satisfactory two-way communication.

At least that's what your author believes it is.

The fact is that there are many different definitions of public relations. American historian Robert Heilbroner once described the field as "a brotherhood of some 100,000, whose common bond is its profession and whose common woe is that no two of them can ever quite agree on what that profession is."[6]

In 1923, the late Edward Bernays described the function of his fledgling public relations counseling business as one of providing "information given to the public, persuasion directed at the public to modify attitudes and actions, and efforts to integrate attitudes and actions of an institution with its publics and of publics with those of that institution."[7]

Today, although a generally accepted definition of public relations still eludes practitioners, there is a clearer understanding of the field. One of the most ambitious searches for a universal definition was commissioned in 1975 by the Foundation for Public Relations Research and Education. Sixty-five public relations leaders participated in the study, which analyzed 472 different definitions and offered the following 88-word sentence:

Public relations is a distinctive management function which helps establish and maintain mutual lines of communications, understanding, acceptance, and cooperation between an organization and its publics; involves the management of problems or issues; helps management to keep informed on and responsive to public opinion; defines and emphasizes the responsibility of management to serve the public interest; helps management keep abreast of and effectively utilize change, serving as an early warning system to help anticipate trends; and uses research and sound and ethical communication techniques as its principal tools.[8]

In 1980, the Task Force on the Stature and Role of Public Relations, chartered by the Public Relations Society of America, offered two definitions that have stood the test of time. Each projects an image of the field at the highest policy-making level and encompasses all its functions and specialties:

Public relations helps an organization and its publics adapt mutually to each other. Public relations is an organization's efforts to win the cooperation of groups of people.[9]

In order to "win the cooperation" of these groups, public relations professionals must initiate a planned process to influence them.

Planned Process to Influence Public Opinion

What is the process through which public relations might influence public opinion? Communications professor John Marston suggested a four-step model based on specific functions: (1) research, (2) action, (3) communication, and (4) evaluation.[10] Whenever a public relations professional is faced with an assignment—whether promoting a client's product or defending a client's reputation—he or she should apply Marston's R-A-C-E approach:

- **Research.** First, research attitudes about the issue at hand.
- **Action.** Second, identify action of the client in the public interest.
- **Communication.** Third, communicate that action to gain understanding, acceptance and support.
- **Evaluation.** Fourth, evaluate the communication to see if opinion has been influenced.

The key to the process is the second step—action. You can't have effective communication or positive publicity without proper action. Stated another way, performance must precede publicity. Act first and communicate later. Positive action communicated straightforwardly will yield positive results.

This is the essence of the R-A-C-E process of public relations.

Public relations professor Sheila Clough Crifasi has proposed extending the R-A-C-E formula into the five-part R-O-S-I-E to encompass a more managerial approach to the field. R-O-S-I-E prescribes sandwiching the functions of objectives, strategies, and implementation between research and evaluation. Indeed, setting clear objectives, working from set strategies, and implementing a predetermined plan is a key to sound public relations practice.

Still others suggest a process called R-P-I-E for research, planning, implementation, and evaluation, which emphasizes the element of planning as a necessary step preceding the activation of a communications initiative.

All three approaches, R-A-C-E, R-O-S-I-E, and R-P-I-E, echo one of the most widely repeated definitions of public relations, developed by the late Denny Griswold, who founded *Public Relations News*, a leading newsletter for practitioners:

Public relations is the management function which evaluates public attitudes, identifies the policies and procedures of an individual or an organization with the public interest, and plans and executes a program of action to earn public understanding and acceptance.[11]

The key words in this definition *management* and *action*. Public relations, if it is to serve the organization properly, must report to top management. Public relations must serve as an honest broker to management, unimpeded by any other group. For public relations to work, its advice to management must be unfiltered, uncensored, and unexpurgated.

Nor can public relations take place without appropriate action. As noted, no amount of communications—regardless of its persuasive content—can save an organization whose performance is substandard. In other words, "You can't pour perfume on a skunk."

The process of public relations, then, as Professor Melvin Sharpe has put it, "harmonizes long-term relationships among individuals and organizations in society."[12] To "harmonize," Professor Sharpe applies five principles to the public relations process:

- Honest communication for credibility
- Openness and consistency of actions for confidence
- Fairness of actions for reciprocity and goodwill
- Continuous two-way communication to prevent alienation and to build relationships
- Environmental research and evaluation to determine the actions or adjustments needed for social harmony

Stated yet another way, the profession is described by public relations Professor Janice Sherline Jenny as "the management of communications between an organization and all entities that have a direct or indirect relationship with the organization, i.e., its publics."

No matter what definition one may choose to explain the practice, few would argue that the goal of effective public relations is to harmonize internal and external relationships so that an organization can enjoy not only the goodwill of all of its publics but also stability and long life.

Public Relations as "Management Interpreter"

The late Leon Hess, who ran one of the nation's largest oil companies and the New York Jets football team, used to pride himself on *not* having a public relations department. Mr. Hess, a very private individual, abhorred the limelight for himself or his company.

But times have changed.

Today, the CEO who thunders, "I don't need public relations!" is a fool. He or she doesn't have a choice. Every organization *has* public relations, whether it wants it or not. The trick is to establish *good* public relations. That's what this book is all about—professional public relations, the kind you must work at.

Public relations affects almost everyone who has contact with other human beings. All of us, in one way or another, practice public relations daily. For an organization, every phone call, every letter, every face-to-face encounter is a public relations event.

Public relations professionals, then, are really the organization's interpreters.

- On the one hand, they must interpret the philosophies, policies, programs, and practices of their management to the public.
- On the other hand, they must convey the attitudes of the public to their management.

Let's consider management first.

Before public relations professionals can gain attention, understanding, acceptance, and ultimately action from target publics, they have to know what management is thinking.

Good public relations can't be practiced in a vacuum. No matter what the size of the organization, a public relations department is only as good as its access to management. For example, it's useless for a senator's press secretary to explain the reasoning behind an important decision without first knowing what the senator had in mind. So, too, an organization's public relations staff is impotent without firsthand knowledge of the reasons for management's decisions and the rationale for organizational policy.

The public relations department in any organization can counsel management. It can advise management. It can even exhort management to take action. But it is management who must call the shots on organizational policy.

It is the role of the public relations practitioner, once policy is established by management, to communicate these ideas accurately and candidly to the public. Anything less can lead to major problems.

Public Relations as "Public Interpreter"

Now let's consider the flip side of the coin—the public.

Interpreting the public to management means finding out what the public really thinks about the firm and letting management know. Regrettably, recent history is filled with examples of powerful institutions—and their public relations departments—failing to anticipate the true sentiments of the public.

- In the 1960s, General Motors paid little attention to an unknown consumer activist named Ralph Nader, who spread the message that GM's Corvair was "unsafe at any speed." When Nader's assault began to be believed, the automaker assigned professional detectives to trail him. In short order, General Motors was forced to acknowledge its act of paranoia, and the Corvair was eventually sacked at great expense to the company.
- In the 1970s, as both the price of gasoline and oil company profits rose rapidly, the oil companies were besieged by an irate gas-consuming public. When, at the height of the criticism, Mobil Oil purchased the parent of the Montgomery Ward department store chain, the company was publicly battered.
- In the 1980s, President Ronald Reagan rode to power on the strength of his ability to interpret what was on the minds of the electorate. But his successor in the early 1990s, George H. W. Bush, failed to "read" the nation's economic concerns. After leading America to a victory over Iraq in the Gulf War, President Bush failed to heed the admonition, "It's the economy stupid," and lost the election to upstart Arkansas Governor Bill Clinton.
- As the 20th century ended, President Clinton forgot the candid communication skills that earned him the White House and lied to the American public about his affair with an intern. The subsequent scandal, ending in impeachment hearings before the U.S. Congress, tarnished Clinton's administration and ruined his legacy.
- In the early years of the 21st century, CEOs of some of the nation's mightiest corporations—among them Enron, Arthur Andersen, Tyco, Sotheby's, and WorldCom—were dragged into court and before Congress for a variety of

A QUESTION OF ETHICS

Interpreting Terror as "Holy War"

The attacks on America in September 2001 established an unusual individual as society's Public Enemy Number One.

Osama bin Laden, thin, soft-spoken son of a wealthy Saudi Arabian businessman, was the architect of a worldwide campaign of terror against the West (Figure 1-2). As warped as bin Laden's objectives were, he proved to be a master of "interpreting" his diabolical campaign to his Islamic followers.

Using modern communications methods to beam charasmatic speeches by satellite TV throughout the Arab world, bin Laden claimed his goal was "holy war" (*jihad*) against the "infidels" (America and the West) responsible for the suffering of Arab peoples in Iraq and elsewhere.

Among bin Laden's 21st century communications appeals were the following:

- He delivered his speeches from his cave hideout in Afghanistan, wearing a turban and camouflage fatigues, signifying both his heritage and the fact that he fought beside his troops.
- He regularly referred in his talks to the two divisions of the world—the faithful and the infidels. (In this bin Laden took a page from his adversary, President George W. Bush, who divided the world into "those who stood with America in rejecting terrorism and those who stood against her.")
- He distributed his taped speeches and pronouncements over a popular Arab satellite channel, Al-Jazeera. From there, the remarks were broadcast around the world.

FIGURE 1-2 **Architect of terror.** Osama bin Laden.

- He timed his communications initiatives to blunt equivalent American efforts. For example, he declared one "Holy War" in October 2001, immediately after President Bush addressed Congress with his own declaration of war.

A host of ethical questions emerged from bin Laden's use of media. Was Al-Jazeera right to give him unlimited use of its airwaves? Were American broadcasters right in playing back the bin Laden propaganda?

Ethical considerations notwithstanding, there was little question that bin Laden was as well versed in modern public relations techniques as he was in delivering terror.

For further information, see Judith Miller, "Bin Laden's Media Savvy: Expert Timing of Threats," *New York Times*, October 9, 2001, B6.

ethical violations that misled the public and, in many cases, ruined their companies. As a consequence, tough new laws were passed to deal with corporate criminals.[13]

Despite being individuals of incalculable wealth, these men and women failed to understand one simple public relations principle. The savviest institutions—be they government, corporate, or nonprofit—understand the importance of effectively interpreting their management and organizational philosophy, policies, and practices to the public and, even more important, interpreting how the public views their organization back to management.

The Publics of Public Relations

The term *public relations* is really a misnomer.

Publics relations, or relations with the publics, would be more to the point. Practitioners must communicate with many different publics—not just the general public—each having its own special needs and requiring different types of communication. Often the lines that divide these publics are thin, and the potential overlap is significant. Therefore, priorities, according to organizational needs, must always be reconciled (Figure 1-3).

Technological change—particularly satellite links for television, the Internet, and World Wide Web, and the computer in general—has brought greater interdependence to people and organizations, and there is growing concern in organizations today about managing extensive webs of interrelationships. Indeed, managers have become interrelationship conscious.

Internally, managers must deal directly with various levels of subordinates, as well as with cross relationships that arise when subordinates interact with one another.

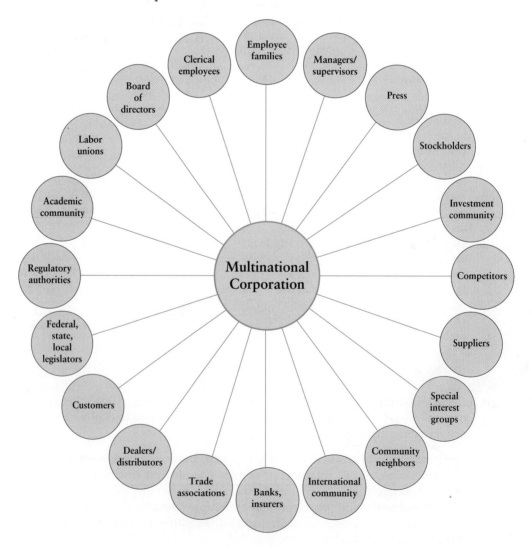

FIGURE 1-3   **Key publics.** Twenty key constituent groups of a typical multinational corporation.

Externally, managers must deal with a system that includes government regulatory agencies, labor unions, subcontractors, consumer groups, and many other independent— but often related—organizations. The public relations challenge in all of this is to manage effectively the communications between managers and the various publics, which often pull organizations in different directions. Stated another way, public relations professionals are very much mediators between client (management) and public (all those key constituent groups on whom an organization depends).

Definitions differ on precisely what constitutes a public. One time-honored definition states that a public arises when a group of people (1) face a similar indeterminate situation, (2) recognize what is indeterminate and problematic in that situation, and (3) organize to do something about the problem.[14] In public relations, more specifically, a public is a group of people with a stake in an issue, organization, or idea.

Publics can also be classified into several overlapping categories:

- **Internal and external.** Internal publics are inside the organization: supervisors, clerks, managers, stockholders, and the board of directors. External publics are those not directly connected with the organization: the press, government, educators, customers, suppliers, and the community.
- **Primary, secondary, and marginal.** Primary publics can most help—or hinder—the organization's efforts. Secondary publics are less important, and marginal publics are the least important of all. For example, members of the Federal Reserve Board of Governors, who regulate banks, would be the primary public for a bank awaiting a regulatory ruling, whereas legislators and the general public would be secondary. On the other hand, to the investing public, interest rate pronouncements of the same Federal Reserve Board are of primary importance.
- **Traditional and future.** Employees and current customers are traditional publics; students and potential customers are future ones. No organization can afford to become complacent in dealing with its changing publics. Today, a firm's publics range from women to minorities to senior citizens to homosexuals. Each might be important to the future success of the organization.
- **Proponents, opponents, and the uncommitted.** An institution must deal differently with those who support it and those who oppose it. For supporters, communications that reinforce beliefs may be in order. But changing the opinions of skeptics calls for strong, persuasive communications. Often, particularly in politics, the uncommitted public is crucial. Many a campaign has been decided because the swing vote was won over by one of the candidates.

Another way of segmenting publics is to do it based on values and lifestyles. Such segmentation regularly is used by marketers to focus product and service appeals on particular socioeconomic levels. Segmentation separates consumers into eight distinct categories:

1. Actualizers are those with the most wealth and power.
2. Fulfilleds have high resources and are principle-oriented professionals or retirees.
3. Believers are Fulfilleds without the resources.
4. Achievers have high resources and are status oriented.
5. Strivers lack the resources of Achievers but are equally status oriented.
6. Experiencers have high resources, are action oriented, and are disposed toward taking risks.

7. Makers also are action oriented but have low resources.
8. Strugglers have the lowest resources.[15]

Applying such lifestyle characterizations to publics can help companies make marketing and public relations decisions to effectively target key audiences.

The typical organization is faced with a myriad of critical publics with which it must communicate on a frequent and direct basis. It must be sensitive to the self-interests, desires, and concerns of each public. It must understand that self-interest groups today are themselves more complex. Therefore, the harmonizing actions necessary to win and maintain support among such groups should be arrived at in terms of public relations consequences.[16]

Whereas management must always speak with one voice, its communications inflection, delivery, and emphasis should be sensitive to all constituent publics.

The Functions of Public Relations

There is a fundamental difference between the functions of public relations and the functions of marketing and advertising. Marketing and advertising promote an individual product or a service. Public relations promotes an entire organization.

The functions associated with public relations work are numerous. Among them are:

● **Writing**—a fundamental public relations skill, with written vehicles from news releases to speeches and from brochures to advertisements falling within the field's purview.
● **Media relations**—dealing with the press is another frontline public relations function.
● **Planning**—of special events, media events, management functions, and the like.
● **Counseling**—in dealing with management and its interactions with key publics.
● **Researching**—of attitudes and opinions that influence behavior and beliefs.
● **Publicity**—the marketing-related function, most commonly misunderstood as the "only" function of public relations, generating positive publicity for a client or employer.
● **Marketing communications**—other marketing-related functions, such as creating brochures, sales literature, meeting displays, and promotions.
● **Community relations**—positively putting forth the organization's messages and image within the community.
● **Consumer relations**—interfacing with consumers through written and verbal communications.
● **Employee relations**—communicating with the all-important internal publics of the organization, those managers and employees who work for the firm.
● **Government affairs**—dealing with legislators, regulators, and local, state, and federal officials—all of those who have governmental interface with the organization.
● **Investor relations**—for public companies, communicating with stockholders and those who advise them.
● **Special publics relations**—dealing with those publics uniquely critical to particular organizations, from African Americans to women to Asians to senior citizens.

Another Way to Define Public Relations

Still confused about the differences among public relations, publicity, advertising, and promotion? This will straighten you out.

Let's say the circus comes to town, and you want people to know about it.

- **Advertising** Displaying a sign announcing that the circus is in town
- **Promotion** Displaying the sign on an elephant and parading the animal through town

- **Publicity** If the elephant carrying the sign tramples through the ornamental garden of the mayor and the newspaper reports it
- **Public Relations** If you are able to get the mayor to laugh about the incident and ride in the circus parade with no hard feelings

Raleigh Pinskey, *The Zen of Hype: An Insider's Guide to the Publicity Game*, Carol Communications, Inc., New York, NY, 1998.

- **Public affairs and issues management**—dealing with public policy and its impact on the organization, as well as identifying and addressing issues of consequence that affect the firm.
- **Web site development and Web interface**—creating what often is the organization's principle interface with the public—its Web site. Also important is monitoring the World Wide Web and responding, when appropriate, to organizational challenge.

This is but a partial list of what public relations does. In sum, the public relations practitioner is a manager/orchestrator/producer/director/writer/arranger and all-around general communications counsel to management. It is for this reason, then, that the process works best when the public relations director reports to the CEO.

The Curse of "Spin"

So pervasive has the influence of public relations become in our society that some even fear it as a pernicious force; they worry about the power of public relations to exercise a kind of thought control over the American public.

Which brings us to "spin."

The propensity in recent years for presumably respected public figures to lie in an attempt to deceive the public has led to the notion that "spinning" the facts is synonymous with public relations practice.

It isn't.

Spin—outright lying to hide what really happened—is antithetical to the proper practice of public relations. In public relations, if you lie once, you will never be trusted again—particularly by the media.

Nonetheless, public relations spin has come to mean the twisting of messages to create the appearance of performance, which may or may not be true. Distortion, obfuscation, even downright lying are fair game as far as spin is concerned.

Spin came into prominence during the administration of President Clinton, largely under the auspices of political communications adviser James Carville (Figure 1-4), who approached issues and opponents with a "go for the jugular" abandon.[17] When

FIGURE 1-4 **Presidential spinner.** James Carville, President Clinton's ragin' Cajun.

Clinton was caught lying to the American public that he "did not have sexual relations" with a young intern, spin reached its low.[18]

Subsequently, in the summer of 2002, corporate spinners were castigated with a series of ethical scandals involving some of the nation's largest companies. Top executives from Enron, WorldCom, Arthur Andersen, Global Crossing, Tyco, and a host of others were found to have twisted facts and shaded comments to deceive shareholders and employees.

Other examples of half truths in the fields of sports, journalism, government, and business further clouded in many people's minds the "ethics" of public relations practice.

All of this high-powered lying, unfortunately, has implications for the field. Indeed, the *New York Times* headlined its review of a popular book on the field, "How Public Relations Tries to Keep the World Spinning."[19] Other critics admonish the field as "a huge, powerful, hidden medium available only to wealthy individuals, big corporations, governments and government agencies because of its high cost."[20]

Faced with such doubts and in an era of spin and unrelenting questioning by the media and the public about the ethics of public relations, practitioners must always be sensitive to and considerate of how their actions and their words will influence the public.

Above all, practitioners should never, ever lie.

What Manner of Man or Woman?

What kind of individual does it take to become a competent public relations professional?

The Report of the Commission on Public Relations Education in 1999 listed a dozen areas of competence that emerging public relations students must have to succeed in the new century:

1. Communication and persuasion concepts and strategies
2. Communication and public relations theories
3. Relationships and relationship building

4. Societal trends
5. Ethical issues
6. Legal requirements and issues
7. Marketing and finance
8. Public relations history
9. Uses of research and forecasting
10. Multicultural and global issues
11. Organizational change and development
12. Management concepts and theories[21]

Beyond these academic areas, in order to make it, a public relations professional ought to possess a set of specific technical skills as well as an appreciation of the proper attitudinal approach to the job (Figure 1-5). On the technical side, the following seven skills are important:

1. Knowledge of the field—the underpinnings of public relations, culture and history, philosophy, and social psychology.
2. Communications knowledge—the media and the ways in which they work, communications research, and, most important, the writing process.
3. Technological knowledge—the computer, the Net, the World Wide Web, cyberspace, all are imperative in the new century.
4. Knowledge of what's going on around you—current events and factors that influence society: history, literature, language, politics, economics, and all the rest—from the Ming Dynasty to Yao Ming, from a unified Germany to a divided Korea; from Dr. Atkins to Dr. Dre; from Kobe Bryant to Bryant Gumbel; from Fat Joe to J Lo to the Squirrel Nut Zippers. A public relations professional must be, in the truest sense, a Renaissance man or woman.
5. Business knowledge—how business works, a bottom-line orientation, and a knowledge of one's company and industry.
6. Knowledge of bureaucracy—how to get things done in a bureaucratic organization, how to use and gain power for the best advantage, and how to maneuver in a politically charged environment.
7. Management knowledge—how public policy is shaped and what pressures and responsibilities fall on senior managers.

In terms of attitude, public relations professionals ought to possess the following four characteristics:

1. Communications orientation—a bias toward disclosing rather than withholding information. Public relations professionals should want to communicate with the public. They should practice the belief that the public has a right to know.
2. Advocacy—a desire to be advocates for their employers. Public relations people must stand up for what their employers represent. Although they should never distort, lie, or hide facts, occasionally it may be in an organization's best interest to avoid comment on certain issues. If practitioners don't believe in the integrity and credibility of their employers, their most honorable course is to quit.
3. Counseling orientation—a compelling desire to advise senior managers. As noted, top executives are used to dealing in tangibles, such as balance sheets, costs per thousand, and cash flows. Public relations practitioners understand the intangibles, such as public opinion, media influence, and communications messages. Practitioners must be willing to support their beliefs—often in

---

Characteristics of a Top CCO

- Acts as a counselor to the leadership team (including the CEO, General Counsel, CFO and business heads) and is seen by all to have good judgment in communications *and* business.

- Offers a perspective gained from broad communications experience (which includes leading -- or working in lockstep with -- Internal/External Communications, Investor Relations, Marketing Communications/Advertising, Community Relations and Charitable Foundations).

- Takes a disciplined approach to communications but has good instincts for what is needed and how to get it done.

- Has a point of view and stands for something.

- Calms people down in tough situations, usually by conveying that the best course of action is to have a position, hold your ground, be responsive and not over react.

- Has operated on big platforms and faced big issues.

- Elevates the comunications function by actively developing his/her team, teaching them the skills required for middle management and the intangibles required for leadership.

- Strong written and verbal skills.

- Has the political agility to get results in a complex environment.

- Is comfortable in conversation at all levels of the organization.

- Has a communications objective in every interaction.

- Sees communications as a means to an end, not as an end in itself.

- Puts things in writing -- even if it is just for the file.

- Understands that we live in an era where information is widely and quickly shared -- and that the action of one employee can put an entire company in the spotlight. Hence, he/she strives to create a culture in which employees care about corporate reputation.

Whitehead Mann

FIGURE 1-5 **Top communicators.** Executive recruiter Whitehead Mann interviewed 200 *Fortune* 500 company communicators who listed these expectations of a chief communications officer. This is their list.

opposition to lawyers or personnel executives. They must even be willing to disagree with management at times. Far from being compliant, public relations practitioners must have the gumption to say "no."

4. Personal confidence—a strong sense of honesty and ethics, a willingness to take risks, and, not unimportant, a sense of humor. Public relations

professionals must have the courage of their convictions and the personal confidence to represent proudly a curious—yet critical—role in any organization.

In recent years many more women have joined the public relations ranks. Women now account for more than 70 percent of all practitioners and, according to the research, are gaining on men in terms of earning power in the field (see Chapter 4).

LAST WORD

Spin, cover-up, distortion, and subterfuge are the antitheses of good public relations.

Ethics, truth, credibility—these values are what good public relations is all about.

To be sure, public relations is not yet a profession like law, accounting, or medicine, in which all practitioners are trained, licensed, and supervised. Nothing prevents someone with little or no formal training from hanging out a shingle as a public relations specialist. Such frauds embarrass professionals in the field and, thankfully, are becoming harder and harder to find.

Indeed, both the Public Relations Society of America and the International Association of Business Communicators have strong codes of ethics that serve as the basis of their membership philosophies (Appendix A).

Meanwhile, the importance of the practice of public relations in a less certain, more chaotic and competitive world cannot be denied.

Despite its considerable problems—in attaining leadership status, in finding its proper role in society, in disavowing spin and earning enduring respect—the practice of public relations has never been more prominent. Approaching its first 100 years as a formal, integrated, strategic thinking process, public relations has become part of the fabric of modern society.

Here's why.

Much more than customers for their products, managers today desperately need constituents for their beliefs and values. In the 21st century, the role of public relations is much more to guide management in framing its ideas and making its commitments. The counsel that management will need must come from advisers who understand public attitudes, public moods, public needs, and public aspirations.

Contrary to what the critics charge, "More often than not, public relations strategies and tactics are the most effective and valuable arrows in the quiver of the disaffected and the powerless."[22] Civil rights leaders, labor leaders, public advocates, and grassroots movements of every stripe have been boosted by proven communications techniques to win attention and build support and goodwill.

Winning this elusive goodwill takes time and effort. Credibility can't be won overnight, nor can it be bought. If management policies aren't in the public's best interest, no amount of public relations efforts can obscure that reality. Public relations is not effective as a temporary defensive measure to compensate for management misjudgment. If management errs seriously, the best—and only—public relations advice must be to get the story out immediately. One public relations leader summed up the responsibilities of public relations professionals as being the organization's "conscience."

There are others in the corporate hierarchy who may possess the same amount or even more of these attributes than the individuals responsible for public relations. But the fact is that being the professional corporate conscience is not part of the job description of other executives. It is part of the job description of the chief public relations officer.[23]

Indeed, this is why the relationship between public relations and other parts of the organization—advertising and marketing, for example—is occasionally a strained one. The function of the public relations department is distinctive from that of any other internal area. Few others share the access to management that public relations enjoys. Few others share the potential for power that public relations may exercise.

No less an authority than Abraham Lincoln once said: "Public sentiment is everything . . . with public sentiment nothing can fail. Without it, nothing can succeed. He who molds public sentiment goes deeper than he who executes statutes or pronounces decisions. He makes statutes or decisions possible or impossible to execute."

Stated another way, no matter how you define it, the practice of public relations has become an essential element in the conduct of relationships for a vast variety of organizations in the 21st century.

Discussion Starters

1. How prominent is the practice of public relations around the world in the 21st century?
2. How would you define the practice of public relations?
3. Why is the practice of public relations generally misunderstood by the public?
4. How would you describe the significance of the planning aspect in public relations?
5. Within the R-A-C-E process of public relations, what would you say is the most critical element?
6. In what ways does public relations differ from advertising or marketing?
7. If you were the public relations director of the local United Way, whom would you consider your most important "publics" to be?
8. What are seven functions of public relations practice?
9. How do professional public relations people regard the aspect of spin as part of what they do?
10. Based on your understanding of the practice, would you expect public relations to grow or diminish in value, power, and importance as the century progresses?

TOP OF THE SHELF

Sheldon Rampton and John Stauber

Trust Us, We're Experts: How Industry Manipulates Science and Gambles with Your Future
New York, NY: J.P. Tarcher/Putnam, 2002

The authors, working from their Center for Media and Democracy and publishing their quarterly newsletter, *PR Watch*, have been thorns in the sides of public relations professionals ever since they came on the scene with the 1995 *Toxic Sludge Is Good for You! Lies, Damn Lies and the Public Relations Industry*.

Their latest book, *Trust Us, We're Experts*, is no less comforting to public relations pros, but its detailed history of spin is an enlightening look at what the public relations industry, through the often unsuspecting mass media, delivers to the American public.

On the book jacket, the authors brag that this book is "destined to be hated by PR firms and corporations everywhere."

Public relations people might not like these two, but they ought to read what they write.

CASE STUDY

Public Relations Leadership on the Nation's Darkest Day

September 11, 2001

8:45 A.M. EDT: A hijacked passenger jet, American Airlines Flight 11 out of Boston, Massachusetts, crashes into the north tower of the World Trade Center in New York City, tearing a gaping hole in the building and setting it afire (Figure 1-6).

9:03 A.M.: A second hijacked airliner, United Airlines Flight 175 from Boston, crashes into the south tower of the World Trade Center and explodes. Both buildings are burning.

9:17 A.M.: The Federal Aviation Administration (FAA) shuts down all New York City area airports.

9:21 A.M.: The Port Authority of New York and New Jersey closes all bridges and tunnels into and out of New York City.

9:30 A.M.: President George W. Bush, speaking from an elementary school classroom in Sarasota, Florida, says the nation has suffered an "apparent terrorist attack."

9:40 A.M.: The FAA, for the first time in U.S. history, halts air traffic at all U.S. airports.

9:43 A.M.: American Airlines Flight 77 crashes into the Pentagon. The Department of Defense is evacuated immediately.

9:45 A.M.: The White House is evacuated.

9:57 A.M.: President Bush departs Florida in Air Force One, bound for an undisclosed "safe location."

10:05 A.M.: The south tower of the World Trade Center collapses, crashing to the street below.

10:10 A.M.: A portion of the Pentagon collapses.

FIGURE 1-6 **The attack.** September 11, 2001.

10:10 A.M.: United Airlines Flight 93, also hijacked, crashes in an open field in Somerset County, Pennsylvania.

10:28 A.M.: The World Trade Center's north tower collapses from the top down, as if it were being peeled apart. Chaos reigns in lower Manhattan. The smell of death and devastation hangs with the enormous cloud of debris and smoke in the air.

The darkest day in the history of the United States was also a moment of heroic public relations leadership.

Most particularly from a most unlikely source—the mayor of New York City, Rudolph Giuliani.

ASSUMING LEADERSHIP

With the nation reeling and the president moving around the nation to evade potential attack, it was New York's controversial mayor who stepped forward to fill the leadership vacuum.

When the first plane hit the tower, Giuliani was uptown giving a speech. He immediately headed downtown to meet his top aides, including communications director Sunny Mindel at the Trade Center. Mindel had organized an impromptu press conference on the street, a block away from the Trade Center, when the buildings began to crumble.

Giuliani, Mindel, and the other key aides had to scramble for their lives, as all hell broke loose in lower Manhattan.

At 11:02 A.M., Mindel organized a belated press conference at the New York Police Academy—announced by the media as "an undisclosed location," for fear of further terrorist attacks. With New York Governor George Pataki by his side, Giuliani immediately took charge of the rescue operation.

Giuliani announced plans for the police, fire, and emergency medical departments; designated hospitals, shelters, and blood centers that would be used; and declared the roads, bridges, and tunnels that would be used officially and closed to the public. He urged New Yorkers to stay at home and ordered an evacuation of all persons south of Canal Street in lower Manhattan.

In subsequent days, Giuliani gave the clear impression that he was listening to many people personally involved with the tragedy. He assumed the role of chief spokesman, to keep the public informed and updated on all the various actions that government was taking to restore order. He led with action, serving as the point man for rescue operations (Figure 1-7).

RESIDING AT THE SCENE OF BATTLE

Giuliani also promised to continue to communicate to the nation from the makeshift command center that he and the governor had established in the very downtown vicinity that had been the focus of the terrorist attack.

Not only did Mayor Giuliani and Governor Pataki continually conduct news conferences at the Ground Zero epicenter of the carnage, but they also both had a narrow escape, departing Building One at the Trade Center 10 minutes before it imploded.

Giuliani understood the importance of "symbolically bonding" with those affected by the tragedy by rushing quickly to the scene of the onslaught. He appeared at Ground Zero numerous times, encouraging rescue workers.

By contrast, President Bush was initially criticized for not returning immediately to Washington to survey the Pentagon attack firsthand.

Mayor Giuliani risked no such criticism.

FIGURE 1-7   **The leaders.** New York City Mayor Rudy Giuliani (holding photo) and New York Governor George Pataki (far left).

This was a principle to which Union Carbide CEO Warren Anderson adhered many years earlier when his company was responsible for thousands of deaths in Bhopal, India, and that Exxon CEO Lawrence Rawl violated when an Exxon ship polluted the Gulf of Valdez in Alaska. Rawl and, by extension, the company he represented were disgraced by the CEO's wrong-headed decision.

COMMUNICATING STEADILY

It is impossible in crisis to keep up with changing facts and information. But it is equally impossible to sit back and wait for all the facts to emerge before communicating. In crisis, uncertainty is the enemy.

Nature abhors a vaccum. Others will fill the crisis information void if official sources don't come forward immediately and continually to set the communications agenda.

Accordingly, Mayor Giuliani set the agenda early, with morning planning meetings of his key aides followed by periodic press briefings to deliver specific messages. At one such meeting he posted photos of the flight recorders that needed to be located. At another he vowed to punish the bogus fund-raisers and bomb scare callers. And at another he pleaded against provocations of people of Arab descent. At all times, he answered questions patiently and became the first information source for a news-hungry world.

By contrast, the White House hesitated. Ironically, the first official national "face" that the nation saw was that of a public relations adviser, White House counselor Karen Hughes, substituting for the incommunicado president.

The White House quickly recovered its crisis communications footing, and the president, secretary of state, secretary of defense, secretary of transportation, and others were made continually available and correctly visible to the nation.

EXHIBITING HUMANITY

Few principles are more important in public relations than showing a human face by exhibiting emotion. But many leaders—corporate CEOs as the most prominent example—mistakenly consider it a sign of weakness to show emotion.

This is another reason public relations professionals are necessary—to counsel their clients and superiors to express humility, caring, and concern in their communications.

As hard-nosed as he is, Rudy Giuliani had no trouble expressing emotion. Among the most poignant portraits amidst the horror was the mayor's hesitant, heartrending acknowledgment early on of the loss of three fire-fighting friends, who had accompanied him to the Trade Center on September 11.

When asked early to speculate on a "death toll" from the tragedy, Giuliani answered, "I don't think any of us want to speculate on that, but there are more than any of us can bear."

Again by contrast, President Bush, neither a gifted speaker nor a comfortable communicator, was at first stiff and formal in the face of calamity. By midweek, however, the president showed himself to be much more human, particularly when he momentarily broke down in an impromptu Oval Office press conference, when addressing the children of the victims.

In any such situation, not only is it not wrong to show emotion—it is imperative to show appropriate concern and sensitivity.

Arrogance is your enemy, humanity your friend.

CITING SYMBOLS

Ours is a visual society. We are galvanized by "symbols," particularly in a crisis.

In the Gulf War, it was yellow ribbons. In Oklahoma City, it was a photo of a fireman carrying the charred remains of a little baby. But in the Trade Center tragedy, the most memorable image was horrific—the sight of a jumbo jet crashing headlong into a steel tower and bringing down a nation.

So here, again, it was left to the mayor to come up with more hopeful, alternative symbolism. And so he did.

With New York City's uniformed personnel the great heroes in the horror and with 300 fire fighters missing and feared dead, the mayor conducted his press conferences in an FDNY baseball cap and an EMS medical worker windbreaker.

In so doing, he transmitted to one and all that hope and heroism and courage and confidence were still very much alive, regardless of the devastation.

EMBRACING OPTIMISM

The final responsibility of a leader in a crisis is to express the clear and unmistakable notion that "this too will pass."

Rudy Giuliani struck that tone early and often.

"We're going to rebuild," he promised at the very first press conference. "We're going to come out of this stronger than we were before. Emotionally stronger, politically stronger, economically stronger."

By the second day, the mayor vowed, "Everything is safe right now in the city," and he exhorted Broadway and businesses to reopen and people to go back to work.

"Returning to normal shows we are not afraid, shows confidence. So do things. Get out. Go to stores. Go to restaurants. Don't feel locked in. This is a horrible thing that's happened, the full dimensions of which we can't begin to understand. But we simply must continue to go about our lives."

Giuliani's language was as simple as it was eloquent—honest, straightforward, apolitical. And perhaps it was this quality, more than anything else, that distinguished him from all the other politicians as a public relations leader.

Questions

1. In assuming public relations leadership, was it more important that Mayor Giuliani communicated or acted?
2. Why was it important for him to go directly to the scene of the tragedy?
3. What is the significance of a leader acting with humanity in such a circumstance?
4. Mayor Giuliani was said by his critics to be arrogant and manipulative. Describe how those characteristics entered into his approach at the Trade Center.
5. Had you been advising Mayor Giuliani at the time, what would you have encouraged him to consider?

For further information, see Kathy Kiely, "Americans Confused: Should We Worry or Go About Our Business," *USA Today*, October 30, 2001, 6A; Wes Pedersen, "The 'Next Big Thing' in Public Affairs," *Public Affairs Review*, 2002, 2–5; Fraser P. Seitel, "Rudy Giuliani's Crisis Communications Leadership," odwyerpr.com, September 14, 2001; and "September 11: Chronology of Terror," CNN.com, September 12, 2001.

TIPS FROM THE TOP

An Interview with Sunny Mindel

Sunny Mindel is communications director of Giuliani Partners LLC. After early experience as an advertising copywriter and TV reporter, she joined the Giuliani administration in 1996. In 1999, she became the mayor's acting press secretary, then press secretary, and then communications director, a position she held on the fateful day of September 11, 2001.

How would you characterize your access to Mayor Giuliani?
Ours was and is an "open door relationship." My access to him is 24/7. That's the way it has to be. A principal has to have 100 percent trust in his communications person. There has to be a comfort level, so that both parties are comfortable calling at any hour and being open and candid.

Does Mayor Giuliani like the press?
Yes, he does. He frequently admits that he misses the mayor's daily press conferences, which kept him and us on our toes.

Where were you on September 11?
I was at my desk at City Hall, two blocks from the Trade Center. I heard the tremendous explosion. A deputy mayor came into my office, said "a plane just

Sunny Mindel and Mayor Giuliani

hit the Towers, let's go." Normally, I'd grab a camera and my tape recorder, but something told me I better not wait the extra two minutes and leave immediately.

What was the scene like?
Total devastation. Falling debris. Chaos. The mayor was enroute downtown, and I knew we had to plan a press conference as soon as he arrived.

(Continued)

And what happened once Mayor Giuliani arrived?

He agreed we needed a press conference and asked me to coordinate a command post with the police department, and to put in land lines so the press could be in contact with their offices.

Then the second plane hit, and I watched people jump from the building. I was surrounded by TV cameras that were shooting the scene. I must say I felt conflicted and thought about asking them to stop or even concealing the lenses. It occurred to me, absolutely not. As awful as it was, it was far too important not to be recorded.

Did you ultimately have the press conference?

We were ready to have the press conference on the street, two blocks from the Trade Center. The mayor desperately wanted to let the people in the buildings and the area know what to do. And I wanted people to know that the government of the City of New York was intact and that the mayor was alive.

At that point, the buildings collapsed, and we all were trapped and had to run.

How did you communicate that the mayor was alive?

We emerged from the chaos with a small band of press people accompanying us. The mayor began relaying information to them, and I told them they would have to "pool" everything with the rest of the media. They immediately agreed. The press was totally cooperative. Their lives were as much in jeopardy as any of the rest of us.

Finally, when we reached our first fire house, we called New York One, a local TV affiliate of CNN, and the mayor spoke with them, to let the world know he was alive and in charge.

Did you counsel the mayor to be compassionate during this difficult period?

There was no need to. He is a very compassionate man. I'd seen that in the four years I'd worked for him. He was concerned though about how to communicate the terrible loss of life. As it turned out, he inherently knew how to do it. We made sure he had the information he needed to convey.

What were the key messages that you wanted to get across to the public?

First, let people know that New York City was still there. Second, let people know the fundamental issues that are so important—what was open, what was closed, what was functioning, and what wasn't.

What lasting lessons did you learn from this crisis?

- First, memorize all your key phone numbers. You never know what you'll be able to grab in a real crisis.
- Second, always bring your tape recorder with you and record what's going on around you for posterity.
- Third, keep a running diary of the details.

What about lessons in working with a person in the spotlight?

You have to know how the principal, thinks, talks, and reacts in situations. One big mistake that people in my position make is that they become "handlers." Ultimately, people pick up that this is disingenuous and not real. I don't have a person who needs "handling." He is who he is. And New Yorkers and Americans needed to hear those messages at that critical moment, not from the communications aide, but from the person elected to run the City of New York.

Suggested Readings

Center, Allen H., and Patrick Jackson, *Public Relations Practices: Managerial Case Studies and Problems*, 5th ed. Upper Saddle River, NJ: Prentice Hall, 2000.

Cutlip, Scott M., Allen H. Center, and Glen M. Broom, *Effective Public Relations*, 8th ed. Upper Saddle River, NJ: Prentice Hall, 2000. (Without question, the first and still most comprehensive textbook in the field.)

Dilenschneider, Robert L., ed., *Dartnell Public Relations Handbook*, 4th ed. Chicago: Dartnell Corp., 1996.

Dozier, David M., Larissa A. Grunig, and James E. Grunig, et al., *Manager's Guide to Excellence in Public Relations and Communication Management*. Hillsdale, NJ: Lawrence Erlbaum Associates, 1995.

Dwyer, Thomas, *Simply Public Relations: Public Relations Made Challenging, Complete and Concise.* Stillwater, OK: New Forums, 1992.

Ewen, Stuart, *PR! A Social History of Spin.* New York: Basic Books, 1996.

Heath, Robert L., *Handbook of Public Relations.* Thousand Oaks, CA: Sage Publications, 2001.

Hutton, James G., "The Definition, Dimensions and Domain of Public Relations," *Public Relations Review* (Summer 1999): 199–214.

Ledingham, John, and Stephen Brunig, *Public Relations as Relationship Management, A Relational Approach to the Study and Practice of Public Relations.* Mahwah, NJ: Lawrence Erlbaum Associates, 2001.

Lesly, Philip, ed., *Lesly's Handbook of Public Relations and Communications*, 5th ed. Lincolnwood, IL: NTC Business Books, 1998.

Rhody, Ron, *The CEO's Playbook: Managing the Outside Forces That Shape Success.* Sacramento, CA: Academy Publishing, 1999.

Wilcox, Dennis, ed., *Public Relations: Strategies and Tactics*, 6th ed. Reading, MA: Addison-Wesley, 1999.

Notes

1. James Carney, "Karen Hughes: Exit the High Prophet," *TIME*.com (July 2, 2002).
2. Occupational Outlook Handbook 2002–2003 Edition, U.S. Department of Labor Bureau of Labor Statistics, see sections on Public Relations Specialists and Advertising, Marketing, Promotions, Public Relations, and Sales Managers.
3. Jack Bergen, "Corporate Communications Spending & Reputations of Fortune 500 Companies," *Ragan's Public Relations Journal* (July/August 1999): 9–32.
4. "2002 Industry Documentation & Rankings," Council of Public Relations Firms, New York, NY.
5. "The Design for Undergraduate Public Relations Education," a study cosponsored by the public relations division of the Association for Education and Journalism and Mass Communication, the Public Relations Society of America, and the educators' section of PRSA, 1987, 1.
6. Cited in Scott M. Cutlip and Allen H. Center, *Effective Public Relations*, 6th ed. (Upper Saddle River, NJ: Prentice Hall, 1985): 5.
7. Edward L. Bernays, *Crystallizing Public Opinion* (New York: Liveright, 1961).
8. Rex F. Harlow, "Building a Public Relations Definition," *Public Relations Review 2*, no. 4 (Winter 1976): 36.
9. Philip Lesly, "Report and Recommendations: Task Force on Stature and Role of Public Relations," *Public Relations Journal* (March 1981): 32.
10. John E. Marston, *The Nature of Public Relations* (New York: McGraw-Hill, 1963): 161.
11. *Public Relations News*, 1201 Seven Locks Road, Suite 300, Potomac, MD 20854.
12. Dr. Melvin L. Sharpe, professor and coordinator of the Public Relations Sequence, Department of Journalism, Ball State University, Muncie, IN 47306.
13. Sandra Sobieraj, "Senate Bans Company Loans to Officials," Associated Press (July 13, 2002).
14. John Dewey, *The Public and Its Problems* (Chicago: Swallow Press, 1927).
15. Linda P. Morton, "Segmenting Publics by Lifestyles," *Public Relations Quarterly* (Fall 1999): 46–47.
16. Sharpe, professor and coordinator of the Public Relations Sequence.

17. Bill Sammons, "President's Pit Bull Goes on the Offensive," *Washington Times National Weekly* (June 22–28, 1998): 4.
18. Aviva Diamond, "Lessons from a Troubled White House," *PR Tactics*, (October 1998): 27–29.
19. Deborah Stead, "How Public Relations Tries to Keep the World Spinning," *New York Times* (November 3, 1996): B8.
20. Derrick Jensen, "The War on Truth: The Secret Battle for the American Mind," interview with John Stauber, mediachannel.org (June 7, 2000).
21. "A Port of Entry: The Report of the Commission on Public Relations Education," Institute for Public Relations (October 1999): 3.
22. Fraser P. Seitel, "Relax Mr. Stauber, Public Relations Ain't That Dangerous," mediachannel.org (June 7, 2000).
23. Harold Burson, "The Role of the Public Relations Professional," *Current Media* (Fall 1996).

Chapter 2

The Growth of Public Relations

Unlike accounting, economics, medicine, or law, public relations is still a young field, which will celebrate its 100th birthday early in the 21st century. Consequently, public relations as a modern American phenomenon is much younger than other disciplines.

The relative youthfulness of the practice means that the field is still evolving, and its status is improving daily. Indeed, the professionals entering the practice today are by and large superior in intellect, training, and even experience to their counterparts decades ago. In many ways, over the past several decades the practice has ascended "from the basement to the penthouse."[1]

The strength of the practice of public relations today is based on the enduring commitment of the public to participate in a free and open democratic society. At least five trends are related to the evolution of public relations:

- *Growth of big institutions*

   The days of the mom-and-pop grocery store, the tiny community college, and the small local bank are rapidly disappearing. In their place have emerged Wal-Marts, Home Depots, and Citigroups, statewide community college systems, and multistate banking networks. The public relations profession has evolved to interpret these large institutions to the publics they serve.

- *Increasing incidence of change, conflict, and confrontation in society*

   Women's rights, senior citizens' rights, gay rights, animal rights, consumerism, environmental awareness, downsizings, layoffs, and resultant unhappiness with large institutions all have become part of day-to-day society. With the growth of the Web, activists have become increasingly more daring, visible, and effective.

- *Heightened awareness and sophistication of people worldwide as a result of technological innovations in communications*

   First came the invention of the printing press. Then came mass communications: the print media, radio, and television. Later it was the development of cable, satellite, videotape, videodisks, video typewriters, portable cameras, word processors, fax machines, cell phones, the World

Wide Web, and all the other communications technologies that have helped fragment audiences. In the 1960s, McGill University Professor Marshall McLuhan predicted the world would become a "global village." In the 21st century, when the acts of homicide bombers in the Middle East are instantaneously communicated around the world, McLuhan's prophesy has become a reality.

- *Growing power of public opinion in the 21st century for positive democratic means, as well as use by those who would repress other people (Figure 2-1)*

    The outbreak of democracy in Latin America, Eastern Europe, the former Soviet Union, and South Africa has heightened the power of public opinion in the world. Public opinion is a powerful force, not only in democracies like the United States but also for oppressed peoples around the world, from Serbia to Afghanistan, who have risen up and spoken out. Accordingly, the practice of public relations as a facilitator for understanding has increased in prominence.

- *Extraordinary growth of the Internet and the World Wide Web, which has made millions of people around the world instant consumers of unlimited communication.*

    With 143 million Americans and countless other millions around the world now on the Net, people are united through linked communications like never before. The change this continues to bring to society is monumental.

Ancient Beginnings

Although modern public relations is a 20th-century phenomenon, its roots are ancient. Leaders in virtually every great society throughout history understood the importance of influencing public opinion through persuasion. For example, archeologists found a farm bulletin in Iraq that told farmers of 1800 B.C. about the latest techniques of harvesting, sowing, and irrigating.[2] The more food the farmers grew, the better the citizenry ate and the wealthier the country became—a good example of planned persuasion to reach a specific public for a particular purpose—in other words, public relations.

Later on, the Greeks put a high premium on communication skills. The best speakers, in fact, were generally elected to leadership positions. Occasionally, aspiring Greek politicians enlisted the aid of Sophists (individuals renowned for both their reasoning and their rhetoric) to help fight verbal battles. Sophists would gather in the amphitheaters of the day and extol the virtues of particular political candidates. Thus, the Sophists set the stage for today's lobbyists, who attempt to influence legislation through effective communications techniques. From the time of the Sophists, the practice of public relations has been a battleground for questions of ethics. Should a Sophist or a lobbyist or a public relations professional "sell" his or her talents to the highest bidder, regardless of personal beliefs, values, and ideologies? When modern-day public relations professionals agree to represent repressive governments, such as Iraq or Libya, or defend the questionable actions of troubled celebrities, such as Robert Blake or O.J. Simpson, these ethical questions remain very much a focus of modern public relations.[3]

The Romans, particularly Julius Caesar, were also masters of persuasive techniques. When faced with an upcoming battle, Caesar would rally public support

FIGURE 2-1   Communicating evil. The communications revolution sweeping the world fueled evil forces as well as good. Terrorists, aware of the media's power to broadcast their message instantaneously around the world, used their acts of destruction to spread their beliefs. (Courtesy of ADL)

through assorted publications and staged events. Similarly, during World War I, a special U.S. public information committee, the Creel Committee, was formed to channel the patriotic sentiments of Americans in support of the U.S. role in the war. Stealing a page from Caesar, the committee's massive verbal and written communications effort was successful in marshaling national pride behind the war effort. According to a young member of the Creel Committee, Edward L. Bernays (later considered by many to be the father of public relations), "This was the first time in our history that information was used as a weapon of war."[4]

Even the Catholic Church had a hand in the creation of public relations. In the 1600s, under the leadership of Pope Gregory XV, the church established a college of propaganda to "help propagate the faith." In those days, the term *propaganda* did not have a negative connotation; the church simply wanted to inform the public about the advantages of Catholicism. Indeed, the roots of public relations lie in the development of propaganda, defined neutrally.[5] Today, the pope and other religious leaders maintain communications staffs to assist relations with the public. Indeed, the chief communications official in the Vatican maintains the rank of Archbishop of the Church. It was largely his role to deal with perhaps the most horrific scandal ever to face the Catholic Church—the clergy pedophilia issue of 2002.[6]

Early American Experience

The American public relations experience dates back to the founding of the republic. Influencing public opinion, managing communications, and persuading individuals at the highest levels were at the core of the American Revolution. The colonists tried to persuade King George III that they should be accorded the same rights as Englishmen. "Taxation without representation is tyranny" became their public relations slogan to galvanize fellow countrymen.

When King George refused to accede to the colonists' demands, they combined the weaponry of sword and pen. Samuel Adams, for one, organized Committees of Correspondence as a kind of revolutionary Associated Press to disseminate speedily anti-British information throughout the colonies. He also staged events to build up revolutionary fervor, such as the Boston Tea Party, in which colonists, masquerading as Indians, boarded British ships in Boston Harbor and pitched chests of imported tea overboard—as impressive a media event as has ever been recorded sans television. Indeed, Adams's precept, "Put the enemy in the wrong and keep him there," is as solid persuasive advice today as it was more than two centuries ago.[7]

Thomas Paine, another early practitioner of public relations, wrote periodic pamphlets and essays that urged the colonists to band together. In one essay contained in his *Crisis* papers, Paine wrote poetically: "These are the times that try men's souls. The summer soldier and the sunshine patriot will, in this crisis, shrink from the service of their country." The people listened, were persuaded, and took action—testifying to the power of early American communicators.

Later American Experience

The creation of the most important document in our nation's history, the Constitution, also owed much to public relations. Federalists, who supported the Constitution, fought tooth and nail with anti-Federalists, who opposed it. Their battle was waged in newspaper articles, pamphlets, and other organs of persuasion in an attempt to influence public opinion. To advocate ratification of the Constitution, political leaders such as Alexander Hamilton, James Madison, and John Jay banded together, under the pseudonym Publius, to write letters to leading newspapers. Today those letters are bound in a document called *The Federalist Papers* and are still used in the interpretation of the Constitution.

A QUESTION OF ETHICS

The Church's Spring of Shame

The spring of 2002 was a bitter and shameful period for the Catholic Church.

Since early January, the American Catholic Church was rocked by a series of articles in the *Boston Globe*, exposing how known pedophile priests had been protected by the Boston Archdiocese and its archbishop, 70-year-old Cardinal Bernard Law, who oversaw 362 parishes serving 2.1 million members (Figure 2-2).

By the spring, the criminal trial of Fr. John Geoghan, a former Boston priest named as a defendant in more than 80 civil lawsuits, became front-page news around the nation. The Geoghan trial shed light on the complicity of Catholic bishops in paying off complainants, sealing records, and moving offending priests from parish to parish to avoid their problems becoming public. Geoghan was defrocked and sentenced to 10 years in prison.

Another former Boston priest, Fr. Paul Shanley, was arrested in California and convicted of even worse and more pervasive offenses. Documents showed that Shanley was moved around various Boston parishes until he was transferred to California. Church officials there were never told of his past problems.

The scandal was, inarguably, the most profound public relations problem in the history of the Roman Catholic Church.

While the floodgates opened and similar cases of pedophilia were reported involving clergy throughout the nation, Cadinal Law remained in his post. Indeed, he was defended by fellow priests, some of whom argued that the U.S. media was "obviously and openly anti-Catholic."

Although Cardinal Law acknowledged that "we were too focused on the individual components of each case, when we should have been more focused on the protection of children," he adamantly refused to resign.

"My desire is to serve this archdiocese and the whole church with every fiber of my being. This I will continue to do as long as God gives me the opportunity," Cardinal Law wrote in an open letter to his "dear brother priests."

After a summer emergency meeting at the Vatican with Pope John Paul II, the Church adopted strict rules to deal with transgressing priests. Nonetheless,

FIGURE 2-2 **Church's shame.** Beleaguered Boston Cardinal Bernard Law.

many wondered why the Archbishop of Boston, who acknowledged mishandling the cases of numerous pedophile priests in his jurisdiction—and, in fact, paid $10 million to settle the case in the fall of 2002—hadn't felt it was his ethical duty to resign.

Finally, nearly a full year after the revelation of the Catholic Church's worst scandal in history, Cardinal Law stepped down.

For further information, see Eric J. Lyman, "Cardinal Blasts U.S. Media for Sex Coverage," *United Press International,* June 8, 2002; Cathy Lynn Grossman, "Church Expected to Settle for $10M," *USA Today,* September 19, 2002; Robert Paul Reyes, "Pope's Response to Sex Scandal Is Inadequate," Aboutpolitics.com, April 1, 2002; and Allyson Smith, "Catholic Organization Grateful to See Boston Pedophile Scandal Exposed," *Culture & Family Report,* March 1, 2002.

After ratification, the constitutional debate continued, particularly over the document's apparent failure to protect individual liberties against government encroachment. Hailed as the father of the Constitution, Madison framed the Bill of Rights in 1791, which ultimately became the first 10 amendments to the Constitution. Fittingly, the first of those amendments safeguarded, among other things, the practice of public relations: "Congress shall make no law respecting an establishment of religion, or prohibiting the free exercise thereof; or abridging the freedom of speech, or of the press, or the rights of the people peaceably to assemble, and to petition the government for a redress of grievances." In other words, people were given the right to speak up for what they believed in and the freedom to try to influence the opinions of others. Thus was the practice of public relations ratified.[8]

Into the 1800s

The practice of public relations continued to percolate in the 19th century. Among the more prominent, yet negative, antecedents of modern public relations that took hold in the 1800s was press agentry. Two of the better-known—some would say notorious—practitioners of this art were Amos Kendall and Phineas T. Barnum.

In 1829, President Andrew Jackson selected Kendall, a writer and editor living in Kentucky, to serve in his administration. Within weeks, Kendall became a member of Old Hickory's "kitchen cabinet" and eventually became one of Jackson's most influential assistants.

Kendall performed just about every White House public relations task. He wrote speeches, state papers, and messages and turned out press releases. He even conducted basic opinion polls and is considered one of the earliest users of the "news leak." Although Kendall is generally credited with being the first authentic presidential press secretary, his functions and role went far beyond that position.

Among Kendall's most successful ventures in Jackson's behalf was the development of the administration's own newspaper, the *Globe*. Although it was not uncommon for the governing administration to publish its own national house organ, Kendall's deft editorial touch refined the process to increase its effectiveness. Kendall would pen a Jackson news release, distribute it for publication to a local newspaper, and then reprint the press clipping in the *Globe* to underscore Jackson's nationwide popularity. Indeed, that popularity continued unabated throughout Jackson's years in office, with much of the credit going to the president's public relations adviser.*

Most public relations professionals would rather not talk about P. T. Barnum as an industry pioneer. Barnum, some say, was a huckster, whose motto might well have been "The Public Be Fooled." More sanguine defenders suggest that although Barnum may have had his faults, he nonetheless was respected in his time as a user of written and verbal public relations techniques to further his museum and circus.

Like him or not, Barnum was a master publicist. In the 1800s, as owner of a major circus, Barnum generated article after article for his traveling show. He purposely gave his star performers short names—for instance, Tom Thumb, the midget, and Jenny Lind, the singer—so that they could easily fit into the headlines of narrow newspaper

---

*Kendall was decidedly not cut from the same cloth as today's neat, trim, buttoned-down press secretaries. On the contrary, Jackson's man was described as "a puny, sickly looking man with a weak voice, a wheezing cough, narrow and stooping shoulders, a sallow complexion, silvery hair in his prime, slovenly dress, and a seedy appearance." (Fred F. Endres, "Public Relations in the Jackson White House," *Public Relations Review* 2, no. 3 [Fall 1976]: 5–12.)

The Legacy of P. T. Barnum

P. T. Barnum's methods to achieve publicity for his museum attractions and circus acts pale in comparison with the efforts of today's entertainment publicists to promote new movies.

With studios investing tens of millions of dollars in movies, which must score at the box office immediately to return the hundreds of millions studios seek, the element of publicity is as important as any other in the movie marketing mix.

So today's movie publicists play hardball.

In one 1996 study, more than half of 61 entertainment writers and film critics said the major Hollywood film studios "put more pressure on them to play by their rules." Nearly one-third said they had been "blacklisted" for not playing by the studio's publicity rules.[9] One writer reported being blacklisted by Disney for trashing the movie *Beauty and the Beast*. The negative review got the writer barred from future Disney screenings, interviews, and junkets.

The study also reported that entertainment publicists make journalists sign agreements as to where a story may run and which sensitive subjects may not be broached in celebrity interviews. The fact is that most magazines will compromise every time to get an interview with Tom Hanks or Matt Damon or Julia Roberts or Ricky Martin or Britney Spears or whoever else is hot at the moment.

That was precisely the case in the summer of 2002 when Tom Cruise's publicity machine went to work to promote the Steven Spielberg film *Minority Report*. Within weeks, Cruise appeared on the covers of *Esquire, Premiere, Entertainment Weekly*, and *Time*. While editors grumbled about "overkill," Pat Kingsley, the chief executive of his public relations agency, PMK/HBH, said, "He's only out there when he has a movie to promote, which is about once a year."[10]

No matter. The Spielberg-Cruise movie broke the magical $100 million box-office barrier three weeks after it opened.

Indeed, modern-day press agents have become so powerful that some publications derisively label such public relations practitioners "flacks." Say what they will, in the 21st century, at least in the area of entertainment publicity, it is the public relations publicist—in the best tradition of P. T. Barnum—who holds all the cards.

columns. Barnum also staged bizarre events, such as the legal marriage of the fat lady to the thin man, to drum up free newspaper exposure. And although today's practitioners scoff at Barnum's methods, some press agents still practice his techniques. Nonetheless, when today's public relations professionals bemoan the specter of shysters and hucksters that still overhangs their field, they inevitably place the blame squarely on the fertile mind and silver tongue of P. T. Barnum.

Emergence of the Robber Barons

The American Industrial Revolution ushered in many things at the turn of the century, not the least of which was the growth of public relations. The 20th century began with small mills and shops, which served as the hub of the frontier economy, giving way to massive factories. Country hamlets, which had been the centers of commerce and trade, were replaced by sprawling cities. Limited transportation and communications facilities became nationwide railroad lines and communications wires. Big business took over, and the businessman was king.

The men who ran America's industries seemed more concerned with making a profit than with improving the lot of their fellow citizens. Railroad owners such as William Vanderbilt, bankers such as J. P. Morgan, oil magnates such as John D. Rockefeller, and steel impresarios such as Henry Clay Frick ruled the fortunes of thousands of others. Typical of the reputation acquired by this group of industrialists was the famous—and perhaps apocryphal—response of Vanderbilt when questioned about the public's reaction to his closing of the New York Central Railroad: "The public be damned!"

Little wonder that Americans cursed Vanderbilt and his ilk as robber barons who cared little for the rest of society. Although most who depended on these industrialists for their livelihood felt powerless to rebel, the seeds of discontent were being sown liberally throughout the culture. It was just a matter of time before the robber barons got their comeuppance.

Enter the Muckrakers

When the ax fell on the robber barons, it came in the form of criticism from a feisty group of journalists dubbed "muckrakers." The "muck" that these reporters and editors "raked" was dredged from the scandalous operations of America's business enterprises. Upton Sinclair's novel *The Jungle* attacked the deplorable conditions of the meatpacking industry. Ida Tarbell's *History of the Standard Oil Company* stripped away the public facade of the nation's leading petroleum firm. Her accusations against Standard Oil Chairman Rockefeller, many of which were grossly untrue, nonetheless stirred up public attention.

Magazines such as *McClure's* struck out systematically at one industry after another. The captains of industry, used to getting their own way and having to answer to no one, were wrenched from their peaceful passivity and rolled out on the public carpet to answer for their sins. Journalistic shock stories soon led to a wave of sentiment for legislative reform.

As journalists and the public became more anxious, the government got more involved. Congress began passing laws telling business leaders what they could and couldn't do. Trust-busting then became the order of the day. Conflicts between employers and employees began to break out, and newly organized labor unions came to the fore. The Socialist and Communist movements began to take off. Ironically, it was "a period when free enterprise reached a peak in American history, and yet at that very climax, the tide of public opinion was swelling up against business freedom, primarily because of the breakdown in communications between the businessman and the public."[11]

For a time, these men of inordinate wealth and power found themselves limited in their ability to defend themselves and their activities against the tidal wave of public condemnation. They simply did not know how to get through to the public effectively. To tell their side of the story, the business barons first tried using the lure of advertising to silence journalistic critics; they tried to buy off critics by paying for ads in their papers. It didn't work. Next, they paid publicity people, or press agents, to present their companies' positions. Often these hired guns painted over the real problems and presented their client's view in the best possible light. The public saw through this approach.

Clearly, another method had to be discovered to get the public to at least consider the business point of view. Business leaders were discovering that a corporation might have capital, labor, and natural resources, yet be doomed to fail if it lacked intelligent management, particularly in the area of influencing public opinion. The best way to influence public opinion, as it turned out, was through honesty and candor. This simple truth was the key to the accomplishments of American history's first successful public relations counselor, Ivy Lee.

Ivy Lee: The Real Father of Modern Public Relations

Ivy Ledbetter Lee was a former Wall Street reporter who plunged into publicity work in 1903. Lee believed in neither Barnum's Public-Be-Fooled approach nor Vanderbilt's Public-Be-Damned philosophy. For Lee, the key to business acceptance and understanding was that The Public Be Informed.

Lee firmly believed that the only way business could answer its critics convincingly was to present its side honestly, accurately, and forcefully.[12] Instead of merely appeasing the public, Lee thought a company should strive to earn public confidence and goodwill. Sometimes this task meant looking further for mutual solutions. At other times, it even meant admitting that the company was wrong. Hired by the anthracite coal industry in 1906, Lee set forth his beliefs in a Declaration of Principles to newspaper editors:

> This is not a secret press bureau. All our work is done in the open. We aim to supply news. This is not an advertising agency; if you think any of our matter ought properly to go to your business office, do not use it. Our matter is accurate. Further details on any subject treated will be supplied promptly, and any editor will be assisted most cheerfully in verifying any statement of fact. . . In brief, our plan is frankly and openly, on behalf of business concerns and public institutions, to supply to the press and public of the United States prompt and accurate information concerning subjects which are of value and interest.

In 1914, John D. Rockefeller Jr., who headed one of the most maligned and misunderstood of America's wealthy families, hired Lee (Figure 2-3). As Lee's biographer Ray

FIGURE 2-3   **Father of public relations.** Ivy Lee. (Courtesy of Seeley G. Mudd Manuscript Library)

Eldon Hiebert has pointed out, Lee did less to change the Rockefellers' policies than to give them a public hearing.[13] For example, when the family was censured scathingly for its role in breaking up a strike at the Rockefeller-owned Colorado Fuel and Iron Company, the family hired a labor relations expert (at Lee's recommendation) to determine the causes of an incident that had led to several deaths. The result of this effort was the formation of a joint labor–management board to mediate all workers' grievances on wages, hours, and working conditions. Years later, Rockefeller admitted that the public relations outcome of the Colorado strike "was one of the most important things that ever happened to the Rockefeller family."[14]

In working for the Rockefellers, Lee tried to "humanize" them, to feature them in real-life situations such as playing golf, attending church, and celebrating birthdays. Simply, Lee's goal was to present the Rockefellers in terms that every individual could understand and appreciate. Years later, despite their critics, the family came to be known as the nation's finest example of philanthropy. Indeed, today's billionaires, from Bill Gates to Warren Buffet to Ted Turner, have attempted to emulate the Rockefellers in terms of generosity.

Ironically, even Ivy Lee could not escape the glare of public criticism. In the late 1920s, Lee was asked to serve as adviser to the parent company of the German Dye Trust, which, as it turned out, was an agent for the policies of Adolf Hitler. When Lee realized the nature of Hitler's intentions, he advised the Dye Trust cartel to work to alter Hitler's ill-conceived policies of restricting religious and press freedom. For his involvement with the Dye Trust, Lee was branded a traitor and dubbed "Poison Ivy" by members of Congress investigating un-American activities. The smears against him in the press rivaled the most vicious ones against the robber barons.[15]

Despite his unfortunate involvement with the Dye Trust, Ivy Lee is recognized as the individual who brought honesty and candor to public relations. Although some may debate whether Lee should be considered "the father of public relations," few question his contribution to the field.

Ivy Lee, more than anyone before him, transformed the field from a questionable pursuit (i.e., seeking positive publicity at any cost) into a professional discipline designed to win public confidence and trust through communications based on openness and truth.

The Growth of Modern Public Relations

Ivy Lee helped to open the gates. After he established the idea that high-powered companies and individuals have a responsibility to inform their publics, the practice began to grow in every sector of American society.

Government

During World War I, President Woodrow Wilson established the Creel Committee, under journalist George Creel. Creel's group, composed of the nation's leading journalists, scholars, press agents, and other assorted press celebrities, mounted an impressive effort to mobilize public opinion in support of the war effort and to stimulate the sale of war bonds through Liberty Loan publicity drives. Not only did the war effort get a boost but also so did the field of public relations. The nation was mightily impressed with the potential power of publicity as a weapon to encourage national sentiment and support.

During World War II, the public relations field received an even bigger boost. With the Creel Committee as its precursor, the Office of War Information (OWI) was established to convey the message of the United States at home and abroad. Under the directorship of Elmer Davis, a veteran journalist, the OWI laid the foundations for the U.S. Information Agency as America's voice around the world.

World War II also saw a flurry of activity to sell war bonds, boost the morale of those at home, spur production in the nation's factories and offices, and, in general, support America's war effort as intensively as possible. By virtually every measure, this full-court public relations offensive was an unquestioned success.

The proliferation of public relations officers in World War II led to a growth in the number of practitioners during the peace that followed. One reason companies saw the need to have public relations professionals to "speak up" for them was the more combative attitude of President Harry Truman toward many of the country's largest institutions. For example, in a memorable address over radio and television on April 8, 1952, President Truman announced that, as a result of a union wage dispute, "the government would take over the steel plants." The seizure of the steel mills touched off a series of historic events that reached into Congress and the Supreme Court and stimulated a massive public relations campaign, the likes of which had rarely been seen outside the government.

Counseling

The nation's first public relations firm, the Publicity Bureau, was founded in Boston in 1900 and specialized in general press agentry. The first Washington, D.C., agency was begun in 1902 by William Wolff Smith, a former correspondent for the *New York Sun* and the *Cincinnati Inquirer*. Two years later, Ivy Lee joined with a partner to begin his own counseling firm.

The most significant counselor this side of Ivy Lee was Edward L. Bernays, who began as a publicist in 1913. He was the nephew of Sigmund Freud and author of the landmark book *Crystallizing Public Opinion* (see interview at the end of this chapter).

Bernays was a giant in the public relations field for nearly the entire century. In addition to contributing as much to the field as any other professional in its history, Bernays was a true public relations scholar. He taught the first course in public relations in 1923 and was also responsible for "recruiting" the field's first distinguished female practitioner, his wife Doris E. Fleischman.

Fleischman, former editor of the *New York Tribune*, was a skilled writer, and her husband was a skilled strategist and promoter. Together they built Edward L. Bernays, Counsel on Public Relations into a top agency. In many ways, Fleischman was the "mother" of public relations, paving the way for a field that is today dominated by talented women (Figure 2-4).

Bernays's seminal writings in the field were among the first to disassociate public relations from press agentry or publicity work. As Bernays wrote later:

> At first we called our activity "publicity direction." We intended to give advice to clients on how to direct their actions to get public visibility for them. But within a year we changed the service and its name to "counsel on public relations." We recognized that all actions of a client that impinged on the public needed counsel. Public visibility of a client for one action might be vitiated by another action not in the public interest.[16]

Historian Eric Goldman credited Bernays with "[moving] along with the most advanced trends in the public relations field, thinking with, around, and ahead of them."[17]

After Bernays's pioneering counseling efforts, a number of public relations firms, most headquartered in New York, began to take root, most notably among them Hill & Knowlton, Carl Byoir & Associates, Newsom & Company, and Burson-Marsteller. One of

FIGURE 2-4 **Dynamic duo.** Edward L. Bernays and his wife, Doris Fleischman, were perhaps history's greatest public relations tandem. (Courtesy of the Museum of Public Relations www.prmuseum.com)

the earliest African American counselors was D. Parke Gibson, who authored two books on African American consumerism and advised companies on multicultural relations.

For many years, Hill & Knowlton and Burson-Marsteller jockeyed for leadership in the counseling industry. One early counselor, Harold Burson, emphasized marketing-oriented public relations, "primarily concerned with helping clients sell their goods and services, maintain a favorable market for their stock, and foster harmonious relations with employees."[18] Burson was named at the end of the past millennium as "the most influential PR person of the 20th century."[19]

In the 1990s, the counseling business saw the emergence of international super-agencies, many of which were merged into advertising agencies. Indeed, both Hill & Knowlton and Burson-Marsteller were eventually merged under one corporation, WPP, which also includes the J. Walter Thompson and Young & Rubican advertising agencies.

In the 21st century, the public relations counseling business boasts a diverse mix of huge national agencies, medium-sized regional firms, and one-person local operations. Public relations agencies may be general in nature or specialists in everything from sports to celebrities to health care to online communications.

As one counseling pioneer put it:

It has been quite remarkable to see the dramatic growth of public relations firms in recent years. I believe that will continue. Specialist firms in technology, investor relations, health, and government relations will continue to play an important role. And, of course, there always will be strong local and regional firms.[20]

Corporations

Problems in the perception of corporations and their leaders dissipated in the United States after World War II. Opinion polls of that period ranked business as high in public esteem. People were back at work, and business was back in style.

Smart companies—General Electric, General Motors, and American Telephone & Telegraph (AT&T), for example—worked hard to preserve their good names through both words and actions. Arthur W. Page became AT&T's first public relations vice president in 1927. Page was a pacesetter, helping to maintain AT&T's reputation as a prudent and proper corporate citizen. Page also was one of the few public relations executives to serve on prestigious corporate boards of directors, including Chase Manhattan Bank, Kennecott Copper, Prudential Insurance, and Westinghouse Electric.[21]

Page's five principles of successful corporate public relations are as relevant now as they were in the 1930s:

1. To make sure management thoughtfully analyzes its overall relation to the public
2. To create a system for informing all employees about the firm's general policies and practices
3. To create a system giving contact employees (those having direct dealings with the public) the knowledge needed to be reasonable and polite to the public
4. To create a system drawing employee and public questions and criticism back up through the organization to management
5. To ensure frankness in telling the public about the company's actions.[22]

Paul Garrett was another person who felt the need to be responsive to the public's wishes. A former news reporter, he became the first director of public relations for mighty General Motors in 1931, working directly for GM's legendary CEO Alfred Sloan. Garrett once reportedly explained that the essence of his job was to convince the public that the powerful auto company deserved trust, that is, "to make a billion-dollar company seem small." Ironically, as good as Garrett was, he still suffered from the universal public relations complaint of "never feeling like an insider" within his organization.[23]

Today, as the nation and the world recover from an era of excess and corporations work to regain the public trust, megacompanies from Microsoft to General Electric and from Mitsubishi to DaimlerChrysler depend on public relations advice to interpret their purposes and actions to the public.

Public Relations Comes of Age

As noted, public relations came of age largely as a result of the confluence of five general factors in our society:

1. The growth of large institutions and their sense of responsibility to the public
2. The increased changes, conflicts, and confrontations among interest groups in society
3. The heightened awareness of people brought about by increasingly sophisticated communications technology everywhere
4. The growing power of public opinion and the spread of global democracy
5. The growth of the Internet and World Wide Web

Growth of Large Institutions

Ironically, the public relations profession received perhaps its most important thrust when business confidence suffered its most severe setback. The economic and social upheaval caused by the Great Depression of the 1930s provided the impetus for corporations to seek public support by telling their stories. Public relations departments sprang up in scores of major companies, among them Bendix, Borden, Eastman Kodak,

Watergate: A Black Eye for Public Relations

On August 8, 1974, President Richard M. Nixon resigned in disgrace and humiliation. His administration had been tarnished by illegal wiretapping, illegal surveillance, burglary, and unlawful use of the law. The president and his men were toppled by the most profound political scandal in the nation's history, which started with a break-in at the Democratic national headquarters in a Washington, D.C., apartment building named Watergate.

Nixon and his advisers steadfastly refused, throughout the long, arduous, and publicly televised Watergate crisis, to acknowledge any role in the break-in.

President Nixon's response, in particular, was bizarre in its obstinacy.

- He ordered preparation of an "Enemies List" of journalists who had written negatively about Watergate.
- He discussed lying about the reasons for the Watergate break-in and another break-in at the office of Daniel Ellsberg's psychiatrist in an attempt to find information to discredit Ellsberg, an administration enemy who had leaked secret Pentagon papers to the *New York Times*.
- He decided to fire Archibald Cox, the special prosecutor appointed to get to the bottom of Watergate (Figure 2-5).
- Attorney General Elliott Richardson refused to carry out Nixon's order to fire Cox, and he, himself, resigned. And Richardson's deputy, William Ruckelshaus, also refused to carry out the order, and Nixon fired him.

Ultimately, as a nation painfully watched on in horror, Nixon's aides appeared at a televised Senate hearing and finally admitted to their role in the break-ins and their subsequent efforts to "cover up."

Nixon's resignation was unprecedented in the nation's history. And many blamed his downfall on one thing: an overriding concern about public relations. Observers argued that the president and his advisers were so consumed with covering up the facts—with public relations—that they orchestrated their own downfall.

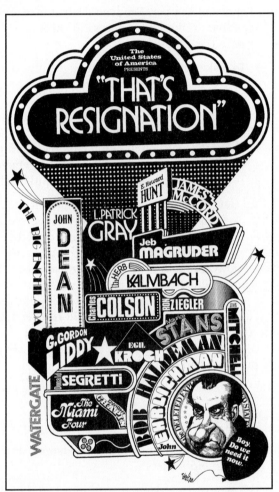

FIGURE 2-5 **Tragicomedy.** Watergate's dubious cast of characters inspired this takeoff on the promotional work done for the movie *That's Entertainment*.

In point of fact, what Nixon and his henchmen wrought was the exact opposite of proper public relations. As we have noted, public relations is neither distortion nor obfuscation nor cover-up but, rather, the communication of truth.

Nonetheless, no event in recent history has given the practice of public relations a blacker eye than Watergate.

Eli Lilly, Ford, General Motors, Standard Oil, and U.S. Steel. The role that public relations played in helping regain post-Depression public trust in big business helped project the field into the relatively strong position it enjoyed during World War II.

The Truman years marked a challenging period for public relations, with government questioning the integrity of large business corporations. The ebbing and flowing conflict between government and business is unique to America. In other nations—Japan and Germany most prominently—government and business work more in concert to achieve common goals. In the United States, many businesses, both large and small, complain that government overregulation frustrates their ability to prosper. Businesses of every size have recognized that aggressively communicating corporate products and positions can help win public receptivity and support and ward off government intrusion.

Change, Conflict, and Confrontation

Disenchantment with big institutions peaked in the 1960s. The conflicts during the early part of the decade between private economic institutions—especially large corporations—and various disenfranchised elements of society arose from long-standing grievances. As one commentator put it: "Their rebellion was born out of the desperation of those who had nothing to lose. Issues were seen as black or white, groups as villainous or virtuous, causes as holy or satanic, and leaders as saints or charlatans."[24]

The social and political upheavals of the 1960s dramatically affected many areas, including the practice of public relations. The Vietnam War fractured society. Ralph Nader began to look pointedly at the inadequacies of the automobile industry. Women, long denied equal rights in the workplace and elsewhere, began to mobilize into activist groups such as the National Organization for Women (NOW). Environmentalists, worried about threats to the land and water by business expansion, began to support groups such as the Sierra Club. Minorities, particularly blacks and Hispanics, began to petition and protest for their rights. Homosexuals, AIDS activists, senior citizens, birth control advocates, and social activists of every kind began to challenge the legitimacy of large institutions. Not since the days of the robber barons had large institutions so desperately needed professional communications help.

Heightened Public Awareness

The 1970s and 1980s brought a partial resolution of these problems. Many of the solutions came from the government in the form of affirmative action guidelines, senior citizen programs, consumer and environmental protection acts and agencies, aids to education, and myriad other laws and statutes.

Business began to contribute to charities. Managers began to consider community relations a first-line responsibility. The general policy of corporations confronting their adversaries was abandoned. In its place, most large companies adopted a policy of conciliation and compromise.

This new policy of social responsibility continued into the 1990s. Corporations came to realize that their reputations are a valuable asset to be protected, conserved, defended, nurtured, and enhanced at all times. In truth, institutions in the 1990s had little choice but to get along with their publics. The general prosperity of the 1990s, fueled by the enormous stock market ascension, helped convey goodwill between organizations and their publics.

By the new century, the vast majority of American homes had television, with millions wired for cable and another 146 million online. As a result of all this communication, publics have become much more segmented, specialized, and sophisticated.

With the stock market pullback of the early 21st century and the public less trusting of institutions in terms of their motives and intentions, organizations face the new reality of communicating with their key publics instantaneously in real time, all the time—in a manner that is believable and trustworthy. Optimizing communications in this environment is a daunting public relations challenge.

Growing Power of Public Opinion and Global Democracy

In the 21st century, the United Nations has reported that two-thirds of the world's people in 140 nations live under some form of democratic government. With a few glaring repressive exceptions, democracy is virtually everywhere.

- The Berlin Wall's destruction was transmitted live around the world. So was the dissolution of the Union of Soviet Socialist Republics.
- In 1993, two longtime archenemies, Nelson Mandela and Frederik Willem DeKlerck, stood together to share the Nobel Peace Prize as free elections were held in South Africa and a black former prisoner of the state became president.
- By the year 2000, the defeat and imprisonment of Slobodan Milosevic in the Balkans allowed the people of Yugoslavia to experience freedom.
- In 2002, the vanquishing in Afghanistan of the repressive Taliban regime, supported by the terrorist Al Queda network, allowed that poor country, too, to begin to experience democratic institutions.
- And in 2003, the defeat of Saddam Hussein signaled the potential for a democratic Iraq.

While problems persist in the Middle East, Africa, and isolated other world hot spots, even in societies slower to pick up the cudgel of democracy, there is change. China celebrates its anniversary by inviting Western business leaders to tour its new economy.

In 2003, in perhaps the most bizarre global media moment of all, Iraq dictator Saddam Hussein sat for a three hour interview with CBS newsman Dan Rather, while the U.S. prepared to attack him.

Today, with the world now truly "safe for democracy," the public relations challenge has grown in intensity.

As discussed in Chapter 3, the best way to deliver public opinion is through mutual understanding and acceptance, built on two-way communication.

Growth of the Internet and the World Wide Web

In the 21st century, true two-way communication has arrived largely as a result of the growth of online access. Not only have cable, satellite, mobile phones, pagers, faxes, bar code scanners, voice mail systems, videodisk technologies, and all the rest revolutionized the information transmission and receiving process but also the emergence of the Internet and the World Wide Web has radically intensified the spread of communications even further.

Beginning during the cold war in 1969 as a U.S. Department of Defense system, the global Internet economy today accounts for more than $800 billion in revenue. More important, with 50 percent of homes in the United States networked and 146 million U.S. online users each month, the Net as a communications medium dwarfs all others.

The impact of the Web on public relations practice has been phenomenal. E-mail dominates internal communications. Journalists now regard the Internet as their second choice of organizational contact—just behind a human source. A new generation of Americans has been weaned and depends on the Internet as its primary source of communication.

In sum, knowledge of and facility with the Internet is no longer an "option" for public relations practitioners. It is a necessity.

Public Relations Education

As the practice of public relations has developed, so too has the growth of public relations education. In 1951, 12 schools offered major programs in public relations. Today well in excess of 200 journalism or communication programs offer concentrated study in public relations, with nearly 300 others offering at least one course dealing with the profession.

In 1999, the Commission on Public Relations Education, chartered by the Public Relations Society of America, recommended a public relations curriculum imparting knowledge in such nontraditional but pivotal areas as relationship building, societal trends, and multicultural and global issues.[25]

Although few data are available on public relations programs in business schools, the number of programs is increasing, especially those related to marketing. As the debate continues about where public relations education should appropriately be housed—either in business or journalism schools—the best answer is that both should offer public relations courses.[26]

In business, the practice of public relations has become an integral part of the way companies operate. Therefore, business students should be exposed to the discipline's underpinnings and practical aspects before they enter the corporate world. In journalism, with more than 70 percent of daily newspaper copy emanating from public relations–generated releases, journalists, too, should know what public relations is all about before they graduate. Wherever it is housed, the profession's role as an academic pursuit has continued to gain strength. This educational dimension has, in turn, contributed to the new respect accorded public relations in modern society.

LAST WORD

Today public relations is big, worldwide business.

- The Public Relations Society of America, organized in 1947, boasts a growing membership of 20,000 in 117 chapters nationwide.
- The Public Relations Student Society of America, formed in 1968 to facilitate communications between students interested in the field and public relations professionals, has 6,500 student members at 220 colleges and universities.
- The International Association of Business Communicators boasts 13,500 members in more than 58 countries.
- More than 5,300 U.S. companies have public relations departments.
- More than 3,000 public relations agencies exist in the United States. The 13 largest list annual fees in the hundreds of millions of dollars.
- More than 2,000 trade associations have public relations departments.
- Top communications executives at major companies and agencies draw six-figure salaries.

The scope of modern public relations practice is vast. Press relations, Web relations, employee communications, public relations counseling and research, local community relations, audiovisual communications, contributions, interactive public relations, and numerous other diverse activities fall under the public relations umbrella. Because of this broad range of functions, many public relations practitioners today seem preoccupied with the proper title for their calling: public relations, external affairs, corporate communications, public affairs, corporate relations, ad infinitum.

Practitioners worry that as public relations becomes more prominent, its function and those who purportedly practice it will be subject to increasingly intense public scrutiny. There are more ardent calls for licensing of practitioners, echoing the sentiment of the late public relations pioneer Edward Bernays, in the "Tips from the Top" interview at the end of this chapter. Professionalism, argue the people who guard the reputation of the practice, is all important. This is not unrelated to the high-profile ethical scandals that have rocked society in recent years—from the sex scandals of the Catholic Church to the political scandals of former Republican Speaker of the House Newt Gingrich and former Demcratic President Bill Clinton to the corporate scandals of Enron, WorldCom, Tyco, and others.

Such ethical transgressions have cast a pall over those in power and, by extension, the practice of public relations.

Indeed, there is no more important characteristic for public relations people to emulate than high ethical character and standards. The field's finest ethical moment occurred when the Johnson & Johnson Company, in the wake of unspeakable tragedy brought about by its lead product Tylenol, didn't hesitate to choose the ethical course. J&J removed its product from circulation not once but twice, both times to preserve its reputation. As the case study at the conclusion of this chapter suggests, the handling of the Tylenol tragedy was public relations' most shining hour.

Then, too, of course, there is the danger that too many uninformed individuals will equate public relations with "spin"—with defending the point of view of the client, whether right or wrong, honest or dishonest, truthful or untruthful. Again, proper, practical, and ethical public relations is not spin. Public relations essentially is about communicating truth, not lies.

Despite these concerns, the practice of public relations in the 21st century stands as a potent, persuasive force in society. Clearly, the public relations field today—whatever it is called and by whomever it is practiced—is in the spotlight. Its senior-most officers serve as members of the management committees that set policy for our great organizations.[27] Its professionals command higher salaries. Its counselors command increased respect. Its practice is taught in increasing numbers, not only in American colleges and universities but around the world.

With 200,000 men and women in the United States alone practicing public relations in some form and thousands of practitioners overseas, the field has become solidly entrenched as an important, influential, and professional component of our society.

Discussion Starters

1. What societal factors have influenced the spread of public relations?
2. Why do public relations professionals think of P. T. Barnum as a mixed blessing?
3. What is the significance to the practice of public relations of American revolutionary hero Samuel Adams?
4. What did the robber barons and muckrakers have to do with the development of public relations?

5. Why are Ivy Lee and Edward Bernays considered two of the fathers of public relations?
6. What impact did the Creel Committee and the Office of War Information have on the development of public relations?
7. What was the significance of Arthur Page to the development of corporate public relations?
8. What did the Legacy of Watergate mean to the practice of public relations?
9. What are some of the yardsticks that indicated that public relations had "arrived" in the latter stages of the 20th century?
10. What are some of the issues that confront public relations in the 21st century?

TOP OF THE SHELF

Larry Tye

The Father of Spin: Edward L. Bernays and the Birth of Public Relations
New York: Henry Holt and Company, 2001

The author's background as a *Boston Globe* journalist, rather than a public relations practitioner or professor, both limits the depth of this biography and offers the refreshing viewpoint of an "outsider."

Tye uses Bernays's life "as a prism to understand the evolution of the craft of public relations and how it came to play such a critical—and sometimes insidious—role in American life." Granted a Nieman Fellowship at Harvard University to write this book, Tye waded into 800 boxes of personal and professional papers Bernays left the Library of Congress, papers that detail cases he worked on and tactics and strategies he employed over a career that spanned eight decades.

Enjoyable, enlightening reading, bolstered by a seven-page bibliography. After four printings in hard cover, *The Father of Spin* is now in paperback.

CASE STUDY

The Tylenol Murders

Arguably, the two most important cases in the history of the practice of public relations occurred within four years of each other to the same company and product.

For close to 100 years, Johnson & Johnson Company of New Brunswick, New Jersey, was the epitome of a well-managed, highly profitable, and tight-lipped consumer products manufacturer.

Round I

That image changed on the morning of September 30, 1982, when Johnson & Johnson faced as devastating a public relations problem as had confronted any company in history.

That morning, Johnson & Johnson's management learned that its premier product, extra-strength Tylenol, had been used as a murder weapon to kill three people. In the days that followed, another three people died from swallowing Tylenol capsules loaded with cyanide. Although all the cyanide deaths occurred in Chicago, reports from other parts of the country also implicated extra-strength Tylenol capsules in illnesses of various sorts. These latter reports were later proved to be unfounded, but Johnson & Johnson and its Tylenol-producing subsidiary, McNeil Consumer Products Company, found themselves at the center of a public relations trauma the likes of which few companies had ever experienced.

Tylenol had been an astoundingly profitable product for Johnson & Johnson. At the time of the Tylenol murders, the product held 35 percent of the $1 billion analgesic market. It contributed an estimated 7 percent to the company's worldwide sales and almost 20 percent to its profits. Throughout the years, Johnson & Johnson had not been—and hadn't needed to be—a particularly high-profile company. Its chairman, James E. Burke, who had been with the company for almost 30 years, had never appeared on television and had rarely participated in print interviews.

Johnson & Johnson's management, understandably, was caught totally by surprise when the news hit. Initially, they had no facts and, indeed, got much of their information from the media calls that inundated the firm from the beginning. The company recognized that it needed the media to get out as much information to the public as quickly as possible to prevent a panic. Therefore, almost immediately, Johnson & Johnson made a key decision: to open its doors to the media.

On the second day of the crisis, Johnson & Johnson discovered that an earlier statement that no cyanide was used on its premises was wrong. The company didn't hesitate. Its public relations department quickly announced that the earlier information had been false. Even though the reversal embarrassed the company briefly, Johnson & Johnson's openness was hailed and made up for any damage to its credibility.

Early on in the crisis, the company was largely convinced that the poisonings had not occurred at any of its plants. Nonetheless, Johnson & Johnson recalled an entire lot of 93,000 bottles of extra-strength Tylenol associated with the reported murders. In the process, it telegrammed warnings to doctors, hospitals, and distributors, at a cost of half a million dollars. McNeil also suspended all Tylenol advertising to reduce attention to the product.

By the second day, the company was convinced that the tampering had taken place during the product's Chicago distribution and not in the manufacturing process. Therefore, a total Tylenol recall did not seem obligatory. Chairman Burke himself leaned toward immediately recalling all extra-strength Tylenol capsules, but after consulting with the Federal Bureau of Investigation, he decided not to do so. The FBI was worried that a precipitous recall would encourage copycat poisoning attempts. Nonetheless, five days later, when a copycat strychnine poisoning occurred in California, Johnson & Johnson did recall all extra-strength Tylenol capsules—31 million bottles—at a cost of more than $100 million.

Although the company knew it had done nothing wrong, Johnson & Johnson resisted the temptation to disclaim any possible connection between its product and the murders. Rather, while moving quickly to trace the lot numbers of the poisoned packages, it also posted a $100,000 reward for the killer. Through advertisements promising to exchange capsules for tablets, through thousands of letters to the trade, and through statements to the media, the company hoped to put the incident into proper perspective.

At the same time, Johnson & Johnson commissioned a nationwide opinion survey to assess the consumer implications of the Tylenol poisonings. The good news was that 87 percent of Tylenol users surveyed said they realized that the maker of Tylenol was not responsible for the deaths. The bad news was that 61 percent still said they were not likely to buy extra-strength Tylenol capsules in the future. In other words, even though most consumers knew the deaths weren't Tylenol's fault, they still feared using the product.

But Chairman Burke and Johnson & Johnson weren't about to knuckle under to the deranged saboteur or saboteurs who had poisoned their product. Despite predictions of the imminent demise of extra-strength Tylenol, Johnson & Johnson decided to relaunch the product in a new triple-safety-sealed, tamper-resistant package (Figure 2-6). Many

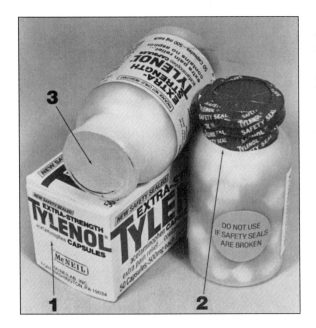

FIGURE 2-6 The triple-safety-sealed, tamper-resistant package for Tylenol capsules had (1) glued flaps on the outer box, (2) a tight plastic neck seal, and (3) a strong inner foil seal over the mouth of the bottle. A bright yellow label on the bottle was imprinted with a red warning: "Do not use if safety seals are broken." As it turned out, all these precautions didn't work.

on Wall Street and in the marketing community were stunned by Johnson & Johnson's bold decision.

So confident was Johnson & Johnson's management that it launched an all-out media blitz to make sure that people understood its commitment. Chairman Burke appeared on the widely watched Phil Donahue network television program and skillfully handled one hour of intense public questioning.

Johnson & Johnson invited the investigative news program *60 Minutes*—the scourge of corporate America—to film its executive strategy sessions to prepare for the new launch. When the program was aired, reporter Mike Wallace concluded that although Wall Street had been ready at first to write off the company, it was now "hedging its bets because of Johnson & Johnson's stunning campaign of facts, money, the media, and truth."

Finally, on November 11, 1982, less than two months after the murders, Johnson & Johnson's management held an elaborate video press conference in New York City, beamed to additional locations around the country, to introduce the new extra-strength Tylenol package. Said the chairman to the media:

> It is our job at Johnson & Johnson to ensure the survival of Tylenol, and we are pledged to do this. While we consider this crime an assault on society, we are nevertheless ready to fulfill our responsibility, which includes paying the price of this heinous crime. But I urge you not to make Tylenol the scapegoat.

In the days and months that followed Burke's news conference, it became clear that Tylenol would not become a scapegoat. In fact, by the beginning of 1983, Tylenol had recaptured an astounding 95 percent of its prior market share. Morale at the company, according to its chairman, was "higher than in years" (Figure 2-7). The euphoria lasted until February 1986, when, unbelievably, tragedy struck again.

Round II

Late in the evening of February 10, 1986, news reports began to circulate that a woman had died in Yonkers, New York, after taking poisoned capsules of extra-strength Tylenol.

The nightmare for Johnson & Johnson began anew.

OUR CREDO

We believe our first responsibility is to the doctors, nurses and patients,
to mothers and fathers and all others who use our products and services.
In meeting their needs everything we do must be of high quality.
We must constantly strive to reduce our costs
in order to maintain reasonable prices.
Customers' orders must be serviced promptly and accurately.
Our suppliers and distributors must have an opportunity
to make a fair profit.

We are responsible to our employees,
the men and women who work with us throughout the world.
Everyone must be considered as an individual.
We must respect their dignity and recognize their merit.
They must have a sense of security in their jobs.
Compensation must be fair and adequate,
and working conditions clean, orderly and safe.
We must be mindful of ways to help our employees fulfill
their family responsibilities.
Employees must feel free to make suggestions and complaints.
There must be equal opportunity for employment, development
and advancement for those qualified.
We must provide competent management,
and their actions must be just and ethical.

We are responsible to the communities in which we live and work
and to the world community as well.
We must be good citizens — support good works and charities
and bear our fair share of taxes.
We must encourage civic improvements and better health and education.
We must maintain in good order
the property we are privileged to use,
protecting the environment and natural resources.

Our final responsibility is to our stockholders.
Business must make a sound profit.
We must experiment with new ideas.
Research must be carried on, innovative programs developed
and mistakes paid for.
New equipment must be purchased, new facilities provided
and new products launched.
Reserves must be created to provide for adverse times.
When we operate according to these principles,
the stockholders should realize a fair return.

Johnson & Johnson

FIGURE 2-7   The Johnson & Johnson credo.

Once again, the company sprang into action. Chairman Burke addressed reporters
at a news conference a day after the incident. A phone survey found that the public
didn't blame the company. However, with the discovery of other poisoned Tylenol capsules two days later, the nightmare intensified. The company recorded 15,000 toll-free
calls at its Tylenol hot line. Once again, production of Tylenol capsules was halted.
"I'm heartsick," Burke told the press. "We didn't believe it could happen again, and
nobody else did either."

A special message from the makers of TYLENOL® products.

If you have TYLENOL capsules, we'll replace them with TYLENOL caplets.

And we'll do it at our expense.

As you know, there has been a tragic event. A small number of Extra-Strength TYLENOL® Capsules in one isolated area in New York have been criminally tampered with.

This was an outrageous act which damages all of us.

Both federal and local authorities have established that it was only capsules that were tampered with.

In order to prevent any further capsule tampering, we have removed all our capsules from your retailers' shelves. This includes Regular and Extra-Strength TYLENOL® capsules, CO-TYLENOL® capsules, Maximum-Strength TYLENOL® Sinus Medication capsules, Extra-Strength SINE-AID® capsules, and DIMENSYN® Menstrual Relief capsules.

And Johnson & Johnson's McNeil Consumer Products Company has decided to cease the manufacture, sale, and distribution of **all** capsule forms of over-the-counter medicines.

If you're a regular capsule user, you may be wondering what to use instead. That's why we'd like you to try TYLENOL caplets.

The caplet is a solid form of TYLENOL pain reliever, which research has proven is the form most preferred by consumers. Unlike tablets, it is specially shaped and coated for easy, comfortable swallowing.

And the caplet delivers a full extra-strength dose quickly and effectively.

So, if you have any TYLENOL Capsules in your home, do one of the following:

1. Return the bottles with the unused portion to us, together with your name and address on the form below. And we'll replace your TYLENOL capsules with TYLENOL Caplets (or tablets, if you prefer). We'll also refund your postage. Or...

2. If you prefer, you can receive a cash refund for the unused capsules by sending the bottle to us along with a letter requesting the refund.

We are taking this step because, for the past 25 years, over 100 million Americans have made TYLENOL products a trusted part of their health care.

We're continuing to do everything we can to keep your trust.

Send to:
TYLENOL® Capsule Exchange
P.O. Box 2000
Maple Plain, MN 55348

Please send my coupon for free replacement caplets or tablets to:

Please print

Name _____

Address _____

City _____

State _____ Zip _____

Offer expires May 1, 1986

(Courtesy of Johnson & Johnson)

FIGURE 2-8   **A special message.**

This time, although Tylenol earned some 13 percent of the company's net profits, the firm decided once and for all to cease production of its over-the-counter medications in capsule form. It offered to replace all unused Tylenol capsules with new Tylenol caplets, a solid form of medication that was less tamper-prone (Figure 2-8). This time the withdrawal of its capsules cost Johnson & Johnson more than $150 million after taxes.

Once again, in the face of tragedy, the company and its chairman received high marks. As President Reagan said at a White House reception two weeks after the crisis hit, "Jim Burke of Johnson & Johnson, you have our deepest appreciation for living up to the highest ideals of corporate responsibility and grace under pressure."

Questions

1. What might have been the consequences if Johnson & Johnson had decided to "tough out" the first reports of Tylenol-related deaths and not recall the product?
2. What other public relations options did Johnson & Johnson have in responding to the first round of Tylenol murders?
3. Do you think the company made a wise decision by reintroducing extra-strength Tylenol?
4. In light of the response of other companies not to move precipitously when faced with a crisis, do you think Johnson & Johnson should have acted so quickly to remove the Tylenol product when the second round of Tylenol murders occurred in 1986?
5. What specific lessons can be derived from the way in which Johnson & Johnson handled the public relations aspects of these tragedies?
6. What was the media environment when the Tylenol crises occurred? How might the results have differed if the crises occurred today?
7. See what information Johnson & Johnson offers for its customers on the Tylenol Web site (www.tylenol.com). Follow the links to the "Care Cards," "House Calls," and "FAQ" sections. How do these sections demonstrate Johnson & Johnson's concern for customers? How do you think Johnson & Johnson would use this Web site to communicate with the public if new health scares surfaced?

For further information on the first round of Tylenol murders, see Jerry Knight, "Tylenol's Maker Shows How to Respond to Crisis," *Washington Post* (October 11, 1982): 1; Thomas Moore, "The Fight to Save Tylenol," *Fortune* (November 29, 1982): 48; Michael Waldholz, "Tylenol Regains Most of No. 1 Market Share, Amazing Doomsayers," *Wall Street Journal* (December 24, 1982): 1, 19; and *60 Minutes*, CBS-TV (December 19, 1982).

For further information on the second round of Tylenol murders, see Irvin Molotsky, "Tylenol Maker Hopeful on Solving Poisoning Case," *New York Times* (February 20, 1986); Steven Prokesch, "A Leader in a Crisis," *New York Times* (February 19, 1986): B4; Michael Waldholz, "For Tylenol's Manufacturer, the Dilemma Is to Be Aggressive—But Not Appear Pushy," *Wall Street Journal* (February 20, 1986): 27; and "Tylenol II: How a Company Responds to a Calamity," *U.S. News & World Report* (February 24, 1986): 49.

For an overall view of Johnson & Johnson and Tylenol, see Lawrence G. Foster, *Robert Wood Johnson: The Gentleman Rebel*. State College, PA: Lillian Press, 1999.

TIPS FROM THE TOP

An Interview with Edward L. Bernays

The late Edward Bernays

Edward L. Bernays, who died in 1995 at the age of 103, was a public relations patriarch. A nephew of Sigmund Freud, Bernays pioneered the application of the social sciences to public relations. In partnership with his late wife, he advised presidents of the United States, industrial leaders, and legendary figures from Enrico Caruso to Eleanor Roosevelt. This interview was conducted with the legendary counselor in his 98th year.

When you taught the first public relations class, did you ever envision the field growing to its present stature?

I gave the first course in public relations after *Crystallizing Public Opinion* was published in 1923. I decided that one way to give the term "counsel on public relations" status was to lecture at a university on the principles, practices, and ethics of the new vocation. New York University was willing to accept my offer to do so. But I never envisioned at that time that the vocation would spread throughout the United States and then throughout the free world.

What were the objectives of that first public relations course?

The objectives were to give status to the new vocation. Many people still believed the term "counsel on public relations" was a euphemism for publicity man, press agent, flack. Even H. L. Mencken, in his book on the American language, ranked it as such. But in his *Supplement to the American Language,* published some years later, he changed his viewpoint and used my definition of the term.

What are the most significant factors that have led to the rise in public relations practice?

The most significant factor is the rise in people power and its recognition by leaders. Theodore Roosevelt helped bring this about with his Square Deal.

Woodrow Wilson helped with his New Freedom, and so did Franklin Delano Roosevelt with his New Deal. And this tradition was continued as time went on.

Do you have any gripes with the way public relations is practiced today?

I certainly do. The meanings of words in the United States have the stability of soap bubbles. Unless words are defined as to their meaning by law, as in the case of professions—for instance, law, medicine, architecture—they are in the public domain. Anyone can use them. Recently, I received a letter from a model agency offering to supply me with a "public relations representative" for my next trade fair at which we might exhibit our client's products. Today, any plumber or car salesman or unethical character can call himself or herself a public relations practitioner. Many who call themselves public relations practitioners have no education, training, or knowledge of what the field is. And the public equally has little understanding of the meaning of the two words. Until licensing and registration are introduced, this will continue to be the situation.

What pleases you most about current public relations practice?

What pleases me most is that there are, indeed, practitioners who regard their activity as a profession, an art applied to a science, in which the public interest, and not pecuniary motivation, is the primary consideration; and also that outstanding leaders in society are grasping the meaning and significance of the activity.

How would you compare the caliber of today's public relations practitioner with that of the practitioner of the past?

The practitioner today has more education in his subject. But, unfortunately, education for public relations varies with the institution where it is being conducted. This is due to the lack of a standard definition. Many institutions of higher learning think public relations activity consists of skillful writing of press releases and teach their students accordingly. This is, of course, not true. Public relations activity is applied social science to the social attitudes or actions of employers or clients.

(Continued)

Where do you think public relations will be 20 years from now?

It is difficult to appraise where public relations will be 20 years from now. I don't like the tendency of advertising agencies gobbling up large public relations organizations. That is like surgical instrument manufacturers gobbling up surgical medical colleges or law book publishers gobbling up law colleges. However, if licensing and registration take place, then the vocation is assured a long lifetime, as long as democracy's.

Suggested Readings

Baskin, Otis. *The Profession and the Practice of Public Relations*, 4th ed. New York: McGraw-Hill, 1996.

Bernays, Edward L. *Crystallizing Public Opinion*. New York: Liveright, 1961.

Bernays, Edward L. *The Later Years: Public Relations Insights, 1956–1986*. Rhinebeck, NY: H & M, 1987.

Burson, Harold. "A Decent Respect to the Opinion of Mankind." Speech delivered at the Raymond Simon Institute for Public Relations (Burson-Marsteller, 866 Third Avenue, New York, NY 10022), March 5, 1987. This speech highlights public relations activities that have influenced the United States from colonial times to the present day.

Cutlip, Scott M. *Public Relations History from the 17th to the 20th Century*. Hillsdale, NJ: Lawrence Erlbaum Associates, 1995.

Cutlip, Scott M. *The Unseen Power—Public Relations, A History*. Hillsdale, NJ: Lawrence Erlbaum Associates, 1994.

Marchand, Roland. *Creating the Corporate Soul: The Rise of Public Relations and Corporate Imagery in American Big Business*. Berkeley and Los Angeles, CA: University of California Press, 2001.

Merk, Frederick. *Fruits of Propaganda in the Tyler Administration*. Cambridge, MA: Harvard University Press, 1971.

Mitroff, Ian I., and Warren Bennis. *The Unreality Industry: The Deliberate Manufacturing of Falsehood and What It Is Doing to Our Lives*. London, England: Oxford University Press, 1993.

Nevins, Allan. "The Constitution Makers and the Public, 1785–1790." An address before the Conference of the Public Relations Society of America, November 13, 1962. Reprinted as "At the Beginning . . . A Series of Lecture-Essays." Gainesville, FL: The Institute for Public Relations Research and Education, 1997.

Newson, Doug, Judy Van Slyke Turk, and Dean Kruckeberg, 7th ed. Belmont, CA: Wadsworth, 1999.

Ni, Chen, and Hugh Culbertson. *International Public Relations, A Comparative Analysis*. Hillsdale, NJ: Lawrence Erlbaum Associates, 1996.

Public Relations News (1201 Seven Locks Road, Potomac, MD 61130). Weekly.

Public Relations Quarterly (P.O. Box 311, Rhinebeck, NY 12572).

Public Relations Review (10606 Mantz Road, Silver Spring, MD 20903).

PR Reporter (P.O. Box 600, Exeter, NH 03833-0600). Weekly.

Public Relations Strategist (PRSA, 33 Irving Place, New York, NY 10003). Quarterly.

Ries, Al, and Laura Ries. *The Fall of Advertising & The Rise of PR*. New York: HarperBusiness, 2002.

Toth, Elizabeth, and Robert Heath. *Rhetorical and Critical Approaches to Public Relations*. Hillsdale, NJ: Lawrence Erlbaum Associates, 1992.

Notes

1. Laurie Freeman, "From the Basement to the Penthouse," *Advertising Age* (September 25, 2000): 40.
2. Scott M. Cutlip, Allen H. Center, and Glen M. Broom, *Effective Public Relations*, 8th ed. (Upper Saddle River, NJ: Prentice Hall, 2000): 102.
3. James D. Sodt, "Why Would I Represent the Serbs," *The Public Relations Strategist* (Spring 1995): 32.
4. Fraser P. Seitel, "The Company You Keep," odwyerpr.com (July 22, 2002).
5. Paul Swift, "The Antecedents," *Public Relations Quarterly* (Summer 1996): 6.
6. "Boston's Cardinal Law Resists Calls for His Resignation," CNN.com (April 12, 2002).
7. Frank Winston Wylie, "Book Reviews," *Public Relations Review* (Fall 1996): 312.
8. Harold Burson, speech at Utica College of Syracuse University, Utica, NY (March 5, 1987).
9. "Film Writers Complain About PR Pressure," *Jack O'Dwyer's Newsletter*, (November 27, 1996): 3.
10. David Carr, "Enough Tom for You? Covers Lose Allure," *New York Times* (July 15, 2002): D1-4.
11. Ray Eldon Hiebert, *Courtier to the Crowd: The Story of Ivy L. Lee and the Development of Public Relations* (Ames: Iowa State University Press, 1966).
12. Rex Harlow, "A Public Relations Historian Recalls the First Days," *Public Relations Review* (Summer 1981): 39–40.
13. Cited in Sherman Morse, "An Awakening in Wall Street," *American Magazine* 62 (September 1906): 460.
14. Hiebert, *Courtier to the Crowd.*
15. Cited in Alvin Moscow, *The Rockefeller Inheritance* (Garden City, NY: Doubleday, 1977): 23.
16. Edward L. Bernays, "Bernays: 62 Years in Public Relations," *Public Relations Quarterly* (Fall 1981): 8.
17. David L. Luis, "The Outstanding PR Professionals," *Public Relations Journal* (October 1970): 84.
18. Burson, speech at Utica College.
19. "Burson Hailed as PR's No. 1 Influential Figure," *PR Week* (October 18, 1999): 1.
20. Address by Daniel J. Edelman, Arthur Page Society, New Orleans, LA (September 21, 1997).
21. Noel L. Griese, *Arthur W. Page: Publisher, Public Relations Pioneer, Patriot* (Tucker, GA: Anvil Publishers, 2001).
22. Cited in Noel L. Griese, "The Employee Communications Philosophy of Arthur W. Page," *Public Relations Quarterly* (Winter 1977): 8–12.
23. "An Afternoon with Peter Drucker," *The Public Relations Strategist* (Fall 1998): 10.
24. James E. Gringo, "Teaching Public Relations in the Future," *Public Relations Review* (Spring 1989): 16.
25. John L. Paluszek, "Public Relations Students: Today Good, Tomorrow Better," *The Public Relations Strategist* (Winter 2000): 27.
26. J. David Pincus, "Changing How Future Managers View Us," *The Public Relations Strategist* (Spring 1997).
27. Harold Burson, "Introduction: The Maturation of Public Relations," *Journal of Corporate Public Relations–Northwestern University* (1994–1995): 6.

PART II / Preparation/ Process

Chapter 3

Communication

English novelist Edward George Earle Lytton Bulwer-Lytton once wrote, that "The pen is mightier than the sword."[1]

In the 21st century, the power of communication through the oral and written word and the images that flash around the world to millions of people in real time is more awesome than any individual or group or even nation.

Consider the following:

In the summer of 2002, after months of Palestinian extremist homicide bombings in Israel, which took the lives of hundreds of innocent civilians, a ray of hope finally appeared amidst the storm clouds.

The political leader of the extremist Hamas party announced that he would consider ending the bombings and reconvening negotiations with its lifelong enemy, if Israel removed its tanks and troops from the West Bank Arab territories it occupied.

Israel seemed ready to agree when tragedy struck.

In the dead of night, an Israeli F-16 fighter jet dropped a one-ton laser-guided bomb into a densely packed Gaza neighborhood, killing the founder of Hamas, whom Israel blamed for many of the attacks on its country. But the bomb also killed 14 others, including nine children.

And the next day, when media around the world flashed video and a single photo of a funeral procession of Palestinians holding aloft the tiny body of a two-month-old baby killed in the bombing (Figure 3-1), even Israel's friends were repulsed in horror.

President Bush, a staunch defender of Israel, condemned it as "a deliberate attack on the site, knowing that innocents would be lost."[2]

The attack—punctuated by the awful photo—destroyed any immediate hope for Arab–Israeli peace.

Such is the power of communications in the 21st century.

As a consequence, communications must be handled with great care.

As noted, first and foremost, the public relations practitioner is a professional communicator. More than anyone else in an organization, the practitioner must know how to communicate. This knowledge sets the public relations professional apart from other employees.

FIGURE 3-1   **Image of war.** This photo of the body of an infant, wrapped in the Palestinian flag, was communicated around the world to remind people of the horrors of the Arab–Israeli confict.

Fundamentally, communication is a process of exchanging information, imparting ideas, and making oneself understood by others. Importantly, it also includes understanding others in return. Indeed, understanding is critical to the communications process. If one person sends a message to another, who disregards or misunderstands it, then communication hasn't taken place. But if the idea received is the one intended, then communication has occurred. Thus, a boss who sends subordinates dozens of memos isn't necessarily communicating with them. If the idea received is not the one intended, then the sender has done little more than convert personal thoughts to words—and there they lie.

Although all of us are endowed with some capacity for communicating, the public relations practitioner must be better at it than most. Indeed, the effectiveness of public relations professionals is determined by their own ability to communicate and to counsel others on how to communicate. Before public relations practitioners can earn the respect of management and become trusted advisers, they must demonstrate a mastery of many communications skills—writing, speaking, listening, promoting, and counseling. Just as the controller is expected to be an adept accountant, and the legal counsel is expected to be an accomplished lawyer, the public relations professional must be the best communicator in the organization. Period.

Goals of Communication

When communication is planned, as it should be in public relations, every communication must have a goal, an objective, a purpose. If not, why communicate in the first place?

What are typical communications goals?

1. *To inform.* Often the communications goal of an organization is to inform or educate a particular public. For example, before the summer travel season begins, the Automobile Association of America (AAA) will often release information providing advice on safe driving habits for long hauls. In so doing, the AAA is performing a valuable information service to the public.
2. *To persuade.* A regular goal of public relations communicators is to persuade people to take certain actions. Such persuasion needn't be overly aggressive; it can be more subtle. For example, a mutual fund annual report that talks about the fund's long history of financial strength and security may provide a subtle persuasive appeal for potential investors.
3. *To motivate.* Motivation of employees to "pull for the team" is a regular organizational communications goal. For example, the hospital CEO who outlines to her managers the institution's overriding objectives in the year ahead is communicating to motivate these key employees to action.
4. *To build mutual understanding.* Often communicators have as their goal the mere attainment of understanding of a group in opposition. For example, a community group that meets with a local plant manager to express its concern about potential pollution of the neighborhood is seeking understanding of the group's rationale and concern.

The point is that whether written release, annual report, speech, or meeting—all are valid public relations communications vehicles to achieve communications goals with key constituent publics. Again, the best way to achieve one's goals is through an integrated and strategically planned approach.

Theories of Communication

Books have been written on the subject of communications theory. Consequently, we won't attempt to provide an all-encompassing discussion on how people ensure that their messages get through to others. But in its most basic sense, communication commences with a source, who sends a message through a medium to reach a receiver who, we hope, responds in the manner we intended.

Many theories exist—from the traditional to the modern—about the most effective ways for a source to send a message through a medium to elicit a positive response. Here is but a sprinkling.

- One early theory of communication, the two-step flow theory, stated that an organization would beam a message first to the mass media, which would then deliver that message to the great mass of readers, listeners, and viewers for their response. This theory may have given the mass media too much credit. People today are influenced by a variety of factors, of which the media may be one but not necessarily the dominant one.
- Another theory, the concentric-circle theory, developed by pollster Elmo Roper, assumed that ideas evolve gradually to the public at large, moving in concentric circles from great thinkers to great disciples to great disseminators to lesser disseminators to the politically active to the politically inert. This theory suggests that people pick up and accept ideas from leaders, whose impact on public opinion may be greater than that of the mass media. The

overall study of how communication is used for direction and control is called cybernetics.

- The communications theories of the late Pat Jackson have earned considerable respect in the public relations field. Jackson's public relations communications models, too, emphasized "systematic investigation—setting clear strategic goals and identifying key stakeholders."[3] One Jackson communications approach to stimulate behavioral change encompassed a five-step process:

  1. *Building awareness.*   First, build awareness through all the standard communications mechanisms that we will discuss in this book, from publicity to advertising to public speaking to word of mouth.

  2. *Developing a latent readiness.*   This is the stage at which people begin to form an opinion, based on such factors as knowledge, emotion, intuition, memory, and relationships.

  3. *Triggering event.*   A triggering event is something—either natural or planned—that makes you want to change your behavior. Slimming down in time for beach season is an example of a "natural" triggering event. Staged functions, rallies, campaigns, or appearances are examples of "planned" triggering events.

  4. *Intermediate behavior.*   This is what Jackson called the "investigative" period, when an individual is determining how best to apply a desired behavior. In this stage, information about process and substance is sought.

  5. *Behavioral change.*   The final step is the adoption of new behavior.

- Many other communications theories abound today, as Internet communication changes the ways and speed at which many of us receive our messages. Professor Everett Rogers talks about the unprecedented "diffusion" of the Net as a communications vehicle that spans cultures and geographies. Others point to the new reality of "convergence" of video, data and voice, mobile and fixed, traditional and new age communications mechanisms with which public relations professionals must be familiar.

- There are even those who focus on the growing import of the "silent" theories of communication. The most well known of these, Elisabeth Noelle-Neumann's theory of the "spiral of silence," suggests that communications that work well depend on the silence and nonparticipation of a huge majority. This so-called "silent majority" fears becoming isolated from and, therefore, ostracized by most of their colleagues. Thus, they invariably choose to "vote with the majority."[4]

All of these theories and many others have great bearing on how public relations professionals perform their key role as organizational communicators.

Grunig-Hunt Public Relations Models

Perhaps the most widely discussed theoretical model of public relations communications is that formulated by Professors James E. Grunig and Todd Hunt. Actually, Grunig and Hunt proposed four models that define public relations communications.[5]

1. *Press agentry/publicity.*   This is essentially one-way communication that beams messages from a source to a receiver with the express intention of persuading the recipient to action. Such an approach is most associated with

"propaganda," the dissemination of messages to persuade public support for positions or actions without seeking feedback.

2. *Public information.*   This is another one-way communication designed not necessarily to persuade but rather to inform. The public relations professional in this model communicates objective information designed to enlighten the public.

3. *Two-way asymmetric.*   This is two-way communication designed to persuade through the classic public relations functions of research, objective setting, communicating, and then evaluating to see if the communication changed atttitudes and opinions as desired. Two-way asymmetric communicators use what they've learned to persuade publics to accept the organization's position.

4. *Two-way symmetric.*   This differs from the two-way asymmetric model in that mutual understanding rather than persuasion is the purpose. In this way, this approach is more "balanced" and, therefore, symmetrical, with the public relations communicator serving as a mediator between the organization and the publics.

Although all four of the Grunig-Hunt models are used in public relations work, it is clearly more advisable—whether attempting to persuade or inform—to seek two-way communication. Feedback, in other words, is critical for true understanding.

Basic S-E-M-D-R Communications Process

Although there are numerous models of communication, one of the most fundamental is the S-M-R approach. This model suggests that the communication process begins with the source (S), who issues a message (M) to a receiver (R), who then decides what action to take, if any, relative to the communication. This element of receiver action, or feedback, underscores that good communication always involves dialogue between two or more parties. The S-M-R model has been modified to include additional elements: (1) an encoding stage (E), in which the source's original message is translated and conveyed to the receiver, and (2) a decoding stage (D), in which the receiver interprets the encoded message and takes action. This evolution from the traditional model has resulted in the S-E-M-D-R process, which illustrates graphically the role of the public relations function in modern communications; both the encoding (E) and the decoding (D) stages are of critical importance in communicating any public relations message.

The Source

The source of a message is the central person or organization doing the communicating. The source could be a politician giving a campaign speech, a school announcing curriculum changes, or even, as one Superior Court judge in Seattle ruled, a topless dancer in the midst of gyrating.

Although the source usually knows how it wants the message to be received, there is no guarantee that it will be understood that way by the receiver. In many cases—a public speech, for example—the speaker is relatively limited in ability to influence the interpretation of the message. Gestures, eye contact, voice tone, and inflection can be used to add special importance to certain remarks, but whether the audience understands what is intended may ultimately depend on other factors, particularly the encoder.

The Encoder

What the source wants to relate must be translated from an idea in the mind to a communication. This is where the public relations practitioner ordinarily enters the picture, adding knowledge, experience, and crediblity to strengthen the message and position it for a greater chance of succeeding.

In the case of a campaign speech, for example, a politician's original message may be subject to translation or reinterpretation by at least three independent encoders.

1. The politician may consult a speech writer to help put ideas into words on paper. Speech writers become encoders in first attempting to understand the politician's message clearly and then in translating that message effectively into language that an audience will understand and, hopefully, accept.
2. Once the speech is written, it may be further encoded into a news release. In this situation, the encoder—perhaps a different individual from the speech writer—selects what seem to be the most salient points of the speech and provides them to media editors in a fairly brief format.
3. A news editor may take the news release and retranslate it before reporting it to the voters, the ultimate audience for the politician's message. Thus, the original message in the mind of the politician has been massaged three separate times before it ever reaches the intended receivers. Each time, in all likelihood, the particular encoder has added new subjective shadings to the politician's original message. The very act of encoding depends largely on the encoder's personal experience.

Words/Semantics

Words are among our most personal and potent weapons. Words can soothe us, bother us, or infuriate us. They can bring us together or drive us apart. They can even cause us to kill or be killed. Words mean different things to different people, depending on their backgrounds, occupations, education, or geographic locations. What one word means to you might be dramatically different from what that same word means to your neighbor. The study of what words really mean is called *semantics,* and the science of semantics, is a peculiar one indeed.

Words are perpetually changing in our language. What's in today is out tomorrow. What a word denotes according to the dictionary may be thoroughly dissimilar to what it connotes in its more emotional or visceral sense. Even the simplest words—*liberal, conservative, profits, consumer activists*—can spark semantic skyrockets. Many times, without knowledge of the territory, the semantics of words may make no sense. Take the word *fat*. In our American culture and vernacular, a person who is fat is generally not associated with the apex of attractiveness. A person who is "thin," on the other hand, may indeed be considered highly attractive. But along came 50 Cent and Ja Rule and Jay-Z and hip-hop, and pretty soon *phat*—albeit with a new spelling—became the baddest of the bad, the coolest of the cool, the height of fetching pulchritudinousness (if you smell what I'm cookin').

Words used in the encoding stage have a significant influence on the message conveyed to the ultimate receiver. Just consider the impact on society of advertising slogans (see Sidebar). Thus, the source must depend greatly on the ability of the encoder to accurately understand and effectively translate the true message—with all its semantic complications—to the receiver (see other Sidebar).

All the Slogans That Fit the Memory . . .

How many of these advertising slogans can you attach to the appropriate products? (No peeking!)

1. "All the News That's Fit to Print."
2. "How Do You Spell Relief?"
3. "The Un-cola."
4. "Takes a Licking and Keeps on Ticking."
5. "Because It's Your Stuff."
6. "Just Do It."
7. "A Different Kind of Company. A Different Kind of Car."
8. "The Pause That Refreshes."
9. "You Deserve a Break Today."
10. "Let Your Fingers Do the Walking."
11. "We're Number Two. We Try Harder."
12. "Come Fly the Friendly Skies."
13. "Have It Your Way."
14. "Don't Leave Home Without It."
15. "We'll Leave the Light On for You."
16. "Be All That You Can Be."
17. "Think Different."
18. "The World on Time."
19. "We Bring Good Things to Life."
20. "Because I'm Worth It."
21. "Please Don't Squeeze the Charmin."
22. "Tell 'Em Charlie Sent You."
23. "A Little Dab'll Do Ya."
24. "Does She or Doesn't She?"
25. "Melts in Your Mouth, Not in Your Hand."
26. "Plop, Plop, Fizz, Fizz."
27. "M'm, M'm, Good."
28. "Get a Piece of the Rock."
29. "Good to the Last Drop."
30. "They're Gr-r-r-r-reat!"

Answers

1. The *New York Times*, 2. Rolaids, 3. 7-Up, 4. Timex, 5. Iomega, 6. Nike, 7. Saturn, 8. Coca-Cola, 9. McDonald's, 10. Bell System Yellow Pages, 11. Avis, 12. United Airlines, 13. Burger King, 14. American Express, 15. Motel 6, 16. U.S. Army, 17. Apple Computer, 18. FedEx, 19. General Electric, 20. L'Oréal, 21. Charmin, 22. StarKist, 23. Brylcreem, 24. Miss Clairol, 25. M&Ms, 26. Alka-Seltzer, 27. Campbell soup, 28. Prudential Insurance, 29. Maxwell House coffee, 30. Kellogg's Frosted Flakes.

The Message

Once an encoder has taken in the source's ideas and translated them into terms a receiver can understand, the ideas are then transmitted in the form of a message. The message may be carried in a variety of communications media: speeches, newspapers, news releases, press conferences, broadcast reports, and face-to-face meetings. Communications theorists differ on what exactly constitutes the message, but here are three of the more popular explanations.

1. *The content is the message.* According to this theory, which is far and away the most popular, the content of a communication—what it says—constitutes its message. According to this view, the real importance of a communication—the message—lies in the meaning of an article or in the intent of a speech. Neither the medium through which the message is being communicated nor the individual doing the communicating is as important as the content.

2. *The medium is the message.* Other communications theorists—the late Canadian professor Marshall McLuhan being the best known—argue that the content of a communication is not the message at all. According to McLuhan, the content is less important than the vehicle of communication. McLuhan's argument stemmed largely from the fact that many people today are addicted to television. He said that television is a "cool" medium—that is, someone can

When in Rome . . .

It's hard enough to understand English words if you speak the language, but if English isn't your first language, it's even more confounding to understand why—when words are apparently put together in the proper construction—they don't exactly mean what they should.

Here are a few overseas examples.

- In a Paris hotel elevator: "Please leave your values at the front desk."
- Outside a Hong Kong tailor shop: "Ladies may have a fit upstairs."
- In a Zurich hotel: "Because of the impropriety of entertaining guests of the opposite sex in the bedroom, it is suggested that the lobby be used for this purpose."

- In a Bangkok dry cleaners: "Drop your trousers here for best results."
- In a Bucharest hotel: "The lift is being fixed for the next day. During that time, we regret that you will be unbearable."
- In a Rome laundry: "Ladies, leave your clothing here and spend the afternoon having a good time."
- Advertisement for donkey rides in Thailand: "Would you like to ride on your own ass?"
- In an Acapulco hotel: "The manager has personally passed all the water served here."
- In a Copenhagen airport: "We take your bags and send them in all directions."
- In a Budapest zoo: "Please do not feed the animals. If you have any suitable food, give it to the guard on duty."

derive meaning from a TV message without working too hard. On the other hand, reading involves hard work to grasp an idea fully; thus, newspapers, magazines, and books are "hot" media. Furthermore, McLuhan argued, a television viewer can easily become part of that which is being viewed. This has particular implications as television—and streaming Internet video for that matter—becomes more and more interactive.

One direct outgrowth of this medium-is-the-message theory was the development of the friendly team style of local television news reporting. Often called the "eyewitness news" approach, this format encouraged interaction among TV newscasters in order to involve viewers as part of the news team family.

The medium of television has become particularly important to U.S. presidents. Commencing with the cool, polished television demeanor of John F. Kennedy and proceeding through modern-day presidents, television has become the great differentiator in terms of presidential popularity. Ronald Reagan, a former movie actor and media spokesman for General Electric, was a magnificent master of the TelePrompTer. Reagan's televised speeches were studies in proper use of the medium. George H. W. Bush, not as good as his predecessor, nonetheless had his moments. Bill Clinton, although not as polished as Reagan with prepared speeches, was greatly skilled in using the medium to suggest a committed, concerned, and undeniably human commander-in-chief. George W. Bush, although not an accomplished public speaker by any means, learned on September 11 that sincerity is the key component in TV communicating, and he improved greatly.

3. *The person is the message.*   Still other theorists argue that it is neither the content nor the medium that is the message, but rather the speaker. For

example, Hitler was a master of persuasion. His minister of propaganda, Josef Goebbels, used to say, "Any man who thinks he can persuade, can persuade." Hitler practiced this self-fulfilling communications prophecy to the hilt. Feeding on the perceived desires of the German people, Hitler was concerned much less with the content of his remarks than with their delivery. His maniacal rantings and frantic gestures seized public sentiment and sent friendly crowds into a frenzy. In every way, Hitler himself was the primary message of his communications, as was Saddam Hussein in Iraq.

Today, in a similar vein, we often refer to a leader's charisma. Frequently, the charismatic appeal of a political leader may be more important than what that individual says. Accomplished speakers, like the Rev. Jesse Jackson and former Gov. Mario Cuomo, for example, can move an audience by the very inflection of their words. Likewise, James Carville on the Democratic side and Oliver North on the Republican side can bring an audience to its feet merely by shaking a fist, picking up the pace, or raising the pitch of their voices. Experienced speakers, from retired military leaders like Norman Schwarzkopf, to business consultants like Tom Peters and Stew Leonard, to sports coaches like Pat Riley and Lou Holtz, can also rally listeners with their personal charismatic demeanor.

Often people cannot distinguish between the words and the person who speaks them. The words, the face, the body, the eyes, the attitude, the timing, the wit, the presence—all form a composite that, as a whole, influences the listener. As political consultant-turned-television-executive Roger Ailes has put it, it comes down to the "like" factor in communication. Ailes points out that some candidates get votes just because people like them. "They forget that you're short, or you're fat, or you're bald . . . they say 'I like that guy.'"[6] In such cases, the source of the communication becomes every bit as important as the message itself.

The Decoder

After a message has been transmitted, it must be decoded by a receiver before action can be taken. This stage is like the encoding stage in that the receiver takes in the

Are You Sure You Saw What You Thought You Saw?

First read the sentence that follows:

FINISHED FILES ARE THE RESULT OF YEARS OF SCIENTIFIC STUDY COMBINED WITH THE EXPERIENCE OF MANY YEARS.

Now, count the *F*s in the sentence. Count them only once, and do not go back and count them again.

Question
How many *F*s are there?

Answer
There are six *F*s. However, because the *F* in OF sounds like a *V*, it seems to disappear. Most people perceive only three *F*s in the sentence. Our conditioned, habitual patterns (mental blocks) restrict us from being as alert as we should be. Frequently, we fail to perceive things as they really are.

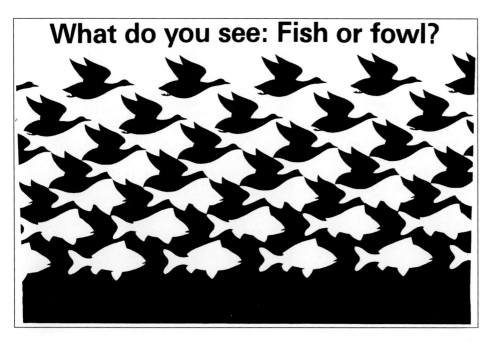

FIGURE 3-2 **Fish or fowl?** Often what we see may not be what others see. (Hint: There are both white fish and black fowl.)

message and translates it into his or her own common terms. Often this is another stage in which public relations counselors help "decode" messages for clients and employers.

Obviously, language again plays a critical role. The decoder must fully understand the message before acting on it; if the message is unclear or the decoder is unsure of its intent, there's probably little chance that the action taken by the receiver will be the action desired by the source. Messages must be understood in common terms.

How a receiver decodes a message depends greatly on that person's own perception. How an individual looks at and comprehends a message is a key to effective communications (Figure 3-2). Remember that everyone is biased; no two people perceive a message identically. Personal biases are nurtured by many factors, including stereotypes, symbols, semantics, peer group pressures, and—especially in today's culture—the media.

Stereotypes

Everyone lives in a world of stereotypical figures. Yuppies, Midwesterners, feminists, bankers, blue-collar workers, PR types, and thousands of other characterizations cause people to think of certain specific images. Public figures, for example, are typecast regularly. The dumb blond, the bigoted right-winger, the computer geek, and the shifty used-car salesman are the kinds of stereotypes our society—particularly television—perpetuate.

Like it or not, most of us are victims of such stereotypes. For example, research indicates that a lecture delivered by a person wearing glasses will be perceived as significantly more believable than the same lecture delivered before the same audience by the same lecturer without glasses. The stereotyped impression of people with glasses is that they are more trustworthy and more believable.

FIGURE 3-3 **What's in a symbol?** Located on Mount Lee in Griffith Park, the Hollywood sign is the most famous sign in the world. Originally built in 1923 for $21,000 as an advertising gimmick to promote home sales, the 45-foot high, 450-foot long, 480,000-pound sign was restored in 1978—Tinseltown's most enduring and instantly identifiable symbol. (Courtesy of Global Icons)

Symbols

The clenched-fist salute, the swastika, and the thumbs-up sign all leave distinct impressions on most people. Marshaled properly, symbols can be used as effective persuasive elements (Figure 3-3). The Statue of Liberty, the Red Cross, the Star of David, and many other symbols have been used traditionally for positive persuasion. On the other hand, the symbols chosen by the terrorists to bomb on September 11, 2001—the World Trade Center, the Pentagon, and probably the Capitol and the White House—were clearly chosen because of their symbolic value as American icons.

Semantics

Public relations professionals make their living largely by knowing how to use words effectively to communicate desired meanings. Occasionally, this is tricky because the same words may hold contrasting meanings for different people. In the 21st century, the contentious abortion debate is couched in the confusing semantic terms pro-life—those against abortion—and pro-choice—those in favor of allowing abortions. Especially vulnerable are politically sensitive phrases such as *capital punishment*, *law and order*, *liberal politician*, *right-winger*, and on and on, until you reach the point where the Oakridge Mall in San Jose, California, demanded that the gourmet hamburger restaurant on its premises, with a logo depicting a smiling hamburger with a monocle and top hat, either change its "suggestive name" or leave the mall. The restaurant's name? *Elegant Buns*.

Controversy also surrounds the semantics associated with certain forms of rap and hip-hop music. To critics, some artists preach a philosophy of violence and hate and prejudice against women. But gangsta rappers claim that they are merely "telling it like it is" or "reporting what we see in the streets." When reporters and record company executives give credence to such misguided rhetoric, they become just as guilty for the often unfortunate consequences that result—for example, the sexual charges posed against singers R&B artist R. Kelly and rapper Mystikal in 2002 and the killings in the late 1990s of enemy rap artists, Tupac Shakur and Notorious B.I.G.[7]

Because language and the meanings of words change constantly, semantics must be handled with extreme care. Good communicators always consider the consequences of the words they plan to use before using them.

Peer Groups

In one famous study, students were asked to point out, in progression, the shortest of the following three lines.

A _____

B _____

C _____

Although line B is obviously the shortest, each student in the class except one was told in advance to answer that line C was the shortest. The object of the test was to see whether the one student would agree with his peers. Results generally indicated that, to a statistically significant degree, all students, including the uncoached one, chose C. Peer pressure prevails.

Media

The power of the media—particularly as an agenda setter or reinforcement mechanism—is also substantial. A common complaint among lawyers is that their clients cannot receive fair trials because of pretrial publicity leading to preconceived verdicts from potential jurors, who read newspapers and watch television. Such was the case in 2000, when the murder trial of four white New York City police officers, who shot and killed an unarmed black man, was moved to upstate Albany and out of the politically volatile atmosphere of the Bronx, where the murder was committed.

It is clear that people often base perceptions on what they read or hear, without bothering to dig further to elicit the facts. Although appearances are sometimes revealing, they are also often deceiving.

The Receiver

You really aren't communicating unless someone is at the other end to hear and understand what you're saying. This situation is analogous to the old mystery of the falling tree in the forest: Does it make a noise when it hits the ground if there's no one there to hear it? Regardless of the answer, communication doesn't take place if a message doesn't reach the intended receivers and exert the desired effect on those receivers.

S I D E B A R

Oops!

If you don't think one little word can make a world of difference, consider the following.

The people of Lauderhill, Florida, were mightily enraged, to say nothing of embarrassed in the early months of 2002. A plaque intended to honor the appearance of award-winning black actor James Earl Jones at a Lauderhill celebration of the life of Martin Luther King, Jr. instead paid tribute to James Earl **Ray,** the man who killed the black civil rights leader.

Over a background featuring stamps of famous black Americans, including Dr. King, the erroneous plaque read, "Thank you, James Earl Ray, for keeping the dream alive."

The mix-up was caused by an error by the plaque's designer, who explained red-faced that it was purely a typographical and not an intentional error.

Oops!

Whaaat?

Extra credit for anyone who can decode the following sentence:

> We respectfully petition, request, and entreat that due and adequate provision be made, this day and the date herein after subscribed, for the satisfying of this petitioner's nutritional requirements and for the organizing of such methods as may be deemed necessary and proper to assure the reception by and for said petitioner of such quantities of baked products as shall, in the judgment of the aforesaid petitioner, constitute a sufficient supply thereof.*

Whaaat?

*Give us this day our daily bread.

Ohhh. Perhaps this one is easier to decode.

1. The Lord is my external-internal integrative mechanism.
2. I shall not be deprived of gratifications for my visogeneric hungers or my need dispositions.
3. He motivates me to orient myself toward a nonsocial object with affective significance.
4. He positions me in a nondecisional situation.
5. He maximizes my adjustment.*

*1. The Lord is my shepherd.
2. I shall not want.
3. He leadeth me beside the still waters.
4. He maketh me to lie down in green pastures.
5. He restoreth my soul.

Even if a communication is understood clearly, there is no guarantee that the motivated action will be the desired one. In fact, a message may trigger several different effects.

1. *It may change attitudes.* This result, however, is very difficult to achieve and rarely happens.
2. *It may crystallize attitudes.* This outcome is much more common. Often a message will influence receivers to take actions they might already have been thinking about taking but needed an extra push to accomplish. For example, a receiver might want to contribute to a certain charity, but seeing a child's photo on a contribution canister might crystallize his or her attitude sufficiently to trigger action.
3. *It might create a wedge of doubt.* Communication can sometimes force receivers to modify their points of view. A persuasive message can cause receivers to question their original thinking on an issue.
4. *It may do nothing.* Often communication results in no action at all. In recent years, the expensive communications campaigns, waged by government and fueled by a $246 billion industry settlement to reduce cigarette sales, have yielded less than stellar results.

As noted, feedback is critical to the process of communication. A communicator must get feedback from a receiver to know what messages are or are not getting through and how to structure future communications. Occasionally, feedback is ignored by professional communicators, but this is always a mistake.

Whether the objectives of a communication have been met can often be assessed by such things as the amount of sales, number of letters, or number of votes obtained. If individuals take no action after receiving a communication, feedback must still be sought. In certain cases, although receivers have taken no discernible action, they may have understood and even passed on the message to other individuals. This person-to-person relay of received messages creates a two-step flow of communications: (1) vertically from a particular source and (2) horizontally from interpersonal contact. The targeting of opinion leaders as primary receivers is based on the hope that they will distribute received messages horizontally within their own communities.

A QUESTION OF ETHICS

Shaking the Negative Effects of "Positive Effects"

After forking over hundreds of billions of dollars for antismoking programs in a 1998 settlement with all 50 states, tobacco companies wanted nothing more than to disappear from the public spotlight.

Alas, for the largest tobacco firm, Philip Morris, it was not to be.

In the summer of 2001, the *Wall Street Journal* reported that a secret Philip Morris study in Czechoslovakia concluded that $1,227 in per person cost savings from smokers' early deaths was one of the "positive effects" of cigarette consumption.

As soon as the *Journal* published those two little words of conclusion, tobacco industry critics jumped out of the woodwork.

- "Tobacco companies used to deny that cigarettes killed people. Now they brag about it," wrote *Boston Globe* columnist Ellen Goodman.
- "Philip Morris is industrial scum. Smoking is a drug. Cigarette companies are the pushers," fumed Bill Maher on ABC's *Politically Incorrect*.
- "This is clear evidence that they haven't changed," sniffed an aide to a Democratic senator.
- The American Legacy Foundation ran a graphic ad that needed no explanation (Figure 3-4).

As soon as the *Wall Street Journal* article appeared, Philip Morris tried to defuse the two-word firestorm.

"We understand that this was not only a terrible mistake, but that it was wrong," said the company's senior vice president for communications.

The CEO of Philip Morris said that the funding and release of the study "exhibited terrible judgment as well as a complete and unacceptable disregard of basic human values."

"All of us at Phillip Morris, no matter where we work, are extremely sorry for this," CEO Geoffrey C. Bible added.

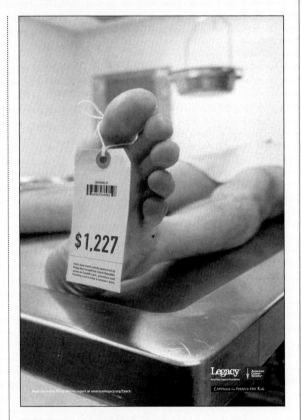

FIGURE 3-4 **Toe tag ad.** This American Legacy Foundation ad was quick to take Phillip Morris to task for its ill-fated secret study.

The company's communications director said that similar studies planned in Poland, Slovakia, Hungary, and Slovenia had been canceled.

"Rest assured, we won't be doing this again," he said.

For further information, see Gordon Fairclough, "Philip Morris Says It's Sorry for Death Report," *Wall Street Journal* (July 26, 2001): B1-6.

L A S T   W O R D

Knowledge of how and when and to whom to communicate is the primary skills base of the public relations practitioner. Above all else, public relations professionals are professional communicators. That means they must understand the theoretical underpinnings of what constitutes a credible message and how to deliver it.

On the doorstep of the 21st century, some communications consultants believed the future might be a "step back in time." The advent of the World Wide Web, narrowcasting, convergence, and communicating to more targeted, smaller audiences would mean a return to more direct communication between people—and, therefore, an increased need for the help of public relations professionals to communicate effectively.[8]

The new century has not kicked off precisely according to plan. With the emergence of worldwide terrorism, turmoil in the Middle East and the deepening cultural chasm between West and East, the puncturing of the dot.com bubble and loss of trillions of dollars of wealth in society, illegal acts on the part of corporate CEOs and the consequent failure of once respected companies—the need for honest, straightforward, and credible communication has never been more important.

There is no trick to effective communication. In addition to some facility with techniques, it is knowledge, experience, hard work, and common sense that are the basic guiding principles. Naturally, communication must follow performance; organizations must back up what they say with action. Slick brochures, a winning Web site, engaging speeches, intelligent articles, and a good press may capture the public's attention, but in the final analysis the only way to obtain continued public support is through proper performance.

Discussion Starters

1. Why is it important that public relations professionals understand communication?
2. What are some principal goals of communication?
3. Why do words such as *liberal, conservative, profits,* and *consumer activist* spark semantic skyrockets?
4. What is the behavioral model of communications?
5. What is meant by the symmetric and asymmetric models of communication?
6. What is the S-E-M-D-R approach to communication?
7. How does perception influence a person's decoding?
8. Why is feedback critical to the communications process?
9. What common mistakes do people make when they communicate?
10. Why do some communications consultants believe that the 21st century may be a "step back in time"?

TOP OF THE SHELF

Ed Krol and Kiersten Conner-Sax

The Whole Internet: The Next Generation, *3rd ed.*
Sebastopol, CA: O'Reilly & Associates, 1999

You cannot talk about communications any longer without talking about the Internet. And you cannot talk about the Internet without knowing your way around it—that is, around more than just your favorite Web site. In a review of this book, Amazon.com (people who should know about these things) said, "For a snapshot of something that is mutating as quickly as the Internet, *The Whole Internet: The Next Generation* exhibits remarkable comprehensiveness and accuracy. It is a good panoramic shot of Web sites, usenet groups, e-mail, mailing lists, chat software, electronic commerce, and the communities that have begun to emerge around all of these."

Just what the communications doctor ordered.

The Whole Internet covers how to minimize junk e-mail, master your mailing lists and customize your mailer, buy and sell on the Internet, and protect your privacy. It also covers some of the newest Internet applications, such as the "push" technologies, conferencing tools, and tools for receiving audio and video broadcasts.

CASE STUDY

Exxon Corporation's Bad Good Friday

In the history of public relations practice, few communications issues have been handled as questionably, received as much global notoriety, and had such far-reaching implications on the profession as those involving the Exxon Corporation in 1989.

At 8:30 A.M. on March 24, 1989—Good Friday, no less—Lawrence G. Rawl, chairman and chief executive of the Exxon Corporation, one of the world's largest companies, was in his kitchen sipping coffee when the phone rang.

"What happened? Did it lose an engine? Break a rudder?" Rawl asked the caller.

"What happened" was that an Exxon tanker had run aground and was dumping gummy crude oil into the frigid waters of Prince William Sound, just outside the harbor of Valdez, Alaska.

What was about to happen to Mr. Rawl and his company—and to the environment—was arguably the worst environmental disaster in the history of the United States.

The facts, painfully portrayed in media across the country, were these: The *Exxon Valdez*, a 987-foot tanker, piloted by a captain who was later revealed to have been legally drunk, ran aground on a reef 25 miles southwest of the port of Valdez. The resulting rupture caused a spill of 260,000 barrels, the largest spill ever in North America, affecting 1,300 square miles of water, damaging some 600 miles of coastline, and killing as many as 4,000 Alaskan sea otters. The disaster also enshrined the name Exxon in the all-time Public Relations Hall of Shame.

Exxon's communications dilemma broke down roughly into five general categories.

To Go or Not to Go

The first problem that confronted Exxon and its top management after news of the Good Friday spill had broken was whether Chairman Rawl should fly to Prince William Sound to demonstrate the company's concern. This was what Union Carbide Chairman Warren Anderson did when his company suffered a devastating industrial explosion in Bhopal, India. It was also what Ashland Oil's Chairman John R. Hall did when his company suffered an oil spill earlier in 1989.

If Rawl went to Alaska, the reasoning went, he might have been able to reassure the public that the people who run Exxon acknowledged their misdeed and would make amends. What could be a better show of concern than the chairman flying to the local scene of the tragedy?

On the other hand, a consensus of executives around Rawl argued that he should remain in New York. "What are you going to do?" they asked. "We've already said we've done it, we're going to pay for it, and we're responsible for it." Rawl's more effective role, said these advisers, was right there at Exxon headquarters in Manhattan.

In the end, the latter view triumphed. Rawl did not go to Alaska. He left the cleanup in "capable hands" and sent a succession of lower-ranking executives to Alaska to deal with the spill. As he summarized in an interview one year after the Prince William Sound nightmare, "We had concluded that there was simply too much for me to coordinate from New York. It wouldn't have made any difference if I showed up and made a speech in the town forum. I wasn't going to spend the summer there; I had other things to do."

Rawl's failure to fly immediately to Valdez struck some as shortsighted. Said one media consultant about Rawl's communications decision, "The chairman should have been up there walking in the oil and picking up dead birds."

Where to Establish Media Central

The second dilemma that confronted Exxon was where to establish its media center.

This decision started, correctly enough, with Exxon senior managers concluding that the impact of the spill was so great that news organizations should be kept informed as events unfolded. Exxon, correctly, wanted to take charge of the news flow and give the public, through the news media, a credible, concerned, and wholly committed corporate response.

It decided that the best place to do this would be in Valdez, Alaska, itself. "Just about every news organization worth its salt had representatives in Valdez," said Exxon's publicity chief. "But in retrospect, we should have sent live broadcasts of news conferences to several points around the country." The problem was that Valdez was a remote Alaskan town with limited communications operations. This complicated the ability of Exxon to disseminate information quickly. As *Oil & Gas Journal* stated later: "Exxon did not update its media relations people elsewhere in the world. It told reporters it was Valdez or nothing."

Additionally, there was a four-hour time difference between Valdez and New York. Consequently, "Exxon statements were erratic and contradictory," said the publisher of another oil bulletin. The phone lines to Valdez quickly became jammed, and even Rawl couldn't find a knowledgeable official to brief him. That left news organizations responsible for keeping the public informed cut off from Exxon information during the early part of the crisis. Because news conferences took place at unsuitable viewing hours for television networks and too late for many morning newspapers, predictable accusations of an Exxon "cover-up" resulted. Said one Exxon official about the decision to put the communications center in Valdez, "It didn't work."

RAPIDITY OF RESPONSE

A cardinal rule in any crisis is: Keep ahead of the information flow—try not to let events get ahead of you. Here Exxon had serious problems.

First, it took Chairman Rawl a full week to make any public comment on the spill. When he did, it was to blame others: The U.S. Coast Guard and Alaskan officials were "holding up" his company's efforts to clean up the spill. But Rawl's words were too little, too late. The impression persisted that, in light of the delay in admitting responsibility, Exxon was not responding vigorously enough.

A full 10 days after the crisis, Exxon placed an apologetic advertisement in 166 newspapers. To some readers, the ad seemed self-serving and failed to address the many pointed questions raised about Exxon's conduct.

"It seems the company was a bit too relaxed in its capabilities," offered the president of the Public Relations Society of America. Meanwhile, one group that wasn't relaxed was the Alaska state legislature, which enacted a tax increase on oil from the North Slope fields within weeks of the Exxon spill. Congressional committees in Washington moved just as quickly to increase liability limits and potential compensation for oil-spill damage and to increase the money available through the industry-financed Offshore Oil Pollution Compensation Fund. When Exxon hesitated, its opponents seized the initiative. Concluded another public relations executive, "They lost the battle in the first 48 hours."

HOW HIGH THE PROFILE

Exxon's communications response in the face of this most challenging crisis in its history was, to put it mildly, muted.

From an operations and logistics viewpoint, Exxon did a good job. The company immediately set up animal rescue projects, launched a major cleanup effort, and agreed to pick up a substantial percentage of the cost. But it made the mistake of downplaying the crisis in public.

Exxon's public statements sometimes contradicted information from other sources. At one point, an Exxon spokesperson said that damage from the oil spill would be minimal. Others watching the industry said the damage was likely to be substantial.

Chairman Rawl, an otherwise blunt and outspoken CEO, seemed defensive and argumentative in his public comments. In one particularly disastrous personal appearance on *CBS Morning News*, Rawl glared at interviewer Kathleen Sullivan and snapped: "I can't give you details of our cleanup plan. It's thick and complicated. And I haven't had a chance to read it yet. The CEO of a major company doesn't have time to read every plan."

Exxon's attempts to calm the public also were criticized. Its ad drew fire for not expressing enough concern. It hired an outside firm to do a series of video news releases to show how the company was cleaning up the spill. At an estimated cost of more than $3 million, a 13-minute tape was shown at the corporation's annual meeting. The video, called *Progress in Alaska*, attracted intense criticism from those attending the conference, as well as from the press. The film implied, argued *Boston Globe* reporter Robert Lenzner, that "the brutal scenes of damage to Alaskan waters seen nightly on television news programs were false." *USA Today* called the tape "Exxon's worst move of the day." When the consultant who devised the video wrote an article in the *New York Times* defending Exxon's approach in Alaska, the Alaskan representative to the National Wildlife Federation responded with a blistering letter to the editor, noting that the consultant omitted in his article that the spill had resulted in the death of more than 15,000 sea birds and numerous otters and eagles.

Exxon then added an environmental expert to its board of directors, but only after pension funds, which control a large chunk of its stock, demanded such a response.

DEALING WITH THE AFTERMATH

Finally, Exxon was forced to deal with all the implications of what its tanker had wrought in Valdez.

The company became embroiled in controversy when it sent a $30,000 contribution to the Alaska Public Radio Network, which covered the crisis on a daily basis. The network, sniffing "conflict of interest," flatly turned down Exxon's attempted largesse. Subsequently, a special appropriations bill was introduced in the Alaskan legislature to forward an identical amount to Alaska Public Radio.

The accident and the company's reaction to it also had consequences for the oil industry. Plans to expand drilling into the Alaskan National Wildlife Refuge were shelved by Congress, and members called for new laws increasing federal involvement in oil spills.

The company's employees, too, felt confused, embarrassed, and betrayed. Summarizing the prevailing mood at the company, one Exxon worker said, "Whenever I travel now, I feel like I have a target painted on my chest."

In 1994, more than five years after the tanker ran aground, Exxon went to court in Anchorage to defend itself against $15 million in civil claims. Early in 1996, the company still battled its past demons, as the company and its new chairman, Lee R. Raymond, were accused of making "side deals" with plaintiffs in the case—even though they denied, under oath, that they had done so.

In November 1996, seven years after the *Exxon Valdez* ran aground, a weary Exxon announced to the world that it was closing the books on its unforgettable disaster. Total cost to Exxon: $2.5 billion.

But that wasn't all. In 1999, a full decade after the *Exxon Valdez* dumped 11 million gallons of oil into Prince William Sound, the Exxon Corporation—rechristened Exxon Mobil—went to court in Alaska to get the courts to overturn an unusual federal restriction. The unique law barred one ship, the *Exxon Valdez*, from ever again sailing into Prince William Sound. Exxon alleged that the ship, renamed the *SeaRiver Mediterranean*, was being unfairly singled out among dozens of tankers that freely sail into Alaska waters. "Nonsense," said a spokesperson for Alaska Senator Ted Stevens, the law didn't single out any ship by name. Rather, she said, the language of the provision bars "vessels that have spilled more than 1 million gallons of oil into the marine environment after March 22, 1989" from entering Prince William Sound. Coincidentally, only one sailing vessel fit that description. Yup.

THE LESSONS

The lessons of the *Exxon Valdez's* Good Friday oil spill would not soon be forgotten by corporate managers. The episode, predicted one, "will become a textbook example of what not to do when an unexpected crisis thrusts a company into the limelight." Said another, "Exxon's response is fast becoming the stuff of PR legend."

Questions

1. What would you have recommended Chairman Rawl do upon learning of the Prince William Sound oil spill?
2. How would you have handled the media in this case?
3. What would have been your timing in terms of public relations responses in this case?
4. What would be your overall public relations strategy—aggressive, low key, and so on—if you were Exxon's public relations director?

5. Do you think this case will ever qualify as a "textbook example" of what not to do in a crisis?
6. Now that Exxon has merged with Mobil, what is the corporation doing about environmental issues? Visit the news release homepage (www.exxon.com/em_newsrelease/index.html) and follow the link to browse the oil giant's recent news releases. What is Exxon Mobil doing about environmental issues? Why would the company continue to issue news releases about environmental activities so many years after the Exxon Valdez incident?

For further information about the *Exxon Valdez* case, see Richard Behar, "Exxon Strikes Back," *Time* (March 26, 1990): 62–63; Claudia H. Deutsch, "The Giant with a Black Eye," *New York Times* (April 2, 1989): B1–4; E. Bruce Harrison, with Tom Prugh, "Assessing the Damage," *Public Relations Journal* (October 1989): 40–45; John Holusha, "Exxon's Public-Relations Problem," *New York Times* (April 21, 1989): D1–4; Peter Nulty, "Exxon's Problem: Not What You Think," *Fortune* (April 23, 1990): 202–204; James Lukaszewski, "How Vulnerable Are You? The Lessons from Valdez," *Public Relations Quarterly* (Fall 1989): 5–6; Phillip M. Perry, "Exxon Falters in PR Effort Following Alaskan Oil Spill," *O'Dwyer's PR Services Report* (July 1989): 1, 16–22; Bill Richards, "Exxon Is Battling a Ban on an Infamous Tanker," *Wall Street Journal* (July 29, 1998): C1; Allanna Sullivan, "Rawl Wishes He'd Visited Valdez Sooner," *Wall Street Journal* (June 30, 1989): B7; Joseph B. Treaster, "With Insurers' Payment, Exxon Says *Valdez* Case is Ended," *New York Times* (November 1, 1996): B2; and Paul Wiseman, "Firm Finds *Valdez* Oil Fowls Image," *USA Today* (April 26, 1990): B1.

TIPS FROM THE TOP

An Interview with Maggie Hughes

Maggie Hughes

As far as Maggie Hughes is concerned, there's nothing unusual about her rise from public relations consultant to president and chief operating officer of a $5.5 billion insurance holding company. As president of Life USA Holding, Inc. of Minneapolis, Minnesota, she was one of the highest-ranking female executives in the nation and certainly the highest-ranking female to emanate from the practice of public relations.

Did you study communications in college?
Yes, I have a degree in journalism. It was the late 1960s, early 1970s. I worked on the college newspaper. I was fairly radical and an activist, so journalism was a must, a way of expressing the emotions of the times.

Do you consider yourself a writer?
I'm a writer, absolutely. That's the easiest form of communication for me. Actually learning to speak in a comprehensive fashion has come over the years, as I became a consultant to business.

Did you like the communications consulting business?
What was interesting to me was finding out what people's business objectives were and then figuring out how to communicate them. In the process of having to put together professional communications that communicated people's projects or services, I began to get a lot of information on business strategy. That led me to believe that I could offer value in terms of helping companies achieve all kinds of objectives, everything from employee relations to crisis management.

What kind of public relations consultant were you?
Well, what I've been told by my board of directors is that I have a knack at getting at the truth of things.

(Continued)

Truth, I have come to understand, is a subjective thing. But I'm a digger and maybe that's my journalistic background. And so I would dig for solutions. I'd also dig for what the issues really were. When you're a public relations consultant, often when management from a company comes to you, they come to you with symptoms of an issue that they would like you to resolve. What I thought I had a special knack for was when people came to me with an issue or problem, I had the ability to get at all the facts behind that symptom, to really define the issue, so we could more effectively put together the strategy to help resolve the situation.

What do you find lacking in public relations consultants?

The problem that I've seen now from the other side of the table is that public relations specialists can come in with a methodology but won't dig far enough. Often they don't have a deep enough business understanding of the environment, the issues, the constituency, to bring real value to what are often fast-moving opportunities. Nothing is more frustrating than to get a canned approach to something that you could plug any company into but that it is not germane to the nuances of my specific industry.

Could you see others in communications areas following your route to top management?

Absolutely, because you learn to operate in a dynamic environment. I mean you never know what's coming at you, be it a crisis or opportunity when you're a public relations consultant. You can make decisions quickly. You can garner different resources to come together with the right answer. The training is very good training for management.

Let's say someone reading this wants to follow your lead. How do they begin?

Okay, two answers. First, silly answer, follow your bliss. But it's not too silly. Second, decide what industry interests you, and then do your research and look for companies that look like they could use a strength you could bring to the table. Don't look for ads in newspapers. Choose. Don't be chosen. Choose. Go after it.

Suggested Readings

Atkin, Charles, and Ronald Rice. *Public Relations Campaigns*. Thousand Oaks, CA: Sage, 2000.

Bell, Arthur H. *Tools for Technical and Professional Communication*. Lincolnwood, IL: NTC Publishing Group, 1995.

Bjorseth, Lillian, *Breakthrough Networking, Building Relationships That Last*. New York, NY: Duoforce Enterprises, 1996.

Bovee, Courtland L., and John V. Thill. *Business Communication Today*, 5th ed. New York: McGraw-Hill, 1998.

Communications Booknotes Quarterly. Mahwah, NJ: Lawrence Erlbaum Associates. A review service for books, reports, documents, and electronic publications on all aspects of mass communication.

Corman, Steven R., et al. *Foundations of Organizational Communication: A Reader*. White Plains, NY: Longman, 1994.

Demers, David, *Communication Theory in the 21st Century*. Mahwah, NJ: Lawrence Erlbaum Associates, 2000.

Edelstein, Alex S. *Total Propaganda: From Mass Culture to Popular Culture*. Mahwah, NJ: Lawrence Erlbaum Associates, 1997.

Ferguson, Sherry Devereaux, *Communication Planning, An Integrated Approach*. Thousand Oaks, CA: Sage, 1999.

Grunig, James E., ed. *Excellence in Public Relations and Communications Management*. Hillsdale, NJ: Lawrence Erlbaum Associates, 1992.

Grunig, Larissa, James Grunig, and David M. Parker, *A Study of Communications in Three Countries*. Mahwah, NJ: Lawrence Erlbaum Associates, 2002.

Heath, Robert L., *Human Communication Theory and Research: Concepts, Context, and Challenges, Lea's Communication Theory*. Mahwah, NJ: Lawrence Erlbaum Associates, 2000.

Hewes, Dean E., ed. *The Cognitive Bases of Interpersonal Communication*. Hillsdale, NJ: Lawrence Erlbaum Associates, 1995.

International Encyclopedia of Communication, vol. 4. New York: Oxford University Press, 1989.

Lutz, William. *The New Doublespeak: Why No One Knows What Anyone's Saying Anymore*. New York: HarperCollins Publishers, 1997.

Mickey, Thomas J. *Sociodrama: An Interpretative Theory for the Practice of Public Relations*. Lanham, MD: University Press of America, 1997.

Perloff, Richard M. *Political Communication: Politics, Press, and Public in America*. Mahwah, NJ: Lawrence Erlbaum Associates, 1997.

Ragan Report. Chicago: Ragan Communications. Weekly. Pointed commentary on current communications issues; particularly pointed columnists.

Sigman, Stuart J., ed. *The Consequentiality of Communication*. Hillsdale, NJ: Lawrence Erlbaum Associates, 1995. Goes beyond the "effects" of communication, exploring the procedures, dynamics, and structures.

Thill, John V., and Courtland L. Bovee. *Excellence in Business Communication*, 5th ed. New York: McGraw-Hill, 2000.

Weiner, Richard. *Webster's New World Dictionary of Media and Communications*. New York: Macmillan, 1996.

Notes

1. George Earle, Lytton Bulwer-Lytton, *Richelieu*, act II, scene II, 1839.
2. David E. Sanger, "Bush Denounces Israeli Airstrike as 'Heavy Handed,'" *New York Times* (July 24, 2002): A1, 6.
3. Patrick Jackson, "The Unforgiving Era," *Currents* (October 1998).
4. Serge Moscovici, "Silent Majorities and Loud Minorities," *Communication Yearbook* 14 (1991): 298–308.
5. James E. Grunig and Todd Hunt, *Managing Public Relations* (New York: Holt, Rinehart and Winston, 1984) 21–27.
6. "The 'Like Factor' in Communications," *Executive Communications* (February 1988): 1.
7. Brent Staples, "The Politics of Gangster Rap," *New York Times* (August 27, 1993).
8. "Communication May Step Back in Time '90s," *IABC Communication World* (February 1990): 9.

Chapter 4

Management

It has been said that the only difference between the public relations director and the CEO is that the latter gets paid more.

In many ways, that's quite true. The CEO, after all, is the firm's top manager, responsible for, in addition to setting strategy and framing policy, serving as the organization's chief spokesperson, corporate booster, and reputation defender—not at all unlike the responsibilities assigned the public relations professional.

As important as communications knowledge and ability are to a public relations professional—equally important are an understanding of and a facility with management.

That means a knowledge of such management functions as planning, budgeting, objective setting, and how top management thinks and operates. That's what this chapter will discuss.

It will also deal with the differences between working as a staff public relations practitioner inside a corporation, nonprofit, or other organization, where the job is to support management to achieve its objectives—as opposed to working as a professional in a public relations agency, where the job is to contribute to the revenue generation of the company. Finally, it will provide some feel of what to expect in terms of income in public relations.

Management Process of Public Relations

Like other management processes, professional public relations work emanates from clear strategies and bottom-line objectives that flow into specific tactics, each with its own budget, timetable, and allocation of resources. Stated another way, public relations today is much more a planned, persuasive social managerial science than a knee-jerk, damage-control reaction to sudden flareups.

Don't get me wrong. As we will learn later, the public relations professionals who have the most organizational clout and get paid the most are those who demonstrate the ability to perform in crisis. Thinking "on your feet" is very much a coveted ability in the practice of public relations.

But so, too, is the ability to think strategically and plan methodically to help change attitudes, crystallize opinions, and accomplish the organization's overall goals.

Managers insist on "results." So the best public relations programs can be measured in terms of achieving results in building the key relationships on which the organization depends.

The relevance of public relations people in the eyes of top management depends largely on the contribution of the public relations group to the management process of the organization.

Top managers are forced to think strategically about reaching their goals. So, too, should public relations professionals think in terms of the strategic process element of their own roles. Specifically, they must constantly ask, in relation to their departments, functions, and assignments:

- What are we attempting to achieve and where are we going in that pursuit?
- What is the nature of the environment in which we must operate?
- Who are the key audiences we must convince in the process?
- How will we get to where we want to be?

It is this procedural mind-set—directed at communicating key messages to realize desired objectives to priority publics—that makes the public relations professional a key adviser to top management.

Reporting to Top Management

The public relations function, by definition, must report to top management.

If public relations, as noted in Chapter 1, is truly to be the "interpreter" for management philosophy, policy, and programs, then the public relations director should report to the CEO.

In many organizations, this reporting relationship has not always been the case. Many times, public relations has been subordinated to advertising, marketing, legal, or human resources. Whereas marketing and advertising promote the product, public relations promotes the entire organization. So if the public relations chief reports to the director of marketing or advertising, the job becomes one of promoting specific products—and not an entire organization.

The fact is you can't correctly "interpret" management's will if you are effectively "blocked" by superiors from getting to top management. That's why, ideally, public relations must report to those who run the organization.

Increasingly, that has become the case. For the public relations function to be valuable to management, it must remain independent, credible, and objective as an honest broker. This also mandates that public relations professionals not only have communication competence but also an intimate knowledge of the organization's business. Without the latter, according to research, public relations professionals are much less effective as top-management advisers.[1]

Whereas the marketing and advertising groups must, by definition, be defenders of their specific products, the public relations department has no such mandated allegiance.

Public relations, rightfully, should be the corporate conscience. An organization's public relations professionals should enjoy enough autonomy to deal openly and honestly with management. If an idea doesn't make sense, if a product is flawed, if the general institutional wisdom is wrong, it is the duty of the public relations professional to challenge the consensus. As the legendary CEO of the Berkshire Hathaway company, Warren Buffet, has put it, "We can afford to lose money—even a lot of money. But we cannot afford to lose reputation—even a shred of reputation."[2]

This is not to say that advertising, marketing, and all other disciplines shouldn't enjoy a close partnership with public relations. Clearly, they must. All disciplines must work to maintain their own independence while building long-term, mutually beneficial relationships for the good of the organization. However, public relations should never shirk its overriding responsibility to enhance the organization's credibility by ensuring that corporate actions are in the public interest.

To perform that function effectively, it needs to report directly to top management.

Planning for Public Relations

Strategic planning for public relations is an essential part of management.

Planning is critical not only to know where a particular campaign is headed but also to win the support of top management. Indeed, one of the most frequent complaints about public relations is that it is too much a seat-of-the-pants activity, impossible to plan and difficult to measure. Clearly, planning in public relations must be given greater shrift. With proper planning, public relations professionals can indeed defend and account for their actions.

Before organizing for public relations work, practitioners must consider objectives and strategies, planning and budgets, and research and evaluation. The broad environment in which the organization operates must dictate overall business objectives. These, in turn, dictate specific public relations objectives and strategies. Once these have been defined, the task of organizing for a public relations program should flow naturally.

Setting objectives, formulating strategies, and planning are essential if the public relations function is to be considered equal in stature to other management processes. Traditionally, the public relations management process involves four steps, echoing the R-A-C-E definition discussed in Chapter 1:

1. *Defining the problem or opportunity.* This requires researching current attitudes and opinions about the issue, product, candidate, or company in question and determining the essence of the problem.
2. *Programming.* This is the formal planning stage, which addresses key constituent publics, strategies, tactics, and goals.
3. *Action.* This is the communications phase, when the program is implemented.
4. *Evaluation.* The final step in the process is the assessment of what worked, what didn't, and how to improve in the future.[3]

Each of these four process steps is important. Most essential is starting with a firm base of research and a solid foundation of planning.

All planning requires thinking. Planning a short-term public relations program to promote a new service may require less thought and time than planning a longer-term campaign to win support for a public policy issue. However, in each case, the public relations plan must include clear-cut objectives to achieve organizational goals, strategies to

A QUESTION OF ETHICS

Jail to the Chief

In the first years of the 21st century, no group needed ethical public relations counsel more than CEOs.

Once revered as the pinnacle of corporate power and respect, by the summer of 2002, "CEO" had become the shadiest three letters in the alphabet.

What a difference a decade makes.

In the 1990s, CEOs—particularly those who ran Internet and telecommunications firms—were revered. The media hung on their every word, and they were surrounded by adoring subordinates. By the 2000s, these same individuals were taking the Fifth Amendment before Congress. And they were still surrounded—but now by FBI agents, who first handcuffed them and escorted them on high-profile, early morning "perp walks," right out of *The Sopranos*.

Although it was unclear whether all the very public arrests and indictments would result in convictions, what was irrefutable was how far and how fast CEOs had fallen. At the heart of the public's anger over CEO performance was the suspicion that investors and employees were grievously misled by individuals who were hired to be stewards of shareholder trust and performance.

Consider a partial Hall of Shame of the miscreants and their malfeasance:

WorldCom. **CEO Bernie Ebbers,** a former teacher and high school basketball coach, miraculously cobbled together the largest telecommunications firm in the United States. How? As it turned out, through improper accounting of $7 billion in expenses, leading to bankruptcy. As its chief financial officer and controller were led away, the company admitted its accounting was fraudulent. (Figure 4-1).

Adelphia. **CEO John Rigas,** together with his sons and other relatives, built a huge cable company and were eminently respected in their Pennsylvania community. Problem was that the family allegedly pilfered $1 billion in hidden loans, lied about number of subscribers, and looted the company. All were charged with fraud.

FIGURE 4-1 **In the dock.** WorldCom CEO Bernie Ebbers (middle) and two fellow executives face the music in the dock of the House of Representatives, as they testify on the company's failure.

ImClone Systems. **CEO Sam Waksal** developed a drug that was rumored to deal effectively with cancer. When Waksal learned the drug would not be approved by the FDA, he allegedly tipped off his father and daughter, and they all dumped their stock before ordinary shareholders ever found out. The CEO was indicted for his efforts.

Tyco International. **CEO Dennis Kozlowski** was known as a master alchemist, who bought hundreds of companies and pieced them together. Less well known was that Kozlowski was allegedly using $135 million in forgiven loans to finance lavish homes, yachts, and a $6,000 gold-and-burgundy, floral patterned shower curtain. Kozlowski was tripped up when he tried to evade state sales taxes on the purchase of priceless artworks (Figure 4-2).

Enron. **CEO Ken Lay** graduated from spirited salesman to proprietor of the world's largest energy trading company. Enron was touted as "a new generation company." It also was exposed for illegal off

(Continued)

FIGURE 4-2 **Man of the shower.** Tyco CEO Dennis Kozlowski outside court.

balance sheet deals to hide debt, inflate earnings, and ultimately kill the company, along with its trusting shareholders and employees.

AOL Time Warner. AOL **Ceo Steve Case** merged the largest online provider with the largest media company to form a content delivery vehicle that promised to set new communications standards. What it really did was fail miserably through a lack of synergy and then was accused of improperly accounting for advertising revenue to inflate its earnings. Case, the darling of the Internet, was guilty of no crime other than being asleep at the switch.

In light of these cases and others that cost shareholders billions of dollars, one had to wonder whether professional, ethical public relations counsel, sitting at the shoulder of the CEO, could have helped prevent such immense financial and reputational tragedies.

reach those objectives, tactics to implement the strategies, and measurement to determine whether the tactics worked.

Among the most important aspects of public relations practice is setting clear goals, objectives, and targets for the tactics applied. Public relations activities are meaningless unless designed to accomplish certain measurable goals.

For example, consider the following elementary public relations plan:

I. *Environment*
We need to increase product sales in the local market. Currently we are number 3 in the market, running close behind the second-place supplier but far behind the market leader.

II. *Business objectives*
Our goal is to build market share for our product in the local area. We seek to surpass the number 2 provider and edge closer to number 1.

III. *Public relations objectives*
- Confirm our company's solid commitment to local customers.
- Convince potential customers that our company offers the staff, expertise, products, and responsiveness that match their needs.
- Position our company as formidable competition to the two market leaders.

IV. *Public relations strategies*
Position our company as the expert in the market through company-sponsored surveys and research directed at local decision makers; media placement of company-related articles; speaking platforms of company executives; and company-sponsored seminars to demonstrate our expertise.

V. *Public relations programs/tactics*
- Seek media placements and bylined articles discussing company products for local media.
- Solicit profile features and interviews with company officials on an exclusive basis with leading trade publications.

- Sponsor a quarterly survey of local companies. Mail the survey to local decision makers, focus on a current topic of concern, and offer information and comment from the customer's view.
- Sponsor four seminars a year for emerging product-using companies in the local area. Tailor each seminar to particular audiences—women, minorities, small businesses, specific industries, not-for-profit groups. Seminars should feature company experts and well-known outside speakers. Thus, they should reinforce our commitment to the local market and also stimulate publicity.
- Launch a company speakers bureau wherein company speakers address important groups throughout the area.

After the adoption of such public relations programs, the success or failure of the campaign must be evaluated. In devising the public relations plan along these lines, an organization is assured that its public relations programs will reinforce and complement its overall business goals.

Activating the Public Relations Plan

Any public relations campaign puts all of the aspects of public relations planning—objectives, strategies, research, budgeting, tactics, and evaluation—into one cohesive framework. The plan specifies a series of "what's" to be done and "how's" to get them done—whatever is necessary to reach the objectives.

Every aspect of the public relations plan should be designed to be meaningful and valuable to the organization. The skeleton of a typical public relations campaign plan resembles the following:

1. *Backgrounding the problem.*   This is the so-called situation analysis, background, or case statement that specifies the major aims of the campaign. It can be a general statement that refers to audiences, known research, the organization's positions, history, and the obstacles faced in reaching the desired goal. A public relations planner should divide the overriding goal into several subordinate objectives, which are the "what's" to be accomplished.

2. *Preparing a proposal.*   The second stage of the campaign plan sketches broad approaches to solve the problem at hand. It outlines the strategies—the "how's"—and the public relations tools to be used to fulfill the objectives. The elements of the public relations proposal may vary, depending on the subject matter, but generally include the following:
   - Situational analysis—description of the challenge as it currently exists, including background on how the situation reached its present state.
   - Scope of assignment—description of the nature of the assignment: what the public relations program will attempt to do.
   - Target audiences—specific targets identified and divided into manageable groups.
   - Research methods—specific research approach to be used.
   - Key messages—specific selected appeals: What do we want to tell our audiences? How do we want them to feel about us? What do we want them to do?
   - Communications vehicles—tactical communications devices to be used.
   - Project team—key players who will participate in the program.
   - Timing and fees—a timetable with proposed costs identified.

The specific elements of any proposal depend on the unique nature of the program itself. When an outside supplier submits a proposal, additional elements—such as cancellation clauses, confidentiality of work, and references—should also be included.

3. *Implementing the plan.* The third stage of a campaign plan details operating tactics. It may also contain a time chart specifying when each action will take place. Specific activities are defined, people are assigned to them, and deadlines are established. This stage forms the guts of the campaign plan.

4. *Evaluating the campaign.* To find out whether the plan worked, evaluation methods should be spelled out here.
   - Did we implement the activities we proposed?
   - Did we receive appropriate public recognition for our efforts?
   - Did attitudes change—among the community, customers, management—as a result of our programs?

Pre- and posttesting of audience attitudes, quantitative analysis of event attendance, content analysis of media success, surveys, sales figures, staff reports, letters to management, and feedback from others—the specific method of evaluative testing is up to the practitioner. But the inclusion of a mechanism for evaluation is imperative.[4]

A public relations campaign plan should always be spelled out—in writing—so that planners can keep track of progress and management can assess results. Although planning in public relations is important and should be taken more seriously than it presently is by public relations professionals, the caveat of management gurus Thomas Peters and Robert Waterman must always be considered: "The problem is that the planning becomes an end in itself."[5] In public relations this cannot be allowed. No mat-

---

S I D E B A R

Potter Planning Parameters

Public relations plans must be spelled out in writing. But how should they be organized and what should they say?

Here's how one communications expert, Les Potter, organizes his strategic communications plans into 10 sections:

1. Executive summary—an overview of the plan.
2. Communication process—how it works, for understanding and training purposes.
3. Background—mission statement, vision, values, events that led to the need for the plan.
4. Situation analysis—major issues and related facts the plan will deal with.
5. Message statement—the plan's major ideas and emerging themes, all of which look to the expected outcome.
6. Audiences—strategic constituencies related to the issues, listed in order of importance, with whom you wish to develop and maintain relationships.
7. Key audience messages—one-or two-sentence messages that you want to be understood by each key audience.
8. Implementation—issues, audiences, messages, media, timing, cost, expected outcomes, and method of evaluation—all neatly spelled out.
9. Budget—the plan's overall budget presented in the organization's accepted style.
10. Monitoring and evaluation—how the plan's results will be measured and evaluated, against a previously set benchmark or desired outcome.[6]

ter how important planning may be, public relations is assessed principally in terms of its action, performance, and practice.

Setting Public Relations Objectives

An organization's goals must define what its public relations goals will be, and the only good goals are ones that can be measured. Public relations objectives and the strategies that flow from them, like those in other business areas, must be results oriented. As the baseball pitcher Johnny Sain used to say, "Nobody wants to hear about the labor pains, but everyone wants to see the baby."

So, too, must public relations people think strategically. Strategies are the most crucial decisions of a public relations campaign. They answer the general question, "How will we manage our resources to achieve our goals?" The specific answers then become the public relations tactics used to implement the strategies. Ideally, strategies and tactics should profit from pretesting.

As for objectives, good ones stand up to the following questions:

- Do they clearly describe the end result expected?
- Are they understandable to everyone in the organization?
- Do they list a firm completion date?
- Are they realistic, attainable, and measurable?
- Are they consistent with management's objectives?

Increasingly, public relations professionals are managing by objectives (MBO) and results (MBR) to help quantify the value of public relations in an organization.

The two questions most frequently asked by general managers of public relations practitioners are, "How can we measure public relations results?" and "How do we know whether the public relations program is making progress?" MBO can provide public relations professionals with a powerful source of feedback. MBO and MBR tie public relations results to management's predetermined objectives—in terms of audiences, messages, and media. Even though procedures for implementing MBO programs differ, most programs share four points:

1. Specification of the organization's goals, with objective measures of the organization's performance
2. Conferences between the superior and the subordinate to agree on achievable goals
3. Agreement between the superior and the subordinate on objectives consistent with the organization's goals
4. Periodic reviews by the superior and the subordinate to assess progress toward achieving the goals

Again, the key is to tie public relations goals to the goals of the organization and then to manage progress toward achieving those goals. The goals themselves should be clearly defined and specific, practical and attainable, and measurable.

The key to using MBO effectively in public relations work can be broken down into seven critical steps:

1. Defining the nature and mission of the work
2. Determining key result areas in terms of time, effort, and personnel
3. Identifying measurable factors on which objectives can be set

4. Setting objectives or determining results to be achieved
5. Preparing tactical plans to achieve specific objectives, including:
   * Programming to establish a sequence of actions to follow
   * Scheduling to set time requirements for each step
   * Budgeting to assign the resources required to reach the goals
   * Fixing individual accountability for the accomplishment of the objectives
   * Reviewing and reconciling through a testing procedure to track progress
6. Establishing rules and regulations to follow
7. Establishing procedures to handle the work.[7]

Budgeting for Public Relations

Forecasting expected activities has always been one of the most uncertain tasks in public relations. Many argue that "measurement" in a practice like public relations is, by definition, an imperfect art. As a consequence, many public relations operations almost routinely overrun planned budget targets.[8]

Nonetheless, like any other business activity, public relations programs must be based on sound budgeting. After identifying objectives and strategies, the public relations professional must detail the particular tactics that will help achieve those objectives. No organization can spend indiscriminately. Without a realistic budget, no organization can succeed. Likewise, public relations activities must be disciplined by budgetary realities.

In public relations agencies responsible for producing revenue, "functional budgeting" is the rule; that is, dollars for staff, resources, activities, and so on, are linked to specific revenue-generating activities. Employees are required to turn in time sheets, detailing hours worked in behalf of specific clients (Figure 4-3). In most other organizations, where public relations is a "staff" activity and not responsible for revenue generation, "administrative budgeting" is the rule; that is, budget dollars are assigned generally against the department's allocation for staff and expenses.

The key to budgeting may lie in performing two steps: (1) estimating the extent of the resources—both personnel and purchases—needed to accomplish each activity and (2) estimating the cost and availability of those resources. With this information in hand, the development of a budget and monthly cash flow for a public relations program becomes easier. Such data also provide the milestones necessary to audit program costs on a routine basis and to make adjustments well in advance of budget crises.

In recent years, public relations budgets have increased. In perhaps the largest public relations budget ever awarded, the American Legacy Foundation—established as a result of the Master Settlement Agreement between 46 states and the tobacco industry in 1999—named Arnold Communications of Boston and its partnering agencies to lead an antismoking public education campaign. The fee? The contract was valued at 50 percent to 85 percent of the $300 million received annually by the foundation.[9]

Whew!

Notwithstanding the huge public relations antitobacco effort, most public relations programs still operate on limited budgets. Therefore, whenever possible, adaptable programs—which can be readily recycled and redesigned to meet changing needs—should be considered. For example, television, magazine, newspaper, and even Internet advertising generally is too expensive for most public relations budgets. On the other hand, special events, personalized literature, direct mail, personal contacts,

```
BURSON-MARSTELLER

            PAYROLL TIME SHEET FOR
               ON CALL EMPLOYEES


                        Employee Name: _____

                        Employee No.: _____

                        Department/Unit: _____

                        Week Ending Sunday: _____
```

DAYS	DATE	TIME IN	TIME OUT	LESS LUNCH	TOTAL TIME
MON.					
TUES.					
WED.					
THURS.					
FRI.					
SAT.					
SUN.					

```
                             TOTAL HOURS       _____

                    EMPLOYEE'S SIGNATURE _____

                    SUPERVISOR'S SIGNATURE _____
```

INSTRUCTIONS: Time Sheets must be completed weekly and submitted to the Payroll Department in New York every Tuesday by 12 noon. Attach a B-M Weekly Time Sheet (yellow) or B-M Word Processing Time Sheet (blue) for client billable hours only, if appplicable. Employee's copy will be returned upon approval.

PAYROLL/WHITE   EMPLOYEE/YELLOW   BUSINESS MANAGER/PINK

FIGURE 4-3   **Agency time sheet.** Public relations agencies, like law firms, ask employees to note the weekly hours they work in behalf of particular clients.

and promotional displays are the kinds of relatively less expensive communications vehicles that can be easily duplicated.

One way to ensure that budgets are adhered to is to practice the process of open bidding for public relations materials and suppliers. An open bidding process allows several vendors to demonstrate how they would fulfill the specifications enumerated for the job. These specifications should take into account programmatic considerations in terms of both quality and quantity. Public relations budgets should be reasonable—ordinarily, a fraction (10 percent or so)—of advertising budgets and flexible enough to withstand midcourse corrections and unexpected cost overruns.

Most public relations agencies treat client costs in a manner similar to that used by legal, accounting, and management consulting firms: The client pays only for services rendered, either on a monthly or yearly retainer basis or on minimum charges based on staff time. Time records are kept by every employee—from chairperson to mail clerk—on a daily basis to be sure that agency clients know exactly what they are paying for. Hourly charges for public relations agency employees can range from low double figures per hour to more than $350 to $500 an hour for agency superstars.

Because agency relationships are based on trust, it is important that clients understand the derivation of costs. In recent years, debate has raged over markups on expenses paid in behalf of clients by public relations firms. Out-of-pocket expenses—for meals, hotels, transportation, and the like—are generally charged back to clients at cost. But when an agency pays in advance for larger expense items—printing, photography, graphics, design—it is standard industry practice to mark up such expenses by a factor approximating 17.65 percent. This figure, which the vast majority of agencies use, was borrowed from the advertising profession and represented the multiplicative inverse of the standard 15 percent commission that ad agencies collected on advertising placement.

The guiding rule in agency budgeting is to ensure that the client is aware of how charges are being applied, so that nasty surprises might be avoided when bills are received.

Implementing Public Relations Programs

The duties and responsibilities of public relations practitioners are as diverse as the publics with whom different institutions deal. Basically, public relations tasks can be divided into four broad categories:

1. Advice—provided to management on organizational decisions and policies, to ensure that they are consistent with the public interest
2. Communications service—including the outward communication of information to various external publics and the inward communication of corporate philosophy, policies, and programs to the employees
3. Public issues research and analysis—identifying, evaluating, and communicating to management the external information that may be most relevant to organizational policies and programs
4. Public relations action programs—designed to generate goodwill through comprehensive programs focused on a particular issue or audience[10]

Specific public relations tasks are as varied as the organizations served. Here is a partial list of public relations duties:

- Reaching the employees through a variety of internal means, including intranet, newsletters, television, and meetings. Traditionally, this role has emphasized news-oriented communications rather than benefits-oriented ones, which are usually the province of personnel departments.
- Coordinating relationships with the online, print, and electronic media, which includes arranging and monitoring press interviews, writing news releases and

related press materials, organizing press conferences, and answering media inquiries and requests. A good deal of media relations work consists of attempting to gain favorable news coverage for the firm.

● Coordinating activities with legislators on local, state, and federal levels. This includes legislative research activities and public policy formation.

● Orchestrating interaction with the community, perhaps including open houses, tours, and employee volunteer efforts designed to reflect the supportive nature of the organization to the community.

● Managing relations with the investment community, including the firm's present and potential stockholders. This task emphasizes personal contact with securities analysts, institutional investors, and private investors.

● Supporting activities with customers and potential customers, with activities ranging from hard-sell product promotion activities to "soft" consumer advisory services.

● Coordinating the institution's printed voice with its public through reprints of speeches, annual reports, quarterly statements, and product and company brochures.

● Coordinating relationships with outside specialty groups, such as suppliers, educators, students, nonprofit organizations, and competitors.

● Managing the institutional—or nonproduct—advertising image as well as being called on increasingly to assist in the management of more traditional product advertising.

● Coordinating the graphic and photographic services of the organization. To do this task well requires knowledge of typography, layout, and art.

● Coordinating the organization's online "face," including Web site design and ongoing counsel, updating, and even management of the site.

● Conducting opinion research, which involves assisting in the public policy formation process through the coordination and interpretation of attitudinal studies of key publics.

● Managing the gift-giving apparatus, which ordinarily consists of screening and evaluating philanthropic proposals and allocating the organization's available resources.

● Coordinating special events, including travel for company management, corporate celebrations and exhibits, dinners, groundbreakings, and grand openings.

● Management counseling, which involves advising administrators on alternative options and recommended choices in light of public responsibilities.

Public relations managers frequently use the visualization tools of Gantt and PERT charts to control and administer these project tasks. The Gantt chart, developed by Charles Gantt in 1917, focuses on the sequence of tasks necessary for completion of the project at hand. Each task on a Gantt chart is represented as a single horizontal bar. The length of each bar corresponds to the time necessary for completion. Arrows connecting independent tasks reflect the relationships between the tasks. PERT charts (Program Evaluation and Review Technique) were first developed in the 1950s by the Navy to help manage complex projects with a high degree of intertask dependency. The PERT chart shows the relationship between each activity. These relationships create pathways through the process. The "critical path" is a series of tasks that must be completed in a certain time period for the project to be completed on schedule (Figure 4-4).

Prototype Gantt Chart
Packaged Goods Product
Target Start of Ship at Start of Year, Retail Availability in March, Marketing Support in April

Category	Activity	Jan	Feb	Mar	Apr	May	Jun	Jul	Aug
Product	Exploratory Research	XXX							
	Concept Development		XXX						
	Quantitative Research			XXX	XXX				
Package	Product Development			XXX	XXX	XXX	XXX	XXX	
	Structural Package Dev			XXX	XXX	XXX	XXX	XXX	
	Graphics Development				XXX	XXX	XXX	XXX	
Financial	Pricing & Profit	XXX							
	Volume Projections	XXX							
	Budget Development					XXX			
Marketing Plan	Sales Promotion				XXX	XXX	XXX	XXX	
	Advertising				XXX	XXX	XXX	XXX	
	Publicity						XXX	XXX	
Purchasing	Produce Ads/Collateral Material								XXX
	Long Lead Supplies				XXX	XXX	XXX	XXX	XXX
	Shorter Lead Supplies						XXX	XXX	XXX
Begin Production	Inventory Build								XXX
Sales Meetings	Ship To Field Warehouses								
	Present To Sales Force								
Start Shipping	Present To Trade								
	Begin Delivery To Trade								

FIGURE 4-4 **Critical path chart.** Daniel Jay Morrison & Associates (www.djmconsult.com) created this prototypical chart to trace the "critical path" of a product coming to market. (Courtesy Daniel Jay Morrison & Associates.)

Public Relations as Boundary Manager

By the end of its first century as a management function, public relations had developed its own theoretical framework as a management system. The work of communications professors James Grunig and Todd Hunt, although not the only relevant management theory, nonetheless has done much to advance this development.[11]

Grunig and Hunt suggest that public relations managers perform what organizational theorists call a "boundary" role; they function at the edge of an organization as a liaison between the organization and its external and internal publics. In other words, public relations managers have one foot inside the organization and one outside. Often this unique position is not only lonely but also precarious.

As boundary managers, public relations people support their colleagues by helping them communicate across organizational lines both within and outside the organization. In this way, public relations professionals also become systems managers, knowledgeable about and able to deal with the complex relationships inherent in the organization.

- They must consider the relationship of the organization to its environment— the ties that unite business managers and operations support staff, for example, and the conflicts that separate them.
- They must work within organizational confines to develop innovative solutions to organizational problems. By definition, public relations managers deal in a different environment from that of their organizational colleagues. Public relations people deal with perceptions, attitudes, and public opinion. Other business managers deal in a more empirical, quantitative, concrete domain. Public relations managers, therefore, must be innovative, not only in proposing communications solutions but also in making them understandable and acceptable to colleagues.
- They must think strategically. Public relations managers must demonstrate their knowledge of the organization's mission, objectives, and strategies. Their solutions must answer the real needs of the organization. They must reflect the big picture. Business managers will care little that the company's name was mentioned in the morning paper unless they can recognize the strategic rationale for the reference.
- Public relations managers also must be willing to measure their results. They must state clearly what they want to accomplish, systematically set out to accomplish it, and measure their success. This means using such accepted business school techniques as management by objectives (MBO), management by objectives and results (MBR), and program evaluation and research technique (PERT).
- Finally, as Grunig and Hunt point out, in managing an organization's public relations system, practitioners must demonstrate comfort with the various elements of the organization itself: (1) functions, the real jobs of organizational components; (2) structure, the organizational hierarchy of individuals and positions; (3) processes, the formal decision-making rules and procedures the organization follows; and (4) feedback, the formal and informal evaluative mechanisms of the organization.[12]

Such a theoretical overview is important to consider in properly situating the practice of public relations as a management system within an organization.

The Public Relations Department

Public relations professionals generally work in one of two organizational structures: (1) as a staff professional in a public relations department of a corporation, university, hospital, sports franchise, political campaign, religious institution, and so on, whose task is to support the primary business of the organization or (2) as a line professional in a public relations agency, whose primary task is to help the organization earn revenue.

Consider the public relations department.

Once an organization has analyzed its environment, established its objectives, set up measurement standards, and thought about appropriate plans, programs, and budgets, it is ready to organize a public relations department. Departments range from one-person operations to far-flung networks of hundreds of people, such as General Motors or Exxon Mobil, with staff around the world, responsible for relations with the press, investors, civic groups, employees, and many different governments.

Today, in the wake of the bursting of the high-tech stock market bubble, many corporate public relations departments have suffered the impact of downsizing and decentralization. The former has led to the shrinkage of once-large operations; the latter has led to the formation of decentralized, line-oriented departments to complement smaller central units. The two together have led many corporate public relations people to fear for the security of positions they once took for granted and a relative cutting back in the number of new positions available.

What's the best way to organize for public relations in an organization? There is no one answer. The strongest public relations department is one led by a communications executive who reports directly to the CEO. This is eminently preferable to reporting to a legal, financial, or administrative executive, who may tend to "filter" top-management messages.[13]

In government, public relations professionals typically report directly to department heads. In universities, the public relations function is frequently coupled with fund-raising and development activities. In hospitals, public relations is typically tied to the marketing function.

As for the names of the departments in which public relations is housed, organizations use a wide variety of names for the function. Ironically, the trend today seems to be away from use of the traditional term *public relations* and toward *corporate communications*.

Whatever the department is called, the pressing need today for chief communications officers and their colleagues is to demonstrate a high level of skills—from writing to counseling to understanding the critical importance of information in the wired world in which we live.

The Public Relations Agency

Now consider the public relations agency.

The biggest difference between an external agency and an internal department is perspective. The former is outside looking in; the latter is inside looking out (often literally for itself). Sometimes the use of an agency is necessary to escape the tunnel-vision syndrome that afflicts some firms, in which a detached viewpoint is desperately needed. An agency unfettered by internal corporate politics might be better trusted to present management with an objective reading of the concerns of its publics.

An agency has the added advantage of not being taken for granted by a firm's management. Unfortunately, management sometimes has a greater regard for an outside specialist than for an inside one. This attitude frequently defies logic but is nonetheless often true. Generally, if management is paying (sometimes quite handsomely) for outside counsel, it tends to listen carefully to the advice.

Agencies generally organize according to industry and account teams. Larger agencies are divided into such areas as health care, sports, fashion, technology, finance, and so on. Account teams are assigned specific clients. Team members bill clients on an hourly basis, with most firms intending to retain two-thirds of each individual's hourly billing rate as income. In other words, if an account executive bills at a rate of $300 per hour—and many senior counselors do—the firm expects to retain $200 of that rate toward its profit. In recent years, as clients have begun to manage resources more rigorously, agencies have gotten much more "systematic" in measuring success and in keeping customers from "migrating" to a competitor. Indeed, if not actively and directly addressed on an ongoing basis, customer satisfaction will inevitably decline.[14]

Public relations agencies today, as noted, are huge businesses. Over the past two decades, most of the top public relations firms have been subsumed by advertising agencies—Burson-Marsteller and Hill & Knowlton by WPP Group; Fleishman-Hillard, Ketchum, and Porter Novelli by Omnicom Group; Weber Shandwick Worldwide and Golin/Harris International by Interpublic Group, among many others. Public relations purists bemoan the incursion by advertising agencies into their field, whereas others point to the potential synergy between the two disciplines. What is indisputable is the tremendous growth in the profession, with the top firms all producing well in excess of $100 million in revenues annually (Table 4-1).

Public relations counsel is, by definition, a highly personalized service. A counselor's prescription for a client depends primarily on what the counselor thinks a client needs and how that assessment fits the client's own perception of those needs. Often an

SIDEBAR

À la Carte Public Relations

Although hourly rates and retainers are standard in the public relations business, at least one Washington, D.C., agency doesn't mess around with such details. It gets paid only when it gets publicity for clients. No publicity—no pay!

Levick Strategic Consulting bills its clients, mostly law firms, by the number of media "opportunities" per month in a program called "Success Billing." Clients identify what they consider "success" in terms of media placement. If a reporter calls for an interview or a story mentions the client, that's an "opportunity."

Clients pay extra for media training, ghost writing, expert coaching, or strategy development. The à la carte cost schedule includes the following:

$10,000 per month: 6 to 8 opportunities
$12,000 per month: 9 to 12 opportunities
$15,000 per month: 13 to 20 opportunities
Ghost writing: $175/hour
Media training: $3,700 to $10,000 per day

Because the Levick "pay for play" system takes great courage—consider the downside—it is safe to say that most public relations agencies will not soon adopt a similar budgeting strategy.

T A B L E 4 - 1

Top 25 Agencies

Ranking 2001	Agency Name	US Revenue($) 2001	2000	% Change	Staff 2001	Revenue($) Per Employee	Global Revenue($) 2001	2000	% Change	Staff 2001	Revenue($) Per Employee	Location
1	Weber Shandwick Worldwide[1]	283,084,398	358,202,702	–21	1,550	182,635	426,572,018	507,438,046	–16	2,838	150,307	New York
2	Fleishman-Hillard[2]	263,345,095	262,406,498	0	1,480	177,936	345,098,241	338,415,880	2	2,288	150,830	St. Louis
3	Hill & Knowlton[3]	190,931,000	174,363,000	10	659	289,728	325,119,000	302,769,000	7	1,117	291,064	New York
4	Ketchum[2]	161,425,000	143,779,000	12	797	202,541	185,221,000	168,247,000	10	1,066	173,753	New York
5	Edelman Public Relations Worldwide	152,385,810	167,485,878	–9	1,073	142,018	223,708,535	233,415,105	–4	1,973	113,385	Chicago
6	Burson-Marsteller[3]	150,417,000	182,259,000	–17	730	206,051	259,112,000	303,860,000	–15	1,613	160,640	New York
7	Porter Novelli[2]	116,764,000	135,888,000	–14	733	159,296	179,294,000	208,157,000	–14	1,553	115,450	New York
8	Ogilvy Public Relations Worldwide[3]	94,904,500	129,063,800	–26	525	180,770	145,949,285	169,453,900	–14	1,110	131,486	New York
9	GCI Group/APCO Worldwide[4]	85,434,598	87,520,051	–2	521	163,982	151,081,645	150,661,643	0	1,282	117,848	New York
10	Golin/Harris International[1]	81,897,283	107,905,495	–24	389	210,533	113,247,644	134,650,000	–16	655	172,897	Chicago
11	MS&L[5]	79,926,519	80,390,676	–1	503	158,900	116,019,465	118,843,522	–2	885	131,095	New York
12	Ruder Finn Group	69,890,000	75,574,000	–8	433	161,409	80,348,000	84,125,000	–4	543	147,971	New York
13	Incepta (Citigate)[6]	68,392,291	79,271,575	–14	389	175,816	266,018,371	243,938,376	9	2,236	118,971	London
14	Waggener Edstrom	57,237,800	56,162,000	2	450	127,195	59,890,800	57,904,000	3	469	127,699	Bellevue, WA
15	Brodeur Worldwide[2]	39,601,900	53,500,000	–26	309	128,161	70,001,900	84,200,000	–17	671	104,325	Boston
16	Cohn & Wolfe[3]	33,785,000	41,945,000	–19	175	193,057	57,779,000	63,580,000	–9	379	152,451	New York
17	Schwartz Communications	30,375,804	33,185,571	–8	156	194,717	30,375,804	33,185,571	–8	156	194,717	Waltham, MA
18	The MWW Group[1]	29,257,830	37,723,000	–22	155	188,760	29,257,830	37,723,000	–22	155	188,760	East Rutherford, NJ
19	Publicis Dialog[5]	28,631,788	29,769,406	–4	161	177,837	28,631,788	29,769,406	–4	161	177,837	New York
20	FitzGerald Communications	22,829,998	21,441,162	6	156	146,346	22,829,998	21,441,162	6	156	146,346	Boston
21	Rowland Communications Worldwide[5]	20,437,000	26,033,000	–22	125	163,496	42,666,000	45,391,000	–6	125	341,328	Dearborn, MI
22	Campbell & Co.	19,998,000	N/A	N/A	168	119,036	19,998,000	N/A	N/A	168	119,036	New York
23	Morgen-Walke Associates[7]	19,973,840	26,826,832	–26	88	226,975	90,655,000	79,810,000	14	633	143,215	New York
24	Magnet Communications[8]	17,830,000	26,652,000	–33	127	140,394	17,830,000	26,652,000	–33	127	140,394	New York
25	Text 100 Public Relations[9]	15,004,479	13,003,773	15	112	133,969	33,676,739	33,681,553	0	405	83,152	San Francisco

Notes: Ownership is noted by the following legend: **1** Interpublic Group **2** Omnicom **3** WPP **4** Grey Advertising **5** Publicis Groupe **6** Incepta **7** Cordiant **8** Havas **9** One Monday **Rankings:** Agencies have been ranked by US revenue, but global revenue and staff have been included in the charts. A ranking by global revenue is available on pp. 8–11. **Revenue:** All revenues are pro forma in this chart. This means that where an agency has made an acquisition, all 2000 revenues from that company are included. Revenue is defined as fee income plus mark-up on billable items. Up to 10% of revenues were also permitted from media commissions on corporate and issues-related advertising; however, media commissions on consumer and b-to-b advertising were not allowed. Per GAAP standards, revenues from subsidiary companies and affiliates were not included if the stake was less than 50; and where the stake was more than 50, the full amount (i.e.100) has been included. **Auditing:** No audit was required for inclusion in the rankings. The CEO/Principal/CFO was required to sign off a statement verifying the accuracy of the data and agreeing to possible participation in a random audit. **Disclaimer:** While every effort has been made to ensure the accuracy of these figures, *PRWeek* cannot accept liability for, nor make financial guarantees based upon, the information in these charts.

Source: *Council of Public Relations Firms*

Public relations agencies, even in recessionary times, have become big business. (Courtesy of PR Week magazine.)

outsider's fresh point of view is helpful in focusing a client on particular problems and opportunities and on how best to conquer or capitalize on them.

On the other hand, because outside agencies are just that—outside—they are often unfamiliar about details affecting the situation of particular companies and with the idiosyncrasies of company management. The good external counselor must constantly work to overcome this barrier. The best client–agency relationships are those with freeflowing communications between internal and external public relations groups so that both resources are kept informed about corporate policies, strategies, and tactics. A well-oiled, complementary department–agency relationship can result in a more positive communications approach for an organization.

Where Are the Jobs?

A not-so-funny thing happened on the way to the anticipated 21st-century boom in public relations high-tech and other corporate positions—the bubble burst.

Although public relations practitioners—particularly in high tech—were in high demand during the 1990s, the crash of the stock market in the first years of the new century affected all aspects of public relations positions—from openings to salaries to most fertile areas.

In companies, layoffs, cutbacks, and diminished income took their toll on public relations departments. As to public relations agencies, the top 10 firms were down 10 percent—nearly $200 million—in revenue in 2001 and collectively cut 2,700 employees, or 24 percent of their staffs.[15]

Although the industry suffered significant casualties, the future of the practice of public relations, like the future of the U.S. and world economy, promises to be steady and strong.

- In terms of areas of specialization, the function of "managing a company's reputation" ranks high on the public relations job scale. So, too, do the areas of investor relations and crisis management. These three specialties, in fact, pay considerably more than other areas of the field.[16]
- Worldwide corporations, faced with increased scrutiny from the media, government, and the general public to act ethically and behave responsibly, have recognized the need for talented, top communications managers.

Many CEOs are willing to pay more for such assistance, but they also demand additional skills beyond the traditional ones. Such new competencies include matrix management, which involves team building and teamwork; virtual management, where one operates at a distance using e-mail, videoconferencing, and other new age tools; business literacy, knowing how a company and industry make money; and working effectively with consultants as more and more tasks get outsourced to conserve internal resources.[17]

- In a related sense, public relations agencies, wiser and more experienced after the boom-bust phenomenon of the 1990s, will continue to expand in the new century. The last three years of the 20th century brought new prominence and success to many in the agency field. Just as a plethora of high-tech public relations agencies emerged in the early 1990s, so, too, is it likely that the move toward public relations specialization among agencies will continue in 2000 and beyond.
- In the nonprofit realm, public relations positions in hospitals, in particular, are likely to grow, as managed care becomes the reality and health care

organizations become more competitive in attracting patients and winning community approval. Other nonprofits—schools, museums, associations—all faced with less resources and more competition for community funding, will also require increased public relations help to attract development and membership funds.

● Even the high-tech industry, which fell further and faster than most others after its unprecedented buildup in the 1990s, will need skilled public relations managers to help it regain a position of prominence, trust, and respect among investors and others.

● Finally, one other public relations skill that will be in increased demand, certainly for the remainder of this decade, is employee communications. Employees in the 21st century, burned by layoffs, pension fund losses, and failures of management to be credible, must be convinced that their organizations deserve their allegiance. This will be a job largely for public relations practitioners—to win back employee trust.[18]

What's It Pay?

Without question the communications function has increased in importance and clout in the new century. Top communications professionals in many large corporations today draw compensation packages well into six figures. According to one recent survey, the average vice president of corporate communications earned almost $190,000 annually.[19]

The same survey indicated that although entry-level jobs for writers and editors generally fall into the $20,000–$30,000 range, more senior writers can expect to earn in the $50,000 range. Managers of public relations units, press relations, consumer relations, and financial communications may earn anywhere from $40,000 to beyond $100,000. Agency account executives fall into a similar range. Public relations directors may earn salaries from $40,000 to more than $500,000.

In the heyday of the 1990s, a fortunate few corporate practitioners, able to profit from corporate stock options, earned in excess of $1 million annually. Agency executives, who either own their firms outright or have significant stock in parent holding companies, also may reach seven-figure earnings. Not bad for public relations work.

In 1996, the Public Relations Society of America (PRSA) conducted a landmark, comprehensive study of public relations salaries. The median public-relations salary, according to that study, was slightly more than $49,000 a year (Table 4-2).[20] A more recent *PR Week* survey put the median public relations salary at $65,860—an increase of 35 percent over five years.[21]

Among other findings, the PRSA study determined:

● Public relations salaries were markedly higher in the Northeast and the West than in the Midwest or South.

● Investor relations was the highest-paying public relations specialty, with a median salary of more than $72,000. (The *PR Week* survey pegged investor relations salaries at nearly $80,000.)

● The lowest-paying public relations jobs were found in government, health care, and nonprofit organizations, with the median salaries approximately $43,000 for each (Table 4-3).

● There was little difference between median salaries in public relations agencies and corporations.

● Members of the Public Relations Society of America had higher salaries than nonmembers.

TABLE 4-2

Overall Public Relations Salaries—1996 PRSA Survey

	Total Respondents %	PRSA Members Total %	APR %	Non-APR %	Nonmembers %
Total Respondents	100	100	100	100	100
Less than $45,000	42	40	23	46	43
Less than $15,000	3	1	2	*	4
$15,000–$24,999	8	4	2	5	10
$25,000–$34,999	14	17	6	21	13
$35,000–$44,999	17	18	13	19	17
$45,000–$74,999	33	34	42	31	3
$45,000–$54,999	15	16	20	15	14
$55,000–$64,999	11	11	14	11	11
$65,000–$74,999	8	7	9	6	
$75,000 or more	21	22	31	19	20
$75,000–$99,999	11	11	16	10	10
$100,000–$149,999	8	7	10	7	8
$150,000 or more	3	3	4	3	3
No answer	4	5	5	4	4
Median	$49,070	$49,830	$58,840	$46,370	$48,660

*Less than 0.5%.

- Entry-level salaries were basically the same from industry to industry, generally in the $20,000 range (Table 4-4). Since getting in the door is often the toughest part of employment in the public relations profession, a lower entry-level salary may be sufficient relative to the potential earnings power later on.

TABLE 4-3

Public Relations Salaries by Organization Type—1996 PRSA Survey

	PR Firms %	Corporations %	Government Health Care/Nonprofit %
Total Respondents	100	100	100
Less than $45,000	39	39	53
Less than $15,000	2	3	1
$15,000–$24,999	9	9	5
$25,000–$34,999	12	13	22
$35,000–$44,999	16	15	25
$45,000–$74,999	24	36	32
$45,000–$54,999	11	15	16
$55,000–$64,999	6	12	9
$65,000–$74,999	6	8	7
$75,000 or more	29	21	12
$75,000–$99,999	11	11	8
$100,000–$149,999	11	8	5
$150,000 or more	7	2	*
No answer	8	4	2
Median	$51,430	$50,770	$43,260

*Less than 0.5%.

TABLE 4-4

Entry-Level Public Relations Salaries by Type of Organization—1996 PRSA Survey			
	PR Firms	**Corporations**	**Government/ Health Care/Nonprofit**
	%	%	%
Total Respondents	100	100	100
Less than $15,000	7	6	3
$15,000–$19,999	27	19	19
$20,000–$24,999	37	29	39
$25,000–$29,999	7	20	19
$30,000 or more	6	17	14
No answer	16	9	5
Median	$21,110	$23,550	$23,210

*Less than 0.5%.

Women and Minorities

Two decades ago, the practice of public relations was overwhelmingly a white male–dominated profession. Today, it is women who predominate in public relations work. And minorities—African Americans, Asians, and Hispanics—have all increased their numbers in the field.

The issue of increased feminization is still a particularly thorny one for the practice of public relations. One area of constant consternation is the traditional discrepancy between men's and women's salaries and upper-management positions.

University public relations programs across the country report a preponderance of female students, outnumbering males by as much as 80 percent. However, the ranks of women executives in public relations, as opposed to their male counterparts, are still relatively thin. Hence, the picture of, on the one hand, public relations becoming a "velvet ghetto" of women workers and, on the other hand, a profession in which women have not achieved upper-management status. This is of paramount concern to the profession.[22] As one educator bluntly put it, "Women in public relations are discriminated against.[23]

The 2001 *PR Week* salary survey indicated that men in the field earned, on average, $83,000 whereas women earned $58,000—a huge 41 percent disparity (Table 4-5). The survey also indicated that whereas 7 percent of all male respondents held the rank of senior vice president, only 2 percent of female respondents held a similar high position. Although some in the field ascribe the disparity to a variety of factors, including age and experience, others, such as Professor Elizabeth Toth, who has studied the gender question extensively, says it's more complicated: "Organizations began to face pressure from affirmative action programs to hire women and train them for management positions, and public relations seemed like a safe place to put women managers. There's a lot of good news in that, but organizational sociologists say it's another way of oppressing women."[24]

Another area of public relations in which remuneration and advancement present a perplexing problem is with respect to African Americans, Asians, and Hispanics.

According to U.S. Census Bureau statistics, the public relations industry is still predominantly white (89 percent), with blacks making up only 4.5 percent of the industry's employees. Hispanics constitute 3 percent of public relations professionals and Asians 2 percent. These numbers are considerably less than the population as a whole.

TABLE 4-5

PRWEEK Salary Survey 2002

Feature	Salaries, benefits, satisfaction	Education, gender, ethnicity, industry	Benefits
Gender differences			

Category	Average	Male	Female
Respondents (%)	N/A	31	69
Age	33.8	37.1	32.4
Years spent in PR	8	10.5	7
Years in current position	3.5	3.3	3.5
Years with current employer	3.5	4.3	3
Graduate degrees (%)	24	31	20
Average no. of times moved home for new job	0.75	1.1	0.59
Average salary now	$65,860	$83,040	$58,150
Average salary this time last year	$66,010	$85,790	$56,960
Raise/decrease on average (%)	−0.22	−3.2	2.1
Expected salary this time next year	$72,050	$89,260	$64,220
Expected % raise	9.4	7.5	10.4
Minimum raise to prompt job move	$15,400	$20,300	$13,400
Salary envisaged as bonus (% this year)	9	11.50	8
Salary envisaged as bonus (% last year)	8.70	10.40	8.10
Respondents currently job seeking in PR (%)	36	38	38
Respondents currently looking to get out of PR (%)	8	8	8
Vacation days (average)	14.98	15.75	14.62
Vacation days last year	16	17	16
Average hours per week	47.13	48.84	46.34
Respondents who are married (%)	45	59	39
Respondents with dependent children (%)	25	38	19−
Respondents members of PRSA (%)	34	36	33
Respondents members of IABC (%)	8	10	8

Gender differential survey. (Courtesy of PR Week *magazine.)*

In terms of salaries, the average pay for African Americans at $50,000 was 36 percent below that for whites. Hispanics earned a slightly higher average salary of $51,670, and Asians received an average of $62,070—still 9 percent below whites.[25]

LAST WORD

In the 21st century, the practice of public relations is firmly accepted as part of the management process of any well-run organization.

Public relations objectives and goals, strategies, and tactics must flow directly from the organization's overall goals. Public relations strategies must reflect organizational strategies, and tactics must be designed to realize the organization's business objectives.

Stated another way, public relations programs are worth little if they fail to further management's and the organization's goals.

Despite its stereotypes and demographic idiosyncrasies, the practice of public relations enjoys a significant management role and challenge in this new century. Coming out of the corporate and accounting scandals of 2002 and the loss of confidence in business in general and CEOs in particular, management must depend on the able assistance of proper public relations practice to help reestablish trust in society's major institutions.

Discussion Starters

1. What is the management process of public relations?
2. Why is it imperative that public relations report to top management?
3. What are the elements that make up a public relations plan?
4. What questions must be answered in establishing valid public relations objectives?
5. What elements go into framing a public relations budget?
6. How is the public relations professional a "boundary manager"?
7. What are the fundamental differences between working as a public relations professional in a corporation versus an agency?
8. What may be the primary areas of opportunity for public relations professionals in the years ahead?
9. Why has the field of public relations been accused of being a "velvet ghetto"?
10. What are primary issues with which the field is grappling today?

TOP OF THE SHELF

Steve Rivkin and Fraser P. Seitel

IdeaWise
New York: John Wiley & Sons, 2002

Whether top manager or public relations practitioner, coming up with creative ideas is the name of the game.

According to these two authors (whose names, frankly, are eerily familiar), anyone is capable of being an innovator.

The book exposes as high-priced charlatans the vast majority of motivational consultants hired annually by desperate, innovation-starved managers. The authors argue that organizations groping to be creative waste millions on off-site retreats and misguided motivational mantras that lead them to such creative catastrophes as Crystal Clear Pepsi, Premier smokeless cigarettes, and Susan B. Anthony dollar coins.

Instead, they suggest that you "steal" to be creative. Collect ideas from your surroundings. Borrow ideas from others. Adapt existing ideas and then apply solutions to substitute, combine, magnify/minimize, exchange, eliminate, and reverse.

Then it's time to apply a six-question checklist to see if a creative suggestion makes sense. If it does, then you, too, can become "IdeaWise."

CASE STUDY

Dow Corning in the Crucible

The sprawling Dow Corning Corporation campus sits peacefully amidst the rolling fields of Midland, Michigan. Thousands of employees, most of them Dow Corning veterans, arrive early, work diligently, and devote themselves happily to a company they consider almost family.

But the pastoral tranquillity of the campus and the friendly devotion of the workers belie a turbulent and uncertain reality. Dow Corning and its management have been involved in a public war of claims and counterclaims, accusations and denials, and public relations judgments that will mean billions of dollars in losses and perhaps, ultimately, the viability of the company itself.

With $5 billion in assets, 50,000 customers, 9,600 products, 8,700 employees, and operations on four continents—Dow Corning is in Chapter 11 bankruptcy, its future by no means clear.

On June 14, 2001, the company reached a settlement with the U.S. government and attorneys representing thousands of women, who claimed that silicone gel-filled breast implants, manufactured by Dow Corning and others, caused, among other ailments, autoimmune disease. Stated simply, Dow Corning and the others were charged with manufacturing dangerous devices, foisted on unsuspecting women.

CBS HATCHET JOB

Dow Corning's precarious situation was the ultimate public relations management crisis.

Breast implants first came on the market in the early 1960s, and the Food and Drug Administration began approving the devices in 1976. Given the long track record of breast implants, the FDA presumed that they were reasonably safe. In 1988, however, the FDA announced that breast-implant manufacturers would henceforth have to submit evidence of safety.

Two years later, on December 10, 1990, Dow Corning was thrust into a spotlight from which it has still not recovered. On her CBS television show, *Face to Face with Connie Chung*, the moderator trotted out a parade of women, seemingly terrified and victimized, who claimed that their silicone breast implants had given them autoimmune disease. Although several supportive breast implant users and doctors were interviewed for the Chung show, none made it on air. Connie Chung never called Dow Corning for comment or participation on the program (Figure 4-5).

FIGURE 4-5 **The hammer.** Connie Chung "lowered the boom" on Dow Corning with a vicious report in 1990.

After the national television broadcast, Dow Corning said nothing publicly but quickly put together a 30-second commercial with women who could speak positively about their experience with breast implants. The company planned to air the spots around the country to follow the rebroadcast of the Chung show and bought time on CBS-owned and operated stations.

A few hours before the program was scheduled to be broadcast, however, the CBS stations notified Dow Corning that the spot would not run because it would open up CBS to "equal time considerations" it couldn't honor.

THE ROOF CAVES IN

After the Chung rebroadcast, the roof caved in for Dow Corning. Congress held public hearings. Ralph Nader's Public Citizen group pressed the issue in the media and the courts. A San Francisco jury awarded more than $7 million to a woman who claimed that her Dow Corning breast implants had caused her to have mixed connective tissue disease. And in April 1992, FDA Commissioner David Kessler banned the sale of silicone gel-filled breast implants, except for use in clinical trials of breast reconstruction after cancer surgery.

The ban, Dr. Kessler took pains to point out, was not because breast implants had been found dangerous—indeed Dow Corning insisted that the implants were safe. He banned the sale because the manufacturers had not "proved scientifically that the products were safe."

This fine distinction—that there was no evidence of danger—was lost on the million or so women who already had implants. Why would the FDA ban a product if it wasn't dangerous? Predictably, women panicked. Large numbers came forward complaining of various illnesses caused by their breast implants. Media-seeking doctors and scientists popped up with evidenceless theories explaining how breast implants affected the immune system. The media, in response, jumped on the story with a vengeance. Plaintiffs' attorneys, capitalizing on the budding crop of "expert witnesses" and media attention, successfully converted the trickle of breast implant lawsuits into a flood.

LOW-KEY RESPONSE

Through the trauma, there was an eerie silence from the people in Midland, Michigan.

Dow Corning management insisted that its product was fundamentally safe. But management wanted to reconfirm that fact with undisputed scientific evidence. Dow Corning committed to spend tens of millions of dollars—upwards of $30 million through 1997—to sponsor independent university research to do the necessary epidemiology studies that would answer the safety questions.

While the company proceeded with the painstaking and prolonged task of scientific research, the media had a field day, in effect, issuing a constant drumbeat of "corporate guilt."

Dow Corning stuck to its guns with a reasoned, low-key public relations response that built up gradually:

- In 1991, it released to the general public more than 10,000 pages of proprietary information on silicone breast implants.
- In 1992, it made available complete sets of its FDA breast implant application to medical schools.
- That same year, it distributed 90 documents—nearly 1,400 pages of internal company memos and scientific studies about the safety aspects of its breast implant product.

● Later, it began to hold news conferences to rebut false allegations, and its new chairman, Richard Hazelton, began to make himself available to the media, including one stormy session facing angry breast implant users on *The Oprah Winfrey Show.*

TOO LITTLE, TOO LATE

Dow Corning's actions couldn't stem the onrushing tide.

In 1993, Dow Corning exited the breast implant business.

In 1994, breast implant manufacturers, desperate to limit their losses, agreed to the largest class-action settlement in history, with $4.25 billion to be set aside for all women with breast implants. The lawyers' take would be $1 billion. Nearly half of all women with breast implants registered for the settlement, with half of the claimants claiming to be suffering from implant-related illnesses.

With so many women opting out of the settlement and deciding to continue with their lawsuits and their attorneys' exorbitant demands, Dow Corning filed for Chapter 11 bankruptcy protection in May 1995. The settlement collapsed shortly thereafter.

In December 1996, Dow Corning filed a proposed $3 billion bankruptcy reorganization plan, $2 billion of which could potentially be set aside to cover breast implant claims. The Dow Corning plan was met by derision among plaintiffs' attorneys, who argued that the settlement fell far short of what was needed.

By 1997, Dow Corning's fate once again rested with the courts. CEO Hazelton, reflecting on the controversy and the decisions that management made throughout, said, "I feel like all of us have done the best we could under the circumstances. Obviously, there are a lot of lessons that everybody has learned that I hope we all take to heart to prevent something like this from ever happening again" (Figure 4-6).

FIGURE 4-6 **Show of support.** Despite its continuing problems, Dow Corning's employees signed off in support of their beseiged management.

In 2001, the U.S. government announced that it had reached a tentative settlement with Dow Corning to compensate women impacted by the company's products. By the summer of 2002, Dow Corning—now a reinvented and much wiser company—was still unsure of exactly how much money it would have to pay out to satisfy the claims against it.

Questions

1. What's your opinion of how *Face to Face with Connie Chung* handled the breast implant story?
2. What options did Dow Corning have in responding to the story?
3. How would you characterize Dow Corning's public relations strategy?
4. What other strategic public relations options did Dow Corning management have in answering the silicone breast implant charges?
5. With the silicon implant controversy now behind it, what kind of public relations strategy should Dow Corning embrace?
6. What has happened to Dow Corning and its breast implant business? See the latest announcements on the company's special Web site (www.implantclaims.com/). Why would the company maintain this special site? Do you agree with the way Dow Corning is using the Internet to communicate with some of its publics?

TIPS FROM THE TOP

An Interview with Richard Hazelton

Richard Hazelton

Richard Hazelton, a lifetime employee of Dow Corning, was named chairman and CEO in 1993, well after the company's breast implant problems began. Mr. Hazelton was at the company's helm when it declared bankruptcy and eventually settled with those who sued over the silicone implants.

Prior to the escalation of the silicone breast implant publicity, how would you describe Dow Corning's approach to communications?

I would describe the company as "reserved" in the sense that our product line and customers are largely other businesses. So we had neither a history nor a tradition of needing to be highly visible, of taking a highly proactive approach to communications.

Did Connie Chung approach you about her program?

We were never approached about the program or asked to participate.

How did you respond to the accusations raised on the Chung show?

We quickly put together a 30-second spot, with people who could speak very positively about the breast implant. And we bought time on CBS-owned and operated stations around the country, to follow the scheduled rebroadcast of the Chung program. But the commercials never aired. Just a few hours before the program was scheduled to be broadcast, we were notified by the CBS stations that it couldn't run the spots because it would open CBS up to "equal time considerations" it couldn't honor.

What was your response after the coverage increased?

In late 1991 and 1992, the whole thing exploded on us. We were unprepared and surprised by how quickly and how intense the whole media storm became. In terms of getting our message out, compared with the message that was hung out by our adversaries, we were pretty much overwhelmed.

What was your "side of the story"? Did you believe the product caused autoimmune problems?

No. Nor do we today. Nor does 99 percent of the scientific community.

So what strategy did you adopt?

The strategy was to put the scientific process in place that would develop our research that would confirm our position. That was the key. We committed to spend tens of millions of dollars—and today we're past $30 million and still counting—to sponsor independent research to do the necessary epidemiology studies that would answer the questions.

Were you concerned in spending millions of dollars to see if the product was safe that this would be interpreted as an admission of guilt?

No. First, it was the right thing to do. Wherever the science would lead, whatever the answers are, we'll deal with the consequences. But, second, we were quite confident in the safety of the product.

What was your communications strategy?

To continue to cooperate as much as possible with the regulatory agencies. To be open and responsive to the media. To keep our business healthy, because this product never constituted more than 1 percent of our sales.

What did this situation teach you about the media?

I don't believe the people in the media are deliberately trying to shade a story to make it more sensational or get more airtime or more column inches, but I do fault the media for developing a herd instinct that quickly forms a conventional wisdom, that builds up such momentum that it's extremely difficult and slow to recover from.

Suggested Readings

Argenti, Paul. *Corporate Communication*. New York, NY, Irwin, McGraw-Hill, paperback, 1997.

Austin, Erica Weintraub, and Bruce E. Pinkleton. *Planning and Managing Effective Communication Programs*. New York, NY, Lawrence Erlbaum Associates, 2001.

Center, Allen H., and Patrick Jackson. *Public Relations Practices, Managerial Case Studies and Problems*, 5th ed. Upper Saddle River, NJ: Prentice Hall, 1995.

Christ, William G. *Leadership in Times of Change*. Mahwah, NJ: Lawrence Erlbaum Associates, 1998.

D'Aprix, Roger. *Communication for Change: Connecting the Workplace with the Marketplace*. San Francisco: Jossey-Bass/Pfeiffer Publishers, 1996.

Galbraith, Jay R. *Designing Organizations*. San Francisco: Jossey-Bass/Pfeiffer, 1995.

Grunig, James E. *Excellence in Public Relations and Communications Management*. Hillsdale, NJ: Lawrence Erlbaum Associates, 1992.

Harris, Thomas L. *Choosing and Working with Your Public Relations Firm*. Lincolnwood, IL: NTC Business, 1992.

Heath, Robert L. *Strategic Issues Management: Organizations and Public Policy Challenges*. Thousand Oaks, CA: Sage, 1997.

Hendrix, Jerry A. *Public Relations Cases*, 2nd ed. Belmont, CA: Wadsworth, 1997.

Ledingham, John A., and Stephen D. Bruning. *A Relational Approach to the Study and Practice of Public Relations*. Mahwah, NJ. Lawrence Erlbaum Associates, 2001.

Mosten, Forrest S., *Mediation Career Guide, A Strategic Approach to Building a Successful Practice*. San Francisco, Jossey-Bass, 2001.

Rice, Ronald E., and Charles K. Atkin. *Public Communication Campaigns*. Thousand Oaks, CA: Sage, 2000.

Simon, Raymond. *Cases in Public Relations Management*. Lincolnwood, IL: NTC Publishing Group, 1994.

Smith, Ronald D., *Strategic Planning for Public Relations*. Mahwah, NJ: Lawrence Erlbaum Associates, 2002.

Spicer, Christopher. *Organizational Public Relations: A Political Perspective*. Mahwah, NJ: Lawrence Erlbaum Associates, 1997.

Trout, Jack, and Steve Rivkin. *Differentiate or Die*. New York: John Wiley, 2000. The future of organizations depends on their ability to separate themselves from the pack—or else, *sayonara*.

Trout, Jack, and Steve Rivkin. *The New Positioning*. New York: McGraw-Hill, 1996.

Notes

1. "Study Results Find Communications Competence Must Be Combined with Knowledge of the Business," Study sponsored by Deloitte & Touche and IABC Research Foundation (June 14, 2001).
2. Internal Berkshire Hathaway memo from Warren Buffet, August 12, 1998, as quoted in *Business Week* (July 5, 1999): 62.
3. Scott Cutlip, Allen Center, and Douglas Broom, *Effective Public Relations,* vol. 8 (Saddle Brook, NJ: Prentice-Hall, Inc., 2000): 340.
4. Anthony Fulginiti, "How to Prepare a Public Relations Plan," *Communication Briefings* (May 1985): 8a, b.
5. Thomas J. Peters and Robert H. Waterman, Jr., *In Search of Excellence* (New York: Harper & Row, 1982): 40.
6. Lester R. Potter, "How to Be a Credible Strategic Counselor to Your Organization," delivered at IABC International Conference, Chicago, (June 2002).
7. George L. Morrisey, *Management by Objectives and Results for Business and Industry*, 2nd ed. (Reading, MA: Addison-Wesley, 1977): 9.
8. H. Lawrence Smith, "Accountability in PR: Budgets and Benchmarks," *Public Relations Quarterly* (Spring 1996): 15.
9. "American Legacy Foundation Board Names Arnold Communications for Multi-Million Dollar Anti-Tobacco Account," American Legacy Foundation news release, September 15, 1999.
10. Charles H. Prout, "Organization and Function of the Corporate Public Relations Department," in *Lesly's Handbook of Public Relations and Communications* (Chicago: Probus Publishing Company, 1991): 228–729.
11. James E. Grunig and Todd Hunt, *Managing Public Relations* (New York: Holt, Rinehart, and Winston, 1984): 89–97.
12. Ibid.
13. Prout, "Organization and Function," 6.
14. Kenneth D. Makovsky, "Seven Strategies to Ensure Quality Control," *Public Relations Strategist* (Summer 1996): 19.
15. Jonah Bloom, "After Years on the Incline, PR Salaries Freeze in 2002," *PRWeek* (March 25, 2002): 1.
16. "Salary Survey 2002," *PR Week* (March 25, 2002):1.
17. William C. Heyman, "Moving On Up in the Year 2000," *Public Relations Strategist* (Summer 1999): 22.

18. Fraser P. Seitel, "Reputation Management," odwyerpr.com (July 9, 2002).

19. "Mercer Releases Corp. Comm Salary Survey," *Ragan Report* (December 10, 2001): 4.

20. *Salary Survey of Public Relations Professionals.* New York: The Public Relations Society of America, 1996.

21. "Salary Survey 2002," *PR Week.*

22. James G. Hutton, "Exploding the Myth of the Public Relations Gender Gap," *Public Relations Strategist* (Fall 1996): 49.

23. Linda Hon, "Feminism and Public Relations," *Public Relations Strategist* (Fall 1995):20.

24. Gary Pallassino, "Tracking the Gender Switch in Public Relations," Syracuse Research Report (Spring 1999).

25. "Salary Survey 2002," *PR Week.*

Chapter 5

Public Opinion

Public opinion is an elusive and fragile commodity. At least one respected public relations practitioner didn't like what he saw of it as the 21st century began. Said Chester Burger, a man who started a greatly successful agency and counseled some of the most powerful corporations of his era:

> *The best public relations campaign in the world can't build trust while reality is destroying it. Reality limits what public relations can accomplish. Today's events are severely damaging the president, the Congress, and the judiciary, but inescapably are damaging the fiber of trust and integrity that is essential to binding together a democratic nation.[1]*

The rationale for Mr. Burger's dismay might have been summarized in one hot summer of 2002, when the following unfortunate public opinion lapses were widely reported.

- *WorldCom Inc., the nation's number-two long-distance provider, filed for Chapter 11 bankruptcy protection, after revealing it had improperly accounted for $3.9 billion to hide losses.[2]*
- *Dennis Kozlowski, the former CEO of an equally powerful corporation, Tyco International, was hauled in on charges that he tried to avoid $1 million in state sales taxes on paintings for which he paid $16 million. Mr. Kozlowski was making $100 million a year at the time of his alleged scam.[3]*
- *Martha Stewart, the doyenne of domesticity and a national TV star, was investigated for "insider trading," when she allegedly dumped a friend's drug stock, right before the government announced its rejection of the the firm's key product. Ms. Stewart made a bit more than $200,000 on the transaction. Meanwhile, her net worth at the time was valued at close to $1 billion.[4]*
- *Michael Jackson, former beloved gloved one, charged his record company with "racism," after Sony refused to aggressively promote his September 11 tribute album. Later it was embarrassingly revealed that Michael had hired a gay porn film producer to produce the record.[5]*
- *Basketball superstar Allen Iverson (Figure 5-1) was arrested on felony gun charges, after brandishing the weapon under the nose of a cousin, suspected of hiding Iverson's wife.[6]*

Event#: 181174087
PID#: 948473
Name: IVERSON
      ALLEN
Arrest Date: 07 / 16 / 02
Age at Arrest: 27
Height: 6'00"
Weight: 165
Hair Color: BLACK
Eye Color: BROWN
Phila. PD ARREST Database:
Printed TFPPHLNT1726: 07/16/02 11:40

FIGURE 5-1 **Public opinion villain.** On the one hand, sports was littered with high-paid athletes like Philadelphia 76er Allen Iverson, who perpetually seemed to get into trouble.

- *Public relations executive Lizzie Grubman—dubbed the "PR Princess" by the tabloid newspapers—sobbed apologetically outside a Long Island courtroom, where she was charged with willfully mowing down night club patrons after an argument.[7]*

And these sordid examples, as tennis star Andre Agassi once muttered, were but "scratching the tip of the iceberg."

So perhaps Mr. Burger has a point after all: Recent times have not been good ones for dealing with the delicate commodity of public opinion.

On the other hand are Michael Jordan and Tiger Woods, the most widely recognized athletes in the world, who are both skillful at managing their public images.

Mr. Jordan had suffered the tragic murder of his father, an ill-fated attempt at playing professional baseball, and assorted accusations of gambling and selfishness. He subsequently retired from professional basketball in 1999 and then made yet another historic comeback in 2001. Meanwhile, his income totaled more than $50 million and his net worth soared to more than $320 million. In terms of public opinion, Michael Jordan continued to be seen in television ads and enjoyed a sky-high image (Figure 5-2).

Mr. Woods, the not yet 30-year-old golfing heir to Mr. Jordan's public image leadership, handled himself generally with grace and dignity—although, at times, he found it difficult to please all the people all the time in terms of fickle public opinion (see A Question of Ethics, p. 107).

Such are the peculiarities of public opinion in a celebrity-dominated culture. Usually it's difficult to move people toward a strong opinion on anything. It's even harder to move them away from an opinion once they reach it. Recent research, in fact, indicates that mass-media appeals may have little immediate effect on influencing public opinion.

Nonetheless, the heart of public relations work lies in attempting to affect the public opinion process. Most public relations programs are designed either to (1) persuade people to change their opinion on an issue, product, or organization; (2) crystallize uninformed or undeveloped opinions; or (3) reinforce existing opinions.

FIGURE 5-2 **Public opinion hero.** On the other hand, there was Michael Jordan, the unretired anti-Iverson, who came back to play basketball in 2001 for the team he co-owned, the Washington Wizards, and performed respectably. Few other indivduals came close to rivaling his worldwide popularity. As spokesman for a diverse range of products, from McDonald's hamburgers to Nike shoes to Kellogg's Wheaties, even to ill-fated MCI WorldCom Communications—people around the world still yearn to "be like Mike."

So public relations professionals must understand how public opinion is formed, how it evolves from people's attitudes, and how it is influenced by communication. This chapter discusses attitude formation and change, and public opinion creation and persuasion.

What Is Public Opinion?

Public opinion, like public relations, is not easily explained. Newspaper columnist Joseph Kraft called public opinion "the unknown god to which moderns burn incense." Edward Bernays called it "a term describing an ill-defined, mercurial, and changeable group of individual judgments."[8] Princeton professor Harwood Childs, after coming up with no fewer than 40 different yet viable definitions, concluded with a definition by Herman C. Boyle: "Public opinion is not the name of something, but the classification of a number of somethings."[9]

Splitting public opinion into its two components, public and opinion, is perhaps the best way to understand the concept. Simply defined, public signifies a group of people who share a common interest in a specific subject—stockholders, for example, or employees or community residents. Each group is concerned with a common issue: the price of the stock, the wages of the company, or the building of a new plant.

An opinion is the expression of an attitude on a particular topic. When attitudes become strong enough, they surface in the form of opinions. When opinions become strong enough, they lead to verbal or behavioral actions.

A QUESTION OF ETHICS

Riding a Wild Public Opinion Tiger

In the 21st century, Michael Jordan's successor as the most recognized athlete in the world was a 6'2", 180-pound Californian named Eldrick T. (Tiger) Woods (Figure 5-3).

It took Woods only two years on the professional golf tour to prove that he was, quite simply, the best golfer who ever lived. Woods began his career by putting against comedian Bob Hope on television at the age of 2 and shooting a 48 for nine holes at the age of 3.

By the time he was 25, young Tiger had set a professional golf single-season earnings record of more than $9 million. And as to his endorsement contracts—well, fugedaboutit!

As skillful and graceful and rich as Woods is, in terms of managing "public opinion," it isn't always that easy being Tiger.

In the summer of 2002, for example, Woods was asked at the British Open if he approved of the host Muirfield Golf Club's men-only membership policy.

Said Tiger, "They're entitled to set up their own rules the way they want them. It would be nice to see everyone have an equal chance to participate if they wanted to but there is nothing you can do about it."

Woods's remarks set off a firestorm of protest around the globe.

Critics felt that Tiger, an African American allowed to play on courses around the world where his predecessors had been barred, had an ethical responsibility to use his stature as the world's best-known sportsman to improve the situation for women and others.

When apprised of the criticism, Tiger was defensive. "I'm trying to do my part so far as trying to

FIGURE 5-3 **Role model.** The greatest golfer who ever lived found that it was difficult to escape tough issues in the spotlight.

get more kids to have access to the game." A day after the controversy erupted, Tiger went out and shot an 81, the worst round of his life, and lost the tournament.

A forest products company executive and an environmentalist from the Sierra Club might differ dramatically in their attitudes toward the relative importance of pollution control and continued industrial production. Their respective opinions on a piece of environmental legislation might also differ radically. In turn, how their organizations respond to that legislation—by picketing, petitioning, or lobbying—might also differ.

Public opinion, then, is the aggregate of many individual opinions on a particular issue that affects a group of people. Stated another way, public opinion represents a consensus. That consensus, deriving as it does from many individual opinions, really begins with people's attitudes toward the issue in question. Trying to influence an individual's attitude—how he or she thinks on a given topic—is a primary focus of the practice of public relations.

What Are Attitudes?

If an opinion is an expression of an attitude on a particular topic, what then is an attitude? Unfortunately, that also is not an easy question to answer. It had been generally assumed that attitudes are predispositions to think in a certain way about a certain topic. But recent research has indicated that attitudes may more likely be evaluations people make about specific problems or issues. These conclusions are not necessarily connected to any broad attitude.[10] For example, an individual might favor a company's response to one issue but disagree vehemently with its response to another. Thus, that individual's attitude may differ from issue to issue.

Attitudes are based on a number of characteristics.

1. *Personal*—the physical and emotional ingredients of an individual, including size, age, and social status.
2. *Cultural*—the environment and lifestyle of a particular country or geographic area, such as Japan versus the United States or rural America versus urban America. National political candidates often tailor messages to appeal to the particular cultural complexions of specific regions of the country.
3. *Educational*—the level and quality of a person's education. To appeal to the increased number of college graduates in the United States today, public communication has become more sophisticated.
4. *Familial*—people's roots. Children acquire their parents' tastes, biases, political partisanships, and a host of other characteristics. Some pediatricians insist that children pick up most of their knowledge in the first seven years, and few would deny the family's strong role in helping to mold attitudes.
5. *Religious*—a system of beliefs about God or the supernatural. Religion is making a comeback. In the 1960s, many young people turned away from formal religion. At the turn of the century, even after several evangelical scandals, religious fervor has reemerged.
6. *Social class*—position within society. As people's social status changes, so do their attitudes. For example, college students, unconcerned with making a living, may dramatically change their attitudes about such concepts as big government, big business, wealth, and prosperity after entering the job market.
7. *Race*—ethnic origin, which today increasingly helps shape people's attitudes. The history of blacks and whites in America—like Arabs and Israelis in the Middle East—has been stormy, with peaceful coexistence often frustrated. Nonetheless, minorities in our society, as a group, continue to improve their standard of living and their relative position in society. Two of the highest-ranking Bush administration executives, Secretary of State Colin Powell and National Security Advisor Condoleeza Rice, for example, are African Americans. So, too, are the CEOs of American Express, AOL Time Warner, and a number of other multinational corporations.

As their lot improves, African Americans, Latinos, Asians, and others have retained pride in and allegiance to their cultural heritage. These characteristics help influence the formation of attitudes. So, too, do other factors, such as experience, economic class, and political and organizational memberships. Again, recent research has indicated that attitudes and behaviors are situational—influenced by specific issues in specific situations. Nonetheless, when others with similar attitudes reach similar opinions, a consensus, or public opinion, is born.

How Are Attitudes Influenced?

Strictly speaking, attitudes are positive, negative, or nonexistent. A person is for something, against it, or neutral. Studies show that for any one issue, most people don't care much one way or the other. A small percentage expresses strong support, and another small percentage expresses strong opposition. The vast majority is smack in the middle: passive, neutral, indifferent. Former Vice President Spiro T. Agnew called them "the silent majority." In many instances—political campaigns being a prime example—this silent majority holds the key to success because they are the group most readily influenced by a communicator's message.

It's hard to change the mind of a person who is staunchly opposed to a particular issue or individual. Likewise, it's easy to reinforce the support of a person who is wholeheartedly in favor of an issue or individual. Social scientist Leon Festinger discussed this concept when he talked about cognitive dissonance. He believed that individuals tend to avoid information that is dissonant or opposed to their own points of view and tend to seek out information that is consonant with, or in support of, their own attitudes.[11] An organization might attempt to remove dissonance to reach its goals. For example, in the face of stinging government attacks against cigarette smoking in the late 1990s, Philip Morris and other leading tobacco companies adopted ambitious antismoking programs. Nonetheless, states' attorneys general and the U.S. Justice Department have continued to go after Big Tobacco for punitive damages.

As Festinger's theory intimates, the people whose attitudes can be influenced most readily are those who have not yet made up their minds. In politics this group is often referred to as the "swing vote." Many elections have been won or lost on last-minute appeals to these politically undecided voters. In addition, it is possible to introduce information that may cause dissonance in the mind of a receiver.

Understanding this theory and its potential for influencing the silent majority is extremely important for the public relations practitioner, whose objective is to win support through clear, thoughtful, and persuasive communication. Moving a person from a latent state of attitude formation to a more aware state and finally to an active one becomes a matter of motivation.

Motivating Attitude Change

People are motivated by different factors, and no two people respond in exactly the same way to the same set of circumstances. Each of us is motivated by different drives and needs.

The most famous delineator of what motivates people was Abraham Maslow. His hierarchy of needs helps define the origins of motivation, which, in turn, help explain attitude change. Maslow postulated a five-level hierarchy:

1. The lowest order is physiological needs: a person's biological demands—food and water, sleep, health, bodily needs, exercise and rest, and sex
2. The second level is safety needs: security, protection, comfort and peace, and orderly surroundings
3. The third level is love needs: acceptance, belonging, love and affection, and membership in a group
4. The fourth level is esteem: recognition and prestige, confidence and leadership opportunities, competence and strength, intelligence and success

5. The highest order is self-actualization, or simply becoming what one is capable of becoming; self-actualization involves self-fulfillment and achieving a goal for the purposes of challenge and accomplishment[12]

According to Maslow, the needs of all five levels compose the fundamental motivating factors for any individual or public.

In the 2000s, as people once again get involved in causes—from corporate accounting scandals to racial profiling to animal rights to environmentalism—motivating attitude change becomes more important (Figure 5-4). Many activist groups, in fact, borrow heavily from psychological research on political activism to accomplish attitude change. Six cardinal precepts of political activism are instructive in attempting to change attitudes:

1. *Don't use graphic images unless they are accompanied by specific actions people can execute.* Many movements—the gay rights campaign and the antiabortion movement, for example—began by relying heavily on graphic images of death and destruction. But such images run the risk of pushing people away rather than drawing them in. Disturbing presentations rarely lead to a sustained attitude change.

2. *Go to the public instead of asking the public to come to you.* Most people will never become directly involved in an activist campaign. They will shy away. But by recognizing the limits of public interest and involvement, you can develop realistic strategies to capitalize on public goodwill without demanding more than people are willing to give.

3. *Don't assume that attitude change is necessary for behavior change.* A large body of psychological research casts doubt on the proposition that the best way to change behavior is to begin by changing attitudes. Indeed, the relationship between attitudes and behavior is often quite weak. Therefore, informing smokers of the link between cigarettes and cancer is far easier than getting them to kick the habit.

4. *Use moral arguments as adjuncts, not as primary thrusts.* Moral views are difficult to change. It is much easier to gain support by stressing the practical advantages of your solution rather than the immorality of your opponent's. For example, it is easier to convert people to a meatless diet by discussing the health benefits of vegetables than by discussing whether the Bible gives people dominion over animals.

5. *Embrace the mainstream.* In any campaign, people from all walks of life are necessary to win widespread approval. No campaign can be won if it is dubbed radical or faddish. That is why the involvement of all people must be encouraged in seeking attitude change.

6. *Don't offend the people you seek to change.* Research on persuasion shows that influence is usually strongest when people like the persuader and see the persuader as similar to themselves. It is impossible to persuade someone whom you have alienated. Or, as my mother used to say, "You can attract more flies with honey than you can with vinegar." The same applies to people.[13]

Power of Persuasion

Perhaps the most essential element in influencing public opinion is the principle of persuasion. Persuading is the goal of the vast majority of public relations programs. Persuasion theory has myriad explanations and interpretations. Basically, persuasion means getting another person to do something through advice, reasoning, or just plain arm-twisting. Books have been written on the enormous power of advertising and public relations as persuasive tools.

Social scientists and communications scholars take issue with the view of many public relations practitioners that a story on network news or the front page of the *New York Times* has a tremendously persuasive effect. Scholars argue that the media have a limited effect on persuasion, doing more to reinforce existing attitudes than to persuade toward a new belief. There is little doubt, however, that the persuasiveness of a message can be increased when it arouses or is accompanied by a high level of personal involvement. In other words, an individual who cares about something and is in fundamental agreement with an organization's basic position will tend to be persuaded by a message supporting that view.

According to classic persuasion theory, people may be of two minds in order to be persuaded to believe in a particular position or take a specific action.

1. First is the "systematic" mode, referring to a person who has carefully considered an argument—actively, creatively, and alertly.
2. Second is the "heuristic" mode, referring to a person who is skimming the surface and not really focusing on the intricacies of a particular position to catch flaws, inconsistencies, or errors.[14]

That is not to say that all systematic thinkers or all heuristic thinkers think alike. They don't. Things are more complicated than that.

Let's say your little brother wants a pair of sneakers and your dad accompanies him to the store to buy them. Both are systematic thinkers. But they have different questions. Your dad asks:

1. How much do they cost?
2. How long will they last?
3. Is the store nearby, so I can get back to watch the ball game?
4. Will they take a personal check?

Your brother asks:

1. Does Kobe Bryant endorse them?
2. Do all my homeboys wear them?
3. Will Wanda Sue go out with me if I buy them?

The point is that all of us are persuaded by different things, which makes the challenge of public relations persuading much more a complex art form than a science.

One much less complex, yet no less profound, notion of persuasion is that of former First Lady Hillary Clinton, whose "Listening Tour" of New York State in her 1999 senate race was built on the proposition that "one of the best ways to persuade others is to listen to them." It worked. She won.

No matter how one characterizes persuasion, the goal of most communications programs is, in fact, to influence a receiver to take a desired action.

How are people persuaded? Saul Alinsky, a legendary radical organizer, had a simple theory of persuasion: "People only understand things in terms of their own experience. . . . If you try to get your ideas across to others without paying attention to what they have to say to you, you can forget about the whole thing."[15] In other words, if you wish to persuade people, you must cite evidence that coincides with their own beliefs, emotions, and expectations.

What Kinds of "Evidence" Persuade People?

1. *Facts.* Facts are indisputable. Although it is true, as they say, that "statistics sometimes lie," empirical data are a persuasive device in hammering home a point of view. This is why any good public relations program will always start with research—the facts.

2. *Emotions.*   Maslow was right. People do respond to emotional appeals—love, peace, family, patriotism. Ronald Reagan was known as "the great communicator" largely as a result of his appeal to emotion. Even when the nation was outraged in 1983, when 200 American soldiers died in a terrorist attack in Lebanon, President Reagan reversed the skepticism by talking of one wounded U.S. marine lying in a Lebanese bed.

> That Marine, and all those others like him, living and dead, have been faithful to their ideals, they've given willingly of themselves so that a nearly defenseless people in a region of great strategic importance to the free world will have a chance someday to live lives free of murder and mayhem and terrorism.[16]

In later years, American presidents have been loath to risk the deaths of so many Americans, so that wars from Kuwait to Kosovo, from Mogadishu to Afghanistan to Iraq, were entered with caution. But in an earlier day, President Reagan could win the support of his countrymen with simple appeals to their patriotism. Such is the persuasive power of emotional appeals.

3. *Personalizing.*   People respond to personal experience.

- When poet Maya Angelou talks about poverty, people listen and respect a woman who emerged from the dirt-poor environs of the Deep South in a day of segregation.
- When *America's Most Wanted* TV host John Walsh crusades against criminals who prey on children, people understand that his son was abducted and killed by a crazed individual.
- When former baseball pitcher Jim Abbott talks about dealing with adversity, people marvel at a star athlete born with only one arm.

    Again, few can refute knowledge gained from personal experience.

4. *Appealing to "you."*   The one word that people never tire of hearing is "you." "What is in this for me?" is the question that everyone asks. So one secret to persuading is to constantly think in terms of the audience and constantly refer to "you."

As simple as these four precepts are, they are difficult to grasp—particularly for business leaders, who frown on emotion or personalizing or even appealing to an audience. Some consider it "beneath them" to show human emotion. This, of course, is a mistake. The power to persuade—to influence public opinion—is the measure not only of a charismatic but also an effective leader.[17]

Influencing Public Opinion

Public opinion is a lot easier to measure than it is to influence. However, a thoughtful public relations program can crystallize attitudes, reinforce beliefs, and occasionally change public opinion. First, the opinions to be changed or modified must be identified and understood. Second, target publics must be clear. Third, the public relations professional must have in sharp focus the "laws" that govern public opinion—as amorphous as they may be.

In that context, the "Laws of Public Opinion," developed many years ago by social psychologist Hadley Cantril, remain pertinent. The attacks on America of September 2001 underscored the relevance of at least six of Cantril's most important "laws:"[18]

1. *Opinion is highly sensitive to important events.*   Events of unusual magnitude are likely to swing public opinion temporarily from one extreme to another.

Opinion doesn't become stabilized until the implications of events are seen in some perspective. For example, after the terrorist attacks of September 11, 2001, President Bush's popularity rose to unprecedented heights, as Americans of every age group and background rallied behind the war effort to combat terrorism.

2. *Opinion is generally determined more by events than by words—unless those words are themselves interpreted as an event.*   For example, in a speech to a joint session of Congress nine days after the terrorist attacks, the president vowed to "lift the dark threat of violence from our people and our future. We will rally the world to this cause by our efforts, by our courage. We will not tire, we will not falter, and we will not fail." Bush's words became a rallying cry for the nation and literally transformed his presidency.[19]

3. *At critical times, people become more sensitive to the adequacy of their leadership. If they have confidence in it, they are willing to assign more than usual responsibility to it; if they lack confidence in it, they are less tolerant than usual.*   For example, relatively few voices rose in protest when, in 2002, the Bush administration, in the cause of fighting terrorism, imposed sweeping changes in privacy rights, regarding such traditional areas as library use and freedom of assembly in houses of worship.

4. *Once self-interest is involved, opinions aren't easily changed.*   For example, a year after the terrorist attacks, Americans still steadfastly supported the president's war on terror. This stood in marked contrast to their support of Bush's economic policy, which fell rapidly as the stock market in the summer of 2002 fell steadily.[20]

5. *People have more opinions and are able to form opinions more easily on goals than on methods to reach those goals.*   For example, few questioned the need for a new U.S. Department of Homeland Security to protect the land within our borders from terrorism. However, the organization, components, and functions of that department were the subject of long and rancorous debate in Congress in the summer of 2002.

6. *By and large, if people in a democracy are provided with educational opportunities and ready access to information, public opinion reveals a hardheaded common sense.*   For example, in the weeks and months following the attacks, as Americans became more enlightened as to the implications and threats of terrorism within the United States, their willingness to accept the opinions and proposals of informed government leaders, such as the attorney general and secretary of defense, increased. Indeed the administration's strategy of continuous communication by these officials helped solidify public opinion.[21]

Polishing the Corporate Image

Most organizations today and the people who manage them are extremely sensitive to the way they are perceived by their critical publics. This represents a dramatic change in corporate attitude from years past. Well into the 1980s, only the most enlightened companies dared to maintain anything but a low profile. Management, frankly, was reluctant to step out publicly, "to stand up for what it stood for."

Today, however, organizations—particularly large ones—have little choice but to go public. The accounting and corporate scandals of the summer of 2002 threatened the confidence of the American capitalistic system. In the wake of the scandals, smart companies realized they simply couldn't "hide" any longer from public scrutiny.

In the 21st century, where news of corporate failings or malfeasance spreads instantaneously via the Internet around the world, smart organizations have learned to stay in touch with their primary publics.

Consider the following corporate "learning experiences" from recent years:

- Bedrock American companies, once the symbols of respected yet silent management decorum, saw their stock prices clobbered as confidence waned in their management, performance, and even ethics. Such stellar firms as General Electric, Hewlett-Packard, and AOL Time Warner experienced unprecedented falls from stock market grace in 2002.
- Executives of two former high-flying billion-dollar corporations, Enron and WorldCom, were villified in the summer of 2002, when their firms crumbled after admissions that they had lied to shareholders—including their own employees—about accounting practices and the financial condition of the companies. Ruined in the fallout was the legendary accounting firm of Arthur Andersen, which saw its franchise destroyed because of its dubious Enron association.
- The CEO of multibillion-dollar Tyco International was charged in 2002 with avoiding New York state sales taxes, after purchasing $13 million in art. According to prosecutors, former CEO Dennis Kozlowski attempted to avoid $1 million in taxes, even though he had earned $300 million in the previous three years. Largely as a result of this revelation, Tyco's stock lost $16 billion in value.
- So sensitive were big companies to public approval that some didn't wait to announce management problems. When Southwest Airlines CEO Herb Kelleher contracted prostate cancer in 1999, he announced it immediately to analysts and the press and even "warned" subordinates that, as a result of sticking around headquarters for treatments, "I'll probably be in the office more than usual."[22]

After such instances, most organizations today understand clearly that it takes a great deal of time to build a favorable image for a corporation but only one slip to create a negative public impression. In other words, the corporate image is a fragile commodity. Yet most firms also believe that a positive corporate image is essential for continued long-term success.

In the 1970s, United Technologies Corporation ran a famous series of ads speaking to the importance of corporate reputation. As Ray D'Argenio, then communications director of United Technologies, put it, "Corporate communications can't create a corporate character. A company already has a character, which communications can reinforce"[23] (Figure 5-5).

Beware the Traps of Public Opinion

Analyzing public opinion is not as easy as it looks. Once a company wins favorable public opinion for a product or an idea, the trick is to maintain it (Figure 5-7 on page 118). The worst thing to do is sit back and bask in the glory of a positive public image; that's a quick route to image deterioration (Figure 5-8 on page 119).

Public opinion is changeable and, in assessing it, communicators are susceptible to a number of subtle yet lethal traps.

Brighten Your Corner

Have you noticed the great difference between the people you meet? Some are as sunshiny as a handful of forget-me-nots. Others come on like frozen mackerel. A cheery, comforting nurse can help make a hospital stay bearable. An upbeat secretary makes visitors glad they came to see you. Every corner of the world has its clouds, gripes, complainers, and pains in the neck—because many people have yet to learn that honey works better than vinegar. You're in control of *your* small corner of the world. Brighten it. . . You *can*.

FIGURE 5-5 **Although many companies attempted to construct a differentiable corporate image through advertising, few succeeded as well as United Technologies, which kept its messages succinct, savvy, and sparkling in a series of historic corporate image ads.**

- **Cast in stone.** This fallacy assumes that just because public opinion is well established on a certain issue, it isn't likely to change. Not true. Consider an issue such as women's liberation. In the early 1960s, people laughed at the handful of women raising a ruckus about equal rights, equal pay, and equal treatment. By the early 1970s, women's liberation pervaded every sector of our culture. By the 1980s, trailblazing women leaders, such as Golda Meir in Israel,

Shredding Her Image Along with the Cabbage

One of the mightiest to suffer public opinion reversals in the troubled summer of 2002 was the nation's "princess of perfection," TV homemaking diva Martha Stewart (Figure 5-6).

When Stewart suspiciously sold $300,000 worth of ImClone Systems stock a day before the company received a government turndown on a key drug, it was suspected that she might have received illegal insider information from her friend, the CEO.

Stewart denied the charge and then refused to discuss the situation further—preferring in one celebrated TV appearance to cut cabbage while ignoring an interviewer's probing questions.

"Now I want to focus on my salad," she indignantly responded to the insider trading queries.

After her cabbage controversy, Martha became fair game for headline writers and TV comedians alike. The generally outspoken Stewart seemed unusually unavailable as the investigation into her stock trading persisted.

Her stockbroker, a former ImClone executive, was called in by the Feds investigating insider trading. Her stockbroker's assistant was called in, presumably to rat on his boss. And all the while, the diva of domesticity stayed silent.

As questions continued to swirl around her, the stock of Martha's own company, Martha Stewart Living Omnimedia, got pummeled; the merchandise she pro-

FIGURE 5-6   **Comfy in the kitchen, but perhaps few other places, as the insider trading scandal swirled around Martha.**

moted at retailer Kmart began to suffer; and her own once wholesome image began to show cracks.

For Martha, alas, there was nothing "wholesome" about insider trading.

had paved the way for the dominant world leadership of Margaret Thatcher in Great Britain. By the year 2000, women were taking leadership roles in the U.S. Congress, running for the U.S. presidency, and starring in collegiate and professional sports. Nobody was laughing anymore.

● **Gut reaction.**   This fallacy assumes that if management feels in its corporate gut that the public will lean strongly in a certain direction, then that must be the way to go. Be careful. Some managements are so cut off from the real world that their knee-jerk reactions to issues often turn out to be more jerk than anything else. One former auto company executive, perhaps overstating the case, described the problem this way: "There's no forward response to what the public wants today. It's gotten to be a total insulation from the realities of the world." Certainly, management's instincts in dealing with the

FIGURE 5-7 **Lemons to lemonade.** The key to a corporate image that gets through to people is a combination of simplicity, unity, and balance. The corporate identity manual of David's Lemonade, the creation of Fulton + Partners, Inc., is an example of a clear corporate image.

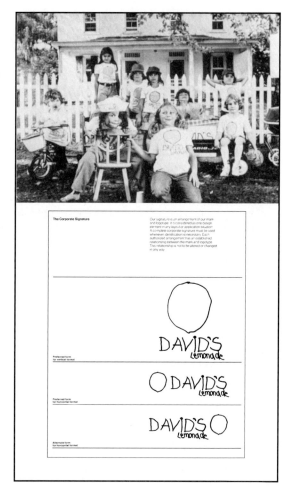

public may be questionable at times. Generally, gut-reaction judgments should be avoided in assessing public opinion.

- **General public.** There may well be a public at large, but there's no such thing as the general public. Even the smallest public can be subdivided. No two people are alike, and messages to influence public opinion should be as pointed as possible rather than scatter shot. Sometimes individuals may qualify as members of publics on both sides of an issue. In weighing the pros and cons of lower speed limits, for example, many people are both drivers and pedestrians. Categorizing them into one general group can be a mistake.

- **Words move mountains.** Perhaps they do sometimes, but public opinion is usually influenced more by events than by words. For example, the rash of child kidnappings and the brutal murder of a 6-year-old California girl in the summer of 2002 triggered nationwide concern about child safety.

- **Brother's keeper.** It's true that most people will rise up indignantly if a fellow citizen has been wronged. But they'll get a lot more indignant if they feel they themselves have been wronged. In other words, self-interest often sparks public opinion. An organization wishing to influence public opinion might be well advised to ask initially, "What's in this for the people whose opinion we're trying to influence?"

FIGURE 5-8 **Lemonade to lemons.** The Xerox Corporation had a unique name and logo problem. The Xerox name was so widely used that it had to fight a continual battle to have the name treated as a proper adjective with a capital *X*, rather than a verb with a lowercase *x*—thus the frustration expressed in this ad. Alas, in the 21st century, Xerox confused its own identity—and lost its copying birthright—when it tried to become "the document company" rather than the "copier company." The public didn't buy it, and the company floundered.

LAST WORD

Influencing public opinion remains at the heart of professional public relations work.

Public opinion is a powerful force that can impact the earnings of enormous corporations through such actions as product boycotts, union strikes, and the misdeeds of key executives; influence government legislation through campaign support, product recalls, and letters and e-mails from constituents; and even unify a nation through calls to action by strong and committed leaders.

In order to influence public opinion, public relations professionals must anticipate trends in our society. Keeping ahead of trends is no easy task. But in the 21st century, trend watching is very much a frontline public relations responsibility. One self-styled prognosticator riding the crest of trend analysis was John Naisbitt, whose book *Megatrends 2000* claimed to predict the new directions that would influence American lives in the 21st century. Among them were the following:

- Inflation and interest rates will be held in check.
- There will be a shift from welfare to workfare.
- There will be a shift from public housing to home ownership.
- There will be a shift from sports to the arts as the primary leisure preference.

Most Respected Companies

More Americans may be doing their business on the Internet, but Internet companies still haven't surpassed more bricks-and-mortar corporations when it comes to commanding the highest public opinion.

According to research reported in 2001, America's "most respected company" was none other than Johnson & Johnson, thanks primarily to the reputation it gained in handling the Tylenol murders.*

The top 10 most respected American companies follow:

1. Johnson & Johnson
2. Maytag
3. Sony
4. Home Depot
5. Intel
6. Anheuser-Busch
7. IBM
8. The Walt Disney Company
9. Microsoft
10. Procter & Gamble

The second annual survey of corporate reputation was conducted by Harris Interactive and polled 26,011 respondents. The reputations of technology firms, in particular, plummeted in terms of trust, admiration, and respect.

The only Internet firms to make the top 30 were Amazon.com at number 23 and Yahoo! at number 27, both dropping several places from the previous year's survey.

The largest Internet firm, America Online, came in 39th, a drop of 13 places. America Online was described by respondents as "the worst thing about the Internet" and its software as "the disk from hell." It was criticized for disappointing service. "Money-hungry sharks" and "evil empire-style monolith" were two of the tamer descriptions of AOL Time Warner.

Such are the vagaries—if not the niceties—of the corporate image.

*Based on research conducted by Harris Interactive and the Reputation Institute as reported in Ronald Alsop, "The Best Corporate Reputations in America," *Wall Street Journal,* February 7, 2001, B–1.

- Consumers will demand more customized products.
- The media will amplify bad economic news.
- The rise of the Pacific Rim will be seen in terms of economic dominance.
- Asia will add 80 million more people.
- CEOs in a global economy will become more important and better known than political figures.[23]

With the first several years of the century behind us and the CEO fallout from the summer of 2002 fresh in mind, Nesbitt's final prediction was particularly ironic. Some might argue that there is nothing revolutionary in these "megatrends" (and they might well be right!). Nonetheless, such trends deserve to be scrutinized, analyzed, and evaluated by organizations in order to deal more effectively with the future. As the late public relations counselor Philip Lesly once pointed out, "The real problems faced by business today are in the outside world of intangibles and public attitudes."[24]

To keep ahead of these intangibles, these public attitudes, and these kernels of future public opinion, managements will turn increasingly for guidance to professional public relations practitioners.

Discussion Starters

1. What is public opinion?
2. What are attitudes, and on what characteristics are they based?

3. How are attitudes influenced?
4. What is Maslow's hierarchy of needs?
5. What is the theory of cognitive dissonance?
6. How difficult is it to change a person's behavior?
7. What are several key "public opinion laws," according to Cantril?
8. What kinds of "evidence" persuade people?
9. What were the elements of Martha Stewart's stock trading problems that influenced public opinion?
10. What are the traps of public opinion?

TOP OF THE SHELF

New York Times
New York: The New York Times Company, www.nytimes.com
Wall Street Journal
Dow Jones & Company, Inc.

Public relations can be practiced only by understanding public opinion, and the best forums in which to study it are the *New York Times* and the *Wall Street Journal*.

Their pages daily reveal the diverse views of pundits, politicians, and plain people. The *Times* is arguably the primary source of printed news in the world. The *Journal*, likewise, is the primary printed source of the world's business and investment news—an area of increasingly dominant importance.

Both papers, through their opinion pages and in-depth stories, express the attitudes of leaders in politics, business, science, education, journalism, and the arts, on topics ranging from abortion rights to genetic engineering to race relations. Occasionally, the *Times* and the *Journal* supplement their usual coverage with public opinion polls to gauge attitudes and beliefs on particularly hot issues. The Sunday *Times*, with features that include the magazine sections "Week in Review" and "Business Forum," is an important resource for public relations professionals.

Read these papers daily, and you'll keep abreast of popular thought on major issues and trends. Or visit their Web sites regularly: At nytimes.com, you can read the day's leading stories for free; at wsj.com, a modest subscription price brings you the *Wall Street Journal* Interactive Edition.

CASE STUDY

Pepsi Punctures the Great Syringe Soda Scare

PepsiCo's worst nightmare began inauspiciously enough on June 10, 1993, when an elderly Fircrest, Washington, couple claimed that they had discovered a syringe floating inside a can of Diet Pepsi.

For the next two weeks, the 50,000 people of PepsiCo—from CEO and corporate communications staff to independent bottlers—worked around the clock to mount a massive public relations offensive that effectively thwarted a potential business disaster for its 95-year-old trademark and a potential devastating blow to one of the world's foremost consumer reputations.

The Pepsi case is a tribute to sound communications thinking and rapid, decisive public relations action in the face of imminent corporate catastrophe. The day after the Fircrest complaint, a nearby Tacoma woman reported finding another hypodermic needle in a can of Diet Pepsi. The story of the two tampered cans—initially labeled "some sort of sabotage" by the local Pepsi bottler—ran on the Associated Press wire nationwide and sent shock waves throughout the country.

PepsiCo, although immediately forming a crisis management team headed by its president and CEO, Craig Weatherup, nonetheless chose to "hold its powder" publicly while first assessing all pertinent facts about the two incidents and devoting attention to the Seattle plant. Pepsi's perceived reluctance to confront the problem in a dramatic way—while it worked "behind the scenes"—drew initial fire from so-called crisis experts. One management communications professor warned, "They are underestimating the potential for rumors to feed off one another." Another crisis management counselor said, "This will be a terrible mistake if it turns out they should have acted in light of later events."

On June 13, the commissioner of the Food and Drug Administration (FDA), David A. Kessler, warned consumers in Washington, Oregon, Alaska, Hawaii, and Guam "to inspect closely cans of Diet Pepsi for signs of tampering and to pour the contents into a glass or cup before drinking."

In the face of criticism and with copycat tamperings accelerating, PepsiCo held its ground. Although critics urged the company to recall its products, the company continued to insist that its cans were virtually tamperproof. "We are 99 percent sure that you cannot open one and reseal it without its being obvious," the company assured its customers. Because there was "no health risk to either of the two consumers who filed the complaints or to the general public," PepsiCo urged its bottlers and general managers not to remove the product from shelves.

On June 14, PepsiCo issued an internal "consumer advisory" to its bottlers and general managers, reporting the results of its initial research on the reported claims:

- "The syringes that were found are those commonly used by diabetics for insulin. We do not have syringes of this type in any of our production facilities."
- "All cans used for Pepsi-Cola products are new packages. They are not reused or refilled at any time. There are two visual inspections during production: the first before cans are filled, the second while cans are on the filling line. The cans are then sealed."

PepsiCo's strong inference was that, first, the speed and security of its bottling production process made it extremely unlikely that any foreign object could appear in an unopened Pepsi container and, second, what was being inserted wasn't being put into cans at the factory.

By June 14, the nation was awash in copycat Pepsi-Cola tamperings. PepsiCo was barraged with reports of syringes in its cans from Louisiana to New York, from Missouri to Wyoming, from Pennsylvania to Southern California. Adding to PepsiCo's nightmare was a media feeding frenzy the likes of which the company had never before encountered.

- "A 'Scared' Firm Fights to Save Its Good Name"—*New York Post*
- "FDA Warns Diet-Pepsi Drinkers"—Associated Press
- "Diet Pepsi Drinkers Warned of Debris"—*USA Today*
- "No Program for a Recall of Diet Pepsi"—*New York Times*

Pepsi tampering stories dominated the national media, leading the evening news and network morning programs for three days. Local crews throughout the nation positioned themselves at local Pepsi bottling plants. PepsiCo's president and six-person public relations staff put in 20-hour days in the company's Somers, New York, headquarters, each fielding 80 to 100 inquiries daily. The company was besieged by syringe-tampering mania.

Late on the evening of June 15, PepsiCo received its first break. A man in central Pennsylvania was arrested on the charge that he had fraudulently reported finding a syringe in a can of Pepsi.

With the first arrest made, PepsiCo seized the offensive.

MEDIA RELATIONS

PepsiCo's media strategy centered on one medium: television. Downplaying traditional print media—"the press conference is a dinosaur"—PepsiCo's communications executives launched daily satellite feeds to the nation's electronic media to get out its side of the tampering allegations.

- An initial video news release (VNR) picturing the high-speed can-filling lines (Figure 5-9), with voice-over narration by a plant manager, conveyed the message of a manufacturing process built on speed, safety, and integrity, in which tampering with products would be highly unlikely. The goal was to show that the canning process was safe. The initial VNR was seen by 187 million viewers (more than watched the 1993 Super Bowl) on 399 stations in 178 markets across the United States.
- A second VNR, picturing PepsiCo President Weatherup and additional production footage, reported the first arrest for a false claim of tampering. It made four critical points: (1) Complaints of syringes reported to be found in Diet Pepsi cans in other cities are unrelated; (2) tampering appears to be happening after cans are opened; (3) the soft drink can is one of the safest packages for consumer food products;

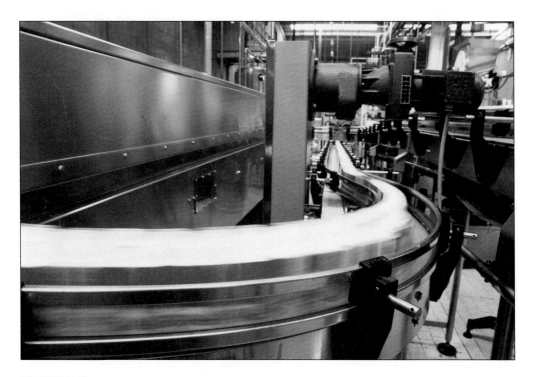

FIGURE 5-9 **Video news release.** The subject of PepsiCo's first VNR to reassure the public about its processing speed and safety was this rapid glimpse of a Pepsi bottling plant.

and (4) a recall is not warranted. This PepsiCo-produced VNR was seen by 70 million viewers on 238 stations in 136 markets.

- A third VNR, narrated by President Weatherup, presented a segment from a convenience store surveillance video (Figure 5-10) in which a woman was caught inserting a syringe into an open Diet Pepsi can. Weatherup thanked consumers for their support, reported additional arrests, and reaffirmed PepsiCo's decision not to recall its product. This surveillance video was broadcast to 95 million viewers on 325 stations in 159 markets and, in effect, "broke the back" of the Pepsi syringe scare.

- In addition to the VNRs, PepsiCo's media offensive included appearances by the company's president and a product safety expert on as many talk shows as could be fit into their schedules—each of the three major network evening newscasts, ABC's *Nightline*, CNN's *Larry King Live*, and so on.

PepsiCo's video media blitz was unparalleled in corporate public relations history.

GOVERNMENT RELATIONS

Meanwhile, PepsiCo cooperated fully with Commissioner Kessler and the FDA. Although other consumer firms have adopted an adversarial position toward the watchdog agency, PepsiCo embraced the FDA's investigation.

SCENES OF AN ALLEGED PRODUCT TAMPERING

FRAME: 08:32:15

An opened can of Diet Pepsi, held by a Colorado woman, appears to be lowered behind the counter of a convenience store, out of the clerk's line of sight.

FRAME: 08:32:27

The woman fumbles with her purse and pulls out what appears to be a syringe.

FRAME: 08:32:34

The woman appears to place the syringe in the opened can of Diet Pepsi while keeping it behind the counter.

FRAME: 08:32:39

The woman places the can back on the counter then asks the clerk for a cup into which she pours the Diet Pepsi and allegedly discovers the syringe.

FIGURE 5-10 **Smoking gun.** The evidence ending the Pepsi tampering hoax was this surveillance video of a woman caught stuffing a syringe into a Pepsi can.

It was the FDA's Office of Criminal Investigation (OCI), in fact, that reported the breakthrough in the arrest of the man in central Pennsylvania. In addition to the FDA's "consumer alert" in the Pacific Northwest, Commissioner Kessler issued a statement on the tampering and the possibility of copycats. Later, Commissioner Kessler appeared with President Weatherup on *Nightline* and took the unprecedented step of declaring that "calm is in order . . . a recall is not necessary."

On June 17, Commissioner Kessler held a press conference in Washington, D.C., unequivocally characterizing the controversy as a hoax—the product of "misguided individual acts, magnified and multiplied by the attendant glare of the media, and a predictable outbreak of copycat behavior."

On June 21, PepsiCo President Weatherup wrote to President Clinton, thanking him for the "excellent work" of Commissioner Kessler and the FDA "in pursuing the recent product tampering hoax."

EMPLOYEE RELATIONS

In the area of employee relations—with its staff and bottlers—PepsiCo adopted a policy of full and immediate disclosure as soon as it had discerned the pertinent facts.

Consumer advisories were dispatched at least once a day, usually twice or three times on each day of the crisis, letting bottlers and general managers in PepsiCo's 400 field locations know what was going on, what had been reported, what the government was doing, and how the company was responding.

Managers were advised on how to "communicate with employees and customers" in the form of "Product Tampering Guidelines," as well as in procedures for reporting alleged tamperings.

President Weatherup also personally wrote to bottlers and general managers periodically during the crisis to keep them advised of breaking developments. When the surveillance video was found, President Weatherup sent all Pepsi bottlers, by overnight mail, a videotape of Commissioner Kessler's news conference, along with the surveillance footage.

"Please share it with your customers," the president suggested.

By June 18, just one week—and what seemed like one millennium—after its product and reputation had been challenged, PepsiCo declared victory in national ads stating, "Pepsi is pleased to announce . . . nothing."

What had begun as the worst kind of national nightmare, with critics and copycats threatening the company at every juncture, ended in a flurry of pervasive public praise. "Media-smart Pepsi" is how *Advertising Age* characterized the company's strategy. The *Milwaukee Sentinel*, in a rare journalistic admission of candor, labeled the media's leap to sensationalism on the Pepsi story "a mistake, a big mistake." *Business Week* credited the company for making "the right moves, Baby." The company was universally heralded for holding the line on a product recall and putting on the line its reputation and credibility.

Perhaps sweetest of all for PepsiCo, after the FDA/OCI's arrest of 55 suspected hoaxers, was the bottom-line aftermath: Not only had PepsiCo weathered the media storm and emerged with its credibility intact, but also the impact on Pepsi's sales was negligible. President Weatherup reported that sales had fallen just 3 percent at the height of the crisis, approximately $30 million. By July and August, Pepsi sales were up 7 percent, the best summer in five years (Figure 5-11).

All in all, as one industry periodical put it, "Pepsi's response constituted nothing less than 'a textbook case' of how to come through a PR crisis" (Figure 5-12).

Pepsi is pleased to announce...

...nothing.

As America now knows, those stories about Diet Pepsi were a hoax. Plain and simple, not true. Hundreds of investigators have found no evidence to support a single claim.

As for the many, many thousands of people who work at Pepsi-Cola, we feel great that it's over. And we're ready to get on with making and bringing you what we believe is the best-tasting diet cola in America.

There's not much more we can say. Except that most importantly, we won't let this hoax change our exciting plans for this summer.

We've set up special offers so you can enjoy our great quality products at prices that will save you money all summer long. It all starts on July 4th weekend and we hope you'll stock up with a little extra, just to make up for what you might have missed last week.

That's it. Just one last word of thanks to the millions of you who have stood with us.

Drink All The Diet Pepsi You Want.
Uh Huh.

DIET PEPSI and UH-HUH are registered trademarks of PepsiCo. Inc

FIGURE 5-11   **Whew.** With its crisis proven to be a hoax, PepsiCo triumphantly proclaimed its victory with this ad.

Questions

1. Do you think PepsiCo erred by not immediately volunteering to recall its product?
2. How would you assess PepsiCo's overall public relations strategy?
3. How would you assess PepsiCo's government relations strategy?

Here's another way Pepsi is saying thank you to millions of Americans this July 4th. Including you.

Thanks America.

Manufacturer's Coupon	Expiration Date: 7/24/93

 SAVE $1.00

on your next purchase of a case of Pepsi products. (Offer valid on 24 cans, 24 16oz. or 20oz. bottles, or 6 2L bottles of Pepsi, Diet Pepsi, Caffeine-Free Pepsi, Caffeine-Free Diet Pepsi, Crystal Pepsi or Diet Crystal Pepsi.)

64100

CONSUMER: Only one coupon per purchase. Cannot be doubled. You pay sales tax and/or deposit charge. Coupon may not be assigned, transferred or reproduced. Any other use constitutes fraud. Cash value: 1/100¢. RETAILER: We will reimburse you for the face value plus 8¢ handling if you and the consumer have complied with our Coupon Redemption Policy available at the redemption address. Mail coupons to: PEPSI-COLA COMPANY; CMS Dept. #12000; 1 Fawcett Dr.; Del Rio, TX 78840. Coupon expires 7/24/93. PEPSI, DIET PEPSI, CAFFEINE-FREE PEPSI, CAFFEINE-FREE DIET PEPSI, CRYSTAL PEPSI and DIET CRYSTAL PEPSI are trademarks of PepsiCo, Inc.

5 12000 00076 3

Let's celebrate July 4th together.

PEPSI and PEPSI-COLA are registered trademarks of PepsiCo, Inc.

FIGURE 5-12   Case closed. Uh huh!

4. What were the pros and cons of ignoring print media and focusing instead on electronic media? Could this strategy backfire on PepsiCo?

5. What were the pros and cons of using PepsiCo's president as chief spokesperson?

6. What public relations lessons can be drawn from PepsiCo's experience for handling future product tampering cases?

7. To learn how PepsiCo is communicating with the public these days, visit its corporate Web site (www.pepsico.com). Follow the links to "Press Releases," then click on "Pepsi Releases." What topics do most of the recent Pepsi press releases focus on? If another syringe soda scare occurred, where on the Web site would you advise PepsiCo to post its position and actions?

For further information about the Pepsi syringe scare case, see Claudia Carpenter, "A 'Scared' Firm Fights to Save Its Good Name," *New York Post* (June 17, 1993): 25; Gerry Hinckley, "'Big Mistake' Acknowledged on Syringe–Pepsi Story," *Milwaukee Sentinel* (June 21, 1993); Thomas K. Grose, "How PepsiCo Overcame Syringe Challenge," *TJFR Business News Reporter* (July 1993): 1; Michael Janofsky, "Under Siege, Pepsi Mounts a TV Counter Offensive," *New York Times* (June 17, 1993): D–1; Charles M. Madigan, "Recipe for National Scare: Pepsi, Media, Me-Too-Ism," *The Record* (June 21, 1993): D–1; Tom Mashberg, "Pepsi Puts Reputation on the Line," *Boston Globe* (June 17, 1993): A–1; "Media-Smart Pepsi," *Advertising Age* (June 28, 1993): 26; "Public Relations Victory Sweep for Pepsi-Cola Officials," *Washington Post News Service* (June 20, 1993); Gary Strauss, "Scare Fails to Flatten Pepsi Sales," *USA Today* (June 23, 1993): B–1; Laura Zinn, "The Right Moves, Baby," *Business Week* (July 5, 1993): 30.

 TIPS FROM THE TOP

An Interview with Craig Weatherup

Craig Weatherup

Craig Weatherup was chairman and chief executive officer of PepsiCo, one of the largest and most successful beverage businesses in the world, with annual sales in excess of $10 billion. Mr. Weatherup served as point man for the company's handling of the 1993 public relations crisis, when syringes were reportedly found in Diet Pepsi cans. He was in the catbird seat, making all of Pepsi's major decisions in the case.

What kind of advice do you seek from public relations professionals?

First, I look for either reaffirmation of my own gut instincts or if I've totally misread a situation. My initial concern is the core thought. Do we have it right in terms of what we're communicating? My public relations director is a great "calibrator" of getting things exactly right. Very secondarily, I look for counsel on the mechanics or the elements that can best be communicated. For me as a CEO, the real value is this constant calibration of what we are doing and ensuring that we are really in touch with our average consumer. I rely on the public relations director to be the primary source of this so that we absolutely have the right stake in the ground. If you have the right stake in the ground, you deal with all the other stuff. If you don't, you're just going to be dangling in the wind, and you'll regret it.

What did you think when you heard that a syringe had been found in a can of Diet Pepsi?

I thought it was legitimate, at least from the standpoint of sabotage. Obviously, somebody had put it in the can. We announced we were doing the things we normally do in terms of checking the product, recalling any product that had specific codes, reexamining inventories, all those kinds of things.

What was your public relations strategy?

The core thing was we had this wonderful advantage: We knew it was a hoax. Every single can has a code on the bottom. As soon as we had the second can and realized these things were produced months apart in different plants, we knew it was fraudulent. And we had an idea to dispatch a crew to Philadelphia and film the can line and get it on the news.

What else did you decide to do?

The other decision we made—because this was the lead story three straight nights on the evening news and there was nothing else happening in the world, unfortunately—was that we would be very open and available. We had honest and credible information that we could share, and we knew we were right. So we decided to take advantage of this media event by using the media. We did hundreds of interviews over those two days. Radio, television, print.

Didn't the *Wall Street Journal* suggest that you recall the product?

Yes, I got hacked up in the *Journal* one morning about how idiotic it was not to recall the product.

Did you consider recalling the product?

No. It would have been an absolute untruth.

What about your relationship with Commissioner Kessler of the FDA?

I think I was able to convince him that this was a hoax. After that, I must have talked to him a couple of times a day, including one very, very heated argument about bringing this to closure. We felt we'd been dangling out there for 72 hours, and another hour was too long. But I would give Kessler great marks. He could have been a lot heavier if he had wanted to. Again, we were cooperating with his agency. We had the technical people talking, the lawyers talking, public relations people talking, and I was talking to Kessler.

How much did you spend on various public relations activities on the syringe problem?

We spent $250,000 on the video news releases, compared to $20 million on the coupon ad we ran immediately after the crisis.

What lessons did you take away from this public relations crisis?

First, stick with the truth. And I don't say that as a platitude either. We didn't have to guess at this. We knew what was happening. So we had to find a way to present these facts so that people would understand them. Second, be clear and totally accessible to the media.

Suggested Readings

Coombs, W. Timothy. *Ongoing Crisis Communications, Planning, Managing & Responding.* Thousand Oaks, CA: Sage Publications, 1999.

Crespi, Irving. *The Public Opinion Process: How the People Speak.* Mahwah, NJ: Lawrence Erlbaum Associates, 1997.

Edelstein, Alex S. *Total Propaganda: From Mass Culture to Popular Culture.* Mahwah, NJ: Lawrence Erlbaum Associates, 1997.

Ferguson, Sherry Devereaux. *Researching the Public Opinion Environment, Theories & Methods.* Thousand Oaks, CA: Sage Publications, 2000.

Glasser, Theodore L., and Charles T. Salmon. *Public Opinion and the Communication of Consent.* New York: Guiford Press, 1995. Anthology of articles spanning the history of the role of public opinion from ancient to contemporary times.

Morley, Michael. *How to Manage Your Global Reputation: A Guide to the Dynamics of International Public Relations.* New York: New York University Press, 1998.

Weissberg, Robert. *Polling, Policy and Pubic Opinion, The Case Against Heeding the "Voice of the People."* New York: St. Martin's Press, 2002.

www.mediainfo.com. *Editor & Publisher* magazine's database offers access to more than 11,000 news Web sites.

www.prnewswire.com. Public Relations Newswire. Features corporate press releases and background, with a link to Expert Contacts.

www.publicagenda.org. Public Agenda Online. "The inside source for public opinion and policy analysis."

Young, Davis. *Building Your Company's Good Name: How to Create and Protect the Reputation Your Organization Wants and Deserves.* New York: AMACOM, 1996.

Notes

1. Chester Burger, Remarks to the Institute for Public Relations, Union League Club, New York, December 2, 1998.
2. Jared Sandberg, Shawn Young, and Deborah Solomon, "WorldCom to File Chapter 11, As Cash Reserves Dwindle Fast, *Wall Street Journal* (July 19, 2002): 1.
3. Fraser P. Seitel, "CEO Ignominious," odwyerpr.com (June 10, 2002).
4. Fraser P. Seitel, "Martha's PR Potpourri," odwyerpr.com (July 15, 2002).
5. Edna Gundersen, "Michael Jackson's Sept. ll Single Produced by Gay-Porn Maker," *USA Today* (July 15, 2002): 2D.
6. "What Not to Do in the Off Season," *Time* (July 22, 2002): 66.
7. Brian Harmon, "Lizzie Drops the Bawl," *New York Daily News* (July 19, 2002): 3.
8. Cited in Edward L. Bernays, *Crystallizing Public Opinion* (New York: Liveright, 1961): 61.
9. Cited in Harwood L. Childs, *Public Opinion: Nature, Formation, and Role* (Princeton, NJ: Van Nostrand, 1965): 15.
10. James E. Grunig and Todd Hunt, *Managing Public Relations* (New York: Holt, Rinehart & Winston, 1984): 130.
11. Leon A. Festinger, *A Theory of Cognitive Dissonance* (New York: Harper & Row, 1957): 163.
12. Abraham Maslow, *Motivation and Personality* (New York: Harper & Row, 1954).
13. S. Plous, "Toward More Effective Activism," *The Animal's Agenda* (December 1989): 24–26.
14. T. C. Brock and S. Shavitt, *Persuasion: Psychological Insights and Perspectives* (Chicago: Allyn & Bacon, 1999).
15. Saul D. Alinsky, *Rules for Radicals* (New York: Vintage Books, 1971): 81.
16. Ronald W. Reagan, Address by the President to the Nation, October 27, 1983.
17. Robert L. Dilenschneider, *Power and Influence* (New York: Prentice Hall, 1990): 5.
18. Hadley Cantril, *Gauging Public Opinion* (Princeton, NJ: Princeton University Press, 1972): 226–230.
19. D. T. Max, "The 2,988 Words That Changed a Presidency: An Etymology," *New York Times* on the web (October 7, 2001).
20. Richard Benedetto, "Business News Alters Perceptions of Bush," *USA Today* (July 10, 2002): 6A.
21. Fraser P. Seitel, "How to Win the Propaganda War," odwyerpr.com (October 29, 2001).
22. "Southwest Airlines Chairman Begins Medical Treatment," Southwest Airlines news release, August 11, 1999.
23. John Naisbitt and Patricia Aburdene, *Megatrends 2000* (New York: Morrow, 1990).
24. Philip Lesly, "How the Future Will Shape Public Relations—and Vice Versa," *Public Relations Quarterly* (Winter 1981–82): 7.

Chapter 6

Ethics

Several years ago, sociologist Raymond Baumhart asked businesspeople, "What does ethics mean to you?" Among their replies:

> *"Ethics has to do with what my feelings tell me is right or wrong."*
> *"Ethics has to do with my religious beliefs."*
> *"Being ethical is doing what the law requires."*
> *"Ethics consists of the standards of behavior our society accepts."*
> *"I don't know what the word means."*

Classical ethics means different things to different people. Ethics theories range from utilitarianism (i.e., "the greatest good for the greatest number") to deontology (i.e., "do what is right, though the world should perish").

Because the meaning of ethics is hard to pin down, the views many people have about ethics are uncertain. Nonetheless, ethical dilemmas are all around us. In many sectors of society today, institutions are sending out mixed signals about the value of moral conduct.

Consider the following:

- *In religion, the Catholic Church, the ostensible symbol of morality and decency in society, was rocked in the spring of 2002 by a priest pedophilia scandal in the United States. In July, Pope John Paul II called the crimes and misdeeds of some priests "a source of shame."[1] The Catholic Church was roundly criticized for its coverup for decades of the activities of rogue priests.*

- *In business, the summer of 2002 was perhaps the most trying in the history of American capitalism. The focus turned to the individuals at the top of the heap—the CEOs—who selfishly, unethically, and in some cases illegally profited while their shareholders and the general public suffered. Top executives from Enron, WorldCom, Global Crossing, Adelphia Communications, Tyco International, Qwest Communications, and a host of others were paraded before the public because of their misdeeds.*

- *In politics, President George W. Bush and Vice President Richard Cheney were both asked about their roles in questionable business practices while*

131

serving in the private sector. Bush was alleged to have engaged in a sweetheart loan arrangement while he was an executive at Harken Energy. Cheney was investigated for accounting matters while serving as CEO of Halliburton Energy.[2]

Meanwhile, on the other side of the aisle, Bush's predecessor in the White House, Bill Clinton, left office in humiliation, after his affair with an intern—which Clinton at first denied—was exposed.

● *In society generally, the first years of the 21st century uncovered a disturbing failure of morality and ethics. Noted historians Stephen Ambrose and Doris Kearns Goodwin were found to have plagiarized the works of others, as parts of their best-selling books. Princeton University was caught accessing arch rival Yale's confidential admissions Web site. Even Little League was found ethically deficient two years in a row, when New York City teams violated age and residence requirements to make the tournament finals.*

The public relations profession was particularly sensitive to the ethical scandals breaking out throughout society in the opening years of the twenty-first century. The heart of public relations counsel is "to do the right thing." The cardinal rule of public relations is to "never lie."

Nonetheless, in one bridling survey of 1,700 public relations executives, it was revealed that 25 percent of those interviewed admitted they had "lied on the job," 39 percent said they had exaggerated the truth, and another 44 percent said they had felt "uncertain" about the ethics of what they did.[3]

Sensing an opening, law firms roared in to fill the breach as crisis managers and "ethical consultants." Typical was Washington, D.C., insider law firm Patton Boggs, which hired a former Clinton apologist, Lanny Davis, to head its crisis management public relations practice.[4] *It mattered not that Mr. Davis had steadfastly defended the former president's ethical lapses—the fields of ethics and public relations had become a new lucrative business.*

That was enough in 2001 to propel the Public Relations Society of America (PRSA) to invest $100,000 in revamping its code of ethics. The new code (Appendix A) was underscored by six fundamental values that the PRSA believed to be vital to the integrity of the profession (Figure 6-1).[5]

Thus was the significance to the practice of public relations of the subject of ethics.

Ethics in Society

Pollster Richard Wirthlin has postulated, "For most organizations, image is determined not only by what goods and services are provided, but also by the persona of the corporation. The first imperative of leadership is 'honesty.' "[6]

So, what constitutes ethics for an organization? Sadly, there is no one answer. Ethical guidelines are just that—guidelines. They don't necessarily provide right answers, just educated guesses. Reasonable people can and do disagree about what is moral, ethical, and right in a given situation.

PRSA Member Code of Ethics 2000

PRSA Member Statement of Professional Values

This statement presents the core values of PRSA members and, more broadly, of the public relations profession. These values provide the foundation for the Member Code of Ethics and set the industry standard for the professional practice of public relations. These values are the fundamental beliefs that guide our behaviors and decision-making process. We believe our professional values are vital to the integrity of the profession as a whole.

ADVOCACY

We serve the public interest by acting as responsible advocates for those we represent. We provide a voice in the marketplace of ideas, facts, and viewpoints to aid informed public debate.

HONESTY

We adhere to the highest standards of accuracy and truth in advancing the interests of those we represent and in communicating with the public.

EXPERTISE

We acquire and responsibly use specialized knowledge and experience. We advance the profession through continued professional development, research, and education. We build mutual understanding, credibility, and relationships among a wide array of institutions and audiences.

INDEPENDENCE

We provide objective counsel to those we represent. We are accountable for our actions.

LOYALTY

We are faithful to those we represent, while honoring our obligation to serve the public interest.

FAIRNESS

We deal fairly with clients, employers, competitors, peers, vendors, the media, and the general public. We respect all opinions and support the right of free expression.

The Public Relations Society of America, 33 Irving Place, New York, NY 10003-2376

FIGURE 6-1   **PRSA's six values.** The values of advocacy, honesty, expertise, independence, loyalty, and fairness form the basis of the PRSA ethical code. *(Courtesy of the PRSA)*

Nonetheless, when previously respected business, government, and religious leaders, as well as other members of society, are exposed as cheaters, con artists, and even crooks, those who would look up to and be influenced by such people are justifiably appalled. Stated another way, when ethical codes are ignored—such as happened with Enron and WorldCom in 2002—faith in the underlying system is jeopardized.

Little wonder then that societal pressure in the area of ethics has never been more intense. In public relations—a practice that is misunderstood by many and even mistrusted by some—no issue is more critical than the ethics of both the practice and the practitioner.

The bigness of most institutions today—where megamergers are commonplace among business organizations, hospitals, media firms, public relations agencies, and other institutions—immediately makes them suspect. All have become concerned about their individual cultures—the values, ideals, principles, and aspirations that underlie their credibility and viability. As the internal conscience of many organizations, the public relations department has become a focal point for the institutionalization of ethical conduct. Increasingly, management has turned to public relations officers to lead the internal ethical charge and to be the keeper of the organizational ethic.

Are We Doing the Right Thing?

What exactly are ethics? The answer isn't an easy one.

The Josephson Institute, which studies ethics, defines ethics as "standards of conduct that indicate how one should behave based on moral duties and virtues."[7]

In general, ethics refers to the values that guide a person, organization, or society—the difference between right and wrong, fairness and unfairness, honesty and dishonesty. An individual's conduct is measured not only against his or her conscience but also against some norm of acceptability that has been societally, professionally, or organizationally determined.[8]

Roughly translated, an individual's or organization's ethics comes down to the standards that are followed in relationships with others—the real integrity of the individual or organization. Obviously, a person's ethical construct and approach depend on numerous factors—cultural, religious, and educational, among others. Complicating the issue is that what might seem right to one person might not matter to someone else. No issue is solely black or white but is rather a shade of gray—particularly in making public relations decisions.

That is not to say that classical ethical distinctions don't exist. They do. Philosophers throughout the ages have debated the essence of ethics.

- Utilitarianism, as noted, suggests considering the "greater good" rather than what may be best for the individual.
- To Aristotle, the golden mean of moral virtue could be found between two extreme points of view.
- Kant's categorical imperative recommended acting "on that maxim which you will to become a universal law."
- Mill's principle of utility recommended "seeking the greatest happiness for the greatest number."
- The traditional Judeo-Christian ethic prescribes "loving your neighbor as yourself." Indeed, this golden rule makes good sense in the practice of public relations.

Because the practice of public relations is misunderstood by so many—even including some of those for whom public relations people work—public relations people, in particular, must be ethical. They can't assume that ethics are strictly personal choices without relevance or related methodology for resolving moral quandaries. Public relations people must adhere to a high standard of professional ethics, with truth as the key determinant of their conduct.

Professional ethics, often referred to as "applied ethics," suggests a commonly accepted sense of professional conduct that is translated into formal codes of ethics, which are monitored, assessed, and enforced through actions taken against those who deviate from the norm.[9]

The essence of the codes of conduct of both the Public Relations Society of America and the International Association of Business Communicators (Appendix A) is that honesty and fairness lie at the heart of public relations practice. Indeed, if the ultimate goal of the public relations professional is to enhance public trust of an organization, then only the highest ethical conduct is acceptable.

Inherent in these standards of the profession is the understanding that ethics have changed and continue to change as society changes. Over time, views have changed on such issues as minority discrimination, double standards in the treatment of women, pollution of the environment, lack of concern for human rights, acceptable standards of language and dress, and so on. Again, honesty and fairness are two critical components that will continue to determine the ethical behavior of public relations professionals.

Boiled down to its essence, the ethical heart of the practice of public relations lies in posing only one question to management: "Are we doing the right thing?"

Often the public relations professional will be the only member of management with the nerve to pose such a question. Sometimes this means saying "no" to what the boss wants to do. Public relations professionals must be driven by one purpose—to preserve defend, sustain, and enhance the health and vitality of the organization always.

Simply translated, that means the bottom line for public relations professionals must always be to counsel and to do what is in the best long-term interests of the organization.

Ethics in Business

For many people today, regrettably, the term *business ethics* is an oxymoron. Its mere mention stimulates images of disgraced CEOs being led away in handcuffs (Figure 6-2), after bilking their shareholders and employees out of millions of dollars. In one period alone, the 2002 "summer of shame," a dizzying array of corporate executives was charged with ethical violations.

- The summer began with executives of Enron Corp. being charged with massive accounting fraud, which effectively destroyed the life savings of shareholders—many of them longtime Enron employees. Chairman Kenneth Lay and Chief Financial Officer Andrew Fastow refused to testify to Congress about their knowledge and actions. CEO Jeffrey Skilling testified and was criticized for his "arrogance."
- In Enron's wake, the bedrock accounting firm of Arthur Andersen was decimated for aiding and abetting in the Enron accounting duplicity.

FIGURE 6-2 **Perp walk.** Adelphia CEO John Rigas is escorted in handcuffs to a waiting police car.

- WorldCom, Global Crossing, and Qwest Communications executives, accused of massive accounting fraud, were charged soon thereafter and later several were taken into custody by the FBI.
- The executives of Adelphia Communications, a leading cable TV company, were charged with using the corporation as their own private "piggy bank."[10] Even worse, the three chief culprits were members of the founding Rigas family. Although they were believed to be pillars of their Pennsylvania community, they were common criminals in the eyes of the law.
- In the months that followed, some of the nation's richest and most celebrated CEOs were called to task for ethical transgressions. Alfred Taubman, multimillionaire chairman of Sotheby's, fixed prices and went to jail. Dennis Kozlowski, who received $300 million in three years as CEO of Tyco International, was charged with trying to avoid $1 million in state sales tax.
- Even Martha Stewart, celebrity homemaking idol, was charged with insider trading violations.

The nation's confidence in its business leaders was so low that in July, President Bush signed a sweeping Corporate Reform Bill, which imposed rigorous sanctions on corporate criminals.

Fraud, venality, discrimination, environmental pollution—all these allegations have made headlines in recent decades. American business, perhaps the most ethical business system in the world, has been shocked—so much so that in 1987, former

Securities and Exchange Commission Chairman John Shad donated $23 million to begin a program at Harvard Business School to make the study of ethics an integral part of the curriculum.*

In one study in the spring of 2002, *Business 2.0* magazine found that some of the most celebrated companies and CEOs of the Internet era were suffering extreme losses in credibility. Although government figures such as President Bush, Secretary of State Powell, and former New York City Mayor Giuliani were deemed "highly credible," business figures, such as the CEOs of Enron, Hewlett-Packard, and Cisco Systems, were found to have "low credibility."[11]

In an earlier study, the Business Roundtable, a leading business group, pointed out the "crucial role of the chief executive officer and top managers in establishing a strong commitment to ethical conduct and in providing constant leadership in tending and reviewing the values of the organization."[12] The Roundtable study debunked the myth that there is an inherent contradiction between ethics and profits. On the contrary, it emphasized that there is a strong relationship between acting ethically, maintaining a good reputation for fair and honest business, and making money.

That became painfully obvious to business in the initial years of the 21st century, when the three most repugnant initials in the English language were *CEO*. One book written by former management consultants described CEOs thusly:

> Among the more than 14,000 publicly registered companies in the U.S. and the even larger number of privately held companies there is a class of people who will lie to the public, the regulators, their employees and anyone else in order to increase personal wealth and power.[13]

To stem the feeling that chief executives and their companies weren't acting ethically, a number of firms increased their efforts to make their activities more "transparent" to the public. In rapid order in the summer of 2002, companies from Coca-Cola to Amazon.com to General Electric announced plans to make accounting procedures more understandable. In June 2002, CEO Henry Paulson of investment banking giant Goldman Sachs called on his fellow CEOs to reform before regulation forced them to do so. "In my lifetime, American business has never been under such scrutiny. To be blunt, much of it is deserved," said Paulson.[14]

The negative perceptions of business organizations and especially of those in charge led some to push for the initials *CEO* standing for something far more important: chief ethical officer.[15]

Corporate Codes of Conduct

In the summer of 2002, in the wake of corporate accounting and executive scandals, the New York Stock Exchange (NYSE) mandated that its member companies, among other corporate governance measures, immediately implement internal corporate codes of conduct to ensure that they act ethically toward all of their key constituents.

Even before the NYSE mandate, codes of ethics, standards of conduct, and similar statements of corporate policies and values have proliferated in recent years. The reasons corporations have adopted such codes vary from company to company.

---

*Ironically Mr. Shad himself was the subject of an embarrassing ethical dilemma. He was called in to head Drexel Burnham Lambert after the firm was fined and discredited for junk bond indiscretions led by Michael Milken. Mr. Shad was duly mortified when Drexel Burnham went belly-up in 1989.

● **To increase public confidence.**   The scandals of recent years have shaken investor confidence and have led to a decline of public trust and confidence in business. Many firms have responded with written codes of ethics.

● **To stem the tide of regulation.**   As public confidence has declined, government regulation of business has increased. Some estimated the cost to society of compliance with regulations at $100 billion per year. Corporate codes of conduct, it was hoped, would help serve as a self-regulation mechanism.

● **To improve internal operations.**   As companies became larger and more decentralized, management needed consistent standards of conduct to ensure that employees were meeting the business objectives of the company in a legal and ethical manner.

● **To respond to transgressions.**   Frequently when a company itself was caught in the web of unethical behavior, it responded with its own code of ethics. For example, Fiat, Italy's biggest private company, sought to extricate itself from a huge corruption scandal in the country by issuing the first Italian corporate code of ethical conduct for employees.[16]

Ralph Waldo Emerson once wrote, "An organization is the lengthened shadow of a man." Today, many corporate executives realize that just as an individual has certain responsibilities as a citizen, a corporate citizen has responsibilities to the society in which it is privileged to operate (Figure 6-3).

Corporate codes of conduct are not without their critics. "Trust has become the overriding concern for America's business executives," according to Stuart Gilman, the president of the Ethics Resource Center. Gilman insists that for companies to "walk the talk" on ethics codes, they must treat them as more than "pieces of paper" by establishing a regular review system to ensure the code is dynamic and updated in light of new developments and implications in society.[17]

Such skepticism notwithstanding, formal ethical codes, addressing such topics as executive compensation, accounting procedures, confidentiality of corporate information, misappropriation of corporate assets, bribes and kickbacks, and political contributions, have become a corporate fact of life.

Corporate Social Responsibility

Closely related to the ethical conduct of an organization is its "social responsibility," which has been defined as a social norm. This norm holds that any social institution, from the smallest family unit to the largest corporation, is responsible for the behavior of its members and may be held accountable for their misdeeds.

In the late 1960s, when this idea was just emerging, initial responses were of the knee-jerk variety. A firm that was threatened by increasing legal or activist pressures and harassment would ordinarily change its policies in a hurry. Today, however, organizations and their social responsibility programs are much more sophisticated. Social responsibility is treated just like any other management discipline: Analyze the issues, evaluate performance, set priorities, allocate resources to those priorities, and implement programs that deal with issues within the constraints of the organization's resources. Many companies have created special committees to set the agenda and target the objectives.

Social responsibility touches practically every level of organizational activity, from marketing to hiring, from training to work standards. In 1996 when Texaco

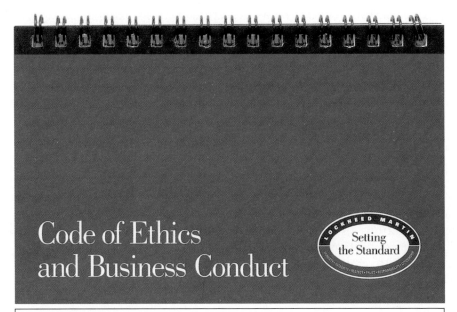

Dear Colleague:

Lockheed Martin aims to "set the standard" for ethical business conduct. We will achieve this through six virtues: Honesty, Integrity, Respect, Trust, Responsibility, and Citizenship.

Honesty: to be truthful in all our endeavors; to be honest and forthright with one another and with our customers, communities, suppliers, and shareholders.

Integrity: to say what we mean, to deliver what we promise, and to stand for what is right.

Respect: to treat one another with dignity and fairness, appreciating the diversity of our workforce and the uniqueness of each employee.

Trust: to build confidence through teamwork and open, candid communication.

Responsibility: to speak up – without fear of retribution – and report concerns in the work place, including violations of laws, regulations and company policies, and seek clarification and guidance whenever there is doubt.

Citizenship: to obey all the laws of the United States and the other countries in which we do business and to do our part to make the communities in which we live better.

You can count on us to do everything in our power to meet Lockheed Martin's standards. We are counting on you to do the same. We are confident that our trust in you is well placed and we are determined to be worthy of your trust.

DANIEL M. TELLEP   NORMAN R. AUGUSTINE   BERNARD L. SCHWARTZ

FIGURE 6-3   **Lockheed Code.** The principles enumerated here represent the obligations that Lockheed Martin Corporation believes it has to its public in the wake of ethical tribulations in the 1990s.

Inc., a worldwide company, discovered its executives were speaking disparagingly of African Americans—a violation of its social responsibility code—it had no alternative but to take prompt and forceful action. The company's CEO fired the executives involved and quickly settled a class-action bias suit against the company.[18] A partial list of social responsibility categories might include the following:

- **Product lines**—dangerous products, product performance and standards, packaging, and environmental impact
- **Marketing practices**—sales practices, consumer complaint policies, advertising content, and fair pricing
- **Corporate philanthropy**—contribution performance, encouragement of employee participation in social projects, and community development activities
- **Environmental activities**—pollution-control projects, adherence to federal standards, and evaluation procedures for new packages and products
- **External relations**—support of minority enterprises, investment practices, and government relations
- **Employment diversity in retaining and promoting minorities and women**—current hiring policies, advancement policies, specialized career counseling, and opportunities for special minorities such as the physically handicapped
- **Employee safety and health**—work environment policies, accident safeguards, and food and medical facilities

More often than not, organizations have incorporated social responsibility into the mainstream of their practice. Most firms recognize that social responsibility, far from being an add-on program, must be a corporate way of life. Beyond this, some studies have indicated that those organizations that practice social responsibility over time rank among the most profitable and successful firms in society.

Ethics in Government

Politics has never enjoyed an unblemished reputation when it comes to ethics. In the early years of the 21st century, politics has developed a particularly sleazy reputation.

As noted, in the midst of the corporate accounting scandals of 2002, the two top executives in the Bush administration were called on to explain their own corporate affiliations, President George Bush at Harken Energy and Vice President Dick Cheney at Halliburton Energy.

Nor did the preceding administration, under Bill Clinton, distinguish itself for high ethical standing. After assuming his second term amidst allegations of questionable campaign contributions from foreign powers, Clinton suffered the ultimate ignominy: being impeached for his inexplicable and embarrassing behavior with a young intern in the White House.

The sleaze factor in government, alas, isn't confined to one party or one level.

- In 2002, Ohio Congressman James Traficant was expelled from the U.S. House of Representatives, after being convicted of racketeering and using his office for political favors.
- That same year, California Congressman Gary Condit was defeated for reelection, after becoming a national pariah for an alleged affair he conducted with an intern, who was later found to have been murdered.

A QUESTION OF ETHICS

You Bet He Didn't Enjoy the Ad

The new mayor of New York wasn't laughing.

"Pot Poster Boy" is how the *New York Daily News* front-page headline described the mayor's debut in an ad to legalize marijuana.

The $105,000 full-page ad in the *New York Times* was the centerpiece in a campaign paid for by the National Organization for the Reform of Marijuana Laws Foundation (NORML) to decriminalize marijuana.

The NORML ad featured a wide-eyed Mayor Bloomberg with the words, "You bet I did and I enjoyed it," appearing in a bubble above the mayor's head. The words stemmed from a premayoral interview five months earlier, in which Bloomberg was asked if he ever smoked marijuana (Figure 6-4).

"At Last, an Honest Politician" headlined the ad. The text applauded Bloomberg's candor and lumped him in with former President Bill Clinton, New York Governor George Pataki, and Supreme Court Justice Clarence Thomas as other public officials who have admitted to smoking pot.

The ad went on to denounce the 50,000 people arrested each year in New York City for smoking pot. "Millions of people smoke marijuana today," said NORML's executive director at a press conference to unveil the ad. "They come from all walks of life, and that includes your own mayor."

Maybe so, but Mayor Bloomberg wasn't a happy camper—or smoker—as the case may be. At a press conference, an obviously unamused Bloomberg questioned the ethics of taking his quote out of context and using it, without seeking permission, in such an advertisement. Said Mayor Bloomberg, "I'm not thrilled, but I suppose there's that First Amendment that gets in the way of me stopping it."

NORML's view of what was "ethical" veered in a different direction. "Is it ethical to speak in a friendly way about your own marijuana use while still arresting thousands of people for it?" asked the NORML executive director.

The NORML executives insisted they were "not trying to hurt the mayor in any way. We did not 'out' the

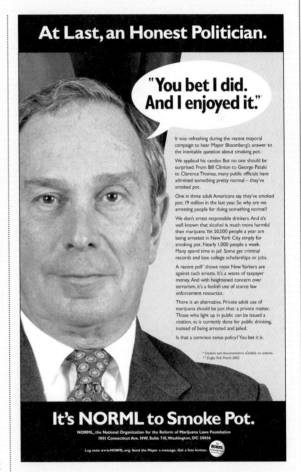

FIGURE 6-4 **Not normal.** New York Mayor Mike Bloomberg cried "foul" over this ad from NORML. *(Courtesy of NORML)*

mayor. All of these people we have mentioned (in the ad) 'outed' themselves."

Outed or not, Mayor Bloomberg may have gotten the last word. He vowed at his rebuttal press conference to "enforce the laws as they are, and the Police Department will do so vigorously."

- Also in 2002, New Jersey Senator Robert Torricelli was "severely admonished" by the Senate Ethics Committee, after he accepted jewelry, a TV set, and a CD player from a shady Korean businessman seeking Congressional influence.
- Earlier, in 1990, five U.S. senators were accused of serious ethical violations in support of Charles Keating, a savings and loan operator convicted of fraud.

S I D E B A R

Short, Sad Saga of the Political Sage

No communications adviser symbolized better the "political ethics"—or lack thereof—of the excesses of the 1990s than Dick Morris (Figure 6-5).

As a strategist for national and local candidates, it apparently made no difference to Mr. Morris which side or inclination his candidates represented. Just as long as they "showed him the money," he was content, working for right-wingers, such as Senators Jesse Helms and Trent Lott, or left-leaners, such as Senator Howard Metzenbaum and President Bill Clinton.

The latter, of course, was Mr. Morris's primary client. Indeed, when President Clinton's popularity sagged in the middle of his first term, he turned immediately to his old strategist to bail him out. Mr. Morris suggested that the president adopt a less liberal, more middle-of-the-road platform. The president took the advice and made great progress.

Adviser Morris, however, let his access and power get the best of him. He flaunted his status, was nasty to others around him, and claimed credit for virtually anything that the administration did right. However, in a classic case of "what goes around comes around," in what should have been his finest hour, the adviser crashed and burned.

On the eve of President Clinton's party "coronation" in Chicago in the fall of 1996, it was revealed in rapid order that presidential confidante Dick Morris had been less than highly ethical with his employer. To wit:

- He secretly signed a lucrative book contract, without telling the White House and in violation of administration ethical standards.
- He regularly employed a D.C. prostitute and let her listen in on the extension as he counseled the Clintons on matters of national importance.
- He alienated most of the president's other associates, so that when it came time to "stick up for Dick," few allies rushed to defend their fallen comrade.

FIGURE 6-5 **Misguided sage.** From Political Guru to public relations casualty, former Clinton adviser-turned-talk-show-host Dick Morris.

Poor Dick.

As he, himself, sadly lamented in his $2.5 million autobiography, "I began life weighing only two pounds, eleven ounces and spent my first three months in incubators, untouched by anyone, even my mother. Only after years of therapy did I begin to understand how this early deprivation affected my personality thereafter."

Poor, whiny Dick.

Ultimately, Mr. Morris was forced to resign from the president's employ. His wife announced she was leaving him. He started a political Web site, vote.com. In the most telling sign of how utterly impoverished his life had now become, Dick Morris became a cable TV political analyst talking head. How low can one go!

Four years later, four of the "Keating Five" senators were gone from the Senate. Ironically, the fifth person involved, Senator John McCain of Arizona, became a strong Republican contender for the presidency in the year 2000 and an ethical reformer in the Senate.

After all the white-collar crime and political scandals that have marked the first few years of the 21st century, the public is less willing to tolerate such ethical violations from their elected officials. It is likely that ethics in government will become an even more important issue as voters insist on representatives who are honest, trustworthy, and ethical.

Ethics in Journalism

The Society of Professional Journalists is quite explicit on the subject of ethics (Figure 6-6).

Journalists at all times will show respect for the dignity, privacy, rights, and well-being of people encountered in the course of gathering and presenting the news.

1. The news media should not communicate unofficial charges affecting reputation or moral character without giving the accused a chance to reply.
2. The news media must guard against invading a person's right to privacy.
3. The media should not pander to morbid curiosity about details of vice and crime.

And so on.

Unfortunately, what is in the code often doesn't reflect what appears in print or on the air. More often than not, journalistic judgments run smack into ethical principles.

- In the new millennium, the proliferation of online media, publishing round the clock, as well as the exponential increase in TV news, cable stations, and programming on the Internet increased the pressure on news outlets to report as much as possible in as entertaining a manner as possible. Icon of a generation of Internet journalists was the intrepid, behatted Matt Drudge, who operated his tell-all Web site from the living room of his Los Angeles apartment. Absolute accuracy, intimated Drudge, was less critical than getting out the news. Other Internet reportorial vehicles were equally cavalier in their treatment of facts, thus introducing a new level of journalistic ethical problems.
- The 21st century is seeing an increase in so-called "reality television," such as MTV's *Real World*. The vast majority of these voyeuristic exercises plumb the depths of human nature, from *Big Brother* and *Fear Factor* to *Survivor* and *Joe Millionaire* to *Anna Nicole* and *I'm a Celebrity, Get Me Out of Here*. Some made interesting TV; all "dumbed down" those who watched. Similarly, "tabloid television" programs featured smarmy hosts, such as Jerry Springer and Jenny Jones, preening over dysfunctional (often toothless) guests. Clearly, the most revealing commentary on TV ethics of the day was the fact that the nation's newest "father figure" was none other than heavy-metal mongering, bat-biting, Black Sabbath–leading Ozzy Osbourne (Figure 6-7), whose dysfunctional family was the hit of MTV.

THE SOCIETY OF PROFESSIONAL JOURNALISTS, SIGMA DELTA CHI

Code
ofEthics

THE SOCIETY of Professional Journalists, Sigma Delta Chi believes the duty of journalists is to serve the truth.

WE BELIEVE the agencies of mass communication are carriers of public discussion and information, acting on their Constitutional mandate and freedom to learn and report the facts.

WE BELIEVE in public enlightenment as the forerunner of justice, and in our Constitutional role to seek the truth as part of the public's right to know the truth.

WE BELIEVE those responsibilities carry obligations that require journalists to perform with intelligence, objectivity, accuracy and fairness.

To these ends, we declare acceptance of the standards of practice here set forth:

RESPONSIBILITY:

The public's right to know of events of public importance and interest is the overriding mission of the mass media. The purpose of distributing news and enlightened opinion is to serve the general welfare. Journalists who use their professional status as representatives of the public for selfish or other unworthy motives violate a high trust.

FREEDOM OF THE PRESS:

Freedom of the press is to be guarded as an inalienable right of people in a free society. It carries with it the freedom and the responsibility to discuss, question and challenge actions and utterances of our government and of our public and private institutions. Journalists uphold the right to speak unpopular opinions and the privilege to agree with the majority.

ETHICS:

Journalists must be free of obligation to any interest other than the public's right to know the truth.

1. Gifts, favors, free travel, special treatment or privileges can compromise the integrity of journalists and their employers. Nothing of value should be accepted.

2. Secondary employment, political involvement, holding public office and service in community organizations should be avoided if it compromises the integrity of journalists and their employers. Journalists and their employers should conduct their personal lives in a manner which protects them from conflict of interest, real or apparent. Their responsibilities to the public are paramount. That is the nature of their profession.

3. So-called news communications from private sources should not be published or broadcast without substantiation of their claims to news value.

4. Journalists will seek news that serves the public interest, despite the obstacles. They will make constant efforts to assure that the public's business is conducted in public and that public records are open to public inspection.

5. Journalists acknowledge the newsman's ethic of protecting confidential sources of information.

ACCURACY AND OBJECTIVITY:

Good faith with the public is the foundation of all worthy journalism.

1. Truth is our ultimate goal.

2. Objectivity in reporting the news is another goal, which serves as the mark of an experienced professional. It is a standard of performance toward which we strive. We honor those who achieve it.

3. There is no excuse for inaccuracies or lack of thoroughness.

4. Newspaper headlines should be fully warranted by the contents of the articles they accompany. Photographs and telecasts should give an accurate picture of an event and not highlight a minor incident out of context.

5. Sound practice makes clear distinction between news reports and expressions of opinion. News reports should be free of opinion or bias and represent all sides of an issue.

6. Partisanship in editorial comment which knowingly departs from the truth violates the spirit of American journalism.

7. Journalists recognize their responsibility for offering informed analysis, comment and editorial opinion on public events and issues. They accept the obligation to present such material by individuals whose competence, experience and judgment qualify them for it.

8. Special articles or presentations devoted to advocacy or the writer's own conclusions and interpretations should be labeled as such.

FAIR PLAY:

Journalists at all times will show respect for the dignity, privacy, rights and well-being of people encountered in the course of gathering and presenting the news.

1. The news media should not communicate unofficial charges affecting reputation or moral character without giving the accused a chance to reply.

2. The news media must guard against invading a person's right to privacy.

3. The media should not pander to morbid curiosity about details of vice and crime.

4. It is the duty of news media to make prompt and complete correction of their errors.

5. Journalists should be accountable to the public for their reports and the public should be encouraged to voice its grievances against the media. Open dialogue with our readers, viewers and listeners should be fostered.

PLEDGE:

Journalists should actively censure and try to prevent violations of these standards, and they should encourage their observance by all newspeople. Adherence to this code of ethics is intended to preserve the bond of mutual trust and respect between American journalists and the American people.

FIGURE 6-6 **Journalists' Code.** The Society of Professional Journalists has elaborated in some detail on the ethical guidelines that should govern all journalists.

FIGURE 6-7 **New family values.**
The new paragon of ethical family virtue in the 21st century was none other than bat-biting, devil-worshipping Ozzy Osbourne.

● So-called more "legitimate" TV news programs also weren't immune from questions of ethics, not to mention taste. The problems of NBC-TV's *Dateline* program tarnished the reputation of television news. *Dateline*'s bogus presentation of exploding General Motors' trucks (see Chapter 7 case study) was one example of the blurring between news and entertainment. CNN's initial collaboration with *Time* magazine resulted in a bogus 1999 report about the U.S. Army's use of nerve gas and led to the inglorious exit of one of the medium's most respected reporters, Peter Arnett. (Arnett was banished by NBC four years later, when he bad-mouthed the U.S. war effort on Iraqi TV.) Beyond this, TV's propensity to explain complicated national issues through screaming adversaries on such shows as *The O'Reilly Factor, Hardball,* and *The McLaughlin Report* added plenty of heat but not much light to the national dialogue.

● Nor has print journalism been immune to ethical scandals in recent years. Plagiarism scandals at three of the nation's leading newspapers—the *Washington Post* and *Boston Globe*—resulted in the firings of high profile journalists.[19] The new century's most embarrassing instance of suspect journalistic ethics involved the vaunted *New York Times.* In the spring of 2003, the "Great Gray Lady" was stunned when one of its promising young reporters, Jayson Blair, was discovered as having fabricated numerous dispatches for the paper over an extended period. The *Times* found out about Blair's fraud only when a reporter from another paper tipped it off. Blair was immediately fired, and the *Times* took a major reputation hit.

The point is that a sense of ethics helps an individual make moral decisions, and journalists have to make their decisions with speed and certainty. They can't usually afford to say "maybe," and they can never say, "We'll have time to get back to this when the dust settles." Their decisions must meet a deadline. Usually, the principles, values, and ideals that get reported depend largely on the individual doing the reporting.

Ethics in Public Relations

In light of numerous misconceptions about the practice of public relations, it is imperative that practitioners emulate the highest standards of personal and professional ethics. Within an organization, public relations practitioners must be the standard bearers of corporate ethical initiatives. By the same token, public relations consultants must always counsel their clients in an ethical direction—toward accuracy and candor and away from lying and hiding the truth.

The public relations department should be the seat of corporate ethics. At least four ethical theories are relevant to the practice of public relations.

- The *attorney/adversary model,* developed by Barney and Black, compares the legal profession to that of public relations in that (1) both are advocates in an adversarial climate and (2) both assume counterbalancing messages will be provided by adversaries. In this model, Barney and Black suggest practitioners have no obligation to consider the public interest or any other outside view beyond that of their client.
- The *two-way communication model,* developed by Grunig, is based on collaboration, working jointly with different people, and allowing for both listening and give-and-take. In this model, Grunig suggests that the practitioner balance his role as a client advocate with one as social conscience for the larger public.
- The *enlightened self-interest model,* developed by Baker, is based on the principle that businesses do well by doing good. In this model, Baker suggests that companies gain a competitive edge and are more respected in the marketplace if they behave ethically.
- The *responsible advocacy model,* developed by Fitzpatrick and Gauthier, is based on the ideal of professional responsibility. It postulates that practitioners' first loyalty is to their clients, but they also have a responsibility to voice the opinions of organizational stakeholders. In this model, Fitzpatrick and Gauthier suggest that the practitioner's greatest need for ethical guidance is in the reconciliation of being a professional advocate versus being a social conscience.

The Public Relations Society of America (PRSA) has been a leader in the effort to foster a strong sense of professionalism among its membership, particularly in its new code of ethics. Its six core values underpin the desired behavior of any public relations professional.

- **Advocacy.** The PRSA Code endorses the Fitzpatrick and Gauthier model in stating: "We serve the public interest by acting as responsible advocates for those we represent." For example, public relations professionals must never reveal confidential or private client information, even if a journalist demands it. The only way such information might be revealed is after a thorough discussion with the client.

- **Honesty.** For example, a client asking a public relations representative to "embellish" the performance the company expects to achieve should be told diplomatically, but firmly, "no." Public relations people don't lie.
- **Expertise.** For example, a client in need of guidance as to whether to accept a sensitive interview invitation for a cable TV talk show must be carefully guided through the pros and cons by a skilled public relations practitioner.
- **Independence.** For example, when everyone in the room—lawyer, human resources, treasurer, and president—all agree with the CEO's rock-headed scheme to disguise bad news, it is the public relations professional's duty to strike an independent tone.
- **Loyalty.** For example, if competing client offers a practitioner more money to abandon his or her original employer, the public relations professional should understand his or her loyalties must remain constant.
- **Fairness.** For example, when a rude and obnoxious journalist demands information, a practitioner's responsibility is to treat even the most obnoxious reporter with fairness.

Among the general public, a 1999 Public Relations Society of America study on credibility indicated that public relations people had suffered in terms of credibility; one presumes they suffered in terms of ethics as well. Whereas Supreme Court justices and teachers ranked highest on the credibility index, public relations specialists ranked near the bottom.[20] Some suggested that in the wake of the Clinton scandals of the late 1990s and the corporate accounting scandals of the early 2000s, public relations became so associated with the evils of "spin" that the field was harshly tarnished. Combating this unethical mind-set poses a great challenge for the field in the 21st century.

L A S T   W O R D

The success of public relations in the 21st century will depend largely on how the field responds to the issue of ethical conduct. Public relations professionals must have credibility in order to practice. They must be respected by the various publics with which they interact. This is as much true overseas as it is in the United States (see Appendix B). To be credible and to achieve respect, public relations professionals must be ethical. It is that simple.

The final arbiter in assessing whether ethics is important is the public. Above all, the public is concerned with the credibility of an organization and of those who serve it. In light of this, the key job for public relations professionals is to "advise clients to adapt to changing conditions and societal expectations, rather than to try to manipulate the environment for the good of the organization."[21]

The bursting of the Internet bubble in 2000 and 2001, followed by the corporate scandals of 2002, did little to enhance the practice of public relations as a force for ethics and decency. The credibility of the field, along with the reputation of business in general, suffered.

For public relations practice in general and individual public relations professionals in particular, credibility in the next few years will depend on how scrupulously they observe and apply the principles and practice of ethics in everything they do.

S I D E B A R

Test Your Workplace Ethics

So you want to enter the workplace? The question of ethics looms larger today than at any previous time, especially with the advent of technology and the potential abuses it brings.

To test how you might measure up as an ethical worker, answer the following questions. And don't cheat!

1. Is it wrong to use company e-mail for personal reasons?
2. Is it wrong to use office equipment to help your family and friends with homework?
3. Is it wrong to play computer games on office equipment during the workday?
4. Is it wrong to use office equipment to do Internet shopping?
5. Is it unethical to visit pornographic Web sites using office equipment?
6. What's the value at which a gift from a supplier or client becomes troubling?
7. Is a $50 gift to a boss unacceptable?
8. Is it okay to take a pair of $200 football tickets as a gift from a supplier?
9. Is it okay to take a $120 pair of theater tickets?
10. Is it okay to take a $100 holiday fruit basket?
11. Is it okay to take a $25 gift certificate?
12. Is it okay to accept a $75 prize won at a raffle at a supplier's conference?

Answers

From a cross section of workers at nationwide companies were compiled by the Ethics Officer Association, Belmont, Massachusetts, and the Ethical Leadership Group, Wilmette, Illinois.

1. 34% said personal e-mail on company computers is wrong.
2. 37% said using office equipment for schoolwork is wrong.
3. 49% said playing computer games at work is wrong.
4. 54% said Internet shopping at work is wrong.
5. 87% said it is unethical to visit pornographic sites at work.
6. 33% said $25 is the amount at which a gift from a supplier or client becomes troubling. Another 33 percent said $50. Another 33 percent said $100.
7. 35% said a $50 gift to the boss is unacceptable.
8. 70% said it is unacceptable to take $200 football tickets.
9. 70% said it is unacceptable to take $120 theater tickets.
10. 35% said it is unacceptable to take a $100 fruit basket.
11. 45% said it is unacceptable to take a $25 gift certificate.
12. 40% said it is unacceptable to take the $75 raffle prize.

Discussion Starters

1. How would you define ethics?
2. How would you describe the state of ethics in business, government, and journalism?
3. How important is the ethical component of the practice of public relations?
4. Why have corporations adopted corporate codes of conduct?
5. What is corporate social responsibility?
6. What were the ethical implications of the Mayor Bloomberg marijuana ad?
7. What are the pros and cons of the attorney/adversary public relations model versus the enlightened self-interest model?
8. Is the public more or less tolerant of ethical violators today? Why or why not?

9. What is the significance of the six ethical values that underscore the Public Relations Society of America Code of Ethics?
10. What are the ethical responsibilities of a public relations professional?

TOP OF THE SHELF

Gerald P. Koocher, ed.

Ethics in Cyberspace
Mahwah, NJ: Lawrence Erlbaum Associates, 1996

Ethics in Cyberspace is a special issue of the journal *Ethics & Behavior*, edited by Gerald P. Koocher of the Harvard Medical School. He writes:

> The scope of topics addressed in this issue is as disparate as the range of interested authors. Electronic communication etiquette, electronic psychotherapy, radiation problems associated with computer use, consequences of pro-

viding and withdrawing Internet access to low-income research participants, and the impact of information technology on social systems are among the themes in the pages that follow. Of particular interest to public relations professionals is "Ethical Dilemmas in the Use of Information Technology: An Aristotelian Perspective," in which the authors discuss privacy, information accuracy, access to information, and intellectual property rights.

CASE STUDY

Doing the Right Thing at Fink, Inc.

It's been only one year since you graduated college and already you are assistant vice president in charge of public relations for the Catfish Division of Fink, Inc., the largest seafood purveyor in the world.

Your Catfish division is the primary income earner in the corporation.

All is going swimmingly at Catfish, until your good friend in purchasing asks you to go to lunch with her. At lunch, she confides that she and another young woman in the purchasing department have been the target of offensive sexual gestures and remarks of one Catfish executive.

The executive, you learn, is none other than Catfish President Boris Swine. Swine, a Catfish veteran of 25 years, is the darling of the securities analysts and the press. His beaming face has appeared on the cover of every seafood trade journal. His magic touch in selling seafood has even named him the industry nickname, "the harpoon king."

Swine's unit continually surpasses profit projections, and his is the best-run subsidiary in the organization. He is the odds-on favorite to replace Fink, Inc. CEO Rhattan Fink, when the kindly founder, who built the company, retires in two years. Indeed, Swine is like a son to the elderly Mr. Fink.

You learn that the women three weeks ago voiced their complaints to Swine's executive assistant, an officious young Ph.D. named Seano Evil. They reminded the executive that Swine's behavior was a violation of the Fink, Inc. "Code of Conduct," for which the company has received numerous awards.

"We have been demeaned and denigrated in the most obscene way," they told Evil. "If the company doesn't take action, we'll be forced to."

Evil, you are told, promised to get back to your friend and the other woman but, as yet, has failed to do so.

A VISIT TO DR. EVIL

You pay a call on Seano Evil, who says he has "looked into the accusations" and found that the women's complaints are "just smoke." He explains, in picturesque fashion, how the two women are "merely frustrated ladies."

He explains to you that the "most important value" at Fink, Inc. is "loyalty." He points out that staff members who show themselves to be "disloyal" are eventually shown the door. "The most loyal employee this place has is Boris Swine," he tells you. "You don't mess with Boris if you know what's good for you."

"These women are making a mountain out of a molehill. Boris says there's nothing to it," he scoffs. "Let it go. We'll handle it here. You just do your job, and let us worry about managing the company."

You leave Evil's office even more concerned than when you entered.

Your mood doesn't improve, after you take a call from local investigative reporter Max Grudge. Grudge says he has received "anonymous calls" from Fink about some kind of "sex scandal involving a top exec—possibly Rhattan Fink himself."

"I get these kinds of calls all the time," he explains. "But this one sounds legit. Have you heard anything about this?"

Your mind is racing. The real answer to Grudge's question, of course, is "yes." But that would "open the gates" for a major scandal at the company. You answer instead, "Let me look into it, Max, and get back to you."

PUNCHING OUT THE CODE

You convene an emergency meeting with Human Resources Director Ophelia Paine and General Counsel Noah Comment. You lay out the facts, as you know them to both.

Paine volunteers that although the two women have exemplary work records, at least one of them is a "known complainer." "Let's try to keep this quiet," she counsels. "You're good at deflecting these obnoxious reporters."

Comment explains that no matter how obnoxious Swine might have been, "he clearly didn't violate any law."

"That might be true," you answer, "but the Fink Code of Conduct says explicitly: "Any employee, who is found to have violated the personal rights of another—most particularly in the realms of racial, religious, and sexual harassment—will be dealt with in the most severe and uncompromising manner.""

Attorney Comment glares at you, "What about Swine's personal rights? The fact is that no law was violated, so it's nobody's business. Period."

As to what you should do with the inquiring reporter, Comment's comment— "Stonewall him."

SEEKING THE ETHICAL COURSE

Now, you've got a real ethical dilemma.

- The four highest-ranking executives in your division have not only failed to follow through on the women's complaints, but they also have expressly forbidden you from further action.
- You've got an aggressive journalist, waiting to learn if the CEO might be involved in a sex scandal.
- You're facing two irate employees, who feel that their legitimate complaints have fallen on deaf ears. "I know who obviously is trying to cover this up," mistakenly concludes your friend in purchasing, "It's that dirty old Rhat Fink himself."

- Finally, the corporate code of conduct, created by the CEO, is being violated, while the CEO himself is being blamed.

As Mr. Fink's speechwriter, you are scheduled to see him today at 3 P.M. to discuss his speech on "corporate responsibility."

Oy vey, do you have a headache.

Questions

1. Do you raise the issue with your CEO?
2. If so, what do you tell him?
3. What do you advise him to do?
4. How do you respond to the journalist?

TIPS FROM THE TOP

An Interview with Joann Killeen

Joann Killeen

Joann E. Killeen was elected president of the Public Relations Society of America in 2002, the first Public Relations Student Society of America member to ascend to the PRSA presidency. With more than 25 years of experience in public relations and investor relations, she has developed strategic public relations plans and applied her skills in investor relations for a variety of industries, from consumer to technology and public service. She is president of Killeen Communications, a public relations practice headquartered in Los Angeles.

How important are ethics in public relations?
Ethics is a critical area. More important than ever before—especially after the corporate scandals over the recent period. Public relations people must be counselors of truth. We're neither "behavior cops" or "ethics cops," but it's our role to make clients understand the consequences of their actions.

What if clients don't listen to ethical counsel?
Our reputations are equally at stake. So our job is to advise CEOs that there are consequences to what they do. I had one client who didn't want to hear this, and he told me, "You're gone." Later, he was arrested. So the point is you've got to be willing to put your job on the line.

Can ethics help differentiate the practice of public relations from other fields?
Absolutely. Our greatest challenge, still, is to help people understand what public relations really is. They think we "reformulate truth." We've got to demonstrate that everything we do is based on ethics and honesty. That will not only help our clients but in the long term will help our field.

What's the key to the new PRSA Code of Ethics?
First, there is a tremendous understanding now as to how ethics impacts every aspect of our business. Ethics has always been part of the public relations business, but its importance today is even greater. Being ethical starts with your own personal behavior and carries over into your practice. Ethical violations may start small, where you don't think much of it, and then it builds, until we have what we've seen with some CEOs. You can't rationalize ethical behavior.

What is the status of women in public relations?
About 80 percent of our PRSA members are women. We're finding that women, by nature, have greater

(Continued)

skills sets in such areas as communications and mediation and are natural leaders and motivators. So public relations has understood the value of women, and now business in general is realizing this, too. I find this myself, that there is no longer that awkwardness when you call on clients. Men are more relaxed now with women in business leadership roles.

What about salary disparities?

Salaries of women are getting there. More men are retiring from leadership positions in the field, and women are replacing them, particularly in corporations. Agencies still lag a bit, but women are definitely catching up.

What about minorities in public relations?

I find a whole new perspective in terms of minorities in public relations. In the past, specific minority groups tended to operate among themselves. Today, there is much more partnership and collaboration—much less of an "us versus them" mentality. We have strong societies of Hispanic practitioners, African Americans and Asians, but there is also a strong initiative to work together and be more open among groups. There have been increased efforts by national associations to "reach out" to minorities. One thing that all groups have in common is bettering the profession. Many professionals understand that.

What advice do you give a student wishing to break into the field?

- First, learn a little bit about everything. It's important to take core courses.
- Second, take a lot of writing courses. Much of public relations is about writing. I find this is an area that, by and large, could use improvement. You've got to have the basics.
- Third, be flexible. Jobs are tight. So be willing to settle for something at first to get experience. Don't worry about becoming vice president right out of the box. Take some time to learn about business and how the system operates. My first job was as a 90-day administrative assistant. Then the public information director suddenly left, and I was promoted. Things have a way of working out.

What's the future of the practice of public relations?

I see only a strong future for this field. People are understanding better the role of public relations. They're trusting us more. Most of all, more CEOs understand the critical role public relations plays, both in providing advice and counsel to them and in communicating key messages to the organization's most important publics. They have begun to see us as business strategists with communications skills.

Suggested Readings

Andron, Scott. "Food Lion Versus ABC," *Quill* (March 1997): 15–21.

Baker, Lee. *The Credibility Factor: Putting Ethics to Work in Public Relations.* Homewood, IL: Business One Irwin, 1992.

Barney, Ralph, and Jay Black. *Ethics and New Media Technology,* Mahwah, NJ: Lawrence Erlbaum Associates, 2002.

Beauchamp, Tom L. *Case Studies in Business, Society and Ethics,* 4th ed. Upper Saddle River, NJ: Prentice Hall, 1999.

Beaucamp, Tom, and Norman E. Bowie, eds. *Ethical Theory and Business,* 6th ed. Upper Saddle River, NJ: Prentice Hall, 2000.

Beder, Sharon. *Global Spin: The Corporate Assault on Environmentalism.* White River Junction, VT: Chelsea Green Publishing, 1998.

Behrman, Jack N. *Essays on Ethics in Business and the Professions.* Upper Saddle River, NJ: Prentice Hall, 1988.

Boatright, John Raymond. *Ethics and the Conduct of Business,* 4th ed. Upper Saddle River, NJ: Prentice Hall, 2002.

Business Ethics, "Corporate Social Responsibility Report," Marjorie Kelly, editor. Bimonthly magazine, Mavis Publications, Minneapolis, MN.

Day, Louis A. *Ethics in Media Communications: Cases and Controversies,* 4th ed. Belmont, CA: Wadsworth, 2002.

DeGeorge, Richard T., *Business Ethics,* 5th ed. Upper Saddle River, NJ: Prentice Hall, 1999.

Donaldson, Thomas L., and Al Gini. *Case Studies in Business Ethics.* Upper Saddle River, NJ: Prentice Hall, 1995.

Fink, Conrad C. *Media Ethics.* Needham, MA: Allyn and Bacon, 1995.

Henderson, Verne E. *What's Ethical in Business.* New York: McGraw-Hill, 1992.

Jensen, J. Vernon. *Ethical Issues in the Communications Process.* Mahwah, NJ: Lawrence Erlbaum Associates, 1997.

Makower, Joel. *Beyond the Bottom Line, Putting Social Responsibility to Work for Your Business and the World.* New York: Touchstone Books, 1995.

Manheim, Joel. *The Death of 1000 Cuts, Corporate Campaigns and the Attack on the Corporation.* Mahwah, NJ: Lawrence Erlbaum Associates, 2000.

McIntosh, Malcolm. *Corporate Citizenship, Successful Strategies for Responsible Companies, Financial Times.* Upper Saddle River, NJ: Prentice Hall, 1998.

Smith, Ron F. *Groping for Ethics in Journalism.* Ames, IA: Iowa State University Press, 1999.

Stauber, John, and Sheldon Rampton. *Toxic Sludge Is Good for You: Lies, Damn Lies and the Public Relations Industry.* Monroe, ME: Common Courage Press, 1996.

Toth, Elizabeth L. *Public Relations Values in the New Millennium,* Special Issue of the *Journal of Public Relations Research,* 2000.

Trevino, Linda K., and Katherine A. Nelson. *Managing Business Ethics: Straight Talk About How to Do it Right.* 2nd ed. New York: John Wiley & Sons, 1999. Discusses not only what business ethics are but also why business should care.

Notes

1. Frank Bruni, "Pope Tells Crowd of 'Shame' Caused by Abusive Priests," *New York Times* (July 29, 2002): A1-8.
2. Jonathan Alter and Howard Fineman, "A Dynasty Dilemma," *Newsweek* (July 29, 2002): 24–29.
3. "In Public Relations, 25% Admit Lying," *New York Times* (May 8, 2000): C20.
4. Elizabeth MacDonald, "Scandal Buster," *Forbes* (November 27, 2000): 80–82.
5. "PR Faces the Nagging Truth: A Code of Ethics," *PR Week* (March 20, 2000): 11.
6. Dennis L. Wilcox, Phillip H. Ault, and Warren K. Agee. *PR Strategies and Tactics,* 5th ed. (New York Longman, 1998): 54.
7. Amanda Holt, "Defining Ethics," PR Ethics Resource Center, April 18, 2002.
8. Scott M. Cutlip, Allen H. Center, and Glen M. Broom. *Effective Public Relations* Upper Saddle River, NJ: Prentice-Hall, 2000): 144.
9. Fraser P. Seitel, "Ethics and Decency," *United States Banker* (April 1993): 58.
10. Alter and Fineman, "A Dynasty Dilemma."
11. Stacy Perman, "Who Do You Believe?" *Business 2.0* (March 2002).
12. "An Overview of a Landmark Roundtable Study of Corporate Ethics," *Roundtable Report* (February 1988): 1.
13. A. Larry Elliott and Richard J. Schroth. *How Companies Lie: Why Enron Is Just the Tip of the Iceberg* (New York, Crown Publishers, NY: 2002).
14. Henry M. Paulson, Address to the National Press Club, Washington, DC, June 5, 2002.

15. Eric Wahlgren, "If Only CEO Meant Chief Ethical Officer," *Business Week Online* (June 13, 2002).

16. Alan Cowell, "Fiat, in Scandal, Adopts Ethics Code," *New York Times* (May 11, 1993).

17. "Corporations Must Walk the Talk on Their Ethics Codes," Ethics Resource Center press release, June 13, 2002.

18. Robert A. Bennett, "Texaco's Bijur: Hero or Sellout," *Public Relations Strategist* (Winter 1996): 18.

19. Howell Raines, "The High Price of Reprieving Mike Barnicle," *New York Times* (August 13, 1998): A22.

20. Jennifer Harper, "Supreme Court Justices Rank Highest in Credibility, Index Says," *Washington Times* (July 8, 1999): 20.

21. Kathie A. Leeper, "Public Relations Ethics and Communitarianism: A Preliminary Investigation," *Public Relations Review* (Summer 1996): 175.

Chapter 7

The Law

Public relations and the law begin with the First Amendment to the Constitution that guarantees freedom of speech in our society. But in the 21st century, ensuring freedom of speech is not as easy as it sounds. One question is, Where does one's freedom start and another's end? Another question is, How much freedom of speech is appropriate—or advisable—in any given situation?

This is the nub of the inherent conflict between public relations advice, on the one hand, and legal advice, on the other.

Ideally, public relations counselors and lawyers should work together to achieve a client's desired outcomes. Indeed, this is often the case. But there is also a fundamental difference in legal versus public relations advice.

- *Lawyers correctly advise clients on what they "must" do, within the letter of legal requirements, to defend themselves in a court of law.*
- *Public relations advisers counsel clients on not what they "must" do—but what they "should" do to defend themselves in a different court—the court of public opinion.*

There is a vast difference between the two.

Nowhere was this more apparent than in the case of California Congressman Gary Condit, which gripped the nation in the summer of 2001.

When a young intern, who had been linked romantically to Condit, was reported missing, the congressman, on the advice of his lawyers, refused to elaborate on their relationship.

Throughout the summer, Condit listened to his lawyers and essentially remained silent, as suspicion mounted that he may have been involved with the young woman's disappearance.

Finally, after weeks of constant negative publicity, Condit's associates leaked word that the congressman may have had an affair with the woman but had nothing to do with her disappearance.

It was too late. Condit was defeated in a reelection primary. And, sadly, the woman's body was found some time later.

If, as he insisted, the congressman was guilty of having an affair with the woman—but of nothing illegal—some wondered why he didn't follow public relations rather than legal advice, acknowledge the relationship from the beginning, and avoid all the negative publicity that led to his political demise.[1]

Thus is the continuing conflict between legal considerations and public relations principles.

Public Relations and the Law: An Uneasy Alliance

The legal and public relations professions have historically shared an uneasy alliance. Public relations practitioners must always understand the legal implications of any issue with which they become involved, and a firm's legal position must always be the first consideration.

From a legal point of view, normally the less an organization says prior to its day in court, the better. That way, the opposition can't gain any new ammunition that will become part of the public record. A lawyer, the saying goes, tells you to say two things: "Say nothing, and say it slowly!"

From a public relations standpoint, though, it may often make sense to go public early on, especially if the organization's integrity or credibility is being called into public question. In the summer of 1997, for example, when respected broadcaster Marv Albert was charged with abusing a woman friend, Albert immediately held a press conference denying the charges, and his advisers followed with questions about the woman's veracity. (Later he pleaded guilty to a lesser charge.)

The point is that legal advice and public relations advice may indeed be different. In an organization, a smart manager will carefully weigh both legal and public relations counsel before making a decision.

It also should be noted that law and ethics are interrelated. The Public Relations Society of America's Code of Professional Standards (see Appendix A) notes that many activities that are unethical are also illegal. However, there are instances in which something is perfectly legal but unethical and other instances in which things might be illegal but otherwise ethical. Thus, when a public relations professional reflects on what course to take in a particular situation, he or she must analyze not only the legal ramifications but also the ethical considerations.[2]

This chapter will examine the relationship between the law and public relations and the more prominent role the law plays in public relations practice and vice versa. The discussion will not be all-encompassing. Rather, it will introduce the legal concerns of public relations professionals today: First Amendment considerations, insider trading, disclosure law, ethics law, privacy law, copyright law, and the laws concerning censorship of the Internet—issues that have become primary concerns for public relations practitioners in the 21st century.

Public Relations and the First Amendment

Any discussion of law and public relations should start with the First Amendment, which states: "Congress shall make no law . . . abridging the freedom of speech or the press." The First Amendment is the cornerstone of free speech in our society: This is what distinguishes America from many other nations.

Saving the Juice

Perhaps never has a legal trial gripped the entire nation so pervasively as the murder charges against Orenthal J. Simpson in the killings of Nicole Brown Simpson and Ron Goldman in 1994. O. J. Simpson was a revered football player, broadcaster, and actor who seemed to be leading a charmed life, until one summer evening he stunned the nation by leading it—via national TV—on a low-speed car chase through the highways and byways of Brentwood, California (Figure 7-1).

The Simpson trial shocked the nation, but the real drama lay in how Simpson's high-powered attorney team of Johnnie Cochran, F. Lee Bailey, and Robert Shapiro used publicity to forward their cause and wallop the hapless Los Angeles District Attorney's Office.

Here's how Mr. Shapiro described the winning public relations approach.

- **Lawyer as public relations person.** "When we are retained for those high-profile cases, we are instantly thrust into the role of a public relations person—a role for which the majority of us have no education, experience, or training. The lawyer's role as spokesperson may be [as] equally important to the outcome of a case as the skills of an advocate in the courtroom."
- **Power of the media.** "The importance and power of the media cannot be overemphasized. The first impression the public gets is usually the one that is most important."
- **"No comment."** "'No comment' is the least appropriate and least productive response. Coming at the end of a lengthy story, it adds absolutely nothing and leaves the public with a negative impression."
- **Lying to the media.** "It is never a good idea to lie to the press. To simply make up facts in the hope that they will later prove correct is too big a risk."
- **Media relationships.** "Initial relationships with legitimate members of the press are very important. Many times a lawyer will feel it is an intrusion to be constantly beset by seemingly meaningless questions that take up a tremendous amount of time. But the initial

FIGURE 7-1   Fallen—but not convicted—hero O. J. Simpson.

headlines of the arrest often make the sacred presumption of innocence a myth. In reality, we have the presumption of guilt. This is why dealing with the media is so important."
- **Responding to the press.** "The wire services depend on immediate updates. Therefore, all calls should be returned as quickly as possible. Wire service reporters can also provide a valuable source of information to you."
- **Framing answers.** "Just as you would do in trial, anticipate the questions a reporter will pose. Think out your answers carefully. My personal preference is to initially talk to a reporter off the record and get an idea what questions the reporter is interested in and where the story is going. I then respond to the questions that are appropriate. Use great care

(Continued)

in choosing your words. Keep your statements simple and concise. Pick and choose the questions you want to answer. You do not have to be concerned with whether the answer precisely addresses the question, since only the answer will be aired."

- **The tabloids.** "My experience is that cooperating with tabloid reporters only gives them a legitimate source of information which can be misquoted or taken out of context and does little good for your client. My personal approach is not to cooperate with tabloid reporters."
- **Dealing with TV hordes.** "The television media, either consciously or unconsciously, create an atmosphere of chaos. Immediately upon arriving at the courthouse, you are surrounded by television crews. We have all

seen people coming to court and trying to rush through the press with their heads down or covering them with newspapers or coats. Nothing looks worse. I always instruct my clients upon arrival at the courthouse to get out in a normal manner, to walk next to me in a slow and deliberate way, to have a look of confidence and acknowledge with a nod those who are familiar and supportive."*

Clearly, the public relations advice of O. J. Simpson's defender must be taken with a large grain of salt. Nonetheless, understanding the importance ascribed to public relations and publicity by a leading defense attorney is ample proof that lawyers, too, are cognizant of the value and power of the practice of public relations.

*Excerpted from Robert Shapiro, "Secrets of a Celebrity Lawyer," *Columbia Journalism Review* (September/October 1994): 25–29.

Recent years have seen a blizzard of First Amendment challenges.

- In the fall of 1999, New York Mayor Rudolph Giuliani threatened to cut off city funding for an art exhibition at the Brooklyn Museum, which featured one painting depicting the Madonna speckled with elephant dung (Figure 7-2). Giuliani called the painting "blasphemous." The American Civil Liberties Union defended the work as "freedom of expression." The court ultimately agreed.
- Mayor Giuliani did better when his administration challenged the right of the Ku Klux Klan to hold a hooded rally in Manhattan in 1999. A federal appellate panel upheld New York's right to block the "white pride" rally. The *New York Times* bemoaned the decision as a "low moment for the First Amendment."[3]
- In the summer of 2002, a federal appeals court in New Hampshire nullified a lower court decision that a former *New York Times* business reporter had intentionally presented the subject of an article in a false light by questioning his real identity. The appeals court rule that the reporter "had not acted with reckless disregard for the truth" when she wrote the article.[4]
- Earlier in 1997, the *Wall Street Journal* wasn't quite as lucky. A Texas court awarded a brokerage firm $222.7 million in damages for a *Journal* article that the company claimed put it out of business.[5] The verdict was later reduced on appeal.
- In the summer of 2002, the Bush administration was livid when a judge ruled that the Justice Department couldn't keep secret the names of more than 1,000 people picked up in connection with the September 11, 2001, attacks.[6]

As these skirmishes suggest, interpreting the First Amendment is no simple matter. One person's definition of obscenity may be someone else's definition of art. Despite continuing challenges to the First Amendment, Americans continue to enjoy broad freedom of speech and expression. Because the First Amendment lies at the heart of the communications business, defending it is a frontline responsibility of the public relations profession.

FIGURE 7-2 **Art or obscenity?** This work, depicting one artist's conception of the Madonna, decorated with elephant dung, touched off a legal battle in New York City.

Public Relations and Defamation Law

The laws that govern a person's privacy have significant implications for journalists and other communicators, such as public relations professionals, particularly laws that touch on libel and slander—commonly known as defamation laws—by the media.

Defamation is the umbrella term used to describe libel—a printed falsehood—and slander—an oral falsehood. For defamation to be proved, a plaintiff must convince the court that four requirements have been met.

1. The falsehood was communicated through print, broadcast, or other electronic means.
2. The person who is the subject of the falsehood was identified or easily identifiable.
3. The identified person has suffered injury—in the form of monetary losses, reputational loss, or mental suffering.
4. The person making the statement was malicious or grossly negligent.[7]

Generally, the privacy of an ordinary citizen is protected under the law. A citizen in the limelight, however, has a more difficult problem, especially in proving defamation of character through libel or slander.

To prove such a charge, a public figure must show that the media acted with actual malice in their reporting. "Actual malice" in a public figure slander case, as noted, means that statements have been published with the knowledge that they were false or with reckless disregard for whether the statements were false. In a landmark case in 1964, *New York Times* v. *Sullivan*, the Supreme Court nullified a libel award of

$500,000 to an Alabama police official, holding that no damages could be awarded "in actions brought by public officials against critics of their official conduct" unless there was proof of "actual malice." And proving actual malice is a difficult task.

Several historic libel cases have helped pave the case law precedent.

- In 1992, the *Wall Street Journal* and its award-winning reporter Bryan Burrough were served with a $50 million libel suit by Harry L. Freeman, a former communications executive of American Express. The suit stemmed from the way Freeman was characterized in Burrough's book, *Vendetta: American Express and the Smearing of Edmund Safra*.[8]

- In 1993, writer Janet Malcolm was sued by Dr. Jeffrey M. Masson over charges that Malcolm fabricated quotations in her *New Yorker* magazine article, which defamed Dr. Masson. Jurors agreed that in several instances Malcolm acted with "reckless disregard" for the accuracy of the quotations and that Masson had indeed been damaged. This clarified an important legal principle that "placing statements materially altered to change their meaning between quotation marks and attributing them to a plaintiff is not an editorial prerogative and can be evidence of actual malice."[9]

- A decade earlier, in a landmark case, the *Washington Post* initially lost a $2 million suit after a federal jury decided that the newspaper had libeled William P. Tavoulareas when it alleged that he had used his position as president of Mobil Oil to further his son's career in a shipping business. The next year a federal judge overturned the verdict against the *Post* because the article in question didn't contain "knowing lies or statements made in reckless disregard of the truth."

  Later, a federal appeals court reinstated the $2 million libel verdict against the *Post*. But later that year, the U.S. Court of Appeals of the District of Columbia agreed to reconsider the reinstatement. Finally, almost six years after the initial verdict, the Supreme Court ruled in favor of the *Post* by throwing out the Tavoulareas suit for lack of merit. A contrary ruling would have restricted the limits of investigative journalism and broadened the interpretation of defamation of character. Reporters breathed a sigh of relief at the decision.

- In another celebrated case, Israeli General Ariel Sharon brought a $50 million libel suit against *Time* magazine. It, too, ended without a libel verdict. However, once again, the jury criticized *Time* for negligent journalism in reporting Sharon's role in a massacre in a Palestinian refugee camp.

- In 1996, Atlanta security guard Richard A. Jewell sued both *NBC News* and the *Atlanta Journal-Constitution* for reporting that he was the lead suspect in the Atlanta Olympic bombing, which led to two deaths. The reports caused a media feeding frenzy, which disrupted Jewell's life and tarnished his name. Late in the year, Jewell was cleared of any involvement in the bombing and reached a settlement with his media accusers, averting a libel lawsuit and presumably compensating the formerly unknown security guard handsomely for the undeserved humiliation.[10]

- In 1997, the *Wall Street Journal* lost a $227 million libel verdict in Texas when it was found to have inaccurately reported on the troubles of MMAR Group, a mortgage-backed securities firm in Houston, which ultimately went out of business after the *Journal* story.[11] Later that year, hedge fund manager Julian Robertson commenced an action against *Business Week* magazine for $1 billion, after a critical cover story on his firm. It, too, was settled before going to trial.

Although most public relations practitioners do little formal "reporting," they, too, must be aware of situations involving libel and slander. Many public relations professionals create, write, and edit internal print and online newsletters. In this context, they must be careful not to "defame" fellow employees or others in what they write. The same caution should be the rule for public relations professionals who make statements to the media on behalf of their organizations. Care must be the watchword in such public speech.

Public Relations and Insider Trading

Every public relations professional should know the laws that govern his or her organization and industry.

1. A practitioner in a hospital should have an understanding of managed care and its ramifications.
2. A practitioner at a nonprofit organization should understand the laws that govern donors and recipients.
3. A practitioner at a college ought to understand the laws that govern privacy of student and faculty records.
4. A practitioner in a particular industry—chemicals, computers, banking, sports—should understand the laws germane to that particular area.

With nearly 100 million Americans as participants in the securities markets, either directly or through company pension plans, nowhere in public relations practice is an understanding of the law more important than in the area of securities law.

Every public company has an obligation to deal frankly, comprehensively, and immediately with any information that is considered material in a decision to buy, sell, or even hold the organization's securities. The Securities and Exchange Commission (SEC)—through a series of court cases, consent decrees, complaints, and comments over the years—has painted a general portrait of disclosure requirements for practitioners (see Appendix C), with which all practitioners in public companies should be familiar. The SEC's mandate stems from the Securities Act of 1933 and the Securities Exchange Act of 1934, which attempted to protect the public from abuses in the issuance and sale of securities.

The SEC's overriding concern is that all investors have an opportunity to learn about material information as promptly as possible. Basically, a company is expected to release news that may affect its stock market price as quickly as possible.[12] Through its general antifraud statute, Rule 10b-5 of the Securities and Exchange Act, the SEC strictly prohibits the dissemination of false or misleading information to investors. It also prohibits insider trading of securities on the basis of material information not disclosed to the public.

Unfortunately, the 20th century ended and the 21st century began with front-page insider trading scandals. In the early part of the 1990s, the public was shocked by a series of celebrated cases involving the use of insider information to amass illegal securities gains. The two most celebrated insider trading cases were those of Ivan Boesky and Michael Milken, Wall Street legends who were both slapped with nine-figure fines and jail terms. Many of their associates, equally guilty of insider trading violations, also were dispatched to the slammer.

In the early years of the 21st century, one celebrated insider trading case involved ImClone Systems CEO Sam Waksal, who, along with family members, unloaded ImClone stock after the CEO learned that the Food and Drug Administration was about to reject a key ImClone drug. The stock was subsequently crushed, as was CEO Waksal, his family, his stockbroker, and his good friend, domestic diva Martha Stewart—all embroiled in an insider trading scandal.[13]

Nor did journalists escape the ignominy of insider trading convictions. In the late 1990s, a columnist at the *Wall Street Journal* was convicted of illegally using his newspaper column to give favorable opinions about companies in which a couple of his stockbroker friends had already invested heavily. He went to jail. In the 2000s, stock commentator James Cramer, a founder of theStreet.com news service, was accused of profiting from advance information from friends at the CNBC financial network. Ironically, when no charges were brought, Cramer became a program host at CNBC.

As to public relations counselors, they, too, must be careful to act only on public information when trading securities. The investor relations director of Dallas-based Carreker Corporation and his brother were fined more than $600,000 in 2002 for netting a combined $209,000 on an insider trading transaction.[14]

No one is immune from the law, least of all the public relations professionals whose job it is to deal with the public.

Public Relations and Disclosure Law

Besides cracking down on insider trading, the SEC has challenged corporations and public relations firms on the accuracy of information they disseminate for clients. The SEC's "Adoption of Integrated Disclosure System" attempts to bring some order to the chaotic SEC requirements by making the instructions governing corporate disclosure of information more uniform. Today, in an environment of mergers, takeovers, consolidations, and the incessant rumors that circulate around them, a knowledge of disclosure law, a sensitivity to disclosure requirements, and a bias toward disclosing rather than withholding material information are important attributes of public relations officials.

In the new millennium, with securities trading extending beyond the traditional 9:30 A.M.–4 P.M. stock market trading day and with instantaneous online trading a reality, the responsibilities on public relations people for full and fair disclosure have intensified. The SEC, in turn, has increased its focus on private meetings between companies and analysts, which are closed to the media and, therefore, to individual investors who rely on the media for financial information.

To combat such selective disclosure, the SEC in 2000 adopted Regulation FD, or fair disclosure. Basically, Regulation FD requires companies to widely disseminate any "material" announcement. A material announcement is one that might cause an investor to buy, hold, or sell a stock.

In the past, companies would share such material news with securities analysts or large investors, who then might act on it before the public found out. Under Regulation FD, even if a material announcement slips out to an analyst, the company is obligated to issue a press release within 24 hours "to provide broad, non-exclusionary disclosure information to the public."[15]

Although many analysts and investors complained that Regulation FD would have a "chilling impact" on companies that previously were willing to communicate, Congress and the regulators were unwilling to yield.[16]

The escalating importance of the stock market to average Americans, coupled with the corporate management and accounting scandals of 2002, increased the necessity of full, fair, and immediate disclosure to all investors.

Public Relations and Ethics Law

The laws on ethical misconduct in society have gotten quite a workout in recent years.

- In 1996, when Swiss banks were accused of making it difficult for the heirs of Jewish Holocaust victims to recover the assets of relatives, the Swiss Bank Association hired Kekst & Co., a New York firm long associated with Jewish causes, to defend the banks. Critics accused the firm of an ethical breach, allowing its clients to exploit it.
- In a celebrated case, translated into the 1999 movie *The Insider*, the late public relations counselor John Scanlon faced a grand jury subpoena, stemming from his efforts to discredit Jeffrey Wigand, an internal critic of Scanlon's cigarette client Brown & Williamson.[17]
- In the political public relations arena, Lyn Nofziger, former White House political director and communications counselor, was sentenced to 90 days in prison and fined $30,000 for violating the Federal Ethics in Government Act, which forbids lobbying former contacts within one year of leaving the government. A related fate was meted out to former White House Deputy Chief of Staff Michael K. Deaver, another well-known public relations professional, who was found guilty of perjury over his lobbying activities. He also faced a jail sentence and a serious fine.

The activities of lobbyists, in particular, have been closely watched by Congress since the imposition of the Federal Regulation of Lobbying Act of 1946. In recent years, however, the practice of lobbying has expanded greatly.

Complicating the lobbyist issue still further, foreign governments are particularly eager to retain savvy Washington insiders to guide them through the bureaucratic and congressional maze and to polish their images in the United States. In 1998, the Clinton administration drew public fire for accepting political contributions from influential representatives of Indonesia and China. Although he violated no law, New Jersey Senator Robert Torricelli was "severely admonished" in 2002 by the Senate Ethics Committee for gifts received from a wealthy Korean constituent. Subsequently, Torricelli was forced to give up his seat.

Public relations counselors are strictly mandated by law to register the foreign entities they represent. However, in recent years, a number of representatives of foreign clients have themselves been the subject of scandals and legal investigations.

The increasing number of government officials who resign to become play-for-pay lobbyists may indicate that those who govern and those who attempt to influence them will in the future be scrutinized more closely for how ethically they do business and how scrupulously they follow the law.

Public Relations and Copyright Law

One body of law that is particularly relevant to public relations professionals is copyright law and the protections it offers writers. Copyright law provides basic, automatic protection for writers, whether a manuscript is registered with the Copyright Office or even published. Under the Copyright Act of 1976, an "original work of authorship" has copyright protection from the moment the work is in the following fixed form.

- literary works
- musical works

A QUESTION OF ETHICS

Out of the Legal Loop

FIGURE 7-3

Maintaining credibility. Presidential Press Secretary Mike McCurry.

In the annals of political ethical violations, few incidents have more morally outraged the nation than President Clinton's transgressions with a White House intern in 1998.

After the walls came closing in on him, Clinton relied on his lawyers to choreograph his every word. Although the president was eventually fined for contempt of court and disbarred in a related case in Arkansas, Clinton—a lawyer himself—deftly provided answers throughout the conflict that were generally evasive but not untruthful.

Meanwhile, most of the president's aides—longtime associates such as James Carville, Lanny Davis, and Paul Begala—kept up a steady public drumbeat defending Clinton against the doubters. All shredded their own credibility in the process.

One Clinton ally, however, maintained his integrity, even though his was among the most difficult and public assignments in the White House. Presidential Press Secretary Mike McCurry, whose job was to meet the press every day to explain the president's actions, drew the line at lying and, as a result, maintained his credibility while all those around him were losing theirs (Figure 7-3).

McCurry realized that although a lawyer tells you what you "must" do to defend yourself in a court of law, a public relations adviser tells you what you "should" do to represent yourself in the court of public opinion. There is often a great ethical difference.

McCurry refused to succumb to the notion—accepted by most of those around the president—that Clinton was "innocent" simply because he claimed to be. When McCurry was asked at White House press briefings if the president "had a relationship with the intern," McCurry's recurring answer was, "The president said he didn't." When McCurry was asked if he, himself, thought the president had had a relationship with the intern, McCurry claimed to be "out of the loop."

Although McCurry argued with Clinton's lawyers to allow the president to make a public confession of what he had done, the attorneys rejected his arguments.

Only once during the controversy did McCurry let down his guard. In an interview with the *Chicago Tribune*, McCurry said he thought the real story of Clinton and the intern "would probably turn out to be a lot more complicated than any of us now know."

He was right, of course, and when the truth came out, many of those who had relied exclusively on the lawyers for guidance were embarrassed and ashamed for defending their boss.

Public relations professional McCurry was not among them. He had nothing to be ashamed about.

For further information, consult Daniel Klaidman and Mark Hosenball, "Are the Walls Closing In?" *Newsweek* (September 14, 1998): 28; Fraser P. Seitel, "Presidential Public Relations Endgame," *Ragan Report* (August 10, 1999): 2; and Roger Simon, "Spinners vs. Lawyers," *AOL Newstalk* (August 4, 1998): 1.

- dramatic works
- pantomimes and choreographic works
- pictorial, graphic, or sculptural works
- motion pictures
- sound recordings

The word *fixed* means that the work is sufficiently permanent to permit it to be perceived, reproduced, or otherwise communicated.[18]

Copyright law gives the owner of the copyright the exclusive right to reproduce and authorize others to reproduce the work, prepare derivative works based on the copyrighted material, and perform and/or display the work publicly. That's why Michael Jackson had to pay $47.5 million for the rights to the Beatles' compositions to the duly sworn representatives and heirs of John, Paul, George, and Ringo.

Copyright law is different from trademark law, which refers to a word, symbol, or slogan, used alone or in combination, that identifies a product or its sponsor—for example, the Nike swoosh.

What courts have stated again and again is that for the purposes of criticism, news reporting, teaching, scholarship, or research, use of copyrighted material is not an infringement but rather constitutes "fair use." Although precise definitions of "fair use"—like everything else in the law—is subject to interpretation, such factors as "the effect on the future market" of the copyrighted work in question or the "volume of quotation used" or even whether the "heart" of the material was ripped off are often considered.[19]

In 1989, the Supreme Court strengthened the copyright status of freelance artists and writers when it ruled that such professionals retain the right to copyright what they create "as long as they were not in a conventional employment relationship with the organization that commissioned their work." The Court's revision of the copyright law set the stage for a wholesale reassessment of the ownership of billions of dollars in reproduction rights for computer programs, fiction and nonfiction writing, advertising copy, drawings, photographs, and so on. As a result of the modification, public relations professionals must carefully document the authorization that has been secured for using freelance material. In other words, when engaging a freelance professional, public relations people must know the law.

Several categories of material are not eligible for copyright protection, such as titles and short slogans; works consisting entirely of information from common sources and public documents, such as calendars, lists, and tables; and speeches and performances that have not been fixed on paper or recorded. Work in the public domain—material that was never covered by copyright or for which the copyright has lapsed, material that lacks sufficient originality, and basic themes and plots—can't be protected by copyright.

Ideas cannot be protected either. This means that an old idea newly packaged is absolutely permissible, legal, and even recommended. Indeed, there are few truly new ideas in the world, only old ideas put together in new and different ways. So a public relations practitioner shouldn't be overly concerned with violating copyright laws when devising a campaign, program, or manuscript in support of a client's activity.

Public Relations and Internet Law

The Internet has introduced a new dimension to the law affecting free speech.

The premise in American law is that "not all speech is created equal."[20] Rather there is a hierarchy of speech, under Supreme Court precedents dating back many decades that calibrate the degree of First Amendment protection with, among other tests, the particular medium of expression. For example, speech that would be perfectly acceptable if uttered in a public park could constitutionally be banned when broadcast from a sound truck.

Dealing with the Internet has introduced new ramifications to this legal principal. Indeed, cyberlaw has brought into question many of the most revered communications law principles.

Censorship

In 1996, Congress passed the Communications Decency Act (CDA) as an amendment to a far-reaching telecommunications bill. The CDA introduced criminal penalties, including fines of as much as $250,000 and prison terms up to two years, for making "indecent" speech available to "a person under 18 years of age." A Philadelphia court a few months later struck down the law, contending that such censorship would chill all discourse on the Internet.[21]

Then, in the summer of 1997, the Supreme Court, in a sweeping endorsement of free speech, declared the CDA unconstitutional. The decision, unanimous in most respects, marked the highest court's first effort to extend the principles of the First Amendment into cyberspace and to confront the nature and the law of this new, powerful medium. In summarizing the Court's finding, Justice John Paul Stevens said the Court considered the "goal of protecting children from indecent material as legitimate and important" but concluded that "the wholly unprecedented breadth of the law threatened to suppress far too much speech among adults and even between parents and children."[22]

In 1998, Congress passed the Child Online Protection Act, which made it a federal crime to "knowingly communicate for commercial purposes material considered harmful to minors."[23] The act called for fines of $150,000 a day for violators. Once again, the law was widely opposed by civil liberties groups and was eventually struck down by the Supreme Court.

In 2002, the high court once again struck down legislation to censor child pornography on the Internet. The Child Online Protection Act was a copy of the 1998 legislation. And once again the Court ruled that it would be unconstitutional to criminalize protected free speech on the Internet.

Intellectual Property

Few cyberlaw cases have drawn more headlines than the case against Napster, the popular application that allowed users to exchange music files. Because Napster ran the file swapping through a central server, it was an easy target for legislation.

In the end—for Napster—the protest, led by those heavy-metal defenders of the First Amendment, Metallica, and backed by the large music companies, convinced the Court that the company was infringing on copyright protections of intellectual property.[24]

Napster's successors, however, such as Gnutella and Kazaa, will prove harder for the courts to handle. The Gnutella model is built on peer-to-peer software. So any intellectual property case involving such a service would require taking actions against the hundreds of thousands of individuals using the program. No easy task.

Cybersquatting

Another complex issue is that of cybersquatting—grabbing domain names in bad faith, expressly for the purpose of tormenting or "shaking down" a rightful registrant.

In 1999, hamburger giant Wendy's International filed a lawsuit against Beswick Adams Corporation for allegedly registering a number of Internet domain names, such as www.wendysrestaurants.com, all closely related to the Wendy's trademark. Earlier, Kmart Corporation successfully mounted a legal challenge to fight a rogue Web site, Kmartsucks.com. Ultimately, the site was forced to change its name to Themartsucks.com.

Current trademark law prohibits a company from registering a name that exactly duplicates a registered trademark, but cybersquatters frequently register names that differ only slightly. They know that Web surfers will type in a variation of a company's name when searching for its site. They then either attempt to sell the names or use the sites to disrupt the company's commerce.[25]

E-Fraud

Fraud is fraud, no matter where it is domiciled. And on the World Wide Web, where anyone who wants to can choose anonymity, fraud runs rampant.

The problem is that e-crooks are difficult to stop. Often it depends on companies policing the Net themselves, frequently to go after former employees. For example:

- Varian Medical Systems of Palo Alto won a $775,000 verdict against two former employees, who posted 14,000 messages on 100 message boards, accusing the firm of being homophobic and of discriminating against pregnant women.
- A California court ruled against a fired Intel employee who sent e-mails to about 35,000 staffers, criticizing the company.[26]

Some companies have even gotten together to form coalitions to fight fraud, such as Merchant Fraud Squad (www.merchantfraudsquad.com), a Web site that informs vendor members about strategies for chasing down cheats.

And these are but a few of the legal issues that surround the World Wide Web.

Web sites even have been sued for not living up to their legal obligation to accommodate the disabled. In virtually every case, corporations have settled out of court when confronted with such challenges. In 1999, the National Federation of the Blind filed a lawsuit against America Online, alleging that the service violated the Americans

S I D E B A R

Public Relations Risks of Squelching Cybersquatters

Verizon, the huge telcom company, learned a valuable lesson in the spring of 2000, when it tried to frustrate incursions by future cybersquatters.

The lesson: Think carefully before threatening.

When Verizon emerged from the merger of Bell Atlantic and GTE, the new firm acted to preempt trademark infringements on the Web. First, prior to the merger, it purchased 500 variations of its new name, including such domain names as www.verizonsucks.com.

In addition, Verizon prepared a legal form letter, threatening any offensive registrants that the company would seek action against them, using the Anticybersquatting Consumer Protection Act. The congressional act prohibited the "bad faith intent to profit from" the registration of domain names that incorporate trademarks or words similar to trademarks.

Sure enough, within three days of the merger announcement, more than 200 variations of Verizon had been registered. The company fired back with a letter to all, demanding that they "cease and desist" or risk lawsuits.

One registrant, a hacker Web magazine—or ezine— that registered the name verizonreallysucks.com, immediately claimed it sought no profit from its registration but merely wanted consumers "to have a place to vent."

The ezine publisher noted that the anticybersquatting bill didn't apply to consumer complaint sites. Furthermore, it charged Verizon with infringing on consumers' right to freedom of expression. To punctuate its point, the ezine registered another domain name, VerizonShouldSpendMoreTimeFixingItsNetworkAndLess MoneyOnLawyers.com.

The embarrassing publicity was enough to make Verizon back off and vow that next time it would be a bit more circumspect before attacking cybersquatters.*

*For further information, see "Legal Lessons: Take a Breath Before You Threaten Cybersquatters," *Ragan's Interactive Public Relations*, vol. 6, no. 9 (September 2000): 2–3.

with Disabilities Act by remaining inaccessible to blind users. The suit could mark a precedent in terms of Internet accessibility to blind users. Smart organizations, therefore, will design Web sites for screen reader accessibility. The readers, which blind users install on their Internet browsers, dictate text on computer screens.

Beyond the matter of sight, of course, is the matter of speech. On the one hand are those who argue that the Internet is the most democratic of democratic institutions, allowing all access to all manner of speech. As such, this argument goes, adults should have every right to exercise their constitutional right to free speech. On the other side are those who contend that the Internet threatens to give children a "free pass into an adult bookstore."[27] Further complicating the issue, of course, is the fact that the Internet is changing every day. A law that applies today may be irrelevant or outdated tomorrow.

This, in essence, is the conundrum that confronts lawmakers as they attempt to construct laws to govern the Internet.

Public Relations and the Legal Profession

What has always been an uneasy alliance between lawyers and public relations professionals has today evolved into a relationship of grudging mutual respect. Lawyers, in fact, are making more use of public relations strategies than ever before.

It is estimated that 75 percent of all major law firms use public relations consultants.[28] Lawyers and legal consultants attribute the increased use of public relations firms to heightened competition within the top tier of the legal profession. Many law firms have grown rapidly in recent years and have to fight harder for clients and for top law school graduates. As a result, public relations has emerged as an important tool to get these firms' names circulated among clients, potential clients, and possible hires.

In 1984, the Supreme Court eased the ban on self-advertisement by lawyers. Although some lawyers are still reluctant to trumpet their capabilities, others are not. The leader of this ilk was Jacoby & Meyers, which, because of its pervasive national advertising, was derided by some as a "fast-food law firm."[29] At its height, Jacoby & Meyers's client roster numbered 175,000 people, with a $42 million business.

Other law firms, such as Searcy Denney Scarola Barnhart & Shipley of West Palm Beach, use community relations techniques to enhance their image in the local area. Searcy Denney, for example, contributes significantly to community causes, provides volunteers for community events, and sponsors public service announcements to promote the good works of particular local charities. The firm's slogan in such endeavors is "Taking Time to Care."

For their part, public relations counselors have become more open to lawyers and have relaxed the tensions that once existed between the two professions. One public relations practitioner offers this advice for working with lawyers:

1. *Become an equal partner with legal counsel.*   At all times, maintain an overview of the legal cases that are before your organization or industry. Take the initiative with legal counsel to discuss those that you believe may have major public relations implications.
2. *Combat the legal "no comment" syndrome.*   Research cases in which an organization has publicly discussed issues without damage.
3. *Take the initiative in making announcements.*   This will help manage the public perception of the issue. If an indictment is pending, consult the legal staff on the advisability of making statements—before you become a target.

4. *Research the background of the jury.*   Past lists of jurors in a particular jurisdiction indicate occupations and other important demographic information.
5. *Winning may not be everything.*   Outside law firms, trained in an adversarial mode and charging fees that depend on the size of the award, always want to "win." For legal counsel the stakes may also include a winning reputation, which helps to secure future cases. Public relations must bring a long-term perspective to strategic decisions.
6. *Beware of leaving a paper trail.*   Any piece of paper that you create may end up in court. That includes desk calendars and notes to yourself. So be careful.[30]

Litigation Public Relations

In court cases, plaintiffs and defendants are often scrupulously warned by judges not to influence the ultimate verdict outside the courtroom.

Forget it.

In the 21st century, with CNN, MSNBC, Fox News Channel, CNBC, and talk radio incessantly jabbering about possible trials, upcoming trials, and current trials, there is little guarantee that any jury can be objective about any high-profile legal case.

That's why litigation public relations has become so important.

Litigation public relations can best be defined as managing the media process during the course of any legal dispute so as to affect the outcome or its impact on the client's overall reputation.[31]

Although court proceedings have certain rules and protocol, dealing in the public arena with a matter of litigation has no such strictures. Although the Sixth Amendment to the Constitution guarantees accused persons "a speedy and public trial, by an impartial jury," TV commentary by knowledgeable—and in many cases, unknowledgeable "experts"—can help influence a potential jury for or against a defendant.

As a result, some litigation communications scholars, such as Lehigh University's Carole Gorney, believe that "litigation journalism is seriously undermining the integrity of our legal process. The role of the courts is being preempted and their procedures undermined as more cases are tried in the public arena long before official hearings can take place."[32]

Nonetheless, smart lawyers understand that with cable TV, in particular, being so pervasive, they have little choice but to engage in litigation public relations to provide their clients with every advantage.

According to one counselor who works exclusively with litigation, there are seven keys to litigation visibility.

1. *Learn the process.*   All involved should be aware of the road map for the case and the milestones ahead, which may lend themselves to publicity.
2. *Develop a message strategy.*   Think about what should be said at each stage of a trial to keep the press and public focused on the key messages of the client.
3. *Settle fast.*   Settlement is probably the most potent litigation visibility management tool. The faster the settlement, the less litigation visibility there is likely to be. This is often a positive development.
4. *Anticipate high-profile variables.*   Often in public cases everybody gets into the act—judges, commentators, jury selection experts, psychologists, and so

on. Always anticipate all that could be said, conjectured, and argued about the case. Always try to be prepared for every inevitability.

5. *Keep the focus positive.* Ultimately, it's a positive, productive attitude that leads to effective negotiations with the other side. So the less combative you can be—especially near settlement—the better.

6. *Try settling again.* Again, this ought to be the primary litigation visibility strategy—to end the agony and get it out of the papers.

7. *Fight nicely.* Wars are messy, expensive, and prone to producing casualties. It is much better to be positive. This will give both sides a greater chance of eventually settling.[33]

L A S T   W O R D

As our society becomes more contentious, fractious, and litigious, public relations must become more concerned with the law.

On the one hand, because management must rely so heavily on legal advice and legal judgments, it is imperative that public relations people understand the laws that govern their organizations and industries. As noted, the public relations view may differ from the legal view. Therefore, it is incumbent on public relations people to be well versed in the legal arguments before stating their own positions.

On the other hand, public relations advisers must depend on "buy-in" from others in management. Lawyers are among the most influential of these associates. Therefore, forming an alliance with legal counselors must be a frontline objective for public relations professionals.

Beyond the working relationship between public relations people and lawyers, the practice of public relations has become involved with the law in many areas of communications beyond those cited in this chapter.

- The Federal Communications Commission (FCC) ruled in 1987 that the *Fairness Doctrine*, the subject of years of debate among broadcasters and others, unconstitutionally restricted the First Amendment rights of broadcasters. The FCC said that broadcasters were no longer obligated to provide equal time for dissenting views on controversial issues. Although this sounds fine on the face of it, questions arise over what constitutes "controversy," "balance," or even "fairness." In recent years, the Radio Television and News Directors Association has sued the FCC to go further to eliminate aspects of the Fairness Doctrine dealing with personal attack and political editorials.[34]

- The *right of publicity* is another legal principle that has come under increased scrutiny in recent years. Deriving from privacy law, the right of publicity makes it unlawful to use another's identity for commercial advantage without permission. Stated another way, it gives individuals, especially celebrities, and their estates the "right to be left alone."[35]

  For example, the estate of Diana, Princess of Wales sued the Franklin Mint Company for producing and advertising jewellery, commemorative plates, sculptures, and dolls depicting Princess Diana. The estates of other dead celebrities, including Charlie Chaplin, W. C. Fields, Mae West, the Marx brothers, and even Elvis, have similarly sued to stop ads, recordings, and other portrayed likenesses without the permission of their heirs.

- The doctrine of *fair use* is another that continually runs up against challenges. Fair use is an exception in copyright law that allows some public access, under certain conditions, to copyrighted material. For example, in 1993, the Supreme Court ruled that the rap group 2 Live Crew could release a vulgar rewrite of the old Roy Orbison hit "Pretty Woman," even though those who copyrighted the original material had refused permission. The Court ruled that the raunchy rappers were entitled to "fair use" of the material for the purpose of parody. But in 1997, Texas became the first state in the nation to prohibit its agencies from investing in companies that produce or distribute music with lyrics that are sexually explicit or extol violence, aka "gangsta rap."[36]

  In 1998, the estate of Martin Luther King, Jr. brought a copyright infringement suit against CBS for its use of about 60 percent of King's famous "I Have a Dream" speech at the Lincoln Memorial in 1963. The Court ruled that the speech is in the "public domain" and, therefore, not protected by copyright law.[37]

- In 1997, in a landmark case with a group of state attorneys general, the tobacco industry agreed to a $368 billion settlement that over time would impose strict limits on tobacco *marketing and advertising*, including a ban on vending machines, outdoor billboards, and even Joe Camel.[38]

In addition to all of these legal areas, the public relations business itself increasingly is based on legal contracts: between agencies and clients, between employers and employees, between purchasers and vendors. All contracts—both written and oral—must be binding and enforceable.

In recent years, controversy in the field has erupted over noncompete clauses, in which former employees are prohibited, within certain time parameters, from working for a competitor or pitching a former account. Time and again, the courts have ruled in favor of public relations agencies and against former clients in noncompete cases.

Likewise, legal challenges have been made relative to the markup of expenses that public relations agencies charge clients. Standard practice in the industry is to mark up by 15 to 20 percent legitimate printing and advertising bills submitted to clients. Legal issues also have arisen over the postal laws that govern public relations people who disseminate materials through the mail.

Add to these the blurring of the lines between public relations advice on the one hand and legal advice on the other, and it becomes clear that the connection between public relations and the law will intensify dramatically in the 21st century.

Discussion Starters

1. What is the difference between a public relations professional's responsibility and a lawyer's responsibility?
2. What have been recent challenges to the First Amendment?
3. How can someone prove that he or she has been libeled or slandered?
4. What is meant by the term *insider trading*?
5. What is the SEC's overriding concern when considering disclosure?
6. What kinds of information must public companies disclose immediately?
7. Whom does copyright law protect?
8. What are some of the dominant issues in laws affecting the Internet?
9. What are several general principles with respect to litigation public relations?
10. What general advice should a public relations professional consider in working with lawyers?

Lawrence Lessig

Code and Other Laws of Cyberspace
New York, NY, Basic Books, 2000

In this book, attorney Lawrence Lessig issues a series of bold arguments for guiding the still evolving regulatory process concerning the Internet.

In the words of the Amazon.com review, "As the former Communist-bloc countries found, a constitution is still one of the best guarantees against the dark side of chaos; and Lessig promotes a kind of document that accepts the inevitable regulatory authority of both government and commerce, while constraining them within values that we hold by consensus."

The New York Times Book Review called *Code and Other Laws of Cyberspace* "a book that's sometimes as brilliant as the best teacher you ever had, sometimes as pretentious as a deconstructionists' conference."

C A S E   S T U D Y

Burned by the Media: General Motors Extinguishes NBC

It is difficult now to believe that a proposal to send a camera crew to Indiana to tape two old Citation cars being driven into two pickup trucks fitted with igniters would be taken seriously.

> Report of Inquiry into Crash Demonstrations Broadcast on *Dateline NBC*
> November 17, 1992, NBC Internal Report, issued March 21, 1993

The estimated 17 million viewers of the November 17, 1992, *Dateline NBC* program couldn't help but be horrified as they observed a General Motors full-size pickup truck burst into flames after being hit broadside by a remote control–operated Citation (Figure 17-4). The clear conclusion for any viewer watching the debacle was that GM trucks were dangerous and ought to be taken off the road—immediately!

There was only one slight problem.

The NBC crash demonstration was a sham. The test was rigged. The segment was flawed from start to finish. And the reporting of *NBC News* was flatly fraudulent, it would soon be learned.

NBC News would have gotten away with its trickery had not GM struck back with a public relations vengeance unprecedented in American corporate history.

Immediately after the damaging NBC broadcast, GM embarked on a painstaking mission to research the facts of the NBC demonstration and expose the network's falsified report. That effort would never have been seen had it not been for a lucky break— a call from a newsman who had discovered witnesses to the rigged demonstration on a rural road near Indianapolis.

Pete Pesterre, editor of *Popular Hot Rodding Magazine*, wrote an editorial criticizing the *Dateline NBC* story. Soon afterward, a reader of the magazine turned up a firefighter who had witnessed the filming of the crash and had filmed his own video of the incident.

GM obtained the firefighter's video, which proved to be the turning point in GM's efforts. The video clearly showed that the test was rigged. GM investigators found the two trucks used in the staged crash at a salvage yard in Indiana and purchased them. In one of the pickups, a used model rocket engine was found.

Between the time the show aired in November 1992 and January 1993, four letters were sent to NBC by GM. When GM received no adequate response, it then threatened suit. NBC continued to state that the story, according to *NBC News* President Michael Gartner, "was entirely accurate." In February 1993, GM filed a lawsuit against the National Broadcasting Company, charging that *Dateline NBC* had rigged the crash. GM also immediately went into crisis mode.

GM's crisis communications program was managed by two members of its recently reorganized communications staff—William J. O'Neill, then director of communications for GM's North American Operations (NAO), and Edward S. Lechtzin, director of legal and safety issues for the NAO communications staff. O'Neill, in fact, had agreed that GM would participate in the original *Dateline NBC* program but hadn't been told during the interview session about NBC's taped test. O'Neill and Lechtzin spearheaded a unique public relations team that also included three GM attorneys and two engineers.

The public relations professionals, attorneys, and engineers together provided a nucleus that could make key decisions quickly and authoritatively.

Lechtzin's boss, GM General Counsel Harry J. Pearce, was selected to face off with the media. At the center of the group's public relations offensive would be a press conference, conducted by Pearce, to lay bare the NBC deception. Furthermore, the GM crisis communications team made a conscious decision to target television as the key medium to deliver GM's strongest message that it had been wronged and wasn't going to take it.

GOING TO WAR WITH NBC

Given the old adage, "Don't pick a fight with the guy who buys ink by the barrel," a large number of "crisis communications consultants" wondered aloud during the days before the Pearce press conference if GM was doing the right thing.

At GM, there was never any doubt that the NBC deception should be publicized—as widely as possible. Briefed during an inaugural event for President Clinton, GM President Jack Smith told his public relations executives, "Don't overplay it, but do what's right."

During the three-week period before the press conference, the group pulling together the case against NBC was asked only two questions: (1) Do we have enough information? and (2) Are we doing the right thing? No presentations. No briefing books. No background meetings. No groups of 15 to 20 people in a room trying to decide what was right. It was left to the small crisis task force to select the right strategy.

Harry Pearce was scheduled to take the stage in the GM showroom at 1 P.M. on February 8, 1993. Only one question remained: How would the media react?

THE PEARCE PRESS CONFERENCE

From the moment Harry Pearce strode onstage until the time he concluded more than two hours later, the assembled media personnel—numbering nearly 150 journalists and 25 camera crews—were mesmerized.

"What I'm about to share with you should shock the conscience of every member of your profession and mine, and I believe the American people as well," Pearce began, speaking to an uncommonly quiet media audience. "I will not allow the good men and women of General Motors and the thousands of independent businesses that sell our products and whose livelihood depends upon our products to suffer the consequences of NBC's irresponsible conduct transmitted via the airwaves throughout this great nation in the November *Dateline* program. GM has been irreparably damaged and we are going to defend ourselves."[1]

For the next two hours, speaking without notes, Pearce systematically shredded any vestiges of defense that NBC might have had. The media audience was transfixed. There was no rushing to phones to call in the story, no shuffling of papers or sighs of boredom. The only sound that interrupted Pearce's devastating dissection of NBC was the intermittent click of camera shutters. Pearce was a skilled trial lawyer weaving a two-hour summation.

The GM attorney concluded by reading a brief statement issued earlier in the day by NBC in which the network said, "We feel that our use of those demonstrations was accurate and responsible." His reply was a challenge of the kind that a good lawyer gives to a jury—in this case, the assembled reporters and thousands of others watching the broadcast. "Well, you decide that one," Pearce said. "And that's going to prove your mettle within your own profession. It's sometimes most difficult to police abuse in one's own profession."

THE CRASH DEMONSTRATION

At the heart of the Pearce press conference was a repeat of NBC's 55-second crash demonstration within a 16-minute broadcast segment. Using videotape, Pearce demonstrated that the segment was flawed from start to finish. It loaded the evidence to prove that GM's full-size C/K pickup trucks, equipped with so-called side-saddle fuel tanks, had a fatal flaw that in a high-speed, side-impact collision caused them to rupture and spew burning gasoline. The clear implication was that the trucks were unsafe. This view was corroborated by the grieving parents of crash victims.

However, no source—not even the internal report generated by NBC after the affair—fully explained what the crashes of two aged Citations being pushed into the sides of two Chevy pickups were supposed to prove. They certainly didn't prove the trucks were dangerous. If anything, the performance of the two old trucks—hit at speeds of 39 and 48 miles per hour, respectively—was superb. The only fire generated, as Pearce showed the reporters, was a 15-second grass fire caused by gasoline spewing from an overfilled filler tube after an ill-fitting gas cap came off on impact.

Careful editing from three views left the impression of a conflagration. As NBC's own investigative report indicated:

> We believe that the combined effect of the shot from the bullet car and the slow motion film creates an impression that the flames are about to consume the cabin of the truck. These images in the edited tape convey an impression quite different from what people saw at the scene. The fire was small, it did not consume the cabin of the truck, and it did not last long.[2]

Although the subsequent filmed truck crash resulted in no holocaust, the program, coupled with a well-orchestrated campaign by the plaintiff's attorneys, helped build public pressure that led the National Highway Traffic Safety Administration (NHTSA) to open an investigation into the safety of GM's trucks just one month after the broadcast.

---

[1]General Motors press conference transcript, Detroit, February 8, 1993.
[2]"NBC Internal Report of Inquiry into Crash Demonstrations Broadcast on *Dateline NBC*, November 17, 1992," issued March 21, 1993.

THE NBC RETRACTION

GM's historic news conference literally brought *NBC News* to its knees.

On the day following Pearce's performance, NBC initiated a negotiating session with the company that lasted for 12 hours. GM would accept nothing less from NBC than a full public retraction of its prior broadcast.

On February 9, 1993, a day after the news conference, that is precisely what NBC did. *Dateline NBC* co-anchors Jane Pauley and Stone Phillips read a four-minute, on-air retraction that put the blame for the bogus broadcast squarely at NBC's door and apologized to GM.

In the aftermath, three *Dateline* producers were fired, the on-air reporter was demoted and reassigned, and ultimately, NBC News President Gartner resigned in humiliation. NBC agreed to reimburse GM the roughly $2 million it had spent in a three-week period investigating the false report. In exchange, GM agreed to drop the defamation suit it had filed against NBC.

For its part, GM was spared years of costly litigation over its suit. The company also was quickly able to put to rest what could have been a nightmarish visual every time GM trucks were mentioned on the evening news.

The cloak-and-dagger story on how GM put its case together remains tantalizingly vague. Nonetheless, what is clear was that in a single day, with a single press conference, GM successfully transformed the pickup truck story from a sensationalized and slanted media feeding frenzy into a serious question of journalistic ethics and integrity.

GM Communications Director O'Neill was blunt in his assessment: "I quite honestly wanted this to happen and I was glad it did happen, because I think these people purposely lied and misrepresented the facts and knew they were doing it. I do not think there is any room for that in this business."[3]

THE AFTERMATH

After NBC's stunning mea culpa, GM increased its public relations offensive to counter concerns about the safety of its trucks.

It sought to show that the plaintiff's bar—the trial lawyers—had a vested financial interest in nurturing the idea that the trucks were dangerous. So did another group, the so-called safety experts, cited by NBC and others, who either were financed by the plaintiff's attorneys or served as expert witnesses in mounting legal action against the company. In the same scrupulous way it had dissected NBC's case, GM systematically discredited the credentials and objectivity of the so-called safety experts.

Apparently galvanized by the publicity, the NHTSA demanded—even before it had completed its own investigation—that GM voluntarily recall its pickup trucks. The company refused. In April 1993, GM sponsored two two-hour shirtsleeve briefings by Pearce with key members of the media, explaining why the company wouldn't recall its trucks and why NHTSA's conclusions were flawed. Interestingly, television representatives were not invited to these sessions because it was felt that the medium could only "enflame the situation further."

In subsequent months, the GM–*NBC News* controversy received lengthy coverage in newspapers and magazines. In most, NBC fared poorly. Summarized one journalist:

> An investigation of past network auto-safety coverage reveals that both CBS and ABC have run the same sorts of material facts about the tests and relied on the same dubious experts with the same ties to plaintiff's bar.[4]

---

[3]Catherine Gates, "NBC Learns a Lesson," *Public Relations Quarterly* (Winter 1993–1994): 42.
[4]"It Didn't Start with *Dateline NBC*," *National Review* (June 21, 1993): 41.

FIGURE 7-4 **The NBC crash set-up.**

The Executive Summary of NBC's internal report concluded, "The story of this ill-fated crash demonstration and its aftermath is rather a story of lapsed judgment—serious lapses—by persons generally well-intentioned and well-qualified. And it is a story of a breakdown in the system for correction and compliance that every organization, including a news organization and network, needs."[5]

One could add that it is also a story that may never have been told had it not been for a gutsy, unyielding public relations initiative by an organization that refused to be dealt with unfairly.

---

[5]"NBC Internal Report," 8.

Questions

1. What other options did GM have in addition to going public in the wake of the *Dateline NBC* report?
2. What was the downside risk for GM of being so public in its response?
3. Do you agree with GM's strategy on sending its general counsel to confront the media?
4. Do you agree with GM's decision not to invite television to its media briefings after the initial Pearce press conference?
5. In terms of reputation and credibility, what do you think its response to the *Dateline NBC* broadcast meant to GM?

6. General Motors, like other auto manufacturers, faces numerous public relations challenges. Scan the list of news releases on the General Motors Web site (www.generalmotors.com/cgi-bin/pr_index.pl) and follow the links to read one or two news releases about product recalls. What publics are being targeted with these news releases? What are the legal implications of such recall announcements?

TIPS FROM THE TOP

An Interview with Harry J. Pearce

Harry Pearce

Harry Pearce was the executive vice president in charge of all corporate staffs at General Motors. He was the automaker's general counsel at the time of the *Dateline NBC* affair in 1992 and 1993. Pearce served as GM's chief spokesman in the *Dateline NBC* crisis.

What were the relative contributions of public relations and the law to GM's handling of the *Dateline NBC* issue?

GM's handling of the *Dateline NBC* issue was unique because the traditional distinctions between the purely legal and public relations lines got blurred. Dedicating key disciplines to a single team allowed each member the ability to focus on the same goal, and the individual contributions of the members became irrelevant.

Because of the litigation aspect of the pickup truck issue, there were some technical issues that only an attorney could address. However, in the larger challenge presented by NBC and the likely media coverage of the dispute, the common goal eliminated a lot of the traditional boundaries between lawyers, engineers, and public relations experts.

What was your objective in going after NBC?

The common goal was at once simple and critical. GM needed to create an environment where facts—not shrill and rhetorical sound bites or sensational video footage—would prevail. In simple terms, we had to neutralize the rhetoric with hard facts, and we needed to shock the media so that it would listen to our message. We knew that we had solid evidence that the *Dateline NBC* segment had crossed the ethical boundaries. And we knew that we had the right facts about the safety of our pickup trucks. We needed to create a climate where that became more, rather than less, important.

Once the facts about NBC's irresponsible conduct were clear to us, the question was really quite easy to answer. The lawsuit was necessary to preserve our legal rights. We then had to ask: "How do we best communicate the truth about the inaccuracies and deception NBC perpetrated against GM and the American people?" It would have been wrong to let the *Dateline NBC* segment go unchallenged. It was obviously a high-stakes decision to go as public as we did, but when you operate on the principle that you are going to do what's right, it really isn't difficult to understand what needs to be done once you have the facts.

How would you characterize the journalistic ethics in the *Dateline NBC* case?

In retrospect, NBC was probably shell-shocked because, as gross as we revealed the segment to be, I'd bet there are dozens of other examples of TV news programs that exhibited a similar bias. The difference in this case was that we were able to obtain the hard physical evidence of the deception—and it was one that we felt the American public would understand. Frankly, the work their so-called experts did was so sloppy and the technical advice they got was so incompetent, that it made our job easy once we knew where to look.

The "ethics" of what *Dateline* did, and failed to do, are manifest throughout the 16-minute segment itself. Though some at the network once would have liked to hide behind a facade that the show was fair except for the "rigged rocket" segment, the fact is

(Continued)

that it was biased from start to finish. It was evident that *Dateline* had already decided the trucks were unsafe before even starting to film the segment and relied heavily on plaintiff attorneys and a family ready to go to trial for much of its input. There was never an attempt to present an objective look at the issue—just to provide sensational footage and grieving parents to gain rating points.

How important is the practice of public relations for a company like GM?

Public relations is a critical function, but we need to be clear how we at GM view this role. These folks aren't just mouthpieces. We will ultimately succeed or fail in any endeavor based on the quality of our products and services. That's as it should be. The role for PR at GM is to help communicate the facts effectively on any given situation. It sounds simple, but when you commit yourself as a company to being straightforward with employees, the public, and the media, you eliminate a lot of unnecessary complication.

What should be the relationship between public relations and the law?

We live in an age when instant communications and sound bites are a way of life, so the link between the law and public relations is both obvious and unavoidable. However, corporations don't often try to win their cases in the media, as do plaintiff attorneys and industry critics. We simply try to neutralize the bombastic rhetoric and distortions to create an environment where the facts can become the focus of the discussion. That's all we ever wanted, and we believe GM was able to achieve that environment in the truck issue.

However, given the media's love of sensationalism and the willingness of members of the legal profession to exploit it, there is a temptation on the part of some on our side of the fence to engage in the same tactics. It's a temptation that both the public relations and legal staffs have to resist.

How would you compare the ethical principles of a lawyer to those of a public relations professional?

In general, the legal duties of a lawyer to a client and to the profession are much higher than the legal or ethical duty of a public relations person. Although there is no code of professional responsibility, with the associated legal consequences, for a member of the public relations profession who fails to follow specific ethical guidelines, PR professionals do have a code of ethics administered by the Public Relations Society of America. It is strict and brings with it consequences for inappropriate actions.

In practical terms, all GM PR professionals must conduct themselves by the highest ethical standards. We will not compromise integrity at GM, and our PR staff is the public face of credibility.

How would you characterize the shift in GM's public relations strategy coming out of this crisis?

It's probably a fair criticism of GM that we've tended to hold back and avoid taking very aggressive public positions when we were unfairly attacked in the press. Maybe it's a function of our history of being the biggest target for such abuse.

However, it makes no sense to us to let false reports and inaccurate statements about our products go unchallenged. We don't seek an unfair advantage with the media, but we fervently believe that GM is entitled to fair treatment. If that means we must be aggressive to get the facts out, so be it.

Suggested Readings

Hiller, Janine. *Internet Law & Policy*. Upper Saddle River, NJ: Prentice-Hall, 2002.

Johnston, David. *Cyberlaw: What You Need to Know About Doing Business Online*. Don Mills, ON: Stoddart Publishing Co. Ltd., 1997.

Lukaszewski, James. "The Other Prosecutors." *Public Relations Quarterly* (Spring 1997): 23–29. Public relations tips for organizations in litigation.

Moore, Roy L. *Mass Communications Law & Ethics*. Mahwah, NJ: Lawrence Erlbaum Associates, 1999.

Moore, Roy L., Ronald T. Farrar, and Erik L. Collins. *Advertising and Public Relations Law*. Mahwah, NJ: Lawrence Erlbaum Associates, 1998.

Poindexter, J. Carl. *Cyberlaw and E-Commerce*. New York, NY: Irwin, McGraw-Hill, 2001.

Roschwalb, Susanne A., and Richard A. Stack. *Litigation Public Relations: Courting Public Opinion*. Littleton, CO: Fred B. Rothman & Co., 1995. This is as good a treatise on legal public relations as currently exists. The authors explore the importance of communications in helping prevail in court.

Rosenoer, Jonathan. *Cyberlaw: The Law of the Internet*. New York: Springer-Verlag, 1997.

Trademark Basics. New York: International Trademark Association, 1995. Defines trademarks, how they differ from patents and copyrights, and spells out the rights and protection of trademark owners.

Notes

1. Fraser P. Seitel, "Following the Lewinsky Rules," odwyerpr.com (August 8, 2001).
2. Gerhart L. Klein, *Public Relations Law: The Basics* (Mt. Laurel, NJ: Anne Klein and Associates, 1990): 1–2.
3. "The Klan Loses," *New York Times* (October 25, 1999): A26.
4. "Court Nullifies Finding Against a Reporter," *New York Times* (June 26, 2002): C15.
5. Iver Peterson, "Firm Awarded $222.7 Million in a Libel Suit vs. Dow Jones," *New York Times* (March 21, 1997): D1.
6. "Bush Administration Condemns Order to Release Detainee Names," Associated Press (August 5, 2002).
7. Dennis L. Wilcox, Phillip H. Ault, Warren K. Agee, and Glen T. Cameron, *Public Relations Strategies and Tactics*, 6th ed. (New York: Addison Wesley Longman, 1999): 265.
8. Thomas K. Grose, "$50 Million Lawsuit Against WSJ and Burrough May Make Some Authors-to-Be Think Twice," *TFJR Report* (April 1992): 3.
9. John J. Walsh, "Dealing with Misbehavior by News Media," Presentation before Annual Meeting of the Arthur W. Page Society, September 1997.
10. "Media Briefs," *Jack O'Dwyer's Newsletter* (December 18, 1996): 3.
11. Larry Reibstein, "One Heck of a Whupping," *Newsweek* (March 31, 1997): 54.
12. "SEC Set to Tighten Disclosure Rules," *O'Dwyer's PR Services Report* (June 1999): 22.
13. Constance L. Hays, "Aide Was Reportedly Ordered to Warn Stewart on Stock Sales," *New York Times* (August 6, 2002): C1–2.
14. Louis M. Thompson, Jr., "SEC Cites Investor Relations Officer for Insider Trading," National Investor Relations Institute release (July 2, 2002).
15. "Managing Tidal Wave of Corporate Disclosure," *Business Wire Newsletter* (April 2002): 2.
16. Jeff D. Opdyke, "Rule of Fair Disclosure Hurts Analysts, House Subcommittee Is Told at Hearing," *Wall Street Journal* (May 18, 2001): C15.
17. Alix M. Freedman and Suein L. Hwang, "Brown & Williamson Faces Inquiry," *Wall Street Journal* (February 6, 1996): A1.
18. Wilcox et al., *Public Relations Strategies and Tactics*, 271.
19. Harold W. Suckenik, "PR Pros Should Know the Four Rules of 'Fair Use,'" *O'Dwyer's PR Services Report* (September 1990): 2.
20. Linda Greenhouse, "What Level of Protection for Internet Speech?" *New York Times* (March 24, 1997): D5.
21. Steven Levy, "U.S. v. the Internet," *Newsweek* (March 31, 1997): 77.
22. Linda Greenhouse, "Decency Act Fails," *New York Times* (June 27, 1997): 1.

23. "In Supreme Court Argument This Wednesday, ACLU to Once Again Battle Internet Censorship Law," American Civil Liberties Union news release (November 26, 2001).

24. Chuck Kapelke, "Cyberlaw 101," *Continental* (May 2001): 42.

25. "In Pursuit of Cybersquatters," *CFO Magazine* (November 1999): 16.

26. "Courts Crack Down on Employees Who Bash Companies Online," *Ragan's Interactive Public Relations* (April 2002): 2.

27. Levy, "U.S. v. the Internet."

28. Ellen Joan Pollock, "Lawyers Are Cautiously Embracing PR Firms," *Wall Street Journal* (March 14, 1990): B1.

29. Robyn Kelley, "Legal Beagles," *Spy* (August 1990): 74.

30. Lloyd Newman, "Litigation Public Relations: How to Work with Lawyers," *PR Reporter Tips and Tactics* (November 23, 1987): 2.

31. "Welcome to the Hotseat: This Is Litigation PR," Lecture by the PR Consulting Group at Ragan's Sixth Annual Strategic Public Relations Conference, Chicago, September 18, 2001.

32. Paul Holmes, "Winning in the Court of Public Opinion and the Court of Law," *Holmes Report* (August 7, 1993).

33. James E. Lukaszewski, "Managing Litigation Visibility: How to Avoid Lousy Trial Publicity," *Public Relations Quarterly* (Spring 1995): 18–24.

34. *RTNDA v. Federal Communications Commission*, Washington D.C. Circuit Court, 98-1305 (October 11, 2000).

35. Russell J. Frackman and Tammy C. Bloofeld, "The Right of Publicity: Going to the Dogs?" The UCLA Online Institute for Cyberspace Law and Policy (September 1996).

36. "Elsewhere," *San Jose Mercury News* (June 21, 1997): A11.

37. *Estate of Martin Luther King, Jr., Inc. v. CBS, Inc.*, U.S. District Court for Northern District of Georgia, 96CV3052-WCO (July 22, 1998).

38. John M. Broder, "Cigarette Makers in a $368 Billion Accord to Curb Lawsuits and Curtail Marketing," *New York Times* (June 21, 1997): A1.

Chapter 8

Research

- *You work for a trade association, and you've been assigned to increase sagging membership. Where do you start?*
- *You work for a hospital that would like to secure publicity for its new cardiovascular care unit. Where do you start?*
- *Your plant manager wants to improve relations with your neighbors in the community. Where do you start?*

The answer in public relations is always the same.

You start with research.

Why?

Frankly, the answer stems from the fact that few managers understand what public relations is and how it works. Managers—particularly those guided by quantitative, empirical measurement—want "proof" that what we advise is based on logic and clear thinking.

In other words, most clients are less interested in what their public relations advisers "think" than in what they "know." The only real way to know your advice is on the right track is by ensuring that it is grounded in hard data whenever possible. In other words, before recommending a course of action, public relations professionals must analyze audiences, assess alternatives, and generally do their homework.

In other words, do research.

Essential First Step

Every public relations program or solution should begin with research. Most don't, which is a shame.

The four-step R-A-C-E, five-step R-O-S-I-E, and four-step R-P-I-E approaches to public relations problem solving, discussed in Chapter 1, all start with research. As noted, the only way to know what to do in any given situation is by researching it

181

first. Indeed, research has become the essential first step in the practice of modern public relations.

Instinct, intuition, and gut feelings all remain important in the conduct of public relations work, but management today demands more—measurement, analysis, and evaluation at every stage of the public relations process. In an era of scarce resources, management wants facts and statistics from public relations professionals to show that their efforts contribute not only to overall organizational effectiveness but also to the bottom line. Why should we introduce a new intranet publication? What should the publication say and how much should it cost? How will we know it's working? Questions such as these must be answered through research.

In a day when organizational resources are precious and companies don't want to spend money unless it enhances results, public relations programs must contribute to meeting business objectives.[1] That means that research must be applied to help segment market targets, analyze audience preferences and dislikes, and determine which messages might be most effective with various audiences. Research then becomes essential in helping realize management's goals.

Research should be applied in public relations work both at the initial stage, prior to planning a campaign, and at the final stage to evaluate a program's effectiveness. Early research helps to determine the current situation, prevalent attitudes, and difficulties that the program faces. Later research examines the program's success, along with what else still needs to be done. Research at both points in the process is critical.

Even though research does not necessarily provide unequivocal proof of a program's effectiveness, it does allow public relations professionals to support their own intuition. It's little wonder, then, that the idea of measuring public relations work has steadily gained acceptance.[2]

What Is Research?

Research is the systematic collection and interpretation of information to increase understanding (Figure 8-1).[3] Most people associate public relations with conveying information; although that association is accurate, research must be the obligatory first step in any project. A firm must acquire enough accurate, relevant data about its publics, products, and programs to answer these questions:

- How can we identify and define our constituent groups?
- How does this knowledge relate to the design of our messages?
- How does it relate to the design of our programs?
- How does it relate to the media we use to convey our messages?
- How does it relate to the schedule we adopt in using our media?
- How does it relate to the ultimate implementation tactics of our program?

It is difficult to delve into the minds of others, whose backgrounds and points of view may be quite different from our own, with the purpose of understanding why they think as they do. Research skills are partly intuitive, partly an outgrowth of individual temperament, and partly a function of acquired knowledge. There is nothing mystifying about them. Although we tend to think of research in terms of impersonal test scores, interviews, or questionnaires, these methods are only a small part of the process. The real challenge lies in using research—knowing when to do what, with whom, and for what purpose.

FIGURE 8-1   **Early research.** An early research effort, albeit a futile one, was the return of the biblical scouts sent by Moses to reconnoiter the land of Canaan. They disagreed in their reports, and the Israelites believed the gloomier versions. This failure to interpret the data correctly caused them to wander another 40 years in the wilderness. (An even earlier research effort was Noah's sending the dove to search for dry ground.)

Principles of Public Relations Research

For years, public relations professionals have debated the standards of measuring public relations' effectiveness. In 1997, the Institute for Public Relations Research and Education offered seven guiding principles in setting standards for public relations research.

- Establishing clear program objectives and desired outcomes tied directly to business goals. what do want to do
- Differentiating between measuring public relations "outputs," quanity generally short-term and surface (e.g., amount of press coverage received or exposure of a particular message), and measuring public relations "outcomes," quality usually more far-reaching and carrying greater impact (e.g., changing awareness, attitudes, and even behavior).
- Measuring media content as a first step in the public relations evaluation process. Such a measure is limited in that it can't discern whether a target audience actually saw a message or responded to it.
- Understanding that no one technique can expect to evaluate public relations effectiveness. Rather, this requires a combination of techniques, from media analysis to cyberspace analysis, from focus groups to polls and surveys.
- Being wary of attempts to compare public relations effectiveness with advertising effectiveness. One particularly important consideration is that

while advertising placement and messages can be controlled, their equivalent on the public relations side cannot be.
- The most trustworthy measurement of public relations effectiveness is that which stems from an organization with clearly identified key messages, target audiences, and desired channels of communication. The converse of this is that the more confused an organization is about its targets, the less reliable its public relations measurement will be. *The more organized the more it coordinates.*

Public relations evaluation cannot be accomplished in isolation. It must be linked to overall business goals, strategies, and tactics.[4]

Types of Public Relations Research

In general, research is conducted to do three things: (1) describe a process, situation, or phenomenon; (2) explain why something is happening, what its causes are, and what effect it will have; and (3) predict what probably will happen if we do or don't take action. Primary, or original, research in public relations is either theoretical or applied. Applied research solves practical problems; theoretical research aids understanding of a public relations process.

Most public relations analysis, however, takes the more informal form called secondary research. This relies on existing material—books, articles, Internet databases, and the like—to form the research backing for public relations recommendations and programs.

Applied Research

In public relations work, applied research can be either strategic or evaluative. Both applications are designed to answer specific practical questions.

- Strategic research is used primarily in program development to determine program objectives, develop message strategies, or establish benchmarks. It often examines the tools and techniques of public relations. For example, a firm that wants to know how employees rate its candor in internal publications would first conduct strategic research to find out where it stands.
- Evaluative research, sometimes called summative research, is conducted primarily to determine whether a public relations program has accomplished its goals and objectives. For example, if changes are made in the internal communications program to increase candor, evaluative research can determine whether the goals have been met. A variant of evaluation can be applied during a program to monitor progress and indicate where modifications might make sense.

Theoretical Research

Theoretical research is more abstract and conceptual than applied research. It helps build theories in public relations work about why people communicate, how public opinion is formed, and how a public is created.

Knowledge of theoretical research is important as a framework for persuasion and as a base for understanding why people do what they do.

Some knowledge of theoretical research in public relations and mass communications is essential for enabling practitioners to understand the limitations of communication as a persuasive tool. Attitude and behavior change has been the traditional goal in public relations programs, yet theoretical research indicates that such a goal may be difficult or impossible to achieve through persuasive efforts. According to such research, other factors are always getting in the way.

Researchers have found that communication is most persuasive when it comes from multiple sources of high credibility. Credibility itself is a multidimensional concept that includes trustworthiness, expertise, and power. Others have found that a message generally is more effective when it is simple, because it is easier to understand, localize, and make personally relevant. According to still other research, the persuasiveness of a message can be increased when it arouses or is accompanied by a high level of personal involvement in the issue at hand.

The point here is that knowledge of theoretical research can help practitioners not only understand the basis of applied research findings but also temper management's expectations of attitude and behavioral change resulting from public relations programs.

Secondary Research

Secondary research is research on the cheap. Basically, secondary research allows you to examine or read about and learn from someone else's primary research, such as in a library.

Also called "desk research," secondary research uses data that have been collected for other purposes than your own. Among the typical sources of secondary research are the following:

- Industry trade journals
- Government
- Web sites
- Informal contacts
- Published company accounts
- Business libraries
- Professional institutes and organizations
- Omnibus surveys
- Census data
- Public records

Because public relations budgets are limited, it always makes sense first to consider secondary sources in launching a research effort.

Methods of Public Relations Research

Observation is the foundation of modern social science. Scientists, social psychologists, and anthropologists make observations, develop theories, and, hopefully, increase understanding of human behavior. Public relations research, too, is founded on observation. Three primary forms of public relations research dominate the field.

- Surveys are designed to reveal attitudes and opinions—what people think about certain subjects.
- Communication audits often reveal disparities between real and perceived communications between management and target audiences. Management may make certain assumptions about its methods, media, materials, and messages, whereas its targets may confirm or refute those assumptions.

● Unobtrusive measures—such as fact-finding, content analysis, and readability studies—enable the study of a subject or object without involving the researcher or the research as an intruder.

Each method of public relations research offers specific benefits and should be understood and used by the modern practitioner.

Surveys

Survey research is one of the most frequently used research methods in public relations. Surveys can be applied to broad societal issues, such as determining public opinion about a political candidate, or to more mundane organizational problems, such as what hotel guests like most and least about their lodging facility (Figure 8-2).

Guest Satisfaction Survey

Our records indicate that you recently had reservations at the hotel shown above on the date indicated.

MARKING INSTRUCTIONS

• Do not use red ink.

• Do not use a marker that will bleed through the page.

• You may use pencil or pen to complete this survey.

Please be sure to fill the response oval completely.

CORRECT MARK

INCORRECT MARKS

Please take a moment and answer the following questions.
If a question is not applicable to your stay, please skip to the next question.

How would you rate our hotel on:

1. QUALITY OF ACCOMMODATIONS...

	EXCELLENT — POOR		EXCELLENT — POOR
Cleanliness of your guest room upon entering	10 9 8 7 6 5 4 3 2 1	Overall maintenance and upkeep	10 9 8 7 6 5 4 3 2 1
Cleanliness and servicing of your room during stay	10 9 8 7 6 5 4 3 2 1	Condition of the grounds	10 9 8 7 6 5 4 3 2 1
Overall cleanliness of bathroom	10 9 8 7 6 5 4 3 2 1	Condition of the lobby area	10 9 8 7 6 5 4 3 2 1
Cleanliness of tub and tile	10 9 8 7 6 5 4 3 2 1	Condition of the restaurants and lounges	10 9 8 7 6 5 4 3 2 1
Overall cleanliness of bedroom	10 9 8 7 6 5 4 3 2 1	Functionality of guest room	10 9 8 7 6 5 4 3 2 1
Condition of bedspread	10 9 8 7 6 5 4 3 2 1	Condition of pool and pool area	10 9 8 7 6 5 4 3 2 1
Overall guest room quality	10 9 8 7 6 5 4 3 2 1		

Everything in your room in working order? ○ Yes ○ No

What was your room number? _____

Please share any comments you may have about the quality of our rooms, lobby, and outside areas.

_____

_____

_____

_____

2. QUALITY OF HOTEL STAFF AND SERVICES...

Did you make your room reservation through the hotel? ○ Yes ○ No

When you arrived at the hotel, was the information the hotel had concerning your reservation correct? ○ Yes ○ No

FIGURE 8-2 Client satisfaction research. Marriott Hotels used this survey to evaluate its facilities, service levels, and people.

Surveys come in two types.

1. *Descriptive surveys* offer a snapshot of a current situation or condition. They are the research equivalent of a balance sheet, capturing reality at a specific point in time. A typical public opinion poll is a prime example.
2. *Explanatory surveys* are concerned with cause and effect. Their purpose is to help explain why a current situation or condition exists and to offer explanations for opinions and attitudes. Frequently, such explanatory or analytical surveys are designed to answer the question "why": Why are our philanthropic dollars not being appreciated in the community? Why don't employees believe management's messages? Why is our credibility being questioned?

Surveys generally consist of four elements: (1) sample, (2) questionnaire, (3) interview, and (4) analysis of results. (Direct-mail surveys, of course, eliminate the interview step.) Because survey research is so critical in public relations, we will examine each survey element in some detail.

The Sample

The sample, or selected target group, must be representative of the total public whose views are sought. Once a survey population has been determined, a researcher must select the appropriate sample or group of respondents from which to collect information. Sampling is tricky. A researcher must be aware of the hidden pitfalls in choosing a representative sample, not the least of which is the perishable nature of most data. Survey findings are rapidly outdated because of population mobility and changes in the political and socioeconomic environment. Consequently, sampling should be completed quickly.

Two cross-sectional approaches are used in obtaining a sample: random sampling and nonrandom sampling. The former is more scientific, the latter more informal.

Random Sampling

In random sampling, two properties are essential—equality and independence in selection. Equality means that no element has any greater or lesser chance of being selected. Independence means that selecting any one element in no way influences the selection of any other element. Random sampling is based on a mathematical criterion that allows generalizations from the sample to be made to the total population. There are four types of random or probability samples.

1. *Simple random sampling* gives all members of the population an equal chance of being selected. First, all members of the population are identified, and then as many subjects as are needed are randomly selected—usually with the help of a computer. Election polling uses a random approach; although millions of Americans vote, only a few thousand are ever polled on their election preferences. The Nielsen national television sample, for example, consists of 4,000 homes. The Census Bureau uses a sample of 72,000 out of 93 million households to obtain estimates of employment and other population characteristics.

   How large should a random sample be? The answer depends on a number of factors, one of which is the size of the population. In addition, the more similar the population elements are in regard to the characteristics being studied, the smaller the sample required. In most random samples, the following population-to-sample ratios apply, with a 5 percent margin of error:

Population	Sample
1,000	278
2,000	322
3,000	341
5,000	355
10,000	370
50,000	381
100,000	383
500,000	383
Infinity	384

Random sampling owes its accuracy to the laws of probability, which are best explained by the example of a barrel filled with 10,000 marbles—5,000 green ones and 5,000 red ones. If a blindfolded person selects a certain number of marbles from the barrel—say, 400—the laws of probability suggest that the most frequently drawn combination will be 200 red and 200 green. These laws further suggest that with certain margins of error, a very few marbles can represent the whole barrel, which can correspond to any size— for example, that of a city, state, or nation.

2. *Systematic random sampling* is closely related to simple random sampling, but it uses a random starting point in the sample list. From then on, the researcher selects every *n*th person in the list. As long as every person has an equal and independent chance to be selected on the first draw, then the sample qualifies as random and is equally reliable to simple random sampling. Random telephone dialing, for example, which solves the problem of failing to consider unlisted numbers, may use this technique.

3. *Stratified random sampling* is a procedure used to survey different segments or strata of the population. For example, if an organization wants to determine the relationship between years of service and attitudes toward the company, it may stratify the sample to ensure that the breakdown of respondents accurately reflects the makeup of the population. In other words, if more than half of the employees have been with the company more than 10 years, more than half of those polled should also reflect that level of service. By stratifying the sample, the organization's objective can be achieved.

4. *Cluster sampling* involves first breaking the population down into small heterogeneous subsets, or clusters, and then selecting the potential sample from the individual clusters or groups. A cluster may often be defined as a geographic area, such as an election district.

Nonrandom Sampling

Nonrandom samples come in three types: convenience, quota, and volunteer.

1. *Convenience samples*, also known as accidental, chunk, or opportunity samples, are relatively unstructured, rather unsystematic, and designed to elicit ideas and points of view. Journalists use convenience samples when they conduct person-on-the-street interviews. The most common type of convenience sample in public relations research is the focus group. Focus groups generally consist of 8 to 12 people, with a moderator encouraging in-

depth discussion of a specific topic. Focus groups generate concepts and ideas rather than validate hypotheses.

2. *Quota samples* permit a researcher to choose subjects on the basis of certain characteristics. For example, the attitudes of a certain number of women, men, blacks, whites, rich, or poor may be needed. Quotas are imposed in proportion to each group's percentage of the population. The advantage of quota sampling is that it increases the homogeneity of a sample population, thus enhancing the validity of a study. However, it is hard to classify interviewees by one or two discrete demographic characteristics. For example, a particular interviewee may be black, Catholic, female, under 25, and a member of a labor union all at the same time, making the lines of demographic demarcation pretty blurry. (A derivative of quota sampling is called purposive sampling.)

3. *Volunteer samples* use willing participants who agree voluntarily to respond to concepts and hypotheses for research purposes.[5]

The Questionnaire

Before creating a questionnaire, a researcher must consider his or her objective in doing the study. What you seek to find out should influence the specific publics you ask, the questions you raise, and the research method you choose. After determining what you're after, consider the particular questionnaire design. Specifically, researchers should observe the following in designing their questionnaire:

1. *Keep it short.* Make a concerted attempt to limit questions. It's terrific if the questionnaire can be answered in five minutes.

2. *Use structured rather than open-ended questions.* People would rather check a box or circle a number than write an essay. But leave room at the bottom for general comments or "Other." Also, start with simple, nonthreatening questions before getting to the more difficult, sensitive ones. This approach will build respondent trust as well as commitment to finishing the questionnaire.

3. *Measure intensity of feelings.* Let respondents check "very satisfied," "satisfied," "dissatisfied," or "very dissatisfied" rather than "yes" or "no." One popular approach is the semantic differential technique shown in Figure 8-3.

4. *Don't use fancy words or words that have more than one meaning.* If you must use big words, make the context clear.

5. *Don't ask loaded questions.* "Is management doing all it can to communicate with you?" is a terrible question. The answer is always no.

6. *Don't ask double-barreled questions.* "Would you like management meetings once a month, or are bimonthly meetings enough?" is another terrible question.

7. *Pretest.* Send your questionnaire to a few colleagues and listen to their suggestions.

8. *Attach a letter explaining how important the respondents' answers are, and let recipients know that they will remain anonymous.* Respondents will feel better if they think the study is significant and their identities are protected. Also, specify how and where the data will be used.

9. *Hand-stamp the envelopes, preferably with unique commemorative stamps.* Metering an envelope indicates assembly-line research, and researchers have found that the more expensive the postage, the higher the response rate. People like to feel special.

10. *Follow up your first mailing.* Send a reminder postcard three days after the original questionnaire. Then wait a few weeks and send a second questionnaire, just in case recipients have lost the first.

NORWOOD RESEARCH GROUP
Market Research for American Industry

March 13, 2001

Good Morning!

Please accept this crisp new bill in exchange for just three minutes of your time.

It's our way of saying "thank you" for your help with a brief survey we've been asked to conduct.

We are interested in your impressions of several firms that provide products, services and grid management systems for the transmission and distribution of electricity.

The enclosed questionnaire lists several of these firms, and several factors involved in purchase decision-making.

Please tell us how you feel about each company or purchasing factor by simply **circling** the number that best reflects your opinion. *For example:*

Company ABC
OVERALL REPUTATION: 1 2 3 4 5 6 7 (8) 9 10
Poor reputation — Excellent reputation

When you're done with the survey, just return it in the stamped envelope that's enclosed.

Your responses are anonymous and confidential. Thank you for being part of this important survey on awareness and attitudes.

Sincerely,

Steve Rivkin
President

B1,B2

P.O. Box 543
Glen Rock, New Jersey 07452-0543
Phone: 201-670-4218 Fax: 201-670-1265
E-mail: research@rivkin.net

FIGURE 8-3 **Measuring intensity and rewarding the respondent.** One common device to measure intensity of feelings is the semantic differential technique, which gives respondents a scale of choices from the worst to the best. Respondents will comply more gladly if a "crisp new bill" is included.

11. *Send out more questionnaires than you think necessary.* The major weakness of most mail surveys is the unmeasurable error introduced by nonresponders. You're shooting for a 50 percent response rate; anything less tends to be suspect.
12. *Enclose a reward.* There's nothing like a token gift of merchandise or money—a $2 bill works beautifully—to make a recipient feel guilty for not returning a questionnaire.[6]

Appendix D gives an example of a full survey questionnaire.

Interviews

Interviews can provide a more personal, firsthand feel for public opinion. Interview panels can range from focus groups of randomly selected average people to Delphi panels of so-called opinion leaders. Interviews can be conducted in a number of ways, including face-to-face, telephone, mail, and through the Internet.

Focus Groups

This approach is used with increasing frequency in public relations today. Such interviews can be conducted one-on-one or through survey panels. These panels can be used, for example, to measure buying habits or the impact of public relations programs on a community or organizational group. They can also be used to assess general attitudes toward certain subjects, such as new products or advertising.

With the focus group technique, a well-drilled moderator leads a group through a discussion of opinions on a particular product, organization, or idea. Participants represent the socioeconomic level desired by the research sponsor—from college students to office workers to millionaires. Almost always, focus group participants are paid for their efforts. Sessions are frequently videotaped and then analyzed, often in preparation for more formal and specific research questionnaires.

Focus groups should be organized with the following guidelines in mind:

1. *Define your objectives and audience.* The more tightly you define your goals and your target audience, the more likely you are to gather relevant information. In other words, don't conduct a focus group with friends and family members, hoping to get a quick and inexpensive read. Nothing of value will result.
2. *Recruit your groups.* Recruiting participants takes several weeks, depending on the difficulty of contacting the target audience. Contact is usually made by phone with a series of questions to weed out employees of competitors, members of the news media (to keep the focus group from becoming a news story), and those who don't fit target group specifications. Persons who have participated in a group in the past year should also be screened out; they may be more interested in the money than in helping you find what you're looking for.
3. *Choose the right moderator.* Staff people who may be excellent conversationalists are not necessarily the best focus group moderators. The gift of gab is not enough. Professional moderators know how to establish rapport quickly, how and when to probe beyond the obvious, how to draw comments from reluctant participants, how to keep a group on task, and how to interpret results validly.
4. *Conduct enough focus groups.* One or two focus groups usually are not enough. Four to six are better to uncover the full range of relevant ideas and opinions. Regardless of the number of groups, however, you must resist the temptation to add up responses. That practice gives the focus group more analytical worth than it deserves.
5. *Use a discussion guide.* This is a basic outline of what you want to investigate. It will lead the moderator through the discussion and keep the group on track.
6. *Choose proper facilities.* The discussion room should be comfortable, with participants sitting around a table that gives them a good view of each other. Observers can use closed-circuit TV and one-way mirrors, but participants should always be told when they are being observed.

7. *Keep a tight rein on observers.* Observers should rarely be in the same room with participants; the two groups ordinarily should be separated. Observers should view the proceedings seriously; this is not "dinner and a show."

8. *Consider using outside help.* Setting up focus groups can be time-consuming and complicated. Often the best advice is to hire a firm recommended by the American Marketing Association or the Marketing Research Association so that the process, the moderator, and the evaluation are as professional as possible.[7]

S I D E B A R

Creatively Measuring Press Coverage

Through the decades, the most tried and true public relations measurement technique was to measure press clipping inches to justify to employers the success of a particular publicity program. In recent years, the techniques surrounding press coverage measurement have become more sophisticated.

The Rowland Company, a New York–based public relations agency, has introduced the Rowland Publicity Index, which applies numerical values to such components as physical characteristics, message, context, and objectives. Measures are applied against such criteria as:

1. **Length**
   How long is the article?
   Is it a brief mention or an extensive story?
   What portion of the article is relevant to the topic?

2. **Position**
   Where does the story appear in the publication? On the page?
   Is it a main story, for example, page one?
   Is there a "teaser" on the front page for the story?

3. **Graphics**
   How big is the headline? One line or two?
   Is there a complementary photo?
   What are the size and quality of the photo?
   Is there a sidebar or similar element?

4. **Key message**
   Were the promotion's key messages included in the article?
   Were they up front or buried in the back?

Was a spokesperson quoted?
Were the messages present in the headline or cutline?

5. **Context**
   Does the story mention a product? In a positive or negative way?
   Does the story offer a substitution for a product?
   Is the story critical of the organization or industry?
   Does the article have a positive or negative tone?

6. **Achieved objectives**
   Did the article accomplish what it set out to achieve?
   Was it covered as a stand-alone or included in a wrap-up mention with other ideas?
   What was the overall impact of the article?

Another agency, Kaiser Associates of Vienna, Virginia, has introduced other media measurement criteria such as:

- Relative costs, such as media relations as a percentage of total revenues or media relations costs as a percentage of total costs.
- Processes, such as cycle times for the creation of news releases and media events.
- Benchmarking media clips against competitors.
- Rating media clips as positive, negative, or neutral in assessing impact on targeted publics.

For further information, see "PR Execs Measure the Worth of Traditional Measurements," *PR News* (February 10, 1997): 7; and Carter Griffin and Aimee P. Martin, "Creatively Measuring Media Relations," *Public Relations Strategist* (Spring 1998): 36–40.

Telephone Interviews

In contrast to personal interviews, telephone interviews suffer from a high refusal rate. Many people just don't want to be bothered. Such interviews may also introduce an upper-income bias because lower-income earners may lack telephones. However, the increasing use of unlisted numbers by upper-income people may serve to mitigate this bias. Telephone interviews must be carefully scripted so that interviewers know precisely what to ask, regardless of a respondent's answer. Calls should be made at less busy times of the day, such as early morning or late afternoon.

With both telephone and face-to-face interviews, it is important to establish rapport with the interview subject. It makes good sense to begin the interview with non-threatening questions, saving the tougher, more controversial ones—on income level or race, for example—until last. Another approach is to depersonalize the research by explaining that others have devised the survey and that the interviewer's job is simply to ask the questions.

Mail Interviews

This is the least expensive approach, but it often suffers from a low response rate. You are aiming for a 50 percent response rate. Frequently, people who return mail questionnaires are those with strong biases either in favor of or (more commonly) in opposition to the subject at hand. As noted, one way to generate a higher response from mail interviews is through the use of self-addressed, stamped envelopes or enclosed incentives such as dollar bills or free gifts.

Drop-off Interviews

This approach combines face-to-face and mail interview techniques. An interviewer personally drops off a questionnaire at a household, usually after conducting a face-to-face interview. Because the interviewer has already established some rapport with the interviewee, the rate of return with this technique is considerably higher than it is for straight mail interviews.

Intercept Interviews

This approach is popular in consumer surveys, where researchers "intercept" respondents on the street, in shopping malls, or in retail outlets. Trained interviewers typically deliver a short (5- to 20-minute) questionnaire concerning attitudes, perceptions, preferences, and behavior.

Delphi Panels

The Delphi technique is a qualitative research tool that uses opinion leaders—local influential persons as well as national experts—often to help tailor the design of a general public research survey. Designed by the Rand Corporation in the 1950s, the Delphi technique is a consensus-building approach that relies on repeated waves of questionnaires sent to the same select panel of experts. Delphi findings generate a wide range of responses and help set the agenda for more meaningful future research. Stated another way, Delphi panels offer a "research reality check."[8]

Internet Interviews

The latest technique of interviewing constituent publics is via the Internet. This is a particularly effective technique in gathering rapid support for a political position. In 1999, disgraced former Clinton adviser Dick Morris created Vote.com to measure voters' attitudes on a variety of arbitrary issues selected by Morris. Because "polling" merely required Internet access, Morris received voluminous responses to his questionnaires and flooded the Clinton White House with e-mail polling results. The White House responded by blocking such e-mail so as not to be overrun by it.

Results Analysis

After selecting the sample, drawing up the questionnaire, and interviewing the respondents, the researcher must analyze the findings. Often a great deal of analysis is required to produce meaningful recommendations.

The objective of every sample is to come up with results that are valid and reliable. A margin of error explains how far off the prediction may be. A sample may be large enough to represent fairly the larger universe; yet, depending on the margin of sampling error, the results of the research may not be statistically significant. That is, the differences or distinctions detected by the survey may not be sizable enough to offset the margin of error. Thus, the margin of error must always be determined.

This concept is particularly critical in political polling, where pollsters are quick to acknowledge that their results may accurately represent the larger universe but normally with a 3 percent margin of error. Thus, the results could be 3 percent more or less for a certain candidate. Consequently, a pollster who says a candidate will win with 51 percent of the vote really means that the candidate could win with as much as 54 percent or lose with as little as 48 percent of the vote.

Political polls are fraught with problems. They cannot predict outcomes scientifically. Rather, they provide a snapshot, freezing attitudes at a certain point in time—like a balance sheet for a corporation. Obviously, people's attitudes change with the passage of time, and pollsters, despite what they claim, can't categorically predict the outcome of an election. Perhaps the most notorious example of this was the political poll sponsored by the *Literary Digest* in 1936, which used a telephone polling technique to predict that Alf Landon would be the nation's next president. Landon thereupon suffered one of the worst drubbings in American electoral history at the hands of Franklin Roosevelt. It was probably of little solace to the *Literary Digest* that most of its telephone respondents, many of whom were Republicans wealthy enough to afford phones, did vote for Landon.

The point is that in analyzing results, problems of validity, reliability, and levels of statistical significance associated with margins of error must be considered before concrete recommendations based on survey data are offered.

Communications Audits

When the gigantic Exxon Corporation merged with the equally gigantic Mobil Oil Corporation in December 1999, it turned to an increasingly important method of research in public relations work: the communications audit. Such audits are used frequently by corporations, schools, hospitals, and other organizations to determine whether a communications group is running effectively and also how the institution is perceived by its core constituents. Communications audits help public relations professionals understand more clearly the relationships between management actions and objectives, on the one hand, and communications methods to promote those objectives, on the other.

Communications audits are typically used to analyze the standing of a company with its employees or community neighbors; to assess the readership of routine communication vehicles, such as annual reports and news releases; or to examine an organization's performance as a corporate citizen. Communications audits often provide benchmarks against which future public relations programs can be applied and measured.

Purpose

The communications audit presents a complete analysis of an organization's internal and external communications, designed to determine communications needs, policies, practices, and capabilities. The data uncovered are used by management to make informed, economical decisions about future communications needs and goals.[9]

A QUESTION OF ETHICS

Assessing an "Unbiased" Testing Agency

In April 2000, a federal jury cleared the publisher of *Consumer Reports* magazine of liability for reporting that Isuzu Troopers were dangerous. But the damage to the research agency's testing procedures and objectivity was done.

For six decades, there was no more trusted research source of information about products and their strengths and weaknesses than *Consumer Reports*. The independent, self-proclaimed bastion of "independent testing and research" was looked upon as one of the most unbiased sources of pertinent product information in the United States. By the end of the century, however, questions emerged as to just how "unbiased" the vaunted research agency was.

What triggered the questions was a *Consumer Reports* attack on Isuzu Motors Limited, maker of the successful Trooper, a popular sport utility vehicle.

The drama started one August morning in 1996 when executives of Isuzu Motors in California were notified by *Consumer Reports* that "an Isuzu product would be discussed at a news conference in 30 minutes." Isuzu executives had no clue as to which product would be discussed and what would be said about it. However, their suspicion was that whatever was said, it wouldn't be very good.

Boy were they right.

At the news conference, *Consumer Reports* played a videotape that showed an out-of-control Isuzu Trooper, unable to negotiate a turn with its right wheels more than 2 feet off the ground, headed for immediate disaster. The conference concluded with a warning from *Consumer Reports'* technical director that, "Consumers shouldn't buy the Isuzu Trooper, and owners of the vehicle should drive it only when necessary."

Five minutes after the news conference, Isuzu received its first call from the media. By day's end, it had received more than 100 press calls, and that night, the incriminating report was prominently featured on CBS and CNN; the next day, it was in all of the nation's most prestigious newspapers. It mattered little that the company adamantly claimed that the Trooper had never experienced any problems. The damage was done.

In the 12 months following the news conference, sales of the Isuzu Trooper declined from 23,000 to 13,000—the dramatic, but not wholly unexpected, impact from a negative piece in a magazine rated as "the most believable and objective source of information about products and services."

Deeply stung, Isuzu fired back. It sued the magazine and questioned its testing methods, claiming that *Consumer Reports* is beholden to its funders, including foundations with specific antibusiness agendas. Specifically, Isuzu charged that *Consumer Reports* and its parent company, Consumers Union, nurtured a long-standing bias against SUVs.

The company alleged that *Consumer Reports'* charges were trumped up as ammunition in its parent company's battle with the federal government over regulation of SUVs. Indeed, prior to the Isuzu offensive, the magazine had run three stories in a year and a half asking, "How safe are SUVs?" Consumers Union even petitioned the National Highway Traffic Safety Administration to tighten standards for SUVs.

In its suit, Isuzu alleged that the Consumers Union test driver purposely tipped the vehicle and also that the driver chose to negotiate around an object in his path rather than hitting the brakes. In other words, Isuzu claimed that *Consumer Reports* rigged the test to increase sales of its magazine.

Consumer Reports denied all charges, and the case went to court in February 2000. Although the jury ruled that nearly half of the statement Isuzu questioned in its suit was in fact false, it decided against awarding monetary damages to Isuzu. While 8 of 10 jurors reportedly wanted to award the company as much as $25 million, the entire jury couldn't be persuaded.

Nonetheless, it was curious that the *Consumer Reports* gave Isuzu only a brief warning before its press conference. In addition, Isuzu claimed it could learn nothing about how the test was conducted until after the damage had been done. This, too, is curious, especially for a revered consumer research testing service that claims to be "unbiased."

For further information, see Jennifer Greenstein, "Testing Consumer Reports," *Brill's Content* (September 1999):70–77; Rhonda H. Kapartkin, "When Attacked CU Will Probably Shut Up," *Consumer Reports* (December 1999); and "Jury Clears *Consumer Reports Magazine* of Liability in Isuzu Case," *Court TV Online* (April 7, 2000).

Scope

The scope of an audit may be as broad or as narrow as the size and complexity of the organization's demands. The audit can measure the effectiveness of communications programs organizationwide or the programs of a single division. It can also hone in on a specific subject—readability of written materials, understanding of an issue, or use of the Intranet, for example. An audit can also uncover misunderstandings and information barriers and bottenecks, as well as opportunities.

Subjects

Typically, communications audits are used to provide information on issues such as the following:

- Objectives and goals—short and long term
- Existing communications programs—methods and media
- Existing communications vehicles—publications, manuals, bulletin boards, closed-circuit TV, videotape, slides, teleconferencing, memos, meetings, Internet, reports, correspondence, and so on
- Uneven communications workloads
- Employees working at cross-purposes
- Hidden information within an organization that is not being used to the detriment of the institution
- Bottlenecked information flows
- Conflicting or nonexisiting notions about what the organization is and does.[10]

Methodology

A communications audit is a straightforward analysis.

1. It begins with a researcher studying all pertinent literature about the organization.
2. Competitive literature is then reviewed for purposes of comparison and contrast.
3. Interviews with top management and the rank and file are then conducted to detect areas of commonality and discontinuity. In other words, what do people agree on and where do they disagree? Interviews with key outsiders, such as the board and customers, also may be included.
4. Recommendations are then presented from the audit knowledge gleaned.

The most effective communications audits start with a researcher who (1) is familiar with the public to be studied, (2) generally understands the attitudes of the target public toward the organization, (3) recognizes the issues of concern to the target public, and (4) understands the relative power of the target public vis-à-vis other publics.

How often should audits be conducted? Generally, an extensive audit should be conducted every five years or so, with "quick and dirty" studies serving in the interim to keep an organization's communications fresh and pertinent.

Unobtrusive Methods

Of the various unobtrusive methods of data collection available to public relations researchers, probably the most widely used is simple fact-finding. Facts are the bricks and mortar of public relations work; no action can be taken unless the facts are known, and the fact-finding process is continuous.

Each organization must keep a fact file of the most essential data with which it is involved. For example, such items as key organization statistics, publications, management biographies and photos, press clippings, media lists, competitive literature, pending legislation, organizational charters, and bylaws should be kept on file and updated. Even better, computerized listings of such facts offer easier access when research is called for in these areas.

Another unobtrusive method is content analysis, the primary purpose of which is to describe a message or set of messages. For example, an organization with news releases that are used frequently by local newspapers can't be certain, without research, whether the image conveyed by its releases is what the organization seeks. By analyzing the news coverage, the firm can get a much clearer idea of the effectiveness of its communications. Such content analysis might be organized according to the following specific criteria:

- **Frequency of coverage.** How many releases were used?
- **Placement within the paper.** Did releases appear more frequently on page 1 or page 71?
- **People reached.** What was the circulation of the publications in which the releases appeared?
- **Messages conveyed.** Did the releases used express the goals of the organization, or were they simply informational in content?
- **Editing of releases.** How much did the newspaper edit the copy submitted? Were desired meanings materially changed?
- **Attitude conveyed.** Was the reference to the organization positive, negative, or neutral?

Another unobtrusive method, the readability study, helps a communicator determine whether messages are written at the right educational level for the audience. Typical measures include the Flesch Formula, the FOG Index, and the SMOG Index—all based on the concept that the greater the number of syllables in a passage, the more difficult and less readable the text.[11]

Closely related is the method of copy testing, in which target publics are exposed to public relations campaign messages to be used in brochures, memos, online, and so on in advance of their publication. This method ensures that compaign messages are understandable and effective.

Finally, case study research that analyzes how other organizations handled similar challenges is a constructive unobtrusive research method.

Clearly, there is nothing particularly mysterious or difficult about unobtrusive methods of research. Such methods are relatively simple to apply, yet they are essential for arriving at appropriate refinements for an ongoing public relations program.

Evaluation

No matter what type of public relations research is used, results of the research and the research project itself should always be evaluated. Evaluation is designed to determine what happened and why by measuring results against established objectives.

The key word in society today is *accountability*, which means taking responsibility for achieving the performance promised. With resources limited and competition fierce, managers at every level demand accountability for every activity on which they spend money. That's what evaluation is all about. Public relations professionals are obligated today to assess what they've done to determine whether the expense was worth it.

Figures and Faces—Lie

If you don't believe the old maxim that "figures lie and liars figure," consider the following: In often repeated research, randomly selected participants are shown the following two faces and asked, "Which woman is lovelier?" Invariably, the answer is split 50-50.

However, when each woman is named, one "Jennifer" and the other "Gertrude," respondents overwhelmingly—more than 80 percent—vote for Jennifer as the more beautiful woman (Figure 8-4).

Why? "Jennifer" is more hip, more happening, more, uh, "phat." (Sorry all you Gertrudes out there!)

The point is that people can't help but introduce their own biases, including even in presumably "objective" research experiments. This factor always should be taken into account in evaluating public relations research.

FIGURE 8-4   Jennifer/Gertrude.

Evaluation of public relations programs depends on several things:

● **Setting measurable public relations program objectives.**   Goals should specify who the target publics are, what impact the program seeks to have on those publics, and when the results are expected.

● **Securing management commitment.**   Public relations people and management should always agree in advance on the program's objectives, so

Reporting back to management

that the results can be clearly evaluated. Without management "buy-in" that the program is objective and well targeted, management may not believe the results.

● **Determining the best way to gather data.** Again, raw program records and observation are a rudimentary but acceptable method of evaluative measurement. Better would be attitude pre- and posttesting to determine if a particular program helped facilitate a shift in attitudes toward a program, company, or issue. Surveys may or may not be called for.

● **Reporting back to management.** Evaluation findings should be shared with management. This reinforces the notion that public relations is contributing to management goals for the organization.

● **Selecting the most appropriate outcomes.** Although public relations "outputs" are important, public relations "outcomes" are more important. Outcome evaluation may be a measurement of the press clippings a program received, that is, the number of column inches or airtime devoted to the program. A more sophisticated evaluation of program effectiveness is a content analysis of the messages conveyed as a result of the program.

Outcome evaluation measures whether targets actually *received* the messages directed to them, *paid attention* to them, *understood* the messages, *retained* those messages, and even *acted* on them.[12]

In many respects, a measurement of public relations outcomes is the most important barometer in assessing success or failure of a program.

Measuring Public Relations Outcomes

What kinds of tools are used to measure public relations outcomes? Here are four of the most common.

Awareness and Comprehension Measurement

This measurement probes whether targets received the messages directed at them, paid attention to them, and understood them. Measuring awareness and comprehension levels requires "benchmarking," or determining preliminary knowledge about a target's understanding, so that the furthering of that knowledge can be tracked. Stated another way, both "before" and "after" research should be conducted. To do this, both quantitative (e.g., surveys and polls) and qualitative (e.g., focus groups and interviews) methods should be applied.

Recall and Retention Measurement

This is a commonly used technique in advertising in which sponsors want to know if their commercials have lasting impact.

Such measurement analysis may be equally important in public relations. It is one thing for a target to have seen and understood a message but quite another for someone to remember what was said. In applying such follow-up research, it is also instructive to see if targets can differentiate between public relations and advertising media. In other words, did the target audience retain the knowledge through media stories, speeches, presentations, or ads?

Attitude and Preference Measurement

Even more important than how much someone retained from a message is a measure of how the message moved an individual's attitudes, opinions, and preferences. This involves the areas of opinion research and attitude research. The former is easier, in that it can be realized simply by asking a few preference questions. The latter, however, is derived from more complex variables, such as predispositions, feelings, and motivational tendencies regarding the issue in question. Preference measurement is often derived by listing alternative choices and asking respondents to make decisions about their relative worth.

Behavior Measurements

This is the ultimate test of effectiveness. Did the message get people to vote for our candidate, buy our product, or agree with our ideas?

Measuring behavior in public relations is difficult, especially in "proving" that a certain program "caused" the desired outcome to occur. In other words, how do we know that it was our input in particular that caused people to contribute more to our charity, or legislators to vote for our issue, or an editor to report favorably on our organization? So although it's difficult to measure causation in public relations behavioral research, it's less difficult to show correlations of outcomes with public relations activity.[13]

Regardless of the evaluative technique, by evaluating after the fact, researchers can learn how to improve future efforts. Were the right target audiences surveyed? Were the correct research assumptions applied to those audiences? Were questions from research tools left unanswered?

Again, research results can be evaluated in a number of ways. Unfortunately, the most common method in public relations may be "seat-of-the-pants" evaluation, in which anecdotal observation and practitioner judgment are used to estimate the effectiveness of the public relations program. Such evaluation might be based on feedback from members of a key public, personal media contacts, or colleagues, but the practitioner alone evaluates the success of the program with subjective observation.

An ongoing system for monitoring public relations activities is yet another way to evaluate programs. Monitoring a public relations campaign, for example, may indicate necessary changes in direction, reallocation of resources, or redefinition of priorities. Another way to evaluate is to dissect public programs after the fact. Such postmortem evaluation can provide objective analysis when a program is still fresh in one's mind. This can be extremely helpful in modifying the program for future use.

In the fiercely competitive, resource-dear 21st century, the practice of public relations will increasingly be called on to justify its activities and evaluate the results of its programs.

Research and the Web

Although to a college student the Internet seems like it's been around forever, it actually is still in its infancy. That means that research techniques in evaluating the effectiveness of programs and products on the Web are also in their infancy.

Evaluating Web Sites

In assessing the impact of the Web, the two most frequent research terms discussed are *hits* and *eyeballs*. The former refers to the number of times a Web site is visited by an individual. The latter refers to the orbital lobes affixed to that hit. Obviously, these are but the most rudimentary of measurement tools in that they don't assess the visitors' interest in the product or service or information conveyed, the duration of their stay at the site, or whether they had the inclination to take the next step—buy the product, subscribe to the service, or vote for the candidate. Indeed, the first 5,000 hits to a new Web site may mean nothing more than the firm's employees checking out the latest communications tool.

In light of this inherent problem in extracting value from Web site measurement data, the best advice is to begin by identifying the key questions the Web site sponsor wants answered. For example:

- How much traffic is coming to the site?
- What pages are people looking at?
- How often do they go beyond the homepage?
- What is it they find most useful and interesting?
- What parts never get looked at?
- Where do visitors come from?
- Is the site functioning as expected—for advertisers, sales leads, requests, and so on?[14]

Value of Web Research

Over time, research sophistication in evaluating Web content and services will develop. Indeed, there has already been a host of Web measurement techniques introduced—from page impressions to chat impressions to stream impressions to interactive impressions—and many others far beyond the scope of this book, not to mention the knowledge of this author!

Like everything else associated with the Internet, measurement techniques will develop rapidly. Consider the additional contributions Web research offers:

- **Intimacy.** Site-based research can bring organizations closer to their constituents.
- **Precision.** Web-based research can provide more detailed answers about consumers than traditional research methods.
- **Timeliness.** Web-based research is eminently more timely than traditional methods.
- **Cost.** Web-based research will reduce costs considerably compared to traditional surveying methods.[15]

Web Research Considerations

The value of Web-oriented research is indisputable. In preparing for such Internet evaluation—just as in preparing for any public relations research—an organization should take several factors into consideration first:

1. *Establish objectives.* Again, implicit in any meaningful measurement is the setting of objectives. Why are we on the Web? What is our site designed to do? What are we attempting to communicate?
2. *Determine criteria.* Define success with tangible data; for example, percentage of people likely to purchase from the site and positive interactive publication mentions that the site will receive.
3. *Determine benchmarks.* Project the hits the site will receive. Base this on competitive data to see how this site stacks up against the competition or other forms of communication.
4. *Select the right measurement tool.* Numerous software packages exist and are being developed to track site traffic. Maybe using a survey on the site is a more meaningful measurement or maybe more than one tool is called for.
5. *Compare results to objectives.* Success of online marketing and communications cannot be concluded in a vacuum. Numbers of visitors, hits, and eyeballs must be correlated with original objectives. If the objective is to

Online Public Relations Resources

You say you want to use the Net for additional public relations knowledge? (How could you need more knowledge, when you're reading the world's greatest public relations textbook?!? Just kidding.)

Well, here is where you might turn.

Free Publicity
6 Horizon Road
Fort Lee, NJ 07024
www.PublicityInsider.com

The Holmes Report
www.holmesreport.com

Interactive Public Relations
316 North Michigan Avenue
Suite 300
Chicago, IL 60601
www.ragan.com/ipr

Media Bridge Newsletter
www.themediabridge.com

Media Relations Insider
5900 Hollis Street
Suite R2
Emeryville, CA 94608
www.infocomgroup.com/mri.html

O'Dwyer's Newsletter
271 Madison Avenue
New York, NY 10016
www.odwyerpr.com

Online PR Workshop
316 North Michigan Avenue
Suite 300
Chicago, IL 60601
www2.ragan.com/onlinepr/4

PR Intelligence Report
316 N. Michigan Avenue
Chicago, IL 60601
www.ragan.com/pri

PR Reporter
P.O. Box 600
Exeter, NH 03833-0600
www.prpublishing.com

PR WEEK (UK)
174 Hammersmith Road
London, ENGLAND W6 /JP
www.prweek.com

PR WEEK (US)
PR Publications Ltd.
220 Fifth Avenue
14th Floor
New York, NY 10001
www.prweek.com

Ragan Report
316 North Michigan Avenue
Suite 300
Chicago, IL 60601
www.ragan.com

The Source and **Strategic Communications Management**
First Floor, Chelsea Reach, 79-89 Lots Road, London SW10 0RN.
www.melcrum.com

The Strategist/PR Tactics
33 Irving Place
New York, NY 10003-2376
www.prsa.org

Web Content Report
316 North Michigan Avenue
Suite 300
Chicago, IL 60601
www.ragan.com/wcr

Courtesy of the Council of Public Relations.

strengthen investor relations, then determine how many visitors made their way to the annual report and how long they stayed reading it. Combine that information with the cost to print the annual report, and this will help determine how much money the Web might save the company.

6. *Draw actionable conclusions.* Research indicates you've received 100,000 visitors to the site. So what? Interpret the significance of the numbers and do something with the data to make progress.[16]

Finally, in terms of researching the Web, consider the aspect of monitoring what is being said about the organization. With the proliferation of rogue sites, antibusiness chat rooms and newsgroups, and chain letter e-mail campaigns, monitoring the Web has become a frontline public relations responsibility. The Internet has been called the "great equalizer," which means that all individuals can have their say—mean, nasty, belligerent—and organizations must constantly keep track of what is being said about them.[17]

Using Outside Research Help

Despite its occasional rough spots, public relations research has made substantial gains in quantifying the results of public relations activities. Counseling firms have organized separate departments to conduct attitude and opinion surveys as well as other types of research projects.

Ketchum Public Relations, for example, has devised a computer-based measurement system that evaluates public relations results on both a quantitative and qualitative basis. The Ketchum system focuses on the differences in placement of publicity, that is, where in a periodical publicity has a better chance of being noticed. Although the Ketchum system cannot predict attitudinal or behavioral change, it is a step forward in providing practitioners with a mechanism to assess the extent to which their publicity has been seen.

Interactive public relations specialists have emerged to help monitor organizational references on the Web. Some outside agencies even volunteer to launch "whisper" campaigns in chat rooms to neutralize negative or inaccurate messages about clients.

It often makes sense to use outside counsel for research assistance. Once a firm is hired, public relations professionals should avoid the temptation of writing the questions or influencing the methodology. The best contribution a public relations practitioner can make to an outside-directed research endeavor is to state the objectives of the project clearly and then stand back and let the pros do the job.[18]

Often, before turning to outside consultants, the best first step is to determine whether research has already been done on your topic. Because research assistance is expensive, it makes little sense to reinvent the wheel. It is much wiser to piggyback on existing research.

LAST WORD

Research is a means of both defining problems and evaluating solutions. Even though intuitive judgment remains a coveted and important skill, management must see measurable results.

Nonetheless, informed managements recognize that public relations may never reach a point at which its results can be fully quantified. Management confidence is still a prerequisite for active and unencumbered programs. Indeed, the best measurement of public relations value is a strong and unequivocal endorsement from management that it supports the public relations effort. However, such confidence can only be enhanced as practitioners become more adept in using research.

Frankly, practitioners don't have a choice. With efficiency driving today's bottom line and with communications about organizations percolating at a 24/7 clip around the world through a variety of media, organizations must always know where they stand. It is the job of public relations to keep track, record, and research changing attitudes and opinions about the organizations for which they work. Therefore, it will become increasingly incumbent on public relations people to reinforce the value of what they do and what they stand for through constantly measuring their contribution to their organization's goals.[19]

Discussion Starters

1. Why is research important in public relations work?
2. What are the differences between primary and secondary research?
3. What are the four elements of a survey?
4. What is the difference between random and stratified sampling?
5. What are the keys to designing an effective questionnaire?
6. What is a communication audit?
7. What kinds of tools are used to measure public relations outcomes?
8. Why is evaluation important in public relations research?
9. What kinds of questions are pertinent in evaluating a Web site?
10. What is the first factor that should be considered in conducting Web-based research?

TOP OF THE SHELF

Internet Search Engines

The Internet and the continuous proliferation of Web sites have revolutionized every aspect of research, including the typical research tasks faced by public relations practitioners. Businesses and organization can even keep tabs on their competitors and opponents. Enormous databases—including those of hundreds of government agencies—are easily accessible, often for free. Most standard directories are also available online, and for obvious reasons they are more up-to-date than their print versions.

A selection of some of the Web sites commonly used by public relations researchers is included in Suggested Readings. Most of them also provide numerous links to related Web sites.

Search engines are the researcher's Holy Grail. Search engines allow you to search the contents of the World Wide Web, usenet groups, and other Internet data. Once you keyboard in a search term, you receive a list of items that match your query. Here are the leading search engines:

- AltaVista. www.altavista.digital.com. (Digital Equipment Corp.)
- HotBot. www.hotbot.com. The favorite search engine of Shel Holtz, author of *Public Relations on the Net* (see Chapter 10).
- InfoSeek. www.infoseek.com. A combination index and engine.
- Lycos. www.lycos.com. A combination index and engine.
- Search.Com. www.search.com. An index of search engines and indexes.
- Yahoo! www.yahoo.com. Considered by many the best of the search indexes, including other elements such as news, weather, and maps.
- Google. www.google.com. Like Yahoo!, Google is a comprehensive and immensely helpful search engine—at times overwhelming unless you know how to refine your search criteria.

CASE STUDY

Researching a Position for Alan Louis General

The administrator at Alan Louis General Hospital confronted a problem that he hoped research could help solve. Alan Louis General, although a good hospital, was smaller and less well known than most other hospitals in Bangor, Maine. In its area alone, it competed with 20 other medical facilities. Alan Louis needed a "position" that it could call unique to attract patients to fill its beds.

For a long time, the Alan Louis administrator, Sven Rapcorn, had believed in the principle that truth will win out. Build a better mousetrap, and the world will beat a path to your door. Erect a better hospital, and your beds will always be 98 percent filled. Unfortunately, Rapcorn learned, the real world seldom recognizes truth at first blush.

In the real world, more often than not, perception will triumph. Because people act on perceptions, those perceptions become reality. Successful positioning, Rapcorn learned, is based on recognizing and dealing with people's perceptions. And so, Rapcorn set out with research to build on existing perceptions about Alan Louis General.

He decided to conduct a communications audit to help form a differentiable "position" for Alan Louis General.

INTERVIEW PROCESS

As a first step, Rapcorn talked to his own doctors and trustees to gather data about their perceptions, not only of Alan Louis General, but also of other hospitals in the community. He did this to get a clear and informed picture of where competing hospitals ranked in the minds of knowledgeable people.

For example, the University Health Center had something for everybody—exotic care, specialized care, and basic bread-and-butter care. Bangor General was a huge, well-respected hospital whose reputation was so good that only a major tragedy could shake its standing in the community. Mercy Hospital was known for its trauma center. And so on.

As for Alan Louis itself, doctors and trustees said that it was a great place to work, that excellent care was provided, and that the nursing staff was particularly friendly and good. The one problem, everyone agreed, was that "nobody knows about us."

ATTRIBUTE TESTING

The second step in Rapcorn's research project was to test attributes important in health care. He did this to learn what factors community members felt were most important in assessing hospital care.

Respondents were asked to rank eight factors in order of importance and to tell Rapcorn and his staff how each of the surveyed hospitals rated on those factors. The research instrument used a semantic differential scale of 1 to 10, with 1 the worst and 10 the best possible score. Questionnaires were sent to two groups: 1,000 area residents and 500 former Alan Louis patients.

RESULTS TABULATION

The third step in the research was to tabulate the results in order to determine community priorities.

Among area residents who responded, the eight attributes were ranked accordingly:

1. Surgical care—9.23
2. Medical equipment—9.20
3. Cardiac care—9.16
4. Emergency services—8.96
5. Range of medical services—8.63

6. Friendly nurses—8.62
7. Moderate costs—8.59
8. Location—7.94

After the attributes were ranked, the hospitals in the survey were ranked for each attribute. On advanced surgical care, the most important feature to area residents, Bangor General ranked first, with University Health Center a close second. Alan Louis was far down on the list. The same was true of virtually every other attribute. Indeed, on nursing care, an area in which its staff thought Alan Louis excelled, the hospital came in last in the minds of area residents. Rapcorn was not surprised. The largest hospitals in town scored well on most attributes; Alan Louis trailed the pack.

However, the ranking of hospital scores according to former Alan Louis patients revealed an entirely different story. On surgical care, for example, although Bangor General still ranked first, Alan Louis came in a close second. Its scores improved similarly on all other attributes. In fact, in nursing care, where Alan Louis came in last on the survey of area residents, among former patients its score was higher than that of any other hospital. It also ranked first in terms of convenient location and second in terms of costs, range of services, and emergency care.

CONCLUSIONS AND RECOMMENDATIONS

The fourth step in Rapcorn's research project was to draw some conclusions to determine what the data had revealed.

He reached three conclusions:

1. Bangor General was still number one in terms of area hospitals.
2. Alan Louis ranked at or near the top on most attributes, according to those who actually experienced care there.
3. Former Alan Louis patients rated the hospital significantly better than the general public did.

In other words, thought Rapcorn, most of those who try Alan Louis like it. The great need was to convince more people to try the hospital.

But how could this be accomplished with a hospital? Other marketers generate trial by sending free samples in the mail, offering cents-off coupons, holding free demonstrations, and the like. Hospitals are more limited in this area. Rapcorn's challenge was to launch a communications campaign to convince prospects to see other area hospitals in a different, less favorable light or to give people a specific reason to think about trying Alan Louis. In other words, he needed to come up with a communications strategy that clearly differentiated Alan Louis—admittedly, among the smallest of area hospitals—from the bigger, less personal hospitals. Rapcorn was confident that the data he had gathered from the research project were all he needed to come up with a winning idea.

He then set out to propose his recommendations.

Questions

1. What kind of communications program would you launch to accomplish Rapcorn's objectives?
2. What would be the cornerstone—the theme—of your communications program?
3. What would be the specific elements of your program?
4. In launching the program, what specific steps would you follow—both inside and outside the hospital—to build support?

5. How could you use the Internet to conduct more research about area hospitals and residents' perceptions of the care at these hospitals? How could you use the Internet to research the effectiveness of the communications program you implement?

TIPS FROM THE TOP

An Interview with Paul Swift

Paul Swift

Paul Swift is editor and publisher of *The Newsletter on Newsletters*, subtitled "News, Views, Trends and Techniques for the Newsletter and Specialized Information Professional." He is also an accomplished editor in the field of public relations, having served for years as managing editor of *Public Relations Quarterly* and as a contributing editor of *Public Relations Strategist*.

As a research vehicle, what do subscription newsletters offer the PR professional?
Subscription newsletters have been called "the purist form of journalism" because they provide highly targeted news, information, and advice underwritten not by advertisers but by the readers themselves through subscriptions. (And that's one reason why newsletters command relatively high subscription prices: Readers are paying for original information in their niche markets.)

What is the value of such newsletters?
Their value falls roughly into two categories: (1) research and (2) professional development. As far as research goes—research at its most basic level—many newsletters keep PR pros up-to-the-minute with media relations contacts and upcoming features.

The Infocom Group (www.infocomgroup.com) publishes *Bulldog Reporter* in Western and Eastern editions, *Lifestyle Media-Relations Reporter*, and *Media Relations Insider*. Lawrence Ragan Communications (www.ragan.com) publishes *Ragan's Media Relations Report* among its 17 newsletters for PR people. These newsletters and others like them save countless hours of research into finding the current contacts and needs of media outlets. No more misguided press releases.

Other newsletters provide professional development in the form of the latest theories and case studies—*PR Reporter*, "The Newsletter of Behavioral Public Relations, Public Affairs & Communications Strategies" (www.prpublishing.com) and *PR News* (www.PBIMedia.com) come easily to mind. For those involved in crisis communications and management, *Jim Lukaszewski's Executive Action* newsletter and Web site (www.e911.com), are very informative.

Why is professional development necessary?
Those PR people who are currently out of work because they didn't keep up with the seismic changes in the industry and in communications in general understand why.

You can increase your Internet IQ with such newsletter titles as *Ragan's Internet Report*, *Ragan's Web Content Report*, and Larry Chase's free online *Web Digest for Marketers* (www.wdfm.com).

Lisa Skriloff's Multicultural Marketing News (www.multicultural.com) is a free newsletter that helps PR pros stay current with media contacts among the nation's "minority" media. Other "publicity leads" newsletters also target specific audiences, such as *Frank Scott's Travel Publicity Leads* (www.scottamerican.com).

Doesn't it cost a lot of money to subscribe to most of these newsletters?
Yes, some of them range from $300 to $500 per year. But compare that with a conference fee (and travel and hotel) that brings you information, which is often dated by the time you get back to your office. With newsletters, the news, information, and advice you receive are today's (and often tomorrow's) news, information, and advice at less than the price—as they used to say even before $3.00 lattes—of a cup of coffee a day.

(Continued)

Isn't most of this type of information available free on the Internet?
There have to be hundreds of free e-newsletters as well as Web sites to satisfy every PR person's needs.

Experts routinely agree that a professional's most precious asset is time, and we all know how much time you can fritter away surfing the Web, sifting through what invariably turn out to be self-promotion efforts disguised as "newsletters." Newsletter editors still believe in the old-fashioned role of an editor—to find and distill today's most pressing news and information and analyze its importance for readers who don't have the time and resources to do this.

What free Web sites do you recommend?
One outstanding example is Jack O'Dwyer's www.odwyerpr.com. I think it ranks at the top of Web sites in any field. Jack offers news stories from his newsletters, hundreds of reviewed books, commentary and advice from industry leaders, PR firm rankings, PR jobs, and much, much more—including, I guess I should add, much advertising.

Another valuable free Web site is Katie Payne's www.themeasurementstandard.com, "the international newsletter of PR measurement."

What's your favorite newsletter?
I'd have to say that *Sex Over Forty* has a certain appeal, but, then again, *The Newsletter on Newsletters* is also dear to my heart.

Suggested Readings

Barzun, Jacques, and Henry F. Graff. *The Modern Researcher*, 6th ed. Ft. Worth, TX: HBJ College Publications, 2002.

Bell, Quentin. "Beware of Sailing into the Shallow Sea of Research," *Marketing* (February 19, 1998): 7. Discusses the superficiality behind surveys and public relations research.

Berger, Arthur Asa. *Media Research Techniques*, 2nd ed. Thousand Oaks, CA: Sage Publications, 1998.

Boyatis, Richard E. *Transforming Qualitative Information*. Thousand Oaks, CA: Sage Publications, 1998.

Broom, Glen M., and David M. Dozier. *Using Research in Public Relations: Applications to Program Management*. Upper Saddle River, NJ: Prentice Hall, 1996.

www.businesswire.com. Business Wire, "The International Media Relations Wire Service," offers news releases on major U.S. corporations, including a majority of Fortune 500 and NASDAQ companies.

Erikson, Robert, and Kent L. Tedin, *American Public Opinion, Its Origin, Contents and Impact*, 6th ed. New York, NY: Longman, 2000.

Fink, Arlene, and Jacqueline Kosecoff. *How to Conduct Surveys: A Step-by-Step Guide*, 2nd ed. Thousand Oaks, CA: Sage Publications, 1998.

Fowler, Floyd J., Jr. *Survey Research Methods*, 2nd ed. Newbury Park, CA: Sage Publications, 2002.

Hoover's Handbooks of: American Business, Major U.S. Companies, World Business, Emerging Companies, and Private Companies. Austin, TX: Hoover's Inc. www.hoovers.com features Hoover's Online: The Business Network. Profiles of more than 12,000 public and private companies.

www.infopls.com. Updated daily, the venerable *Information Please Almanac's* Web site also includes data from *Information Please Sports Almanac, Entertainment Almanac, Columbia Encyclopedia*, and *Infoplease Dictionary*. It also offers hyperlinks to key subject areas.

Lehman, Carol M., William Himstreet, and Wayne Baty. *Business Communications*, 11th ed. Cincinnati, OH: South-Western College Publishing, 1996.

Marcoulides, George A., ed. *Modern Methods for Business Research*. Mahwah, NJ: Lawrence Erlbaum Associates Inc., 1998.

www.marketingsource.com/associations. The Marketing Resource Center's Associations Database provides a directory of business-related associations around the world.

The Markets Directory. Dobbs Ferry, NY: Dobbs Directories, 1993.

www.mediainfo.com. *Editor & Publisher* magazine makes it easy to find online news pages anywhere in the world, and its database offers access to more than 11,000 Web sites.

Nos, Danny. *Public Relations Research, An International Perspective*. London, England: International Thomson Business Press, 1997.

www.odwyerpr.com. *Jack O'Dwyer's Newsletter* offers online logos, agency statements, and complete listings of 550 PR firms. There is no cost for accessing any part of the Web site, including news from the newsletter and other publications, hyperlinks to articles on PR, job listings, and more than 1,000 PR services in 58 categories.

Pavlik, John V. *Public Relations: What Research Tells Us*. Newbury Park, CA: Sage Publications, 1987. Old but a classic in the field.

Rea, Louis M., et al. *Designing and Conducting Survey Research: A Comprehensive Guide*. San Francisco: Jossey-Bass Publishers, 1997.

Rossi, Peter H., and Howard E. Freeman. *Evaluation: A Systematic Approach*, 5th ed. Newbury Park, CA: Sage Publications, 1999.

Rubenstein, Sondra Miller. *Surveying Public Opinion*. Belmont, CA: Wadsworth Publishing, 1995.

Schwab, Donald P. *Research Methods for Organizational Studies*. Mahwah, NJ: Lawrence Erlbaum Associates, 1998.

Stacks, Don W. *Primer of Public Relations Research*. New York, NY: Guilford Press, 2002.

Sudman, Seymour. *Thinking About Answers: The Application of Cognitive Process to Survey Methodology*. San Francisco: Jossey-Bass Publishers, 1996.

Tourangeau, Roger, Lance Rips, and Kenneth Rasinski. *The Psychology of Survey Response*. Cambridge Universisty Press, 2000.

www.world-chambers.com. The World Network of Chambers of Commerce and Industry features a global index of chambers of commerce and chambers for international business development.

Notes

1. Jennifer Nedeff, "The Bottom Line Beckons: Quantifying Measurement in Public Relations," *Journal of Corporate Public Relations Northwestern University* (1996–1997): 34.
2. Lisa Richter and Steve Drake, "Apply Measurement Mindset to Programs," *Public Relations Journal* (January 1993): 32.
3. John V. Pavlik, *Public Relations: What Research Tells Us* (Newbury Park, CA: Sage, 1987): 16.
4. Walter K. Lindenmann, "Setting Minimum Standards for Measuring Public Relations Effectiveness," *Public Relations Review* (Winter 1997): 394–395.
5. Walter K .Lindenmann, "Opinion Research: How It Works; How to Use It," *Public Relations Journal* (January 1977): 13.

6. Walter K. Lindenmann, *Attitude and Opinion Research: Why You Need It, How to Do It*, 3rd ed. (Washington, D.C.: Council for Advancement and Support of Education, 1983): 35–38.

7. David L. Nasser, "How to Run a Focus Group," *Public Relations Journal* (March 1988): 33–34.

8. "The Delphi: A Forecasting Methodology You Can Use to Generate Expert Opinion on Any Subject," *PR Reporter* (June 29, 1992): 3.

9. Joseph A. Kopec, "Tips and Techniques: The Communications Audit," Public Relations Society of America Professional Practice Center.

10. Seymour Hamilton, "Selling the CEO on a Communication Audit," *IABC Communication World* (May 1988): 33.

11. Pavlik, *Public Relations*, 39.

12. "Guidelines and Standards for Measuring and Evaluating PR Effectiveness," The Institute for Public Relations Commission on PR Measurement and Evaluation (1997): 5.

13. Ibid.

14. Bill Zoellick, "Who, What, Why Important to Know about Web Visitors," *The Boulder County Business Reporter* (Summer 2000).

15. Michael Krauss, "Research and the Web: Eyeballs or Smiles?" *Marketing News* (December 7, 1998): 18.

16. Katherine D. Paine and Beth Roed, "The Basics of Internet Measurement," *Ragan's Interactive PR* (March 1999): 7.

17. Don Middleberg, "The Dark Side of the Net," *Reputation Management* (October 1997): 70–72.

18. Andrea L. Simpson, "Ten Rules of Research," *Public Relations Quarterly* (Summer 1992): 27–28.

19. Nedeff, "The Bottom Line Beckons."

When was the last time I have referred to it

Does I have some legal work to it

PART III The Publics

Chapter 9

Print Media Relations

To most people, the term public relations *is synonymous with two things: dealing with the press and getting publicity.*

Indeed, modern public relations practice got its start as an adjunct to journalism, with former press people, such as Ivy Lee, hired to refine the image of well-to-do clients. In the old days (before 1990), most of the professionals who entered the practice of public relations were former journalists.

Today, of course, with public relations professionals emanating from many different fields of study and directly from the university, the field is no longer dominated by former journalists. Nonetheless, the importance of the media to the practice of public relations cannot be denied.

Put simply, if you're in public relations, you must know how to deal with the press.

Therein lies the problem, because in the 21st century, the "press" has changed, often for the worst. As Presidential Press Secretary Ari Fleischer has said:

> *I think we've reached a point where the press, in pursuit of its devil's advocate role, would do well to ask itself, are they "informing" the public or are they being so negative about the institutions they cover, that they're not covering all the news, but only the "bad news."*[1]

This "devil's advocate" role is the key to why many don't like the press.

The media, by definition, challenge authority with pointed, nasty, even hostile questions. Their proper role in a democracy is to independently ferret out the truth. Often this means "breaking eggs" in the process.

Consider the following:

- *In 2001, the media were unmerciful in hounding an obscure California congressman suspected of having an affair with a missing intern. Eventually, the scrutiny caused the downfall of Rep. Gary Condit, who bitterly denounced the press on his way out of Washington.*[2]

- *Also in 2001 when celebrity public relations counselor Lizzie Grubman crashed her $70,000 Mercedes-Benz into a crowd of people outside a Long Island night club, the press dubbed her the "PR princess" and headlined*

FIGURE 9-1   **Facing the music.** Dubbed the "PR princess" by the tabloids, public relations executive Lizzie Grubman arrives in court.

each clumsy step she took to get off the hook as "The Curse of the PR Gal"[3] (Figure 9-1).

● *In 2002, when baseball slugger Ted Williams passed away and his son, against the wishes of the rest of the family, had the body shipped to a cryonics lab in Arizona, the media made a mockery of the family's travails. Williams's daughter Claudia was incensed, and called the press reports "terribly hurtful and simply not true."[4] The media weren't fazed.*

● *And when CEOs were cornered in the scandals of the summer of 2002, the press refused to let up on the likes of Enron's Ken Lay, Global Crossing's Gary Winnick, WorldCom's Bernie Ebbers, and Martha Stewart's Martha Stewart.*

What all this means is that dealing with the press has never been more challenging. When one adds the growing impact of Internet journalism, where 70 percent accuracy is considered acceptable, dealing with the media has become a high-risk business.

This is the business of the public relations professional, who serves as the first line of defense and explanation with respect to the media. It is the public relations practitioner who meets the reporter head-on. In the 21st century, this is not a job for the squeamish.

Number One Medium

Despite the growth of the Internet and electronic media, print still stands as the number one medium among public relations professionals.

Why?

The answer probably lies in the fact that many departments at newspapers and magazines use news releases and other publicity vehicles compared to the limited opportunities on network TV. Because online databases also use wire service material destined for print usage, the Internet often serves as a residual target compared to print.

In this context, the media—particularly the print media—constitute a critically important public for public relations professionals. Print sets the media agenda.

It is no secret that as the Internet and MTV generations have become dominant members of society, newspaper readership has slipped in the United States and around the world. The world's two biggest economies, the United States and Japan, both have experienced declines in readership, as has the European Union.[5]

The better news, though, is that after September 11, 2001, newspapers in the United States experienced a resurgence. People were eager to learn of developments in the aftermath of the tragedy and to be updated on the government's response. While some of the nation's largest circulation papers, among them *USA Today*, the *Wall Street Journal*, and the *New York Times*, all showed gains, others such as the *Los Angeles Times* and *San Francisco Chronicle* slipped in circulation[6] (Table 9-1).

Although the media's image also improved, after its supportive posture, after September 11, 2001 public confidence in the media dissipated as time wore on. Less than a year after the terrorist attacks, research indicated that Americans had become considerably disenchanted with the media.

- 49% considered the media "highly professional," compared to 73% after 9/11.
- 49% rated the media "patriotic," compared to 69% after 9/11.
- 59% considered the media "politically biased," compared to 47% after 9/11.
- 35% believed the news media "don't care" about the people they report on, while 47% found them compassionate after 9/11.[7]

The significance of these data is that although the public is reading and listening and viewing the media, its faith and trust in the press are limited.

In the United States today, 1,772 daily newspapers are published, with a total circulation of 55 million daily. In terms of readership, according to the Newspaper Association of America, total daily readership is more than 76 million and total Sunday readership is more than 89.5 million.[8]

There are 17,321 magazines published in the United States today, according to the National Directory of Magazines. After a rough stretch in the mid-1990s, magazine readership is on the increase again with specialty publications leading the way.

With so many print outlets—newspapers, magazines, and online publications—the waterfront for public relations publicity is broad and deep.

Power of Publicity

Whether the mass media have lost relative influence to other proliferating alternative communications vehicles or not, the fact remains that securing positive publicity through the media still lies at the heart of public relations practice.

TABLE 9-1

Top 100 Daily Newspapers in the United States by Circulation

Rank	Newspaper	Daily	Sunday	Rank	Newspaper	Daily	Sunday
1.	USA Today[1]	2,120,357	2,575,423	51.	(Oklahoma City) Daily Oklahoman	217,523	290,742
2.	Wall Street Journal[1]	1,820,525	None	52.	Hartford Courant*	203,306	288,814
3.	New York Times*	1,176,762	1,735,059	53.	(Norfolk) Virginian-Pilot*	199,984	232,139
4.	Los Angeles Times*	985,798	1,394,544	54.	Cincinnati Enquirer*	198,869	310,279
5.	Washington Post*	799,159	1,069,656	55.	Omaha World-Herald	193,727	241,892
6.	(New York) Daily News*	705,510	810,112	56.	Richmond Times-Dispatch	193,582	232,117
7.	Chicago Tribune*	618,006	1,016,103	57.	St. Paul Pioneer Press*	190,786	247,517
8.	Newsday (Long Island, NY)*	553,182	664,288	58.	Arkansas Democrat-Gazette (Little Rock)	190,543	291,453
9.	Houston Chronicle	545,727	738,456	59.	(Nashville) Tennessean*	188,128	258,323
10.	New York Post*	537,812	403,195	60.	Austin American-Statesman	187,754	238,714
11.	Dallas Morning News*	529,617	776,868	61.	(Bergen County, NJ) Record	187,247	230,889
12.	San Francisco Chronicle*	516,939	536,816	62.	Riverside (CA) Press-Enterprise	184,562	189,095
13.	(Phoenix) Arizona Republic	495,373	601,885	63.	Contra Costa (CA) Times	184,440	192,340
14.	Boston Globe*	473,406	705,017	64.	Palm Beach (FL) Post	180,081	223,569
15.	Chicago Sun-Times*	459,098	382,471	65.	Rochester Democrat & Chronicle	175,194	235,779
16.	Atlanta Journal-Constitution[2]	430,981	660,445	66.	(Memphis) Commercial Appeal*	175,035	235,596
17.	(Newark) Star-Ledger*	393,998	608,511	67.	(Los Angeles) Daily News*	174,278	200,161
18.	Detroit Free Press[2]	393,574	740,513	68.	Las Vegas Review-Journal[2]	173,915	223,922
19.	(Minneapolis) Star Tribune*	375,807	669,290	69.	Raleigh News & Observer*	172,332	210,922
20.	Philadelphia Inquirer*	370,108	760,026	70.	Florida Times-Union (Jacksonville)	172,011	231,085
21.	(Denver) Rocky Mountain News*	369,696	795,049	71.	Asbury Park Press	167,658	227,606
22.	(Cleveland) Plain Dealer	368,322	479,355	72.	Fresno Bee	164,815	194,551
23.	San Diego Union-Tribune	367,629	450,489	73.	Providence Journal	165,065	232,040
24.	Denver Post*	364,497	795,049	74.	Seattle Post-Intelligencer*	161,638	473,232
25.	St. Petersburg Times	352,772	440,049	75.	Birmingham News*	157,240	190,259
26.	(Portland) Oregonian*	345,058	425,498	76.	Des Moines Register	152,326	243,752
27.	Miami Herald	327,105	443,752	77.	Dayton Daily News*	150,999	203,381
28.	Orange County (CA) Register	314,759	370,838	78.	Honolulu Advertiser	150,277	170,009
29.	Sacramento Bee	307,238	358,087	79.	Tulsa World	146,323	205,191
30.	Baltimore Sun*	295,870	468,377	80.	Akron Beacon Journal	143,429	187,349
31.	St. Louis Post-Dispatch	290,372	472,322	81.	Salt Lake City Tribune	142,567	162,250
32.	Detroit News[2]	289,130	740,513	82.	Grand Rapids Press	140,048	189,486
33.	San Jose Mercury News*	275,312	301,346	83.	Toledo Blade	139,766	189,981
34.	Investor's Business Daily[1]	272,563	None	84.	Philadephia Daily News*	138,347	None
35.	Kansas City Star*	271,062	379,664	85.	Tacoma News Tribune	129,219	145,868
36.	Orlando Sentinel	265,365	387,728	86.	La Opinion*	124,536	72,752
37.	South Florida Sun-Sentinel (Ft. Lauderdale)	261,822	371,957	87.	Allentown Call	123,142	167,048
38.	New Orleans Times-Picayune	259,635	290,100	88.	Syracuse (NY) Post-Standard	122,659	177,729
39.	Columbus Dispatch	253,063	372,305	89.	Knoxville News-Sentinel*	122,246	157,428
40.	Indianapolis Star	253,020	366,496	90.	Wilmington News Journal	121,264	141,969
41.	Milwaukee Journal Sentinel*	246,939	434,056	91.	The State (Columbia, SC)	120,576	153,928
42.	Boston Herald*	246,443	162,497	92.	Lexington (KY) Herald-Leader*	120,150	148,347
43.	Pittsburgh Post-Gazette*	245,423	412,271	93.	Sarasota Herald-Tribune	117,960	147,778
44.	Charlotte Observer	240,324	291,938	94.	Greensburg (PA) Tribune-Review	117,052	190,387
45.	San Antonio Express-News*	240,227	360,341	95.	East Valley Tribune (Mesa, AZ)	113,270	90,665
46.	Fort Worth Star-Telegram*	233,326	325,747	96.	Albuquerque Journal	111,714	155,929
47.	Louisville Courier-Journal	227,467	283,503	97.	Tucson (AZ) Star	106,708	177,883
48.	Seattle Times*	226,037	473,232	98.	(Spokane) Spokesman-Review*	106,651	133,272
49.	Tampa Tribune	224,921	298,623	99.	Daytona Beach (FL) News-Journal	106,078	123,218
50.	Buffalo News	220,345	302,400	100.	Charleston (SC) Post & Courier	105,667	115,858

The top 100. The nation's leading circulation newspapers, according to Luce Press Clippings.

This chapter focuses on how to coexist with the print media, with which public relations professionals deal the most. Chapter 10 addresses the electronic media. We explore here what it takes to work with the media to convey the most effective impression for an organization—that is, to attract positive publicity.

Why attract publicity?

The answer, as we will see, is that publicity is regarded as more credible than advertising. To attract positive publicity requires establishing a good working relationship with the media. This is, of course, easier said than done. In the 21st century, faced with intense competition from on-air and online journalists, print reporters are by and large more aggressive, some would argue more hostile. As National Basketball Association coach Doug Collins once put it to a reporter:

> I know what this business is all about. Let's find something we can stir up. A good story isn't fun. How many good stories do you read? How many times do you pick up something and say, "Boy, wasn't that nice," where there wasn't a slant to it? How many good stories do you read anymore?[9]

Ironically, Collins became an outstanding broadcast journalist when he stopped coaching, before returning to the bench to coach Michael Jordan's last hurrah. There is truth in Coach Collins's words.

When the media take aim at a particular individual or institution, the results can be devastating. Indeed, in 1997, it took nothing less than a $1 billion lawsuit from legendary Wall Street investor Julian Robertson to get *Business Week* magazine to acknowledge in print the inaccuracy of its hatchet job about the stock picker, sympathetically titled, "The Fall of the Wizard of Wall Street."[10] Other companies, similarly singed, have also resorted to taking legal action against news organizations.

On the other hand, when the media go to bat for an organization or individual, the rewards can be substantial. Former boxer Rubin Carter, for example, the subject of a 2000 movie, *The Hurricane*, was freed from prison after a wave of publicity called into question his murder conviction.

When the United States waged its war on terrorism in 2001, its most unlikely publicity hero was Secretary of Defense Donald Rumsfeld. A former corporate CEO who kept away from the media, Rumsfeld turned into a media darling with a candid, no nonsense, straightforward style. His weekly press conferences helped keep the media in check as the Bush administration waged its continuing war.[11]

A primary responsibility of a public relations professional vis-à-vis the media, then, is to help promote the organization when times are good and help defend the organization in times of attack. This requires a ready working knowledge of what drives the press.

Objectivity in the Media

The presumed goal of a journalist is objectivity—fairness with the intention of remaining neutral in reporting a story. But total objectivity is impossible. All of us have biases and preconceived notions about many things. Likewise, in reporting, pure objectivity is unattainable; it would require complete neutrality and near-total detachment in reporting a story. Reporting, then, despite what some journalists might suggest, is subjective. Nevertheless, scholars of journalism believe that reporters and editors should strive for maximum objectivity (Figure 9-2).

By virtue of their role, the media view officials, particularly business and government spokespersons, with a degree of skepticism. Reporters shouldn't be expected to accept on faith the party line. By the same token, once a business or government official effectively substantiates the official view and demonstrates its merit, the media should be willing to report this accurately without editorial distortion.

Stated another way, the relationship between the media and the establishment—that is, public relations people—should be one of "friendly adversaries" rather than of bitter enemies. Unfortunately, this is not always the case. According to one *Washington Post* columnist, the fault may lie with the American public:

> We are only incidentally bringing truth to the world—although don't get me wrong, from time to time we manage to do just that. But most journalists most of

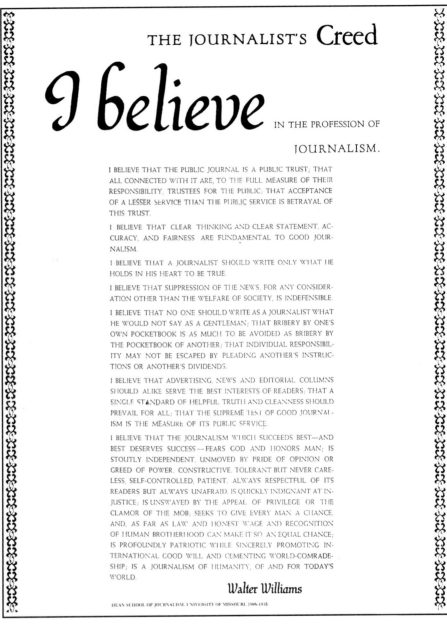

FIGURE 9-2 **Code of objectivity.** "The Journalist's Creed" was written after World War I by Dr. Walter Williams, dean of the School of Journalism at the University of Missouri.

the time are just trying to give the public what it wants—and much of the time, the public wants trash.[12]

That is not to say that the vast majority of journalists don't try to be fair. They do. Despite the preconceived biases that all of us have, most reporters want to get the facts from all sides. An increasing number of journalists acknowledge and respect the public relations practitioner's role in the process. (Some don't, but there are rotten apples in any profession.) If reporters are dealt with fairly, most will reciprocate in kind.

However, some executives fail to understand the essential difference between the media and their own organizations. That is:

1. The reporter wants the "story" whether bad or good.
2. Organizations, on the other hand, want things to be presented in the best light.

Because of this difference, some executives consider journalists to be the "enemy," dead set on revealing all the bad news they can about their organization. These people fear and distrust the media.

The Internet Factor

Further complicating the relationship between journalists and those in the news is the Internet.

To some, the Internet has ushered in a new age of journalistic reporting: immediate, freewheeling, unbridled. To others, the Internet is responsible for the collapse of journalistic standards and the ascendancy of rumor mongering.

The credit—or blame—for the rise in Internet reporting may lie with a particular journalistic creation of the late 1990s: Matt Drudge (Figure 9-3).

Mr. Drudge, a fedora-wearing, tough-talking, "new-age journalist," reported both fact and fiction parading as fact on his Web site, which at its height ranked near the top 200 sites in Web traffic each day. Occasionally, Mr. Drudge broke some big stories;

FIGURE 9-3 **Drudge as in sludge.** Be he journalistic curse or blessing, Matt Drudge had a profound influence on how the Internet impacted journalistic coverage.

for example, he was the first to report that Monica Lewinsky had retained an incriminating blue dress from her liaisons with President Clinton. The story was quickly picked up throughout the nation and turned out to be the smoking gun leading to President Clinton's impeachment.

In the end, Matt Drudge was dumped from the Fox News program he hosted when the network refused to air a photo of an unborn fetus that he wanted to display. He continued on the radio and his Web site. But the door Drudge helped open and the challenge he introduced to public relations people and the organizations they work for will not soon go away. As he put it:

> We have entered an era vibrating with the din of small voices. I envision a future where there'll be some 300 million reporters, where anyone from anywhere can report for any reason.[13]

Indeed, Internet reporters from every political bias and ulterior motive were busy 24 hours a day, seven days a week, churning out continuous stories—some true, others not—about corporations, government agencies, nonprofits, and prominent individuals.

What this suggests is that the media and the organizations they cover will likely remain on different philosophical wavelengths for some time to come. The challenge for public relations professionals is to foster a closer relationship between their organizations and those who present the news. The key, once again, is fairness, with each side accepting—and respecting—the other's role and responsibility.

Dealing with the Media

It falls on public relations professionals to orchestrate the relationship between their organizations and the media. To be sure, the media can't ordinarily be manipulated in our society. They can, however, be confronted in an honest and interactive way to convey the organization's point of view in a manner that may merit being reported. First, an organization must establish a formal media relations policy (Figure 9-4). Second, an organization must establish a philosophy for dealing with the media, keeping in mind the following dozen principles:

1. *A reporter is a reporter.*   A reporter is never "off duty." Anything you say to a journalist is fair game to be reported. Remember that and never let down your guard, no matter how friendly you are.
2. *You are the organization.*   In the old days, reporters disdained talking to public relations representatives, who they derisively labeled "flacks" (as in "catching flak" or bad news). Public relations people, therefore, were rarely quoted. Today the opposite is true. The public relations person represents the policy of an organization, so every word out of the public relations professional's mouth must be carefully weighed in advance.
3. *There is no standard issue reporter.*   The fact is that most business managers want nothing to do with the press. They believe them to be villains. But that isn't necessarily true. As noted, most are simply trying to do their jobs, like anyone else. So each should be treated as an individual, unless known to be unworthy of trust.
4. *Treat journalists professionally.*   As long as they understand that your job is different than theirs and treat you with deference, you should do likewise. A journalist's job is to get a story, whether good or bad. A public relations

Organization and Policy Guide

**Unit with Primary
Responsibility for Review** Corporate Communications

It is frequently in Chase's best interest to take advantage
of interest from the media to further the reputation and
services of the bank. In dealing with the media, Chase
officers must be careful to protect the best interests of
the bank, particularly with regard to the area of customer
confidence.

The following policies will serve as a guideline for media
relationships. Specific questions regarding the media
should be addressed to the Public Relations Division.

Inquiries from the Media

Most journalists call the Public Relations Division when
they need information about the bank or wish to arrange
an interview with a bank officer. Many times, public
relations officers are able to handle inquiries directly.
Occasionally, however, more complex questions require input from appropriate bank officers. In these cases, inas-
much as journalists are often under deadline pressures,
it is important that bank officers cooperate as fully and
respond as promptly as possible. Such cooperation enhances
Chase's reputation for integrity with the news media.

Less frequently, reporter inquiries will go directly to
line officers. In this case, either one of two responses
may be appropriate:

1. If a journalist seeks simple, factual information
   such as Chase's current rate on a particular
   savings instrument or the factual details of a
   new bank service, officers may provide it directly.

2. If a reporter seeks Chase policy or official opinion on such subjects as trends in interest rates,
   legislation, etc., responses should be reviewed
   with the Public Relations Division. If an officer
   is unfamiliar with a particular policy or requires
   clarification of it, he or she should always
   check first with the Public Relations Division
   before committing the bank in print.

In talking with a reporter, it is normally assumed that
whatever a bank officer says may be quoted and attributed
directly to him or her by name as a spokesperson for the
bank. An officer not wishing to be quoted must specify
that desire to the journalist.

FIGURE 9-4 **Media relations policy.** Every organization should have a formal policy such as the one
shown here to guide its activities with the press. Public relations should have the primary responsibility of
liaison with the media *(continued on next page)*.

person's job is to present the organization in the best light. That difference
understood, the relationship should be a professional one.

5. *Don't sweat the skepticism.* Journalists aren't paid to ask nice questions.
   They are paid to be skeptical. Some interviewees resent this. Smart
   interviewees realize it comes with the territory.

Most reporters with whom the bank deals will respect an officer's wishes to maintain anonymity. Most journalists recognize that it is as important for them to honor the wishes of their sources at the bank as it is for the bank to disseminate its comments and information to the public through the news media. Chase's policy toward the media should be one of mutual trust, understanding and benefit.

Interviews With the Media

In order to monitor the bank's relationships with journalists, all requests for interviews with bank officers by journalists must be routed through the Public Relations Division.

As a rule, public relations officers check the credentials of the journalist and determine the specific areas of inquiry to be examined. The public relations officer will then decide whether the interview is appropriate for the bank. When the decision is affirmative, the public relations officer will discuss subject matter with the recommended interviewee and together they will decide on a course of action and Chase objectives for the interview.

A member of the public relations staff is normally present during any face-to-face interview with an officer of the bank. The purpose of the public relations staffer's attendance is to provide assistance in handling the interview situation as well as to aid the reporter with follow-up material.

When a reporter calls an officer directly to request an interview, the officer should check with the Public Relations Division before making a commitment.

Authorized Spokespersons

Vice presidents and above are normally authorized to speak for the bank on matters in their own area of responsibility.

Normally, officers below the level of vice president are not authorized to speak for attribution on behalf of the bank except where they are specialists in a particular field, such as technical directors, economists, etc.

Exceptions may be made in special situations and in concert with the Public Relations Division.

Written Material for the Media

Chase articles bylined by officers may either be written by the officer approached or by a member of the public relations staff. If an officer decided to author his or her own article, the public relations division must be consulted for editing, photographic support and policy proofing.

Occasionally, customers or suppliers may wish to include Chase in an article or advertisement they are preparing. This material too must be routed through the Public Relations Division for review.

FIGURE 9-4 **(Continued)**

6. _Don't "buy" a journalist._ Never try to threaten or coerce a journalist with advertising. The line between news and advertising should be a clear one. No self-respecting journalist will tolerate someone trying to, in effect, "bribe" him or her for a positive story.

7. _Become a trusted source._ Journalists can't be "bought" but they can be persuaded by becoming a source of information for them. A reporter's job is to report on what's going on. By definition, a public relations person knows more about the company and the industry than does a reporter. So become a source and a positive relationship will follow.

8. *Talk when not "selling."*   Becoming a source means sharing information with journalists, even when it has nothing to do with your company. Reporters need leads and story ideas. If you supply them, once again a positive relationship will follow.

9. *Don't expect "news" agreement.*   A reporter's view of "news" and an organization's view of "news" will differ. If so, the journalist wins. (It's the reporter's paper, after all!) Don't complain if a story doesn't make it into print. Sometimes there is no logical reason. So never promise an executive that a story will "definitely make the paper."

10. *Don't cop a 'tude.*   Meaning, don't have an attitude with reporters. They need the information that you possess. If you're coy or standoffish or reluctant to share, they will pay you back. Although reporters vary in look and type, they all share one trait: They remember.

11. *Never lie.*   This is the cardinal rule. As one *Wall Street Journal* reporter put it, "Never lie to a reporter or that reporter will never trust you again."[14]

12. *Read the paper.*   The number-one criticism of public relations people by journalists is that they often don't have any idea what the journalist writes about. This is infuriating, especially when a journalist is approached on a story pitch. Lesson: Read the paper.

Although some may deny it, reporters, are human beings. So there is no guarantee that even if these principles are followed, that all reporters will be fair or objective. Most of the time, however, following these dozen rules of the road will lead to a better relationship between the journalist and the public relations professional.

Attracting Publicity

Publicity, through news releases and other methods, is eminently more powerful than advertising.

Publicity is most often gained by dealing directly with the media, either by initiating the communication or by reacting to inquiries. Although most people—especially CEOs!—confuse the two, publicity differs dramatically from advertising.

First and most important, advertising costs money—tens of thousands of dollars for a full-page ad in newspapers such as the *New York Times* and *Wall Street Journal*. Since you pay for your ad, advertising allows you to control the following:

- **Content:**   what is said and how it is portrayed and illustrated
- **Size:**   how large a space is devoted to the organization
- **Location:**   where in the paper the ad will appear
- **Reach:**   the audience exposed to the ad, that is, how many papers the ad is in
- **Frequency:**   how many times the ad is run

Frequency is extremely important. Today, with 500 cable and broadcast television channels, thousands of newspapers and magazines, and millions more Internet sites, people often skip over or surf by the ads or commercials. The only way to get through is to repeat the ad over and over again. In that manner, the largest advertisers—McDonald's, Microsoft, IBM—blast their way into public consciousness.

Publicity, on the other hand, offers no such controls. Typically, publicity is subject to review by news editors, who may decide to use all of a story, some of it, or none of it. Many news releases, in fact, never see the light of print.

When the story will run, who will see it, and how often it will be used are all subject to the whims of a news editor. However, even though attracting publicity is by no means a sure thing, it does offer two overriding benefits that enhance its appeal far beyond that of advertising:

- First, although not free, publicity costs only the time and effort expended by public relations personnel and management in conceiving, creating, and attempting to place the publicity effort in the media. Therefore, relatively speaking, its cost is minimal compared to advertising; rough rule of thumb is 10 percent of equivalent advertising expenditures.
- Second and more important, publicity, which appears in news rather than in advertising columns, carries the implicit—third-party—endorsement of the news source that reports it. In other words, publicity is perceived not as the sponsoring organization's self-serving view but as the view of the objective, neutral, impartial news source. For years, for example, when surveys asked people to name their "most trusted American," respondents invariably answered not the president or first lady but rather Walter Cronkite, the former news reader at CBS. Today, NBC's Tom Brokaw has become equally "trusted."

That is the credibility that a news reporter or publication enjoys. So when publicity is reported by such a source, it becomes more credible, believable, and, therefore, valuable "news."

That, in essence, is the true benefit of publicity over advertising.

Value of Publicity

For any organization, then, publicity makes great sense in the following areas:

- **Announcing a new product or service.** Because publicity can be regarded as news, it should be used before advertising commences. A new product or service is news only once. Once advertising appears, the product is no longer news. Therefore, one inflexible rule—that most organizations, unfortunately break—is that publicity should precede advertising.
- **Reenergizing an old product.** When a product has been around for a while, it's difficult to make people pay attention to advertising. Therefore, publicity techniques—staged events, sponsorships, and so on—may pay off to rejuvenate a mature product.
- **Explaining a complicated product.** Often there isn't enough room in an advertisement to explain a complex product or service. Insurance companies, banks, and mutual funds, which offer products that demand thoughtful explanation, may find advertising space too limiting. Publicity, on the other hand, allows enough room to tell the story.
- **Little or no budget.** Often organizations don't have the budget to accommodate advertising. To make an impact, advertising requires frequency—the constant repetition of ads so that readers eventually see them and acknowledge the product. In the case of Samuel Adams Lager Beer, for example, the company lacked an advertising budget to promote its unique brew. So it used public relations techniques to spread the word about this different-tasting beer. Over time, primarily through publicity about its victories at beer-tasting competitions, Samuel Adams grew in popularity. Today its advertising budget is robust, but the company's faith in publicity endures.
- **Enhancing the organization's reputation.** Advertising is, at its base, self-serving. When a company gives to charity or does a good deed in the

community, taking out an ad is the wrong way to communicate its efforts. It is much better for the recipient organization to commend its benefactor in the daily news columns.

- **Crisis response.**   In a crisis, publicity techniques are the fastest and most credible means of response. In 1996, when Texaco was charged with racism, the company took to the public airwaves to dispel the criticism. Earlier, when PepsiCo suffered its tampering scare (see Chapter 5 case study), the company launched an immediate publicity response. Only when the crisis was resolved and Pepsi had won did the company authorize ads thanking its employees and customers for their loyalty amid the turmoil.

These are just a few of the advantages of publicity over advertising. A smart organization, therefore, will always consider publicity a vital component in its overall marketing plan.

Pitching Publicity

The activity of trying to place positive publicity in a periodical—of converting publicity to news—is called "pitching." After writing the release, the following hints may help achieve placement:

1. *Know deadlines.*   Time governs every newspaper. Even with the flexibility of the computer, newspapers have different deadlines for different sections of the paper. For example, the *New York Times* business section essentially closes down between 6:00 and 7:00 P.M. News events should be scheduled, whenever possible, to accommodate deadlines. An old and despised practice (at least by journalists) is to announce bad news close to deadline time on Friday afternoon, the premise being that newspaper journalists won't have time to follow up on the story and that few people will read Saturday's paper anyway. Although this technique may work on occasion, it leaves reporters and editors feeling hostile.

2. *Generally write, don't call.*   Reporters are barraged with deadlines. They are busiest close to deadline time, which is late afternoon for morning newspapers and morning for afternoon papers. Thus, it's preferable to mail or send news releases by messenger rather than try to explain them over the telephone. Follow-up calls to reporters to "make sure you got our release" also should be avoided. If reporters are unclear on a certain point, they'll call to check.

3. *Direct the release to a specific person or editor.*   Newspapers are divided into departments: business, sports, style, entertainment, and so on. The release directed to a specific person or editor has a greater chance of being read than one addressed simply to "Editor." At smaller papers, one person may handle all financial news. At larger papers, the financial news section may have different editors for banking, chemicals, oil, electronics, and many other specialties. Public relations people should know who covers their beat and target releases accordingly.

4. *Determine how the reporter wants to be contacted.*   E-mail, mail, fax, paper, and so on. Treat the reporter as the client. How he or she prefers to get the news should guide how you deliver it.

5. *Don't badger.*   Newspapers are generally fiercely independent about the copy they use. Even a major advertiser will usually fail to get a piece of puffery published. Badgering an editor about a certain story is bad form, as is

complaining excessively about the treatment given a certain story. Worst of all, little is achieved by acting outraged when a newspaper chooses not to run a story.

6. *Use exclusives but be careful.* Reporters get credited for getting "scoops" and citing "trends." So public relations people might promise exclusive stories to particular newspapers. The exclusive promises one publication or other news source a scoop over its competitors. For example, practitioners frequently arrange to have a visiting executive interviewed by only one local newspaper. Although the chances of securing a story are heightened by the promise of an exclusive, the risk of alienating the other papers exists. Thus, the exclusive should be used sparingly.

7. *When you call, do your own calling.* Reporters and editors generally don't have assistants. Most do not like to be kept waiting by a secretary calling for the boss. Public relations professionals should make their own initial and follow-up calls. Letting a secretary handle a journalist can alienate a good news contact. Above all, be pleasant and courteous.

8. *Don't send clips of other stories about your client.* This will just suggest to the journalist that others have been there before him or her and make the story potential less attractive.

9. *Develop a relationship.* Relationships are the name of the game. The better you know a reporter, the more understanding and accommodating to your organization he or she will be.

10. *Never lie.* The cardinal rule.

Although cynics continue to predict "the end of reading as we know it," newspapers and magazines continue to endure. Although some predicted a decline in the magazine business in the 1990s, today almost 11,000 magazines are published in the United States. They range from the mainstream *Time* and *Newsweek*; to the trendy *O*, the Oprah Winfrey magazine; from the gossipy *People* and *Vanity Fair*, to publications further afield, such as *OUT*, catering to the upscale gay and lesbian market, and *Murder Dog* and *Kronick*, magazines of the hip-hop community.

The fact remains that dealing with the print media is among the most essential technical skills of the public relations professional. Anyone who practices public relations must know how to deal with the press.

Pitching Online

With online outlets increasing in numbers and use, it is important to consider nuances in terms of pitching publicity online.

- In pitching online, the place to start is with a techno-savvy media database. Such firms as Newstips, Global Internet News Agency, and the Internet News Bureau all offer services that deliver releases to cyberspace audiences.
- Don't assume that just because a reporter has an e-mail address that he or she wants to get spammed (i.e., receive unsolicited e-mail). It's best to first send a brief e-mail message, identifying yourself and inquiring whether e-mail is the preferred route to send news announcements.
- Ideally, the more you can target to a particular reporter, the better the chance the story will be used. The Internet, after all, is a more personalized medium. So the more personal the pitch, the better.

A QUESTION OF ETHICS

Stone Cold Media Burnout

In October 1999, amidst all the newfangled dot-com companies going public for zillions of investor dollars, one unique enterprise stood out among all of the other initial public offerings: the World Wrestling Federation (WWF).

The WWF was the creation of Vince McMahon, a third-generation, take-no-prisoners wrestling promoter, whose questionable "scorched-earth" policy included crushing smaller wrestling promoters and maximizing outrageous stunts to hype media attention for his 400-pound goliaths.

Under McMahon, the WWF became the biggest of big media business in the 1990s—with the highest-rated cable TV show, *Raw Is War*; the top-rated UPN Network show, *SmackDown*; the number-one home videos; high-selling action figures; and even best-selling biographies by such WWF intellectuals as Mankind and the Rock.

Through it all, McMahon and the WWF weathered publicity storms, generated by a steroid scandal, allegations of sexual misconduct, and charges (later confirmed) of how the whole thing was rigged.

By the summer of 2002, McMahon's operation—now rechristened the WWE, World Wrestling Entertainment—had decidedly hit the mat.

TV ratings plummeted. Arena attendance shrunk. One top draw in the sport, The Rock aka Dwayne Johnson, became an actor. The other top draw, Stone Cold Steve Austin aka Steve Williams, was charged with beating his wife (Figure 9-5). Worst of all, wrestling's most important viewers, 14-year-old boys, began losing interest in the whole media extravaganza.

McMahon's response to the loss of interest was to pull out all the stops. He plugged murder in to plotlines and featured more and more explicit sex. But still the decline continued. Finally, McMahon resorted to such media motivators as wrestlers simulating urinating on one another and eating their own vomit.

FIGURE 9-5 **Choke hold.** Stone Cold Steve Austin in happier times.

Although such low-brow, ethically challenged media responses may have saved the day in the past, there was real question whether this time professional wrestling may have been down for the count.

For further information, see "Wrestling Down for the Count," On the Media, National Public Radio (August 2, 2002).

● Links are vehicles that transport readers to Web sites. On the surface, a link is an image or a word that, once clicked, retrieves a file for the reader. When a link is activated, a new Web site appears on screen. Links are important publicity vehicles in that they immediately and automatically deliver audiences to a Web site being promoted. Indeed, links are the simplest way to get potentially interested parties to visit Web sites.

- E-mail newsletters in publicity efforts. Such services as AnchorDesk, Netsurfer Digest, TechWeb, InfoBeat, and IDG all deliver e-mail announcements to target publics.
- Don't ignore Web-based news sites, such as ZDNet, Mecler, and CMPNet. The online news outlets may or may not duplicate standard wire services such as Dow Jones or Reuters.
- By the way, Reuters shouldn't be ignored either. Many Web sites use Reuters as a principal news feed.
- Web libraries are but another publicity tool. The ability of the Web to cheaply store vast quantities of information online is a clear advantage over print. Online news releases or announcements can be backed up with a library of supporting data at a Web site—support files, product brochures and facilities statements, backgrounders, press kits, frequently asked questions (FAQ files), newsletters, events calendars, interview transcripts, help files, audio sound bites, video clips, press clips, and so on.[15]
- Don't forget discussion forums, where individuals discuss products and companies. Increasingly, discussion forums create the buzz for a product. Hollywood, for example, is often accused of "salting" chat rooms and discussion groups with "ringers," who will recommend a particular film.[16] Also possible are "dead chats," where guests (still very "live") answer questions that have been solicited in advance and posted in the form of an interview.
- Finally, consider the cyber-media tour, another wrinkle in online publicity. Traditional media tours link a spokesperson in a studio with TV stations around the nation. The cyber-media tour links the spokesperson with television, radio, Web site, and print journalists via satellite, the Web, and telephone simultaneously. Thus, the cyber-media tour takes advantage of streaming video and audio, both gaining exponentially in Web usage.

Although establishing a relationship with online reporters may not be as easy as with print journalists because of the physical remoteness, the same principle still holds: The closer you are to reporters, the more fairly they will treat you.

Dealing with the Wires

Wire services are a compulsory vehicle for distributing news.

The Associated Press, with more than 15,000 clients worldwide, is the most traditional of wire services. It and the three primary financial wires—Dow Jones, Reuters, and Bloomberg—actively report news of the largest companies around the clock. However, these wires are selective in the news they choose to use.

Accordingly, because the onslaught of 21st-century competition to make news is so ferocious, organizations of even moderate size should consider using one of the paid wire services to make their voices heard. These are wires that guarantee use of your material (you pay them!), and then they, in turn, distribute your material to media outlets. Although PR Newswire and Business Wire are the two primary paid wires, Internet Wire is another paid wire that specializes in reaching Web sites and online databases. All charge a flat fee for a release—normally $200 to $800, depending on distribution—with an additional fee for more words.

In preparing copy for paid wires, public relations professionals must consider the following:

SIDEBAR

One-Minute Media Relations

How well would you do if you were asked to go toe-to-toe with a reporter? Take this yes-or-no quiz and find out. Answers follow.

1. When addressing a print reporter or electronic medium moderator, should you use his or her first name?
2. Should you ever challenge a reporter in a verbal duel?
3. Are reporters correct in thinking that they can ask embarrassing questions of anyone in public office?
4. Should you answer a hypothetical question?
5. Should you ever say "No comment"?
6. When a reporter calls on the telephone, should you assume that the conversation is being taped?
7. Do audiences remember most of the content of a TV interview 30 minutes after it is broadcast?
8. Should you ever admit you had professional training to handle the media?
9. If you don't know the correct answer to a reporter's question, should you try to answer it anyway?

Bonus Question
What did Henry Kissinger say at the start of his press briefings as secretary of state?

Answers
1. Yes. In most cases, using first names is the best strategy. It makes the discussion much more conversational and less formal than using "Mr." or "Ms."
2. No. Most people should try to gain goodwill in an interview. This is rarely achieved by getting into an acrimonious debate.
3. Yes. Journalists must be suspicious of any claim by a public person that he or she is telling not only the truth but also the whole truth. Anyone in public office must be prepared to respond to such questions.
4. No. Avoid hypothetical questions. Rarely can you win by dealing with them.
5. No. It is tantamount to taking the Fifth Amendment against self-incrimination. You appear to be hiding something.
6. Yes. Many state laws no longer require the "beep" that signals a taped call. Always assume that everything you say is being recorded and will be used.
7. No. Studies have found that audiences remember only 60 percent of the content after 30 minutes. They remember 40 percent at the end of the day and 10 percent by the end of the week.
8. Yes. By all means. You should point out that good communication with the public is a hallmark of your organization and that you're proud it has such a high priority.
9. No. Don't be afraid to say, "I don't know." Offer to find the answer and get back to the interviewer. Don't dig yourself into a hole you can't get out of.

Bonus answer: "Does anyone have any questions . . . for my answers?"

- **Always include headlines.** This is essential. Most editors receive wire service copy over their computers, and all they initially see is the headline. So it must be eye-catching and provocative.
- **The "lead" is critical.** The lead or first paragraph will generally indicate whether the release will be used. Include the dateline of the release, so the editor knows the place and date of release.
- **Identify the stock symbol.** One purpose of the release is to get it into as many online databases as possible. Therefore, public companies must list right after the first mention of their name the stock symbol of the release originator

and the symbol of any other public entity mentioned, for example (Nasdaq MSFT) for Microsoft. This is the key to database entry.

- **Include contact names and numbers at the end.** Reporters must know whom to call for accuracy and follow-up.
- **Specify timing.** The busiest times of day are 8:00 to 10:00 A.M. and 4:00 to 5:00 P.M. So if you can, avoid these busy periods, and announce news via the wires in off-hours to encourage pickup.
- **Specify targets.** The list of targeted recipients is up to you. Part of a paid wire's service is to feed the release to any media outlet you indicate.
- **Check for accuracy.** Wires make mistakes. In the final analysis, the wire copy is your responsibility.

In terms of online distribution, there are numerous other services, besides www.prnewswire.com and www.businesswire.com, that will distribute releases. Among them are Newstips (www.newstips.com), Techwire (www.ezwire.com), and Press Flash (www.pressflash.com).

Beyond the wire services, feature syndicates, such as the Washington Post Syndicate, North American Newspaper Alliance, and King Features, are another source of editorial material for newspapers and magazines. They provide subscribing newspapers with a broad spectrum of material, ranging from business commentaries to comic strips to gossip columns. Some of their writers—such as Art Buchwald, Dave Barry, and Jane Bryant Quinn—have built national reputations. Many such columnists depend heavily on source material provided by public relations personnel.

Measuring Publicity

After an organization has distributed its press materials, it needs an effective way to measure the results of its publicity. A variety of outside print and online services can help.

Beware the Bogus Wire Copy

In public relations, as in life, never take anything for granted.

That especially includes paid wire service copy.

Consider the case of Internet Wire, the newest of the paid wire services specializing in distributing copy quickly over the World Wide Web.

In August 2000 at 9:30 A.M. upon the opening of the stock markets, Internet Wire mistakenly put out a fake press release that contained fictional news that the CEO of Emulex Corp. had resigned. The story was immediately relayed over Bloomberg and Dow Jones.

The problem was that the release was bogus—concocted and relayed to the wire service by a 23-year-old day trader, looking to get rich on a falling stock.

And fall Emulex did. The stock lost a whopping $2.2 billion in market value—falling from $110 to $43 per share—in one day.

Days later, the FBI arrested the man, who was later sent to prison. And Internet Wire, and presumably public relations people who deal with paid wires, had learned a valuable lesson.

Media Directories

A variety of directories exist that describe in detail the various media. From *Editor & Publisher* that lists newspapers across the United States to *Bacon's Publicity Checker* that focuses on trade and business publications to specialized directories, such as *Hudson's Washington News Media Directory* and the *Anglo-Jewish Media List*—these resources help public relations people target their publicity efforts.

Press Monitoring Bureaus

Press clipping bureaus monitor company mentions in the press, supplying newspaper and magazine clippings on any subject and about any company. The two largest, Burrelle's and Luce, each receive hundreds of newspapers and magazines daily. Both services dispatch nearly 50,000 clippings to their clients each day, subscribing to about 1,700 daily newspapers, 8,300 weeklies, 6,300 consumer and trade magazines, as well as providing online monitoring.

Other Web-only monitoring services include eWatch (www.ewatch.com) and Deja News (www.dejanews.com). Both track Web hits for customer names across the World Wide Web.

Broadcast Transcription Services

Specialized transcription services monitor broadcast stories. A handful of such broadcast transcription services exist in the country, with Radio-TV Reports and the Video Monitoring Service the largest, monitoring major radio and TV stations around the clock, checking for messages on client companies.

Media Distribution Services

Public relations people often resort to outside agencies to assist in distributing releases and other press materials. Media Distribution Services Mediamatic database contains more than 250,000 editorial contacts by name and "beat" covered. PR Newswire offers a related service, Profnet, an online service that notifies subscribers several times daily with leads about journalists working on specific topics.

S I D E B A R

Homemade Headlines

Headlines are critical in influencing editors to use publicity releases. But sometimes even the editors get confused when it comes to constructing a clear and coherent headline.

Consider this confusing cross section gleaned from the daily paper.

- "Include Your Children When Baking Cookies"
- "Something Went Wrong in Jet Crash, Experts Say"
- "Police Begin Campaign to Run Down Jaywalkers"
- "Iraqi Head Seeks Arms"

- "Prostitutes Appeal to Pope"
- "Panda Mating Fails; Veterinarian Takes Over"
- "Teacher Strikes Idle Kids"
- "Clinton Wins Budget; More Lies Ahead"
- "Miners Refuse to Work after Death"
- "Stolen Painting Found by Tree"
- "Man Struck by Lightning Faces Battery Charge"
- "New Study for Obesity Looks for Larger Test Group"
- "Juvenile Court to Try Shooting Defendant"
- "Never Withhold Herpes from Loved One"

Content Analysis Services

A more sophisticated analysis of media results is supplied by firms that evaluate the content of media mentions on clients. Firms such as Ketchum Public Relations, Carma International, Delahaye Medialink, and PR Data use computer analysis to find positive and negative mentions about organizations. Although this measurement technique is rough and somewhat subjective, it helps an organization obtain a clearer idea of its portrayal by the media.

Handling Interviews

Another primary task of public relations people is to coordinate interviews for their executives with the media.

Most executives are neither familiar with nor comfortable in such interview situations. For one thing, reporters ask a lot of searching questions, some of which may seem impertinent. Executives aren't used to being put on the spot. Instinctively, they may resent it and, thus, the counseling of executives for interviews has become an important and strategic task of the in-house practitioner, as well as a lucrative profession for media consultants.

In conducting interviews with the media, the cardinal rule to remember is that such interviews are not "intellectual conversations." Neither the interviewee nor the interviewer seek a lasting friendship. Rather, the interviewer wants only a "good story," and the interviewee wants only to convey his or her key messages.

Accordingly, the following 10 do's and don'ts are important in newspaper, magazine, or other print interviews:

1. *Do your homework in advance.* An interviewee must be thoroughly briefed—either verbally or in writing—before the interview. Know what the interviewer writes, for whom, and his or her opinions. Also determine what the audience wants to know
2. *Relax.* Remember that the interviewer is a person, too, and is just trying to do a good job. Building rapport will help the interview.
3. *Speak in personal terms.* People distrust large organizations. References to "the company" and "we believe" sound ominous. Use "I" instead. Speak as an individual, as a member of the public, rather than as a mouthpiece for an impersonal bureaucracy.
4. *Welcome the naive question.* If the question sounds simple, it should be answered anyway. It may be helpful to those who don't possess much knowledge of the organization or industry.
5. *Answer questions briefly and directly.* Don't ramble. Be brief, concise, and to the point. An interviewee shouldn't get into subject areas about which he or she knows nothing. This situation can be dangerous and counterproductive when words are transcribed in print.
6. *Don't bluff.* If a reporter asks a question that you can't answer, admit it. If there are others in the organization more knowledgeable about a particular issue, the interviewee or the practitioner should point that out and get the answer from them.
7. *State facts and back up generalities.* Facts and examples always bolster an interview. An interviewee should come armed with specific data that support general statements. Again, the practitioner should furnish all the specifics.

8. *If the reporter is promised further information, provide it quickly.*   Remember, reporters work under time pressures and need information quickly to meet deadlines. Anything promised in an interview should be granted soon. Forgetting (conveniently) to answer a request may return to haunt the organization when the interview is printed.

9. *There is no such thing as being off the record.*   A person who doesn't want to see something in print shouldn't say it. It's that simple. Reporters may get confused as to what was off the record during the interview. Although most journalists will honor an off-the-record statement, some may not. It's not generally worthwhile to take the risk. Occasionally, reporters will agree not to attribute a statement to the interviewee but to use it as background. Mostly, though, interviewees should be willing to have whatever they say in the interview appear in print.

10. *Tell the truth.*   It sounds like a broken record but telling the truth is the key criterion. Journalists are generally perceptive; they can detect a fraud. So don't be evasive, don't cover up, and, most of all, don't lie. Be positive but be truthful. Occasionally, an interviewee must decline to answer specific questions but should candidly explain why. This approach always wins in the long run. Remember, in an interview, your integrity is always on the line. Once you lose your credibility, you've lost everything.[17]

S I D E B A R

Confessions of a Media Maven

Dealing with the media for fun and profit, even for an experienced public relations hand, is a constant learning experience. Often such learning is achieved the hard way. Consider the real-life case of an up-and-coming, daring, but wet-behind-the ears public relations trainee.

In the 1980s, many of the nation's largest banks were a bit jittery about negative publicity on their loans to lesser developed countries. One of the most vociferous bank bashers was Patrick J. Buchanan, a syndicated columnist who later became President Reagan's communications director and still later ran for president.

After one particularly venomous syndicated attack on the banks, the young and impetuous bank public affairs director wrote directly to Buchanan's editor asking whether he couldn't "muzzle at least for a little while" his wild-eyed columnist. The letter's language, in retrospect, was perhaps a bit harsh.

Some weeks later, in a six-column article that ran throughout the nation, Buchanan wrote in part:

> Another sign that the banks are awaking to the reality of the nightmare is a screed that

lately arrived at this writer's syndicate from one Fraser P. Seitel, vice president of Chase Manhattan.

> Terming this writer's comments "wrong," "stupid," "inflammatory," and "the nonsensical ravings of a lunatic," Seitel nevertheless suggested that the syndicate "tone down" future writings, "at least 'til the frenetic financial markets get over the current hysteria."[*]

The columnist went on to describe the fallacy in bankers' arguments and ended by suggesting that banks begin immediately to cut unnecessary frills—such as "directors of public affairs"!

Moral: Never get into a shouting match with somebody who buys ink by the barrel.

Secondary moral: Just because you write a textbook doesn't mean you know everything!

[*]Patrick J. Buchanan, "The Banks Must Face Up to Losses on Third World Loans," *New York Post* (July 12, 1984): 35.

Press Conferences

Press conferences, the convening of the media for a specific purpose, are generally not a good idea (Figure 9-6).

Unless an organization has real news to communicate, press conferences can flop. Reporters don't have the time for meetings that offer little news. They generally don't like to shlep across town to hear news they could have received through a release. They also don't like learning of the news at the same time as their competitors.

Before attempting a conference, ask this question: Can this information be disseminated just as easily in a news release? If the answer is yes, the conference should be scratched.

Eventually, though, every organization must face the media in a conference—in connection with an annual meeting or a major announcement or a presentation to securities analysts. The same rules and guidelines that hold true for a one-on-one interview hold true for dealing with the press in conference. Be honest, forthright, and fair. Follow these additional guidelines in a press conference:

1. *Don't play favorites.*   Invite representatives from all major news outlets. Normally, it makes sense to alert wire services, which in turn may have the resources to advise their print and broadcast subscribers. For example, the AP carries daily listings, called the "Daybook," of news events in major cities.
2. *Notify the media by mail well in advance.*   Ordinarily, the memo announcing the event should be straightforward and to the point, listing the subject, date, time, and place. If possible, the memo should reach the editor's desk at least seven to 10 days before the event.
3. *Follow up early and often.*   Journalists are notorious "no shows." They say they'll be somewhere and they don't make it. So follow up frequently to get an accurate expected count.
4. *Schedule the conference in midmorning.*   Journalists get to work late and leave work later. They are on deadline in the afternoon. So 11:00 A.M. to noon is about right for most press conferences.

FIGURE 9-6   **Enter laughing.** For some executives, "meeting the press" is their least favorite pastime.

"Just tell the press the Ambassador feels it would be inappropriate to comment until he's had time to study the complete text."

5. *Hold the conference in a meeting room, not someone's office.* You want enough space but not too much space. There's nothing worse than a sparsely attended event in an oversized room.

6. *The time allotted for the conference should be stated in advance.* Reporters should be told at the beginning of the conference how much time they will have. That will help avoid people drifting out at various intervals.

7. *Keep the speaker away from the reporters before the conference.* Mingling prior to the conference will only give someone an edge. Keep all reporters on equal footing in their contact with the speaker.

8. *Prepare materials to complement the speaker's presentation.* Just because journalists are there doesn't mean they'll write the story the way you'd like it. Therefore, press kits and releases are a must.

9. *Remember TV.* This means prepare your executives for the entry of the Cro-Magnon man. TV reporters, light men, and soundmen are notorious for knocking things over, disrupting organized proceedings, and generally being slobs. Prepare for the worst if you want TV coverage. (And you do!)

10. *Let the reporters know when the end has come.* Just before the stated time has elapsed, the practitioner should announce to the reporters that the next question will be the last one.

11. *Cue the reinforcements.* The worst thing that can happen to you is that 10 minutes before the press conference, there is one bored reporter sitting among 30 empty chairs. When that happens (and, alas, it will), get on the phone to the public relations department and summon every last man, woman, and child to get upstairs with pads, pens, and trench coats to save your job.

LAST WORD

When journalists were asked at the end of the 20th century "how much respect" they had for public relations people, less than half answered in the affirmative. That's the bad news. The better news is that the scores accorded public relations professionals ranked higher in the eyes of these scribes than did lawyers, salespeople, celebrities, or politicians.[18] So there's always hope. On the other hand, it must be acknowledged that journalists still regard public relations people with suspicion and maybe even (though they won't admit it) envy.

As is true of any other specialty in public relations work, the key to productive media relations is professionalism. Because management relies principally on public relations professionals for expertise in handling the media effectively, practitioners must not only know their own organization and management but must also be conversant in and respectful of the role and practice of journalists.

Indeed, public relations professionals must understand the pressures a reporter faces daily—deadlines, spotty information, frequently uncooperative sources, and sometimes even danger (Figure 9-7).

All that has been discussed in this chapter must be practiced: sending journalists information that is newsworthy, knowing how to reach reporters most expeditiously, understanding that journalists have become more pressured to produce material that is "entertaining" and, therefore, more potentially flammable for most organizations; and recognizing that a journalist has a job to do and should be treated with professional respect.

FIGURE 9-7 **The
death of a journalist.
Wall Street Journal
reporter Daniel Pearl
was abducted and
killed in Pakistan in
2002 while covering
the war on terrorism.

FIGURE 9-7 **The death of a journalist.** Wall Street Journal reporter Daniel Pearl was abducted and killed in Pakistan in 2002 while covering the war on terrorism.

At the same time, all public relations practitioners should understand that their role in the news-gathering process has become more respected by journalists. As Fred Andrews, the former business/finance editor of the *New York Times*, once said:

> PR has gotten more professional. PR people can be a critical element for us. It makes a difference how efficiently they handle things, how complete the information is that they have at hand. We value that and understand all the work that goes into it.[19]

Indeed, the best public relations–journalist relationship today—the only successful one over the long term—must still be based on mutual understanding, trust, and respect.

Discussion Starters

1. What is meant by the "devil's advocate" role of the media?
2. What is the current state of the newspaper industry?
3. What is the importance of objectivity to a reporter?
4. What are some of the key principles in dealing with the press?
5. What is the difference between advertising and publicity?
6. What is the value of publicity?
7. What are some of the keys in pitching publicity?
8. What are the several dos and don'ts of interviews?
9. Why are press conferences not advisable in most cases?
10. What are several keys to pitching online media?

Carole M. Howard and Wilma K. Matthews

On Deadline: Managing Media Relations, *3rd edition*
Prospect Heights, IL: Waveland Press Inc., 2000

The best media relations guidebook available.

This new, expanded edition of *On Deadline* includes the latest on Internet and e-mail media relations. The first chapter sets the new tone: "Technology and Tabloids: How the New Media Is Changing Your Job."

Throughout the book the authors give hints on taking advantage of the Internet. For example, in crisis situations establish a crisis update center online, put spokespersons in chat rooms, create multilingual sites if reporters covering the news speak other languages than English, and do keyword searches regularly so that you are not sabotaged by negative or erroneous information that could have been corrected or explained.

This expanded edition also presents strategy and practical guidelines on all aspects of developing and implementing a successful media relations program, drawing on case histories and the authors' extensive experience practicing media relations in the United States and around the world.

CASE STUDY

Bagging the Elusive Exclusive

"How can we maximize publicity on the new survey?" asked Sarah Jane Persimmon, vice president for public relations of Quagmire, Inc.

Quagmire, one of the nation's largest asset management firms, catering to the wealthiest Americans, had finished conducting its first survey of the "Attitudes of the Affluent." The survey had been the brain child of Quagmire President R. Ulrich Widmee.

President Widmee had been hopeful that by maximizing publicity on the survey's findings, Quagmire would be linked positively to its target audience.

"What would be great," he told Sarah Jane as they discussed the survey, "would be a major piece in the *Wall Street Journal* that our clients would notice."

He left it to Sarah Jane and her public relations department to figure out how to achieve the firm's publicity goals.

"I've got it," breathlessly responded Samantha Shram, one of the department's newest associates. "Let's have a press conference and have the president preside."

Sarah Jane was loath to stage a press conference, aware of the liabilities that press conferences always evoked. But this time, in light of the company's new survey data, she was intrigued.

The survey had revealed that despite terrorist attacks and stock market declines, affluent Americans were still optimistic about the economy and the market.

"This should be big news," Sarah Jane said. "The entire business press will be interested, and I'm certain we can get R.U. on the cable channels too. So we need a splash, and a press conference may just be the ticket. Samantha, you take charge."

"Gladly," answered Samantha.

THE MEDIA PLAN

Samantha's first step was to devise the media plan, including targets and literature. She decided to invite all the leading business dailies and periodicals, as well as CNN, CNBC, Fox News, MSNBC, and the local Chicago affiliates. She planned to notify the media with a "Media Advisory" on Tuesday, alerting them to a "news conference of major significance on next Monday."

She recommended and Sarah Jane agreed that President R.U. Widmee would host the conference and reveal the findings of the survey. It would be held in the wood-paneled Quagmire boardroom. Canapes, finger sandwiches, and assorted cookies would be available. (Samantha knew the press had a "nose for news" and a "stomach for food.")

Samantha carefully worded the advisory, so as not to give away the primary findings. She wrote:

> The results of Quagmire, Inc.'s first survey of the most affluent Americans will be revealed by President R. Ulrich Widmee at 11 A.M. Monday in Quagmire's boardroom.

Among the findings that will be reported include:

1. Affuent attitudes post terrorist attacks and stock market losses
2. Affluent confidence or lack thereof in the economy and the administration
3. Affluent investment strategy in an uncertain time
4. Affluent primary concerns for their children and themselves

We know this will be a much-discussed survey, and we hope you can be with us.

In light of the subject matter, the prestige of Quagmire, and the fact that the company's president would preside made Samantha feel confident she would draw a full house on Monday. She messengered the advisories to every top journalist in town.

THE EXUBERANT RESPONSE

By Thursday, Quagmire had already received 10 acceptances to the press conference, including the *New York Times*, CNN, *Chicago Tribune*, and *Chicago Sun Times*, among others.

"This is going to be great," Sarah Jane exulted to Samantha. "You're doing a great job."

And Samantha, in all humility, agreed with her superior officer's assessment, particularly when she got the encouraging voice mail from Max Womflash, the *Wall Street Journal*'s asset management editor.

"I got your note about the new survey. It sounds intriquing. Please call me."

"Bingo," shouted Samantha. "The *Journal* is hot to trot."

She dialed back immediately to reel in the big fish.

THE FLY IN THE PUNCH BOWL

"Max, hi, Samantha Shram returning your call."

"Hey Samantha. Listen, this survey of yours sounds fascinating. We're very interested and would like to take a look at it."

"Great, Max. But I'm afraid you'll have to wait till Monday for that. But I know R.U. would love to speak with you personally about it, maybe just after the press conference."

"Samantha, you don't understand. We really need to see the survey *before* the press conference. If we like it and can have it exclusively before the press conference, then we'll run a piece in the *Journal* on Monday morning."

"But, Max, that's the day of our press conference. If you run the story in advance of the press conference, I'm going to have 20 very upset journalists on my hands."

"I guess that's why they pay you the big bucks, Samantha. Anyway, the only way we'll use the story is if we run it in advance. If we can't get it early, then we won't be at the press conference. Sorry. But them's the rules."

"Max, you're putting me in an impossible box."

"Sorry about that. But I don't need a decision on it right now. But I will need one in an hour. Lemme know."

Questions

1. What are Samantha's options in deciding on a response?
2. What are the pros and cons of each option?
3. What are the key questions that must be asked in seeking to determine an appropriate response?
4. What would you do if you were Samantha?

TIPS FROM THE TOP

An Interview with Jesse Ventura

Jesse Ventura was elected the 38th governor of Minnesota in 1998, the first-ever Reform Party candidate to win statewide office. Born James Janos, Governor Ventura was a professional wrestler for 11 years. After his wrestling career, the governor was an actor and radio talk show host. While hosting his radio show, somebody suggested he run for governor. He did. He won.

In your book, *Do I Stand Alone,* one gets the distinct impression that you don't have a high opinion of the media. Do you?
Well, it's not the case of having a high opinion of the media necessarily, high or low, it's just what they're doing. They are a bit dishonest in the fact that they aren't telling the public they're strictly a moneymaker and that ratings points are all that matter to them. And whatever they feel will sell to the public is what they will focus on.

What would you cover if you were a newspaper publisher?
Well, I haven't been in that business, and you realize you have a bottom line. You know you've got to make money and profits and you answer to shareholders and you answer to a board and all that stuff. But what I

Your friendly author greets Governor Jess Ventura, right (as if you had to ask!).

would try to do is get out of the private lives—get out of this *National Enquirer*-type journalism, this Jerry Springer mentality of worrying about whether somebody did something at age 20. Well, when you

(Continued)

reach age 50, who can't look back and say, "Boy, I did some stupid things when I was 20." Well, that's part of growing up. And it doesn't have any bearing on how you think and how you operate at age 50.

So I say, judge us by how we govern, by the jobs we're doing, the initiatives and things we're trying to accomplish. Don't go back and say, "Oh, my goodness, Governor Ventura doesn't wear underwear because it's a Navy SEAL tradition."

Is that true?
Absolutely, it is. And I'm proud of it. But they'd rather focus in on things like that that are truly meaningless to people, other than being titillating.

Do you take the media criticism personally or do you ignore it?
I take it personally if it's a lie.

In terms of coverage, is anybody better or worse?
I think print can be the worst, because print offers no emotions. In print, you can make a joke and unless it's clearly written that "the governor was joking" they'll simply say what you said. No one knows if you were laughing or winking as you said it. Now with the media, I say to them, "That was a joke, joke, joke." And I say it three times so that they are clear that I was joking.

How do you look at the media process that has come to be known as "spin doctoring?"
I think it's terrible. It takes us to a point where we can't make up our own minds when we hear something. You mean we need someone to give us the pros and cons of what we just heard—"He said this but he meant this." Well, what is that?

The last word many people equate with politicians is *honesty*.
Not with this one.

In your job, could you envision a situation in which you would have to lie?
No, because if I lied I would lose all my credibility. I would be betraying everyone who elected me. One of the major reasons I think I was elected was the fact that I am candid. Even my critics will say, "You know, I don't agree with all of Governor Ventura's positions, but I respect the fact that he's honest and he tells us what he feels. So we at least know where he's coming from."

Suggested Readings

American Society of Journalists and Authors Directory (1501 Broadway, New York, NY 10036). Freelance writers.

Bacon's Media Alerts. Chicago: Bacon Publishing Co. (332 S. Michigan, Chicago 60604). Bimonthly.

Charity, Arthur. *Doing Public Journalism.* New York: Guilford Press, 1995.

Downing, John, et al. *Questioning the Media*, 2nd ed. Thousand Oaks, CA: Sage Publications, 1995.

Edelstein, Alex S. *Total Propaganda: From Mass Culture to Popular Culture.* Mahwah, NJ: Lawrence Erlbaum Associates, 1997.

Helitzer, Melvin. *The Dream Job: Sports Publicity, Promotion and Marketing*, 3rd ed. Mansfield, OH: University Sports Press, 1999.

International Directory of Special Events and Festivals. Chicago: Special Events Reports (213 W. Institute Place, Chicago, IL (60610).

Loeffler, Robert. *A Guide to Preparing Cost-Effective Press Releases.* Binghamton, NY: The Haworth Press, Inc. 1996.

Marconi, Joe. *The Complete Guide to Publicity: Maximize Visibility for Your Product, Service or Organization.* Lincolnwood, IL: Contemporary Books, 1999.

Merritt, Davis "Buzz." *Public Journalism and Public Life: Why Telling the News Is Not Enough*. Mahwah, NJ: Lawrence Erlbaum Associates, 1998.

Miller, Peter. *Media Marketing: How to Get Your Name and Story in Print and On the Air*. New York: Harper Collins, 1987.

National Research Bureau. *Working Press of the Nation* (Available from the author, 242 N. 3rd St.,Burlington, IA 52601.) Each volume covers a different medium: newspapers, magazines, radio-TV, feature syndicates, and in-house newsletters.

Network Futures (Television Index, 40–29 27th St., Long Island City, New York 11101). Monthly.

Newsletter on Newsletters (P.O. Box 348, Rhinebeck, NY 12572). Semimonthly.

O'Dwyer, Jack, ed. *O'Dwyer's Directory of Corporation Communications*. New York: J. R. O'Dwyer, annually. This guide provides a full listing of the public relations departments of thousands of public companies and shows how the largest companies define public relations and staff and budget for it.

O'Dwyer, Jack, ed. *O'Dwyer's Directory of PR Firms*. New York: J. R. O'Dwyer, annually. This directory lists thousands of public relations firms. In addition to providing information on executives, accounts, types of agencies, and branch office locations, the guide provides a geographical index to firms and cross-indexes more than 8,000 clients.

Parkhurst, William. *How to Get Publicity (And Make the Most of It Once You've Got It)*. New York: HarperBusiness, 2000.

Rein, Irving, Philip Kotler, and Martin Stoller. *High Visibility: The Making and Marketing of Professionals into Celebrities*. Lincolnwood, IL: NTC Business Books, 1997.

Rodgers, Joann Ellison, and William C. Adams. *Media Guide for Academics*. Los Angeles: Foundation for American Communications, 1994.

Ross, Marilyn, ed. *National Directory of Newspaper Op-Ed Pages*. Buena Vista, CO: Communication Creativity, annual. Description, contact information, and comments.

Salzman, Jason. *Making the News: A Guide for Non-Profits and Activists*. Boulder, CO: Westview Press, 1998.

Schudson, Michael. *The Power of News*. Cambridge: Harvard University Press, 1996. Describes news coverage as a culture with its own conventions.

Silverblatt, Art. *Media Literacy*. Westport, CT: ME Sharpe, 1999.

Sohn, Ardyth, et al. *Media Management: A Casebook Approach*, 2nd ed. Mahwah, NJ: Lawrence Erlbaum Associates, 1998.

Surmanek, Jim. *Media Planning: A Practical Guide*. Lincolnwood, IL: Contemporary Books, 1996.

Van Ginneken, Jaap. *Understanding Global News: A Critical Introduction*. Thousand Oaks, CA: Sage Publications, 1998.

Wallack, Lawrence, Katie Woodruff, Lori Dorfman, and Iris Diar. *News for a Change, An Advocate's Guide to Working with the Media*. Thousand Oaks, CA: Sage, 1999.

Weiner, Richard. *Webster's New World Dictionary of Media and Communications*. Foster City, CA: IDG Books Worldwide, 1996.

"What to Do When the Media Contact You." (New York State Bar Association, Department of Communications and Public Affairs, One Elk St., Albany, NY 12207).

Whetsel, Tripp. "Nothing Beats a Good Pitch Letter." *Public Relations Tactics* (October 1998): 18 ff.

Yale, David R. *Publicity and Media Relations Checklists: 59 Proven Checklists to Save Time, Win Attention, and Maximize Exposure with Every Public Relations and Publicity Contact*. Lincolnwood, IL: NTC Business Books, 1995.

Notes

1. Interview with Ari Fleischer, for *The Practice of Public Relations,* 9th ed. (August 7, 2002).
2. Fraser P. Seitel, "An Open Letter to Marina Ein," odwyerpr.com (July 23, 2001).
3. Fraser P. Seitel, "Grubman Crash Crisis Is a PR Classic," odwyerpr.com (July 16, 2001).
4. Bill Frederick, "It's Cold in Here!" *ExpertPR from MediaMap,* vol. 3, no. 14 (July 25, 2002).
5. "World Newspaper Sales Also Falling Like the U.S.," *Business Wire Newsletter* (January 1999): 1
6. "9/11 Does Not Boost All Daily Circulations; Several Lose Big," Business Wire (June 2002): 1.
7. "News Media's Improved Image Proves Short-Lived," The Pew Research Center for the People and the Press (August 4, 2002).
8. "Top Daily Newspapers in the U.S," *The Luce Media Report* (June 1, 2002):1.
9. Jo-Ann Barnas, "The Drive Never Ends," *The Sporting News* (April 14, 1997): 21.
10. Peter Truell, "Investor Settles Libel Suit Against *Business Week,*" *New York Times* (December 18, 1997): D3.
11. Fraser P. Seitel, "Wanted: An Anthrax Rummy," odywerpr.com (November 5, 2001).
12. David T. Z. Mindichi, "The New Journalism," *Wall Street Journal* (July 15, 1999): A18.
13. Lee Berton, "Avoiding Media Land Mines," the *Public Relations Strategist* (Summer 1997): 16.
14. Alex Kuczynski, "Several Media Companies Form Web Site Partnership," *New York Times* (February 2, 2000): C6.
15. Steve O'Keefe, *Complete Guide to Internet Publicity.* New York: John Wiley & Sons, Inc., 2002, 363.
16. "Online Media Relations: How to Take Full Advantage," *Ragan's Interactive Public Relations,* vol. 5, no. 6, 1999.
17. Robert T. Gilbert, "What to Do When the Press Calls," *Wall Street Journal* (June 17, 1996).
18. "Adam Leyland, "Journalists Grudging Respect for PR Execs," *PR Week* (September 20, 1999): 1.
19. "Getting into the Times: How Andrews Views PR," *Across the Board* (August 1989): 21.

Chapter 10

Electronic Media Relations

In the early years of the 21st century, TV rules.

The power of television has proven itself eminently capable of taking on all comers—newspapers, magazines, radio, even the Internet. TV dominates them all. Consider the following:

- *According to a Roper Center for Public Opinion Research study, 50 percent of the nation gets most of its news from TV, as opposed to 24 percent from newspapers and 14 percent from radio.[1]*

- *The jarring impact of international news events—September 11, the war with Iraq, skirmishes around the globe—has recharged network newscasts, all of which have gained audience, beyond their approximately 30 million viewers per night, with the spate of earthshaking events in the news.*

- *Meanwhile, cable networks also have boomed—with Fox News Channel regularly attracting 1 million viewers a night and with CNN drawing slightly less. Although these numbers pale in comparison to the broadcast networks, they do show remarkable growth.[2]*

- *TV news anchors have replaced professional wrestlers as best-selling authors, with both Tom Brokaw and Bill O'Reilly authoring books that hit number one.*

- *Finally, underscoring the tremendous power of television, in 2002 former Playboy playmate/full-size model Anna Nicole Smith played herself in a weekly reality series and became the nation's biggest TV star (Figure 10-1).*

Such is the power in our society of television and, right behind it, radio—especially talk radio.

In the 21st century, few communications forces are more pervasive and prominent than the electronic media.

Television and radio are everywhere, which is both good and bad for society.

- *Once, three TV news networks dominated the airwaves; today, in addition to NBC, CBS, and ABC, CNN, Fox News Channel, and MSNBC all hum along 24/7, keeping the nation and the world posted on the breaking news of the day.*

FIGURE 10-1 **Anna Nicole Smith.** Former full-size model turned reality TV star.

- *The effect is that Americans are provided with a continuous loop of unrelated national events that seem to all run together in perpetual images, from terrorism and kidnapped children to insider trading scandals and pending murder verdicts.*
- *Specialized cable networks, offering everything from food and fashion to weather and history, beam nonstop across the land. In the financial area alone, CNBC, CNNfn, Bloomberg Television,* PBS Nightly Business Report, *and other similar efforts have become enormously popular barometers of the nation's stock market appetite.*
- *By the time the average child graduates from elementary school, he or she will have witnessed at least 8,000 murders and more than 100,000 other assorted acts of violence on television.*[3]
- *Meanwhile, talk radio has become an enormous political and social force. Each week, tough-love advocates, like Dr. Laura Schlessinger, spew out take-no-prisoners advice; infantile "shock jocks," like Howard Stern, unleash trash-mouth venom; and political pundits, like Rush Limbaugh, let fly conservative bombast—as millions of loyal listeners stay glued to their radios.*[4]

What makes the electronic media's news dominance so disconcerting—some would say scary—is that the average 30-minute TV newscast would fill, in terms of words, only one-half of one page of the average daily newspaper! That means that if you're getting most of your news from television, you're <u>missing</u> *most of the news.*

Moreover, in recent years, especially prior to September 11, 2001, TV news was wracked by scandals—for example, Dateline NBC's *exploding General Motors trucks, discussed in Chapter 7, and* ABC Prime Time Live's *contaminated Food Lion supermarket story, which used hidden cameras and deception; and journalists serving as "pitchmen" for products.*

Since the attacks on America, the credibility of TV newscasters has increased, with 54 percent of the public, according to a Harris poll, now trusting newscasters, compared with 44 percent three years earlier. The study, done prior to the Catholic Church scandal, showed the clergy, teachers, doctors, and the president all ranking 80 percent or better.[5]

The electronic media undoubtedly will remain a force in the new millennium. Given the extent to which the electronic media dominate society, public relations people must become more resourceful in understanding how to deal with TV and radio.

24/7 TV News

Video news, in particular, has overwhelmed society.

In the 21st century, no situation comedy, ensemble drama, miniseries, movie, or documentary—not even programs about becoming a 30-second celebrity or marrying a millionaire!—dominate American TV the way news and talk shows do.

After the terrorist attacks on America in 2001, according to the Pew Internet and American Life Project, more than 80 percent of Americans relied primarily on TV for coverage of the unfolding drama. Indeed, on Tuesday, September 11, 2001, 77 million viewers turned to TV news to find out the worst.

In the daytime, it's wall-to-wall stock market coverage on CNBC, CNNfn, and Bloomberg TV and sports coverage on ESPN, ESPN 1, 2, 3, and so on. In the evening, it's the nightly network news on ABC, CBS, and NBC; the perpetual news cycle on CNN, MSNBC, and Fox News; the news-oriented gabfests of *Crossfire, Hardball, The O'Reilly Factor, Larry King Live,* ad nauseum; and the news magazines of *60 Minutes, 20/20,* and *NBC Dateline.* Even the weekends are loaded with news/talk shows, such as *Meet the Press, Face the Nation,* and *ABC's This Week.* Moreover, in times of national crisis—for example, a kidnapping, a car chase, a terrorist attack, an airplane crash—TV news is there immediately and nonstop.

The credit for the rise of TV news around the world has been the growth of the Cable News Network (CNN), the brainchild of controversial entrepreneur Ted Turner (see A Question of Ethics). CNN—which competitors mocked as "Chicken Noodle Network" when it began more than two decades ago—today reaches hundreds of millions of people around the world and is part of AOL Time Warner, the world's largest media empire.

The growth of cable television has created enormous new publicity placement possibilities for public relations professionals. Cable networks offer so-called "narrowcasting" opportunities for everyone—on the Food Channel, the Game Show Channel, the History Channel, Black Entertainment Television, MTV, VHI, National Empowerment Television, and others.

On the other hand, the push toward breathless investigatory reporting, nonstop issues discussion, and inflammatory commentary on television has created additional problems for public relations professionals assigned to ensure their organizations are treated with fairness.

- News magazine programs have been attacked in recent years for occasional bias and distortion. *ABC's Prime Time Live* drew great fire for using devious methods, including falsified employee applications and hidden cameras, to infiltrate Food Lion stores in the Carolinas in 1992. CNN's "Tailwind" report of 1998 falsely accused the United States of dropping nerve gas in Laos. The report turned out to be bogus, embarrassing both *Time* magazine and CNN, which collaborated on it, and skewering the reputation of Pulitzer Prize journalist Peter Arnett, who moderated the fiasco.[6]
- Talk shows, hosted by such personalities as Oprah Winfrey, Ricki Lake, Maury Povich, Greta Van Susteren, Geraldo Rivera, and Larry King, have become standard stomping grounds for politicians, authors, and anyone else seeking to sell a product or an issue.
- Sleazy talk show knockoffs, such as offerings from Jerry Springer, Howard Stern, and Jenny Jones, have proliferated.
- Finally, vying for the bottom of the TV barrel was the gaggle of reality-based shows, pushing the boundaries of taste and tolerance, from *Unsolved Mysteries* and *Cops*, which staged reenactments of real-life events; to *Fear Factor, Dog Eat Dog*, and *Survivor*, which pit would-be actors against each other in cutthroat competition for million-dollar payoffs; to *The Osbournes, The Anna Nicole Show, Joe Millionaire,* and *Celebrity Boxing*, which. . . . well, never mind.

As NBC's *Today Show* moderator Katie Couric put it, "Some news coverage has become more salacious, more sensationalistic, less intelligent, more giving people what they want to hear or what you think they want to hear, rather than what you think they need to or should ideally hear."[7] Organizations have gone to great lengths to protect themselves from "ambush interviews" and unfair exposure on national television. The most famous case in public relations history occurred in 1979, when Illinois Power Company followed *60 Minutes* reporter Harry Reasoner with its own camera and produced a video that clearly indicated the CBS program's one-sided presentation.

Today, the "dumbing down" of TV news has put added pressure on public relations people to deal cautiously when contemplating coverage of the organizations they represent.

Handling TV Interviews

Although appearing on television may indeed be dangerous for one's health, it nonetheless can also be most persuasive. Accordingly, as television has become a more potent channel of news, executives from all fields are being called on to air their views on news and interview programs. For the uninitiated and the unprepared, a TV interview can be a harrowing experience. This is particularly true now, when even TV veterans such as Dan Rather warn of "sleaze and glitz replacing quality and substance" on the airwaves.[8] To be effective on TV takes practice. Executives must accept guidance from public relations professionals on how to act appropriately in front of a camera that never blinks. The following do's and don'ts may help:

1. *Do prepare.* Preparation is the key to a successful broadcast appearance. Executives should know the main points they wish to make before the interview begins. They should know the audience. They should know who the reporter is and something about the reporter's beliefs. They should also

A QUESTION OF ETHICS

Reeling in the Mouth of the South

Say what you will about Robert Edward "Ted" Turner III (Figure 10-2). He's a self-made man, who worked his way up from selling outdoor billboards into presiding over a communications empire.

In the process, he got rich—very rich.

The brash billionaire, known as the "Mouth of the South" and "Captain Outrageous," founded the Cable News Network and Turner Network Television. He bought the Atlanta Braves baseball team and Atlanta Hawks basketball team. He won the America's Cup yachting race—and then showed up drunk to collect the prize. He started the Goodwill Games in Moscow, and donated $1 billion to support the United Nations—the largest single donation by a private individual in history.

As off the wall as Turner always has been, his mouth landed him in particularly hot water in the summer of 2002.

In the midst of a rash of Palestinian suicide bombings in Israel, Turner told a British newspaper that Israel's response to the bombings was, itself, a form of "terrorism." The *London Guardian* headlined the story, "CNN Accuses Israel of Terror."

"The Palestinians are fighting with human suicide bombers, that's all they have," Turner said. "The Israelis have got one of the most powerful military machines in the world. The Palestinians have nothing. So who are the terrorists?"

Reaction to the CNN founder's words was immediate. "CNN's pro-Palestinian bias cannot be tolerated," screamed Israeli commentators. "CNN must go."

CNN's reaction to the onslaught was just as immediate.

- The network issued a disclaimer that "Ted Turner has no operational or editorial oversight

FIGURE 10-2   **The mouth that roared.** Ted Turner.

of CNN. Mr. Turner's comments are his own and definitely do not reflect the views of CNN in any way."

- CNN's chief news executive was immediately dispatched to Israel to soothe ruffled feathers.
- Finally, the Mouth himself apologized. "I regret," said Turner one day later, "any implication that I believe the actions taken by Israel to protect its people are equal to terrorism."

But the damage to CNN was done. With sympathetic Fox News Channel newly arrived in the country, Israel's three cable companies received permission from the Israeli Satellite and Cable Council to pull CNN from their systems.*

*For further information, see Craig Offman, "Israeli Cable Operators Can Pull CNN," *Reuters/Variety* (August 2, 2002); and Fraser P. Seitel, "Ted Strikes Again," odwyerpr.com (June 24, 2002).

rehearse answering tough hypothetical questions before entering the studio (Figure 10-3).

2. *Do be yourself.* Interviewees should appear relaxed. Smiles are appropriate. Nonverbal signs of tension (clenching fists, gripping the arms of a chair, or tightly holding one hand with the other) should be avoided. Gesturing with the palms opened, on the other hand, suggests relaxation and an eagerness to discuss issues. Giggling, smoking, or chewing gum should be avoided. Proper posture also is important.

LOS ANGELES   NEW YORK

LARRY KING LIVE
CONDIT BREAKING SILENCE   CNN

FIGURE 10-3   **Just chatting.** Or at least that's the way it ought to seem in a TV interview, even though the key for an interviewee is to be prepared.

3. *Do be open and honest.*   Television magnifies everything, especially phoniness. If facts are twisted, it will show. On TV, a half-truth becomes a half-lie. Credibility must be established early.
4. *Do be brief.*   TV and radio have no time for beating around the bush. Main points must be summarized at the beginning of sentences. Language must be understandable. Neither the reporter nor the public is familiar with technical jargon, so avoid it.
5. *Do play it straight.*   An interviewee can't be giddy, vacuous, or irreverent. Attempts to be a comic may be interpreted as foolishness. Natural and relaxed use of appropriate humor may be a big plus in getting a point across. If humor doesn't come naturally, interviewees should play it straight. That way, they won't look stupid.
6. *Do dress for the occasion.*   Bold patterns, checks, or pinstripes should be avoided; so should jewelry that shines or glitters. Skirts should fall easily below a woman's knees. Men's socks should be high enough to prevent a gap between socks and pants. Colors of shirts, socks, suits, and accessories generally should be muted.
7. *Don't assume the interviewer is out to get you.*   Arguments and hostility come through clearly on TV, and the guest frequently comes out looking like the villain. Therefore, all questions, even naive ones, should be treated with respect and deference.
8. *Don't think everything you say will be aired.*   TV is a quick and imperfect medium—very imperfect. A guest might be interviewed for 45 minutes and

appear as a 10-second segment on a newscast. That's why an interviewee must constantly hammer home his or her main points.

9. *Don't let the interviewer dominate.* Interviewees can control the interview by varying the length and content of their responses. If a question requires a complicated answer, the interviewee should acknowledge that before getting trapped in an incomplete and misleading response. If interviewees make mistakes, they should correct them and go on. If they don't understand the question, they should ask for clarification.

10. *Don't say "No comment."* "No comment" sounds evasive, and most Americans assume it means "guilty." If interviewees can't answer certain questions, they should clearly explain why. Begging off for competitive or proprietary reasons is perfectly all right as long as some explanation is offered.

11. *Do stop.* One common broadcast technique is to leave cameras running and microphones on even after an interviewee has responded to a question. Often the most revealing, misleading, and damaging statements are made by interviewees embarrassed by the silence. Don't fall for the bait. Silence can always be edited out later. Interviewers know this and interviewees should, too, especially before getting trapped.

These are just a few hints in dealing with what often becomes a difficult situation for the uninitiated. The best advice for a TV interviewee is to be natural, straightforward, and, most of all, prepared.

Video News Releases

If it is true that most Americans get most of their news from television—and it is—then public relations people must try to get their organizations covered on the tube.

News releases in video form, known as video news releases (VNRs), have become standard tools in the practice of public relations. The best VNRs are those that cover "breaking" news—a press conference or news announcement that broadcasters would cover themselves if they had the resources. Such "breaking" news VNRs are delivered by satellite directly to TV newsrooms (Figure 10-4).

FIGURE 10-4   **The real thing.** Once a VNR makes it into a newsroom like CNN's and over the airwaves, few viewers question the story's authenticity or origination. (Courtesy of CNN)

Satellite feeds of unedited footage, called B-roll, include a written preamble-story summary and sound bites from appropriate spokespersons. The TV stations then assemble the stories themselves, using as much or as little of the VNR footage as they see fit.

The second method of VNR delivery is for stories without a breaking news angle. These "evergreen" VNRs are usually delivered by cassette to broadcasters and are more timeless in terms of content.

Before a VNR is attempted then, the following questions must be considered:

1. *What is a reasonable expectation of a VNR?*   A well-done, timely VNR should receive 40 to 50 station airings with an audience of 2.5 to 3 million viewers. Some may reach more; others may not be used by stations at all.

2. *How should a VNR be distributed?*   The answer is the same as with a print news release: any way the reporters want it. If a station prefers satellite or hard-copy cassette, give them what they want.

3. *Are you out of luck if a VNR doesn't get picked up?*   Not necessarily. It can be lightly edited, removing the "breaking news" aspect and redistributed as an "evergreen."

4. *How important is it to localize a VNR?*   Localization—tailoring for local interest—is quite important. Anything that can be done to include local personalities, contacts, or statistics will help potential usage.

5. *Do all stations use VNRs?*   Some say they don't. But virtually every TV station nationwide will use a VNR, at least in part. Much depends on the subject matter.

6. *What makes a good VNR?*   It has to tell a story and tell it in television format: effective sound bites, graphics, and a short, punchy style. In other words, it has to look and feel just like the evening news.

7. *What kinds of subjects should a VNR treat?*   The short answer is anything newsworthy and visual—a legitimate medical, scientific, or industrial breakthrough in which the video will clarify or provide a new perspective and help a news department create a better story.

8. *When is a VNR not appropriate?*   If a story has no visuals to complement it, save your money. Television is a visual medium. Without the pictures, you have little chance for making the airwaves. Also, you need a wide enough audience and a large enough budget.

9. *How much should a VNR cost?*   They're not cheap. A nationally distributed VNR should cost $20,000 at a minimum. So the point is that it must be worth the expense.[9]

VNR Caveats

As noted, VNRs are not without risks.

For one thing, they are expensive. They must be created, produced, packaged, and distributed professionally. Before one creates a VNR—and because a good one is expensive—the following questions must be asked:

- Is the VNR needed?
- How much time do we have?
- How much do we have to spend to make the VNR effective?
- What obstacles must be considered, including bad weather, unavailability of key people, and so on?
- Is video really the best way to communicate this story?

Then, too, there is the controversy surrounding VNRs in general. In 1992, *TV Guide*, angered primarily by the Kuwaiti VNR distributed by Hill & Knowlton to build support for the Desert Storm offensive, labeled VNRs "fake news—all the PR that news can use." *TV Guide*'s researchers reported that, although broadcasters used elements from VNRs, rarely were they labeled so that viewers could know their sponsor's identity.

On the heels of the *TV Guide* controversy, the PR Service Council for VNR Producers issued a "Code of Good Practice" for VNRs, which called for putting the source of the material on every VNR issued. Still, the controversy persists.

Despite their problems, the fact remains that if an organization has a dramatic and visual story, using VNRs may be a most effective and compelling way to convey its message to millions of people.

Satellite Media Tours

The 21st-century equivalent to the sit-down, in-studio interview is the satellite media tour (SMT), which is a series of preset interviews, conducted via satellite, between an organization's spokesperson and TV station personalities across the nation or around the world.

An SMT originates with a subject speaking from one location, who is then whisked electronically from station to station where he or she enjoys on-air, one-on-one discussions. A derivative of the in-studio SMT is a remote SMT, which originates on location from a site outside the studio.

Corporate executives, celebrities, and "experts" of every stripe have taken advantage of the privatization of satellites and downlink dishes at local TV stations by conducting these rapid-fire "personalized" television interviews.

A successful SMT relies on the immediate relevance of an organization's issue and message. In addition, several steps must be taken to ensure the viability of an SMT:

1. *Defining objectives.*   As in any public relations program, the organization's objectives must first be considered. What is the "news hook" required to interest stations? Who is the target audience? In which markets do we want interviews? What stations do we prefer? Within which programs on these stations will our interviews play best?
2. *Pitching the SMT.*   Television producers must be contacted, first by letter and then by phone, about the availability of the organization's spokesperson. The key issue that must be stressed is news value. Press kits and background material should be sent to the stations at least two weeks in advance of the interview.
3. *Last-minute juggling.*   Stations often request time changes. Maintain contact with station personnel, even when placed on a waiting list, so that any scheduling "holes" can be filled if a station cancels an interview close to the SMT date.
4. *Satellite time.*   Satellite time needs to be contracted for well in advance to ensure that the SMT is aired when the organization wants.
5. *B-roll. Background footage.*   B-roll video should be available to further illustrate the topic and enhance the interest of stations.
6. *Availability of dedicated phone lines.*   Several dedicated phone lines to communicate with stations should be available, especially in case of interrupted feedback audio—in other words, static.
7. *Spokespersons briefing.*   It is essential to brief spokespersons to avoid potential confusion on the names and locations of interviewers during an SMT. All names should be written out on a studio TelePrompTer or on large

cue cards, which the spokesperson should refer to before the interview. In addition, the spokesperson should become accustomed to the earpiece because the director's voice can be distracting initially.

8. *Consider controversy.*   Don't worry about stirring up a storm; it often makes news.

9. *Avoid becoming too commercial.*   Of course, the spokesperson is there to "plug" the organization or product, but don't overdo it or you won't be invited back. SMTs can save time and streamline logistics for any organization. But they are expensive—costing $9,000 for a two-hour studio-produced tour reaching 12 to 14 outlets.[10]

Public Service Announcements

The public service announcement (PSA) is a TV or radio commercial, usually 10 to 60 seconds long, that is broadcast at no cost to the sponsor. Nonprofit organizations are active users of PSAs. Commercial organizations, too, may take advantage of PSAs for their nonprofit activities, such as blood drives, voter registration drives, health testing, and the like. The spread of local cable TV stations has expanded the opportunity for placing PSAs on the air.

In the United States, radio and TV stations allot a limited amount of airtime to PSAs and other service-oriented programming. In other countries, there may be opportunities for nonprofit organizations to purchase media time and space at a reduced cost.

Because broadcast and cable stations survive on advertising and PSAs are free, precious little time is devoted to them. The top four broadcast networks donate an average of 17 seconds an hour (5 seconds in prime time) to PSAs. Cable networks donate an average of 7 seconds an hour in prime time. Univision, the dominant Spanish-language network, donates 48 seconds per hour to PSAs. A significant portion of all PSAs—43 percent—are aired during the late night hours between midnight and 6 A.M.[11]

PSAs can be grouped loosely into three categories:

1. *Public affairs:*   information about environmental or public policy issues, such as voter registration campaigns.

2. *Public relations:*   information about free-of-charge government, association, or corporate services, such as blood drives.

3. *Marketing communications:*   information about safety, health, or lifestyle issues within a context that allows brand identification and even promotion of products and services in a generic way, such as in the areas of food, fitness, and nutrition.

Unlike news releases, PSAs are generally written in advertising-copy style: punchy and pointed. The essential challenge in writing PSAs is to select the small amount of information to be used, discard extraneous information, and persuade the listener to take the desired action. The following is a typical 20-second PSA:

President Bush asked all Americas to volunteer their time for the service of others. By giving of yourself, you are helping to improve yourself, your community, and doing your part to make a difference in the world.

The Volunteers of America need your help. Sign up today, and make someone's life a lot more fulfilling—yours.

This message is brought to you by the Advertising Council.

According to survey research, broadcasters use three primary criteria in determining which PSAs make the air: (1) sponsorship, (2) relevance of the message to the community, and (3) message design. In terms of sponsorship, the reputation of the sponsor for honesty and integrity is critical.

As to the relevance of the message, urgent social problems, such as health and safety issues and education and training concerns, all rank high with broadcasters. In message design, the more imaginative, original, and exciting the message, the better the chance of its getting free play on the air.

Videoconferences

A more recent phenomenon of the video revolution is the videoconference, which connects audiences throughout the United States or around the world in a satellite-linked meeting.

Long-distance meetings via videoconferences are now becoming much more popular. Videoconferences may originate from hotel ballrooms or offshore oil platforms, from corporate headquarters or major trade shows. They can be used for information or motivation. All have the benefit of conveying a message—internally to employees or externally to the news media, investors, or consumers—instantly.

In considering a videoconference, the following factors should be addressed:

- **Origination site.**   Videoconferences may originate from a broadcast studio. However, their impact can be increased by choosing a remote location that adds authenticity to the proceedings.
- **Visuals.**   Because a videoconference is a live TV show, graphics must be considered to heighten the visual excitement of the presentation. When General Motors exposed *Dateline NBC*'s fraudulent reporting of GM trucks in 1993, the company used a host of visuals at its media videoconference. GM not only made use of extensive video at the conference, but it also displayed one of the actual trucks used in the bogus broadcast.
- **Interactivity.**   A videoconference also may be enhanced by allowing viewers to ask questions. Two-way audio linkups are now common in videoconferences. Again, these add a note of immediacy and spontaneity that enhances the interest and impact of the videoconference.

Growth of Talk Radio

Talk radio has become an influential communications medium in contemporary America. Today, nearly one-quarter (22 percent) of American adults listen to news/talk radio, according to Scarborough Research.

With many downsized and outsized Americans working from home and many others on the road, the radio has returned as a primary communications medium. All-news, all-sports, and talk have become a steady communications diet for many Americans.

Talk radio really emerged as a result of the 1987 repeal of the Fairness Doctrine, which opened the door to uninhibited discussion of controversial issues on the radio. Prior to that, opposing views had to be given equal time out of "fairness." The next year Rush Limbaugh entered national syndication, and talk radio was off and running.

Part of the appeal of talk radio is that it offers almost every shade of opinion. And it's unfiltered; that is, talk radio cuts out the "middleman." There is no reporter interceding between the listener and the speaker. Communication on talk radio, then, can be considered "purer" than other methods.

Talk radio is also among the only media in which the voices of "everyday people" can be heard immediately. No wonder: Talk radio must fill 24 hours of airtime each

Top 10 Talk Radio People/Stories of the 1990s

Talker's Magazine, the bible of the talk radio business, selected its top 10 people and stories of the decade just passed.*

What the list proves is the fleeting nature of fame and the narrow nature of attention spans in the 21st century. How many of these events do you recall? How many of these people do you even remember?

Top 10 Stories

1. Presidential sex scandal/impeachment
2. O. J. Simpson murder case
3. Presidential election of 1992
4. Persian Gulf war
5. Oklahoma bombing
6. Congressional election of 1996
7. Death of Princess Diana
8. Clarence Thomas–Anita Hill hearings
9. Presidential election of 1996
10. Rodney King/L.A. riots

Top 10 People

1. Bill Clinton
2. Hillary Clinton
3. O. J. Simpson
4. Newt Gingrich
5. Monica Lewinsky
6. George Bush (the elder)
7. Ross Perot
8. Saddam Hussein
9. Ken Starr
10. Princess Diana

*For further information, see "Talk Radio Research Project," *Talker's Magazine* Online (Spring 2002).

day, 168 hours a week, 8,736 hours a year. That's a lot of talk! Says talk show host and former Ronald Reagan associate Oliver North, himself no stranger to controversy, "Talk radio is interactive. Listeners know that what they're hearing is authentic."[12]

With FM radio dominated by music, talk radio has resurrected AM radio. Talk radio is still dominated by conservative viewpoints; it's estimated that 70 percent of talk radio hosts nationally are conservatives.[13] But for every Rush Limbaugh "ditto head"—and there are 14.5 million per week—there is a devoted lovelorn fan of Dr. Laura Schlessinger or Dr. Joy Browne, or a hormone-happy, loyal, leering listener of Howard Stern. Indeed, the combined audiences of those four talkers alone is 37 million every week. The medium is nothing if not controversial. But controversy sells, and talk radio is booming.

Penetrating the Radio Marketplace

What makes radio especially effective for public relations people is the sheer number of radio outlets in the United States: There are 10,304 radio stations versus 1,500 broadcast TV and 9,000 cable TV stations in the U.S., according to World Factbook 2002.

All-news radio stations—"You give us 20 minutes, we'll give you the world"—are regularly consulted for quick updates by people on the go. After the terrorist attacks on September 11, 2001, 11 percent of the public got most of their information from radio.[14]

Beyond all news, of course, radio disc jockeys are an excellent source of product promotion, through on-the-air mentions, contests and giveaways tied to product, and even remote broadcasts to promote venues or events.

Four aspects must be considered paramount in penetrating the radio market.

1. *Strong, focused message.* Stations must be given valuable information that will enhance the lives of listeners.
2. *Localization.* The local angle is key. The message must be tailored to suit the needs of targeted listeners.
3. *Positive spokespersons.* Spokespersons must radiate enthusiasm and goodwill. They, after all, are representing the organization and must reflect on it positively.
4. *Timeliness.* Finally, the message must be timely and topical. If not, a radio station won't be interested.

Although radio, broadcasting 24 hours a day, is difficult to monitor, the growth in listenership makes the medium a prime choice for public relations professionals.

LAST WORD

The pervasiveness of TV and radio in society has made it even more important for public relations professionals to be conversant with the electronic media. Adding to the challenge is the aforementioned trend of softer news and heightened sensationalism. If much of journalism today has become "entertainment," TV and radio are the most guilty of the media.

As generations weaned on TV enter the public relations field, familiarity with broadcast methods will increase. Indeed, one significant broadcast challenge is to attract younger viewers to the broadcast networks' nightly news. Younger viewers are not tuning in in appreciable numbers. More than one out of every two network news viewers is still over the age of 55. The hope lies in the fact that younger viewers are flocking back to broadcast reality programs.[15]

As cable television stations in particular proliferate, the need for additional programming—for more material to fill news and interview holes—also will expand. Then, too, the growth of streaming audio and video on the Internet only adds to the necessity that public relations professionals master the electronic media. Finally, the future prospect of linking personal computer, telephone, and TV in one interactive medium makes it even more important for public relations practitioners to master the nuances of the electronic media.

This will open the door to a new breed of public relations professional, comfortable with and proficient in the art of writing for, dealing with, and mastering the art of electronic communication.

Discussion Starters

1. Why has video become more important for public relations professionals?
2. How has the definition of news changed because of video?
3. What are the pros and cons of so-called reality television?
4. What are several keys to handling a TV interview?
5. Is it a good idea for an executive to be spontaneous in a TV interview?
6. Should an interviewee always try to be humorous?
7. When should an organization consider using a video news release?
8. What are the benefits of a public service announcement?
9. What is a satellite media tour and when does it make sense?
10. How important to a public relations initiative is talk radio?

60 Minutes

CBS Television News magazine program *www.sixtyminutes.com*

For decades, the most widely watched TV program in the nation has been a Sunday night news magazine program that is the subject of fear and loathing for politicians, presidents, and corporate potentates.

60 Minutes, as the saying goes, has been often imitated, never duplicated—although weekdays, *60 Minutes II* now appears. The brainchild of news producer Don Hewitt, the show and its correspondents—Mike Wallace, Morley Safer, Dan Rather, Diane Sawyer, Lesley Stahl, Steve Croft, the late Harry Reasoner, Ed Bradley, and others—have become synonyms for investigative TV journalism.

In its first decade, *60 Minutes* was despised and avoided by most business organizations. They feared the consequences of a national TV skewering, and most refused to be interviewed. Invariably, this cost them, because *60 Minutes* correspondents ordinarily don't accept "not available" or "no comment" for an answer.

In recent years, smart organizations have realized that, in some cases, it makes sense to cooperate with *60 Minutes*. Adolph Coors Company and Johnson & Johnson, for example, found that the program treated them fairly in the midst of terrible crisis.

Today, *60 Minutes* has become so incontestable that a spin-off, *60 Minutes II*, is now on the air.

CASE STUDY

They're Heeere!

Suppose you gave a party and *60 Minutes* showed up at the door. Would you let them in? Would you evict them? Would you commit hara-kiri?

Those were the choices that confronted the Chase Bank at the American Bankers Association convention, when *60 Minutes* came to Honolulu to "get the bankers."

The banking industry was taking its lumps. Profits were lagging. Loans to foreign governments weren't being repaid. Financings to bankrupt corporations were being questioned. And it was getting difficult for poor people to open bank accounts.

Understandably, few bankers at the Honolulu convention cared to share their thoughts on camera with *60 Minutes*. Some headed for cover when the cameras approached. Others barred the unwanted visitors from their receptions. In at least one case, a *60 Minutes* cameraman was physically removed from the hall. By the convention's third day, the *60 Minutes* team was decrying its treatment at the hands of the bankers as the "most vicious" it had ever been accorded.

By the third night, correspondent Morley Safer and his *60 Minutes* crew were steaming and itching for a confrontation.

That's when *60 Minutes* showed up at our party.

For 10 years, with your intrepid author as its public affairs director, Chase Manhattan had sponsored a private convention reception for the media. It combined an informal cocktail party, where journalists and bankers could chat and munch hors d'oeuvres, with a more formal, 30-minute press conference with the bank's president. The press conference was on the record, no-holds-barred, and frequently generated news coverage by the wire services, newspapers, and magazines that regularly sent representatives. No TV cameras were permitted.

But when we arrived at Honolulu's scenic Pacific Club, there to greet us—unannounced and uninvited—were Morley and the men from *60 Minutes*, ready to do battle.

The ball was in our court. We faced five questions that demanded immediate answers.

- **First, should we let them in?** What they wanted, said Safer, was to interview our president about "critical banking issues." He said they had been "hassled" all week and were "entitled" to attend our media reception. But we hadn't invited them. And they hadn't had the courtesy to let us know they were coming. It was true that they were members of the working press. It was also true that our reception was intended to generate news. So we had a dilemma.
- **Second, should we let them film the press conference?** Chase's annual convention press conference had never before been filmed. TV cameras are bulky, noisy, and intrusive. They threatened to sabotage the normally convivial atmosphere of our party. Equally disconcerting would be the glaring TV lights that would have to be set up. The *60 Minutes* crew countered that their coverage was worthless without film. Theirs, after all, was a medium of pictures, and without pictures, there could be no story. As appetizing as this proposition sounded to us, we were worried that if we refused their cameras, what they might film instead would be us blocking the door at an otherwise open news conference. So we had another problem.
- **Third, should we let them film the cocktail party?** Like labor leader Samuel Gompers, TV people are interested in only one thing: "More!" In the case of our reception, we weren't eager to have CBS film the cocktails and hors d'oeuvres part of our party. We were certain the journalists on hand would agree with us. After all, who wants to see themselves getting sloshed on national television when they're supposed to be working?
- **Fourth, should we let them film a separate interview with our president?** Because few top people at the convention were willing to speak to CBS, *60 Minutes* was eager to question our president in as extensive and uninterrupted a format as possible. Safer wanted a separate interview before the formal press conference started. So we also had to deal with the question of whether to expose our president to a lengthy, one-on-one, side-room interview with the most powerful—and potentially negative—TV news program in the land.
- **Fifth, should we change our format?** The annual media reception/press conference had always been an informal affair. Our executives joked with the journalists, shared self-deprecating asides, and generally relaxed. Thus, in light of the possible presence of *60 Minutes*, we wondered if we should alter this laid-back approach and adopt a more on-guard stance.

We had 10 minutes to make our decisions. We also had splitting headaches.

Questions

1. Would you let *60 Minutes* in?
2. Would you let them film the press conference?
3. Would you let them film the cocktail party?
4. Would you let them film a separate interview with the president?
5. Would you change the format of the party?

6. How does the American Bankers Association (ABA) deal with the media today? Visit its online press room (www.aba.com/aba/PressRoom/PR_mainmenu.asp). What resources can members of the press access on this site? How does ABA make it easy for reporters to make contact?

TIPS FROM THE TOP

An Interview with Jackson Bain

Jackson Bain

Jackson Bain is one of America's top communications counselors to executives, government leaders and celebrities. He is a 30-year veteran journalist, communications and media expert. He was senior anchor and managing editor at television stations in Texas, Georgia, and Washington, DC. In the mid-1970's, Bain joined NBCNews, where he covered the White House under four administrations, the State Department, Congress, and many other domestic and overseas assignments.

What should be the proper relationship between PR people and broadcast journalists?

Despite what you may hear publicly, PR people are frequently considered trusted inside sources by television and radio producers and reporters. The key word is *trust*. Broadcast journalists at any level have nanoseconds to hear what you say, read what you send, and consider its importance and relevance to their viewers or listeners. They have a very short attention span for nonstory, meaningless drivel in the offerings from PR people, but they have a very long memory of the names of those PR people.

What builds trust?

You build a relationship of trust with broadcast journalists by:

1. Thinking through your story or event before you call or e-mail. Is it visual? Is it a story of con-flict or change? Which TV/radio outlets and reporters/producers are right for this story? Is there a follow-up story potential? How can I help them explain it for their viewers?

2. Is the timing right for my offering this story? Is tomorrow the "news" day or is it today or the day after tomorrow? The definition of "news" day for broadcast journalists shifts with every story.

3. Always measure your words and phrases with the "hype-o-meter"—stay away from superlatives and astronomical descriptions of the story or your client. Keep it simple, straight, and honest.

4. Never, ever lie. To anybody.

How do electronic and print reporters differ?

Electronic journalists differ very little from their print colleagues in the 21st century. Almost all are reporting for multiple outlets, including the online audience. Some print journalists are now being thrust (some kicking and screaming) in front of television cameras to promote their paper or magazine.

Television journalists still need moving pictures—active events and interactive people to make good TV.

What are the keys to a successful broadcast interview?

There are two general types of broadcast interview: taped and live. Taped interviews are cut down and one or two sound bites are extracted to fit the story. Live interviews will run from 3 to 30 minutes (think *Nightline*) and give you the opportunity (I call it a gift) to put your hands on the steering wheel of the information vehicle.

The key to success in either venue is *control*. I know that can be tough with Ted Koppel or Bill O'Reilly on the other end of your earpiece. But you gain control by *responding* to the question, not just answering it.

In short, steer the *response* where you want it to go. Your client must be trained and rehearsed in some hard-hitting rehearsal sessions to do this naturally and comfortably.

How important is media training?

We live in an expanding universe—not just of galaxies but also of media outlets. The new sign held by the prophet down on the street corner reads: "Prepare to meet thy camera!" When that camera shows up, it will also likely be a critically important moment in the lives of those individuals—and they should be ready. Media training simply provides basic tools to help them get their story across in a medium that is very two-dimensional and yet very intimate. It helps them hone their key messages, understand a little of the technology so they can use its oddments to their advantage, and *calm down* so they appear confident and honest.

What are the keys to a successful radio interview?

Radio is still the "theater of the mind" because listeners depend on audio imagery to construct the missing information in a one-dimensional medium about the interview subject. The three tools for that construction are (1) the proper use of your voice, (2) the stories you tell, and (3) the words you choose.

Radio interviews can frequently be trial by telephone, with callers asking sharp and intelligent, mildly irrelevant, or crushingly idiotic questions to which you are expected to respond. Your job is to handle each with an appropriate response, steering to a key message, wrapping it up in a nice package of analogy, simile, metaphor, or experience.

How effective are PSAs?

Public service announcements can be very effective—if they are good enough and relevant enough to be selected for air by station public (or community) service directors.

Here's the hard part: The window of opportunity for PSAs has been narrowing to a slit since the FCC lightened its minimum requirements for PSA airings, and there is huge competition for those few slots. Who gets them? The Ad Council, for the most part, which produces rich, compelling, and powerful PSAs your client could probably not afford. They are important and deserve to be aired—but so does your client's PSA.

You can achieve "airdom" by creating PSAs that are demonstrably relevant to a significant segment of the station's viewing audience, then (using your outstanding creative instincts) producing them in a way that delivers powerful messages in simple (read inexpensive) ways.

What is the key to the relationship between communicator and client?

The key to the relationship between the communicator and the client is honesty and trust. The best, longest-lasting client relationships are not about the organizations—they are about the *personal* relationship between the client decision maker and the communicator and his or her colleagues. If there is enough honesty between them to make the truth a requisite starting point in discussing PR planning, and if there is enough trust to ensure that sensitive information will always be treated with respect and care, then a great PR relationship is born.

Suggested Readings

Associated Press. *Broadcast News Stylebook.* (Available from the author, 50 Rockefeller Plaza, New York, NY 10020.) This has a more generalized style than that presented in the UPI stylebook. Suggestions of methods and treatment for the preparation of news copy and information pertinent to the AP broadcast wire operations are given.

Broadcasting Publications. *Broadcasting.* (Available from the author, 1735 DeSales Street, NW, Washington, D.C. 20036; published weekly on Mondays.) This basic news magazine for the radio, TV, and cable TV industries reports all activities involved in the entire broadcasting field.

Common Sense Guide to Making Business Videos. (Available from Creative Marketing Corporation, 285 S. 171 Street, New Berlin, WI 53151-3511.) Anyone not familiar with business videos will benefit from this booklet, which zeros in on the planning needed to make a successful video.

Cronkite, Walter. *A Reporter's Life.* New York: Knopf, 1996. Reminiscences of the "most trusted man in America."

Daily Variety. (Available from 1400 N. Cahuenga Blvd., Hollywood, CA 90028.) This trade paper for the entertainment industries is centered mainly in Los Angeles, with complete coverage of West Coast production activities; it includes reports from all world entertainment centers.

Howard, Carol, and Wilma K. Mathews. Prospect Heights, IL *On Deadline: Managing Media Relations.* Waveland Press, 2000.

Jankowski, Gene F., and David C. Fuchs. *Television Today and Tomorrow.* New York: Oxford University Press, 1996.

Lewis, Lidj Ernest. "When Two Tours Are Better Than One," *Public Relations Tactics* (July 1997): 20 ff. Combine satellite and radio media tours—twice the exposure for one reasonable price.

Marconi, Joe. *The Complete Guide to Publicity: Maximize Visibility for Your Product, Service or Organization.* Lincolnwood, IL: Contemporary Books, 1999.

Mathis, Mark. *Feeding the Media Beast, An Easy Recipe For Great Publicity.* West Lafayette, IN Purdue U. Press, 2002.

Shingler, Martin. *On Air: Methods and Meanings of Radio.* New York: Oxford University Press, 1998.

www.Gebbieinc.com. Web sites listing an estimated 4,600 radio stations with Web sites and an estimated 1,020 TV stations with Web sites.

www.MediaPost.com. Web site listing of 4,993 radio stations in 260 markets, 2,188 TV stations in 21 markets, and 125 cable networks.

www.NewsDirectory.com. Web site listing 1,070 TV stations.

Notes

1. "How Americans Use the News," Roper Center for Public Opinion Research, The Freedom Forum Media Studies and the Newseum (January 1997).
2. Terrence Smith, "Cable News Wars," *NewsHour with Jim Lehrer* (March 5, 2002).
3. William F. Baker, "The Lost Promise of American Television," *Vital Speeches of the Day* (June 5, 1998): 684.
4. Ruth Bayard Smith, "Absolute Talk on the Radio," *Media Studies Journal* (Spring/Summer 1998): 73.
5. Humphrey Taylor, "Whom Do We Trust to Tell the Truth?" *Harris Interactive* (December 12, 2001).
6. Bill Carter, "CNN Excludes Arnett from War and Future," *New York Times* (April 19,1999): C1–2.
7. Peter Johnson, "NBC's Couric Reflects on the State of TV News," *USA Today* (February 19, 1997): D3.
8. "Rather to TV News Heads: Fight 'Sleaze and Glitz,'" *O'Dwyer's PR Services Report* (November 1993): 1, 22–26.
9. "Answers to the Most Frequently Asked VNR Questions," *PR Tactics* (June 1999): 21.
10. "The Experts Reveal the Secrets to Successful Satellite Media Tours," *Interactive Public Relations* (September 1, 1995): 1.
11. "Most PSAs Run After Midnight," *O'Dwyer's PR Services Report* (March 2002): 39.
12. "Radio Is One Way PR Pros Can Reach a Lot of People," *Interactive Public Relations* (August 1, 1995): 8.
13. Smith, "Absolute Talk on the Radio," 73.
14. "Nation Turns to TV for News," *Jack O'Dwyer's Newsletter* (September 26, 2001): 3.
15. Elizabeth White, "Nightly News Soars but Not Among Young," *Medialife Magazine* (October 1, 2001).

estyles of the Rich and Healthy
(And   They're Famous!)

ALSO INSIDE:
Ivory Felix Packs It In
Linda Gartner Loses It
NOT INSIDE:
Vegetarian Gives Birth To Green Baby

ARCO/July 1990

Chapter 11

Employee Relations

The headline in the summer of 2002 said it all:

"Unhappy Campers Growing in Number"[1]

The story, which ran coast to coast, described the increasing disenchantment of the nation's workers with what they do for a living and their employers. In fact, only 51 percent were satisfied with their jobs. Only about one worker in five was satisfied with his or her company's promotion policy and bonus plans. Even among higher-paid workers, job satisfaction levels dropped to 55 percent from 67 precent in a study done in 1995.

The clear conclusion from the Conference Board research was that workers were less content, more suspicious, and less trusting than at any time in recent history.

It also underscored the notion that there is no job in public relations more important than employee communications.

Strong Employee Relations = Solid Companies

According to *Fortune* magazine, the top 200 "most admired" corporations in America spent a significantly larger share of their communications budgets—more than 50 percent—on employee relations. These firms spent three times as much on communicating with employees, in fact, as the 200 companies ranked "least admired."[2]

In the 21st century, employee relations matters—a lot. This was not always the case. For years, internal communications was considered less important than the more glamorous and presumably more critical functions of media, government, and investor relations. No more. For a variety of reason communicating with employees has become increasingly important for organizations in the new millennium.

● First, the wave of downsizings and layoffs that dominated business and industry both in the United States and worldwide after the high-tech bubble burst in the early years of the 21st century has taken its toll on employee loyalty. Although employees once implicitly trusted their organizations and superiors, today they are much more "brittle," hardened to the realities of a job market dominated by technological change that reduces human labor.

259

Today, when companies lay off workers, they are often rewarded by the stock market for becoming more productive and efficient. This phenomenon has caused employees to understand that in today's business climate, every employee is expendable and there is no such thing as "lifetime employment." Consequently, companies must work harder at honestly communicating with their workers.

● The widening gulf between the pay of senior officers and common workers is another reason why organizations must be sensitive to employee communications. One 1999 study of CEO compensation found that "the line between pay and any objective standard of performance has been all but severed."[3] Some examples of bloated CEO pay are scandalous. Occidental Petroleum CEO Ray Irani received $101.5 million in total 1997 compensation, after the company lost—lost!—$390 million. Foundation Health Systems CEO Malik Hasan collected more than $28 million during a five-year period, during which the company's stock declined by 2 percent. Procter & Gamble's failed CEO Durk I. Jager was handed a $9.5 million bonus in 2000, after being booted out after only 17 months at the helm.

In the initial years of the 21st century, as their companies' stocks plummeted, the following list of fat cats cashed out of their own company holdings to the following phat tune:

1. Qwest Communications CEO Philip Anschutz—$1.57 billion
2. Gateway CEO Ted Waitt—$1.10 billion
3. Global Crossing CEO Gary Winnick—$508 million
4. AOL CEO Steve Case—$475 million
5. i2 Technologies CEO Sanjiv Sidhu—$447 million
6. Schwab CEO Charles Schwab—$353 million
7. Cisco Systems CEO John Chambers—$239 million

No wonder employee trust was at an all-time low. Examples such as these couldn't help but breed contempt among rank-and-file workers.

Not surprisingly, the notion of "job stability" for most workers has disappeared in the 21st century. Most employees no longer expect cradle-to-grave employment. They're eager to develop work skills to pursue more money, better hours, and greater job satisfaction but not necessarily at the same company. The name of the game today is job mobility. New employment opportunities fueled by the high-tech revolution, coupled with labor shortages in many industries, has led to unprecedented mobility among workers. So, in the new century, the notion of employee loyalty is as out-moded as a manual typewriter.[4] Companies must communicate to keep employees interested.

The move toward globalization, including the merger of geographically dis-persed organizations, is another reason for increased focus on internal communica-tions. Technology has hastened the integration of business and markets around the world. Customers on far-away continents are today but a mouse click away. Alliances, affiliations, and mergers among far-flung companies have proliferated. Organizations have become much more cognizant of the importance of communicat-ing the opportunities and benefits that will enhance support and loyalty among worldwide staffs.[5]

In light of these phenomena, the value of intellectual capital has increased in importance. In the new information economy, business managers have realized that the assets of their companies exist "very much in the heads of their employees."[6] Employee communications, then, has become a key way to nourish and transfer that intellectual capital among workers.

All of these changes pose a significant challenge for employee communicators. Consequently, internal communications has become a "hot ticket" in public relations. With fewer employees expected to do more work, staff members are calling for empowerment—for more of a voice in decision making. Just about every researcher who keeps tabs on employee opinion finds evidence of a "trust gap" that exists between management and workers.

One Roper Starch Worldwide study for the Public Relations Society of America found that attitudes toward work have declined over time, just as morale has gotten lower. In response, one CEO suggests, "If employees are to share in greater risk, they should also have a greater share of the rewards."[7] Whatever the solution, increased employee communications must play a pivotal role.

Dealing with the Employee Public

Just as there is no such thing as the "general public," there is also no single "employee public."

The employee public is made up of numerous subgroups: senior managers, first-line supervisors, staff and line employees, women and minority workers, union laborers, per diem employees, contract workers, and others. Each group has different interests and concerns. A smart organization will try to differentiate messages and communications to reach these segments.

Indeed, in a general sense, today the staff is younger, increasingly female, more ambitious and career oriented, less complacent, and less loyal to the company than in the past. Today's more hard-nosed employee demands candor in communications. Internal communications, like external messages, must be targeted to reach specific subgroups of the employee public.

According to research, communications must be continuous, respectful, and candid to reinforce a consistent management message.

- A survey of 700 employees at 70 companies found that 54 percent felt that management didn't explain its decisions well, and another 64 percent said they didn't believe what management told them.[8]
- A survey by Deloitte & Touche found that 81 percent of health care respondents said "employee morale" was the top human resources issue in hospitals today—compared to 75 percent only one year earlier.
- A survey of American Management Association member companies that cut jobs revealed that declining morale was a problem for three out of four of them.[9]

Clearly, organizing effective, believable, and persuasive internalcommunications in the midst of organizational change is a core critical public relations responsibility in the 21st century.

Communicating Effectively in a Sea of Doubt

An organization truly concerned about "getting through" to its employees in an era of downsizing, displacement, and dubious communications must reinforce five specific principles:

- **Respect.**   Employees must be respected for their worth as individuals and their value as workers. They must be treated with respect and not as interchangeable commodities.
- **Honest feedback.**   By talking to workers about their strengths and weaknesses, employees know where they stand. Some managers incorrectly assume that avoiding negative feedback will be helpful. Wrong. Employees need to know where they stand at any given time. Candid communications will help them in this pursuit.
- **Recognition.**   Employees feel successful when management recognizes their contributions. It is the duty of the public relations professional to suggest mechanisms by which deserving employees will be honored.
- **A voice.**   In the era of talk radio and television talk shows, almost everyone wants their ideas to be heard and to have a voice in decision making. This growing "activist communications" phenomenon must be considered by public relations professionals seeking to win internal goodwill for management.
- **Encouragement.**   Study after study reveals that money and benefits motivate employees up to a point, but that "something else" is generally necessary. That something else is encouragement. Workers need to be encouraged. Communications programs that can provide encouragement generally produce results. What distinguishes the communication effort at a "better place to work"?

According to Milton Moskowitz, coauthor of the *100 Best Companies to Work For in America,* six criteria, in particular, are important:

1. *Willingness to express dissent.*   Employees, according to Moskowitz, want to be able to "feed back" to management their opinions and even dissent. They want access to management. They want critical letters to appear in internal publications. They want management to pay attention.
2. *Visibility and proximity of upper management.*   Enlightened companies try to level rank distinctions, eliminating such status reminders as executive cafeterias and executive gymnasiums. They act against hierarchical separation,

says Moskowitz. He adds that smart CEOs practice MBWA—"management by walking around."

3. *Priority of internal to external communication.* The worst thing to happen to any organization is for employees to learn critical information about the company on the 10 o'clock news. Smart organizations always release pertinent information to employees first and consider internal communication primary.

4. *Attention to clarity.* How many employees regularly read benefits booklets? The answer should be "many" because of the importance of benefit programs to the entire staff, but most employees never do so. Good companies will write such booklets with clarity—to be readable for a general audience rather than for human resources specialists.

5. *Friendly tone.* According to Moskowitz, the best companies "give a sense of family" in all that they communicate. One high-tech company makes everyone wear a name tag with the first name in big block letters. These little things are most important, declares Moskowitz.

6. *Sense of humor.* People are worried principally about keeping their jobs. Corporate life for many is grim. Moskowitz says this is disastrous. "It puts people in straitjackets, so they can't wait to get out at the end of the day."[10]

What internal communications comes down to—just like external communications—is, in a word, credibility. The task for management is to convince employees

A QUESTION OF ETHICS

One of a Kind

With all the abuse heaped (properly) on CEOs in the first years of the 21st century, the story of Malden Mills CEO Aaron Feuerstein stands out as a tribute to doing what's right—even at great personal cost.

On the night of December 11, 1995, a fire engulfed much of the Malden Mills Industries complex in Lawrence, Massachusetts.

Twenty-four people were injured, and the company's manufacturing facilities were substantially affected. It was one of the largest factory fires in New England history. The next day, as the embers still smoldered, CEO Feuerstein vowed, "The tragedy will not derail Malden Mills' leadership position in either the local community or the world textile market."

Most people probably took the CEO's vow with a grain of salt. At 70 years old and his factory fully insured, the Malden Mills chief could have been excused for taking the insurance money, retiring to a warmer climate, and leaving his 2,400 workers to fend for themselves.

But CEO Feuerstein was built better than that.

He and his family kicked in $15 million to keep paying salaries and benefits for the full three months

it took to get the factory back to speed. When the employees returned, their productivity skyrocketed, and union workers rose to support the executive who had stood up for them.

Alas, by late 2001, the company again faced a crisis, this time because of skyrocketing debts, and was forced into filing for bankruptcy protection. Once more, CEO Feuerstein vowed, "This company will survive."

And once again, less than a year later, Malden Mills emerged from bankruptcy. Said the chairman:

> Today there's some kind of crazy belief that if you discard the responsibility to your country, to your city, to your community, to your workers, and think only of the immediate profit, that somehow not only your company will prosper but the entire economy will prosper as a result.
>
> I think it's dead wrong.*

*For further information, see Lynnley Browning, "Fire Could Not Stop a Mill, but Debts May," *New York Times* (November 28, 2001): C1-5; "Malden Mills to File Plan to Emerge from Bankruptcy," *New York Times* (August 6, 2002): C4; Jeffrey L. Seglin, "A Boss Saved Them. Should They Save Him?" *New York Times on the Web* (January 20, 2002).

that it not only desires to communicate with them but also wishes to do so in a truthful, frank, and direct manner. That is the overriding challenge that confronts today's internal communicator.

Credibility: The Key

The employee public is a savvy one. Employees can't be conned because they live with the organization every day. They generally know what's going on and whether management is being honest with them. That's why management must be truthful.

Employees want managers to level with them. They want facts, not wishful thinking. The days when management could say "Trust us, this is for your own good" are over. Employees like hearing the truth, especially in person. Candor works best when it's "not slipped inside a memorandum or—worst of all—in an e-mail or voice mail message broadcast to the troops."[11]

Employees also want to know, candidly, how they're doing. Research indicates that trust in organizations would increase if management (1) communicated earlier and more frequently, (2) demonstrated trust in employees by sharing bad news as well as good, and (3) involved employees in the process by asking for their ideas and opinions. Employees desperately want to know in what direction an organization is headed and what their own role is in getting it there. Without management feedback, employees are left to gauge for themselves how they are doing, which ultimately creates the feeling that "they must not care so I must not be meeting expectations."[12]

Today, smart companies realize that well-informed employees are the organization's best goodwill ambassadors. Managements have become more candid in their communications with the staff. Gone are the days when all the news coming from the communications department was good. In today's environment, being candid means treating people with dignity and giving them the opportunity to understand the realities of the marketplace.[13]

IBM, for example, gutted its award-winning, four-color magazine, *Think,* with the arrival of new CEO Lou Gerstner Jr. in 1993. The new *Think* was smaller and more candid than its predecessor, discussing such formally taboo topics as "avoiding getting swallowed up in bureaucracy" and "working without the warmth of a corporate security blanket." The new *Think* was most successful.

So, too, was *The Spark*, the no-holds-barred monthly publication of ARCO (Figure 11-1).*The Spark* poked fun at the company, encouraged blunt feedback from employees, and generally promoted an environment of candor and openness at ARCO. Alas, when BP Amoco purchased ARCO in 1999, *The Spark* was replaced by BP Amoco's less lively *Horizon.*[14]

One reason that organizations such as Hewlett-Packard, which cut out its magazine for employees in 2001 after 58 years, opt out of print publications is the tremendous growth of e-mail and intranets. These instant, direct devices provide greater opportunity today to increase the frequency and candor of communications. A major part of the challenge that confronts internal communicators is to reflect a credibility in communicating that underscores the level of respect with which employees should be held by management.

There is little worse than management being condescending to employees. For example, when the former CoreStates Financial Corporation downsized 7,000 people in 1998, it treated the wrenching event like a high school graduation—distributing going-away yearbooks and disposable cameras to take parting snapshots. The imbecilic attempt to assuage feelings failed miserably.[15]

FIGURE 11-1 **Snuffing a spark.** The (ARCO) Spark, discontinued after a 1999 merger, was legendary among employee publications for its candor and openness. The Spark freely published taboo subjects—everything from photos of refinery fires to employee letters criticizing management. Few similar publications would have had the chutzpah to feature their own employees in a National Enquirer "Lifestyles of the Rich and Famous" motif.

Most employees desperately want to be treated as important parts of an organization; they should not be taken for granted, nor should they be shielded from the truth. Thus, the most important ingredient of any internal communications program must be credibility.

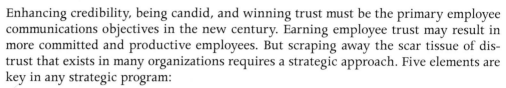

Employee Communications Strategies

Enhancing credibility, being candid, and winning trust must be the primary employee communications objectives in the new century. Earning employee trust may result in more committed and productive employees. But scraping away the scar tissue of distrust that exists in many organizations requires a strategic approach. Five elements are key in any strategic program:

1. *Survey employees' attitudes regularly.* Ironically, it is organizations that audit their financial resources on a daily basis that regularly fail to take the temperature of their own employees. They "fly blind." Internal communications audits and attitude surveys can identify problems before they become crises. Employees who are audited about their attitudes, consulted on what the surveys reveal, and then shown action as a result of the survey findings will be much more willing to accept management's policies.

2. *Be consistent.* Management that promises open and honest communications must practice it. An open door must remain open—not just partly open part of the time. Communications must be consistent to be believed. That means conveying both good and bad news on a regular basis.

3. *Personalize communications.* One study found that 80 percent of corporate chief executives believed that "personally communicating with employees benefits the bottom line." But only 22 percent of them did it on a regular basis. Workers want personal attention from those for whom they work, particularly their immediate supervisor. Indeed, the best internal communications are those that are personal and face-to-face.

4. *Be candid.* Employees today are younger, less well educated, less loyal, and include more women, minorities, and immigrants than workers of the past. These new, more skeptical, less trusting employees demand honesty in everything management says.

5. *Be innovative.* New employees in the workforce and increased skepticism in the workplace demand new communications solutions. This means resorting to new technology—voice, video, data transmission on PCs, and so on—to reach workers. Today's workforce, fiercely loyal to the Internet and weaned on a daily diet of high-resolution, mind-numbing television, demands innovative solutions to counteract the trust gap[16] (Figure 11-2).

Employee Communications Tactics

Once objectives are set, a variety of techniques can be adopted to reach the staff. The initial tool again is research. Before any communications program can be implemented, communicators must have a good sense of staff attitudes.

Internal Communications Audits

Both a strategy and a tactic, the internal communications audit is the most beneficial form of research on which to lay the groundwork for effective employee communications.

Ideally, this starts with old-fashioned, personal, in-depth interviews with both top management and communicators. It is important to find out from top management what they "want" from the communications team. It is also important to find out what

AOL Time Warner

January 22, 2001

Dear AOL Time Warner Colleague,

At last our new Company, AOL Time Warner, is a reality. As well as sharing our excitement at the beginning of this historic venture, we want to take this occasion to express our appreciation to you.

Your unwavering focus on serving our millions of readers, viewers, listeners, members and subscribers makes us more confident than ever that AOL Time Warner will be of tremendous benefit to consumers.

In recognition of the dedicated and extraordinarily talented women and men who are joining together in AOL Time Warner, our board has decided to mark the company's launch in a special way. The board has authorized a Founders Grant of stock options designed to create the broadest possible participation in the dynamic growth we expect to achieve. In the next few days, you will hear from your senior management about your eligibility for one of these grants.

The world's premier Internet-powered company, AOL Time Warner is positioned to be the most valued and respected enterprise in the century ahead. Just as important as being the first to deliver the full benefits of the Digital Age, we intend to make a significant difference in the communities of which we are part.

AOL Time Warner is making its debut at a time when the Internet is generating profound possibilities for us to connect, inform and entertain people in new and innovative ways. Thanks to you and the rest of our teammates -- thanks to your resources of heart and mind -- we believe there's no limit to what AOL Time Warner can achieve.

With deep appreciation and high hopes,

Steve Case
Chairman of the Board

Gerald M. Levin
Chief Executive Officer

AOL Time Warner Inc. 75 Rockefeller Plaza New York, NY 10019

FIGURE 11-2 **The best strategy: cash.** There is still one employee communications strategy that can't be beat—money. With the creation of the world's largest media company in 2001, the CEOs of merging AOL and Time Warner authorized stock options for all employees.

communicators "think" management wants. Often the discontinuities are startling. The three critical audit questions to probe are:

1. How do internal communications support the mission of the organization?
2. Do internal communications have management's support?

3. How responsive to employee needs and concerns are internal communications?[17]

Audits help determine staff attitudes about their jobs, the organization, and its mission, coupled with an analysis of existing communications techniques. The findings of such audits are often revealing, always informative, and never easily ignored.

Internal audits can be conducted by organizational personnel or consultants. Sometimes consultants provide a more objective analysis of the situation and what is required to improve it. (But, then, as a consultant, I'm biased.)

Once internal communications research is completed, the public relations practitioner has a clearer idea of the kinds of communications vehicles that make sense for the organization.

Online Communications

The age of online communications has ushered in a whole new set of employee communications vehicles—from e-mail to voice mail to tailored organizational intranets. Such vehicles are more immediate than earlier print versions. They reach employees at their desks and are more likely to be read, listened to, and acted on.

Online communications also have the capability of reaching virtual employees at their desks in their homes or on their Palm Pilots, in their cars, or wherever they remotely may be.

As print publications become fewer and fewer, tailored online newsletters have begun to replace them. Every Friday, for example, Honeywell International dispatches an electronic publication called *Honeywell Headlines*, a roundup of key news and events involving the firm. Honeywell also issues "e-mail on demand" to employees wishing to keep abreast of changing corporate information and developments, for example, by summary reports of management meetings.[18]

Many organizations, from traditional companies such as Xerox, Exxon, and Ford, to the new high-tech giants such as Cisco Systems, Intel, and Oracle, increasingly rely on intranets to exchange information quickly and effectively. Miller Brewing Company's intranet, "Miller Time," sponsors an interactive forum through which employees offer suggestions to and ask questions of management. Everyone who offers an idea through the Miller intranet is guaranteed a response (not a beer). Such feedback is critical to corporate credibility.[19]

The Intranet

In 1997 Forrester Research predicted that within the first few years of the 21st century the vast majority of American companies would have intranet capability.[20] In many organizations, the intranet has overtaken and even emulsified print communications. At IBM, where just about everyone is computer savvy, the company has eliminated every other internal communications medium but the corporate intranet to reach IBM's 300,000 employees.[21]

Unfortunately, having an intranet site doesn't mean employees will necessarily go there for information. Sites high in visual appeal but low in usefulness will likely be ignored. To prevent that, intranet creators should keep in mind several important considerations:

1. *Consider the culture.* If the organization is generally collaborative and collegial, it will have no trouble getting people to contribute information and

materials to the intranet. But, if the organization is not one that ordinarily shares, a larger central staff may be necessary to ensure that the intranet works.

2. *Set clear objectives and then let it evolve.* Just as in setting up a corporate Web site, intranets must be designed with clear goals in mind: to streamline business processes, to communicate management messages, and so on. Once goals are established, however, site creators ought to allow for growth and evolution as new intranet needs become apparent.

3. *Treat it as a journalistic enterprise.* Company news gets read by company workers. That's a truism throughout all organizations. Employees must know what's going on in the company and complain bitterly if they are not given advance notice of important developments. In this way, the intranet can serve as a critical journalistic communications tool within the organization.

4. *Market, market, market.* The intranet needs to be "sold" within the company. Publicize new features or changes in content. Weekly e-mails can be used to highlight noteworthy additions and updates. Just as with any other internal communications vehicle, the more exposure the site gets, the more frequently it will be used.

5. *Link to outside lives.* Some CEOs may not recognize it, but employees have lives outside the corporation. An intranet site that recognizes that simple fact can become quite popular. Links to classified ads, restaurant and movie reviews, and information on local concerts are ways to reinforce both the intranet's value and the organization's concern for its staff.

6. *Senior management must commit.* Just like anything else in an organization, if the top executive is neither interested nor supportive, the idea will fail. Therefore, the perceived value of an organization's intranet will increase dramatically if management actively supports and uses it.[22]

SIDEBAR

Beware That E-Mail

Stop. Do not press "Send."

Sure, online communications may be most employees' choice mode of communications in the 21st century. Even so, be careful what you e-mail. It could be dangerous to your job. More and more, companies are cracking down on employees for inappropriate use of e-mail. Ergo, this cautionary tale:

In the spring of 2001, a recently hired banking analyst in the South Korea office of the international private equity firm Carlyle Group e-mailed 10 former colleagues at Merrill Lynch about the wonders of his new job. He wrote in part:

"I know I was a stud in NYC, but I pretty much get about, on average, 5–8 phone numbers a night and at least three hot chicks who say that they want to go home with me every night I go out."

The exuberant 24-year-old e-mailer went on to describe his "spanking brand-new 2,000-square-foot, three-bedroom apartment with a 200-square-foot terrace" and bragged that he used one bedroom for his "harem."

Unfortunately for the young man, his e-mail was forwarded to thousands of people on Wall Street and wound up being sent to his bosses at Carlyle.

Two days later, he was fired.

Contacted by the *New York Times* at his Seoul apartment, the once deliriously happy former banking analyst mumbled, "It's devastating. I really can't comment. Sorry."

The moral: Beware that e-mail.

For further information, see Andrew Ross Sorkin, "An E-Mail Boast to Friends Puts Executive Out of Work," *New York Times* (May 22, 2001): C2.

Print Publications

The advent of online internal communications has been hard on print publications.

It's happening all over corporate America: Print editors are being told to either kill their publication entirely or move it onto the company's intranet.[23]

- At Tennessee's Eastman Chemical Company, for example, the CEO's drive to convert the firm to a Web-based organization tolled the death knell for the *Inside Eastman* newsletter, after 50 years of publication.
- At another Eastman, New York's Eastman Kodak Company, the internal publication was not used when the company announced that it would lay off 16,600 workers and save $1 billion. Supervisors were briefed by special e-mails and then directed to personally relay the bad news to their subordinates.
- When Michigan's Fel-Pro Inc. agreed to be acquired by Federal-Mogul Corporation, it "cascaded" the information down from departmental managers to supervisors to staff.

To print critics, what all these instances suggest is that "the time-honored or worn corporate newsletter with its stiff 'message from the chairman' and months-old articles is becoming passé."[24]

Thus saith the critics.

Print defenders, on the other hand, argue that there is still a complementary role for a management-driven-publication that unites employees within divisions or around the world (Figure 11-3). They argue that print and online communications should complement each other—with online communications used to transmit information immediately and print publications used to convey more comprehensive information.[25]

Indeed, a traditional job for an entry-level public relations professional is working on the employee newsletter. Whether print or online, in approaching the writing or editing of an employee newsletter, the professional should ponder the following questions:

1. Who is this publication designed to reach?
2. What kinds of articles should be featured?
3. What is the budget for the newsletter?
4. What is the appropriate format for the newsletter?
5. How frequently should the newsletter be published?
6. What is the desired approval process for the newsletter?

The answers to these questions, of course, vary from one organization to another, but all should be tackled before approaching the assignment. Whether print or online, employee newsletters should appear regularly, on time, and with a consistent format. Employees should expect them and even look forward to them.

One reason that many such publications will likely survive is that they serve as a ready vehicle for management to explain the company's philosophy and policies. In the 21st century, it is especially important that such newsletters provide two-way communications, expressing not only management wishes but staff concerns as well.

Desktop Publishing

One reason print publications won't go the way of the buggy whip and Vanilla Ice so quickly is the emergence of desktop publishing. Desktop publishing enables a public relations professional to produce a newsletter at his or her own desk.

FIGURE 11-3 **First line of defense.** Print is by no means dead in a besieged company like cigarette manufacturer Philip Morris, which used its international newsletter to rally the troops.

Introduced in 1985, desktop publishing allows an editor to write, lay out, and typeset a piece of copy. (The term *desktop publishing* is a misnomer; *desktop layout* or *desktop page layout* is more accurate.) Desktop publishing requires a personal computer, a laser printer, and software for word processing, charts, drawings, if desired, and publishing applications such as layout.

Desktop publishing allows a user to control the typesetting process in-house, provides faster turnaround for clients, and saves money on outside design. The desktop operation allows scanning photos and drawings, incorporating those images into page layouts, using the computer to assign color in design elements, and producing entire color-separated pages of film, from which a printer can create plates for printing.

Most who have switched to desktop publishing to gain control and curb the costs of printed materials combine the new technology with more conventional editing methods.

Specifically, a typical newsletter editor must consider the following steps in approaching the task:

1. *Assigning stories.*   Article assignments must focus on organizational strategies and management objectives. Job information—organizational changes, mergers, reasons behind decisions, and so on—should be stressed.
2. *Enforcing deadlines.*   Employees respect a newsletter that comes out at a specific time. An editor, therefore, must assign and enforce rigid copy deadlines. Deadline slippage can't be tolerated if the newsletter is to be respected.

FIGURE 11-4 **Alien crowd.** Publicity photos don't have to be mundane. At least that's the view of Sue Bohle Public Relations and Infogrames Entertainment, which decked out these Southwest Airlines passengers in out-of-this-world masks on the way to the E3 Entertainment Trade Show.

3. *Assigning photos.* People like photographs. Because internal publications compete with glossy, high-tech newspapers and magazines and the Internet, organizational photos can't be dull (Figure 11-4).
4. *Editing copy.* An editor must be just that: a critic of sloppy writing, a student of forceful prose, a motivator to improve copy style. This is especially true now that the computer does at least part of the job for you. However, spelling checks aren't foolproof, especially when it comes to context.
5. *Formatting copy.* An editor, particularly a desktop editor, must also make the final decisions on the format of the newsletter: how long articles should run, where to put photos, how to crop artwork, what headlines should say, and so on.
6. *Ensuring on-time publication.* In publishing, timeliness is next to godliness. It is the editor's responsibility to ensure that no last-minute glitches interfere with on-time publication.
7. *Critiquing.* After the fact, the editor's job must continue. He or she must scrupulously review copy, photos, placement, content, philosophy, and all the other elements to ensure that the next edition will be even better.

One organization devoted originally to internal communications, the International Association of Business Communicators, has come to rival the older Public Relations Society of America. With more than 13,500 members throughout the United States and in 58 countries, this association helps set journalistic standards for communicators for both print and online publications.[26]

Employee Annual Reports

It often makes sense to print a separate annual report just for employees. Frequently, the lure of this report—published in addition to the regular corporate shareholder annual report—is that it is written for, about, and by the employees.

Most employees do care about how their organization functions and what its management is thinking. The annual report to the staff is a good place to discuss such issues informally, yet candidly. The report can be both factual, explaining the performance of the organization during the year, and informational, reviewing organizational changes and significant milestones during the year. It can also be motivational in its implicit appeal to team spirit and pride. Southwest Airlines does perhaps the best job in America in keeping its staff loose and making it feel special through a constant barrage of innovative and fun communications (Figure 11-5).

Staff reports observe few hard-and-fast rules about concept and format. Staff annuals can be as complex as the shareholder annual report itself or as simple as a brief outline of the company's highlights of the year. Typical features of the employee annual report include the following:

1. *Chief executive's letter:* a special report to the staff that reviews the performance and highlights of the year and thanks employees for their help
2. *Use-of-funds statement:* often a graphic chart that describes how the organization used each dollar it took in
3. *Financial condition:* frequently a chart that describes the assets and liabilities of the corporation and the stockholders' equity
4. *Description of the company:* simple, graphic explanation of what the organization is and where its facilities are located
5. *Social responsibility highlights:* discussion of the organization's role in aiding society through monetary assistance and employee participation during the year
6. *Staff financial highlights:* general description, usually in chart form, of salaries, benefits, and other staff-related expense items
7. *Organizational policy:* discussion of current issues about which management feels strongly and for which it seeks employee support
8. *Emphasis on people:* in-depth profiles of people on the job, comments from people about their jobs, and/or pictorial essays on people at work to demonstrate, throughout the report, the importance of the people who make up the organization

Employees appreciate recognition. The special annual report is a measure of recognition that does not go unnoticed—or unread—by a firm's workers.

Bulletin Boards

Bulletin boards, among the most ancient of employee communications vehicles, have made a comeback in recent years.

For years, bulletin boards were considered second-string information channels, generally relegated to the display of federally required information and policy data for such activities as fire drills and emergency procedures. Most employees rarely consulted them. But the bulletin board has experienced a renaissance and is now being used to improve productivity, cut waste, and reduce accidents on the job. Best of all, employees are taking notice.

How come?

For one thing, yesterday's bulletin board has become today's news center. It has been repackaged into a more lively visual and graphically arresting medium. Using

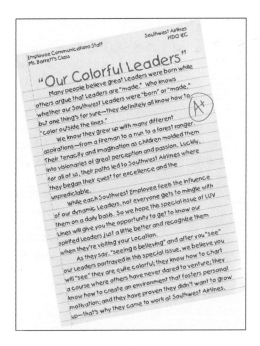

FIGURE 11-5 **One of a kind.** Southwest Airlines is "another" kind of company. Its irrepressible founder and former chairman, Herb Kelleher, created a climate of creativity and productivity through spirited communications that encourage airline employees to adopt a "happy family" attitude. Even when CEO Kelleher stepped down in 2001, his successor vowed to continue the tradition.

ETHICS

QUESTIONS OR CONCERNS

Setting the Standard — LOCKHEED MARTIN

For help...

STEP 1

Contact your supervisor. If necessary, take it up the chain of command at your location.

STEP 2

Contact your Company Ethics Officer in person, by phone, or by mail.

LMASC Ethics Director:	Tom Salvaggio
Location:	B-2, 2nd Floor, Col. 28
Phone:	Helpline Coordinator, (770) 494-3999
Mailing Address:	LMASC Ethics Office
	P O Box 1771
	Marietta, GA 30061

STEP 3

If the first two steps do not resolve the matter, contact the Corporate Office of Ethics and Business Conduct for confidential assistance:

Helpline:	800 LM ETHIC (800 563-8442)
Fax:	(818) 876-2082
Or Write:	Corporate Office of Ethics and Business Conduct
	Lockheed Martin Corporation
	P O Box 34143
	Bethesda, MD 20827-0143

STEP 4

Contact the Department of Defense Hotline to report fraud, waste and abuse, and/or security violations.

Hotline:	800 424-9098
Or Write:	Defense Hotline
	The Pentagon
	Washington, DC 20301-1900

IDENTITIES OF WRITERS AND CALLERS ARE FULLY PROTECTED.

LOCKHEED MARTIN

FIGURE 11-6   **Comeback kid.** Among important announcements included on organizational bulletin boards are updates on key corporate issues such as ethical questions and concerns.

enlarged news pictures and texts, motivational messages, and other company announcements—all illustrated with a flair—the bulletin board has become an important source of employee communications (Figure 11-6). Hospitals, in particular, have found that a strategically situated bulletin board outside a cafeteria is a good way to promote employee understanding and cooperation.

One key to stimulating readership is to keep boards current. One person in the public relations unit should be assigned to this weekly task.

Suggestion Box/Town Hall Meetings

Two other traditional staples of employee communication are the suggestion box and the town hall meeting.

In the old days, suggestion boxes were mounted on each floor, and employees, often anonymously, deposited their thoughts on how to improve the company and its processes and products. Often rewards were awarded for the most productive or profitable suggestions.

Town hall meetings are large gatherings of employees with top management, where no subject is off limits, and management–staff dialogue is the goal. That was the conclusion of one study of 200 employees, some of whom labeled these vehicles "charades, phony, management games and a joke."[27]

Two immediate new-day necessities for suggestion boxes are (1) guaranteed feedback for suggestions and (2) guaranteed rewards for good suggestions. Employees must have responses to their efforts, and rewards are never frowned on.

Town hall meetings must encourage unfettered two-way communication. Too often, questions from the floor are "screened" by public relations people, thus causing suspicion from the crowd. The more open the format of meeting is the greater management and the organization will be trusted.

In the 21st century, with employees increasingly suspect of all in charge, only candid, open, and honest communications work.

Internal Video

As important as broadcast and cable TV are as communications media in society today, video has had an up-and-down history as an internal communications medium.

On the one hand, internal television can be demonstrably effective. A 10-minute videotape of an executive announcing a new corporate policy imparts hundreds of times more information than an audiotape of that same message, which, in turn, contains hundreds of times more information than a printed text of the same message.

A number of organizations work skillfully with internal video:

- Burger King produced a video in an in-house studio and soundstage to train workers in its 5,000 restaurants.
- Miller Brewing Company produced a 20-minute video magazine and distributed it to all company locations. It featured new company commercials, brand promotions, happenings at Miller plants, and employee human interest stories.
- The Ford Motor Company took the unprecedented step of stopping work on assembly lines to show videotapes to workers.
- The most unique internal video ever produced was the legendary "Southwest Shuffle," in which the employees of Southwest Airlines—from maintenance crews to pilots—chimed in on a rap video extolling the virtues of their innovative carrier. Deejay for the rap extravaganza was—who else?—former Southwest CEO Herb Kelleher!

On the downside, internal video is a medium that must be approached with caution. Unless video is of broadcast quality, few will tolerate it—especially an audience of employees weaned on television. Consequently, a public relations professional must raise at least a dozen questions before embarking on an internal video venture:

1. Why are we doing this video?
2. Whom are we trying to reach with this video?
3. What's the point of the video?
4. What do we want viewers to do after seeing the video?
5. How good is our video script?
6. How sophisticated is the quality of our broadcast?
7. How innovative and creative is the broadcast? Does it measure up to regular television?
8. How competent is our talent?

9. How proficient is our crew?
10. Where will our viewers screen the video?
11. With what communications vehicles will we supplement the video?
12. How much money can we spend?

The keys to any internal video production are, first, to examine internal needs; then to plan thoughtfully before using the medium; and, finally, to reach target publics through the highest-quality programming possible. Broadcast quality is a tough standard to meet. If an organization can't afford high-quality video, it shouldn't get involved.

Face-to-Face Supervisory Communications

First and foremost, employees want information face-to-face from their supervisors.

Supervisors, in fact, are the preferred source for 90 percent of employees, making them the top choice by far. The reason is obvious. You report to your supervisor, who awards your raise, promotes you, and is your primary source of corporate information.

That's the good news.

The bad news is that despite paying attention to enhanced supervisory communications, most companies are still inconsistent when it comes to supervisors relaying important information. Thus, even though most employees vastly prefer information from their supervisor over what they learn through rumors, many still rely on the grapevine as a primary source of information.

What can public relations departments do to combat this trend?

Some departments formalize the meeting process by mixing management and staff in a variety of formats, from gripe sessions to marketing/planning meetings. Many organizations embrace the concept of skip-level meetings, in which top-level managers meet periodically with employees at levels several notches below them in the organizational hierarchy. As with any other form of communication, the value of meetings lies in their substance, their regularity, and the candor managers bring to face-to-face sessions. In any event, one key to improved internal communications clearly is increased face-to-face communications between supervisor and subordinate.[28]

S I D E B A R

The Oy Vey Bulletin Board

Bulletin boards can be most effective as a communications medium, but one must make certain that messages are clear and unambiguous. For example, these bloopers appeared on various synagogue bulletin boards.

1. The rabbi spoke briefly, much to the delight of the congregation.
2. Low Self-Esteem Group will meet Thursday at 7 P.M. Please use back entrance.
3. Remember in prayer the many who are sick of our synagogue and community.

4. The 8th graders will be presenting *Hamlet* in the auditorium on Monday at 7 P.M. The congregation is invited to attend this tragedy.
5. The flowers this morning are to announce the birth of David Alan Belzer, the sin of Rabbi and Mrs. Julius Belzer.
6. Don't let worry kill you. Let the synagogue help.
7. The concert in the Schwartz Auditorium was a great success. Special thanks are due to the rabbi's daughter, who labored the whole evening at the piano, which as usual fell upon her.

Dealing with the Grapevine

In many organizations, it's neither the Internet nor cyberspace that dominates communications but rather the company grapevine. The rumor mill can be devastating. As one employee publication described the grapevine:

> It's faster than a public address announcement and more powerful than a general instruction. It's able to leap from LA to San Francisco in a single bound. And its credibility is almost beyond Walter Cronkite's.

Rumors, once they pick up steam, are difficult to stop. Because employees tend to distort future events to conform to a rumor, an organization must work to correct rumors as soon as possible.

Identifying the source of a rumor is often difficult, if not impossible, and it's usually not worth the time. However, dispelling the rumor quickly and frankly is another story. Often a bad-news rumor—about layoffs, closings, and so on—can be dealt with most effectively through forthright communication. Generally, an organization makes a difficult decision after a thorough review of many alternatives. The final decision is often a compromise, reflecting the needs of the firm and its various publics including, importantly, the workforce.

In presenting a final decision to employees, management often overlooks the value of explaining how it reached its decision. By comparing alternative solutions so that employees can understand more clearly the rationale behind management decisions, an organization may make bad news more palatable.

As diabolical as the grapevine can become, it shouldn't necessarily be treated as the enemy of effective communications with employees. Management might even consider using it as a positive force. A company grapevine can be as much a communications vehicle as internal publications or employee meetings. It may even be more valuable because it is believed, and everyone seems to tap into it.

LAST WORD

The best defense against damaging grapevine rumors is a strong and candid communications system. Employee communications, for years the most neglected strategic opportunity in corporate America, is today much more appreciated for its strategic importance. Organizations that build massive marketing plans to sell products have begun today to apply that same knowledge and energy to communicating with their own employees.

A continuing employee relations challenge for public relations communicators is to work hand-in-hand with human resources officials. In the 1950s, personnel departments began to change their name to "human resources" to more accurately reflect the personal focus of their responsibilities. Over the past half century, human resources functions have concentrated on such areas as organization, staffing, benefits, and recruitment rather than communications.

The responsibility for communicating to employees has largely fallen on the public relations function, which must coordinate its initiatives with human resources priorities to create a culture of professionalism, accountability, and candor.

In the 21st century, organizations have no choice but to build rapport with and morale among employees. The shattering of morale that accompanied the early years of the century will take time to repair. Building back internal credibility is a long-term process that depends on several factors—among them, listening to employees, developing information exchanges to educate employees about changing technologies and processes, providing the strategic business information that employees require, and adapting to the new culture of job "mobility" that is replacing job "stability."

Most of all in this new century, effective employee communications requires openness and honesty on the part of senior management. As legendary Berkshire Hathaway CEO Warren Buffet has said, "We can afford to lose money—even a lot of money. We cannot afford to lose reputation—even a shred of reputation."[29]

Public relations professionals must seize this initiative to foster the open climate that employees want and the two-way communications that organizations need.

Discussion Starters

1. What societal factors have caused internal communications to become more important today than in the past?
2. What is the general mood of the employee public today?
3. what are the key elements to effective employee relations?
4. What are some important employee communications strategies today?
5. What are the key questions of an employee communications audit?
6. What is the status of internal print communications?
7. What are the key considerations in communicating through an intranet?
8. What are the primary tasks of an employee newsletter's editor?
9. What questions should be raised before communicating through internal video?
10. What is the best way to combat the grapevine?

TOP OF THE SHELF

Jim Harris

Getting Employees to Fall in Love with Your Company
New York: AMACOM, 1996

Author Jim Harris asks, "What's love got to do with it?"

Here's what: Airline pilots voluntarily cleaning their planes on their days off! Employees voluntarily giving back their bonuses to pay down corporate debt! Hard to believe in today's cynical, bottom-line, downsizing, job-shifting environment?

Harris says, "Believe it! Learn how over 140 of today's most profitable and progressive organizations go beyond the bottom line to build commitment, trust . . . and even love with their employees."

Every supervisor should read *Getting Employees to Fall in Love with Your Company*.

CASE STUDY

The Chairman's E-Mail

From.   Solomon Doophis, Chairman
To.   All Doophis Corp. Headquarters Managers
Re.   Work Standards

I have had it. I have been making this point to most of you for the better part of a year, and I'll take it no longer.

We are getting less than 40 hours of work from a large number of headquarters employees.

The parking lot is sparsely used at 8 a.m., when I arrive, and likewise at 7 p.m., when I depart. At 4:30 p.m. each day, it starts to empty out.

My point is that as managers, you either don't know what YOUR employees are doing or YOU simply don't care. You have created expectations of the work effort, shich allowed this to happen inside Doophis, creating a very unhealthy environment.

In either case, you have a problem, and you will fix it or you will be replaced.

NEVER in my career have I allowed a team which worked for me to think they had a 40-hour job. I, personally, work 12 hours a day, everyday. I don't expect YOUR employees to work as hard as I do, but I will permit this no longer.

At the end of next week, I will implement the following:

1. Closing of the cafeteria to employees between the hours of 9-12 and 2-5 each day.
2. Implementing a hiring freeze on all headquarters positions. Exceptions must be granted by one person, ME.
3. Implementing a time clock system, requiring ALL EMPLOYEES to "punch in" and "punch out" to work. Any unapproved absences will be charged to the EMPLOYEE'S vacation.
4. Last month, the Board passed a Stock Purchase Program, allowing for employees to purchase Doophus stock at a 15% discount. HELL WILL FREEZE OVER before this CEO allows another employee benefit in this culture.
5. Implement a 5% reduction of staff at headquarters.
6. I am deferring all promotions and raises currently scheduled, until such time as I am convinced that the ones being promoted are the solution, not the problem. (If YOU are the problem, pack your bags!)

Believe me, I think this parental type action SUCKS. Ordinarily, I am a good and kind boss. But what you are doing as managers with this company makes me SICK. It makes me sick to have to write this directive.

We have a big vision. It will take a big effort. Too many at headquarters are not making this effort.

I STRONGLY suggest that you call some 7 AM, 6 PM AND SATURDAY AM team meetings with the employees who work directly for you. Discuss this serious issue with them, and if they balk or complain, don't be reluctant to fire their butts. I suggest that you call your first Meeting TONIGHT. I suggest that STRONGLY.

I will give you two weeks to fix this. My measurement will be the parking lot; it should be substantially full at 7:30 a.m. and 6:30 p.m. The pizza girl should show up at 7:30 p.m. to feed the starving peasants working late. The lot should be half full on Saturday mornings.

Folks, this is a MANAGEMENT problem not an EMPLOYEE problem.

Congratulations, you are management. And you aren't working HARD enough. You have the responsibility for our EMPLOYEES. I will hold you accountable. You have allowed this to get to this state. You have two weeks.

Tick tock.

Sol

Solomon Doophis
Chairman and Chief Executive
Doophis Corporation
"We Treat You Right"

Questions

1. How would you rate this letter as an employee communication?
2. How would you rate the CEO's language, grammar, punctuation?
3. What would you imagine would be the reaction to this e-mail from those who receive it?
4. How would you "improve" this correspondence?
5. Do you think a "real" CEO could ever send such an e-mail?

TIPS FROM THE TOP

Interview with Alvin Wong

Alvin Wong

Alvin Wong is the Internal Communications Leader at Royal & Sun Alliance Australia, one of the leading insurance companies in the country. He is an internal communications veteran of Australian companies, including NRMA Insurance and American Express in Sydney.

What is the state of employee communications in companies today?

There is a growing recognition that employee communication is no longer a luxury in organizations, particularly in companies where there is a need for a complex restructure or a fast rate of change. Many companies now realize that employee communication tools and activities can make a difference to the culture and performance of an organization and that it's a strategic function, not just a form of tactical support. In effect, employees are now seen as a 'market', just like consumers.

What are some of the most common problems with internal communication?

One of the most common problems facing internal communications today is our weakness in showing how we add value to the company's performance. While we may be able to prove the effectiveness and efficiency of our communications, we need to be able to translate that into how that adds value to the organization—in hard data. So while we can prove that X per cent of employees received, read and understood a message, we need to be able to show what that comprehension means to the bottom line.

How has online communications affected the state of internal communication?

Online communications has dramatically changed the way we communicate in organizations today. Employees now expect instant communication and we should aim to provide it. Why? Because we are often forced to compete with the Internet to ensure our employees find out about important company news before they hear it elsewhere. More than ever, we need to ensure the information is relevant and easy to find. And importantly, it must add value, not just volume.

What is the status of internal print communications in organizations?

Internal print publications definitely have a role to play in today's organizations. We need to remember that print and on-line channels each have their pros and cons and we should exploit the best from each medium. Lengthier and more detailed analytical articles are more appropriate in printed publications as they are more portable and allow the audience to read in their own time. However, an online article is best suited to shorter, snappier communication that requires a fast delivery. The two mediums can work hand in hand to complement each other, rather than compete with each other.

(Continued)

How can internal communications help the state of employee morale?

Internal communication can improve employee morale by helping to celebrate the successes of a company. Tell and show how well something was done and how it helped the company, its customers and other stakeholders achieve a desired outcome.

Internal communications can also help morale by painting the big picture of the company—communicate the strategy to employees to ensure they are all on the same page, heading towards the same destination and on the same journey. Then detail how they each contribute to that vision and that they have a voice to direct that vision. Make them feel heard, make them feel valued.

What should management do to improve communications with employees?

Management needs only to do three things—communicate, communicate and communicate. Do it effectively and communicate with an outcome in mind. One thing management can do to start the process is to understand communications—what it is and what it isn't.

Managers at all levels must understand that communications is a two way process. Feedback must be sought as part of this process, not an afterthought. Management can specifically improve employee communications by providing, developing, and constantly refining mechanisms to allow communication and feedback to happen.

What is the single most important challenge to internal communicators in the 21st century?

I believe a major issue for internal communications is getting a seat at the board table alongside the CEO. The importance of internal communications will only be realized once there is high level recognition and buy-in.

Suggested Readings

Aud, Jody Buffington. "What Internal Communicators Can Learn from Enron," *Public Relations Strategist* (Spring 2002): 11–12.

Cohen, Allan. *Effective Behavior in Organizations,* 7th ed. New York: McGraw-Hill, 2001.

Flannery, Thomas P. *People, Performance and Pay: Dynamic Compensation for Changing Organizations.* New York: The Free Press, 1995. Traditional methods of compensation may simply not cut it in an era of employee skepticism and quest for empowerment.

Freeland, David B. *Company Policy Manual Special Report: Effective Communication Strategies.* New York: Aspen Publishers, 1998. Discusses the rising skepticism of employees and offers solutions.

Grossman, Jack, and Robert Parkinson. *Becoming a Successful Manager: How to Make a Smooth Transition from Managing Others to Managing Yourself.* New York: Contemporary Books, 2001.

Hammer, Michael, and Steven Stanton. *The Reengineering Revolution.* New York: Harper Business, 1995. Reengineering gurus explain why work and workers will differ materially in the 21st century.

Kreitner, Robert, and Angelo Kinicki. *Organizational Behavior,* 5th ed. New York: McGraw Hill College Division, 2001.

Lundin, Kathleen, and William Lundin. *When Smart People Work for Dumb Bosses: How to Survive in a Crazy and Dysfunctional Workplace.* New York: McGraw-Hill, 1998.

Miller, Debra A. "Measuring the Effectiveness of Your Intranet" *Public Relations Strategist* (Summer 2001): 35–39.

Mogel, Leonard. *An Insider's Guide to Career Opportunities,* 2nd ed. Lawrence Erlbaum, 2002.

Penzias, Arno. *Harmony: Business Technology and Life After Paperwork.* New York: Harper Business, 1995. Deals with the uncertainty resulting from technology replacing people and the challenges of the technical workforce.

Ragan's Intranet Report. Chicago: Ragan Communications Inc. Monthly newsletter. www.ReportGallery.com. This Web site features annual reports for more than 1,000 publicly traded companies, including most of the Fortune 500 companies. Also links to the companies' homepages.

Sack, Steven Mitchell. *From Hiring to Firing: The Legal Survival Guide for Employers in the '90s.* New York: Alliance House, 1995. The first best defense for a public relations professional: Know the law.

Taylor, Winnifred. *The Dragon Complex, Identifying and Conquering Workplace Abuse.* Leawood, KS: Cypress Publishing, 2002.

Ward, Peter, and Rae Andre. *The 59-Second Employee: How to Stay One Second Ahead of Your One-Minute Manager.* Lincoln, NE: iUniverse.com, 2000.

Notes

1. Robert O'Neill, "Unhappy Campers Growing in Number," *The Record* (August 22, 2002): B1-5.
2. "Employee Communications Today: It's New, It's Different, and It Has Bottom Line Impact," *Positioning Newsletter* 10, no. 2, (1999). Heyman Associates, Inc., 11 Penn Plaza, Suite 1105, New York, NY 10001.
3. Denis B. K. Lyons, "CEO Compensation: The Whole Truth," (1999). Spencer Stuart, 401 N. Michigan Ave., Chicago, IL.
4. Erin Arvedlund, "Jumping Careers," *Kinko's Press* 1 (2000): 22.
5. Jeffrey Ball, "Daimler Chrysler's Transfer Woes," *Wall Street Journal* (August 24, 1999): B1, 12.
6. "Employee Communications Today: It's New, It's Different, and It Has Bottom Line Impact," *Positioning Newsletter* 10, no. 2. (1999). Heyman Associates, Inc., 11 Penn Plaza, Suite 1105, New York, NY 10001.
7. "The Dream in Danger," *Public Relations Strategist* (Spring 1995): 43.
8. Steve Rivkin, "Mutiny in the Cafeteria," *Public Relations Strategist* (Winter 1998): 20.
9. Bryan W. Armentrout, "The Five Best Gifts to Give Your Employees," *HR Focus* (December 1995): 3.
10. "An Employee's Eye View of Business," *Ragan Report* (November 25, 1991): 1, 2.
11. Thomas W. Hoog, "A Strategy to Retain Your Best People," *Public Relations Strategist* (Summer 1999): 16.
12. Rivkin, "Mutiny in the Cafeteria."
13. Fraser P. Seitel, "Leaping the 'Trust Gap,'" *U.S. Banker* (November 1990): 61.
14. "After More Than 25 Years, the ARCO Spark Is Snuffed," *Ragan Report* (November 15, 1999): 4.
15. "Putting the Fun Back in Downsizing," *Ragan Report* (May 18, 1998): 1.
16. Fraser P. Seitel, "Leaping the Trust Gap."
17. Jerry Stevenson, "How to Conduct a Self-Intranet Audit," *Ragan Report* (August 19, 2002): 7.
18. Karen Bachman, "Does Anybody Do It Better?" *Across the Board* (January 1997): 55.
19. "Two Ways to Pull People to the Intranet," *Ragan Report* (October 18, 1999): 6.
20. Scott Rodrick, "Use Intranets to Connect Employee Owners," *Interactive Investor Relations* (January 1997): 3.
21. "All Intranet, All the Time," *Ragan Report* (May 14, 2001): 6.

22. John R. Kessling, "Maintaining a Successful Intranet: The KGN Experience," *PR Tactics* (November 1999): 20.

23. "Kissing Off Your Print Publication," *Ragan Report* (October 11, 1999): 6.

24. Joanne Cleaver, "An Inside Job," *Marketing News* (February 16, 1998): 1, 14.

25. "On Why the Battle Between Print and Online Must End—Finally," *Ragan Report* (April 19, 2002): 3.

26. For further information about the International Association of Business Communicators, write to IABC, One Hallidie Plaza, Suite 600, San Francisco, CA 94102, www.iabc.com, phone 800-776-4222, fax 415-544-4747.

27. John Guiniven, "Suggestion Boxes and Town Hall Meetings: Fix 'Em or Forget 'Em," *Tactics* (February 2000): 22.

28. Wilma K. Mathews, "What the CEO Can Do About It," *Public Relations Strategist* (Spring 1995): 49.

29. "Talking to the Troops," *Business Week* (July 5, 1999): 62.

Chapter 12

Multicultural Community Relations

Most people overlooked the story in August 1998, but it was very big news nonetheless. Fortune *magazine had just announced its selection of "The 50 Best Companies for Asians, Blacks, and Hispanics." There, incredibly, at number two on the list of corporate models of diversity was Advantica Restaurant Group, parent company of Denny's.*[1]

Six years earlier, both Denny's and its sister company Shoney's were synonymous with mistreatment of minorities and bigotry. In 1992, Shoney's paid $132.8 million to settle a class-action discrimination suit brought by 20,000 employees and rejected job applicants. Two years later, Denny's paid $54.4 million to settle two class-action suits brought by black customers who claimed some restaurants refused to seat or serve them (see the case study at the conclusion of this chapter).

Fortune's recognition of the Denny's/Advantica turnaround epitomized how seriously organizations today consider multicultural communities.

Women, senior citizens, African Americans, Latinos, gays, and other groups formerly overlooked are today focused on, marketed to, and targeted by organizations of all types, especially mainstream corporations.

In today's society, multiculturalism has become big business.

America has always been a melting pot, attracting freedom-seeking immigrants from countries throughout the world. Never has this been more true than today, as America's face continues to change. Consider the following:

- *In 2000, the U.S. population of 281 million was approximately 75 percent Anglo. Latinos and African Americans represented about 70 million people. By the year 2050, Latinos alone are projected to represent 25 percent of the population with African Americans accounting for about 15 percent, and Asians 2 percent.*[2] *Today ethnic minorities spend $600 billion a year out of a total U.S. economy of $4.4 trillion. This amount is certain to increase substantially.*[3]

- *In 1940, 70 percent of U.S. immigrants came from Europe; today the vast majority of immigrants arrive from Asia, Latin America, and the Caribbean.*

- *In 1976, there were 67 Spanish-language radio stations in the United States; today that number has increased fivefold. There are also 100 Spanish-language TV stations, 350 Spanish-language newspapers, and a potential audience of 30 million.*
- *In New York City alone, 12 percent of the population under 18 is foreign-born, and that percentage continues to increase.*
- *The Internet, a broad canvas of interactive communities uniting the world, has spawned numerous microcommunity sites, such as iVillage for women, Africana.com and BlackPlanet.com for blacks, SeniorNet for senior citizens, and CollegeClub for Generation Xers.*

Such is the multicultural diversity enjoyed today by America and the world. The implications for organizations are profound. Almost two-thirds of the new entrants into the workforce now are women. People of color make up nearly 30 percent of these new entrants. Meanwhile, the Hispanic population has spread out across the nation faster and farther than any previous wave of immigrants.[4]

Community Diversity

In light of the increasing diversity of U.S. society, both profit and nonprofit organizations must become more diverse as well and learn to deal and communicate with those who differ in work background, education, age, gender, race, ethnic origin, physical abilities, religious beliefs, sexual orientation, and other perceived differences.

Those organizations that waver in responding to the new multicultural communities do so at their own peril. Community activism, so prominent in prior decades, has returned. To wit:

- In 2000, the New York City Police Department was attacked by the African American community and its leaders after four officers were acquitted in the killing of an unarmed African immigrant, Amadou Diallo. The community refused to accept the court's verdict and kept the issue alive as a police brutality cause célèbre.
- Meanwhile, in neighboring New Jersey, activists prosecuted the state police, who were found guilty of racial profiling in police stops on the state's highways.
- On the West Coast, the chief of the Los Angeles Police Department was forced to step down and police officers were jailed after an African American motorist, Rodney King, was beaten following a high-speed chase. The King beating triggered a massive riot and focused attention on the department's problems in dealing with minorities (Figure 12-1). In 2002, the police force of the Inglewood suburb of Los Angles came under scrutiny when a violent beatdown of a black teenager was secretly videotaped and distributed to the national media.
- In 2001, two high-powered black attorneys, Cyrus Mehri and Johnnie Cochran, Jr., launched a massive suit against Johnson & Johnson, alleging discrimination against more than 1,000 black and Hispanic employees. In earlier similar suits, Mehri collected $176 million from Texaco and $192.5 million from Coca-Cola.[5] In the Texaco case, incriminating tapes, in which

FIGURE 12-1 **Healing community conflicts.** Los Angeles was sorely tested in the spring of 1992, when the Rodney King beating led to riots. Southern California Edison published a special issue of its *SCE News* to report on the company's response to the disturbances and to salute employees who worked through the crisis. The issue was called "Time to Heal."

executives disparaged minorities, were made public. The company's CEO, Peter Bijur, settled the suit, he said, so that the offensive comments of the executives would not be construed to represent Texaco.[6]

As the arbiters of communications in their organizations, public relations people must be sensitive to society's new multicultural realities. This is a particular challenge with respect to an increasingly disenfranchised Muslim community in the wake of September 11, 2001 and the war with Iraq. Dealing in an enlightened manner with multicultural diversity and being sensitive to nuances in language and differences in style are logical extensions of the social responsibility that has been an accepted part of American organizational life since the 1960s.

Social Responsibility in the Community

The Enron/WorldCom/Global Crossing/ImClone et al. corporate scandals of 2002 underscored the importance of organizations to build a reservoir of goodwill within their host communities.

More and more, companies and other organizations acknowledge their responsibilities to the community: helping to maintain clean air and water, providing jobs for minorities, enforcing policies in the interests of all employees, and, in general, enhancing everyone's quality of life. This concept of social responsibility has become widely accepted among enlightened organizations.

For example, most companies today donate a percentage of their profits to non-profit organizations—schools, hospitals, social welfare institutions, and others. The best companies donate as much as 2 percent or more of pretax profits.

Corporate philanthropy and social responsibility is a uniquely American concept. U.S. firms feel an obligation to support thousands of community-based groups working to expand affordable housing, create economic opportunity, improve public schools, and protect the environment.

On the other hand, corporate contributions to the community very much depend on profits. If a company earns little, it can't give much to the community. Lucent Technologies, for example, whose foundation annually contributed more than $50 million, is among those that scaled back considerably after hitting had times (Figure 12-2). Indeed, on the heels of the nation's recession in 2001, corporate giving fell 12 percent to $9 billion in 2001. This equated to an average of 1.3 percent of corporate pretax profits.[7]

After September 11, 2001, companies responded across the board with community generosity. Among them:

- Marsch & McLennan Companies, an insurer that lost hundreds of employees in the World Trade Center, donated $20 million to its Victims' Relief Fund.
- ExxonMobil Corporation donated $16.25 million to support various relief and recovery organizations.
- Citigroup Foundation donated $15 million to support relief efforts and provide scholarships for the children of victims.
- Deutsche Bank, a German financial power with offices at the Trade Center, donated $13 million to aid the families of New York City police and firemen.[8]

Another element of "giving back to the community" is voluntarism. Many firms, which have given generously to their communities, have begun to become more directly involved by actively encouraging executives and employees to roll up their sleeves and volunteer to help out in their communities. At the Walt Disney Company, for example, Disney VoluntEARS spent more than 800,000 hours in volunteer services over a two-year span. A national effort to spur voluntarism was launched in 1998, under the leadership of Colin Powell. Called "America's Promise—The Alliance for Youth," Secretary of State Powell's initiative was designed to "give back" to the community by connecting 2 million children from poorer neighborhoods with adult mentors and "hope for a brighter future" (Figure 12-3).

Such initiatives reject the oft-quoted notion of University of Chicago economics professor Milton Friedman that a corporation's only responsibility is to make money and sell products, so that people can be hired and paid. It is the job of the individual, not the company, Professor Friedman argued, to serve society through philanthropy. Most companies today flatly reject the Friedman argument. They understand that in the 21st century an organization must be a "citizen" of the community in every respect and accept its role as an agent for social change in the community.

For an organization to coexist peacefully in its community, three skills in particular are required: (1) determining what the community knows and thinks about the organization, (2) informing the community of the organization's point of view, and (3) negotiating or mediating between the organization and the community and its constituents, should there be a significant discrepancy.

Basically, every organization wants to foster positive reactions in its community. This becomes increasingly difficult in the face of protests from and disagreements with

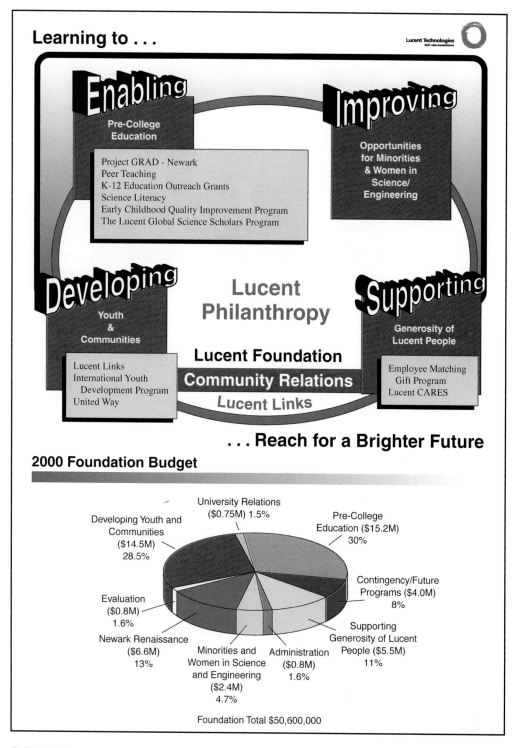

FIGURE 12-2 **Enlightened self-interest.** Until the fall of the telcom sector in 2000, Lucent Technologies was one of the most "enlightened" of corporations, annually donating more than $50 million to a wide variety of worthwhile charitable endeavors in the fields of education and youth development.

FIGURE 12-3

America's Promise. Secretary of State Colin Powell, President George W. Bush, and the symbol of America's Promise— The Alliance for Youth, the little red wagon.

community activists. Community relations, therefore—to analyze the community, help understand its makeup and expectations, and communicate the organization's story in an understandable and uninterrupted way—are critical.

Community Relations Expectations

The community of an organization can vary widely, depending on the size and nature of the business. The 7-Eleven grocery store may have a community of only a few city blocks, the community of a Buick assembly plant may be the city where the plant is located, and the community of a multinational corporation may embrace much of the world.

What the Community Expects

Communities expect from resident organizations such tangible commodities as wages, employment, and taxes. But communities have come to expect intangible contributions, too:

- **Appearance.** The community hopes that the firm will contribute positively to life in the area. It expects facilities to be attractive, with care spent on the grounds and the plant. Increasingly, community neighbors object to plants that belch smoke and pollute water and air. Occasionally, neighbors organize to oppose the entrance of factories, coal mines, oil wells, drug treatment centers, and other facilities suspected of being harmful to the community's environment. Government, too, is acting more vigorously to punish offenders and to make sure that organizations comply with zoning, environmental, and safety regulations.
- **Participation.** As a citizen of the community, an organization is expected to participate responsibly in community affairs, such as civic functions, park and recreational activities, education, welfare, and support of religious institutions.

- **Stability.** A business that fluctuates sharply in volume of business, number of employees, and taxes paid can adversely affect the community through its impact on municipal services, school loads, public facilities, and tax revenues. Communities prefer stable organizations that will grow with the area. Conversely, they want to keep out short-term operations that could create temporary boom conditions and leave ghost towns in their wake.
- **Pride.** Any organization that can help put the community on the map simply by being there is usually a valuable addition. Communities want firms that are proud to be residents. For instance, to most Americans, Battle Creek, Michigan, means cereal; Armonk, New York, means IBM; and Hershey, Pennsylvania, means chocolate. That's why the residents of Hershey were fearful when, in 2002, Nestle-Corporation offered to buy the pride of Hershey for $11.5 billion. Organizations that help build the town generally become revered symbols of pride.

What the Organization Expects

Organizations, in turn, expect to be provided with adequate municipal services, fair taxation, good living conditions for employees, a good labor supply, and a reasonable degree of support for the business and its products. When some of these requirements are missing, organizations may move to communities where such benefits are more readily available.

The great inner-city exodus of the 1970s is a case in point. New York City, for example, experienced a substantial exodus of corporations, when firms fled to neighboring Connecticut and New Jersey, as well as to the Sun Belt states of the Southeast and Southwest. New York's state and city legislators responded to the challenge by working more closely with business residents on such issues as corporate taxation. By the new century, not only had the corporate flight to the Sun Belt been arrested, but also many firms reconsidered the Big Apple and returned to the now more business-friendly city and state.

After the terrorist attacks of September 11, 2001, New York Governor George Pataki and New York City Mayor Michael Bloomberg teamed with the federal government to encourage companies to return to their Lower Manhattan offices that had been devastated.

The issue for most urban areas faced with steadily eroding tax bases is to find a formula that meets the concerns of business corporations while accommodating the needs of other members of the community.

Community Relations Objectives

Research into community relations indicates that winning community support for an organization is no easy matter. Studies indicate difficulty in achieving rapport with community neighbors, who expect support from the company but object to any dominance on its part in community affairs.

One device that is helpful is a written community relations policy that clearly defines the philosophy of management as it views its obligation to the community. Employees, in particular, must understand and exemplify their firm's community relations policy; to many in the community, the workers are the company.

A QUESTION OF ETHICS

Sierra Club Sizzles as Ford Eco Standards Fizzle

You had to sympathize with Ford Motor Company CEO William C. Ford, Jr., who found himself in hot water with the Sierra Club, environmental advocate, in 2002.

Under Ford's leadership, the car company was the first to publish an annual corporate citizenship report, frankly discussing such taboo subjects as the impact of sport utility vehicles on global warming and smog-forming pollutants (Figure 12-4).

While competitors bristled at the Ford social responsibility innovations, CEO Ford and his company earned great credit from environmental groups. In the first report, Mr. Ford himself acknowledged that some

FIGURE 12-4 **No one doubted that new Ford CEO William Clay Ford was sincere about his desire to act responsibly.** Unfortunately, declining business conditions made him put some environmental pledges on hold. (Courtesy of Ford Motor Company)

of his peers regarded him as a "Bolshevik" for his pro-environmental stance.

By 2002, however, Ford Motor Company had fallen into difficult times. The year before, it suffered a loss of $5.5 billion. While foreign imports like Honda and Toyota threatened Ford's cars, German-backed Chrysler put additional pressure on Ford by launching a price war.

Things became so dicey for the historic auto manufacturer that Ford had to scale back certain of its environmental commitments in order to make more money.

Its old friend the Sierra Club was outraged.

"This report takes a giant step in the wrong direction for Ford Motor Company, for American consumers, and for the environment," huffed the Sierra Club's executive director.

After two years of proudly issuing its corporate citizenship report, Ford delayed publication of its 2002 installment for four months. CEO Ford was apologetic in explaining the less ambitious tone of its initiatives.

"Difficult business conditions make it harder to achieve the goals we set for ourselves in many areas, including corporate citizenship. But that doesn't mean we will abandon our goals or change our direction."

The Sierra Club wasn't buying it and questioned Ford's ethics. "It moves the ball backwards . . . and raises troubling questions about Ford's commitment to improving its environmental performance."

One couldn't help but wonder if Ford, too, was questioning the ethics, not to mention the understanding, of its former environmental friend.*

*For further information, see Danny Hakin, "Ford Stresses Business but Disappoints Environmentalists," *New York Times* (August 20, 2002): xx.

This plan focuses on three key elements: products, cost reduction and aligning our manufacturing capacity with worldwide demand. It lets us get back to the basics of building great products, and doing so profitably.

A legitimate question to ask is whether our intense focus on the economic side of our business will distract us from our environmental and social efforts. As we said in last year's report, corporate citizenship can only be achieved in the context of a strong and profitable business. But it's also true that businesses can only be as successful as the communities, and the world, that they exist in. That makes ongoing corporate citizenship efforts essential.

Difficult business conditions make it harder to achieve the goals we set for ourselves in many areas, including

corporate citizenship. But that doesn't mean we will abandon our goals or change our direction.

Our revitalization plan is working. Although it includes many short-term actions, the plan gains momentum over the next several years as we launch new products. By mid-decade, we will generate billions of dollars of improved profitability.

> *Difficult business conditions make it harder to achieve the goals we set for ourselves in many areas, including corporate citizenship. But that doesn't mean we will abandon our goals or change our direction.*

Our environmental efforts also build momentum as we introduce new products. In the United States, we are committed to continuous improvement in the fuel economy of all of our vehicles. In Europe, we have agreed, along with others, to reduce the average CO_2 emissions of the vehicles we sell there.

The Company also has set a global target to reduce energy use at its facilities on a production-normalized basis.

And we are proceeding on schedule with the development of the Ford Rouge Center, which will transform our historic Rouge manufacturing complex in Dearborn, Michigan, into a global model of lean and sustainable manufacturing.

Socially, we continue to have a major impact as a large company with a worldwide presence. In 2001, for example, our total charitable giving reached an all-time high of $139 million for projects focused on education, the environment and community development.

Unfortunately, our efforts to strengthen our business economically will have an adverse effect on some employees and communities. We expect to reduce our workforce by 35,000 people worldwide, on a base of 350,000, when all our actions are completed — including closing five plants in North America by mid-decade. We will make every effort to make the changes as non-disruptive and mutually beneficial as possible.

We realize that some of the things that must be done will be painful and will impact people's lives in difficult ways. But I sincerely believe that these actions will do the most good for the most people in the long term.

2001 Corporate Citizenship Report — Our Learning Journey   3

FIGURE 12-4   (Continued)

Typical community relations objectives may include the following:

1. To tell the community about the operations of the firm: its products, number of employees, size of the payroll, tax payments, employee benefits, growth, and support of community projects
2. To correct misunderstandings, reply to criticism, and remove any disaffection that may exist among community neighbors
3. To gain the favorable opinion of the community, particularly during strikes and periods of labor unrest, by stating the company's position on the issues involved
4. To inform employees and their families about company activities and developments, so that they can tell their friends and neighbors about the company and favorably influence opinions of the organization
5. To inform people in local government about the firm's contributions to community welfare and to obtain support for legislation that will favorably affect the business climate of the community
6. To find out what residents think about the company, why they like or dislike its policies and practices, and how much they know of its policy, operations, and problems
7. To establish a personal relationship between management and community leaders by inviting leaders to visit the plant and offices, meet management, and see employees at work
8. To support health programs through contributions of both funds and employee services to local campaigns
9. To contribute to culture by providing funds for art exhibits, concerts, and drama festivals and by promoting attendance at such affairs
10. To aid youth and adult education by cooperating with administrators and teachers in providing student vocational guidance, plant tours, speakers, films, and teaching aids and by giving financial and other support to schools
11. To encourage sports and recreational activities by providing athletic fields, swimming pools, golf courses, or tennis courts for use by community residents and by sponsoring teams and sports events
12. To promote better local and county government by encouraging employees to run for public office or to volunteer to serve on administrative boards; by lending company executives to community agencies or to local government to give specialized advice and assistance on municipal problems; and by making company facilities and equipment available to the community in times of emergency (Figure 12-5)
13. To assist the economy of the community by purchasing operating supplies and equipment from local merchants and manufacturers whenever possible
14. To operate a profitable business in order to provide jobs and to pay competitive wages that increase the community's purchasing power and strengthen its economy
15. To cooperate with other local businesses in advancing economic and social welfare through joint community relations programs financed and directed by the participating organizations

Community Relations on the Internet

At the heart of the Internet is a sense of community. Indeed, the Internet links people of like-minded interests in a virtual community, although "community members" may live continents away.

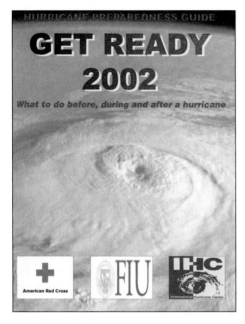
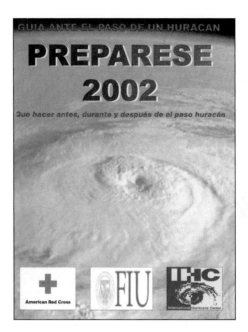

FIGURE 12-5 **Cooperative citizenship.** Florida International University's Public Relations Student Society of America has, for many years, teamed with BP Amoco and the International Hurricane Center to provide a valuable "Hurricane Alert Program" to the community—in both English and Spanish.

From this concept of community has emerged an effort to use the Internet for social good, to expand educational and commercial opportunities for minority communities as well as provide a philanthropic forum for the less fortunate. For example:

- Black Entertainment Television created BET.com to bring "connectivity, content, and commerce" to African Americans, a community decidedly underrepresented in cyberspace. Although 74 percent of white college and high school students own computers, only 32 percent of African American students own computers. So armed with $35 million, the largest online investment ever aimed at African Americans, BET.com hopes to help African Americans become more computer savvy and bring "connectivity, content, and commerce" to the global black online population.[9] "Although some black-oriented sites, among them the NetNoir.com pop culture portal and the hip, urban Volume.com portal, suffered layoffs when the Internet bubble burst, such sites still showed great potential. As proof, in 2000, Time Warner paid $10 million for Africana.com in an effort to attract more African American users to AOL.[10]

- In a more global community effort, Cisco Systems launched "NetAid" in 1999 to raise awareness of and cash for the 1 billion people living in extreme poverty throughout the world. NetAid's initially webcast live concerts from New Jersey with the Black Crowes and Mary J. Blige, from London with David Bowie and the Eurythmics, and from Geneva with Bryan Ferry and Ladysmith Black Mambazo, among others. Cisco kicked in $22 million to make sure that "the Internet would serve as a bootstrap mechanism to improve people's lives."[11]

- Perhaps the most ambitious socially responsible undertaking on the Internet was GreaterGood.com, one of a number of Internet firms that introduced a cause orientation to e-commerce. GreaterGood.com was aimed at America's 650,000 registered not-for-profit charities—from Big Brothers/Big Sisters to Special Olympics to Elizabeth Glaser Pediatric AIDS Foundation. It helped fund these charities by arranging the sale of name-brand retail items on not-for-profit Web sites and then donating part of the purchase price back to the charity.[12]

Although the Internet may be characterized by some as metallic and heartless, efforts such as these underscore the Internet's immense potential in furthering human relations and progress—across common communities and for the larger society.

Serving Diverse Communities

What were once referred to as "minorities" are rapidly becoming the majority.

The U.S. Census Bureau reports that more than two-thirds of current U.S. and future population growth is and will be the result of immigration. The 11.2 milliion immigrants who indicated they arrived in the United States between 1990 and 2000, plus the 6.4 million children born to immigrants in the United States during the 1990s, are equal to almost 70 percent of the U.S. population growth over the last 10 years.[13]

According to the Census Bureau, Latinos will soon overtake African Americans as the largest minority group, but the fastest-growing segment of minorities will be Asians and Pacific Islanders, whose numbers will increase fivefold.[14]

For many years, women were considered a minority by public relations professionals. This is no longer the case; women now dominate not only the public relations field but also many service industries. Women, African Americans, Latinos, Asians, gays, and a variety of other groups have become not only important members of the labor force but also important sources of discretionary income.

Public relations professionals must be sensitive to the demands of all for equal pay, promotional opportunities, equal rights in the workplace, and so on. Communicating effectively in light of the multicultural diversity of society has become an important public relations challenge.

Women

In the 21st century, women have made great strides in "leveling the playing field" between their roles and compensation schedules and those of their male counterparts. The days of "mommy tracks" and "mommy wars," glass ceilings, and pink-collar ghettos are rapidly falling by the wayside.

Women today head large corporations, especially in the high-tech area, where Carly Fiorina was recruited in 1999 to become CEO of powerful Hewlett-Packard; Meg Whitman is given great credit as eBay's CEO; and Anne Mulcahy was named CEO by Xerox Corporation in 2001 and charged with the formidable task of rescuing that once great company.

In public relations as well, women have increasingly graduated into middle-management and upper-management positions, particularly at public relations agencies. In the corporate area, there is still a disparate number of men holding top public relations jobs.

Although some disparities also may linger in compensation schedules in public relations and other fields, equality of the sexes in the workplace is clearly an imminent reality.[15]

African Americans

Today, 25 of the nation's largest cities—including Chicago, Detroit, and Los Angeles—have a majority population of African Americans, Latinos, and Asians. In addition, foreign-born blacks have increased materially in numbers. In Miami, the West Indian population makes up 48 percent of the black population. In New York, nearly a third of the black population is foreign-born.

The socioeconomic status of African Americans has improved markedly, with disposable income increasing fivefold over the past decade.

Despite their continuing evolution in the white-dominated workplace, the nation's 29 million African Americans can still be reached effectively through special media:

- Black Entertainment Television is a popular TV network that has done well.
- Local African American radio stations have prospered.
- Pioneering Internet sites, such as BlackFamilies.com, Blackvoices.com, NetNoir.com, and The Black World Today (www.tbwt.com) have created a culture of acceptance and desirability for Web access among African Americans.
- Magazines such as *Black Enterprise* and *Essence* are national vehicles. *Ebony,* the largest African American–oriented publication in the world, has a circulation of 1.3 million.
- Newspapers, such as the *Amsterdam News* in New York City and the *Daily Defender* in Chicago, also are targeted to African Americans. Such newspapers are controlled by active owners whose personal viewpoints dominate editorial policy.

All should be included in the normal media relations functions of any organization. In recent years, companies have made a concerted effort to understand the family structure, traditions, and social mores of the black community through sponsorship of programs targeted to pressing community needs.

One area of frustration in improving the livelihood of African Americans is the practice of public relations. The field has failed to attract sufficient numbers of African American practitioners to its ranks. In recent years, the Public Relations Society of America has increased outreach efforts to attract and retain African Americans. It established the D. Parke Gibson Pioneer Award in 1994 to recognize a practitioner who increases awareness of public relations within multicultural communities. Parke Gibson was a pioneer in multicultural relations and author of two books on African American consumerism.

The National Black Public Relations Society was created to increase the participation of and resources available to black public relations professionals. It has seven chapters and sponsors an annual conference.

Attracting African Americans to the field remains a great challenge to public relations leaders in the new century.

Latinos

There is little question why companies need to reach Latinos. Currently 38 million strong, the group is growing three times faster than the rest of the country. The Census Bureau predicts that the Latin population will jump from 11 to 14 percent in the next 10 years. At the same time, the African American population is expected to level off at approximately 12.5 percent. Thus, Latinos will soon be the nation's most prominent minority group, and by 2050, Latinos will comprise one-third of the population, nearly 100 million people.[16]

The U.S. Hispanic population already ranks as the fifth largest in the world, behind Mexico, Spain, Columbia and Argentina. There are more than 7.6 million Hispanic households in the United States, with 74 percent of Hispanics residing mainly in five states—California, Texas, New York, Florida, and Illinois.

New York City has the largest Latin population with 1.8 million residents. Los Angeles rates second with more than 1 million.[17] The majority of U.S. Latinos—62 percent—are of Mexican origin. About 13 percent are of Puerto Rican origin, and 5 percent are of Cuban origin. In Los Angeles, Latino kindergarten enrollment is 66 percent and rising. The Anglo enrollment is 15 percent and falling.

Accordingly, Latinos comprise a potent political and economic force. Between 1994 and 1998, Latino voting in nationwide midterm elections jumped 27 percent, even as overall voter turnout dropped. In terms of commerce, U.S. Latinos pump $400 billion a year into the economy.[18]

Latinos are voracious media consumers, relying heavily on TV and radio to stay informed (Figure 12-6). Two large Spanish-programming networks, Univision and Telemundo, dominate the airwaves, with Univision drawing 83 percent of the country's adult, prime-time, Spanish-language viewing audience.[19] CNN also offers a daily program in Spanish for its Latin American viewers.

Magazines also are a great source of entertainment to the Latino community, so recent years have seen a plethora of new offerings, from *LatinCEO* for top executives to *Latina* magazine for teenage girls to *Healthy Kids en Español* for parents to the general-interest *Latina* and *People en Espanol*.

In addition, radio stations and newspapers that communicate in Spanish, such as New York City's *El Diario* and *La Prensa*, are prominent voices in reaching this increasingly important community.

Other Ethnic Groups

Beyond Latinos, other ethnic groups—particularly Asians—have increased their importance in the American marketplace.

Japanese, Chinese, Koreans, Vietnamese, and others have gained new prominence as consumers and constituents. Asians and Pacific Islanders account for 4 percent of the U.S. population. At about 7 million today, that number is expected to nearly quintuple—to 32 million by 2050.[20]

FIGURE 12-6 Todas las Noticias. Television is a key medium for reaching Latinos. News anchors Edwardo Quezada and Andrea Kutyas delivered "Noticias 34" for KMEX-TV.

The formation of the Asian American Advertising and Public Relations Alliance in California underscored the increasing prominence of Asian Americans in the public relations profession.

Gays, Seniors, and Others

In the 21st century, a diverse assortment of special communities has gravitated into the mainstream of American commerce.

One such group is the gay market. To some, homosexuality may remain a target of opprobrium, but in the new century, the gay market, estimated at 12 to 20 million Americans, comprises a major target of opportunity.

An increasing number of marketers, including IBM, United Airlines, and Anheuser-Busch, run ads with gay themes. Generally, marketers confine such advertising to the gay press. However, in 2000, Gfn.com devoted $6 million to advertise its Gay Financial Network Internet Web site in the mainstream media. This groundbreaking campaign indicated that gay advertising was ready to cross over into the more widely read and seen media.[21]

The clear conclusion is that the gay market—average age 36, household income six times higher than the national average and with more discretionary income than average, three times more likely to be college graduates than the national average, and 86 percent of whom saying they would purchase products specifically marketed to them—has become extremely attractive to all kinds of marketers.

In addition to gay men and women, senior citizens also have become an important community for public relations professionals and the organizations they represent. The baby boomer generation has passed 50 years of age. Together, the over-50 crowd controls more than 50 percent of America's discretionary income. The AARP, founded in 1958, has a membership of more than 35 million members, about half of whom work.

As the American population grows older, the importance of senior citizens—as consumers, voters, and opinion leaders—will increase. Public relations professionals must be sensitive to that reality and to the fact that other special communities in society will increasingly demand specialized treatment and targeted communications.

At no time was this fact more apparent than when actor Christopher Reeve was paralyzed in 1996 after falling off a horse. Mr. Reeve, who gained fame as the movie hero Superman, became an effective and outspoken advocate for people with disabilities, calling for an additional $40 million a year in congressional funding.[22]

Growing Community Advocacy

One outgrowth of the increased voice in society of minority groups and other special communities is a willingness on the part of community groups to speak out and object to what they perceive as wrongs.

One popular tactic in raising public awareness, particularly among community groups, is so-called "media advocacy." Media advocacy is public relations without resources. It is using the media to attract attention and shake the established order.[23] Examples abound:

- In 1999, antibiotech activists around the world used the Internet and the media to challenge genetically modified foods. In the face of the attack, the world's biggest biotech companies mounted a massive public relations

S I D E B A R

Tuning Out Dr. Laura

Dr. Laura Schlesinger, known to her faithful radio fans as "Dr. Laura," was no pushover.

She scolded, chided, and bridled her callers. She dressed them down if they admitted to extramarital affairs, bullied them if they weren't stern with their children, and mocked them if they were single with child. And the 18 million strong radio audience ate it up. So much so that Paramount signed her to a $3 million TV contract.

But then Dr. Laura ran into a force the likes of which she had never encountered—the gay community.

Led by the Gay and Lesbian Alliance Against Defamation, the gay community and feminist groups teamed up to oppose Dr. Laura going on television. Full-page newspaper ads quoted her as saying, "I always told people who opposed homosexuality that they were homophobic, bad, bigoted and idiotic. I was wrong."

Dr. Laura was further quoted as saying that homosexuality was a "biological error—where a huge portion of the male homosexual populace is predatory on young boys."

But she was no match for the gay community. The gay activists created a Web site, StopDrLaura.com, and began targeting specific advertisers as "bad guys," going so far as to publish the personal telephone numbers, e-mail addresses, and fax numbers of key executives. Other anti-Laura Web sites began to proliferate (Figure 12-7).

Soon after the protests began, Procter & Gamble canceled plans to advertise on the TV program. The company said it had decided "to place our commercials in less polarizing environments." P&G was followed by Sears, Gateway, and Red Lobster, all of whom repudiated Dr. Laura's language against gays.

In all, 170 advertisers reportedly shunned the Dr. Laura TV show, which was unceremoniously dropped after one season. The result: Gay community 1, Dr. Laura 0.

For further information, see David France, "Tuning Out Dr. Laura," *Newsweek,* (September 18, 2000): 80; and Aimee Grove, "GLAAD Ups Attack on Dr. Laura's TV Debut," *PR Week* (August 28, 2000): 1.

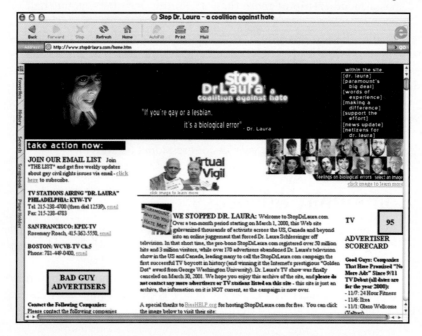

FIGURE 12-7 **Dr. Laura exposed.** The fighting got ugly when allies joined the gay community in opposing Dr. Laura's TV show.

Do you feel ripped off having to pay over $100 for a pair of sneakers?

How do you think the men and women who made your sneakers feel?

Most of NIKE's sneakers are made in Indonesia, Vietnam, and China. They make up to 100 shoes and get paid between $2 and $4 per day.

How do you think Philip Knight feels? He's the Chief Executive Officer of NIKE and the 6th richest man in America worth over $5 billion dollars!

Join the SNEAKER GIVE-BACK and protest.

SATURDAY, SEPTEMBER 27, 11:00 A.M.
at
NIKE TOWN, USA
6 East 57th Street off 5th Ave.

Join Youth from community centers in NYC as they turn in sneakers and speak out to protest NIKE business practices here and overseas.

Tell Philip Knight (NIKE's CEO) to pay a decent "LIVING WAGE" to employees in southeast Asia and to stop overcharging and misleading youth here. Reinvest profits in our communities and youth.

Participating Organizations (list in formation, call to participate):

Citizen's Advice Bureau	*East Side House*
Edenwald Gun Hill Neighborhood Center	*Forrest Hills Community House*
Goddard Riverside Community Center	*Hartley House*
James Weldon Johnson Comm. Center	*Kingsbridge Heights Community Center*
School Settlement	*United Community Center*
United Neighborhood Houses Of NYC	

For additional information:

Edenwald GunHill Neighborhood Center	**Goddard Riverside Community Center**
1150 East 229th Street, Bronx, N.Y. 10466	**593 Columbus Ave, N.Y., N.Y. 10024**
Phone: (718) 652-2232	**Phone: (212) 873-6600 ext. 204**

Labor donated

FIGURE 12-8 **Power to the people.** Huge corporations such as Nike are sensitive when their policies and public image are questioned by protests and placards (continued on next page).

campaign to counter a campaign that vilified firms like Monsanto, labeling it "Mutanto" and "Monsatan."[24]

● The mighty Nike Corporation came under attack for selling astronomically priced sneakers while underpaying its workers (Figure 12-8). The protest centered on the company's flagship retail outlet, Nike Town USA in New York City.

**Settlement House Youth
NIKE Give Back Campaign**

Its a New Year, We're Still Here

It's 1998 and Nike has not changed:
-Your still being charged $75 - $200 for $6 sneakers.
-Nike workers are still underpaid.
-They're still not giving back to your community.

In the spirit of Martin Luther King Jr. we protest
these practices!

January 19, 1998
12:00 noon - 1:00 pm
at Niketown
6 East 57th Street

Bring your old Nike sneakers and apparel.

For more information:

Edenwald - Gun Hill	Goddard Riverside
Neighborhood Center	Community Center
(718) 652-2232	(212) 873-6600, ext. 204

Labor donated

FIGURE 12-8 (Continued)

● In 2000, the group People for the Ethical Treatment of Animals (PETA) had to apologize to New York Mayor Rudy Giuliani for using his face on a billboard that linked milk consumption to prostate cancer, from which Giuliani was recovering (Figure 12-9). PETA was eminently more successful the next year, when it convinced the big three burger makers, McDonald's, Burger King, and Wendy's, to bolster their animal welfare standards. Although the burger makers denied PETA had anything to do with them strengthening the oversight of suppliers, most people thought differently.[25]

FIGURE 12-9
Milk militants. PETA sought to defend the rights of milk cows with this campaign. (Courtesy of PETA)

The Internet has been a tremendous boon to activists, magnifying the clout and reach of resource-challenged groups around the world. Undoubtedly enhancing the spread of activism in the years ahead will be the increased access to and proficiency with the Internet as a tool of social discontent. Nontheless, the grandaddy of all social activists, legendary labor organizer Saul Alinsky, is probably still the final word on activism three decades after publishing his radical manifesto (see Sidebar).

Nonprofit Public Relations

Among the most important champions of multiculturalism in any community are nonprofit organizations. Nonprofit organizations serve the social, educational, religious, and cultural needs of the community around them. So important is the role of public relations in nonprofit organizations that this sector is a primary source of employment for public relations graduates.

The nonprofit sector is characterized by a panoply of institutions: hospitals, schools, trade asociations, labor unions, chambers of commerce, social welfare agencies, religious institutions, cultural organizations, and the like. The general goals of nonprofit agencies are not dissimilar to those of corporations. Nonprofits seek to win public support of their

13 Rules for Radicals

Want to know how to organize a winning protest on campus?

Here are the time-honored suggestions of labor leader Saul Alinsky, from his 1971 classic, *Rules for Radicals*. They are just as relevant now as they were then. (Just don't tell anybody where you learned 'em!)

1. Power is not only what you have but what the enemy thinks you have.
2. Never go outside the experience of your people.
3. Whenever possible, go outside the experience of the enemy.
4. Make the enemy live up to its own book of rules.
5. Ridicule is a person's most potent weapon.
6. A good tactic is one that your people enjoy.
7. A tactic that drags on too long becomes a drag.
8. Keep the pressure on.
9. The threat is usually more terrifying than the thing itself.
10. The major premise for tactics is the development of operations that will maintain a constant pressure on the opposition.
11. If you push a negative hard and deep enough, it will break through to its counterside.
12. The price of a successful attack is a constructive alternative.
13. Pick the target, freeze it, personalize it, and polarize it.

mission and programs through active and open communications. Unlike corporations, though, nonprofits also seek to broaden volunteer participation in their efforts, often through the use of controversial communications (Figure 12-10).

Master of Many Trades

Also unlike corporations, nonprofits generally don't have much money for key activities. That's why public relations professionals in nonprofits must be masters of many functions, key among them are the following:

FIGURE 12-10

Nonprofit communicators. The Campaign for Tobacco-Free Kids was chaired by former public relations executive William Novelli, who aggressively spoke out about the evils of cigarette smoking. (Courtesy of Campaign for Tobacco-Free Kids)

Positioning the Organization

With thousands of competitors vying for support dollars, a nonprofit must stand out from the rest. This positioning initiative depends largely on the public relations function. To successfully position the organization, a practitioner must ask:

1. What position do we own; that is, who are we?
2. What position do we want?
3. Who else is out there and what is their position?
4. Do we have the funds to get us where we wish to go?
5. Can we stick it out over time?
6. Do all our communications line up with each other?

No organization, particularly a resource-challenged nonprofit, can afford to be "all things to all people." The best nonprofits, like the best corporations, stand for something. And they are unafraid to "break a few eggs" in order to achieve a clear and differentiable identity (Figure 12-11).

FIGURE 12-11   **Communications hardball.** Nonprofits must make every communications dollar count. So when the American Cancer Society, American Heart Association, American Lung Association, and Campaign for Tobacco-Free Kids got together against big tobacco, they pulled no punches.

Developing a Marketing/Promotional Plan

Often in nonprofits the public relations director is the marketing director is the advertising director is the promotion director. The job, simply, is marketing the organization to raise its profile, respect, and levels of support. This requires planning in terms of audiences, messages, and vehicles to deliver those messages to those audiences. Crucial in framing these messages is to recognize the "cause-related" quotient—that is, what the organization stands for—around which the marketing campaign is based.

Strategic Planning

Nonprofit public relations campaigns must depend on clear and coherent messages, which articulate well-formulated strategies. What that implies is that the nonprofit public relations professional must (1) plan, (2) define issues, (3) build strategies, (4) frame issues, (5) develop talking points, (6) choose appropriate spokespersons,(7) develop communications materials, and (8) target messages.

Media Relations

Because most nonprofits lack sufficient resources for advertising or formal marketing, the use of "free" media is a critical public relations function. As broadcaster Daniel Schorr once put it, "If you don't exist in the media, for all practical purposes you don't exist." Nonprofits desperately need media advocates, who champion their cause and mission. Advocacy strategy can take the form of a variety of initiatives:

- **Talk radio.** The extensive audience of this medium is a natural way to spread the nonprofit gospel.
- **Cable TV.** So, too, is the nonstop menu of nightly cable talk television programs, all hungry for outspoken, opinionated, articulate guests.
- **Op eds.** Opinion editorials drafted by nonprofit executives are another prominent—and cheap!—way of getting points of view aired to an influential audience.
- **Cable access.** Community channels are generally willing repositories for nonprofit programming and talent.

Supporting Fund-Raising

Nonprofits depend on donors for support. Fund-raising, therefore, is a key nonprofit challenge that must engage the attention of the organization's key executives. Public relations professionals must be intimately involved in fund-raising communications and appeals, so that messages can be targeted and consistent with the organization's general position.

Clearly, there are many other duties of the nonprofit public relations professional. Nonprofit public relations and marketing are described by some as "performing, pleading, petitioning, and praying." To be sure, the falloff in the stock market and the recession in the United States in the early years of the 21st century have made the challenge for many nonprofits that much more difficult.

Nonetheless, because America is a nation of joiners and belongers, nonprofit organizations in our society will most certainly continue to proliferate. And the need for competent public relations help will continue to be central to their existence and vitality.

Fund-Raising

Fund-raising—the need to raise money to support operations—lies at the heart of every nonprofit institution. Schools, hospitals, churches, and organizations—from the mighty United Way to the smallest block association—can't exist without a constant source of private funds. Frequently, the fund-raising assignment becomes the province of public relations professionals. Like other aspects of public relations work, fund-raising must be accomplished in a planned and programmatic way.

A successful fund-raising campaign should include the following basic steps:

1. *Identify campaign plans and objectives.* Broad financial targets should be set. A goal should be announced. Specific sectors of the community, from which funds might be extracted, should be targeted in advance.
2. *Organize fact-finding.* Relevant trends that might affect giving should be noted. Relations with various elements of the community should be defined. The national and local economies should be considered, as should current attitudes toward charitable contributions.
3. *Recruit leaders.* The best fund-raising campaigns are ones with strong leadership. A hallmark of local United Way campaigns, for example, is the recruitment of strong business leaders to spearhead contribution efforts. It is the responsibility of the nonprofit itself to direct its leaders, particularly outside directors, so that their efforts can be targeted in the best interests of the organization.[26]
4. *Plan and implement strong communications activities.* The best fund-raising campaigns are also the most visible. Publicity and promotion must be stressed. Special events should be organized, particularly featuring national and local celebrities to support the drive. Updates on fund-raising progress should be communicated, particularly to volunteers and contributors.
5. *Periodically review and evaluate.* Review the fund-raising program as it progresses. Make midcourse corrections when activities succeed or fail beyond expectations. Evaluate program achievements against program targets. Revise strategies constantly as the goal becomes nearer.

Because many public relations graduates enter the nonprofit realm, a knowledge of fund-raising strategies and techniques is especially important. Beginning practitioners, once hired in the public relations office of a college, hospital, religious group, charitable organization, or other nonprofit organization, are soon confronted with questions about how public relations can help raise money for the organization.

LAST WORD

The increasing cultural diversity of society in the 21st century has spawned a wave of "political correctness," particularly in the United States. Predictably, many have questioned whether sensitivity to women, people of color, the physically challenged, seniors, and other groups has gone too far. One thing, however, is certain. The makeup of society—of consumers, employees, political constituents, and so on—has been altered inexorably. The number of discrete communities with which organizations must be concerned will continue to increase.

Intelligent organizations in our society must be responsive to the needs and desires of their communities. Positive community relations must begin with a clear understanding of community concerns, an open door for community leaders, an open and honest flow of information from the organization, and an ongoing sense of continuous involvement and interaction with community publics.

Community relations is only as effective as the support it receives from top management. Once that support is clear, it becomes the responsibility of the public relations professional to ensure that the relationship between the organization and all of its multicultural communities is one of mutual trust, understanding, and support.

Discussion Starters

1. How is the atmosphere for community relations different today than it was in the 1960s?
2. What is meant by the term *multicultural diversity*?
3. In general terms, what does a community expect from a resident organization?
4. What are typical community relations objectives for an organization?
5. What was the philosophy of corporate responsibility espoused by economist Milton Friedman?
6. What is meant by the term *media advocacy*?
7. Why do companies need to reach the Latino community?
8. What are the primary responsibilities of a nonprofit public relations professional?
9. What is meant by the term *corporate social responsibility*?
10. What are the basis steps of a fund-raising campaign?

TOP OF THE SHELF

Saul D. Alinsky

Rules for Radicals: A Practical Primer for Realistic Radicals
New York: Vintage Books, 1989

As ancient as it is, Alinsky's *Rules for Radicals* is still the classic handbook for those bent on organizing communities, rattling the status quo, and effecting social and political change as well as for those who wish to learn from a legendary master.

Alinsky, a veteran community activist who fought on behalf of the poor from New York to California, provides strategies for building coalitions and for using communication, conflict, and confrontation advantageously.

In "Of Means and Ends," Alinsky lists 11 rules of ethics that define the uses of radical power. His discussion of tactics suggests 13 ways to help organizers defeat their foes. Rule 3, for instance, tells activists to go outside the experience of their enemy to "cause confusion, fear, and retreat."

Alinsky supports his principles with numerous examples, the most colorful of which occurred when he wanted to draw attention to a particular cause in Rochester, New York. To do so, Alinsky and his group attended a Rochester Symphony performance—after a meal of nothing but beans. The results were hilarious.

Alinsky died in 1972, but his lessons endure in this offbeat guide to seizing power. Whether your goal is to fluster the establishment or defend it, *Rules for Radicals* is must reading. So read it!

CASE STUDY

Guess Who's Coming to Denny's

Few allegations are more damaging to a company's reputation than charges of racism.

When systemic racism is revealed in the ranks, strong—and often momentarily painful—remedial action must be taken. This is precisely what Denny's restaurants did—to the tune of $54 million—in the spring of 1994.

Denny's was vilified as a symbol of racial discrimination. But in the years immediately following the company's embarrassing and painful publicity, Denny's became a model of progressive diversity.

PAINFUL BREAKFAST AT DENNY'S

With more than 1,500 company and franchise restaurants located throughout the United States, Denny's is the nation's largest full-service family restaurant chain. On April Fool's Day 1993, 21 members of the Secret Service, preparing for a Naval Academy visit by President Clinton, stopped for breakfast at a Denny's outside Annapolis, Maryland.

Fifteen of the officers were served quickly, but one table of six uniformed men—all black—never received the food they had ordered. As it turned out, although their food was ready for a full 20 minutes, neither the waitress nor her manager felt compelled to serve the black agents until they got around to it.

The officers' subsequent discrimination suit unleashed a tidal wave of damning national publicity and legal actions against the 43-year-old company. Dan Rather summarized the situation on *CBS News*: These agents "put their lives on the line every day, but they can't get served at Denny's."

Denny's paid $54 million to settle all suits and adopted a far-reaching affirmative action program to hire minority managers, recruit minority franchise owners, and roust out racists in its ranks (Figure 12-12).

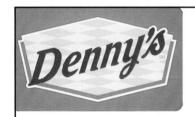

STATEMENT BY C. RONALD PETTY
DENNY'S PRESIDENT AND CHIEF EXECUTIVE OFFICER

As the settlement payout process is completed, Denny's, our managers and our employees will be able to look ahead. We will be able to focus our attention on providing all our restaurant guests with quality, value and excellent service.

All of us at Denny's regret any mistakes made in the past. But I want to emphasize that Denny's does not tolerate racial discrimination. Our company policy is clear and simple: If employees discriminate, they will be fired. If franchisees discriminate, they will lose their franchises.

I am proud to say Denny's and our parent company, Flagstar, have already made important strides in recent years. In fact, Denny's is becoming a model in our industry.

Let me be specific:

Dr. Vera King Farris, an African-American, president of Richard Stockton College in Pomona, N.J., joined the Flagstar board of directors two years ago. Mr. Michael Chu, a Hispanic and Asian-American, has been a board member since 1992. Minorities hold 27 percent of Flagstar restaurant and multi-restaurant supervisory positions. Almost half of Flagstar's 94,000 employees are minorities.

FIGURE 12-12 **Cleansing the company.** Denny's confronted charges of blatant racism at its restaurants with a comprehensive and well-publicized program.

LESSONS LEARNED

"All of us at Denny's regret any mistakes made in the past," said C. Ronald Petty, president and chief executive officer, when Denny's announced its settlement (Figure 12-13).

"Our company policy is clear and simple: If employees discriminate, they will be fired. If franchisees discriminate, they will lose their franchises."

After the flare-up, Denny's worked at becoming "a model in the industry." It recruited an African American woman to join its parent company board of directors. It promoted minorities to supervisory positions, and it introduced a "Fast Track" program to help prepare minority candidates for restaurant ownership. In 1993, there was

FIGURE 12-13 Lessons learned. Advantica CEO James Adamson announced a series of diversity ads to symbolize the hard lessons that Denny's learned about diversity.

ADVANTICA
restaurant group

STATEMENT BY JAMES B. ADAMSON
CHAIRMAN & CEO ADVANTICA RESTAURANT GROUP, INC.
NATIONAL PRESS CLUB

We will begin this week to air three television messages on the topic of racial diversity, spending nearly $2 million between now and June to get these important messages out to the American public. The messages are intended to spark thinking and honest discussion about the importance of America's racial diversity. We at Denny's have learned some difficult, but valuable, lessons about race in the last few years and are committed to spending our time and money sharing those lessons with America.

Contact: Karen Randall
              864-597-8440

                                                              1/12/99

• ADVANTICA RESTAURANT GROUP, INC. •
203 East Main Street • Spartanburg, South Carolina 29319 • 864-597-8000

Citigate
communications

TV 30:   I'm Black

I want to let you in on a little secret. I'm black.

There are some people who never notice another person's color.

But most of us do. And that's OK. Don't feel guilty. Noticing a person's color doesn't make you a racist. Acting like it matters does.

Some flowers are roses. Some are daisies.

One's not automatically better than another. Just different.

America is a garden. The more variety, the better.

AVO: Diversity. It's about all of us.

only one Denny's restaurant owned by an African American. By 1995, the number had risen to 26, with plans to reach 65 within two years.

Said Karen Randall, public relations director of Denny's new parent Advantica Restaurant Group, "We decided to look inside the organization and focus on 'substance' and change our makeup and management philosophy and the way we serve our customer base. In just a few years, this effort has changed the company."

DIVERSITY ROLE MODEL

When Advantica CEO Jim Adamson took over Denny's in 1995, he made no secret of his intent. "I am a complete supporter of affirmative action because I don't believe the playing field is level." To ensure that a diverse slate of candidates is presented for every senior Advantica job, Adamson employs minority-owned search firms in addition to more traditional companies.

In 1992, there were no Asians, blacks, or Latinos in top corporate management and only one minority group member on the company's board. Today, minorities account for a third of its directors. Nearly one in three Advantica officers and managers is a minority group member.

Purchases from minority suppliers accounted for less than $2 million in 1989. By 1997, that number had increased to more than $36 million. In terms of franchises, minorities own 35 percent of the 737 franchised restaurants. An African American, Akin Olajuwon (brother of professional basketball player Hakeem Olajuwon), is the company's second-largest franchisee.

The company's chief diversity officer coaches diversity training sessions, specifically geared toward serving customers and managing Denny's restaurants. Managers are required to attend two-day sessions to learn how to communicate to their employees about diversity issues and to better meet the needs of customers.

Has it worked? Well, *60 Minutes* was impressed enough to give Denny's glowing marks in 1999. And *Fortune* magazine, in compiling its "50 Best Companies for Asians, Blacks, and Hispanics" in 1998, ranked Denny's first in contributions to minority organizations, second in spending with minority vendors, and second in overall diversity consciousness.

It was, indeed, a miraculous turnaround (Figure 12-14).

FIGURE 12-14
The new Denny's.

Questions

1. Should Denny's have capitulated so quickly to charges of racism in its restaurants?
2. How would you assess the company's response to the accusations?
3. How wise was Denny's to appoint a chief diversity officer?
4. With Denny's now having proven itself relative to diversity efforts, can it feel free to devote less resources to the effort?
5. Read the company philosophy posted on its Web site, (www.dennys restaurants.com/who/philosophy_main.html). Why would Denny's use the Internet to publicize its approach to diversity?

TIPS FROM THE TOP

Two Perspectives on Diversity and Community Relations

Pat Tobin

I. *The African American: An Interview with Pat Tobin*
Pat Tobin is cofounder and president of the National Black Public Relations Society. When she founded Tobin & Associates, few in the industry had ever heard of an African American–owned, woman-operated, public relations firm. In the year 2000, she celebrated her 18th year in business, and Tobin & Associates has become one of the most prominent African American–owned public relations firms in the nation. In addition to assisting major corporations in communications work, she is a member of the board of directors of Women in Film (WIF) and serves on the Planning Committee for the Children's Defense Fund.

What is the state of community relations in American industry today?
Community relations should be a way of life for everyone. You must ensure that you are involved in your community and that you're "giving back" to it, no matter who you are. And I think people are giving back more today. After Sept. 11, people are more aware of their community and their neighbors.

Have companies gotten that message?
More and more, they have. We've worked for Toyota Motor Sales for 14 years. I've watched that company become more and more involved with an entire diversity program. This effort includes minority participation from procurement to advertising to employment to retail initiatives. It is very comprehensive. They sponsor Hispanic conferences and scholarships. They're active in the United Negro College Fund, the Urban League, the NAACP. That's what I'm talking about.

How important is the African American market today?
African American spend $600 billion a year in this economy. That's $600 billion with a "b." We are a market to be reckoned with, not to be taken for granted. If we're buying your product, then you have to give back to our community. Smart companies are getting that message.

How did you get started?
Twenty years ago, I left the CBS media department, and I became an entrepreneur. I opened an agency to reach the minority community. I told people, "Look, I'm black. I've been black all my life. You can't tell me about reaching blacks." So I worked with people like Spike Lee to promote his movies and kept going. We've always tried to exceed our client's expectations. I say, "I don't like excuses. I like results." That's how we've been successful.

What is the status of African Americans in the public relations field today?
It's getting better, although there is still a long way to go. I've been in my own firm for 20 years. Twenty years ago, African Americans couldn't even get a job

in public relations. There are still far too few people of color employed at the top public relations firms. But that is changing. But groups like the National Black Public Relations Association are changing that. Many African Americans are starting their own public relations firms. And many more African Americans are starting to hired in public relations jobs in major corporations.

What about African American public relations people in companies?
More and more people of color are becoming employed and getting positions in these companies. You can't talk about "diversity" and then look around and see no people who look like me. They know they have work to do. Organizations like the National Black PR Association have to keep their "feet to the fire."

How would you recommend a young person develop his or her public relations skill?
Number one, get a good education. That's first. You have to be articulate. You have to be able to communicate. Writing, especially, is an extremely valuable skill. I was fortunate to have mentors, like Barbara Harris when I worked for Sun Oil. She is now the first black woman Episcopalian Bishop.

What is the future of minority public relations?
This is a growing field with growing opportunities for young men and women of color. My daughter, Lauren, is a young woman, who has had extensive public relations experience and is now director of publicity for ABC entertainment. And I think opportunities will become much more plentiful. Companies all talk about "diversity," but you can't be diverse unless you have the "rainbow" in your own staff. So inclusion and diversity are the name of the game.

What are you, personally, looking forward to in the field?
My goal is to leave a legacy in public relations, marketing and advertising. If I can help young people to be successful, that's what I want to do. I have a 10-year-old grandson, who I hope might run Tobin & Associates when he is older. He won't have to go knocking on doors. Of course, he'll be experienced, because he is already working for me now, answering phones and stuffing envelopes. So he's got a head start.

Ray Durazo

II. *The Latino: An Interview with Ray Durazo*
Ray Durazo is president of Los Angeles–based Durazo Communications and a nationally recognized authority on Latino public relations. Before forming his own firm, Durazo was a partner in the Latino public relations firm of Moya, Villanueva & Durazo. Earlier, he headed the Los Angeles office of Ketchum Public Relations. Before returning to his native Southern California, Durazo headed Ketchum's Washington, DC, office.

How important is the ethnic market in the United States?
The United States receives two-thirds of the world's immigrants. Two-thirds of those immigrants will settle in California and Texas. Soon "minorities" will be the "majority" in Los Angeles, Dallas, Denver, Houston, and 23 other major U.S. cities. In Los Angeles, the Latino kindergarten enrollment is 66 percent and rising; Anglo enrollment is 15 percent and falling. Latino, Asians, and African Americans constitute more than half the population of Los Angeles County. In short, the U.S. ethnic market has become too large to ignore.

Why deal specially with ethnic markets?
Addressing ethnic audiences is simply another form of market segmentation, a recognition that the lifestyles, the life experiences, and the attitudes and outlooks of ethnic persons may influence their receptivity to certain messages, and to the way in which products and ideas are presented to them. As to why it's worth doing, all you have to do is look at the numbers, the buying power, the proportion of the population made up by ethnics, and you conclude that it's worth the effort.

What should a practitioner do to become conversant with the ethnic market?
The market isn't going to come to you. You have to go out and find it, experience it, learn it. And it isn't hard. Next time there's a Cinco de Mayo festival, or a Chinese New Year celebration, or an African American

(Continued)

heritage celebration, or any other ethnic event in your community, get out of your home or office, get in your car, drive over there, and participate!

What is the future of minority-oriented public relations?
The world is becoming a more competitive place every day. Recent history has shown that only the strong, the smart, the courageous will survive in this new international arena. If you are too timid even to venture into your own backyard to reach important new audiences, I hate to think what will happen to you in the future! Aggressive, progressive companies have already concluded that the U.S. ethnic audience is too big to ignore. It isn't about being politically correct. It isn't about being touchy-feely. It's about the bottom line, about profits, about market share, about winning.
Wake up and smell el cafe!

Suggested Readings

Costa, Jeanne Arnold, and Gary J. Bamossy, eds. *Marketing in a Multicultural World: Ethnicity, Nationalism and Cultural Identity.* Thousand Oaks, CA: Sage Publications, 1995.

Dines, Gail, and Jean M. Humez. *Gender, Race and Class in Media.* Thousand Oaks, CA: Sage Publications, 1995.

Ferguson, Robert. *Representing Race: Ideology, Identity and the Media.* London: Oxford University Press Inc., 1998.

Gibson, Dirk C., editor. *American Hispanic Public Relations* (Spring 2002). Special issue of *Public Relations Quarterly* featuring six articles on the subject.

Godfrey, Joline. *No More Frogs to Kiss.* New York: HarperBusiness, 1995. Offers a guide to empowering women economically and avoiding economic dependence on men.

Kalbfleisch, Pamela J., and Michael J. Cody. *Gender Power and Communications in Human Relationships.* Hillsdale, NJ: Lawrence Erlbaum Associates, 1995. Focuses on understanding differences in uses of communication by males and females.

Kelly, Kathleen S. *Fund Raising and Public Relations: A Critical Analysis.* Mahwah, NJ: Lawrence Erlbaum Associates, 1991.

Lukenbill, Grant. *Untold Millions: Secret Truths about Marketing to Gay and Lesbian Consumers.* New York: Haworth, 1999. Uncovers truths and debunks myths behind the gay and lesbian consumer patterns and lifestyles.

McLaughlin, Shane. "Communicating Across the Gender Gap in Corporate Leadership," *Public Relations Strategist* (Spring 2002): 20–24.

McLaughlin, Shane. "Diversity Drives Dollars for Corporate Communications," *Public Relations Strategist* (Summer 2002): 25–29.

Newsom, Doug A., and Bob J. Carrell. *Silent Voices.* Lanham, MD: University Press of America, 1995. A collection of articles examining issues concerning the status of women worldwide.

Rao, C. P. *Marketing and Multicultural Diversity.* Westport, CT: Quorum Books, 2002.

Schreiber, Alfred L. *Multicultural Marketing.* New York, NY: Contemporary Books, 2000.

Source Book of Multicultural Experts, annual. New York: Multicultural Marketing Resources Inc., 1999. Lists hundreds of resources and experts in the African American, Asian American, Hispanic, gay and lesbian, women's, and multicultural markets.

Tharp, Marye C. *Marketing and Consumer Identity in Multicultural America.* Thousand Oaks, CA: Sage Publications, 2001.

Tingley, Judith C. *Genderflex: Men and Women Speaking Each Other's Language at Work*. New York: AMACOM, 1995. Author refers to the phenomenon of adapting to the language gap between men and women as "genderflexing."

U.S. Census Bureau Staff, eds. *Hispanic-Latinos: Diverse People in a Multicultural Society* (Marketing Guideposts Series). Carlsbad, CA: WPR Publishing, 1998.

Valdivia, Angharad L. *Feminism, Multiculturalism and the Media*. Thousand Oaks, CA: Sage Publications, 1995.

Wilson, Clint C. II. *Race, Multiculturalism and the Media: From Mass to Class Communication*. Thousand Oaks, CA: Sage Publications, 1995. Examines the historical relationship between the four largest racial groups and the mainstream media in the United States.

Notes

1. Anne Faircloth, "Guess Who's Coming to Denny's," *Fortune* (August 3, 1998).
2. "Profiles of General Demographic Characteristics," 2000 Census of Population and Housing, U.S. Department of Commerce, May 2001.
3. Bob Weinstein, "Ethnic Marketing: The New Numbers Game," *Profiles* (May 1994): 51–52.
4. Lynette Clemetson, "Latino Population Growth Is Widespread, Study Says," *New York Times* (July 31, 2002): A14.
5. Elisabeth Preis, "Taking Aim at J&J," *Minority Law Journal* (Spring 2002).
6. Robert A. Bennett, "Texaco's Bijur: Hero or Sellout?" *Public Relations Strategist* (Winter 1996).
7. "Charitable Giving Reaches $212 Billion," American Association of Fundraising Counsel news release (June 20, 2002).
8. "Corporate Foundations Ranked by 9/11 Response Funding of $5 Million or More," The Foundation Center (February 2002).
9. Ann Marie Gothard, "The African-American Online Community: A Portal to the Global Black Diaspora," *Public Relations Tactics* (November 1999): 18.
10. Daniel Golden, "Time Warner to Buy Henry Gates's Africana.com," *Wall Street Journal* (September 7, 2000): B1-4.
11. "Cisco Enlists Net in War on Poverty," *O'Dwyer's PR Services Report* (November 1999): 8.
12. Peter Santucci, "Giving a Heart to E-Commerce," *Washington CEO* (October 1999).
13. Steven A. Camarota, "Immigrants in the United States — 2000," Center for Immigration Studies (January 2001).
14. "The First Black Face I Ever Saw in Public Relations Was in the Mirror," *Inside PR* (March 1993): 25.
15. Elizabeth L. Toth, "Confronting the Reality of the Gender Gap," *Public Relations Strategist* (Fall 1996): 51.
16. "Reaching the Hispanic Audience," *fastforward* (Fall 1999): 1.
17. Ignasi B. Vendrell, "What Is Hispanic Public Relations and Where Is It Going?" *Public Relations Quarterly* (Winter 1994–95): 33.
18. "2002 U.S. Hispanic Market," Strategy Resource Corporation (June 2002).
19. Dana Calvo, "As the Channels Turn: Soaps Draw Viewers to Telemundo," *Washington Post* (December 25, 1999): C2.
20. "America 2000: A Map of the Mix," *Newsweek*.

21. Ronald Alsop, "Web Site Sets Gay-Themed Ads for Big, National Publications," *Wall Street Journal* (February 17, 2000): B4.
22. Kendall Hamilton, "Fighting to Fund an 'Absolute Necessity,'" *Newsweek* (July 1, 1996): 56.
23. Michael Pertschuk, "Progressive Media Advocacy," *Public Relations Strategist* (Winter 1995): 55.
24. David Barboza, "Biotech Companies Take On Critics of Gene-Altered Food," *New York Times* (November 12, 1999): A1, 12.
25. Bruce Horovitz, "Wendy's Steps Up Animal Welfare Standards," *USA Today* (September 6, 2001): 28.
26. Gary Stern, *Marketing Workbook for Nonprofit Organizations* (St Paul, MN: Amherst H. Wilder Foundation, 1990).

Chapter 13

Government Relations

"The American people are appreciative of the forthrightness of the government. I think the government has an obligation to be forthright."

—White House briefing by Press Secretary Ari Fleischer
October 1, 2001

After September 11, 2001, the communications stakes for President Bush and his team changed forever.

The war on terrorism depended on candid, frank, and informative communications with the American people and the world.

"Why do they hate us?" the president asked rhetorically about the Muslim attackers and their sympathizers in his historic speech before Congress the week after the terrorist attacks.[1] To combat such hate and to reassure the American people about the goodness of the war effort, the government's public relations initiatives took center stage.

Among them:

- *The White House created a permanent Office of Global Communications to coordinate the administration's foreign policy message and supervise America's image abroad.[2]*
- *Bush mounted the "bully pulpit" of the American presidency first to deliver a riveting speech before Congress and the nation, in which he vowed: "I will not yield. I will not rest. I will not relent in waging this struggle. We will not tire. We will not falter, and we will not fail."[3]*

The president then used the vehicle of frequent news conferences to keep the public informed.

- *The Bush cabinet, particularly Defense Secretary Donald Rumsfeld, Attorney General John Ashcroft, and Secretary of State Colin Powell, regularly conducted press conferences of their own to keep the country apprised of developments in their spheres and to cut off critics suspicious of secrecy.*
- *The position of Undersecretary for Public Diplomacy and Public Affairs was created in the State Department, immediately after September 11, 2001, to work to convince the Muslim world of the true values and ethics of America.*

All of these measures and more underscored the critical function that open and honest communications played in the government's intention to fight an extended war against terrorism.

Although the war magnified the role of strategic communications, the fact remains that the smartest politicians recognize the importance of the practice of public relations to their own success in getting themselves elected, their programs supported, and their policies adopted.

As such, the practice of public relations is represented throughout government—in each government branch, in all government agencies, on the state and local levels, and also in lobbying the government to maintain or change legislation. All of these functions are part of the multiple levels of communications professionals employed in and around government.

SIDEBAR

Surprise Public Relations Superstar

Of all the members of the Bush cabinet, the one least likely to become a public relations superstar was Defense Secretary Donald Rumsfeld (Figure 13-1).

A crusty, former corporate CEO, Rumsfeld played things close to the vest, shared little, and reportedly harbored a deep suspicion of the press. But once the terrorists struck and the war started, the hard-nosed defense secretary turned into something of a public relations pussy cat. Well, almost.

Three times every week, Rumsfeld conducted Pentagon press conferences that the *Wall Street Journal* labeled "must viewing." He was informative, thought provoking, inspiring, and always categorical.

"There is no question we have a job to do as a country to make sure the entire world understands that this war is not against any religion or country or people," Rumsfeld answered one reporter, who questioned the standing of the United States overseas. "We are fighting against terrorists. To the extent that people who understand that aren't happy that we're against terrorists—then that's just too bad."

No wonder CNN called the 69-year-old secretary "a virtual rock star," and Fox News dubbed him "a babe magnet."

Rumsfeld, like former Mayor Rudy Giuliani before him, demonstrated that people in power have little to fear from the media, as long as they know their facts, do their homework, and tell the truth.

The defense secretary was confident enough even to second guess his own policy directives. He elimi-

FIGURE 13-1   **Babe magnet.** Secretary of Defense Donald Rumsfeld with Chairman of the Joint Chiefs of Staff Richard Myers.

nated a planned office intended to influence public opinion overseas, when people objected that it might spread inaccurate and misleading information.

When asked if to protect American soldiers in harm's way, Rumsfeld would ever use "disinformation" with the press, the secretary replied simply, "There may be things we will refuse to tell you—but we will never, ever lie."

For further information, see Eric Schmitt, "Rumsfeld Says He May Drop New Office of Influence," *New York Times* (February 25, 2002): A13; and Fraser P. Seitel, "Public Relations Winners of 2001," odwyerpr.com (January 7, 2002).

Public Relations in Government

The growth of public relations work both with the government and in the government has exploded in recent years. Although it is difficult to say exactly how many public relations professionals are employed at the federal level, it's safe to assume that thousands of public relations–related jobs exist in the federal government and countless others in government at state and local levels. Thus, the field of government relations is a fertile one for public relations graduates.

Since 1970, more than 20 new federal regulatory agencies have sprung up—including the Office of Homeland Security, the Environmental Protection Agency, the Consumer Product Safety Commission, the Department of Energy, the Department of Education, and the Drug Enforcement Administration. Moreover, according to the Government Accounting Office (GAO), more than 120 government agencies and programs now regulate business.

Little wonder that today American business spends more time calling on, talking with, and lobbying government representatives on such generic issues as trade, interest rates, taxes, budget deficits, and all the other issues that concern individual industries and companies. Also, little wonder that political interest groups of every stripe—from Wall Street bankers to Asian influence seekers to friends of the Earth—contribute more to political coffers than ever before. Thus, today's organizations continue to emphasize and expand their own government relations functions.

Beyond this, the nation's defense establishment offers some 7,000 public relations jobs, although none are labeled "public relations," in Department of Defense military and civilian positions. Indeed, with military service now purely voluntary, the nation's defense machine must rely on its public information, education, and recruiting efforts to maintain a sufficient military force. Thus, public relations opportunities in this realm of government work should continue to expand.

Ironically, the public relations function has traditionally been something of a "poor relation" in the government. In 1913, Congress enacted the Gillette Amendment, which almost barred the practice of public relations in government. The amendment stemmed from efforts by President Theodore Roosevelt to win public support for his programs through the use of a network of publicity experts. Congress, worried about the potential of this unlimited presidential persuasive power, passed an amendment stating: "Appropriated funds may not be used to pay a publicity expert unless specifically appropriated for that purpose."

Several years later, still leery of the president's power to influence legislation through communication, Congress passed the gag law, which prohibited "using any part of an appropriation for services, messages, or publications designed to influence any member of Congress in his attitude toward legislation or appropriations." Even today, no government worker may be employed in the "practice of public relations." Public affairs, yes. But public relations, no. Indeed, the government is flooded with "public affairs experts," "information officers," "press secretaries," and "communications specialists."

Government Practitioners

Most practitioners in government communicate the activities of the various agencies, commissions, and bureaus to the public. As consumer activist Ralph Nader has said, "In this nation, where the ultimate power is said to rest with the people, it is clear that a free and prompt flow of information from government to the people is essential."

It wasn't always as essential to form informational links between government officials and the public. In 1888, when there were 39 states in the Union and 330 members in the House of Representatives, the entire official Washington press corps consisted of 127 reporters. Today there are close to 4,000 full-time journalists covering the capital.

In 1990, the U.S. Office of Personnel Management reported nearly 15,000 public relations–related jobs in the federal government. The National Association of Government Communicators, which has 500 members from all levels of government, estimated there were about 40,000 government communicators in the United States.[4] The vast majority of government communicators are engaged in public affairs tasks, such as dealing with the media and other layers of government, as well as writing, editing, and the other public relations tasks.

The closest thing to an audit of government public relations functions came in 1986 when former Senator William Proxmire, a notorious gadfly, asked the GAO to tell him "how much federal executive agencies spend on public relations."

The GAO reported that the 13 cabinet departments and 18 independent agencies spent about $337 million for public affairs activities during fiscal 1985, with almost 5,600 full-time employees assigned to public affairs duties. In addition, about $100 million was spent for congressional affairs activities, with almost 2,000 full-time employees assigned. Also, about $1.9 billion—that's $1.9 billion—was spent, primarily in the Department of Defense, "for certain public affairs–related activities not classified as public affairs." These included more than $65 million for military bands, $13 million for aerial teams, $11 million for military museums, and more than $1 billion for advertising and printing regarding recruitment.

Lead Voices at State and Defense

Even before the War on Terrorism, the most potent public relations voices in the federal government, exclusive of the president, were the U.S. Departments of State, first, and Defense, second. After September 11, 2001, the communications importance of both increased, but their relative positions were reversed.

The State Department

The State Department, like other government agencies, has an extensive public affairs staff, responsible for press briefings, maintaining secretary of state homepage content, operating foreign press centers in Washington, New York, and Los Angeles, as well as managing public diplomacy operations abroad.

In October 1999, as part of the Foreign Affairs Reform and Restructuring Act of 1998, the State Department inherited the United States Information Agency (USIA), for many years the most far-reaching of the federal government's public relations arms. USIA had been an independent foreign affairs agency within the executive branch created in 1953 by President Dwight Eisenhower. Its job was to explain and support American foreign policy and promote U.S. national interests through a wide range of overseas information programs and educational and cultural activities.

The State Department consolidated USIA's 6,352 employees, of whom 904 are Foreign Service personnel and 2,521 are locally hired Foreign Service nationals overseas. There are 2,927 civil service employees based in the United States, of whom 1,822 work in international broadcasting and 1,105 are engaged in USIA's educational and informational programs.

The director of the USIA had reported directly to the president and received policy guidance from the secretary of state. Under the 1999 integration plan, an undersecretary for public diplomacy and public affairs, within the State Department, was chosen to head the operation.[5] The USIA's annual appropriation has exceeded $1 billion since the late 1980s.

In the 21st century, with America's motives for the war on terrorism challenged around the world, the former USIA's mission—"to support the national interest by conveying an understanding abroad of what the United States stands for"—has been modified to include new challenges:

- Build the intellectual and institutional foundations of democracy in societies around the globe
- Support the war on drugs in producer and consumer countries
- Develop worldwide information programs to address environmental challenges
- Bring the truth to any society that fails to exercise free and open communication

In its 46-year history, the USIA was a high-level public relations operation and not without controversy. Under the direction of such well-known media personalities as Edward R. Murrow, Carl Rowan, Frank Shakespeare, and Charles Z. Wick, the agency prospered.

Among its more well-known communications vehicles are the following.

1. *Radio*   Voice of America broadcasts 660 hours of programming weekly in 52 languages, including English, to an international audience. In addition to Voice of America, the USIA in 1985 began Radio Marti, in honor of José Marti, father of Cuban independence. Radio Marti's purpose is to broadcast 24 hours a day to Cuba in Spanish and "tell the truth to the Cuban people" about ruler Fidel Castro and communism. TV Marti telecasts four-and-a-half hours daily. Although some in Congress claim that the telecasts are a waste, because the Castro government blocks the TV signal, the effort continues.
2. *Film and television.*   The agency annually produces and acquires an extensive number of films and videocassettes for distribution in 125 countries.
3. *Media.*   About 25,000 words a day are transmitted to 214 overseas posts for placement in the media.
4. *Publications.*   Overseas regional service centers publish 16 magazines in 18 languages and distribute pamphlets, leaflets, and posters to more than 100 countries.
5. *Exhibitions.*   Approximately 35 major exhibits are USIA-designed annually for worldwide display, including in Eastern European countries and the former Soviet Union.
6. *Libraries and books.*   The agency maintains or supports libraries in more than 200 information centers and binational centers in more than 90 countries and assists publishers in distributing books overseas.
7. *Education.*   The agency is also active overseas in sponsoring educational programs through 111 binational centers where English is taught and in 11 language centers. Classes draw about 350,000 students annually.
8. *Electronic information.*   Electronic journals were created to communicate with audiences overseas on economic issues, political security and values, democracy and human rights, terrorism, the environment, and transnational information flow. The journals are transmitted in English, French, and Spanish. They are also transmitted on a domestic World Wide Web site at www.usia.gov.[6]

The Defense Department

The importance of Department of Defense (DOD) communications has been intensified in war time.

The DOD's public affairs network is massive—3,727 communicators in the Army, 1,250 in the Navy, 1,200 in the Air Force, 450 in the Marines, and 200 at headquarters. The DOD public affairs department is headed by an assistant secretary of defense for public affairs, one of six direct reports to the deputy secretary of defense (Figure 13-2).

With the DOD consisting of more than 3 million active duty forces, reserves, and civilian employees, information is the strategic center of gravity. Communications must be organized, secure, and rapid to fulfill the deparment's mission.

Although each service has its own public affairs organization and mission, DOD's American Forces Information Service (AFIS) promotes cooperation among the various branches (Figure 13-3). AFIS is responsible for maintaining the Armed Forces Radio and Television Service, *Stars and Stripes* newspaper, communications training at the Defense Information School, and a variety of other functions.

As with any communications operation, the DOD public affairs effort is subject to periodic audits and refinements. Most observers agree, however, that the wars in Afghanistan and Iraq have served to focus the DOD communications operation in a more targeted and effective manner. Ironically, prior to September 11, 2001, DOD's chief communicator, Secretary Rumsfeld, was criticized as a "fumbler," who lacked "the power to persuade."[7] What a difference a war makes.

Government Agencies

Nowhere has government public relations activity become more aggressive than in federal departments and regulatory agencies. Many agencies, in fact, have found that the quickest way to gain recognition is to increase their public relations aggressiveness.

The Federal Trade Commission (FTC), which columnist Jack Anderson once called a "sepulcher of official secrets," opened up in the late 1970s to become one of the most active government communicators. In an earlier heyday, a former FTC director of public information described the agency's attitude: "The basic premise underlying the commission's public information program is the public's inherent right to know what the FTC is doing."[8] When the FTC found a company's products wanting in standards of safety or quality, it often announced its complaint through a press conference. Although corporate critics branded this process "trial by press release," it helped transform the agency from a meek, mild-mannered bureau into an office with real teeth.

The late 1990s' successor to the FTC was the Food and Drug Administration, particularly under President Clinton appointee Dr. David Kessler. Dr. Kessler was an unbridled critic of products from fat substitutes and cigarettes to silicone breast implants. When he stepped down in 1997, consumer advocates groaned while business groups cheered.

The business cheering stopped in the early years of the 21st century, when a new round of business and accounting scandals caused both the Justice Department and the Securities and Exchange Commission to increase their public role in tracking down corporate fraud. Part of the Justice Department offensive was to round up alleged business perpetrators, and then arrest and handcuff them in full view of tipped-off TV and print cameras.

Other government departments also have stepped up their public relations efforts. The Department of Health and Human Services has a public affairs staff of 700 people. The Departments of Agriculture, State, and Treasury each have communications staffs in excess of 400 people, and each spends more than $20 million per year in public

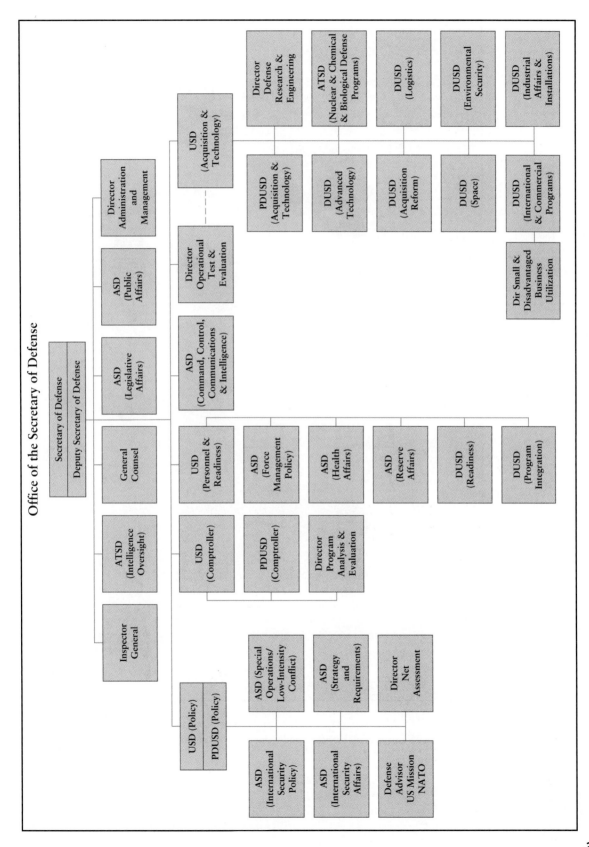

Office of the Secretary of Defense

FIGURE 13-2 DOD organization. Assistant Secretary of Defense for Public Affairs Victoria Clarke was one of six who reported to the Defense Secretary's chief deputy, Deputy Secretary of Defense Paul Wolfowitz.

FIGURE 13-3 **AFIS.** The primary mission of the American Forces Information Service is to integrate the various military branches under one communications umbrella.

About AFIS

Mission

Provide high-quality news, information, and entertainment to U.S. Forces worldwide in order to promote and sustain unit and individual readiness, quality of life and morale.

AFIS trains public affairs, broadcast and visual information professionals, and provides communications services to support the informational needs of commanders and combat forces through the entire range of military operations and contingencies.

Vision

Keep America's Armed Forces the best informed Armed Forces in the world.

Initiatives

- Take a leadership role in promoting cooperation among the Military Services in all aspects of internal communications.
- Ensure that access to AFIS products by internal audiences is free (or lowest possible cost) and consistent among all commands/Services.
- Identify and promote AFIS products to all audiences.
- Develop integrated AFIS website for DefenseLINK.

FIGURE 13-3   **(Continued)**

A QUESTION OF ETHICS

Answering Anthrax Accusations

One federal agency that increased its communications initiatives in the early years of the 21st century was the embattled Federal Bureau of Investigations.

The FBI was taken to task, rightly or wrongly, for not acting more decisively in anticipation of the September 11, 2001, terrorist attacks. In the summer of 2002, with the FBI assigned to capture the killer who used the U.S. mail to send lethal anthrax, the bureau vowed it would get its target.

By August, attention centered on a former government scientist, Dr. Steven J. Hatfill. Although he wasn't charged as the anthrax killer, Hatfill's name was prominently leaked as a Justice Department target, and news photographers camped outside his home.

Then the doctor struck back.

Much against lawyers' advice, he called a press conference and denounced the government's shadowy, strong-armed tactics (Figure 13-4).

"This assassination of my character appears to be part of a government-run effort to show the American people that it is proceeding vigorously and successfully with the anthrax investigation.

"I want to look my fellow Americans directly in the eye and declare to them, I am not the anthrax killer. I know nothing about the anthrax attacks. I had absolutely nothing to do with this terrible crime."

Hatfill accused the FBI and Attorney General John Ashcroft of singling him out in a desperate attempt to divert attention from their lack of progress in the case. He said he would waive privacy rules to allow the release of the results of a blood test he took to determine anthrax. He offered to compare his handwriting to that appearing on the anthrax letters. And he vowed to keep his targeting public and held another press conference two weeks later.

FIGURE 13-4   Seizing the offense. Dr. Steven Hatfill declares his innocence in anthrax attacks.

The Justice Department was stunned by Dr. Hatfill's vigorous public relations campaign. In muted public statements, the department would only acknowledge that Dr. Hatfill was one of many "persons of interest" in the case.

By questioning the government's ethics in going after him, Dr. Hatfill had succeeded in putting the FBI and the Justice Department on the defensive.

For further information, see Ron Kampeas, "Hatfill: Tests Will Prove Innocence," Associated Press (August 26, 2002).

relations–related activities. Even the U.S. Central Intelligence Agency has three spokespersons. Out of how many CIA public relations people? Sorry, that's classified.

The President

Despite early congressional efforts to limit the persuasive power of the nation's chief executive, the president today wields unprecedented public relations clout. The president controls the "bully pulpit." Almost anything the president does or says makes news. The broadcast networks, daily newspapers, and national magazines follow his every move. His press secretary provides the White House press corps (a group of national reporters assigned to cover the president) with a constant flow of announcements supplemented by daily press briefings. Unlike many organizational press releases that seldom make it into print, many White House releases achieve national exposure.

Ronald Reagan and Bill Clinton were perhaps the most masterful presidential communicators in history. Reagan gained experience in the movies and on television, and even his most ardent critics agreed that he possessed a compelling stage presence. As America's president, he was truly the "Great Communicator." Mr. Reagan and his communications advisers followed seven principles in helping to "manage the news":

1. Plan ahead.
2. Stay on the offensive.
3. Control the flow of information.
4. Limit reporters' access to the president.
5. Talk about the issues you want to talk about.
6. Speak in one voice.
7. Repeat the same message many times.[9]

So coordinated was Reagan's effort to "get the right story out" that even in his greatest public relations test—the accusation at the end of his presidency that he and his aides shipped arms to Iran and funneled the payments to support Contra rebels in Nicaragua, in defiance of the Congress—the president's "Teflon" image remained largely intact. The smears simply washed away.

George H. W. Bush was not as masterful as his predecessor in communicating with the American public. Indeed, Mr. Bush met his communications match in 1992, when Bill Clinton beat him soundly in the presidential race.

The press had a love-hate relationship with President Clinton. On the one hand, Mr. Clinton's easygoing, "just folks" demeanor, combined with an unquestioned intelligence and grasp of the issues, was praised by the media. On the other hand, the president's legendary "slickness," accentuated by his false statements and downright lying to the American people during the Lewinsky affair caused many journalists to treat him warily.[10]

Next to the booming economy, President Clinton's accessibility to the media—except during the Lewinsky saga—and his commonsense approach to dealing with media were greatly responsible for his popularity, despite a series of embarrassing scandals afflicting his administration during both terms of his presidency.

George W. Bush, like his father, wasn't particularly comfortable with the press and public speaking. However, the second President Bush came of age as a communicator with the events of September 11, 2001. After the terrorist attacks, President Bush delivered an historic speech before Congress, addressed workers at the World Trade Center site through a bullhorn, and conducted frequent press conferences in Washington and at his ranch in Crawford, Texas. Ironically, the terrorist challenge had awakened the communications instincts in the president.

Beginning with the presidency of Lyndon Baines Johnson, the president's wife, the first lady, also has borrowed the "bully pulpit" of public relations to promote pet causes. In Lady Bird Johnson's case, it was national beautification. Betty Ford promoted mental health, Nancy Reagan fought drug abuse, and Barbara Bush and her daughter-in-law Laura both spoke against illiteracy. First Lady Hillary Clinton, however, superseded all others by taking an active role in education and health care policy, first as an agent of the president and then as a U.S. Senator from New York (Figure 13-5).

Bye Bye Bluebird

In 2000, First Lady Hillary Clinton made the unprece-dented announcement of her intention to run for the senate in the state of New York. A resident of Arkansas, the first lady and her husband bought a house in Westchester County, New York, and set out for the senate (Figure 13-5).

But to do it, she had to face up to one of New York's most feared political analysts, David Letterman. Mr. Letterman, the lovable, goofy, acid-tongued late-night TV host was all ready for the candidate when she arrived to boost her candidacy.

And she, evidently, was ready for him.

So ready, in fact, that she scored 100 percent on a "pop quiz" that supposedly was sprung on her at the last minute.

Or was it?

One question she was asked: "What is New York's state bird?"

"The bluebird," she replied without hesitation.

New Yorkers were stunned and also suspicious. Few residents could have even guessed "the bluebird" as the New York State bird. The pigeon, maybe. Or the sparrow. Or even the herring! But the bluebird??

"Was Hillary given the questions in advance?" her spokesperson was asked.

The sheepish answer—tantamount to "not exactly"—underscored the fact that just as in war, in political public relations, anything goes, especially since Mrs. Clinton was elected senator a few months later.

FIGURE 13-5 **The candidate.** First Lady Hillary Clinton was history's most visible first lady, lending her name and presence to a variety of causes, such as helping children fight asthma.

The President's Press Secretary

Some have called the job of presidential press secretary the second most difficult posi-tion in any administration. The press secretary is the chief public relations spokesper-son for the administration. Like practitioners in private industry, the press secretary must communicate the policies and practices of the management (the president) to the public. Often it is an impossible job.

In 1974, Gerald terHorst, President Ford's press secretary, quit after disagreeing with Ford's pardon of former President Richard Nixon. Said Mr. terHorst, "A spokesman should feel in his heart and mind that the chief's decision is the right one, so that he can speak with a persuasiveness that stems from conviction."[11] A contrasting view of the press secretary's role was expressed by terHorst's replacement in the job, former NBC reporter Ron Nessen. Said Mr. Nessen, "A press secretary does not always have to agree with the president. His first loyalty is to the public, and he should not knowingly lie or mislead the press."[12] A third view of the proper role of the press secretary was offered by a former public relations professional and Nixon speechwriter who became a *New York Times* political columnist, William Safire:

> A good press secretary speaks up for the press to the president and speaks out for the president to the press. He makes his home in the pitted no-man's-land of an adversary relationship and is primarily an advocate, interpreter, and amplifier. He must be more the president's man than the press's. But he can be his own man as well.[13]

In recent years, the position of press secretary to the president has taken on increased responsibility and has attained a higher public profile. Jimmy Carter's press secretary, Jody Powell, for example, was among Carter's closest confidants and frequently advised the president on policy matters. He went on to found his own Washington public relations agency. James Brady, the next press secretary, who was permanently paralyzed in 1981 by a bullet aimed at President Reagan, later joined his wife, Sarah, to lobby hard for what would be called the "Brady Bill," establishing new procedures for licensing handguns, which was passed by Congress.

In addition, the position of press secretary has been awarded more to career public relations people rather than to career journalists. Larry Speakes, who followed Mr. Brady, was a former Hill & Knowlton executive and was universally hailed by the media for his professionalism. During President Reagan's second term, Mr. Speakes apparently was purposely kept in the dark by Reagan's military advisers planning an invasion of the island of Grenada. The upset press secretary later apologized to reporters for misleading them on the Grenada invasion.

The next press secretary was a low-key, trusted, and respected lifetime government public relations professional, Marlin Fitzwater. His successor was another career political public relations professional, Dee Dee Myers, who was respected by the media and brought a refreshing perspective to her role as President Clinton's press secretary. She went on to become a cable talk show host and magazine editor.

The trend toward retaining experienced communications people continued in the second Clinton White House, with the president hiring political public relations veteran Mike McCurry. When Mr. McCurry left in 1998 to help form a new Washington public affairs agency, he was replaced by another public relations veteran, Joe Lockhart.

President George W. Bush appointed another government communications veteran, Ari Fleischer, as his press secretary. Upon taking over, Fleischer looked at the challenge optimistically, "I may be crazy, but I like working with reporters."[14] It was Fleischer who served as the administration's principal liaison with the media during the wars on terrorism and with Iraq (see "Tips from the Top" at the end of this chapter).

Over the years, the number of reporters hounding the presidential press secretary— dubbed by some "the imperial press corps"—has grown from fewer than 300 reporters during President Kennedy's term to around 3,000 today. Salaries approaching six figures, rare in most media offices in prior years, are today common in Washington bureaus. TV network White House correspondents command higher incomes, with each major network assigning two or three correspondents to cover the White House simultaneously.

Dealing with such a host of characters is no easy task. And the role of press secretary is neither easy nor totally satisfactory. As former press secretary McCurry put it, "Having a single person standing at a podium and answering questions and trying to explain a complicated world is not a very efficient way to drive home the idea that government can make a difference."[15] Perhaps President Johnson, the first chief executive to be labeled an "imperial president" by the Washington press corps, said it best when asked by a TV reporter what force or influence he thought had done the most to shape the nature of Washington policy. "You bastards," Johnson snapped.[16]

Lobbying the Government

The business community, foundations, and philanthropic and quasi-public organizations have a common problem: dealing with government, particularly the mammoth federal bureaucracy. Because government has become so pervasive in organizational and personal life, the number of corporations and trade associations with government relations units has grown steadily in recent years.

In 1999, the nation's 21,000 registered lobbyists spent a whopping $1.45 billion to speed up or slow down legislation in Washington. In 2000, the leading industry lobbying groups were those representing finance, insurance, and real estate spending $229 million; health care organizations spending $209 million; and communications and electronics companies spending $201 million.[17]

Government relations people are primarily concerned with weighing the impact of impending legislation on the company, industry group, or client organization. Generally, a head office government relations staff complements staff members who represent the organization in Washington, DC, and state capitals. These representatives have several objectives:

1. To improve communications with government personnel and agencies
2. To monitor legislators and regulatory agencies in areas affecting constituent operations
3. To encourage constituent participation at all levels of government
4. To influence legislation affecting the economy of the constituent's area, as well as its operations
5. To advance awareness and understanding among lawmakers of the activities and operations of constituent organizations

Carrying out these objectives requires knowing your way around the federal government and acquiring connections. A full-time Washington representative is often employed for these tasks.

To the uninitiated, Washington (or almost any state capital) can seem an incomprehensible maze. Consequently, organizations with an interest in government relations usually employ a professional representative, who may or may not be a registered lobbyist, whose responsibility, among other things, is to influence legislation. Lobbyists are required to comply with the federal Lobbying Act of 1946, which imposed certain reporting requirements on individuals or organizations that spend a significant amount of time or money attempting to influence members of Congress on legislation.

In 1995, the Lobbying Disclosure Act took effect, reforming the earlier law. The new act broadened the activities that constitute "lobbying" and mandated government registration of lobbyists. Under the new law, a "lobbyist" is an individual who is paid by a third party to make more than one "lobbying contact," defined as an oral or written communication to a vast range of specific individuals in the executive and legislative branches of the federal government.[18] In addition, lobbyists are prohibited from paying for meals for members of Congress or their aides. The law also broadened the definition of "lobbying activities" to include research and other background work prepared for a lobbying purpose.[19]

In fact, one need not register as a lobbyist in order to speak to a senator, congressional representative, or staff member about legislation. But a good lobbyist can earn the respect and trust of a legislator. Because of the need to analyze legislative proposals and to deal with members of Congress, many lobbyists are lawyers with a strong Washington background. Lobbying ranks are loaded with former administration officials and congressional members, who often turn immediately to lobbying when they move out of office.

Lobbyists, at times, have been labeled everything from influence peddlers to fixers to downright crooks. In 1999, in fact, the American League of Lobbyists—the lobbyist's lobby—sent out an open letter asking for "kinder treatment." Fat chance!

Despite the slings and arrows, the fact is that today's lobbyist is likely to be a person who is well informed in his or her field and who furnishes Congress with facts and information necessary to make an intelligent decision on a particular issue. This task—the lobbyist's primary function—is rooted in nothing less than the First Amendment right of all citizens to petition government.

What Do Lobbyists Do?

The number of lobbyists registered with the U.S. Senate has increased from just over 3,000 in 1976 to more than 40,000 today. Lobbying has become big business.

But what exactly do lobbyists do?

In the spring of 1994, the Treasury Department issued a 30-page definition of lobbying that confounded most of those engaged in the arcane profession. Among other decisions, the department ruled that anyone employed to "follow" federal or even state issues—say, by reading newspapers or magazines—is not engaged in lobbying. However, if the articles are clipped and filed as part of research intended to influence legislation, then that, the department ruled, is lobbying.[20]

The fact of the matter is the essence of a lobbyist's job is to inform and persuade.

The contacts of lobbyists are important, but they must also have the right information available for the right legislator. The time to plant ideas with legislators is well before a bill is drawn up, and skillful lobbyists recognize that timing is critical in influencing legislation. The specific activities performed by individual lobbyists vary with the nature of the industry or group represented. Most take part in these activities:

1. *Fact-finding.*   The government is an incredible storehouse of facts, statistics, economic data, opinions, and decisions that generally are available for the asking.
2. *Interpretation of government actions.*   A key function of the lobbyist is to interpret for management the significance of government events and the potential implications of pending legislation. Often a lobbyist predicts what can be expected to happen legislatively and recommends actions to deal with the expected outcome.
3. *Interpretation of company actions.*   Through almost daily contact with congressional members and staff assistants, a lobbyist conveys how a specific group feels about legislation. The lobbyist must be completely versed in the business of the client and the attitude of the organization toward governmental actions.
4. *Advocacy of a position.*   Beyond the presentation of facts, a lobbyist advocates positions on behalf of clients, both pro and con. Hitting a congressional representative early with a stand on pending legislation can often mean getting a fair hearing for the client's position. Indeed, few congressional representatives have the time to study—or even read—every piece of legislation on which they are asked to vote. Therefore, they depend on lobbyists for information, especially on how the proposed legislation may affect their constituents (Figure 13-6).
5. *Publicity springboard.*   More news comes out of Washington than any other city in the world. It is the base for thousands of press, TV, radio, and magazine correspondents. This multiplicity of media makes it the ideal springboard for launching organizational publicity. The same holds true, to a lesser degree, in state capitals.

Sample Letter to the Editor 1

SAMPLE

RE: Response to Address of Joint Session of Congress

Dear Editor,

It was marvelous to hear our new president, George W. Bush, outline his ideas for America so eloquently in his Address to a Joint Session of Congress last night. Just watching him filled me with a sense of opportunity I have not felt for the past eight years.

His plan for tax relief is particularly inspiring. Everyone who pays income taxes gets relief. The Bush tax relief plan meets key budget priorities, pays down the debt and helps families put aside more money for their children's future and for those unexpected things – car repairs, a new roof, or medicine – that life seems to throw a family's way.

Some Democrats in Congress have snidely suggested that the Bush tax relief plan won't help all taxpaying families. Maybe their large salaries have caused them to forget how significant an extra $1,600 is to the average American's budget.

Sincerely,
XXXXXXX

Sample Letter to Editor 2

RE: Response to Address of Joint Session of Congress

Dear Editor,

Watching President Bush speak to Congress Tuesday night, I began to have my faith in government renewed. He outlined policies that focus on the concerns of the American people, not Washington politicians. I particularly like his tax relief plan that will reduce income taxes for everyone who pays them.

President Bush's plan to replace the five current tax rates with four lower rates is a smart move to get our economy moving again. And his proposals to reduce the marriage penalty tax, end the death tax on family-owned farms and businesses, and increase the child tax credit are refreshing signs that he remembers those of us who live outside the Washington Beltway.

Finally, we can be proud again. Thank you President Bush!

Sincerely,
XXXXXXX

FIGURE 13-6 **Advocating a position.** One function of lobbyists is to stimulate and communicate the advocacy of a position among constituents.

6. *Support of company sales.*   The government is one of the nation's largest purchasers of products. Lobbyists often serve as conduits through which sales are made. A lobbyist who is friendly with government personnel can serve as a valuable link for leads to company business.

In recent years, there has been no shortage of controversy surrounding lobbyists and influence peddling in Washington. A number of close advisers to President Clinton, including the late Secretary of Commerce Ron Brown and former Justice Department official Webster Hubbell, were accused of courting influence in a questionable manner. Brown was killed in a Bosnian air crash and Hubbell went to jail. Both New Jersey Senator Robert Torricelli and Ohio Congressman James Traficant were accused in 2002 of shaking down contributors. Torricelli was "severely reprimanded" by the Senate, and Traficant was sent to the slammer.

With the stakes of political power so high, the temptation to abuse the privileges of lobbying remains a risk in our democratic society.

Emergence of E-Lobbying

As it has in every other area of society and public relations work, the Internet has influenced the practice of lobbying as well.

In 1999, disgraced former Clinton adviser Dick Morris, a veteran of old-fashioned political hardball, turned his attention to the new area of e-politics to get across his messages.

Mr. Morris's company, Vote.com, asked Web site visitors to vote "yes" or "no" on particular issues. The votes were then converted into e-mail messages sent to elected officials. In its early days out of the box, the technique created an uproar among

SIDEBAR

The "Be" List of Getting Through to Legislators

One Washington lobbying veteran offered the following most sensible "be" list for anyone wishing to get through to legislators:

- **Be independent.**   Policymakers value an independent view.
- **Be informed.**   Government thrives on information. Timely facts, a deep knowledge of the subject, and specific examples are invaluable.
- **Be bipartisan.**   Matters are more likely to be addressed on merit if approached in a bipartisan manner. Although it is necessary to be sensitive to political nuances, politics is best left to the politicians.
- **Be published.**   Clear and cogent thinking, in articles and op-ed pieces, is noticed in Washington and at the state house.

- **Be broad-minded.**   Don't peddle petty self-interest. Address the broader interests and your counsel will be sought.
- **Be persistent.**   A long-term, persistent commitment of time is mandatory in dealing with legislators.
- **Be practical.**   Politicians value practical recommendations they can defend to their constituents.
- **Be honest.**   Politicians and the press are skilled at spotting phonies. Honesty is the best policy. It works.

For further information, see Cindy Skrzycki, "Possible Leaders Abound in Business Community," *Washington Post* (January 24, 1988): D2.

elected officials and Internet experts, because Mr. Morris—and not the visitors to his site—set the question agenda and then flooded politicians' e-mail with his votes. In one barrage of 82,000 such messages to the White House, Mr. Morris's former employer effectively blocked the correspondence from getting through.[21]

In terms of political campaigning and grassroots lobbying, the presidential campaign of 2000 indicated that the role of the Web was growing. The Bush–Gore campaign was politics at cyberspeed. Gore's camp, in particular, regularly barraged 1,200 reporters and news editors on their e-mail list with positive references to Gore positions and negative critiques of their opponents' proposals. Ironically, just as e-mail grew as a direct communications electioneering mechanism, the more voters used the new technology—voice mail, caller ID, satellite dishes, remote controls, and digital programming—to shut out political messages.[22]

Candidates at every level create sophisticated Web sites to discuss issues, provide biographies, offer campaign schedules, solicit funds, and recruit volunteers and support. One candidate for president, in fact, wealthy publisher Steve Forbes, became the first to declare his candidacy on the Internet and conduct his campaign largely over the Web.

Beyond these measures, the Internet has become a pivotal tool to inform voters about election issues (Figure 13-7). Such election-oriented sites as FAQvoter.com promise to proliferate in the years ahead, as the World Wide Web becomes a more prominent tool in the election process.

Political Action Committees

The rise of political action committees (PACs) has been among the most controversial political developments in recent years. Thirty years ago, there were about 600 PACs. Today, the number is well in excess of 4,000 representing labor unions, business groups, corporations, nonprofit organizations, and so on.

Each PAC can give a maximum of $5,000 to a federal candidate in a primary election and another $5,000 for the general election. The top 50 PACs contribute in excess of $60 million annually. The four largest PACs in the nation are those controlled by (1) U.S. realtors, $2.5 million; (2) trial lawyers, $2.4 million; (3) state, county, and municipal employees, $2.4 million; and (4) American Medical Association, $2.3 million. An organization with many individual PACs, then, can have a tremendous monetary influence on an election. In the 1996 presidential campaign, the AFL-CIO labor union spent about $35 million through its various PACs.[23]

The increased influence of such groups on candidates is one reason why Senators John McCain and Russ Feingold led the Congress in 2002 to pass new strictures on campaign financing and particularly advertising for or against a candidate just prior to an election. Some would like to go further to see PACs severely curtailed or even banned. Indeed, over the years, Congress has limited what its members could accept in the form of trips and other niceties from the sponsors of PACs.

Critics of campaign finance reform argue that the First Amendment allows the freedom to speak out for or against any candidate. The tobacco industry, they note, was one of the most prominent PAC contributors to Congress, but the industry still got hammered. Although the number and size of PACs have increased, evidence of PAC-inspired indiscretions or illegalities has been minimal. Nonetheless, the furor over the heightened role of PACs in funding elections is bound to continue, even as campaign finance reform becomes the law of the land.

"*We must give over-charged taxpayers some of their own money back.*"
-President George W. Bush

The Bush Tax Relief Plan
www.bushtaxrelief.com

Dear Friend:

In his address to a Joint Session of Congress, President Bush made clear his intention to pass a tax relief plan that will reinvigorate our economy and put money back in the pockets of hardworking Americans. The Bush plan:

✓ Gives a tax cut to every family that pays income taxes.
✓ Replaces the current five-rate tax structure with four lower rates.
✓ Doubles the child tax credit to $1,000.
✓ Reduces the marriage penalty.
✓ Eliminates the death tax.
✓ Expands the charitable tax deduction.

While the President's plan is based on common-sense principles, some groups are determined to keep our government--and the tax bills that feed it--large. Please join me in contacting our state's U.S. Senators and your Member of Congress (202-224-3121) to ask them to support the Bush plan to reduce taxes on America's families and small businesses. Learn more at www.bushtaxrelief.com.

Sincerely,

Paid for by Republican National Committee.

FIGURE 13-7   **Internet lobbying.** Web sites promoting government programs of all sorts have become the first line of communications for politicians.

Dealing with Local Government

In 1980, Ronald Reagan rode to power on a platform of New Federalism, calling for a shift of political debate and public policy decisions to state and local levels. Presidents Clinton and Bush picked up the same initiative when they assumed power. Senator McCain seized the grassroots spirit when he won the New Hampshire Republican primary in 2000 and made the nomination a horserace. Thus, it has become more important for public relations people to deal with local, state, and regional governments.

Dealing with local entities, of course, differs considerably from dealing with the federal government. For example, opinion leaders in communities (those constituents with whom an organization might want to affiliate to influence public policy decisions) might include such sectors as local labor unions, teachers, civil service workers, and the like. Building a consensus among such diverse constituents is pure grassroots public relations. The very nature of state and local issues makes it impossible to give one all-encompassing blueprint for successful government relations strategies.

Although the federal government's role in wielding power and employing public relations professionals is significant, state and local governments also are extremely important. Indeed, one viable route for entry-level public relations practitioners is through the local offices of city, county, regional, and state government officials.

Local agencies deal directly—much more so than their counterparts in Washington—with individuals. State, county, and local officials must make themselves available for local media interviews, community forums and debates, and even

S I D E B A R

Do-It-Yourself Lobbying

You say you can't afford to hire a professional lobbyist to do your bidding on the local level. No problem. You can be your own "advocate."

Here's how to ensure your issue gets the consideration it deserves.

1. **Call your legislator.**
   - Keep your message brief, polite, and focused on one issue.
   - Identify yourself as a constituent.
   - Get beyond the receptionist and talk to the legislative aide. He or she is the person who advises the legislator.
2. **Write your legislator.**
   - Keep your message brief and focused on one issue.
   - Identify yourself as a constituent.

   - Be polite, no matter what the voting record has been on your issue.
   - Don't use form letters or preprinted postcards. They lack impact.
   - Cite the bill number along with the title of the bill when writing about specific legislation.
3. **Meet face-to-face with your legislator.**
   - Request meetings in writing. Send a letter or fax to request your appointment with a follow-up phone call if you don't get a response within several days.
   - Keep your visit brief, polite, and focused.
   - Bring relevant printed material to your visit, so that staff members have a printed record of what you discussed.
   - Be passionate about your issue to leave a lasting impression with your legislator.

door-to-door campaigning. In recent years, local and state officials have found that direct contact with constituents—often through call-in radio programs—is invaluable, not only in projecting an image but also in keeping in touch with the voters.

Indeed, the public information function at state and local levels—to keep constituents apprised of legislative and regulatory changes, various government procedures, and notices—is a frontline public relations responsibility on the local level.

Local government officials, assigned to ensure the quality of local schools, the efficiency of local agencies, and the reliability of local fire and police departments, increasingly require smart and experienced public relations counsel. State and local information officer positions, therefore, have become valued and important posts for public relations graduates.

LAST WORD

The pervasive growth of government at all levels of society may not be welcome news for many people. However, government's growth has stimulated the need for increased public relations support and counsel. Indeed, in recent years, the once overwhelming power of television advertising on political campaigns has declined, and the importance of individuals has increased.[24] So the importance of communicating directly with individual voters has become paramount for politicians.

The massive federal government bureaucracy, organized through individual agencies that seek to communicate with the public, is a vast repository for public relations jobs. The most powerful position in the land—that of president of the United States—has come to rely on public relations counsel to help maintain a positive public opinion of the office and the incumbent's handling of it.

On state and local levels, public relations expertise also has become a valued commodity. Local officials, too, attempt to describe their programs in the most effective manner. In profit-making and nonprofit organizations alike, the need to communicate with various layers of government also is imperative.

Like it or not, the growth of government in our society appears unstoppable, particularly now that the United States is engaged in a long-term military struggle. As a result, the need for public relations support in government relations will clearly continue to grow in the 21st century.

Discussion Starters

1. Why is the public relations function regarded as something of a stepchild in government?
2. What is the current status of the USIA and what are its responsibilities?
3. What is meant by "trial by press release"?
4. Why was Ronald Reagan called the "Great Communicator?"
5. What is the function of the White House press secretary?
6. What are the objectives of government relations officers?
7. What are the primary functions of lobbyists?
8. What impact has the Internet had on lobbying?
9. What are the pros and cons of PACs?
10. What are the key considerations in individually lobbying a legislator?

C A S E   S T U D Y

The Condit Calamity

The tale of Congressman Gary Condit's fall from power in the summer and fall of 2001 is a classic public relations case study in how not to deal with a front-page issue.

Until the summer of 2001, few people out of his Modesto, California, congressional district had ever heard of the 53-year-old Democratic congressman, who had served in the House for 13 years. He was an obscure politician, whose most notable claim to fame was being cited by journalists as one of the "Hunks of the House."

But in the spring of 2001, a young Washington, DC intern named Chandra Levy mysteriously disappeared on the very day she was supposed to return home to her parents in Modesto.

Levy was last seen at a Washington health club. Soon after, rumors spread that Condit and Levy were having an affair. Over the next 13 months, Condit remained high in the media spotlight surrounding the case, while police investigators continued to search for clues. The congressman's reputation for having a bizarre sexual history was reported in gruesome—yet gleeful—detail in the tabloid press.

No Comment Congressman

As soon as the Levy disappearance began to pick up publicity steam, Congressman Condit went into a shell (Figure 13-8).

He refused to acknowledge any affair with the intern, saying only that he had a "friendship" with Levy. As the congressman's denials increased, so, too, did the number of reporters tailing his every move.

Robert and Susan Levy, the missing woman's parents, by contrast, were vocal and public about their doubts that Condit was telling the truth about his relationship with their missing daughter. Furthermore, the Levys said, Condit might be the key to the investigation.

"I don't feel he has been very truthful to me. And I think someone out there knows where my daughter is," Mrs. Levy said to the cameras.

FIGURE 13-8   **No comment congressman.** Gary Condit.

Two and a half months after the disappearance, Condit took a privately adminis-tered polygraph test. His attorney announced that the congressman passed the test and, therefore, did not know anything about Chandra Levy's disappearance.

The press snickered, and the cable TV focus on Gary Condit intensified. Still, Condit remained silent. "We are not gonna feed the media frenzy," repeated Condit spokesperson Randy Groves as the media shadowed his boss.

PUBLIC RELATIONS ADVICE FROM LAWYERS
After Condit appeared for two meetings with the District of Columbia police, the media scrutiny intensified. Although the police repeatedly said they did not consider him "a suspect," the media camped out at his door and trailed Condit wherever he went.

In retaliation, he turned to lawyers for public relations advice.

When several papers quoted unidentified law enforcement sources as saying Levy slept at the congressman's condominium apartment, his spokesperson fiercely denied he had said any such thing.

When a Levy relative later claimed the intern was romantically involved with Condit, Condit's lawyer appeared on *Good Morning America* and measured his words carefully. While reiterating that his client had never "told police" that Levy spent the night, he added, "If she did, she had to spend it on a couch, because Cong. Condit's wife was in Washington the entire week."

Later, when the *Washington Post* ran a damning piece on the Condit–Levy rela-tionship, pieced together largely from anonymous sources, Condit's lawyer angrily fired off an eight-page letter demanding a retraction and threatening suit.

His words were hollow. There was no suit, and the media had a field day.

The problem confronting Cong. Condit—and anyone else caught in the media crosshairs—was articulated succinctly by Mike Lynch, Condit's chief of staff.

Said Mr. Lynch, "We have witnessed a series of newspaper articles and broadcast reports citing unidentified sources, including anonymous police sources, which have conveyed partial, misleading and, at times, outright inaccurate or irrelevant information."

In such a chaotic, unrestrained, media-frenzied environment, a lawyer's legal letters and litigious threats were not only meaningless—they were counterproductive.

FINALLY, DISASTROUSLY, GOING PUBLIC

After months of nonstop, unchallenged cable TV accusations, Condit finally permitted his team to go public.

He hired public relations counsel and, after yet another interview with D.C. police, his public relations person announced the congressman had hit "a home run." The press bridled at the choice of words.

Worse, Salon.com Internet webzine reported that Condit's public relations team was spreading stories about Chandra Levy's "own sordid sexual history."

Adding to the parade of surrogates speaking in Condit's behalf were his son and daughter, both of whom were interviewed about former friends turning on their father. Although the children were believable and persuasive, Condit, himself, still needed to come forward.

And so, finally, in August 2001, Gary Condit agreed to break his silence with a nationally televised interview with Connie Chung on ABC. Chung was chosen for the fact that she was a woman and would presumably be compassionate.

She wasn't.

Over and over again, the interviewer asked the uncomfortable, rigid congressman if he "had had an affair with Chandra Levy."

Over and over again, Condit refused to confirm that affair.

As much as Chung persisted, Condit refused. While his heart went out to the Levys, he said, he had nothing to apologize for.

The interview was disastrous.

A few months later, Condit was trounced in a primary campaign for reelection.

In May 2002, a man walking his dog in Washington's Rock Creek Park, where Chandra Levy was known to go jogging, found a skull in the weeds. Dental records later confirmed that the skeletal remains were Levy's.

The mystery of her death remains unsolved.

Questions

Assuming Gary Condit was innocent of the murder of Chandra Levy:
1. How would you have altered his public relations strategy?
2. Would you have used your attorney as public relations spokesperson?
3. How would you rate the performance of Condit's public relations team?
4. What messages would you have recommended the congressman deliver during the Connie Chung interview?
5. What are the primary public relations lessions that can be derived from the Condit calamity?

TIPS FROM THE TOP

An Interview with Ari Fleischer

Ari Fleischer

Ari Fleischer was the first press secretary to President George W. Bush, serving as the official liaison between the White House and members of the media and acting as the primary spokesperson for the president. He resigned in 2003. Mr. Fleischer served in a similar capacity in Mr. Bush's 1999 campaign for the presidency. Prior to that, Mr. Fleischer served as communications director for Elizabeth Dole's presidential campaign, press secretary to Senator Pete Dominici of New Mexico, and spokesperson for the House Ways and Means Committee.

What is the primary mission of the president's press secretary?
At its core, the press secretary job is a straight and simple job—to articulate what the president thinks.

What is President Bush's feeling about communications?
He understands the vital nature of explaining to the public what he's doing, why he's doing it, and what it means to the country.

How much access do you have to the president?
Extensive. I have "walk-in rights" any time I need to. I probably spend one-quarter to one-third of my day in meetings with the president. Every day, I will tell him what the press is asking, and we'll talk about it.

He takes advice well. By far the best way to speak for the president is to listen to him.

How important is it for any press secretary to "know" his or her principal?
It's the sine qua non of the job. To speak for the president, you need to be able to "read" him, pick up the nuances, and also what to leave behind in the Oval Office.

How would you characterize the White House press corps?
They're inquisitive. The press has a job to do—essentially to play the "devil's advocate" and to question whoever is in power, keeping the government honest and accountable.

Is the press "fair" in its coverage?
I think we've reached a point where the press, in pursuit of this devil's advocate role, would do well to ask itself if they are "informing" the public or are they being so negative about the institutions they cover that they're not covering all the news but only the "bad news." Shades of grey ought to be better reflected, particularly in headlines and leads. There's a tendency to simplify. In the process, a lot of depth gets lost. That's why press secretaries are forced sometimes to speak cautiously, in diplobabble and gobbledygook.

Has the press gotten better or worse over your career?
The cynicism has gotten worse. On the other hand, one of the reasons this country is free is that we have a free press. So despite the occasional tension, the system has worked very well for our country for 225 years.

What should be the proper relationship between the White House and the press?
It should be highly interactive, free flowing, and marked by a small, inherent amount of tension—the press wants to know "everything" and sometimes, in the national interest, we can't tell them—but always in a spirit of professionalism and politeness.

(Continued)

How much of your job is "selling" the president's agenda versus "informing"?

I happen to believe that, by informing, the public will make up its own mind. If the public agrees with the information provided, then it will "sell" itself. The public is savvy and able to cut to the bottom line. That means they're able to tune out the "spin" from Washington as well as the cynicism of the press.

Does President Bush like the media?

He respects what they do. He understands the power and importance of informing the public. I think he agrees there are too many games being played by the press, that there is too much cynicism and negativism. But he's got a wonderful intuition and gut—that he probably picked up from watching his father—that tells him what counts with the public and what trades at a discount with the media.

What's been your toughest challenge?

Bar none, the days after September 11 and also the anthrax attacks. Nothing prepares you for the country being attacked and 3,000 lives being taken. Nothing.

So how do you respond in the face of the magnitude of this tragedy?

You're still guided by the most fundamental guidance of all. First, learn the facts and then inform the country of what the president thinks.

What is the most rewarding part of your job?

One, working for someone in whom you believe so deeply, like President Bush, is rewarding in itself. Two, the honor of working in an institution as hallowed as the White House is fantastic. Every day you walk through the gates, you say to yourself how lucky you are to have this job. One of my predecessors, Marlin Fitzwater, advised me to once in a while "stop and smell the roses." It's the best advice I've gotten.

How does one become the president's press secretary?

You do something wrong and you get punished! Actually, the best route for a young person is to become a press secretary in politics. Start out learning the ropes. The truth is there is no difference between answering a small town reporter's question in a congressman's office and answering a question from the podium of the president's press secretary.

Suggested Readings

Browning, Graeme. *Electronic Democracy: Using the Internet to Influence American Politics.* Information Today Inc., 1996.

Crawford, Alan Pell. "D.C. Clients: A Capital Challenge," *Public Relations Strategist* (Summer 2002), 18–21.

Dennis, Lloyd. *Practical Public Affairs in an Era of Change.* New York: The Public Relations Society of America, 1995. A comprehensive guide to contemporary public affairs practice, offering the latest thinking and action programs impacting government and public policy.

Eggers, William D., and John O'Leary. *Revolution at the Roots: America's Quest for Smaller, Better Government.* New York: The Free Press, 1995. Maintains that a revolution is sweeping across America to return power and influence to states and municipalities.

Elster, Jon, ed. *Local Justice in America.* New York: Russell Sage Foundation, 1995. Justice plays a central role in public relations practice, and this book, which is now out of print, examines aspects of justice, including government relations principles.

Fitzwater, Marlin. *Call the Briefing! Reagan and Bush, Sam and Helen: A Decade with Presidents and the Press.* New York: Times Books, 1995. The trials and tribulations of a longtime political press secretary, done occasionally humorously but also with deadly seriousness in other spots.

Greenberg, Mike. *The Poetics of Cities: Designing Neighborhoods That Work*. Columbus: Ohio State University Press, 1995. Examines the politics of municipalities, including communications aspects on the local level.

Grossman, Lawrence K. *The Electronic Republic: Reshaping Democracy in the Information Age*. New York: Penguin USA, 1996. A discussion of government relations in a democracy rooted in information technology. How times will change.

Howard, Elizabeth, moderator, "Capital Gains," *Public Relations Strategist* (Summer 2002), 6–13.

Howard, Philip K. *The Death of Common Sense: How Law Is Suffocating America*. New York: Warner Books, 1996. Posits the view that regulation at all levels is breeding contempt for the governmental system of the United States.

Somerby, Bob. www.dailyhowler.com. This Web site features The Daily Howler, comedian and former *Baltimore Sun* reporter Bob Somerby, who comments on the Washington news corps' "astonishing combination of dishonesty and foolishness."

Stateman, Alison. "Life at the Pentagon," *Public Relations Strategist* (Summer 2002), 22–24.

Susskind, Lawrence, and Patrick Field. *Dealing with an Angry Public: The Mutual Gains Approach to Resolving Disputes*. New York: The Free Press, 1996. Outlines the six key elements of the "mutual gains approach" to help business and government get along.

Walsh, Kenneth T. *Feeding the Beast: The White House Versus the Press*. New York: Random House, 1996. The press that covers the executive branch of government is characterized by a surly, snarling bunch of pit bulls. And those are the pleasant ones! Or at least that's what Kenneth Walsh argues in this book. A former senior correspondent for *U.S. News and World Report,* he knows whereof he speaks.

Yinger, John. *Closed Doors, Opportunities Lost: The Continuing Costs of Housing Discrimination*. New York: Russell Sage Foundation, 1997 paperback. Another aspect of government relations—dealing with the important issue of housing and the lack thereof among certain groups in society.

Notes

1. Karen De Young, "Bush to Create Formal Office to Shape U.S. Image Abroad,"*Washington Post* (July 30, 2002): A1.

2. Sonya Ross, "White House Opens Office to Put a Better Face on U.S. Policy and Messages Abroad," Associated Press (July 30, 2002).

3. Fraser P. Seitel, "Words of Speech = Weapons of War," odwyerpr.com (October 15, 2001).

4. Robin-Pan Lener, "There's Room to Grow," *Government Communications*, National Association of Government Communicators (March 1992): 3.

5. Press statement by James P. Rubin, U.S. Department of State, October 1, 1999.

6. "Fact Sheet," February 1999, United States Information Agency, 301 4th Street, S.W., Room 602, Washington, D.C. 20647.

7. Fareed Zakaria, "The Myth of the Super-CEO," *Newsweek* (September 3, 2001): 33.

8. David H. Buswell, "Trial by Press Release?" *NAM Reports* (January 17, 1972): 9–11.

9. Mark Hertsgaard, "Journalists Played Dead for Reagan—Will They Roll Over Again for Bush?" *Washington Journalism Review* (January–February 1989): 31.

10. "Give Him an 'F,'" *The Scudder Media Report* (October 1998): 1, 6.

11. Robert U. Brown, "Role of Press Secretary," *Editor & Publisher* (October 19, 1974): 40.

12. William Hill, "Nessen Lists Ways He Has Improved Press Relations," *Editor & Publisher* (April 10, 1975): 40.

13. William Safire, "One of Our Own," *New York Times* (September 19, 1974): 43.

14. Laurence McQuillan, "Ari Fleischer Warms Up for Grillings," *USA Today* (January 23, 2001): 6A.

15. Remarks by Mike McCurry, "A View from the Podium," New York, NY, May 5, 1999.

16. Michael J. Bennett, "The 'Imperial' Press Corps," *Public Relations Journal* (June 1982): 13.

17. "Lobbyists Database," The Center for Responsive Politics, 2000.

18. "PR Is Lobbying? Read the New Law," *Next*, no. 2 1996, Edelman Public Relations Worldwide, 1500 Broadway, New York, NY 10036.

19. "Spin Doctors Try to Spin New Image Despite All Evidence to the Contrary," *Modern Healthcare* (December 20–27, 1999): 84.

20. Robert D. Hershey Jr., "In Very Fine Print the Treasury Defines a Lobbyist," *New York Times* (May 11, 1994): A16.

21. Rebecca Fairley Raney, "In E-Politics, Clinton's Ex-Adviser Still Plays by His Rules," *New York Times* (November 12, 1999): A16.

22. Bob Davis and Jeanne Cummings, "A Barrage of E-Mail Helps Candidates Hit Media Fast and Often," *Wall Street Journal* (September 21, 2000): A1,16.

23. Dennis L. Wilcox, Phillip H. Ault, and Warren K. Agee, *Public Relations Strategies and Tactics* (New York: Addison-Wesley Educational Publishers, 1998): 329.

24. Adam Nagourney, "TV's Tight Grip on Campaigns Is Weakening," *New York Times* (September 5, 2002): A1-19.

Chapter 14

Consumer Relations

Dear Amazon.com Customer,

On behalf of everyone here at Amazon.com, I'd like to thank you for ordering from us in the last few months. To put it simply, Amazon.com wouldn't be Amazon.com without customers like you.

If you're like me, you're always keeping your eye out for your next great read. We think we might be able to help. . . . [1]

Thus began the e-mail from one of the most savvy e-commerce marketers: a subtle, soft-sell, yet successful direct e-mail attempt to sell books to a targeted consumer. Pure, positive, pointed public relations.

The Amazon.com e-mail underscored one indisputable fact of business—a company can't exist without customers. That simple truth—that you need to sell your products and services to stay in business—underscores the importance of practicing positive, friendly, and helpful consumer relations.

Consequently, companies constantly are working to improve their image with consumers. Complicating this task are the hundreds of thousands of products and services from which consumers may choose (Figure 14-1).

The trick is to differentiate your product from all the others. Often it is public relations techniques and sensitivities that help distinguish a company and its products from the competition.

- *In the spring of 1997, the* Wall Street Journal's *lead story proclaimed, "Old-Fashioned PR Gives General Mills Advertising Bargains." The story chronicled how the venerable General Mills, Inc. had hearkened back to tried-and-true public relations techniques—Betty Crocker Cook-Offs, newspaper Q&A food columns, and pancake breakfasts for presidential candidates—to win recognition. One expert quoted in the story concluded that "a third-party endorsement is almost always more effective than a paid commercial."[2]*
- *In 2000, the California Prune Board petitioned the Food and Drug Administration for permission to use the term* dried plums *as an*

FIGURE 14-1 **So many products.** So important to differentiate.

alternative to prunes *on packages of the fruit.* Prunes, *it was felt, hurt the more youthful image of the prune—uh, plum—people wished to convey to attract younger consumers.*[3]

- *In 2001, Yahoo! announced it would remove adult-oriented products from its shopping, auctions, and classified sections because many of its users complained about the raunchy nature of the merchandise. Said Yahoo!'s president, "We value the strong relationships we have with our members and have consistently listened to them."*[4]

As Bruce Springsteen has put it, with "500 channels and nothing on," all offering commercial after commercial, it has become increasingly difficult for consumers to penetrate the advertising clutter to identify winning products and services.

In an era overwrought with advertising "noise"—tens of thousands of blaring messages beamed in the direction of a single consumer—public relations solutions can help cut through the clutter and distinguish one company from the next, enhancing the sale of a firm's products.

This chapter will examine how public relations helps attract, win, and keep consumers.

Consumer Relations Objectives

Building sales is the primary consumer relations objective. A satisfied customer may return; an unhappy customer may not. Here are some typical goals:

- **Keeping old customers.** Most sales are made to established customers. Consumer relations efforts should be made to keep these customers happy. Pains should be taken to respond to customers' concerns. For example, telephone companies will typically suspend normal charges in areas of natural disasters to make calls to loved ones.
- **Attracting new customers.** Every business must work constantly to develop new customers. In many industries, the prices and quality of competing products are similar. In choosing among brands, customers may base decisions on how they have been treated.

- **Marketing new items or services.**   Customer relations techniques can influence the sale of new products. Thousands of new products flood the market each year, and the vast array of information about these products can confuse the consumer. When General Electric's research revealed that consumers want personalized service and more information on new products, it established the GE Answer Center, a national toll-free, 24-hour service that informed consumers about new GE products and services. Building such company and product loyalty lies at the heart of a solid consumer relations effort.
- **Expediting complaint handling.**   Few companies are free of complaints. Customers protest when appliances don't work, errors are made in billing, or deliveries aren't made on time. Many large firms have established response procedures. Often a company ombudsman can salvage a customer relationship with a speedy and satisfactory answer to a complaint.
- **Reducing costs.**   To most companies, an educated consumer is the best consumer. Uninformed buyers cost a company time and money—when goods are returned, service calls are made, and instructions are misunderstood. Many firms have adopted programs to educate customers about use of their products.

Office of the Ombudsperson

Research indicates that only a handful of dissatisfied customers—4 percent—will ever complain. But that means that there are many others with the same complaint who never say anything. And the vast majority of dissatisfied customers won't repurchase from the offending company.

In the old days, a frequent response to complaint letters was to dust off the so-called "bedbug letter." This stemmed from occasional letters to the railroads complaining about bedbugs in the sleeper cars. To save time, railroad consumer relations personnel simply dispatched a prewritten bedbug letter in response. Today, with the volume of mail, e-mail, and faxes at a mountainous level, an occasional bedbug letter still appears from time to time (Figure 14-2).

At many companies the most immediate response to complaints has been the establishment of ombudsman offices. The term *ombudsman* originally described a government official—in Sweden and New Zealand, for example—appointed to investigate complaints about abuses made by public officials. In most firms, the office of the ombudsperson investigates complaints made against the company and its managers. Such an office generally provides a central location that customers can call to seek redress of grievances.

Typically, the ombudsperson monitors the difficulties customers are having with products. Often he or she can anticipate product or performance deficiencies. Ombudspersons are in business to inspire customer confidence and to influence an organization's behavior toward improved service. They accomplish this by responding, more often than not, in the following manner:

- "We'll take care of that for you."
- "We'll take full responsibility for that defect."
- "We want your business."
- "Thank you for thinking of us."
- "Consider it done."

Alas, in these days of voice mail, e-mail, and recorded sequential answering systems, such personalized "magic words" seem to be in short supply. Pity. The companies that express such understanding and courtesy will be the ones that keep the business.

12 King Place
Closter, New Jersey
07624
June 2, 1993

President Clinton
The White House
Washington, D.C. 205000

Dear President Clinton:

My name is David Seitel, and I am a sixth grader. I'm writing about a very important topic. This topic is SMOKING. Our tobacco companies in the U.S. are setting a bad example for us kids today. They are going to other countries, and encouraging people in their teens especial my age, to smoke.

Please, won't you try to help stop American tobacco companies from addicting the world's children. Thank you.

Sincerely,
David Seitel

Thank you for writing to me. I enjoy hearing from young people because you are the future of our country. I am honored to be your President.

Bill Clinton

FIGURE 14-2 **Bedbug letter.** Even in these days of direct-mail sophistication, a young consumer still risks the disappointment of his sincere missive being answered with a cursory bedbug letter.

The Consumer Movement

Although consumerism is considered to be a relatively recent concept, legislation to protect consumers first emerged in the United States in 1872, when Congress enacted the Criminal Fraud Statute to protect consumers against corporate abuses. In 1887, Congress established the Interstate Commerce Commission to curb freewheeling railroad tycoons.

However, the first real consumer movement came right after the turn of the century when journalistic muckrakers encouraged legislation to protect the consumer. Upton Sinclair's novel *The Jungle* revealed scandalous conditions in the meatpacking industry and helped usher in federal meat inspection standards as Congress passed the Food and Drug Act and the Trade Commission Act. In the second wave of the movement, from 1927 to 1938, consumers were safeguarded from the abuses of manufacturers, advertisers, and retailers of well-known brands of commercial products. During this time, Congress passed the Food, Drug, and Cosmetic Act.

By the early 1960s, the movement had become stronger and more unified. President John F. Kennedy, in fact, proposed that consumers have their own bill of rights, containing four basic principles:

1. *The right to safety:* to be protected against the marketing of goods hazardous to health or life
2. *The right to be informed:* to be protected against fraudulent, deceitful, or grossly misleading information, advertising, labeling, or other practices and to be given the facts needed to make an informed choice

A QUESTION OF ETHICS

So You Want to Be an Ombudsperson . . .

The mantra of consumer relations officers, like that of public relations officers, is not necessarily that "the customer is always right" but rather "do the right thing."

With that in mind, consider the following random selection of complaints received by the consumer affairs division of a local bank. How would you handle each?

1. A businesswoman carrying an attaché case made a deposit at a midtown branch before going to her office. Inadvertently, she left her case on the main banking floor. By the time she discovered that it was missing, the police bomb squad had smashed the innocent case and cordoned off the area. The owner asked the bank for a replacement. Would you have given it to her?

2. After making a deposit and leaving the bank, a woman reported that a huge icicle fell from the bank's roof and nearly hit her. She complained bitterly to consumer affairs. How would you appease her?

3. A young installment loan customer claimed that his car had been taken because of delinquent loan payments. He claimed that he had paid the loan on time and objected to the illegal

seizure. On checking, it was determined that several loan payments were, in fact, delinquent. The car is returned but in a damaged condition. The young man sought reimbursement for the repairs. What would you recommend?

4. A customer complained that she had received no response to her numerous letters concerning the hostile treatment accorded her at her local branch. After investigation, it was learned that the woman was a nuisance to branch officers, yet she kept a very healthy balance in her savings account. Furthermore, all the correspondence to which she referred was written on the backs of checks she submitted in loan payments. How would you handle this problem?

5. A new depositor complained that he was not given a promised toaster for making his deposit. After checking, it was learned his deposit was made the day after the premium offer ended. What would you do?

6. The executor of an estate complained that his deceased brother, who had been a bank customer, received a card reading, "Best wishes in your new residence." What remedial action would you suggest?

---

3. *The right to choose:* to be assured access, whenever possible, to a variety of products and services at competitive prices
4. *The right to be heard:* to be assured that consumer interests will receive full and sympathetic consideration in the formulation of government policy

Subsequent American presidents have continued to emphasize consumer rights and protection. Labeling, packaging, product safety, and a variety of other issues continue to concern government overseers of consumer interests.

Federal Consumer Agencies

Today a massive government bureaucracy attempts to protect the consumer against abuse: more than 900 different programs administered by more than 400 federal entities. Key agencies include the Justice Department, Federal Trade Commission, Food and Drug Administration, Consumer Product Safety Commission, and Office of Consumer Affairs.

- **Justice Department.**   The Justice Department has had a consumer affairs section in its antitrust division since 1970. Its responsibilities include the enforcement of such consumer protection measures as the Truth in Lending Act and the Product Safety Act. The Justice Department is particularly concerned with antitrust and monopolistic activities. This was the root of the initiative against the world's largest computer company, Microsoft, in the early years of the 21st century.

- **Federal Trade Commission.** The FTC, perhaps more than any other agency, has vigorously enforced consumer protection. Its national advertising division covers television and radio advertising, with special emphasis on foods, drugs, and cosmetics. Its general litigation division covers areas not included by national advertising, such as magazine subscription agencies, door-to-door sales, and income tax services. Its consumer credit and special programs division deals with such areas as fair credit reporting and truth in packaging.

- **Food and Drug Administration.** The FDA is responsible for protecting consumers from hazardous items: foods, drugs, cosmetics, therapeutic and radiological devices, food additives, and serums and vaccines. Under Dr. David Kessler, the FDA waged an all-out war against cigarette advertising to children, in particular. After years of fighting, the industry finally capitulated and removed its teenager-targeted Joe Camel symbol from its ads (Figure 14-3).

- **Consumer Product Safety Commission.** This bureau is responsible for overseeing product safety and standards and has been particularly aggressive in recent years in the area of seat belt restraints, strollers, blankets, and other products for small children.

- **Office of Consumer Affairs.** This agency, the central point of consumer activities in the government, publishes literature to inform the public of recent developments in consumer affairs.

The corporate scandals of 2002 reenergized the federal bureaucracy to safeguard consumers from unscrupulous practices. The Justice Department, FDA, and SEC (discussed at length in Chapter 15) all increased their scrutiny of company management after the revelations of corporate fraud that came to light in 2002.

In the 21st century, clearly the best policy for any public company is to communicate directly and frequently with regulators in Washington, ultimately to win their understanding and support.

Consumer Activists on the Internet

The consumerist movement has attracted a host of activists in recent years. Although private testing organizations that evaluate products and inform consumers about potential dangers have proliferated, the most significant activity to keep companies honest has occurred on the Internet.

Perhaps the best-known testing group, Consumers Union was formed in 1936 to test products across a wide spectrum of industries. It publishes the results in a monthly magazine, *Consumer Reports*, which reaches about 3.5 million readers. Often an evaluation in *Consumer Reports*, either pro or con, greatly affects how customers view particular products. Consumers Union also produces books, a travel newsletter, a column for 450 newspapers, and monthly features for network television. It has an annual budget of $70 million.

The Consumer Federation of America was formed in 1968 to unify lobbying efforts for proconsumer legislation. Today the federation consists of 200 national, state, and

Does RJR Nabisco Lie About Marketing To Kids?

In public they say:

"I do not want to sell tobacco to children. I'd fire anyone on the spot if I found they were doing it." (Steven Goldstone, CEO, RJR Nabisco Holdings Corp., 12/6/96).

But a 1976 RJR internal memo stated:

"Evidence is now available to indicate that the 14-to-18-year-old group is an increasing segment of the smoking population. RJR-T must soon establish a successful new brand in this market if our position in the industry is to be maintained over the long term."

You Decide.

In 1988, RJR introduced Joe Camel. Subsequently, Camel's share of the kids' market quadrupled. Camel is now the second most popular cigarette among children, and kids were found to be as familiar with Joe Camel as Mickey Mouse.

Tell your elected officials to support restrictions on tobacco marketing to children, including the Food and Drug Administration rule.

Tobacco vs. Kids. Where America draws the line.

CAMPAIGN for TOBACCO-FREE Kids

To learn more, call 1-800-284-KIDS.

This ad supported by: American Cancer Society; American Lung Association; American Heart Association; Center for Women Policy Studies; National Federation of State High School Associations; Committee for Children; Intercultural Cancer Council; Interreligious Coalition on Smoking OR Health; Youth Service America; American College of Preventive Medicine; Girl Scouts USA; Child Welfare League of America; National Association of Secondary School Principals; National Association of Elementary School Principals; American Federation of Teachers; Women's Legal Defense Fund; Association of State and Territorial Health Officials.

The National Center for Tobacco-Free Kids, 1707 L Street NW, Suite 800, Washington, DC 20036

FIGURE 14-3 **Good-bye, Joe.** For years, Joe Camel was the too-cool symbol that helped lure teenage smokers. Ultimately, the industry, at the government's insistence, killed old Joe.

local consumer groups, labor unions, electric cooperatives, and other organizations with consumer interests.

Probably most effective, though, in actively dealing with corporate abuse is the emergence of the Internet. From the Yahoo! Boycott Board, which lists actions being taken against organizations, to so-called rogue Web sites, which air the gripes of dissatisfied consumers, to wildfire e-mail campaigns and discussion groups directed at product abuse—the Internet has become a prime source of consumer activism.

Smart companies take Internet challenges seriously and act on them immediately. When a disgruntled Buy.com customer began a Web site in 1999, www.buycrap.cjb.net, to complain about purchasing a mispriced computer, the company flew him across the country to meet top executives.[5] Accordingly, companies have found that word-of-mouth criticism, aided and abetted by the Internet, must be dealt with—quickly.

Although companies often find such activists' criticism annoying, the emergence of the consumer watchdog movement has generally been a positive development for consumers. Ralph Nader, the dean of consumer activists, and others have forced organizations to consider, even more than usual, the downside of the products and services they offer. Smart companies have come to take seriously the pronouncements of consumer activists.

Business Gets the Message

Obviously, few organizations can afford to shirk their responsibilities to consumers. Consumer relations divisions have sprung up, either as separate entities or as part of public relations departments. The title of vice president for consumer relations is showing up with more frequency on corporate organization charts.

In many companies, consumer relations began strictly as a way to handle complaints, an area to which all unanswerable complaints were sent. Such units have frequently provided an alert to management. More recently, companies have broadened the consumer relations function to encompass such activities as developing guidelines to evaluate services and products for management, developing consumer programs that meet consumer needs and increase sales, developing field-training programs, evaluating service approaches, and evaluating company effectiveness in demonstrating concern for customers.

The investment in consumer service apparently pays off. Marketers of consumer products say that most customer criticism can be mollified with a prompt, personalized reply. Throw in a couple of free samples and consumers feel even better. In any case, consumers are impressed when a company takes the time to drop them a line for whatever reason (Figure 14-4).

On the other hand, failing to answer a question, satisfy a complaint, or solve a problem can result in a blitz of bad word-of-mouth advertising. More typical of the increased concern shown today by most business organizations are the following:

- In 1999, a revitalized Apple Computer, backed off a decision to retroactively raise prices on some computers that customers already had ordered and paid for.[6]
- When Alamo Rent A Car experienced a shortage of vehicles in a busy vacation season at certain locations, it eagerly reimbursed customers for the difference between their reserved Alamo rate and the upgraded one they were forced to pay.
- When the Swingline Company received numerous complaints about its Tot Stapler, it reconstituted the product and sent new models, free of charge, to people who complained.
- When Newman's Own Microwave Popcorn received complaints that its bags were leaking, it hired a technical consulting organization to reevaluate the bag sealing system. It also refunded the cost of the purchase.

CNN AMERICA, INC.
1271 Avenue of the Americas, 4th Floor
New York, NY 10020

CONNIE CHUNG
212.522.2676
Fax: 212.522.2723
connie.chung@cnn.com

August 9, 2002

Fraser Seitel
Emerald Park
177 Main Street
Suite 215
Fort Lee, NJ 07024

Dear Fraser,

Thank you so much for coming on our program. It was a pleasure talking to you, and I hope that we made you feel welcome and comfortable through the entire production process.

I just wanted to let you know how much I appreciated the time you spent with me. I certainly hope that our interview was a positive experience for you as well.

I wish you the very best for the future.

Very best regards,

Connie Chung

Connie Chung

FIGURE 14-4 Nice touch. Whether thanking or apologizing, a short note to a consumer always makes good sense.

In adopting a more activist consumerist philosophy, firms like these have found that consumer relations need not take a defensive posture. Consumer relations professionals must themselves be activists to make certain that consumers understand the benefits and realities of using their products.

The consumer philosophy of the DaimlerChrysler Corporation is typical of the more enlightened attitude of most companies today. Its "Car Buyer's Bill of Rights" states:

1. Every car buyer has the right to quality.
2. Every buyer has the right to long-term protection.
3. Every buyer has the right to friendly treatment, honest service, and competent repairs.
4. Every buyer has the right to a safe vehicle.
5. Every buyer has the right to address grievances.
6. Every buyer has the right to satisfaction.

LAST WORD

Without consumers, there would be no companies. Despite periodic legislative setbacks and shifting consumerist leadership, the cause of consumerism seems destined to remain strong. The increasing use of seat belts and air bags, increased environmental concerns about packaging and pollution, rising outrage about secondhand smoke and

FIGURE 14-5 **Teaming up for the planet.** In 2002, the founders of ice cream maker Ben & Jerry's teamed up with the Dave Matthews Band to support the campaign to fight global warming.

all smoking in general, and numerous other causes indicate that the push for product safety and quality will likely increase in the years ahead.

Indeed, the smartest companies are those that tie their products and services to larger societal causes, thus establishing a link in the minds of consumers that represents "loftier" goals than merely making money (Figure 14-5).

That is not to say there is anything wrong with making money. Companies depend on their profits to exist. Without profitability, corporations can't contribute to bettering society.

Safeguarding the relationship with consumers of products and services is fundamental to continuing to earn profits. That's why the efforts of public relations professionals, assigned to maintaining, sustaining, and enhancing a company's standing with its customers, is a core communications challenge in the 21st century.

Discussion Starters

1. Why is dealing with consumers so important for public relations?
2. What are typical consumer relations objectives?
3. What is the office of the ombudsperson?
4. What was President Kennedy's role in consumerism?
5. What key federal agencies are involved in consumerism?
6. What is the purpose of the FDA?
7. What is a consumer bill of rights?
8. What is the impact of the Internet on a company's consumer relations?
9. Who is Ralph Nader and what is his significance to consumerism?
10. What constitutes a quality consumer-oriented company?

TOP OF THE SHELF

Christopher Locke, Rick Levine, Doc Searls, and David Weinberger

The Cluetrain Manifesto: The End of Business as Usual *Cambridge, MA: Perseus Books, 2001*

The Cluetrain Manifesto began as a Web site, www.cluetrain.com, in 1999 when the authors, who have worked variously at IBM, Sun Microsystems, the *Linux Journal*, and NPR, posted 95 theses that pronounced what they felt was the new reality of the networked marketplace.

Examples include thesis 2: "Markets consist of human beings, not demographic sectors"; thesis 20, "Companies need to realize their markets are often laughing"; and of particular interest to PR professionals, thesis 62, "Markets do not want to talk to flacks and hucksters. They want to participate in the conversations going on behind the corporate firewall."

Another one of their theses you might appreciate is thesis 70: "We are immune to advertising. Just forget it."

This book, which elaborates on their theses through seven essays, is quite controversial, but anyone interested in managing a business and reaching out to consumers in the coming years should hear these authors out.

CASE STUDY

Tobacco Wars

The manufacturers of cigarettes, among the most powerful corporations in the world, learned a valuable lesson in the first years of the 21st century:

If you violate the faith of consumers, you will lose—big time.

In the final years of the last century and the first years of this one, cigarette companies have seen their products and advertising restricted, their executives denigrated before national panels, and their reputations tarnished with accusations of lying and worse.

The enemies of smoking have recast the pastime as nothing short of sin. Today, smokers can no longer light up on airplanes, in restaurants, offices, or stadiums. They have been branded as outcasts, forced to vacate the premises if they wish to light up.

As recently as the 1980s, congressional and business deals were still made in smoke-filled rooms. Even the first Americans, Christopher Columbus wrote, carried a "fire brand in the hand, and herbs to drink the smoke thereof, as they are accustomed."

Smoking had always been politically sacrosanct, like guns. Tobacco companies produced jobs for workers and profits for shareholders and, not coincidentally, also financed political campaigns. Tobacco was untouchable, right up until 1994.

And then the roof caved in.

PERMANENT POLITICAL SHIFT

As more activist politicians spoke out against the dangers of smoking, particularly to young people, the political landscape began to shift. Some believe the shift is irreversible.

- President Clinton proposed steep excise taxes on cigarettes as part of health care reform efforts.
- The Environmental Protection Agency classified secondhand smoke as a serious health risk. The House approved legislation barring smoking from most

public places. The Department of Defense prohibited smoking in its workplaces worldwide.

● FDA Commissioner Dr. David A. Kessler, considered public enemy number one by tobacco companies, proposed treating tobacco products as drugs, based on "accumulating evidence" that the industry was using unnecessarily high levels of nicotine to create and maintain smokers' addiction.

● Lawsuits began to be filed around the country, including one by Mississippi's attorney general, seeking reimbursement for the estimated tens of millions of dollars that the state spent on medical care for tobacco-related illness. Other states, like Florida, initiated similar efforts.

The major manufacturers of tobacco products increasingly found themselves under pressure and under the spotlight.

FATAL CONGRESSIONAL TESTIMONY

In February 1994, tobacco makers appeared before Congress, denying that nicotine is addictive and that cigarettes have been proved to cause disease and more than 400,000 deaths a year. It was the first of many bitter confrontations.

As part of the hearing process, internal company documents were made public that shed light on the approach of cigarette companies in selling their product.

Among the documents was one detailing minutes of a meeting of Brown & Williamson executives held just before tobacco advertising was banned from radio and television in 1971. Code-named "Project Truth," the text of the presentation made at the meeting read in part:

> Doubt is our product, since it is the best means of competing with the "body of fact" that exists in the minds of the general public. With the general public, the consensus is that cigarettes are in some way harmful to their health.
>
> Unfortunately, we cannot take a position directly opposing the anti-cigarette forces and say that cigarettes are a contributor to good health. No information that we have supports this claim.

The objective of Project Truth was to "lift the cigarette from the cancer identification as quickly as possible and restore it to its proper place of dignity and acceptance in the minds of men and women in the marketplace of American free enterprise."

By the mid-1980s, according to the documents revealed at the hearing, the companies had forsaken attempts to exonerate smoking as a health hazard and seemed to shift to a legal concern "about what would happen if the years of studies on biological hazards of cigarettes were to become available to plaintiffs in court cases."

In later testimony, Commissioner Kessler revealed information that Brown & Williamson developed a genetically engineered tobacco that would more than double the amount of nicotine delivered in some cigarettes. The company responded by calling Dr. Kessler's testimony "exaggerated."

PUBLIC PERCEPTION GROWS NEGATIVE

The confusion and disputes resulting from the cigarette manufacturers' testimonies before Congress began to build up.

The American Heart Association, American Cancer Society, American Lung Association, and American Medical Association began to work together to win smoking bans. Activists began to get access to caches of internal tobacco industry documents through lawsuits, such as the one filed by the family of Rose Cipollone, who died in 1984 at age 58. Her family won initially but dropped its suit in 1992 after years of costly litigation. The cigarette companies refused to acquiesce.

Perhaps the most damning report was the EPA document on secondhand smoke, which said that environmental tobacco smoke causes 3,000 lung cancer deaths each year. When incoming Clinton administration EPA Administrator Carol Browner was apprised of the findings, she said, "Let that thing rip," and she began promoting the report heavily.

In the latter years of the 1990s, tobacco manufacturers slid further into the public abyss:

- In February 1997, the FDA implemented regulations that forbade merchants from selling tobacco to minors.
- Cigarette advertising was the next to be attacked, with critics vowing to rid such advertising from the airwaves, where minors are exposed to it. The primary target was R. J. Reynolds' Joe Camel advertising campaign. Joe Camel, it was charged, represented a seductive appeal to young people.
- The Campaign for Tobacco-Free Kids was begun with a vigorous public relations and advertising barrage that mobilized children in the pursuit against big tobacco (Figure 14-6).
- Cigarette package labeling became more restrictive. U.S. legislators looked toward Great Britain, where cigarette advertising is more tightly regulated and packs are labeled with dire warnings (Figure 14-7).
- In 1997, the Liggett Group tobacco company agreed that its tests had indicated that cigarette smoking was in fact harmful to health and agreed to label its

FIGURE 14-6   Kids against cancer. The Campaign for Tobacco-Free Kids was relentless in its attacks on smoking.

FIGURE 14-7 **Smoking Kills.** Warnings posted on cigarettes sold in Great Britain left nothing to the imagination in terms of the relative danger.

products accordingly. Liggett also acknowledged that it had consciously marketed its products to children.

COMPANY CAPITULATION

For their part, the cigarette companies themselves remained adamant in their fight—at least at first. Said the Philip Morris public affairs director, "There are risk factors in smoking. But 50 million adults have chosen to smoke, and they have the right to make that decision."

In the wake of the Liggett bombshell, however, the industry was on shaky ground. In 1998, the tobacco industry settled a battery of legal cases with 46 individual states' attorneys general. The settlement was expected to total $246 billion over 25 years. As part of the settlement with the states, $1 billion was devoted to a multiyear public relations program to fight tobacco use. Nonetheless, more suits loomed, and the Justice Department readied further litigation as the drumbeat against tobacco increased (Figure 14-8).

In 1999, Philip Morris, the largest tobacco company, announced plans to repair its tarnished image. Centerpiece was a $100 million Philip Morris Youth Smoking Prevention Initiative public relations program. By 2000, the Philip Morris stock, once one of the bluest of all blue chips, had plunged by more than half.

Faced with an unprecedented loss of public opinion and a tide against cigarettes that now swept around the world, the companies could have but one overriding objective as they faced the new century: to restore their public image.

ROAD TO RESURRECTION

By the new century, most cigarette companies had gotten the message.

Although still vigilantly fighting antismoking lawsuits in court, tobacco manufacturers were no longer equally vigorous in promoting their primary products. Those with food-oriented subsidiaries, such as Philip Morris, became much more eager to promote that side of the business, as opposed to the cigarette side. Philip Morris, in fact, wound up spinning out its Kraft food division to separate it from the tarnished tobacco name.

By 2002, while the Campaign for Tobacco-Free Kids still attacked aggressively (Figure 14-9) and states' attorneys general still occasionally railed against tobacco companies, the pressure had died down considerably.

Ironically, many states used their 2002 tobacco settlement payments of $8.9 billion to balance their sagging budgets. This was in direct contradiction to the states' promise to use settlement funds for tobacco prevention.

Nontheless, the cigarette manufacturers themselves had learned their lesson. As proof, in 2002, the world's largest tobacco company, Philip Morris, changed its name to Altria (meaning "higher" in Latin), once and for all shedding the stigma that had cost it so much with consumers.

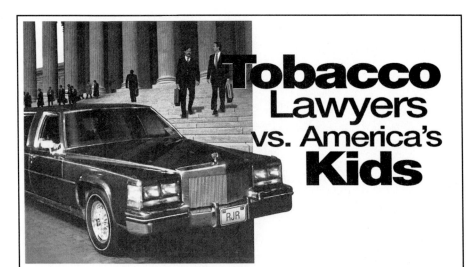

Tobacco companies claim they don't target kids. Yet they're in court, right now, trying to block a sensible Food and Drug Administration rule to protect kids from tobacco marketing and sales.

Three thousand children start smoking every day. One-third will eventually die from their addiction. If the tobacco industry's lawyers get their way in court, thousands of kids will be sentenced to an early death.

Where's the justice in that?

Tobacco vs. Kids.
Where America draws the line.

CAMPAIGN for TOBACCO-FREE Kids

To learn more, call 1-800-284-KIDS.

This ad sponsored by: American Cancer Society; American Heart Association; American Lung Association; Association of Black Cardiologists, Inc.; YWCA of the U.S.A.; American Federation of Teachers; General Board of Church and Society of the United Methodist Church; Intercultural Cancer Council; Women's Legal Defense Fund; Committee for Children; Interreligious Coalition on Smoking OR Health; National Middle School Association; American College of Preventive Medicine; Association of State and Territorial Health Officials; American College of Cardiology.

The National Center for Tobacco-Free Kids,
1707 L Street, NW, Suite 800, Washington, DC 20036

FIGURE 14-8   **Pitched battle.** The wave of antismoking advertising continued, even after huge industry class-action settlements.

Questions

1. How would you assess the credibility of the cigarette industry today?
2. If you were hired as public relations counsel to the tobacco industry, what would you advise it to do?
3. What do you think of Philip Morris changing the name of its company?

No matter how often a snake sheds its skin... **It's still a snake.**

Altria *is* Philip Morris.

Why is Philip Morris changing its name? After decades of marketing to kids, deceiving the public and manipulating its products, Philip Morris now wants to hide from its past. But it can't hide this: More kids still smoke "Altria's" Marlboros than all other brands combined. 2,000 kids still get hooked on tobacco every day. 1 in 3 will die prematurely. Philip Morris may be changing its name, but it's not changing its ways.

CAMPAIGN for TOBACCO-FREE Kids

AMERICAN LUNG ASSOCIATION. American Cancer Society. American Heart Association. Fighting Heart Disease and Stroke

New Name. Same Deadly Habits. www.PhilipMorrisCantHide.org

FIGURE 14-9 **Still a snake.** Even after humongous settlement payments, cigarette companies could not escape the wrath of the Campaign for Tobacco-Free Kids.

4. Visit the Philip Morris tobacco Web site (www.philipmorris.com/tobacco_bus/index.html). Read the homepage and then follow the link to "Tobacco Issues." How is Philip Morris using this Web site to boost its credibility?

For further information on the Tobacco Wars, see "Defending an Embattled Industry," *Public Relations Strategist* (Summer 1999): 7; Stuart Elliott, "When the Smoke Clears, It's Still Reynolds," *New York Times* (September 13, 1995): D1; Suein L. Hwang, "Philip Morris Plans to Take Steps to Mend Its Image," *Wall Street Journal* (June 29, 1999): B9; Youssef M. Ibrahim, "Cigarette Makers Cope with British Ad Restrictions," *New York Times* (April 18, 1997): D5; Mary Kuntz and Joseph Weber, "The New Hucksterism," *Business Week* (July 1, 1996); Otto Lerbinger, "Branding vs. Identity," *PR Reporter* (June

24, 2002): 1; William D. Novelli, "Waging War on Tobacco," Public Relations Strategist (Fall 1999): 15; Tara Parker-Pope, "Danger: Warning Labels May Backfire," *Wall Street Journal* (April 28, 1997): B1; "Philip Morris Launches $100M Anti-Smoking Pitch," *O'Dwyer's PR Services Report* (January 1999): 1, 20; Eben Shapiro, "RJR Nabisco's Tobacco Unit Escapes Fight with FTC Over Joe Camel Ads," *Wall Street Journal* (June 2, 1994); John Schwartz, "Double Blow for Tobacco Industry: Waxman Assails Research Council, Justice Dept. Probe Sought," *Washington Post* (May 27, 1994): A1.

TIPS FROM THE TOP

Tobacco Wars Postscript: The View from the Bunker
An Interview with Murray H. Bring

Murray Bring

Murray H. Bring was vice chairman for external affairs and general counsel of Philip Morris Companies, Inc. In addition to being the top lawyer at the world's leading cigarette manufacturer, Mr. Bring was also responsible for the company's public affairs function.

The industry has lost a number of court cases. Why do you think these cases have gone against you?

It's hard to say. It's probably a combination of things, which started in 1994 with Commissioner David Kessler's congressional testimony before the Waxman Committee, and a series of events that transpired at about that time, including a program in which *ABC Day One* made the false allegation that the tobacco companies spiked their cigarettes with additional nicotine to keep smokers hooked.

What was your response to that broadcast?

We sued ABC for libel. We ended up settling after ABC agreed to pay all of our costs and issued a retraction and apology indicating its allegation was inaccurate.

Isn't the industry to blame to some degree for its willingness to remain silent?

That's an interesting question and a subject of discussion internally. We try very hard to counteract these false allegations whenever we can.

What about your approach toward litigation public relations?

For many years, we refused to engage in a public relations discussion of the issues that were involved in litigation. That began to change in the *Cipollone* case in New Jersey

in 1988, when the other side was offering things to the press virtually every day at the end of court. So we decided we needed to be a player in that arena.

We hired a public relations consultant to work with the lawyers in that case, and he was an integral part of the effort by the industry to get our side of the story across—to the public at large, who was reading about the case.

And your public relations strategy today?

From that point forward, we have concluded that it is important to have a public relations component to our litigation activities. We now have public relations people in the company who have experience in the media and work with the trial lawyers. We also have outside consultants present during the course of important trials and make an effort on a daily basis to communicate to the press about what's going on in the courtroom from our perspective. We now realize this is an important function for us.

What's the Philip Morris approach to its adversaries?

We've had critics and adversaries out there for a long time. We obviously have to be mindful of what they're saying. I think we need to correct the record when we can if we think what they're saying is inappropriate. But I think it's important for us to try and develop a dialogue. In the earlier days of this industry, there was probably not enough of an effort made to try to communicate with our critics and to try to find common ground.

What lessons have you learned from being in the spotlight in recent years?

I think we have learned that when you are in the spotlight and subject to intense scrutiny, you have to listen to others, including your critics. You need to try to engage in a dialogue and work with others to find common ground and reasonable solutions.

TIPS FROM THE TOP

An Interview with Laura Ries

Laura Ries

Laura Ries is the coauthor of two bests-selling books with her partner and father, Al Ries: *The Fall of Advertising and the Rise of PR* (2002) and *The 22 Immutable Laws of Branding* (1998). A recognized marketing expert in her own right, she speaks and consults with companies around the world. Her Web site is www.ries.com.

How effective is advertising in reaching consumers?
Advertising is effective in reminding consumers of something they already know. Volvos are safe or Coke is the real thing. Advertising is not nearly as effective in trying to change the minds of consumers. Advertising that tells consumers Volvo makes great convertibles or you should "always" drink Coke are simply unbelievable in consumers' minds.

How effective is PR in reaching consumers?
PR is effective because it has credibility with consumers. While people don't believe everything they see or read, they are much more receptive to a new idea when presented by the media than they are when the idea is presented in an advertisement.

Why do you think advertising has lost its effectiveness?
Advertising has lost effectiveness for two reasons. First, there is just too much of it. We are bombarded with advertisements everywhere from ATM machines to toilet stalls. Second, advertising has no credibility. Why believe what companies say about themselves?

What kind of PR do consumers appreciate?
Consumers appreciate finding out about new categories. The first energy drink, the first direct-to-consumer personal computer, the first oversized driver, the first impotence drug. They don't really care about Red Bull, Dell, Callaway, or Viagra as brands. They care about the new categories represented by these brands.

Does a company's reputation influence buying decisions?
A company's reputation definitely influences buying decisions. Most people are more likely to buy from a company they know than from a company they don't know. On the other hand, the brand is more important to consumers than the company that makes the brand. Cadillac is more important than General Motors.

What companies emulate the best consumer qualities?
Companies that stand for something in the mind are most meaningful to consumers. If consumers cannot put what your company does into one or two words, you are unlikely to be successful.

What percentage of a marketing budget should go for advertising? For PR?
It all depends on where a brand is in its life cycle. For new brands almost no money should be spent on advertising and the entire budget should go to PR efforts. For established brands, advertising should make up the majority of the marketing budget.

Suggested Readings

Barlow, Janelle, and Claus Moller. *A Complaint Is a Gift*. San Francisco: Berett-Koehler, 1996. Provides feedback mechanisms.

Caywood, Clarke L., ed. *The Handbook of Strategic Public Relations and Integrated Communications*. New York: McGraw-Hill, 1997.

Crego, Edwin T., Jr., and Peter D. Schriffin. *Customer-Centered Reengineering Remapping for Total Customer Value*. Burr Ridge, IL: Irwin Professional Publishing,

1995. Focuses on the failures of many reengineering efforts to make effective long-range change.

Del Vecchio, Gene. *Creating Ever-Cool: A Marketer's Guide to a Kid's Heart,* Gretna, LA: Pelican Publishing Co., 1997.

Dyche, Jill, *The CRM Handbook: A Business Guide to Customer Relationship Management.* Boston, MA Addison Wesley, 2001.

Greenberg, Paul. *CRM At the Speed of Light, Capturing and Keeping Customers in Internet Real Time.* New York: McGraw-Hill, 2001.

Hartman, Jason. *Become the Brand of Choice: How to Earn Millions Through Relationship Marketing.* Greensboro, NC: Lifestyles Press, 1999.

Lewis, Jordan D. *The Connected Corporation: How Leading Companies Win Through Customer–Supplier Alliances.* New York: The Free Press, 1995. Finds customers and suppliers forming alliances for their mutual benefit instead of engaging in adversarial wrangling.

Peppers, Don, and Martha Rogers. *The One to One Future: Building Relationships One Customer at a Time.* New York: Bantam Doubleday Dell Publishers, 1997.

Ries, Laura, and Al Ries. *The Fall of Advertising and the Rise of PR.* New York, NY: Harper Business, 2002.

Notes

1. Customer e-mail from Allison Demeritt, product manager, Amazon.com, January 19, 2000.
2. Kevin Helliker, "Old-Fashioned PR Gives General Mills Advertising Bargains," *Wall Street Journal* (March 20, 1997): 1.
3. Richard Peterson, "Rejuvenating the Humble Prune," *New York Times* (August 13, 2000): D2.
4. Yahoo! Removing Adult Products," Thestreet.com (April 13, 2001).
5. Rachel Beck, "On-line Gripe Pays Off," *The Record* (May 6, 1999): B1, 2.
6. Apple's Selling Practices Called Rotten to Core," *Boston Herald* (October 18, 1999): 31.

Chapter 15

Investor Relations

In the two years prior to the 21st century, buying and selling stock became the nation's number one sport, and companies both new and old flooded to Wall Street to attract investors.

Then, suddenly, the bubble burst, and companies and investors alike learned an age-old lesson: There's no such thing as a free lunch.

The turn of the century brought a number of jarring realities to investors. Among them:

1. *In August 2000, a 23-year-old hoaxer placed a false news release on an Internet wire service that cost investors more than $2.5 billion in market value (see the case study at the end of this chapter). The perpetrator of the hoax was ultimately fined $241,000 and sent to prison.[1]*

2. *In September 2000, a 15-year-old New Jersey high school student masterminded a stock manipulation scheme on the Internet that earned him $273,000 in illegal gains. The scheme centered around spurious optimistic messages about companies that the boy sent to Internet chat rooms. People believed the phony messages and bought the stock, while the boy sold the same stock at higher prices.[2]*

3. *Finally, in 2002, the disclosure of accounting fraud and stock selling shenanigans at once revered companies, such as Enron, WorldCom, and Global Crossing, sent investor confidence to an all-time low.*

"In my lifetime," said one corporate CEO, "American business has never been under such scrutiny. To be blunt, much of it is deserved."[3]

The fallen promises of high-tech and other companies and the shaken spirits of formerly trusting investors have increased the scrutiny on and importance of the function of investor relations in the new century. The images of corporate executives being dragged away in handcuffs in the summer of 2002 underscored the reality that companies today must be especially careful of how they communicate with investors for a variety of reasons but one in particular:

The government is watching.

In this chapter, we will explore the importance of investor relations and introduce the rudiments of the practice in the 21st century.

Dealing with Investors

Investor relations (IR) increased in importance as the stock market of the late 1990s climbed ever higher.

Investor relations was born in the mid-1930s, shortly after the passage of the Securities Act of 1933 and the Securities Exchange Act of 1934, which attempted to protect the public from abuses in the issuance and sale of securities.

Who exactly are investors?

The simple answer is that they are the owners of the company. When individuals buy shares of stock, they become owners in the particular corporation in which they've invested. So they're entitled to fair and honest treatment from IR.

What exactly is IR?

Basically, it is the effort to narrow the gap between the perception of a company and the reality—in other words, helping the firm's securities reach their appropriate market price. To do this, IR professionals must encourage stockholders to buy and hold company shares and persuade Wall Street financial analysts and institutions to take an interest.

A company's stock price is its currency. Premium stock prices allow an organization to acquire others, whose low stock prices encourage raids from competitors. For example, in the most talked about venture of the new century, upstart America Online announced in 2000 that it would merge with venerable Time Warner Inc., owner of Time and Warner Brothers and CNN. The $120 billion deal was the biggest combination ever of a major Internet company with a traditional company.[4] Two years after it was formed, the new AOL Time Warner was beset with massive problems that clobbered its stock price and infuriated investors who had believed its early promise.

If a company's shares are fairly priced in relation to current or future expectations, the company has a better chance of raising money for future expansion. A strong shareholder base is necessary to support management's objectives. Helping build a strong shareholder base is the duty of investor relations officers. Once again, integrity and credibility must form the basis of professional IR practice.[5]

One way to win shareholder support is through timely and valuable communications. This is the job of investor relations.

Investor Relations Philosophy

The essence of investor relations lies in a public company's obligation to disclose information that may impact an investor's decision to buy, sell, or hold a stock.

This means that a company must disclose information that is adjudged to be "material." The legal standard of what is "material" is any fact that would be important to an investor making an investment decision. Typical examples of "materiality" are the following:

- Proposed mergers or acquisitions
- Change in dividend policy
- Determination of earnings
- Acquisition or loss of a significant business contract
- Major management changes
- Significant change in capital investment plans
- Purchase or sale of a significant asset
- Incurring a significant debt or sale of a significant amount of equity securities
- Pending significant legislation

- A major discovery or invention
- The marketing of significant new products[6]

When such realities exist, the law expects the company to release the information fully, fairly, and quickly to the widest audience possible in order that all market participants be given the same opportunity to act on the news.

Today, with the ability of the Internet to disseminate material news immediately, the Securities and Exchange Commission (SEC) has expressed great concern about "selective disclosure" to some investors and not to others. In particular, corporate "conference calls" with securities analysts increasingly let out news not known to the wider investing public. This is the practice that the SEC has vowed to stop.[7]

As explained in Chapter 7, the SEC has taken significant action to limit so-called "insider trading" and facilitate "disclosure." The passage of Regulation FD—Fair Disclosure—in 2000 was a step to shore up disclosure regulations for companies to ensure that some investors were not being given favored treatment on information.

A QUESTION OF ETHICS

Chainsawing an Investor Cheat

FIGURE 15-1
Rusted chainsaw. Al Dunlap, before the fall.

Well before all the disgraced corporate executives of the year 2002, there was Al Dunlap.

"Chainsaw Al" was the man famous for joining companies in the 1990s as CEO and then obliterating thousands of jobs and firing managers (Figure 15-1).

CEO Dunlap earned a faithful following on Wall Street for his take-no-prisoners ways. Among those Dunlap particularly delighted in firing were public relations staff members. As he noted in his 1998 autobiography, *Mean Business*, public relations departments are of limited value, especially when they work for a CEO as public as the author.

True to his history, when Chainsaw Al took the helm at Sunbeam Corporation in 1997, he began by slashing 12,000 jobs and getting rid of, among others, the internal public relations department. He also pocketed tens of millions of dollars for himself (proving, if nothing else, he was ahead of his time!). Dunlap then proceeded to go on a one-man investor relations campaign, assuring his loyal followers on Wall Street that he was once again about to turn around a lagging company. The analysts lapped up the CEO's predictions and Sunbeam's stock soared.

But contrary to the chairman's statements, financial results began to worsen. Mr. Dunlap continued to provide thumping assurances that he would work his magic. But while he courted the financial community, the CEO virtually ignored Sunbeam's employees and customers. Morale sagged and sales soured.

So in June 1998, approximately one year after Chainsaw Al had ridden to the rescue, he, himself, was fired after an emergency board meeting.

That was just the beginning. Three years later, the SEC filed a federal suit, charging Dunlap with reporting fraudulent profits that cost investors billions of dollars. And in the fall of 2002, Chainsaw Al agreed to pay a $500,000 fine and was banned from ever again serving as an officer or director of a public company. Oh, yes, earlier he also agreed to pay $15 million to settle a shareholder suit.

It was an inglorious end for a man who gloated in his disdain for the practice of public relations. (But frankly, not all that painful for the rest of us.)

For further information, see Martha Branigan and James R. Hagerty, "Sunbeam, Its Prospects Looking Ever Worse, Fires CEO Dunlap," *Wall Street Journal* (June 15, 1998): A1-14; Floyd Norris, "SEC Accuses Former Sunbeam Official of Fraud," *New York Times* (May 16, 2001): A1, C2; Floyd Norris, "Former Sunbeam Chief Agrees to Ban and a Fine of $500,000," *New York Times* (September 5, 2002): C1-9; and "Sunbeam: Lack of PR Hurts Image in Wake of Financial Crisis," *PR News* (July 13, 1998): 1–6.

In 2002, the New York Stock Exchange, which governs the large companies that are its members, announced a similar tightening of standards, increasing the role and authority of independent directors, estalishing new control and enforcement mechanisms, and giving shareholders greater opportunity to participate in the governance of companies.[8]

Appendix E references one public relations agency's attempt to quantify all the reporting requirements to which a public company is subject.

Investor Relations Activities

The typical corporate investor relations office is staffed by two or three individuals. The average budget, according to the National Investor Relations Institute, is just under $500,000.[9] Investor relations professionals are responsible for a variety of communications activities.

1. *Annual report.*   The annual report is a company's key financial communications tool. The annual report, both in printed and online versions, generally include the following elements:
   - *Company description.*   This includes the company's name, headquarters address, description of its overall business, and a summary of operations.
   - *Letter to shareholders.*   This incorporates a photo of the firm's CEO, an account of last year's performance, and a forward-looking view of the industry, environment, and company's prospects for the future. The best shareholder letters are those that are frank, fun, and straightforward (Figure 15-2).
   - *Financial review.*   In light of the SEC's increased demand for financial disclosure, companies have expanded financial sections to include required filings and registration statements.
   - *Explanation and analysis.*   This complement to the financial review is a general discussion of the factors influencing the financial results.
   - *Management/marketing discussion.*   The annual report has a narrative section that allows the company to expand on its products and prospects.
   - *Graphics.*   Photos and charts are critical to help bring to life the company and its performance.

     In recent years, as companies have suffered credibility problems, some corporations have tried to break the traditional mold, à la Southwest Airlines, and offer fresh and innovative annual reports (Figure 15-3).
2. *Quarterly report.*   Quarterlies or interim reports are issued every quarter to keep shareholders abreast of corporate developments, particularly earnings, between annual reports. In general, companies compare their performance during the current quarter with their performance over the same period of time in the previous year.
3. *Annual meeting.*   Once a year, the management of public companies is obligated to meet with the shareholders, in person, to discuss the firm. Occasionally, this annual "mating dance" between management and shareholders is greeted with fear and loathing by CEOs, particularly if the company has had problems. Nonetheless, shareholders are the "owners" of the company and deserve answers. In addition to question-and-answer sessions, the annual meeting also consists of management speeches updating the shareholders on corporate performance and stockholder voting on proposals

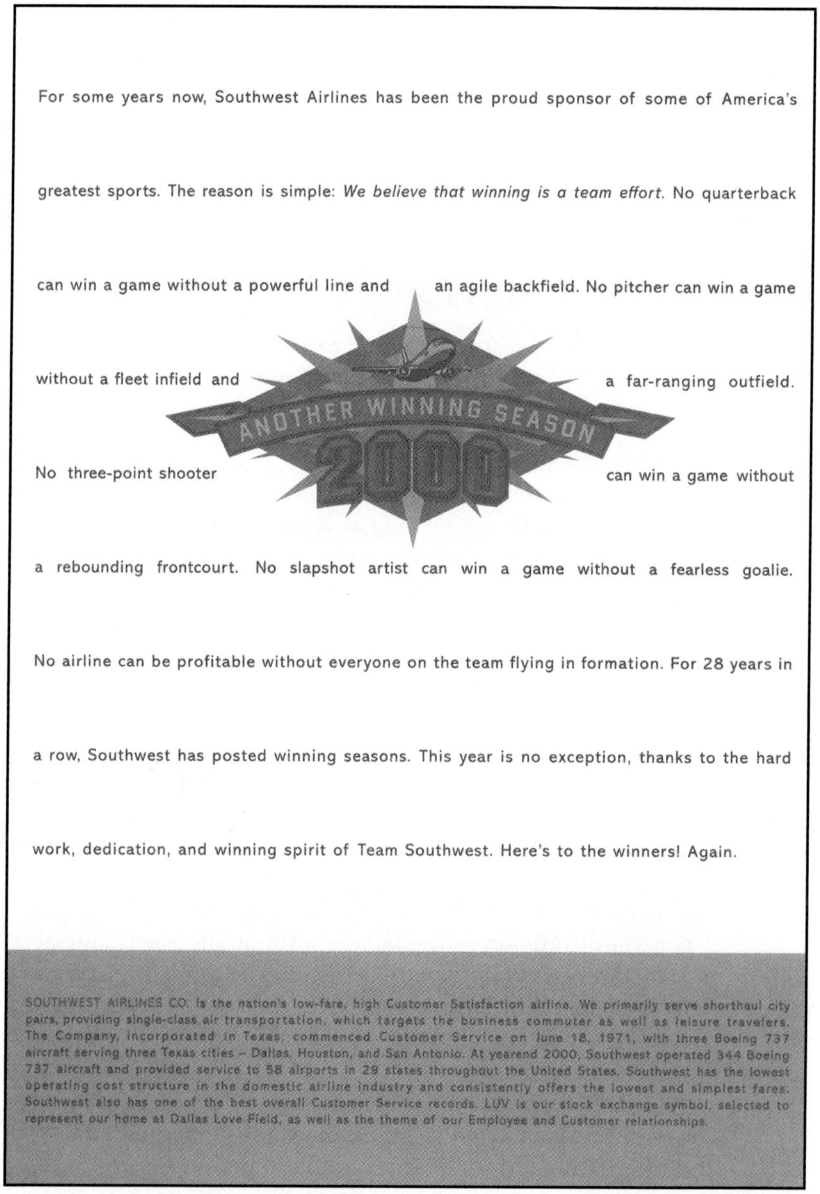

For some years now, Southwest Airlines has been the proud sponsor of some of America's

greatest sports. The reason is simple: *We believe that winning is a team effort.* No quarterback

can win a game without a powerful line and   an agile backfield. No pitcher can win a game

without a fleet infield and   a far-ranging outfield.

ANOTHER WINNING SEASON
2000

No three-point shooter   can win a game without

a rebounding frontcourt. No slapshot artist can win a game without a fearless goalie.

No airline can be profitable without everyone on the team flying in formation. For 28 years in

a row, Southwest has posted winning seasons. This year is no exception, thanks to the hard

work, dedication, and winning spirit of Team Southwest. Here's to the winners! Again.

SOUTHWEST AIRLINES CO. is the nation's low-fare, high Customer Satisfaction airline. We primarily serve shorthaul city pairs, providing single-class air transportation, which targets the business commuter as well as leisure travelers. The Company, incorporated in Texas, commenced Customer Service on June 18, 1971, with three Boeing 737 aircraft serving three Texas cities – Dallas, Houston, and San Antonio. At yearend 2000, Southwest operated 344 Boeing 737 aircraft and provided service to 58 airports in 29 states throughout the United States. Southwest has the lowest operating cost structure in the domestic airline industry and consistently offers the lowest and simplest fares. Southwest also has one of the best overall Customer Service records. LUV is our stock exchange symbol, selected to represent our home at Dallas Love Field, as well as the theme of our Employee and Customer relationships.

FIGURE 15-2 **CEO quarterback.** Southwest Airlines former CEO Herb Kelleher set the tone for frankness and fun in his annual letter to shareholders. (Courtesy Southwest Airlines)

spelled out in previously mailed proxy statements. Appendix F offers an annual meeting checklist.

4. **Conference calls.** An increasing number of companies—73 percent according to one survey—are releasing quarterly corporate earnings information with a conference phone call to analysts, institutions, and now, as a result of Regulation FD, individual shareholders. Top management conducts the call, explains earnings, and answers tough questions.[10]

Companies must be careful about making forecasts on sales and earnings during such calls. Such forecasts require immediate disclosure, so that those not

We will commence service to West Palm Beach on January 21, 2001, and expand our available seat mile capacity by approximately 11 percent for the year.

The year 2000, and particularly its fourth quarter, proved to be a very trying time for much of the airline industry but a triumphant time for the "fans" of Southwest, our Employees – Shareholders – Customers. This championship performance was produced by our Employees' diligent dedication to maintaining low costs, and thus low fares, and to providing high-spirited and winning Customer Service to themselves and to our passengers. The unity, altruism, and results-oriented focus of our People are both my joy and my pride as we enter our 30th year of commercial air service – and as we herald the commencement of the millenium with our new "Canyon Blue" exteriors and "Canyon Blue" and "Saddle Tan" full-leather interiors on our growing fleet of aircraft. We have introduced a new aesthetic for a new millennium, and an integral part of its purpose is to refresh and honor our People who, without doubt, are the Greatest Generation in the History of the Airline Industry!

Most sincerely,

Herbert D. Kelleher

Herbert D. Kelleher
Chairman, President, and Chief Executive Officer
January 20, 2001

FIGURE 15-2   (Continued)

in on the call have an equal opportunity to act on the material information. This is why, as per Regulation FD, firms should consider including members of the media on the call, so that charges of selective disclosure can be rebutted.

5. **Media contact and monitoring.**   Visit a business establishment or a doctor's office or even a health club anywhere in America these days and a television set is tuned—often with sound off—to CNBC, CNNfn, or Bloomberg TV. These financial news networks, which broadcast live during each business day, keep investors aware of current market developments. Savvy investor relations specialists must also keep current through regular contact with and monitoring of these important financial news outlets.

6. **Proxy mailings.**   Infrequently, corporations become involved in contentious shareholder issues that must be resolved by a vote of the shareholders. In these contests—called "proxy fights"—investor relations professionals participate in mailings to shareholders expressing management's point of view as to the direction of the vote.

FIGURE 15-3 **Not your mother's annual report.** The 2001 annual report of Cognex Corp. featured CEO Dr. Robert J. Shillman's "10-K rap" and a tour of his crib. (Courtesy Cognex)

Dealing with Analysts

The principal investor relations contact is the stock market analyst.

In the sea of jargon that is Wall Street, analysts are pretty easy to understand. Analysts "analyze." They are responsible for determining the value of a stock, based on its current valuation in the market and their expectations of the company's future earnings per share.[11]

Analysts are divided into two types: sell-side analysts and buy-side analysts. Approximately 4,000 *sell-side* or Wall Street analysts are employed by brokerage firms to sell their investment ideas and picks, via brokers, to individual investors. Sell-side analysts research specific stocks in particular industry groups and attempt to predict future earnings. In so doing, they place a recommendation on each stock to buy, sell, or hold.

In the past, such analysts also cultivated investment banking opportunities with the companies they followed. These opportunities to help with initial public offerings, mergers, or other strategic acquisitions could result in millions of dollars for brokerage firms. But this was a practice that led to conflicts of interest. And, in 2003, analysts at Merrill Lynch and Solomon Smith Barney, two of the largest firms on the street, were both called to task by the government for potential conflicts and paid heavy fines.

Merrill Lynch settled with the New York State attorney general for $100 million and got rid of its high-profile, high-tech analyst Henry Blodgett. Solomon Smith Barney, meanwhile, bid adieu to its equally high-profile telecom analyst, Jack Grubman, as it, too, struggled with government investigations.[12] As a consequence, the widespread suspicions regarding sell-side analysts were not likely to disappear soon.

Buy-side analysts, on the other hand, work for large institutional money management firms, such as mutual funds, investment advisers, family trusts, and pension funds. The duty of these 22,000 buy-side analysts is to find stocks that their institutions can purchase and make a profit on. Because buy-side analysts work for only one institutional entity and are "selling" nothing to the public, they have escaped government inquiries unscathed.

The recent hard reputational times of analysts notwithstanding, they still compose a critical public for investor relations professionals. Institutional investors, who are the buyers of a company's securities, also are critical. Although it is difficult to have extended contact with individual shareholders, it is not uncommon for IR professionals to speak frequently with specific brokers who closely follow a particular stock.

The essence of the IR job, then, is candid and trustworthy communication.

Internet Investor Relations

Just as it has affected most areas of public relations work, the Internet has revolutionized investor relations. In the 21st century, companies must use the Internet to reach investors.

- It has become expected of a forward-looking company to have a homepage providing investment information.
- A well-designed Web site provides a service to investors and potential investors that they can receive nowhere else. At any time of day, anywhere in the world, a potential investor can learn about the company as an investment.
- The firm can better control its messages to investors through an integrated Web site than it can through randomly distributed news releases and investor packets.
- Today's investor not only often invests by using online mechanisms but also prefers to research personal investments on the Internet (Figure 15-4).[13]

A strong investor site will include all of the staples of investor relations work: news releases, SEC documents, links to corporate filings powered by Edgar Online, executive profiles, annual and quarterly reports, even analyst recommendations and stock price data. In addition, a section of frequently asked questions (FAQs) should be linked to financial data within tables on the site. All material should be able to be downloaded, and a feedback e-mail mechanism should be incorporated to hear from investors.[14]

Beyond the Web site itself, investor relations professionals must monitor and be in contact with the most widely consulted online investor sites. CBSMarketWatch.com, Fool.com, CNNfn.com, Thestreet.com, and CNBC.com are just some of the sites to which investors turn on a daily basis to learn what's going on in the market. A sudden report or rumor broadcast online on one of these services could torpedo a company's securities. That's why they must be monitored.[15]

FIGURE 15-4

Investing in sites online. Tech Central Station.com was sponsored by AT&T and hosted by stock market author James Glassman. It provided commentary and insights on issues of interest to tech investors.

Once a firm's Web site has been established satisfactorily, Internet search services, such as Yahoo! and AOL, should be notified, so that the company can be included in their directories. Finally, great care should be taken with keeping information and technology current. Online investor relations is a good way to showcase one's firm and differentiate it from all others. That's why the data must be fresh and the technology state of the art.

L A S T   W O R D

Despite the stock market downturn of the early years of the 21st century, investors are among a company's most important and influential publics.

The nation—and much of the world for that matter—has never been more heavily invested through pension plans, retirement plans, and mutual funds. The corporate management failings of 2002 make it imperative that investors receive ever-increasing amounts of information from which to make intelligent investment choices. The government, cognizant of the public's suspicion of the markets, will certainly increase its scrutiny of disclosure and other practices designed for investors.

All of this suggests that in the new century, communications to investors will become even more important. The need for intelligent investor relations professionals—knowledgeable about both finance and communications—will increase over time. The area of investor relations, therefore, will continue to develop as a fertile ground for public relations practitioners.

Discussion Starters

1. Why has investor relations become so important?
2. What is meant by the term *materiality*?

3. How does the SEC define *full disclosure*?

4. What are the principle activities of an investor relations professional?

5. What are the key elements of an annual report?

6. What is the difference between buy-side and sell-side analysts?

7. What are important considerations for investor conference calls?

8. What are proxy contests?

9. What is the importance to investors of the Internet and electronic financial media?

10. What is the role of the Internet with respect to investor relations?

TOP OF THE SHELF

Jeffrey P. Parker and Robert J. Adler

Investor Relations in the Internet Age
Naperville, Panacea Press Inc., 2001

As the founder and CEO of several successful financial services companies over the past 20 years, coauthor Jeffrey P. Parker brings an operating perspective to the companies in which he invests, as well as a wealth of financial expertise. He shares that expertise in this book, offering practical guidance for corporate communications and investor relations executives.

The authors also share observations, insights, and best practices gathered from their experience in pro-

viding Web-based investor communication services to more than 6,000 public companies and 700 leading institutional investment firms.

Investor Relations in the Internet Age also features rich examples and hands-on case studies on complying with Regulation Fair Disclosure, creating and managing IR Web sites, webcasting, and leveraging the Internet to reach institutional and individual investors.

CASE STUDY

Fake News, Real Losses

At 10:13 A.M., Eastern Standard Time, on August 26, 2000, investors in Emulex, a California company that made fiber-optic equipment, received some terrible news.

Bloomberg News, a leading financial news service, reported that the company's chief executive had resigned and that Emulex planned to restate its earnings for the last two years.

Investors rushed to unload the stock, and shares plunged from $103 to $45 in 15 minutess. The drop stripped more than $2 billion from the company's market valuation before the Nasdaq stock market halted trading in the stock about 20 minutes after the original announcement.

All the other financial wires and networks soon joined Bloomberg in reporting Emulex's woes.

There was just one problem.

The news was bogus.

The statement was a hoax, perpetrated by a 23-year-old college dropout, who formerly worked for Internet Wire, Inc., the relatively new, paid news release wire service that unwittingly dispatched the fake release.

Bad Trade Gone "Badder"

The young man responsible for the fraud was Mark S. Jakob, who reportedly had placed a bet against Emulex stock, which had gone against him. By sending the stock into a tailspin, Jakob made money closing out his position. He made even more by scooping up Emulex stock after it cratered.

Until, of course, he was fingered by the FBI.

Jakob was able to file the release by e-mailing Internet Wire, identifying himself as the company's investor relations professional, and providing billing instructions and Internet Wire internal code information. Jakob had obtained the necessary code information while employed by Internet Wire.

Internet Wire, with no reason to doubt the veracity of the news about the California-based company, immediately issued the release at the opening bell of the stock market, 9:30 A.M. in New York. This equated to 6:30 A.M. California time, well before Emulex management would arrive at work.

Bloomberg picked the news up shortly after it appeared on Internet Wire. And the other wire services and cable financial news stations picked it up shortly thereafter. The stock meanwhile began its meltdown.

By the time Emulex officials arrived at their offices shortly after 7 A.M. Pacific Time, they found their stock in unexplained freefall. "I walked in," said the firm's senior vice president, "and my administrative assistant immediately said to me, 'The stock is down 45 points.'"

Emulex's CEO called the stock exchange and asked for a halt in trading. But the damage was done.

The Dust Settles

A week later, after tracing e-mails to Internet Wire and scouring the company's records for recently departed employees, the FBI arrested Mr. Jakob and charged him with criminal securities fraud.

Meanwhile, a red-faced Internet Wire was hit by numerous lawsuits for the millions lost by investors, who acted immediately on the bogus reports. Bloomberg, too, was sued by irate investors.

Bloomberg's editor-in-chief acknowledged that he was "disappointed" in his organization's handling of the episode. He said the wire service should have clearly explained in its reports that it had been unable to confirm information firsthand from the company. "The way it was handled was not up to the standards that we normally apply," he said.

As to Internet Wire, its CEO explained that his company had fallen victim to a "sophisticated fraud." He reasoned that the people responsible "were successful in convincing somebody from the nighttime shift that they had authorization from the daytime shift."

Older rival paid wire services gloated at Internet Wire's dilemma. Said Business Wire, "Fully experienced, veteran wires like Business Wire and PR Newswire are subject to fakery, too. But the likelihood of it happening in the quarter million releases each one carries is remote."

As to Mr. Jakob, his flight of fraudulent fancy cost him the $241,000 he made trading Emulex stock, plus another $97,000 interest, plus a penalty of $102,642.

Oh yes, he was also sentenced to 44 months in federal prison.

Questions

1. If you were the Emulex director of pubic relations, what action would you recommend the company take as a result of this hoax?
2. If you were the Internet Wire director of public relations, what action would you recommend the company take?
3. If you were the Bloomberg director of public relations, what action would you recommend the company take?

For further information on the Emulex case, see Alex Berenson, "On Hair-Trigger Wall Street, A Stock Plunges on Fake News," *New York Times* (August 26, 2000): A1, C4; Terzah Ewing, Peter Waldman, and Matthew Rose, "Bogus Report Sends Emulex on a Wild Ride," *Wall Street Journal* (August 28, 2000): C1, 6; Terzah Ewing and Mattew Rose, "E-Mail Trail Leads to Emulex Hoax Suspect," *Wall Street Journal* (September 1, 2000): C1-2; and "SEC Settles Press Release Hoax Case," *Jack O'Dwyer's Newsletter* (August 1, 2001): 2.

T I P S   F R O M   T H E   T O P

An Interview with Andrew S. Edson

Andy Edson

Andrew S. Edson is president and chief executive of the public and investor relations consultancy of the same name, which he founded in June 1996, and won the prestigious Silver Anvil award bestowed by the PR industry in 2002. He has also served as a senior counselor in the corporate and financial relations practice at Manning, Selvage & Lee, Inc. (MS&L), a global communications company.

What training does investor relations work require?

You need not be a numbers cruncher to enjoy investor relations; however, comprehending what the numbers say and do isn't all bad either. Still, a CPA is not requisite for IR. A broad set of disciplines, including liberal arts, effective writing skills, adherence to deadline pressure, stick-to-itiveness, and a probing mind are essential training for this craft. The ability to withstand sleepless nights is another consideration.

How important is the ability to communicate in investor relations?

Very, very important. It cannot be emphasized enough. Next to the CEO and the CFO, the IR officer is often the key communications ingredient with the investment community, shareholders—both institutional and individual, the financial media, and the regulators. If the IR professional cannot communicate properly with good and organized verbal and written skills, then the company is in for trouble. The first opinion that many will form about a company is usually from perceptions derived from dealing with the IR officer. The IR professional, therefore, must be in the informational loop.

How important is financial knowledge in investor relations?

It is important because the IR professional must be able to interpret and put financial information in proper perspective. What's more, putting this in simple and understandable language is a necessity and part of the job description. Fortunately, if you don't have this body of knowledge when you enter the field, there are many colleges and universities that offer courses, along with the National Investor Relations

(Continued)

Institute (www.niri.org), the leading trade association, which has inspired an entire series of continuing education courses. And there's nothing wrong with asking if you don't know the answer.

What are the essential skills of an investor relations professional?

An understanding of the corporate process, being able to detect sensitive issues and the need to communicate or not, and the ability to interface with others internally or externally are mandatory skills. Being organized, responsive to ever-changing demands and time dictates, and flexibility are equally important. The IR pro is not necessarily a "yes" person, but a team member whose opinion is valued or should be. Bridging the gap between corporate wants and shareholder and Street needs demands a lot. The more astute IR officer can readily provide this.

How has the investor relations assignment changed as a result of the corporate scandals of 2002?

To a large and unfortunate degree, many corporations have become suspect when earnings are filed or any type of big announcement made, largely because of the sins committed by Enron, Andersen, and others. Corporate governance and accountability are the new buzzwords. If anything, there is a greater need to be forthcoming.

How does one break into investor relations work?

In the early days of the craft, out-of-work securities analysts faded in and out of investor relations. To a large degree, IR was the purview of the public relations or corporate communications executive. This changed, however, over time, as IR became almost a separate discipline, and oddly enough, there are those who are imploring IR types to assume control of the PR discipline. Perhaps the best way to break into the field is to contact an IR firm and pay sweat equity. You'll be exposed to many different industry sectors, the various components exercised to realize objectives, time pressures, and even excitement. It's a real juggling act, but if you're a quick learner, you will mature in a hurry. I think it's easier, too, to work on the consulting side before making the transition, if desired, to the corporate side.

What is the future of investor relations practice?

The future looks robust. IR is a well-accepted discipline today. IR officers are a growing part of senior management rank. Their counsel gets heard, their work is appreciated by top management, and, in many instances, they serve as a corporation's voice to its many targeted publics. Titles are inching up, remunerative packages are on the rise, and it's only a matter of time before we see IR officers assume the CEO spot.

Suggested Readings

Chambers, Larry. *The Guide to Financial Public Relations: How to Stand Out in the Midst of Competitive Clutter.* Boca Raton, FL: St. Lucie Press, 1999.

Higgins, Richard, and Mark W. Begor. *Best Practices in Global Investor Relations: The Creation of Shareholder Value.* Westport, CT: Greenwood Publishing, 2000.

Marcus, Bruce W., and Sherwood Lee Wallace. *New Dimensions in Investor Relations: Competing for Capital in the 21st Century.* New York: John Wiley and Sons, 1997.

Raish, Warren. *The Emarketplace—Strategies for Success in B2B Commerce.* New York: McGraw-Hill, 2000.

Turnock, Madeline. "IR and PR: Come Together," *Public Relations Strategists* (Spring 2002), 13–15.

Notes

1. "Hoaxer's Fake Release on 'Fledgling' Internet Wire Raises Market Havoc," *Business Wire Newsletter* (September 2000): 1.

2. Gretchen Morgenson, "SEC Says Teenager Had After-School Hobby: Online Stock Fraud," *New York Times* (September 21, 2000): A1, C10.

3. Henry M. Paulson, Jr., "Restoring Investor Confidence: An Agenda for Change," Remarks before the National Press Club, Washington, DC (June 5, 2002).

4. Alex Berenson, "Minimal Research Prepared on AOL-Time Warner Deal," *New York Times* (February 18, 2000): C2.

5. "National Investor Relations Institute Code of Ethics," National Investor Relations Institute, Washington, DC.

6. Alan J. Berkeley, "Some FAQs and Answers about Corporate Disclosure," Kirkpatrick & Lockhart, LLP, Washington, DC, August 1998.

7. "SEC Proposes New Disclosure Rules," *Jack O'Dwyer's Newsletter* (January 26, 2000): 6.

8. "NYSE Issues Additions to Disclosure Standards," *Business Wire Newsletter* (August 2002): 1.

9. Standards of Practice for Investor Relations, National Investor Relations Institute (January 2001).

10. Charles Nekvasil, "Getting the Most Out of Your Investor Relations Conference Calls," *PR Tactics* (August 1999): 10, 11.

11. Bob Dunn, "What in the World Is a Buy-Side/Sell-Side Analyst?" Bankrate.com (May 30, 2002).

12. Merrill Lynch Announces Agreement with New York State Attorney General," Merrill Lynch news release (May 21, 2002).

13. Allan Feinstein, "Investor Relations on the Internet: A Step-by-Step Guide to Getting Started," *Interactive Investor Relations* (July 1999): 8.

14. "24 Items to Supplement Your Online Annual Report," *Interactive Investor Relations* (July 1999): 9.

15. Felicity Barringer, "Financial Sites Are Said to Seek Merger," *New York Times* (February 17, 2000): C11.

Chapter 16

International Relations

The practice of public relations is very much an international phenomenon.

As Professor Daniel Awodiya has written, "The opportunities for public relations are increasing in the face of phenomenal growth in information technology and the pace-setting trend of corporate mergers and acquisitions."[1]

Former PRSA President Joe Epley identified three reasons for the increased interaction among organizations and publics in the world, which, in turn, has necessitated the need for international public relations:

1. *The expansion of communications technology has increased the dissemination of information about products, services, and lifestyles around the world, thus creating global demand.*
2. *The realignment of economic power, caused by the formation of multinational trading blocs, such as the North American Free Trade Agreement (NAFTA), Asia Pacific Economic Conference (APEC), Organization of African Unity (OAU), and the European Economic Community (EEC). Such alliances have brough global producers and consumers closer.*
3. *People around the world are uniting in pursuit of common goals, such as reducing population growth, protecting the environment, waging the war against terrorism, and fighting disease, particularly AIDS.[2]*

As trade and information flows have become borderless, so, too, has public relations. Indeed, the International Public Relations Association, founded in 1955, has members in 95 countries.

Although the reality of peoples and nations of the world becoming more closely connected is largely positive for society, there is also a dark side. The images beamed across satellite technology and the Internet have, in some quarters, served to foment misunderstandings and jealousies, as the chasm between rich and poor, haves and have-nots, comes more sharply into focus.

The terror attacks on America of September 11, 2001, served to exacerbate these problems, particularly with respect to understanding the practice of Islam and relations with people of Middle Eastern descent. Repairing these rifts will take time, as well as thoughtful action and communication from all sectors of society. This is a key international public relations challenge in the 21st century.

In this chapter, we will briefly explore the state of public relations practice around the world and the opportunities available for international public relations practice.

Operating Around the Globe

Communications Professor Marshall McLuhan's vision nearly a half century ago that we would all be operating in a "global village" today has come to pass.

The actions of individuals and organizations in one part of the world are felt instantly and irrevocably by people around the globe. As a consequence, multinational corporations, in particular, must be sensitive to how their actions might affect people of different cultures in different geographies.

Companies, in fact, have become the most prominent standard bearers of their countries. And American companies, with nine of the 10 most powerful brands in the world (see Sidebar) are the most prominent of the prominent.

Consider the challenges multinational companies face.

- In 2001, when Muslim restaurant owners took to the streets of Bombay, India, to demonstrate against America's military action in Afghanistan, they didn't burn the Stars and Stripes—they vented their anger by pouring bottles of Coke and Pepsi out into the road. Worse, a Coca-Cola bottling plant in Buntur, India, was bombed.[3]
- McDonald's has been singled out around the world, mostly because of its visibility as a symbol of America. In Hong Kong, the company was attacked for using genetically modified food. In Paris, demonstrators protested working conditions at McDonald's restaurants. In Chile, McDonald's was torched in protest of the Inter-American Development Bank meeting in the country in 2001.[4]
- Nike billboards in Pakistan were defaced in protest of the company's alleged use of low-paid, underage workers.

What can multinational companies do to avert such trouble and reinforce the notion that they are responsible and concerned residents of local communities? The answer is to resort to the public relations philosophy of leading with proper action and then communicating it. KFC, for example, has 158 franchises in Indonesia, most of which are locally owned and operated. Indeed, a poster in the window of the Jakarta McDonald's reads:

> *In the name of Allah, the merciful and the gracious, McDonald's Indonesia is owned by an indigenous Muslim Indonesian.*

Smart multinationals also support local causes and incorporate international audiences and celebrities in their philanthropic efforts. Among intelligent multinational concerns, the overriding mantra must be "thinking global, acting local" in order to win lasting friendship and support in other countries.

The Brand Leaders

When one talks about global consumer brands, they're usually American companies.

According to Interbrand, which annually publishes the 100 most valuable global brands, 62 are U.S. based. American companies account for nine of the 10 most powerful brands in the world. Here's the Interbrand 2001 top 10.

1. Coca-Cola
2. Microsoft
3. IBM
4. General Electric
5. Nokia—Finland
6. Intel
7. Disney
8. Ford
9. McDonald's
10. AT&T

Hopscotching the World for Public Relations

In the 21st century, public relations has become a global phenomenon.

Major political shifts toward democracy throughout the world, coupled with the rapidity of worldwide communications and the move to form trading alliances of regional nations, have focused new attention on public relations. The collapse of communism, the coming together of European economies, and the outbreak of democracy everywhere from Eastern Europe to South Africa have brought the global role of public relations into a new spotlight.

In 2000, the Global Alliance for Public Relations and Communications Management was formally established at a meeting in Bled, Slovenia, linking 24 member organizations and representing more than 75,000 practitioners around the world. The purpose of the alliance was to provide a forum to share ideas and best public relations practices, seek common standards, and provide a better understanding of each culture in which practitioners operate.[5]

Here, in globe-trotting summary, are developments depicting the state of public relations beyond the boders of the United States.

Canada

Canadian public relations is the rival of American practice in terms of its level of acceptance, respect, sophistication, and maturity. The Canadian Public Relations Society (CPRS), formed in 1948, is extremely active, representing more than 1,500 public relations professionals in 17 member societies throughout the country.

Like its American counterparts, the CPRS maintains a code of professional standards that revolves around "dealing fairly and honestly with the communications media and the public." A professional accreditation progam, job registry, and affiliations with Canadian university public relations programs are included in CPRS offerings.

Canadian public relations professionals must be conversant not only in the English-speaking parts of their country but also in the French-speaking markets, such as

NATURAL VACATION
60 and 30 Second PSAs
Icelandic Tourist Board

Narrator: Many Americans are searching for a vacation in a place

that is pure, natural, and unspoiled.

Iceland, the closest European country, uses geothermal steam to heat homes

and outdoor swimming pools—which leaves the air clean and clear.

The seafood is ocean-fresh, caught daily in the cold waters of the North Atlantic. Game and lamb are raised organically.

Reykjavik is a charming and safe city to walk, with a small town flavor and warmth, and beautiful historic buildings and churches.

The fashion sense is edgy and emerging.

Unspoiled nature is nearby, abundant, and breathtaking.

"In Iceland we use super jeeps to travel out to the nature. It's a great adventure."

One travel writer summed up his visit to this unusual nation as follows: "Everyone is so polite it breaks your heart."

Come see for yourself. Iceland naturally.

Iceland
www.icelandnaturally.com

SALO PRODUCTIONS

FIGURE 16-1   The Icelandic Tourist Board called on Salo Productions to introduce the country's many wonders to its southern neighbors. (Courtesy Salo Productions)

Quebec. Also, Canada in recent years, like America, has become a nation of nations, with great multicultural diversity. Dealing with diverse ethnicity also becomes a public relations challenge. Beyond Canada, America's other neighbors to the north also have become active in public relations efforts (Figure 16-1).

Europe

The emergence of a more unified Europe, through the EEC, has major implications on the practice of public relations in Europe.

Like Canada, public relations developed more or less simultaneously in Europe and the United States during the 20th century. In Germany, in particular, public relations writings appeared in the early 1900s.

In the new century, privatization and the synthesis of the European Economic Community into a more unified bloc have spurred increased public relations action in many European countries. Public relations has experienced tremendous growth in Great Britain, employing 30,000 practitioners and growing at a rate of 20 percent annually.[6] The largest U.K.-based public relations operations, the Shandwick and Brunswick Groups, are challenged by significant offices of the largest American firms.

The Institute of Public Relations, headquartered in London and 50 years old, is the largest professional organization in Europe, with 7,500 public relations practitioner members. It encompasses 13 regional groups, has a Web site at www.ipr.org.uk, and produces a monthly magazine.

The world's economic setbacks in the first years of the 21st century had a dampening impact on the growth of the practice in Europe. Nonetheless, as European organizations pay increased attention to their reputations and how they are perceived, public relations is certain to be at the forefront of European commercial concern in the years ahead.

Latin America

Latin America is expanding at a faster rate than virtually any other region in the world. In terms of public relations development in Latin America, the scene is more chaotic than in the United States, Canada, or Europe.

The field is most highly developed in Mexico, where public relations practice began in the 1930s. Mexican corporations all have communications and public relations departments, and many employ local or U.S. public relations agencies. Mexican schools of higher learning also teach public relations. The passage of NAFTA under President Clinton and the reinforcement of solid relations with Mexico under President Bush signal increasing opportunities for U.S–Mexican trade and, therefore, for public relations growth.

In the other countries of Latin America, public relations is not as well developed. Here again, current economic and political problems in Argentina, Brazil, Venezuela, and Chile have slowed the growth of public relations practice. Once economic stability is restored, Latin American public relations practice will clearly increase. Chile, with its robust economy and approach to capitalism, is a particularly prominent candidate for increased public relations activity in the initial years of the new century.

Further indication of potential Latin American public relations expansion is the fact that the *Wall Street Journal Americas* edition, nestled amidst the pages of 20 Latin American newspapers, reaches more than 2.5 million readers.

Asia

Public relations in Asia has experienced sharp growth in recent years.

In Japan, the practice of public relations, by definition, is contrary to the nation's cultural heritage. Japanese culture values modesty and promotes silence over eloquence. Public relations, mistakenly equated with self-publicity, has, therefore, not traditionally been valued in Japanese society. As one Japanese professional put it, "In Japan, companies have had the attitude that they should keep as quiet as possible."[7]

The public relations profession in Japan was established after World War II. Although the Japanese take a low-key approach to public relations work—especially self-advocacy—the field is growing, particularly as the six major national newspapers and four national networks become more aggressive in investigating a proliferation of national scandals. By far, the most important aspect of Japanese public relations is dealing with the media.

Japanese public relations differs markedly from that of the West. For example, *keiretsu* business associations, or press clubs, which bring together individual firms, operate with enormous influence as intermediaries in arranging press events. In recent years, television in general and talk shows in particular have become increasingly popular in Japan.

In India, the antecedents of modern public relations practice have been traced to around 300 B.C., when the Indian Emperor Asoka used rock and pillar edicts as effective communications tools.

Modern-day Indian public relations emerged during World War II, as public opinion became more important and mass-circulation newspapers proliferated. It was at this time that the powerful Tata industrial conglomerate formed the first public relations department in India.[8]

In 1958, eight years after India became a republic, the Public Relations Society of India was formed. Today, public relations practice in India is largely a subordinate of the marketing function. This is not uncommon in Asia and around the world.

Elsewhere in Asia, public relations also has begun to take root. It is important to remember that every Asian country is different. In certain Asian nations, as opposed to the United States, news releases are printed verbatim. Korea has an active public relations community, as do Indonesia, Taiwan, and Singapore. In Singapore, public relations was boosted in the late 1990s by new companies raising funds through a booming stock market and active economy. Technology, financial services, and real estate development also are burgeoning areas of public relations growth.[9]

China, after a number of false starts, holds great potential for public relations expansion. By 2020, some predict that 70 percent of the world will speak Mandarin as their principal language. China is the world's fastest-growing economy, second only to the United States, which it should pass soon. As the nation with the largest consumer population, China ranks eleventh in world trade and holds magnificent promise. Even with government control, some 8.9 million Chinese log onto the Internet every day.[10]

Western-style public relations was introduced to China only two decades ago in 1980, by way of a foreign joint venture. Today, there are 1,200 public relations firms in China, employing more than 30,000 people, including more than 5,000 professionals.[11] The China Public Relations Association attracted more than 300 practitioners to its 1998 meeting in Beijing. Public relations courses are offered at leading universities, such as China's Institute of International Relations in Beijing, Nankai University in Tianjin, and Zhongshan University in Guangzhou.

As China modernizes its way into the 21st century, one of the greatest challenges for indigenous business enterprises will be increased foreign and domestic competition in everything from soap products to household appliances, and from cars to banking to telecommunications.[12] Public relations will be called on to help differentiate these enterprises from the competition. Already major U.S. public relations agencies have moved into the country (Figure 16-2). All of this suggests that the public relations business in China has a bright future in the 21st century.

Even in Vietnam, opportunities for public relations work promise to emerge, as it rejoins the world community. Indeed, increasing numbers of U.S. business and trade missions to the country suggest the public relations potential of a newly rediscovered Vietnam.

FIGURE 16-2

Entry celebration.
Edelman Worldwide's entry into China was celebrated at a gala Beijing banquet honoring the Chicago-based firm.

Eastern Europe

There are 370 million consumers in recently democratized Eastern Europe. The prospects for public relations expansion are enticing.

- More than 80 percent of all Eastern Europeans watch television daily. Nearly 100 percent watch several times a week.
- In Hungary, about 20 percent of the population have TV sets connected to satellite dishes.
- In Poland, 13 percent of the population report owning VCRs.
- In Hungary, Serbia, and Croatia, about two-thirds of the population read newspapers daily.

Russia

Although newly capitalist Russia has suffered fits and starts—not to mention scandals and bloody internal conflicts—the practice of public relations will likely build in the years ahead. AT&T, Intel, Coca-Cola, and many other companies are already ensconced in Russia. Large American public relations firms have also set up bases. PR Newswire, in combination with the news agency TASS, distributes news releases from U.S. companies to locations in the Commonwealth of Independent States. Releases are translated into Russian and reach 40 newspapers in Moscow alone.

Australia/New Zealand

Public relations in the land "down under" is also alive and thriving.

The Public Relations Institute of Australia is an extremely active organization and the practice is widespread, particularly in the country's two commercial centers, Melbourne and Sydney. Australian public relations practice, like Australians themselves, is more low key and less flashy than American practice but no less competent and sophisticated.

In New Zealand, too, public relations is practiced through local and international public relations agencies and communications practitioners at major banks and companies.

Middle East

Although the public relations profession is less active in the Middle East, the power of public relations is well known and understood.

During the 1990 invasion of Kuwait, Iraq's leader Saddam Hussein was quick to harness the world's communications apparatus to spread his views. He tried again a decade later on his way out of the country.

In 2001, Saudi Arabia resorted to public relations communications, when 15 of the 19 hijackers dispatched by another Saudi, Osama bin Laden, crashed planes into the World Trade Center, the Pentagon, and a Pennsylvania field. Saudi Arabia, one of the most traditional and closed of the world's societies, immediately hired Washington, D.C.–based Qorvis Communications—for $200,000 a month—to give the country a media makeover.[13] (See A Question of Ethics.)

One positive sign in the growth of Middle Eastern public relations was the admission of 20 women students into the public relations major program at the United Arab Emirates University in Al-Ain in 1995.[14]

Africa

In Africa, too, the practice of public relations is growing.

In 1990, the largest public relations meeting in the history of the continent was held in Abuja, Nigeria, with 1,000 attendees from 25 countries. In 1994, as a result of an extensive worldwide communications and public relations campaign, Nelson R. Mandela became the first democratically elected president of the nation of South Africa.

As the most developed country in sub-Saharan Africa, South Africa led the continent in sophisticated public relations. It boasted more than 30 public relations–related companies and a professional association, the Institute for Public Relations and Communication Management.

Africa, too, has discovered the power of public relations.

Communicating to the "Global Village"

Communications media around the world have truly converted the globe into one large "village," united by satellite and Internet technology. What happens in one corner of the globe is instantly transmitted to another.

Secretary of State Colin Powell learned this the hard way in September 2002, when he was shouted down by dozens of activists at the World Summit in Johannesburg, South Africa. The activists had been lying in wait for the American representative for three days. "Shame on Bush," they chanted as Powell attempted to address the crowd of 1,500 government leaders. The activists had achieved their purpose—to beam their message around the world via satellite and the Internet—for the cost of a plane ticket and a banner.[15]

Tens of thousands of nongovernmental organizations (NGOs) operate in most countries—from Greenpeace to Friends of the Earth, from Africa Action to the World Rainforest Movement. As globalization and international trade impact societies, such nongovernmental organizations have become increasingly influential in world affairs. They are consulted by governments as well as international organizations, such as the

A QUESTION OF ETHICS

Public Relations Saudi Style

After the four planes crashed into the World Trade Center, the Pentagon, and the Shanksville, Pennsylvania, field, the world was shocked to learn that 15 of the 19 hijackers on September 11, 2001, were from Saudi Arabia.

And no one was more surprised than the leadership in Saudi Arabia itself.

For six decades, the Kingdom of Saudi Arabia was a strong ally of the United States. But in one dreadful day in world history, the two nations were pulled apart.

In the months that followed the attacks, the Saudis were roundly criticized in American media. The nation's ruling family government was labeled as "repressive," and Saudi leaders were denounced for not speaking out forcefully enough against Osama bin Laden—himself the son of a wealthy Saudi Arabian—and his Al Queda terrorist network.

To fight back, Saudi Arabia turned to a time-honored weapon in the battle for public opinion—public relations.

The Saudis hired Qorvis Communications, an affiliate of the kingdom's Washington law firm, Patton Boggs, to create issue advertising and advise on public relations responses. The theme of the Qorvis campaign was to reassert Saudi Arabian denunciation of terrorism and support of the United States.

"Unlike other countries here, Saudi Arabia has no political base in the U.S.," said Qorvis CEO Michael Petruzzello.* "In one fell swoop, the strong U.S.–Saudi relationship was cast into doubt."

The Qorvis campaign consisted of several elements:

1. *Ad campaign*, running in the top 26 U.S. markets, depicting the kingdom as a staunch ally in the global fight against terrorism. All the major TV networks, from A&E and USA to Bravo and the History Channel, however, refused to run the Saudi spots.

2. *Media spokesmanship*, through the ready availability of an intelligent, telegenic Saudi Embassy executive and University of North Texas graduate. The Saudi spokesman appeared frequently on cable talk shows.

3. *Positive media leaks*, including a well-publicized idea offered by Saudi Arabia's Crown Prince Abdullah to columnist Thomas Friedman of the *New York Times*, in which a new plan for Middle East peace was offered.

Despite Qorvis's best efforts, the Saudis continued to play "ethics catch-up" in the press:

1. A 2002 report, disputed by spokespersons, that the Saudis gave money to the families of Palestinian suicide bombers received extensive national attention.

2. So, too, did a "secret" Pentagon briefing that the United States would seize Saudi oil fields, if the kingdom didn't crack down on terrorism.

3. Meanwhile, the country continued to be criticized for allowing religious leaders to preach anti-American hatred in Saudi Arabia's mosques.

Complicating the Qorvis task was the call in the fall of 2002 by the influential editor of Saudi Arabia's English-language newspaper, *Arab News*, that the kingdom cease its "PR drivel."

"Let us not be lured into placing full-page advertisements in U.S. newspapers that in the same edition write horrid untruths about us," he wrote. The editor urged his country's leaders to "abandon those fancy public relations firms whose own executives look at us unfavorably but are doing the job for the dollars."

Said CEO Petruzello of Qorvis, "Restoring American public opinion will be a difficult road back for Saudi Arabia."

* Interview with Michael Petruzzello, September 3, 2002.

S I D E B A R

Think Multilingual—Or Else . . .

According to America's foremost "nameologist," Steve Rivkin, organizations dealing overseas better think multilingual—or else.

Or else what? Or else this:

- A food company named its giant burrito a "Burrada." Big mistake. The colloquial meaning of that word in Spanish is "big mistake."
- Estée Lauder was set to export its Country Mist makeup when German managers pointed out that *mist* is German slang for, uh, well, to put it gently, "manure." (The name became Country Moist in Germany.)
- When General Motors introduced the Chevrolet Nova in South America, it was shocked to learn that *no va* is Spanish for "does not go." After GM realized it wouldn't sell many of the "go-less" cars, it renamed the vehicle Caribe in Spanish markets.
- Ford had a similar problem in Brazil when it introduced the Pinto. The name turned out to be Brazilian slang for "tiny male genitals."

Red-faced Ford pried off all the nameplates and renamed the car, Corcel, which means "horse."
- Colgate introduced a toothpaste in France called Cue, the name of a notorious French porno magazine.
- The name Coca-Cola in China was first rendered as "ke-kou-ke-la." Unfortunately, Coke did not discover until after thousands of signs had been printed that the phrase means "bite the wax tadpole." Coke then researched 40,000 Chinese characters and found a close phonetic equivalent, "ko-kou-ko-le," which loosely translates as "happiness in the mouth." Much better.
- A leading brand of car de-icer in Finland will never make it to America. The brand's name: Super Piss.
- Ditto for Japan's leading brand of coffee creamer. Its name: Creap.*

*Courtesy of Rivkin & Associates, 233 Rock Road, Glen Rock, NJ 07452

S I D E B A R

Straighten Out Your English—Or Else

On the other hand, it might be equally beneficial for our friends in foreign lands to make sure of their own English.

Consider these actual signs posted in various establishments around the world.

- In a Copenhagen airline ticket office: "We take your bags and send them in all directions."
- In a Norwegian cocktail lounge: "Ladies are requested not to have children in the bar."
- At a Budapest zoo: "Please do not feed the animals. If you have any suitable food, give it to the guard on duty."
- In a doctor's office in Italy: "Specialist in women and other diseases."

- In a Paris hotel elevator: "Please leave your values at the front desk."
- From the brochure of a Tokyo car rental firm: "When passenger of foot heave in sight, tootle the horn. Trumpet him melodiously at first, but if he still obstacles your passage then tootle him with vigor."
- In an advertisement by a Hong Kong dentist: "Teeth extracted by the latest Methodists."
- In an Acapulco hotel: "The manager has personally passed all the water served here."
- In a Bucharest hotel lobby: "The lift is being fixed for the next day. During that time we regret that you will be unbearable."

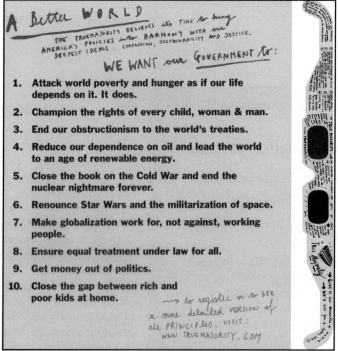

FIGURE 16-3 **Worldview.** Nongovernmental organizations such as True Majority, started by the founders of Ben & Jerry's Ice Cream, are united in generally seeking "a better world." (Courtesy True Majority)

United Nations (see Tips from the Top at the end of this chapter), which have created associative status for them. These organizations are not directly affiliated with any national government but often have a significant impact on the social, economic, and political activity of the country or region involved.

NGOs have been reenergized by the Internet. For minimal expense, such organizations can spread their views—often criticisms of multinationals—across the globe (Figure 16-3).

What have smart organizations done to deal with such international challenges?

More often than not, they've "joined" rather than "fought" them. After Monsanto was battered by a coalition of worldwide NGOs for genetically modified crops, the company's new CEO reversed his predecessor's policy of "holding the line." "We found that doesn't work," said Hendrik Verfaillie, Monsanto's former CEO. Henceforth, Monsanto began a program of meeting frequently with relevant NGOs.[16]

In the 21st century, as the world continues to get "smaller" in a communications sense, public relations professionals, knowledgeable about foreign customs and cultures and skilled in the practice of communication will be in great demand.

LAST WORD

The "brave new world" that emerged after September 11, 2001, promises to remain the reality well into the 21st century. At the same time, the world is getting "smaller," with phenomena such as MTV, CNN, basketball, baseball, hip-hop, and Madonna knowing no geographic boundaries.

The conflicts around the globe—between Arabs and Israelis in the Middle East, Catholics and Protestants in Ireland, and warring factions in Africa, Asia, and Eastern Europe—make it even more imperative that companies, governments, and individuals reach out to communicate with each other.

Stated another way, organizations desperately need professional communicators to navigate through this "brave new world" of instantaneous communication. As the world's companies continue to expand across borders, they must be sensitive to local customs and people. As global competition intensifies, so will global communications, making it easier to communicate around the world but much more difficult to be heard.

Faced with such a formidable global reality, smart organizations will deal honestly, forthrightly, and frequently with world media. Indeed, new United Nations guidelines specify how its leadership "is committed to being open and transparent in its dealings with the press."[17] In the past, U.N. officials were forbidden to give interviews, but under Secretary General Kofi Annan, "Every member of the Secretariat may speak to the press, within limits."

The U.N.'s new initiative toward openness was just the latest evidence that public relations has become a growth industry around the world.

Discussion Starters

1. What evidence can you point to that indicates the increased stature of public relations practice around the world?
2. What factors have necessitated the need for increased international public relations?

3. What is meant by the term global village?
4. What kinds of public relations practices should be observed by multinationals operating in a foreign country?
5. What is the state of public relations in the Western Hemisphere?
6. What is the state of public relations in Europe?
7. What is the state of public relations in Asia?
8. What is the state of public relations in Latin America?
9. What is the significance to public relations practice of NGOs?
10. What public relations initiatives has Saudi Arabia attempted to ease harsh feelings in the West?

TOP OF THE SHELF

Ni Chen and Hugh Culbertson

International Public Relations, A Comparative Analysis
Lawrence Erlbaum Associates Inc., 1996

A wide variety of practitioners and university professors have contributed to this comprehensive treatment of public relations, edited by Ni Chen and the legendary professor of public relations Hugh Culbertson.

Chapters cover specific countries and regions, always with an eye on comparing practices from one country to another and comparing them to the profession as practiced in the United States. Nor does this book shy away from theory: Chapter 1, for example, is "Interdisciplinary Theoretical Foundations for International Public Relations," by University of Maryland professor Robert I. Wakefield.

CASE STUDY

Selling Uncle Sam

Perhaps the most difficult revelation to emerge from September 11, 2001, was that there are people in the world who hate America and that for which it stands (Figure 16-4).

In the wake of the terrorist attacks, the American government focused its attention on Muslims at airports and border crossings, flight schools, and religious institutions. With 2 billion Muslims in the world and the religion being the globe's fastest-growing one, the backlash among Muslims was of great concern to the U.S. government.

Condemnation as "the Great Satan" was an image the United States needed desperately to counter.

And so, in the months following the attack, the United States acted by launching a public relations offensive, promoting the benefits of freedom and democracy to win the hearts and minds of the world's Muslim population.

FROM MADISON AVENUE TO THE FIRING LINE

In November, Secretary of State Colin Powell appointed Charlotte Beers, a former Madison Avenue advertising executive, as Undersecretary for Public Diplomacy, to lead the State Department's public relations efforts.

Explained Powell, "Well, she got me to buy Uncle Ben's rice and so there is nothing wrong with getting somebody who knows how to sell something."

FIGURE 16-4   **The challenge.**
The people who hate America.

Beers, a master of product branding, faced a more difficult task: to brand Osama bin Laden as a mass murderer to millions of Muslims who had never seen a 767 airliner or a skyscraper, much less one flying into the other.

Beyond that, Beers's challenge included speaking to people who understood only their own language, arcane tongues such as Pashto and Dari.

Finally, Beers faced the difficult task of counteracting wildfire-like rumors that followed September 11, 2001, in Muslim countries. The most pervasive was that it wasn't Muslim terrorists at all but rather the Israeli Mossad secret service that crashed the plane into the Trade Center. Another was that Purim pastry for the Jewish holiday was made out of the blood of adolescent Muslims.

BOOKLETS, BREAKFASTS, AND BEAMING DIRECT
The American propaganda war to change Muslim attitudes took a number of initiatives.

Terrorist Booklet
The first product of the campaign was a 24-page booklet, in print and on the Internet, in 14 languages, which featured graphic pictures of the September 11, 2001, attacks. The booklet used bin Laden's own words to accuse him of masterminding the murderous attacks.

Wanted Poster
A poster was created and plastered around the Arab world, offering $25 million for information leading to the arrest of the Most Wanted Terrorists, including bin Laden and his key aides (Figure 16-5).

FIGURE 16-5 **The enemy.** America's Most Wanted.

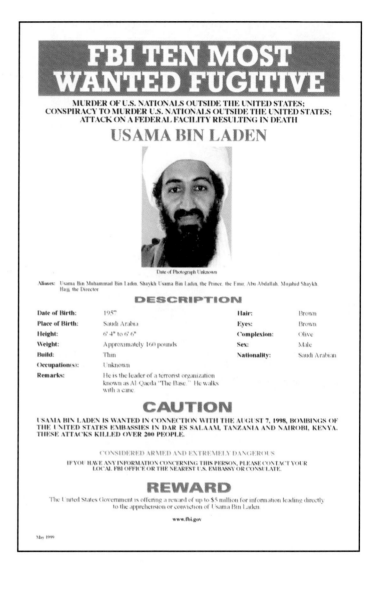

FIGURE 16-5 **The enemy.** America's Most Wanted.

Breakfast Meetings
Undersecretary Beers held a series of meetings with prominent Muslim Americans to gauge which messages might promote a more positive image of the United States. She hired as a consultant former Ambassador Christopher Ross, a fluent speaker of Arabic, who served in Syria and Algeria. Additional marketing research was conducted with younger Muslims. This latter research was particularly important, in light of the overwhelming numbers of Arab Muslims under the age of 30.

Entering the Lion's Den
The most visible part of the public relations initiative was meeting the Muslim world on its home turf.

The Middle Eastern satellite TV network Al Jazeera, with 35 worldwide bureaus, was the primary source of Osama bin Laden videos and Al Queda propaganda, reaching 35 million Arabs and Muslims around the world. Although the Bush administration first condemned the network for its biased coverage, that standoffish policy quickly changed.

When the network played a bin Laden tape, consultant Ross was rushed over to Al Jazeera's Washington studio to rebut the terrorist's claims.

Secretary Powell, Defense Secretary Donald Rumsfeld, and National Security Advisor Condoleeza Rice all sat for interviews with Al Jazeera correspondents.

In 2003, Beers stepped down as Undersecretary for Public Diplomacy.

Her initiatives were but the earliest salvos in a long-term battle to win the understanding of millions of people around the world who, for whatever reason, harbored grave suspicions about America and its people.

Questions

1. What is your appraisal of the early stages of America's war to win Muslim understanding and acceptance?
2. If you were the Undersecretary for Public Diplomacy, what other programmatic elements would you recommend be instituted?

TIPS FROM THE TOP

An Interview with Shashi Tharoor

Shashi Tharoor was named the first director of communications and special projects of the United Nations in 1998. He later served as interim director of the U.N.'s 735-person Department of Public Information. He is the author of five books, the most recent of which, *India: From Midnight to the Millennium*, was selected as a *New York Times* Notable Book of the Year and cited by former President Clinton in his address to the Indian Parliament in 2000. One of his novels, *Show Business*, was filmed as the motion picture *Hollywood*.

What did Secretary General Annan want you to do as the U.N.'s first communications director?
Principally two things. First, he felt we needed to coordinate the external message of the organization. He felt that the U.N. message was being slightly lost in the routine, in the shuffle. Second, he also felt— and this was recommended by a task force that he had appointed in 1997—that he should have somebody on his immediate team, directly reporting to him, who would be concerned about the way in which the world saw the U.N. and would help put the secretary general's own point of view across to those conveying the message of the organization.

Shashi Tharoor (right) with UN Secretary General Kofi Annan.

How do you answer the criticism that the U.N. is little more than a glorified debating society?
We need to let Americans know that the U.N. is not merely this "talking shop." It is a "talking shop" part of the time, when there is the General Assembly meeting every year. As Churchill put it,

(Continued)

"Isn't jaw jaw better than world war?" I mean wouldn't you rather have these countries boring each other to death, if necessary, in the General Assembly chamber than boring holes into each other on the battlefield?

How have you organized the U.N.'s media relations policy?

We have made more systematic use of op-eds. We've had more press conferences. One of the first things I was able to do—but really, it wasn't me but the secretary-general—was the issuance for the first time in the 55 years of the United Nation of media guidelines, which authorize every single U.N. official to speak to the press, on the record within his or her area of competence. Never existed before.

What was the prior policy?

The prior practice, frankly, was that bureaucrats were not supposed to speak to the press. And if they sometimes did, they did so very quietly and anonymously, on background or off the record, and they were just reluctant to tell the story. People felt that if they saw their name in the paper, it was actually "bad news." There's been a 180-degree change.

How important is the communications function at the U.N.?

I see communications as integrally linked to the substantive work. It's not just a question of people doing what they want, and we then have to sell it to the world. It's that needing to be accountable to the world should help determine that we do the right thing. We must ask, in shaping our conferences, "What do we expect the world public to get out of this meeting? What is the story we have to tell them? Why do we expect them to care?" Our job is to help shape such conferences more constructively.

What does the term public relations mean to you?

Public relations is telling the truth, often to people who don't have the time to hear it. It's also about using the public to help shape what you really are doing, because the fact is that the public ultimately is why you're doing it. I've told my colleagues in the U.N. that communications and information is not an end in itself. It exists to make your substantive work successful. Therefore, our communications philosophy has to be to tell the world what we're doing, truthfully and transparently, and use communications to be accountable for the faith the world's peoples have placed in us as an institution.

Suggested Readings

Cavusgil, Tamer, and Michael R. Czinkota. *International Perspective on Trade Promotion and Assistance.* Westport, CT: Greenwood Press, 1990.

Drobis, David R. "The New Global Imperative for Public Relations," *Public Relations Strategist* (Spring 2002): 36–37.

Hackley, Carol Ann, and Qingwen Dong. "American Public Relations Networking Encounters China's *Guanxi,*" *Public Relations Quarterly* (Summer 2001): 16–19.

Howard, Carole M. "Ten Strategies to Avoid Global Gaffes in Media Relations," *Public Relations Strategist* (Fall 2001): 34–37.

Howard, Elizabeth. "A 'World' of PR Opportunities," *Public Relations Strategist* (Winter 2002): 38–39.

Ihator, Augustine. "Understanding Cultural Patterns of the World—An Imperative in Implementing Strategic International PR Programs," *Public Relations Quarterly* (Winter 2000): 33–37.

McKinney, Bruce C. "Public Relations in the Land of the Ascending Dragon: Implications in Light of the U.S./Vietnam Bilateral Trade Agreement," *Public Relations Quarterly* (Winter 2000): 23–26.

Mintu-Wimsatt, Alma, and Hector R. Lozada, eds. *Green Marketing in a Unified Europe.* Binghamton, NY: The Haworth Press, 1996. This book gives public relations professionals insights into the opportunities for positioning in an environmentally aware Europe.

Ritchey, David. "The Changing Face of Public Relations in China and Hong Kong," *Public Relations Quarterly* (Winter 2000): 27–32.

Wu, Xu. "Doing PR in China—Concepts, Practices and Some Misconceptions," *Public Relations Quarterly* (Summer 2002): 10–18.

Notes

1. Daniel O. Awodiya, "In International Public Relations, What Is Good for the Goose is Good for the Gander," Suffolk County Community College, Brentwood, NY (March 11, 2000).

2. K. Sriramesh, "The Mass Media and Public Relations: A Conceptual Framework for Effective International Media Relations," paper submitted to the Public Relations Division, Association for Education in Journalism and Mass Communication (August 2000).

3. Connor Digman, "Brand Builders vs. Flag Burners," *Ad Age Global* (December 2001): 4–5.

4. Sarika Gupte, "McDonald's Averts a Crisis," *Ad Age Global* (July 2001): 4.

5. "Global Alliance for Public Relations Announces 2003 Executive Board," news release of the Global Alliance (July 16, 2002).

6. "Champions of Accountability Seek to Reclaim Their Crown," *The London Sunday Herald* (June 5, 2002).

7. K. Sriramesh and Mioko Takasaki, "The Impact of Culture on Japanese Public Relations," *Journal of Communication Management*, Vol. 3, No. 4 (1999): 343.

8. Krishnamurthy Sriramesh, "The Models of Public Relations in India," *Journal of Communication Management*, Vol. 4, No. 3 (2000): 229.

9. "Gavin Anderson Moves into Growing Singapore Market," *PR News* (February 10, 1997): 1.

10. Steven L. Lubetkin, "China's Growth Makes Understanding of Media Crucial," *Public Relations Tactics* (December 1996): 18.

11. James B. Strenski and Kung Yue, "China: The World's Next Public Relations Superpower," *Public Relations Quarterly* (Summer 1998): 25.

12. Carole Gorney, "Why China Is Ripe for 'Professional' Public Relations," *International Review* (May 2000).

13. "Saudi Arabia: Allies Against Terrorism," On the Media, National Public Radio (May 25, 2002).

14. Pamela J. Creedon, Mai Abdul Wahed Al-Khaja, and Dean Kruckeberg, "Women and Public Relations Education and Practice in the United Arab Emirates," *Public Relations Review* (Spring 1995): 59.

15. Alexandra Zavis, "Activists Mar Powell's Summit Talk," Associated Press (September 4, 2002).

16. "McDonald's Has Beef with Global Image; Monsanto Reaches Out to NGOs," *O'Dwyer's PR Services Report* (March 2001): 8.

17. Barbara Crossette, "U.N. Issues Guidelines on Dealing with the Press," *New York Times* (August 9, 1999): B9.

PART IV Execution

Chapter 17

Public Relations Writing

Even in the age of the computer, writing remains the key to public relations.

Public relations practitioners are professional communicators. And communications means writing.

All of us know how to write and speak. But public relations professionals should write and speak better than their colleagues. Communication—that is, effective writing and speaking—is the essence of the practice of public relations.

There is no substitute for clear and precise language in informing, motivating, and persuading. The ability to write and speak with clarity is a valuable and coveted skill in any organization.

What this means is that the ability to write easily, coherently, and quickly distinguishes the public relations professional from others in an organization. It's not that the skills of counseling and marketing and judgment aren't just as important; some experts argue that these skills are far more important than knowing how to write. Maybe. But not knowing how to write—how to express ideas on paper— may reduce the opportunities to ascend the public relations success ladder.

Senior managers usually have finance, legal, engineering, or sales backgrounds, where writing is not stressed. But when they reach the top, they are expected to write articles, speeches, memos, and testimony. They then need advisers, who are often their trusted public relations professionals. That's why it's imperative that public relations students know how to write—even before they apply public relations techniques to cyberspace. Beginning public relations professionals are expected to have mastery over the written word. Chapters 17 and 18, properly preceding discussions of the Internet and Integrated Marketing, focus on public relations writing.

What does it take to be a public relations writer? For one thing, it takes a good knowledge of the basics. Although practitioners probably write for a wider range of purposes and use a greater number of communications methods than do other writers, the principles remain the same, whether writing for the Internet, an annual report or a case history, an employee newsletter, or a public speech. This chapter and the next will explore the fundamentals of writing: (1) discussing public relations writing in general and news releases in particular, (2) reviewing writing for reading, and (3) discussing writing for listening.

Writing for the Eye and the Ear

Writing for a reader differs dramatically from writing for a listener. A reader has certain luxuries a listener does not have. For example, a reader can scan material, study printed words, dart ahead, and then review certain passages for better understanding. A reader can check up on a writer; if the facts are wrong, for instance, a reader can find out pretty easily. To be effective, writing for the eye must be able to withstand the most rigorous scrutiny.

On the other hand, a listener gets only one opportunity to hear and comprehend a message. If the message is missed the first time, there's usually no second chance. This situation poses a special challenge for the writer—to grab the listener quickly. A listener who tunes out early in a speech or a broadcast is difficult to draw back into the listening fold.

Public relations practitioners—and public relations students—should understand the differences between writing for the eye and the ear. Although it's unlikely that any beginning public relations professional would start by writing speeches, it's important to understand what constitutes a speech and how it's prepared and then be ready for the assignment when opportunity strikes. Because writing lies at the heart of the public relations equation, the more beginners know about writing, the better they will do. Any practitioner who doesn't know the basics of writing and doesn't know how to write—even in the age of the Internet—is vulnerable and expendable.

Fundamentals of Writing

Few people are born writers. Like any other discipline, writing takes patience and hard work. The more you write, the better you should become, provided you have mastered the basics. Writing fundamentals do not change significantly from one form to another.

What are the basics? Here is a foolproof, four-part formula for writers, from the novice to the novelist:

1. *The idea must precede the expression.* Think before writing. Few people can observe an event, immediately grasp its meaning, and sit down to compose several pages of sharp, incisive prose. Writing requires ideas, and ideas require thought. Ideas must satisfy four criteria:

   - They must relate to the reader.
   - They must engage the reader's attention.
   - They must concern the reader.
   - They must be in the reader's interest.

   Sometimes ideas come quickly. Other times, they don't come at all. But each new writing situation doesn't require a new idea. The trick in coming up with clever ideas lies more in borrowing old ones than in creating new ones. What's that, you say? Is your author encouraging "theft"? You bet! The old cliché, "Don't reinvent the wheel," is absolutely true when it comes to good writing. Never underestimate the importance of maintaining good files.[1]

2. *Don't be afraid of the draft.* After deciding on an idea and establishing the purpose of a communication, the writer should prepare a rough draft. This is a necessary and foolproof method for avoiding a mediocre, half-baked product. Writing, no matter how good, can usually be improved with a second look. The draft helps you organize ideas and plot their development before you commit them to a written test. Writing clarity is often enhanced if you know

where you will stop before you start. Organization should be logical; it should lead a reader in a systematic way through the body of the text. Sometimes, especially on longer pieces, an outline should precede the draft.

3. *Simplify, clarify, aim.*   In writing, the simpler the better. Today, with more and more consumers reading from computer screens, simplicity is imperative. The more people who understand what you're trying to say, the better your chances for stimulating action. Shop talk, jargon, and "in" words should be avoided. Standard English is all that's required to get an idea across. In practically every case, what makes sense is the simple rather than the complex, the familiar rather than the unconventional, and the concrete rather than the abstract. Clarity is another essential in writing. The key to clarity is tightness; that is, each word, each passage, each paragraph must belong. If a word is unnecessary, a passage redundant, a paragraph vague—get rid of it. Writing requires judicious editing; copy must always be reviewed with an eye toward cutting.

4. *Finally, writing must be aimed at a particular audience.*   The writer must have the target group in mind and tailor the message to reach them. To win the minds and hearts of a specific audience, one must be willing to sacrifice the understanding of certain others. Writers, like companies, can't expect to be all things to all people. Television journalist Bill Moyers offers this advice for good writing:

> Strike in the active voice. Aim straight for the enemy: imprecision, ambiguity, and those high words that bear semblance of worth, not substance. Offer no quarter to the tired phrase or overworn idiom. Empty your knapsack of all adjectives, adverbs, and clauses that slow your stride and weaken your pace. Travel light. Remember the most memorable sentences in the English language are also the shortest: "The King is dead" and "Jesus wept."[2]

Flesch Readability Formula

Through a variety of writings, the late Rudolf Flesch staged a one-man battle against pomposity and murkiness in writing.* According to Flesch, anyone can become a writer. He suggested that people who write the way they talk will be able to write better. In other words, if people were less inclined to obfuscate their writing with 25-cent words and more inclined to substitute simple words, then not only would communicators communicate better but also receivers would receive more clearly.

In responding to a letter, Flesch's approach in action would work as follows: "Thanks for your suggestion, Tom. I'll mull it over and get back to you as soon as I can." The opposite of the Flesch approach would read like this: "Your suggestion has been received; and after careful consideration, we shall report our findings to you." See the difference? In writing for the Internet, such straightforward writing is the only approach.

There are countless examples of how Flesch's simple dictum works.

● Few would remember William Shakespeare if he had written sentences such as "Should I act upon the urgings that I feel or remain passive and thus cease to

---

*Among the more significant of Flesch's books are *Say What You Mean, The Art of Plain Talk, The Art of Readable Writing* and *How to Be Brief: An Index to Simple Writing*.

S I D E B A R

Speaking Like the Suits

Worried about fitting in a corporate environment? Concerned that the suits speak and write a different language than do you—more convoluted, hyperextended, and obtuse?

Relax. Thanks to a former corporate communicator at a Virginia bank, you can rely on the following "Jargon Master Matrix," a chart consisting of three columns of jargon words that can be mixed and matched for any occasion.*

Just select any three words from the three columns, such as *value-based process model* or *overarching support centralization*, and you will fit right in.

1. overarching	visionary	objectives
2. strategic	support	alternatives
3. special	customer-oriented	expectations
4. specific	stretch	mechanisms
5. core	planning	assessment
6. long-term	marketing	update
7. defined	service	model
8. technology-based	process	product
9. formal	fundamental	centralization
10. exceptional	sales	incentive
11. value-based	budget	initiatives
12. executive	operating	feedback
13. immediate	discretionary	infrastructure
14. interactive	tracking	proposition

*Eileen Kinsella, "After All, What's a News Article but a Formalized Update Process?" *Wall Street Journal* (August 1, 1996): C1.

exist?" Shakespeare's writing has stood the test of centuries because of sentences such as "To be or not to be?"

● A scientist, prone to scientific jargon, might be tempted to write, "The biota exhibited a 100 percent mortality response." But, oh, how much easier and infinitely more understandable to write, "All the fish died."

● One of President Franklin D. Roosevelt's speechwriters once wrote, "We are endeavoring to construct a more inclusive society." FDR changed it to "We're going to make a country in which no one is left out."

● Even the most famous book of all, the Bible, opens with a simple sentence that could have been written by a 12-year-old: "In the beginning, God created the heaven and the earth."

Flesch gave seven suggestions for making writing more readable.

1. Use contractions such as *it's* and *doesn't*.
2. Leave out the word *that* whenever possible.
3. Use pronouns such as *I*, *we*, *they*, and *you*.
4. When referring back to a noun, repeat the noun or use a pronoun. Don't create eloquent substitutions.
5. Use brief, clear sentences.

SIDEBAR

Nonreadability

Although Rudolf Flesch stressed the "readability" of writing, every day we see numerous examples of writing that seeks to be anything but readable. To wit, the following, "Accident Report."

> The party of the first part hereinafter known as Jack and the party of the second part hereinafter known as Jill ascended or caused to be ascended elevation of undetermined height and degree of slope, hereinafter referred as "hill." Whose purpose it was to obtain, attain, procure, secure, or otherwise gain acquisition to, by any and/or all means available to them a receptacle or container, hereinafter known as "pail," suitable for the transport of a liquid whose chemical properties shall be limited to hydrogen and oxygen, the proportions of which shall not be less than or exceed two parts for the first mentioned element and one part for the latter. Such a combination will hereinafter be called "water."
>
> On the occasion stated above, it has been established beyond a reasonable doubt that Jack did plunge, tumble, topple, or otherwise be caused to lose his footing in a manner that caused his body to be thrust in a downward direction. As a direct result of these combined circumstances, Jack suffered fractures and contusions of his cranial regions. Jill, whether due to Jack's misfortune or not, was known to also tumble in a similar fashion after Jack. (Whether the term, "after," shall be interpreted in a spatial or time passage sense, has not been determined.)

6. Cover only one item per paragraph.
7. Use language the reader understands.

To Flesch, the key to all good writing was getting to the point. Stated another way, public relations writers, in writing for the Internet or any other medium, should remember their A's and B's:

- Avoid big words.
- Avoid extra words.
- Avoid clichés.
- Avoid Latin.
- Be specific.
- Be active.
- Be simple.
- Be short.
- Be organized.
- Be convincing.
- Be understandable.[3]

In addition to Flesch, a number of other communications specialists have concentrated on how to make writing more readable. Many have developed their own instruments to measure readability. The most prominent, the Gunning Fog Index, designed by Robert Gunning, measures reading ease in terms of the number of words and their difficulty, the number of complete thoughts, and the average sentence length in a piece of copy. Good writing can't be confusing or unclear. It must be understandable.

The Beauty of the Inverted Pyramid

Newspaper writing is the Flesch formula in action. Reporters learn that words are precious and are not to be wasted. In their stories every word counts. If readers lose interest early, they're not likely to be around at the end of the story. That's where the inverted pyramid comes in. Newspaper story form is the opposite of that for a novel or short story. Whereas the climax of a novel comes at the end, the climax of a newspaper story comes at the beginning. A novel's important facts are rolled out as the plot thickens, but the critical facts in a newspaper story appear at the start. In this way, if readers decide to leave a news article early, they have already gained the basic ideas.

Generally, the first tier, or lead, of the inverted pyramid is the first one or two paragraphs, which include the most important facts. From there, paragraphs are written in descending order of importance, with progressively less important facts presented as the article continues—thus, the term *inverted pyramid*.

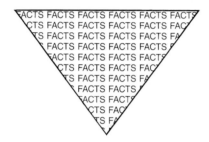

The lead is the most critical element, usually answering the questions concerning who, what, why, when, where, and occasionally how. For example, the following lead effectively answers most of the initial questions a reader might have about the subject of the news story.

> Columbia Pictures announced today it had signed Britney Spears to a three-film deal for $60 million.

That sentence tells it all; it answers the critical questions and highlights the pertinent facts. It gets to the point quickly without a lot of extra words. In only 17 words it captures and communicates the essence of what the reader needs to know.

After the lead, the writer must select the next most important facts and array them in descending order with the most important facts earlier in the story. In this way, the inverted pyramid style is more the "selection and organization" of facts than it is an exercise in creative "writing."

This same style of straightforward writing forms the basis for the most fundamental and ubiquitous of all public relations tools: the news release.

The News Release

A valuable but much-maligned device, the news release is the granddaddy of public relations writing vehicles. Most public relations professionals swear by it. Some newspaper editors swear about it. Indeed, PR Newswire, a paid wire service used by public relations people to distribute releases, issues about 1,500 news releases every day.[4]

The reason is that everyone uses the release as the basic interpretive mechanism to let people know what an organization is doing. There is no better, clearer, more persuasive way to announce news about an organization, its products, and their applications than by issuing a news release.[5]

A news release may be written as the document of record to state an organization's official position—for example, in a court case or in announcing a price or rate increase. More frequently, however, releases have one overriding purpose: to influence a publication to write favorably about the material discussed. Each day, in fact, professionals e-mail and mail releases to editors in the hope of stimulating favorable stories about their organizations.

Most news releases are not used verbatim, although there are occasional exceptions. Rather, they may stimulate editors to consider covering a story. In other words, the release becomes the point of departure for a newspaper, magazine, radio, or television story. Why, then, do some editors and others describe news releases as "worthless drivel"?[6] The answer, says researcher Linda Morton of the University of Oklahoma's Herbert School of Journalism, is threefold:

1. *Releases are poorly written.* Professor Morton found that most news releases are written in a more complicated and difficult-to-read style than most newspaper stories. "This could be the result of pressure from administrators as they review and critique press releases," she reasoned.

2. *Releases are rarely localized.* Newspapers focus largely on hometown or regional developments. The more localized a news release, the greater the chance it has of being used. However, according to Professor Morton, "Practitioners may not want to do the additional work that localization requires." This is a bad decision because research indicates that a news release is 10 times more likely to be used if it is localized.

3. *Releases are not newsworthy.* This is the grand dilemma. An editor will use a public relations release only if he or she considers it news. If it's not newsworthy, it won't be used. What determines whether something is news? Professor Morton suggests five requisites:

   * *Impact:* a major announcement that affects an organization, its community, or even society

   * *Oddity:* an unusual occurrence or milestone, such as the one-millionth customer being signed on (Figure 17-1).

   * *Conflict:* a significant dispute or controversy, such as a labor disagreement or rejection of a popular proposal

   * *Known principal:* the greater the title of the individual making the announcement—president versus vice president—the greater the chance of the release being used

   * *Proximity:* how localized the release is or how timely it is, relative to the news of the day.[7]

Beyond these characteristics, **human interest** stories, which touch on an emotional experience, are regularly considered newsworthy.[8] Research, however, indicates that the vast majority of public relations releases don't contain any of these elements, limiting their chances of "seeing the light of print."[9]

With these findings as backdrop, it is not surprising that research also indicates that less than 10 percent of all news releases are published.[10] Nonetheless, each day's *Wall Street Journal, New York Times, USA Today*, CNN, CNBC, Thestreet.com, CBSmarketwatch.com, Google News, and other daily media around the nation and world are filled with stories generated from news releases issued by public relations professionals.

UNITED STATES
POSTAL SERVICE

POSTAL NEWS

USPS Contact: Sue Brennan
(202) 268-6353
Pager: (800) SKY-PAGE PIN 573-1647
E-Mail: sbrennan@email.usps.gov
USPS Web Site: http://www.usps.gov
Release Number 97-053

FOR IMMEDIATE RELEASE
July 7, 1997

DOLLED UP POSTAGE STAMPS
COMMEMORATE PRECIOUS COLLECTIBLES

WASHINGTON - Providing comfort and delight to millions of children of all ages for the past century, dolls not only continue to be favorite childhood playthings today, but the hobby of doll collecting has become an international pastime, surpassed only by stamp and coin collecting in this country and abroad.

The U.S. Postal Service will pay tribute to this collectible with the issuance of the Classic American Dolls stamps, featuring 15 special dolls that reflect the tradition, heritage, culture and artistic style from various geographical regions of this country.

Postal Service Governor LeGree Daniels and the president of the United Federation of Doll Clubs (UFDC), Patricia Gosh, will officially dedicate the stamps on Monday, July 28, at a 7 p.m. ceremony held at the Anaheim Hilton and Towers Hotel in Anaheim, California. This ceremony will be held in conjunction with the annual membership meeting of the UFDC and subsequent week long convention.

"These delightful, charming stamps illustrate the joys of collecting, appreciating and cherishing classic dolls," said Daniels. "I believe these images will recall memories of many sweet, tender moments of our youth."

The dolls featured on the stamps are identified by either the doll's maker, designer, trade name or common name and include:

<u>"Alabama Baby" and Martha Chase</u>. Ella Smith designed the cloth Alabama Baby doll with molded and painted features. These dolls were originally named "The Alabama Indestructible Doll" and were made from 1900-1925. The second doll was created by Martha Chase and is an all-cloth doll made between 1890-1925.

- more -

FIGURE 17-1 **Oddity sells.** The U.S. Postal Service announcement of Classic American Dolls stamps is an example of a unique newsworthy event (continued on next page).

So the fact is that the news release—despite the harsh reviews of some—remains the single most important public relations vehicle.

News Release News Value

The key challenge for public relations writers is to ensure that their news releases reflect news. What is "news"? That's an age-old question in journalism. Traditionally, journalists said that when "dog bites man, it's not news," but when "man bites dog,

FIGURE 17-1 (Continued)

that's news." The best way to learn what constitutes "news value" is to scrutinize the daily press and broadcast news reports and see what they call news. In a general sense, news releases ought to include the following elements:

- Have a well-defined reason for sending the release
- Focus on one central subject in each release
- Make certain the subject is newsworthy in the context of the organization, industry, and community
- Include facts about the product, service, or issue being discussed
- Provide the facts "factually"—with no puff, no bluff, no hyperbole
- Rid the release of unnecessary jargon
- Include appropriate quotes from principals but avoid inflated superlatives that do little more than boost management egos
- Include product specifications, shipping dates, availability, price, and all pertinent information for telling the story
- Include a brief description of the company (aka "boilerplate") at the end of the release, what it is, and what it does
- Write clearly, concisely, forcefully[11]

Just the Facts

Writing in news release style is easy. It is less a matter of formal writing than it is of selecting, organizing, and arraying facts in descending sequence.

Here are 10 facts:

Fact 1: Attorney General John Ashcroft will speak in Madison, Wisconsin, tomorrow.

Fact 2: He will be keynote speaker at the annual convention of the American Bar Association.

Fact 3: He will speak at 8 p.m. at the Kohl Center.

Fact 4: His speech will be a major one.

Fact 5: His topic will be capital punishment.

Fact 6: He will also address university law classes while in Madison.

Fact 7: He will meet with the university's chancellor while in Madison.

Fact 8: He is serving his first term as attorney general under President Bush.

Fact 9: He is a former U.S. senator from Missouri.

Fact 10: He has, in the past, steadfastly avoided addressing the subject of capital punishment.

Organize these facts into an American Bar Association news release for tomorrow morning's Lansing newspaper. One right answer appears later in this chapter. Just don't peek.

News Release Style

The style of writing, particularly news release writing, is almost as critical as content. Alas, many in the public relations profession overlook the importance of proper writing style. Sloppy style can break the back of any release and ruin its chances for publication. Style must also be flexible and evolve as language changes.

Most public relations operations follow the style practiced by major newspapers and magazines rather than that of book publishers. This news style is detailed in various guides published by such authorities as the Associated Press and the *New York Times*.

Because the press must constantly update its style to conform to changing societal concepts, news release style is subjective and ever changing. However, a particular firm's style must be consistent from one release to the next. The following are examples of typical style rules:

- **Capitalization.** Most leading publications use capital letters sparingly; so should you. Editors call this a down style because only the most important words begin with capital letters.
- **Abbreviations.** Abbreviations present a many-faceted problem. For example, months, when used with dates, should be abbreviated, such as Sept. 2, 2003. But when the day of the month is not used, the month should be spelled out, such as September 2003. Days of the week, on the other hand, should never be abbreviated. In addition, first mention of organizations and agencies should be spelled out, with the abbreviation in parentheses after the name, such as Securities and Exchange Commission (SEC).
- **Numbers.** There are many guidelines for the spelling out of numbers, but a general rule is to spell out numbers through nine and use figures for 10 and up. Yet figures are perfectly acceptable for such things as election returns,

speeds and distances, percentages, temperatures, heights, ages, ratios, and sports scores.

● **Punctuation.**   The primary purpose of punctuation is to clarify the writer's thoughts, ensure exact interpretation, and make reading and understanding quicker and easier. Less punctuation rather than more should be the goal. The following are just some of the punctuation marks a public relations practitioner must use appropriately.

1. The colon introduces listings, tabulations, and statements and takes the place of an implied "for instance."
2. The comma is used in a variety of circumstances, including before connecting words, between two words or figures that might otherwise be misunderstood, and before and after nonrestrictive clauses.
3. In general, exclamation points should be resisted in releases. They tend to be overkill!
4. The hyphen is often abused and should be used carefully. A single hyphen can change the meaning of a sentence completely. For example, "The six-foot man eating tuna was killed" means the man was eating tuna; it should probably be punctuated "The six-foot, man-eating tuna was killed."
5. Quoted matter is enclosed in double or single quotation marks. The double marks enclose the original quotation, whereas the single marks enclose a quotation within a quotation.

● **Spelling.**   Many words, from *adviser* to *zucchini*, are commonly misspelled. The best way to avoid misspellings is to have a dictionary always within reach. When two spellings are given in a dictionary, the first spelling is always preferred.

These are just a few of the stylistic stumbling blocks that writers must consider. In the news release, style should never be taken lightly. The style, as much as any other part of the release, lets an editor know the kind of organization that issued the release and the competence of the professional who wrote it.[12]

News Release Format

The format of a news release is also important, whether print or online. Editors complain that releases are often "sloppy," thrown together with misspellings, incorrect grammar, and even wrong facts. No way will such shoddy products be used by the media.

Because the release is designed to be used in print, it must be structured for easy use by an editor. Certain mechanical rules of thumb should be followed.

● **Spacing.**   News releases should always be typed and double-spaced on $8\frac{1}{2} \times 11$" paper. No editor wants to go rummaging through a handwritten release or a single-spaced, oversized piece of paper. Although most releases are typed on only one side, in these days of environmental concern, releases typed on both sides of a page are acceptable.

● **Paper.**   Inexpensive paper stock should be used. Reporters win Pulitzer prizes with stories written on plain copy paper. Nothing irritates an editor more than seeing an expensively embossed news release while watching newspapers die due to soaring newsprint costs.

● **Identification.**   The name, address, and telephone number of the release writer should appear in the upper part of the release in case an editor wants

News Release Taboo Terms

Back in the old days of 1978, comedian George Carlin found himself in deep turbulence for uttering seven "dirty words" that the Supreme Court found to be "patently offensive" to radio listeners. (Because this is a "family textbook," we will leave the seven words to your imagination.)

In the 21st century, there is nothing more "patently offensive" to a reporter than a news release that contains the following taboo terms.

Leading. For example, "Goniff & Co., a *leading* public relations agency, today named 16 new vice chairpersons."

The problem is that everyone considers themselves "leading." Unless the agency is bigger, more profitable, or more highly recognized than others, the term is meaningless and, worse, embarrassing.

Going Forward. For example, "Gazbak said that *going forward* the company would rely more on generally accepted accounting principles in deriving earnings."

Can you ever go any other direction but "forward"? Answer: yes but. . . . So "going forward," like "in the future," is one of those redundancies that means nothing and takes up space. Lose it.

Unique. For example, "Dr. Delaruprup's *unique* laser technology allows a patient to discard his eyeglasses."

C'mon. That ain't "unique." Lots of others may perform the same technological accomplishment. And that's the point. For something to be labeled as "unique," you must be ready to demonstrate its individuality and distinctiveness. If you can't, don't use the word.

Breakthrough. For example, "Professor Kleinswort's *breakthrough* research proves conclusively that we are not alone."

Like "unique," it must be a demonstrable "breakthrough" to be labeled as such. Anybody can call their research or invention or product or process a "breakthrough." But few can prove it. The overused word has become the worst of clichés.

Revolutionary. For example, "Sol Seymour's *revolutionary* hair-restoral method can grow a luxurious mane on a pomegranate."

Well, perhaps if it can do that, it is *"revolutionary."* But like "unique" and "breakthrough," most new products or services or methods or models may in fact be "evolutionary" advancements of what came before, but they can't be fairly construed as "revolutionary."

Cutting-edge. For example, "Bilgebracket's *cutting-edge* radiology department keeps the hospital ahead of the curve in delivering health care services."

This one has really gotten out of hand in the press release business. Everything, it seems, is "cutting edge." But is what you're pitching really precedent setting or original? If not, then it can't be considered "cutting edge." Forget it.

State-of-the-Art. For example, "Poobah's *state-of-the-art* measurement system allows you to empirically evaluate the benefits of the publicity you attain."

See "Cutting-Edge."

World Class. For example, "Ms. Lung Lung, a *world class* yodeler of immense proportions, has performed in concert with Shaggy and the Smyrna Philharmonic Orchestra."

Like "world-renowned" and "world famous," this self-serving superlative should be reserved only for the most unique, revolutionary, and cutting edge of our society.

In writing a news release, then, forget these terms. Use some originality. Be more creative.

further information. It's a good idea to list two names, with office and home telephone numbers. For online releases, printing contact information at both the top and bottom of the release reduces the need for scrolling.

- **Release date.**   Releases should always be dated, either for immediate use or to be held until a certain later date, often referred to as an embargoed date. In this day of online communication, however, publications frown on embargoes. Only in the most extreme cases—for example, proprietary or confidential medical or government data—will they be honored. Therefore, the best policy is to plan on immediate release.
- **Margins.**   Margins should be wide enough for editors to write in, usually about 1 to 1½ inches.
- **Length.**   A news release is not a book. It should be edited tightly so that it is no more than two to two-and-a-half pages long, or, for e-mail, two online screens. Words and sentences should be kept short.
- **Paragraphs.**   Paragraphs should also be short, no more than six lines. A single sentence can suffice as a paragraph. Because typographical composers may type exactly what they see, words should not be broken at the end of a line. Likewise, paragraphs should be completed before a new page is begun to ensure that a lost page in the news or composing room will not disrupt a particular thought in the release.
- **Slug lines.**   Journalistic shorthand, or slug lines, should appear on a release—for example, "more" at the bottom of a page when the release continues to another page and "30" or "###" to denote the end of the release. Page numbers and one-word descriptions of the topic of the release should appear on each page for quick editorial recognition.
- **Headlines.**   Headlines are a good idea and help presell a print or online editor on the news release that follows. Releases should be folded with the headline showing.
- **Boilerplate.**   In the old days, syndicated copy was distributed to thousands of weekly newspapers in matrix or plate form. Such "boilerplate" copy became synonymous with fomulaic or standardized material. So, too, in releases, should a final paragraph be included that describes the organization, what it is and what it does. This not only informs an editor but also might well be picked up in the story.
- **Proofreading.**   Grammar, spelling, and typing must be perfect. Misspellings, grammatical errors, or typos are the quickest route to the editorial wastebasket.
- **Timing.**   News release writers must be sensitive to editorial deadlines. Newspapers, magazines, and broadcast stations work under constant deadline pressure. Because stale news is no news, a release arriving even a little late may just as well never have been mailed. This is particularly the case today, where faxes and e-mail deliver documents immediately.
- **Internet prudence.**   Increasingly, journalists use technology for news collection. However, many journalists have two sets of e-mail: one for correspondence they seek and the other for extraneous material that is normally discarded. So it is important for a public relations writer to recognize that e-mailing releases, stating the lead over voice mail, or messengering a disk won't guarantee that a reporter will even see a release. The best advice is to check a particular reporter's preferred way of receiving news releases before dispatching them.

A QUESTION OF ETHICS

Bad Taste News Release

In the winter of 2001, the *Washington Post Magazine* took public relations firm Porter Novelli International to task for what the paper called a tasteless news release for client Chef America's "Hot Pockets" sandwiches.

In the aftermath of the September 11, 2001, attacks, the release said:

Although the last few weeks have been a challenging time for everyone both personally and professionally, I know that we are all striving to return to "normal."

In the coming weeks as you begin to return to your regular areas of focus, I want you to be familiar with Chef America, makers of HOT POCKETS brand sandwiches.

The *Post* ripped Porter Novelli for the release. Said columnist Gene Weingarten, sarcastically, "This release cannot possibly be tasteless because it issues from no less distinguished a source than Porter Novelli International, a company that is, to quote its website, 'a world leader in the field of brand building and reputation management'."

Weingarten reasoned, "People don't buy HOT POCKETS because they are grateful to the manufacturers for their humanitarian gestures. They buy HOT POCKETS because they're scared of Osama."

Porter Novelli defended itself to Weingarten, contending it was not trying to capitalize on the terrorist attacks but rather "trying to introduce the product to different people, and after September 11 less people are eating out."

News Release Content

Again, the cardinal rule in release content is that the end product must be newsworthy. The release must be of interest to an editor and readers. Issuing a release that has little chance of being used by a publication serves only to crush the credibility of the writer.

When a release is newsworthy and of potential interest to an editor, it must be written clearly and concisely in proper newspaper style. It must get to the facts early and answer the six key questions. From there it must follow the inverted pyramid structure to its conclusion. For example, consider the following lead for the John Ashcroft news release posed earlier in this chapter.

MADISON, WISCONSIN—Attorney General John Ashcroft will deliver a major address on capital punishment at 8 p.m. tomorrow in the Kohl Field House before the annual convention of the American Bar Association.

This lead answers all the pertinent questions:

1. who—Attorney General John Ashcroft
2. what —a major address on capital punishment
3. where—Kohl Field House
4. when—tomorrow at 8 p.m.
5. why—American Bar Association is holding a convention

In this case, how is less important. Whether or not the reader chooses to delve further into the release, the gist of the story has been successfully communicated in the lead.

To be newsworthy, news releases must be objective. All comments and editorial remarks must be attributed to organization officials. The news release can't be used as the private soapbox of the release writer. Rather, it must appear as a fair and accurate representation of the news that the organization wishes to be conveyed.

News releases can be written about almost anything. Three frequent subjects are product and institutional announcements, management changes, and management speeches.

The Product Announcement

Frequently, practitioners want to announce a new product or institutional development, such as earnings, mergers, acquisitions, or company celebrations. The announcement release should have a catchy yet significant lead to stimulate an editor to capitalize on the practitioner's creative idea.

"Tennis whites," the traditional male court uniform, will yield to bright colors and fashion styling this spring as Jockey spearheads a new wave in tennis fashion with the introduction of a full line of tennis wear for men.

Typically, in an announcement release, after the lead identifies the significant aspects of the product or development, a spokesperson is quoted for additional product information. Editors appreciate the quotes because they then do not have to interview a company official.

The new, lightweight plastic bottle for Coca-Cola began its national rollout today in Spartanburg, S.C. This two-liter package is the nation's first metric plastic bottle for soft drinks. "We are very excited about this new package," said John H. Ogden, president, Coca-Cola U.S.A. "Our two-liter plastic bottle represents an important advancement. Its light weight, toughness, and environmental advantages offer a new standard of consumer benefits in soft drink packaging."

The subtle product "plug" included in this release is typical of such announcements. Clearly, the organization gains if the product's benefits are described in a news story. But editors are sensitive to product puffery, and the line between legitimate information and puffery is thin. One must always be sensitive to the needs and concerns of editors. A professional avoids letting the thin line of product information become a short plank of puffery.

The Management Change

Newspapers are often interested in management changes, but editors frequently reject releases that have no local angle. For example, the editor of the Valdosta, Georgia, *Citizen* has little reason to use this announcement:

NEW YORK, NY, April 5, 2004—Ronald O. Schram has been named manager of the hosiery department at Bloomingdale's Paramus, NJ, store.

On the other hand, the same release, amended for local appeal, would almost certainly be used by the *Citizen*.

NEW YORK, NY, Arpil 5, 2004—Ronald O. Schram, son of Mr. and Mrs. Siegfried Schram of 221 Starting Lane, Valdosta, has been named manager of the hosiery department at Bloomingdale's Paramus, NJ, store.

Sometimes one must dig for the local angle. For example, suppose Mr. Schram was born in Valdosta but went to school in Americus, Georgia. With this knowledge, the writer might prepare the following release, which would have appeal in the newspapers of both Georgia cities.

NEW YORK, NY, April 5, 2004—Ronald O. Schram, son of Mr. and Mrs. Siegfried Schram of 221 Starting Lane, Valdosta, and a 1976 graduate of Americus High School, was named manager of the hosiery department of Bloomingdale's Paramus, NJ, store.

Penetrating local publications with the management change release is relatively easy once the local angle has been identified, but achieving publication in a national newspaper or magazine is much harder.

For national consumption it is the importance or uniqueness of the individual or company that should be emphasized. For example, an editor might not realize that the following management change is unique:

> WASHINGTON, D.C., JUNE 6, 2004—Howie Barmad of Jersey City, NJ, today was promoted to the rank of admiral in the United States Navy.

However, the same release stands out clearly for its news value when the unique angle is played up.

> WASHINGTON, D.C., JUNE 6, 2004—Howie Barmad, born in Yugoslavia, today was named the first naturalized admiral in the history of the United States Navy.

One can never go wrong by being straightforward in a news release, but a local or unique angle to help sell the story to an editor should always be investigated.

The Management Speech

Management speeches are another recurring source of news releases. The key to a speech news release is selecting the most significant portion of the talk for the lead. A good speech generally has a clear thesis, from which a lead naturally flows. Once the thesis is identified, the remainder of the release simply embellishes it.

> BOONEVILLE, MO, OCT. 18, 2004—Booneville Mining Company is "on the verge of having several very profitable years," Booneville Mining President J. Kenneth Kelinson said today.
>
> Addressing the Booneville Chamber of Commerce, the Missouri mining company executive cited two reasons for the positive projections: The company's orders are at an all-time high, and its overseas facilities have "turned the corner" on profitability in the current year.

Normally, if the speechmaker is not a famous person, the release should not begin with the speaker's name but rather with the substance of the remarks. If the speaker is a well-known individual, leading with the name is perfectly legitimate.

> Federal Reserve Chairman Alan Greenspan called today for a "new attitude toward business investment and capital formation."

The body copy of a speech release should follow directly from the lead. Often the major points of the speech must be paraphrased and consolidated to conform to a two-page release. In any event, it is frequently a significant challenge to convert the essence of a management speech to news-release form.

Internet News Releases

The Internet has revolutionized news releases and news release writing. Before the Internet, public companies would issue news releases only when they had newsworthy announcements to make. Today, companies regularly issue releases merely to be included on online databases. Why? This indicates to the consumers and investors who access the Web directly that the company is progressing.

In addition, the numerous online news sources—including e-zines, Internet radio programs, bulletin boards, Web-based discussion groups, newsgroups, online services, and mailing lists—make targeting the Internet with news releases an obligatory assignment for public relations writers.

In terms of writing for the Internet, brevity and succinctness are paramount. Reading from a computer screen is more difficult and tedious than extracting from paper. Therefore, Internet writing must appeal to the eye with:

1. Short paragraphs
2. Short sentences
3. Frequent lists
4. Bullets, dashes, numbers

According to Business Wire, another paid news release service used by public relations people, the average news release is 500 words in length.[13] Releases tailored to the Internet, particularly if they are delivered as e-mail, must be even shorter—confined to one or two screens, no more.

As to Internet releases themselves, they must, like print releases, interest the recipient early in the news value of the subject matter. That means making sure the release's headline and lead explain, up front and without hyperbole, what is new and different. Ideally, Internet releases should tailor messages to the individual recipient's needs or interests. Also, keywords in the release should be linked to a glossary defining industry terms and other jargon.

The Importance of Editing

Editing is the all-important final touch for the public relations writer. You must edit your work. One error can sink a perfectly worthwhile release.

In a news release, a careful self-edit can save the deadliest prose. An editor must be judicious. Each word, phrase, sentence, and paragraph should be weighed carefully. Good editing will "punch up" dull passages and make them sparkle. For instance, "The satellite flies across the sky" is dead, but "The satellite roars across the sky" is alive.

SIDEBAR

In Style with the Internet

The Internet, of course, has a writing style all its own.

In chat rooms, a correctly spelled word may be a sign of the inarticulate. Consider, for example, this conversation:

> Wuzup?
> n2m
> well g/g c ya

Literal translation by anyone who spends 8 to 10 hours a day in chat rooms: Not too much is up with the respondent, and so the writer has got to go and will see his friend later.

Indeed, in terms of e-mail vocabulary, the following shortened vernacular can be adjudged as "chat ready":

- pls — please
- flfre — feel free
- btw — by the way
- brb — be right back
- irl — in real life
- IMHO — in my humble opinion
- lol — laughing out loud
- rotfl — rolling on the floor laughing
- u r — you are
- info — information
- doc — document
- convo — conversation
- latr — later

Latr.

In the same context, good editing will get rid of passive verbs. Invariably, this will produce shorter sentences. For example, "George Washington chopped down the cherry tree" is shorter and better than "The cherry tree was chopped down by George Washington."

A good editor must also be gutsy enough to use bold strokes—to chop, slice, and cut through verbiage, bad grammar, misspellings, incorrect punctuation, poorly constructed sentences, misused words, mixed metaphors, non sequiturs, clichés, redundancies, circumlocutions, and jargon. Sentences such as "She is the widow of the late Marco Picardo" and "The present incumbent is running for reelection" are intolerable to a good editor.

A good unabridged dictionary and a thesaurus provide the practitioner with significant writing and editing support. To these might be added *Bartlett's Familiar Quotations*, the *World Almanac*, and an encyclopedia. Editing should also concentrate on organizing copy. One release paragraph should flow naturally into the next. Transitions in writing are most important. Sometimes it takes only a single word to unite two adjoining paragraphs. Such is the case in the following example, which uses the word *size* as the transitional element.

> The machine works on a controlled mechanism, directed by a series of pulleys. It is much smaller than the normal motor, requiring less than half of a normal motor's components. Not only does the device differ in size from other motors, but it also differs in capacity.

Writing, like fine wine, should flow smoothly and stand up under the toughest scrutiny. Careful editing is a must.

S I D E B A R

Deobfuscating Obfuscatory Proverbs

Test your editing skills by tightening up these annoyingly verbose proverbs.

1. Avian entities of identical plummage inevitably congregate.
2. Pulchritude possesses profundity of a merely cutaneous nature.
3. It is fruitless to become lachrymose over precipitately departed lacteal fluid.
4. It is inefficacious to indoctrinate a superannuated canine with innovative maneuvers.
5. Eschew the implement of correction and vitiate the scion.
6. Visible vapors that issue from ignited carbonaceous materials are a harbinger of simultaneous or imminent conflagration.
7. Lack of propinquity causes an effulgence of partiality in the cardiac area.
8. A revolving mass of lithic conglomerate does not accumulate a congery of small green bryophitic plants.
9. Presenter of the ultimate cachinnation thereby obtains the optimal cachinnation.
10. Ligneous or petrous projectiles may have the potential to fracture my osseous structure, but perjorative appellations remain eternally innocuous.

Answers

1. Birds of a feather flock together.
2. Beauty is only skin deep.
3. There's no use crying over spilt milk.
4. You can't teach an old dog new tricks.
5. Spare the rod and spoil the child.
6. Where there's smoke, there's fire.
7. Absence makes the heart grow fonder.
8. A rolling stone gathers no moss.
9. He who laughs last laughs best.
10. Sticks and stones may break my bones, but names can never hurt me.

LAST WORD

Writing is the essence of public relations practice, whether involved with print or online work. The public relations professional, if not the best writer in his or her organization, must at least be one of the best. Writing is the communications skill that sets public relations professionals apart from others.

Or should.

The fact is that the most frequent complaint of employers is that "public relations people can't write." That's why any public relations student who "can write" is often ahead of the competition.

Some writers are born. But most are not.

Writing can be learned by understanding the fundamentals of what makes interesting writing; by practicing different written forms; and by working constantly to improve, edit, and refine the written product. When an executive needs something written well, one organizational resource should pop immediately into his or her mind: public relations.

Discussion Starters

1. What is the difference between writing for the ear and for the eye?
2. What are several of the writing fundamentals one must consider?
3. What is the essence of the Flesch method of writing?
4. What is the inverted pyramid and why does it work?
5. What is the essential written communications vehicle used by public relations professionals?
6. Why is the format of a news release important to a public relations professional and the organization?
7. What are common purposes of news releases?
8. Should a news release writer try to work his or her own editorial opinion into the release?
9. What are the keys in writing releases for the Internet?
10. What is the purpose of editing?

TOP OF THE SHELF

Helen Cunningham and Brenda Greene

The Business Style Handbook
New York: McGraw-Hill, 2002

The Business Style Handbook is subtitled "An A-to-Z Guide for Writing on the Job with Tips from Communications Experts at the Fortune 500."

It was authored by two public relations professionals, who created a 33-question survey for corporate communications departments at the Fortune 500 to gauge how major corporations approach writing.

Among the 21st-century standards that the new PR style book declares are the following random rules:

1. **Dot-com.** Use a hyphen, which is what most U.S. business publications use, instead of *dot.com* or *dotcom*.
2. **FAQ.** Frequently asked questions.
3. **Internet.** Capitalize and use in the first reference. Use the *Net* interchangeably afterward. On the other hand, *intranet* is lowercased.
4. **JPEG.** Use JPEG in all references. It stands for Joint Photographic Experts Group and is a file format for Web-based images, particularly photos.

CASE STUDY

The Raina, Inc. News Release

Background: The Raina, Inc., carborundum plant in Blackrock, Iowa, has been under pressure in recent months to remedy its pollution problem. Raina's plant is the largest in Blackrock, and even though the company has spent $5.3 million on improving its pollution-control equipment, black smoke still spews from the plant's smokestacks, and waste products are still allowed to filter into neighboring streams. Lately, the pressure on Raina has been intense.

- On April 7, J. K. Krafchik, a private citizen, called to complain about the "noxious smoke" fouling the environment.
- On April 8, Mrs. Janet Greenberg of the Blackrock Garden Club called to protest the "smoke problem" that was destroying the zinnias and other flowers in the area.
- On April 9, Clarence "Smoky" Salmon, president of the Blackrock Rod and Gun Club, called to report that 700 people had signed a petition against the Raina plant's pollution of Zeus Creek.
- On April 10, WERS Radio editorialized that "the time has come to force area plants to act on solving pollution problems."
- On April 11, the Blackrock City Council announced plans to enact an air and water pollution ordinance for the city. The council invited as its first witness before the public hearing Leslie Sludge, manager of the Raina Carborundum Blackrock plant.

NEWS RELEASE DATA

1. Leslie Sludge, manager of Raina's Carborundum Blackrock plant, appeared at the Blackrock City Council hearing on April 11.
2. Sludge said Raina had already spent $5.3 million on a program to clean up pollution at its Blackrock plant.
3. Raina received 500 complaint calls in the past three months protesting its pollution conditions.
4. Sludge said Raina was "concerned about environmental problems, but profits are still what keeps our company running."
5. Sludge announced that the company had decided to commit another $2 million for pollution-abatement facilities over the next three months.
6. Raina is the oldest plant in Blackrock and was built in 1900.
7. Raina's Blackrock plant employs 10,000 people, the largest single employer in Blackrock.
8. Raina originally planned to delay its pollution-abatement program but speeded it up because of public pressure in recent months.
9. Sludge said that the new pollution-abatement program would begin in October and that the company projected "real progress in terms of clean water and clean air" as early as two years from today.
10. Five years ago, Raina, Inc., received a Presidential Award from the Environmental Protection Agency for its "concern for pollution abatement."
11. An internal Raina study indicated that Blackrock was the "most pollutant laden" of all Raina's plants nationwide.
12. Sludge formerly served as manager of Raina's Fetid Reservoir plant in Fetid Reservoir, New Hampshire. In two years as manager of Fetid Reservoir, Sludge

was able to convert it from one of the most pollutant-laden plants in the system to the cleanest, as judged by the Environmental Protection Agency.

13. Sludge has been manager of Blackrock for two months.

14. Raina's new program will cost the company $2 million.

15. Raina will hire 100 extra workers especially for the pollution-abatement program.

16. Sludge, 35, is married to the former Polly Yurathane of Wheeling, West Virginia.

17. Sludge is author of the book *Fly Fishing Made Easy*.

18. The bulk of the money budgeted for the new pollution-abatement program will be spent on two globe refractors, which purify waste destined to be deposited in surrounding waterways, and four hyperventilation systems, which remove noxious particles dispersed into the air from smokestacks.

19. Sludge said, "Raina, Inc., has decided to move ahead with this program at this time because of its long-standing responsibility for keeping the Blackrock environment clean and in response to growing community concern over achieving the objective."

20. Former Blackrock plant manager Fowler Aire was fired by the company in July for his "flagrant disregard for the environment."

21. Aire also was found to be diverting Raina funds from company projects to his own pockets. In all, Aire took close to $10,000, for which the company was not reimbursed. At least part of the money was to be used for pollution control.

22. Aire, whose whereabouts are presently not known, is the brother of J. Derry Aire, Raina's vice president for finance. *not good —*

23. Raina's Blackrock plant has also recently installed ramps and other special apparatus to assist employees with disabilities. Presently, 100 workers with disabilities are employed in the Raina Blackrock plant.

24. Raina's Blackrock plant started as a converted garage, manufacturing plate glass. Only 13 people worked in the plant at that time.

25. Today the Blackrock plant employs 10,000 people, covers 14 acres of land, and is the largest supplier of plate glass and commercial panes in the country.

26. The Blackrock plant was slated to be the subject of a critical report from the Private Environmental Stabilization Taskforce (PEST), a private environmental group. PEST's report, "The Foulers," was to discuss "the 10 largest manufacturing polluters in the nation."

27. Raina management has been aware of the PEST report for several months.

Questions

1. If you were assigned to draft a news release to accompany Sludge to the Blackrock City Council meeting on April 11, which items would you use in your lead (i.e., who, what, why, where, when, how)?

2. Which items would you avoid using in the news release?

3. If a reporter from the *Blackrock Bugle* called and wanted to know what happened to former Blackrock manager Fowler Aire, what would you tell the reporter?

4. How could Raina use the Internet to research public opinion of the pollution problem? How could the company use the Internet to communicate its position in advance of the Blackrock City Council meeting?

TIPS FROM THE TOP

An Interview with Bill Adams

Bill Adams

William C. Adams was associate professor at the School of Journalism and Mass Communication at Florida International University (FIU). Prior to joining FIU in 1990, Professor Adams spent 25 years in corporate public relations, including management positions with Amoco Corporation, Phillips Petroleum Company, and ICI Americas. Professor Adams died in 2003.

How important is writing in public relations?

Good writing is the essence of public relations. It's the lifeblood of our profession and is often what sets us apart from others in the organizations we serve. It's also a balancing act. By "good," I'm referring to well-thought-out, grammatically correct, targeted, purposeful, and effective writing. Writing to communicate effectively both inside and outside the organization is the most critical thing a student can learn when studying the many elements of public relations.

By "balancing act," I mean that public relations writers are both translators and interpreters of concepts and ideas, while also being the organization's advocates/persuaders. It's skillfully achieving that fine balance between news and advocacy that gets your writing looked at and read by internal and external audiences alike.

What's the quality of public relations writing?

Unfortunately, much of it is not very good. And what is good—or even passable—is often mundane and perfunctory, devoid of even a whiff of humor or cleverness. News releases, for example, too often miss their target audiences, are loaded with jargon and legalese, aren't newsy and interesting, or offer nothing but hype. Many simply are not well written. (Ask any journalist.)

The same goes for other public relations communications tools, such as newsletters, brochures, memos, and even letters. I see too much sloppiness in sentence construction, a lack of smooth-flowing transitions between paragraphs and thoughts, and an overall carelessness in editing and proofing (and don't blame Spell-Check!).

Are news releases still worthwhile?

It depends on whom you ask. Some reporters and editors claim never to use news releases, while others find them indispensable for covering their beats. The trick, much like targeting audiences you wish to reach with your communications program, is to find out who prefers what. For example, one writer on a specific beat may prefer "fact sheets" or even a phone call, while another wants news releases.

Research has shown that the reasons most releases don't get used is because they have poor-quality writing, are full of hype, or are not newsy enough. A well-prepared, professional-appearing, and targeted release has an excellent chance of being used—or at least getting the reporter's or editor's attention. A daily newspaper columnist once told one of my public relations writing classes not to "bother him" with "junk mail" (news releases) when they went out into the "real world." They were stunned until a reporter from that same newspaper followed by saying, "Don't believe him . . . he couldn't write his column without help from public relations people and their news releases."

What's the key to writing a good news release?

You and the reporters and editors should ask basically the same questions: "Is it news?" "Is it timely?" "Is it localized?" The newsperson asks a critical fourth question: "Is it important to my readers/listeners/viewers?" If the answer to all four of the questions is "yes," there's an excellent chance that your release will be used or at least provide a basis from which a reporter will call you for further information.

Also important as a "use factor" is a well-crafted informational lead and the overall quality of the release itself, which includes grammar, punctuation, sentence structure, and style—free from jargon and hype.

(Continued)

What's the secret to effective public relations writing?

Clarity and conciseness are the keys to successful public relations writing (correct grammar goes without saying). You also must be able to grab a journalist's attention with a newsy and interesting opening statement (it is a "pitch," after all), followed with a reason that reporter should be interested in your story idea.

Does writing remain important throughout one's career?

The answer is a solid "yes." Even at the managerial level, writing remains a crucial part of the public relations profile.

First of all, to get to that level of success, public relations managers generally move through the "technician" stage, wherein they hone their communication skills, increasing their value to the organization.

Writing well is an art, however, and often scares young people just entering the profession. For example, once after speaking to a group of students, I was approached by a potential public relations major who asked, timidly, "If I go into PR, do I have to do all that writing stuff?" The answer remains "yes."

Suggested Readings

Bivins, Thomas. *The Handbook for Public Relations Writing: The Essentials of Style and Format.* Lincolnwood, IL: NTC Business Books, 1999.

Bivins, Thomas, and William E. Ryan. *How to Produce Creative Publications: Traditional Techniques and Computer Applications.* Lincolnwood, IL: NTC Publishing Group, 1992.

Block, Mervin. *Writing Broadcast News—Shorter, Sharper, Stronger, Revised and Expanded.* Chicago: Bonus Books, 1997.

Braden, Marie, with Richard Ross. *Getting the Message Across: Writing for the Mass Media.* Boston: Houghton Mifflin Company, 1996. Includes in-depth treatment of persuasive writing.

Crystal, David. *The Cambridge Encyclopedia of the English Language.* Cambridge, England: Cambridge University Press, 1995.

Fensch, Thomas. *Sports Writing Handbook,* 2nd ed. Hillsdale, NJ: Lawrence Erlbaum Associates, 1995. Updates a special type of writing for sports information.

Fink, Conrad C. *Writing Opinion for Impact.* Ames, IA: Iowa State University Press, 1999.

Hudson, Howard Penn. *Publishing Newsletters,* 3rd ed. Rhinebeck, NY: H&M Publishers, 1997.

LaRocque, Paula. *Championship Writing: 50 Ways to Improve Your Writing.* Oak Park, IL: Marion Street Press Inc., 2000. Master writing coach Paula LaRoque's book on grammar and composition is directed mainly to journalists, but anyone who writes for a living will find this very interesting and even entertaining.

Newsom, Doug, and Bob Carrell. *Public Relations Writing,* 6th ed. Belmont, CA: Wadsworth Publishing Company, 2000.

Nunberg, Gregory. *The Way We Talk Now: Commentaries on Language and Culture from NPR's "Fresh-Air."* Boston, MA: Houghton Mifflin Company, 2001.

Simon, Raymond, and Joseph Zappala. *Public Relations Workbook: Writing and Techniques.* Lincolnwood, IL: NTC Publishing Group, 2001.

Smith, Peggy. *Letter Perfect: A Guide to Practical Proofreading.* Alexandria, VA: EEI Press, 1996 paperback.

Smith, Ronald D. *Becoming a Public Relations Writer: A Writing Process Workbook for the Profession,* 2nd ed. Mahwah, NJ: Lawrence Erlbaum Associates, 2003.

Strunk, W., and E. B. White. *Elements of Style.* New York: Allyn & Bacon, 1999.

Wilcox, Dennis L., and Lawrence W. Nolte. *Public Relations Writing and Media Techniques,* 4th ed. New York: Longman, 2000.

Writing That Works: The Business Communications Report. Springfield, VA: Communications Concepts Inc. Monthly newsletter.

Wysocki, Patria M. *The Ultimate Guide to Newsletter Publishing.* Arlington, VA: The Newsletter & Electronic Publishers Association, 1999.

Notes

1. Fraser P. Seitel, "Steal!" *United States Banker* (1992): 44.
2. Bill Moyers, "Watch Your Language," *The Professional Communicator* (August–September 1985): 6.
3. Fraser P. Seitel, "Getting It Write," *United States Banker* (December 1991): 54.
4. "PRN Averages 1,500 News Releases a Day," *Jack O'Dwyer's Newsletter* (September 15, 1999): 4.
5. G. A. Marken, "Press Releases: When Nothing Else Will Do, Do It Right," *Public Relations Quarterly* (Fall 1994): 9.
6. "J-Prof Says PR Releases Are 'Worthless,' " *Jack O'Dwyer's Newsletter* (July 14, 1993): 4.
7. "How to Get Editors to Use Press Releases," *Jack O'Dwyer's Newsletter* (May 26, 1993): 3.
8. "What Makes a Story Newsworthy," *Communicator* (September 1997): 1.
9. "Researcher Finds Complaints Against Press Releases Are Justified," *Editor & Publisher* (May 8, 1993): 42, 52.
10. Linda P. Morton, "Producing Publishable Press Releases," *Public Relations Quarterly* (Winter 1992–1993): 9–11.
11. Marken, "Press Releases: When Nothing Else Will Do, Do It Right."
12. "Tired Words to Ban from Press Releases," *Ragan's Media Relations Report* (March 17, 1997): 3–5.
13. "In 36 Years, Releases Are Longer and the Competition Is All but Gone," *Business Week Newsletter* (March 1998): 1.

Chapter 18

Writing for the Eye and Ear

On September 20, 2001, President George W. Bush came before a joint session of Congress and the nation to deliver a very special State of the Union speech.

> *My fellow citizens, for the last nine days, the entire world has seen for itself the state of our union, and it is strong.*
>
> *Tonight, we are a country awakened to danger and called to defend freedom. Our grief has turned to anger and anger to resolution. Whether we bring our enemies to justice or bring justice to our enemies, justice will be done. . . .*
>
> *Our nation, this generation, will lift the dark threat of violence from our people and our future. We will rally the world to this cause by our efforts, by our courage. We will not tire, we will not falter, and we will not fail.[1]*

Bush's speech, more than any other action, rallied the nation in the war against terrorism.

Such is the power of the word.

Writing for reading and speaking is a hallmark of the practice of public relations.

Writing for reading emphasizes the written word. Writing for listening emphasizes the spoken word. The two differ significantly.

Writing for the eye traditionally has ranked among the strongest areas for public relations professionals. Years ago, most practitioners entered public relations through print journalism. Accordingly, they were schooled in the techniques of writing for the eye, not the ear. Today, of course, a background in print journalism is not necessarily a prerequisite for public relations work.

Just as important today is writing for the ear—writing for listening. The key to such writing is to write as if you are speaking. Use simple, short sentences, active verbs, contractions, and one- and two-syllable words. In brief, be brief.

This chapter will focus on two things: first, the most frequently used communication vehicles designed for the eye, beyond the news release; and second, the most widely used methods for communicating through the ear, particularly speeches and presentations.

Today's public relations professional must be conversant in writing for both the eye and the ear.

Writing for the Eye

The Media Kit

Beyond the news release, the most ubiquitous print vehicle in public relations work is the media or press kit.

Press kits—in print or online format—incorporate several communications vehicles for potential use by newspapers and magazines. A bare-bones media kit consists of a news release, backgrounder, biography, photo, perhaps a CD-ROM, and any other item that will help a reporter understand and tell a story. The kit is designed to answer all of the most likely questions that the media might ask about the organization's announcement.

In effect, the media kit serves as a "calling card" to intoduce the organization to the media.

Media kits may also require fact sheets or Q&A (question-and-answer) sheets. The public relations professional must weigh carefully how much information is required in the media kit. Journalists don't appreciate being overwhelmed by too much copy and too many photos.

In preparing a media kit, public relations professionals must keep the following points in mind:

- Be sure the information is accurate and thorough and will answer a journalist's most fundamental questions.
- Provide sufficient background information material to allow the editor to select a story angle.
- Don't be too commercial. Offer balanced, objective information.
- Confine opinions and value judgments to quotes from credible sources.
- Never lie. That's tantamount to editorial suicide.
- Visually arresting graphics may mean the difference between finding the item in the next day's paper or in the same day's wastebasket.

The Biography

Next to the news release, the most popular tool is the biography, often called the biographical summary or just plain bio. The bio recounts pertinent facts about a particular individual. Most organizations keep a file of bios covering all top officers. Major newspapers and wire services prepare standby bios on well-known people for immediate use on breaking news—including sudden deaths, which they file in the paper's "morgue."

Straight Bios

The straight bio lists factual information in a straightforward fashion in descending order of importance, with company-oriented facts preceding more personal details. For example, the straight biography of New York Yankees Manager Joe Torre might begin this way:

> *On November 2, 1995, Joe Torre was named manager of the New York Yankees. In becoming the 31st manager in team history, he joined Casey Stengel, Yogi Berra, and Dallas Green as the fourth skipper to wear both Yankees and New York Mets uniforms.*
>
> *During his 17-year playing career, Torre compiled a .297 batting average, 2,342 hits, 252 home runs, and 1,185 RBI's while playing for Milwaukee, Atlanta, St. Louis, and the Mets. He hit over .300 five times in his career and was a nine-time All-Star.*

As a manager, Torre led the 1996 Yankees to their first World Series title since 1978. He was named Sportsman of the Year by The Sporting News *and Co-American League Manager of the Year by the Baseball Writers Association of America.*

After a return to postseason competition in 1997, he led the Yankees to 114 wins during the 1998 regular season, an American League record, and a four-game sweep of the San Diego Padres in the 1998 World Series. Once again, Torre was named American League Manager of the Year, and the season earned him his second AP Manager of the Year Award.

Torre led the 1999 Yankees to their third World Series title in four years, and the first team to win back-to-back championships since the 1977–78 Yankees. In sweeping the Atlanta Braves, the Yankees won 12 straight World Series games, tying a record set by the dominating Yankee teams of the late 1920s and early 1930s.

This biography is written straightforwardly, a chronology of the subject's work history and accomplishments, with little editorializing.

Narrative Bios
The narrative bio, on the other hand, is written in a breezier, more informal way. This style gives spark and vitality to the biography to make the individual come alive. For example, in the case of Joe Torre, the narrative bio might read thusly:

Joe Torre, a nine-time All Star player, has become one of baseball's all-time great managers.

In piloting the New York Yankees to six World Series appearances, Torre has earned a reputation as a savvy strategist, wise counselor, and emotional leader. He is living proof that "nice guys" do, indeed, finish first.

The narrative bio, in addition to bringing the individual to life, doubles as a speech of introduction when that individual serves as a featured speaker. In effect, the narrative bio becomes a speech.

The Backgrounder

Background pieces, or backgrounders, provide additional information generally to complement the news release. Backgrounders can embellish the announcement, or they can discuss the institution making the announcement, the system behind the announcement, or any other appropriate topic that will assist a journalist in writing the story.

Backgrounders are longer and more general in content than the news release. For example, a two-page release announcing the merger of two organizations may not permit much description of the companies involved. A four- or five-page backgrounder provides editors with more depth on the makeup, activities, and history of the merging firms. Backgrounders are usually not used in their entirety by the media but are excerpted.

Subject matter dictates backgrounder style. Some backgrounders are written like a news release, in a snappy and factual manner. Others take a more descriptive and narrative form.

In devising a backgrounder, a writer enjoys unlimited latitude. As long as the piece catches the interest of the reader/editor, any style is permissible.

Fact Sheets, Q&As, Photos, Etc.

Beyond bios and backgrounders, media kits may contain any other information that will help a journalist tell story. Increasingly today, journalists are accessing organizational media kits online. They want information in a hurry, without being delayed by voice mail or foot-dragging. Therefore, the following make great sense to include in media kits.

DODGER STADIUM FOOD FACTS

What does it take to feed the suites, private clubs and club level seating at Dodger Stadium for the 2000 baseball season?

Here's a taste:

Sushi	75,000 pieces
Chinois Chicken Salad	6,100 pounds
Jumbo Crab	2,500 pounds
Seasoned Beef Tenderloin	10,000 pounds
Spago Pizzas/Flatbread	4,200 each
Jumbo Shrimp	6,500 pounds
Chinois Rack of Lamb	1,650 pounds
Smoked Salmon	500 pounds
Giant Taffy Apples	3,000 apples
Beer	97,200 bottles
Wine	9,500 bottles

Slammin' Salads
Whether its Spago Caesar Salad or Chinois Chicken Salad, more than 12,000 pounds of salad will be provided to guests of Dodger Stadium throughout the year.

Wolfgang's MVP – Most Valuable Pizzas
Guests of the Stadium Club will enjoy more than 4,200 gourmet pizzas and flatbreads created Spago-style in the brick-oven. Featured pizzas include Smoked Salmon with dill cream fraiche, red onions and salmon caviar and Prosciutto with leeks, roasted tomatoes, thyme and goat cheese.

An Apple A Day . . .
How about an apple a day for the next 8 years! Guests will enjoy more than 3,000 Jumbo Taffy Apples over the course of the season, courtesy of the Levy Restaurants trademarked Dessert Cart.

No Wining Allowed
The competition may be tough, but the Dodgers can be sure that their fans are enjoying themselves. More than 9,500 bottles of the finest wines will be poured in the private clubs and suites at Dodger Stadium.

We Want a Pitcher...of Beer
Dodger fans know that a baseball game isn't complete without a cold beer. Premium fans will enjoy more than 97,200 bottles of beer, which also equates to approximately 21,000 pitchers.

Levy Restaurants
Sports & Entertainment
www.levyrestaurants.com

FIGURE 18-1 **Just the facts.** Fact sheets allow reporters to extract pertinent morsels to include in stories or complementary boxes. (Courtesy Levy Restaurants)

- **Fact sheets,** which compile the most relevant facts concerning the product, issue, organization, or candidate discussed in quick and easily accessible fashion (Figure 18-1).
- **Q&As,** which present the most probable questions posed about the subject matter at hand and then the answers to those questions. Again, this preempts a reporter having to ask questions of a live—and often unavailable—public relations person.

FIGURE 18-2 **Killer photos.** Provocative photos ready for print, such as this of Shamu the killer whale, should always be included in print and online media kits. (Courtesy of Sea World of California)

● **Photos,** which illustrate the subject. The popularity of *USA Today,* a national full-color newspaper, has stimulated virtually every competitor to move to full-color printing. With photo editors now downloading from the Web, online color media kit photos are a necessity (Figure 18-2). Although a detailed discussion of photographic terms and techniques is beyond the scope of this book, public relations practitioners should be relatively conversant with photographic terminology and able to recognize the attributes of good photos:
  1. Photos should be taken "live," in real environments with believable people, instead of in studios with stilted models.
  2. They should focus clearly on the issue, product, image, or person that the organization wishes to emphasize, without irrelevant, visually distracting clutter in the foreground or background.
  3. Photos should be eye-catching, using angles creatively—overhead, below, to the side—to suggest movement.
  4. They must express a viewpoint—an underlying message.
  5. Most of all, photos must make a visual impact. The best photos are those that remain in a person's mind long after written appeals to action have faded. These are the pictures that are "worth 10,000 words."[2]
● **Etc., etc., etc.** What other material should be included in media kits? Additional pertinent photos, advertising schedules and slicks, CD-ROMs, speeches—there is no hard-and-fast rule. However, journalists have little patience for being overwhelmed with extraneous material. Therefore, as with news releases, in media kits, less is more (Figure 18-3).

Contact: Felicia Roff
Vorhaus & Company Inc.
212.554.7438 – telephone
888.639.9857 – pager
froff@vorhaus.com

**Peanut Butter and Jelly
Fun Facts**

Everybody Loves Peanut Butter and Jelly

- **Jack Nicholson** told *Marie Claire Magazine* that peanut butter and jell
  he needs in the bedroom.*
- During the Senate Impeachment hearings, **Senator Mike DeWine** (R-(
  brown bag containing a peanut butter and jelly sandwich.
- While on the campaign trail for re-election, **Governor George Bush** w
  butter and jelly sandwich.

A Longtime Favorite

- Peanut butter and jelly sandwiches are the 3rd most frequently eaten ma
- Peanut butter and jelly sandwiches ranked 5th out of 100 favorite Amer
- In a six month period, it is estimated that 131 million adults will eat jel

Restaurants Are Catching On...

- A restaurant in New York City, called Peanut Butter and Company, is (
  dishes only made with peanut butter, including the favorite peanut butt
- East of Chicago Pizza Company boasts a popular pizza topped with pe

A Nutritional Choice

- A peanut butter and jelly sandwich provides 18 percent of the daily val
  useful in the prevention of birth defects.***

* * *

* *Marie Claire Magazine*, February 1999
** *March of Dimes and Southeastern Peanut Farmers Brochure*
*** NET, 52 weeks ending 11/22/97

Russell Stover Candies, 4900 Oak Street, Kansas City, Missouri

Contact: Felicia Roff
Vorhaus & Company Inc.
212.554.7438 – telephone
888.639.9857 – pager
froff@vorhaus.com

What Do Bill Clinton and Marilyn Monroe Have In Common?

New York, September 7, 1999 – According to a nationwide survey, Americans most want to eat peanut butter and jelly with President Clinton and Marilyn Monroe. The nationwide survey was conducted by Yankelovich Partners[1] for Russell Stover Candies to announce their new candy, *Peanut Butter and Jelly Cups*. Other favorites include Jimi Hendrix, Sophia Loren and Albert Einstein.
Some highlights of the Peanut Butter and Jelly Survey include:

What television show reminds you of peanut butter and jelly?

- Americans are torn between the 50's classic, *Leave it to Beaver* and the 70's favorite, *The Brady Bunch*.

Baby Boomers want to hold onto their youth...with food:

- Three in four adults believe that the world would be a better place if everyone took time out of their day to remember their childhood.
- Seven out of ten Americans say peanut butter and jelly was among their favorite foods as a child.
- 75% of Americans ate their first peanut butter and jelly sandwich before age 7 and two out of three Americans still savor peanut butter and jelly today.

Peanut butter and jelly is...

- 46% said "an American tradition"
- 36% said "fun"
- 26% said "nostalgic"
- 7% said "sexy" (including Jack Nicholson)

In addition to being the nation's largest manufacturer of boxed chocolates, Russell Stover produces America's favorite candy bars including The Pecan Delight Bar and The Mint Dream Bar with plans to introduce more candy bars and other exciting products in the coming months. The third largest chocolate manufacturer in the country, Russell Stover has been producing *only the finest* candy for over 75 years. The company is headquartered in Kansas City, Missouri and remains a family owned business, run by co-presidents, Scott and Tom Ward.

Missouri, 64112-2702, 1-800-777-4004

FIGURE 18-3   **Filling in the blanks.** When Russell Stover announced its Peanut Butter & Jelly Cups, it offered this fact sheet and survey report to complement media kit information.

The Case History

Beyond the news release and the media kit, another popular and foolproof public relations writing vehicle to attract publicity is the case history.

The case history is frequently used to tell about a customer's favorable use of a company's product or service. Generally, the case history writer works for the company whose product or service is involved. Magazines, particularly trade journals, often welcome case histories, contending that one person's experience may be instructive to another.

Case histories generally follow a five-part formula:

1. They present a problem experienced by one company but applicable to many other firms.
2. They indicate how the dimensions of the problem were defined by the company using the product.
3. They indicate the solution adopted.
4. They explain the advantages of the adopted solution.
5. They detail the user company's experience after adopting the solution.

Trade book editors, in particular, are often willing to share a case that can be generalized—and is, therefore, relevant—to the broader readership. Done skillfully, such a case history is soft sell at its best: beneficial to the company and interesting and informative to the editor and readers.

The Byliner

The bylined article, or byliner, is a story signed and ostensibly authored by an officer of a particular firm. Often, however, the byliner is ghostwritten by a public relations professional. In addition to carrying considerable prestige in certain publications, byliners allow corporate spokespersons to express their views without being subject to major reinterpretation by the publication.

Perhaps the major advantage of a byliner is that it positions executives as experts. The fact that an organization's officer has authored an informed article on a subject means that not only are the officer and the organization credible sources, but also, by inference, they are perhaps more highly regarded on the issues at hand than their competitors. The ultimate audience exposed to a byliner may greatly exceed the circulation of the periodical in which the article appears, because organizations regularly use byliner reprints as direct-mail pieces to enhance their image with key constituent groups.

The Op-Ed

Similar to the byliner, the op-ed article is an editorial written by an organizational executive and then submitted for publication to a leading newspaper or magazine. Most leading newspapers include a page opposite their editorial pages for outside opinions, thus "op-ed."

Being included on a publication's op-ed page is a prestigious publicity forum, and op-ed submissions are, therefore, plentiful. Op-ed pieces then must be written in a style that attracts attention. According to writing counselor Jeffrey D. Porro, the good ones contain the following elements:

Grabber, which starts off the piece and "grabs" attention
Point, which hammers home the thesis of the article
Chain of evidence, which gives the facts that support the argument
Summation, which summarizes the argument
Good-bye zinger, which leaves the reader with something to think about[3]

The Roundup Article

Reporters get rewarded for two things in particular: scoops and trends. The former refers to breaking a story before anyone else. The latter concerns breaking a story that speaks of an emerging trend afoot or relevant to an industry. Although many publications discourage publicity about a single company, they encourage articles that summarize, or "round up," the experiences of several companies within an industry. These trend articles may be initiated by the publications themselves or at the suggestions of public relations people. Weaker or smaller companies, in particular, can benefit from being included in a roundup story with stronger, larger adversaries. Thoroughly researching and drafting roundup articles is a good way to secure stories that mention the practitioner's firm in favorable association with top competitors. The *Wall Street Journal, New York Times, USA Today*, and CNN—all regularly use roundups.

The Pitch Letter

The pitch letter is a sales letter, pure and simple. Its purpose is to interest an editor or reporter in a possible story, interview, or event. Although letter styles run the gamut, the best are direct and to the point, while being catchy and evocative.

Pitch letters, like sales letters, may contain elements that seek to entice a reader's active participation in attending an event or covering a story. Among approaches that work are the following:

- **Challenge.** "Are you prepared to unravel the mysteries of. . . ?"
- **Question.** "Will you do your readers a favor?"
- **News.** "An important announcement for all those concerned. . . . "
- **Invitation.** "We are pleased to inform you that you have been. . . . "
- **Urgency.** "We have now decided to hold an emergency session. . . . "
- **Narrative.** "You don't have to suffer it firsthand to know the. . . . "
- **Action.** "If you can be with us, we need to reserve your place immediately so. . . ."[4]

Pitch letters that sell generally contain several key elements. First, they open with a grabber, an interesting statement that impels the reader to continue reading. Next, they explain why the editor and/or publication should be interested in the pitch, or invitation, and why it is relevant to their readership. That means it must allude to the scope and importance of the story. Finally, they are personally written to specific people rather than being addressed to "editor" (which is the journalistic equivalent of "occupant").

Related to the pitch letter is the "media advisory," a more straightforward listing of facts to interest an editor or news director, usually into attending an event (Figure 18-4). This format eschews the use of long paragraphs in favor of short, bulleted items highlighting the "5Ws" used by journalists: who, what, when, where, and why. The premise of the media advisory is that it "talks to the media in a language it has been trained to accept."[5]

The Newsletter

Another written vehicle that is used for external promotional purposes is the newsletter.

Personal service practitioners, in particular, such as accountants, physicians, lawyers, and investment counselors, use newsletters to subtly promote their services and advise clients and potential clients of needs and possibilities.

FIGURE 18-4 **To the point.** Media advisories are straightforward memos to editors, requesting their presence at an event, such as this unveiling of PSAs for the National Breast Cancer Coalition. (Courtesy of National Breast Cancer Coalition)

For Wednesday, October 2, 2002

MEDIA ADVISORY

The National Breast Cancer Coalition
Unveils New Initiative to Fight Pink Ribbon Complacency

WHEN: Wednesday, October 2, 2002
9:30 – 10:30 a.m.

WHERE: United States Capitol, Room HC-8
Washington, DC
Press Entrance: South Door at New Jersey and Independence Avenues

WHAT: The National Breast Cancer Coalition (NBCC)—the nation's largest advocacy organization dedicated to ending breast cancer—will unveil its first Public Service Announcement (PSA) campaign, designed specifically to move the public from complacency to activism. The campaign, entitled "Not just ribbons," was created by McCann-Erikson, and is NBCC's first PSA campaign in its 11-year history.

WHY: Symbols alone will not eradicate breast cancer. Symbols must be backed by a real commitment from Congress and the public to do the substantive work: finding the cause through research, developing the best treatments, and ensuring access to quality care for all patients.

WHO:
- **Fran Visco,** President, The National Breast Cancer Coalition
- **Senator Tom Harkin,** (D, IA)
- **Representative Anna Eshoo** (D, CA)
- **Representative Sue Myrick** (R, NC)
- **Dr. Susan Love, MD,** Breast cancer surgeon, author of "Susan Love's Breast Book"

NOTE: Speakers will be available for interviews upon request.

Contact Stephanie Sherman at (202) 973-0569 for further details.

# # #

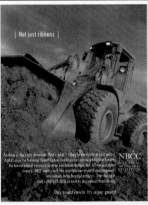

NBCC "Not Just Ribbons" Publicity Campaign

For the first time in its 11-year history, the National Breast Cancer Coalition is undertaking an extensive national publicity campaign. Titled "Not Just Ribbons," it is a call to action to the public to become involved in the fight to end breast cancer.

The campaign includes three print ads (above), which will appear in national publications, and two on-air PSAs featuring well-known celebrities, which will air on cable. The print campaign uses various symbols of power and strength, including a bulldozer, tool belt and hardhat to communicate NBCC's message that "pushing in the right direction," "using all the tools at our disposal" and "working relentlessly" are the most effective means to stopping breast cancer.

Our advocacy has increased federal spending for breast cancer by more than one billion dollars, launched new research models that speed innovative treatments, and changed public policy to include access to treatment for thousands of uninsured women with breast and cervical cancer. But, the fight is far from won.

If we are to succeed, we must increase our ranks of activists. As we pledge in our campaign tagline, we can "Stop breast cancer. It's in our power!"

For more information, call 800/622-2838 or visit us online at www.stopbreastcancer.org.

NBCC
NATIONAL
BREAST CANCER
COALITION

Newsletter copy often takes the form of anecdotal stories that are generalizeable to a large group of readers. They frequently are framed around the following elements.

1. *Point.*   Newsletter items must have a point, meaning, and significance to this broad body of communications recipients. Every story—be it about a product, issue, organization, or person—must be relevant to readers.
2. *Purpose.*   Every item also must have a purpose to the organization; that is, it must be written to achieve a specific organizational objective.
3. *Perspective.*   Every item also must be put in perspective. The reader must be given some sense of where this story fits into the overall scheme of his or her own experience.
4. *Proof.*   Newsletter items must have sufficient "proof"—data, detail, description, facts, statistics, figures, comparisons, contrasts—that overwhelmingly support the points made.
5. *People.*   People love to read about people. Therefore, the best newsletter items are those that refer to case studies of others who have benefited in some way from the product or service being discussed.

Newsletters may be originally produced but, more often than not, they are prepackaged and syndicated by third-party firms and then "personalized" locally.

 A QUESTION OF ETHICS

Congratulations. You're a Big Winner! (NOT)

"You've just been positively identified as our $1,000,000 mystery millionaire from Florida."

Junk mail from a sweepstakes promoter seems to address you personally and often makes it sound as if you will soon receive money in your bank account. Most of the time, you won't.

In recent years, sweepstakes companies, such as Publishers Clearing House, American Family Publishers, and *Reader's Digest,* have been called to task for composing pitch letters that sound too good to be true and usually are.

Most of the letters clearly indicate that "No Purchase Is Necessary," but thousands of people still believe that a purchase helps win all that cash. In 1999, as a result of class-action suits filed against the biggest sweepstakes companies, some questionable practices are being altered.

For example, it was always fair game for your sweepstakes letter to list your past orders and indi-cate that you are either "meeting the criteria for winning" or imply that "you're not ordering enough." Nonbuyers might have to use a reply envelope that says, "No Reward Entitled."

Older people make up a disproportionate number of players, and sweepstakes companies regularly use such trusted figures as Ed McMahon and Dick Clark to hawk their contests. In recent years, state attorneys general have received increasing complaints from families whose gullible, elderly relatives are squandering their limited incomes reaching for the sweepstakes brass ring.

In response to growing litigation and government scrutiny, companies like Publishers Clearing House have developed education and assistance programs to protect consumers and have taken out ads to explain their philosophy. Clearly, no company should profit from people who can't understand what they are reading.

Internal Writing Tools

In addition to writing vehicles expressly designed for external use, a variety of tools are written to be distributed internally. Among them:

The E-Mail Memorandum

Humorist Art Buchwald tells of the child who visited his father's office. When asked what his dad did, the son replied, "He sends pieces of paper to other people, and other people send pieces of paper to him." Most people who work know a great deal about memoranda, which these days is most likely to be distributed via e-mail. E-mail today is by far the number-one internal communications vehicle and may just be the number-one communications vehicle externally as well.

E-mail memos are written for a multitude of purposes and take numerous forms. Even though almost everyone gets into the memo-writing act, writing memos correctly takes practice and hard work.

The keys to writing good e-mail memos are clear thinking and brevity. Many memos reflect unclear thinking and are plagued by verbosity and fuzzy language. Inverted pyramid style is often a good way to compose a memo. More often, rewriting turns out to be the key.

Public relations people are expected to write good e-mail and print memos. This is no easy feat. The key is to keep in mind the six primary elements of a meaningful memo:

1. *State the issue.* Don't dilly dally. Memos don't require preambles. Get right to the issue at hand.
2. *Back it up with data.* Put the issue into a clear, snappy context so that the recipient understands your thought processes.
3. *Present alternatives.* List all the possibilities that must be considered before rendering a decision. Again, brevity is a virtue.
4. *Offer your solution or recommendation.* Be decisive. Stick your neck out. Suggest a clear course of action.
5. *Back it up with detail.* Explain, again briefly, why you believe the action you've recommended is justifiable.
6. *Call for the question.* Always end with a question that demands action.

Don't leave things up in the air. Memos, particularly e-mails, can't end by drifting into space. Avoid this. Make the recipient get back to you by asking a question to which he or she must respond, such as "Do you agree with this?" or "Can we move on this?"

The Position Paper

Public relations people are frequently called on to write a "position paper," also called a "white paper." Written primarily for internal background purposes, position papers are long and rigorously document the facts and assumptions that lead to a particular "position" that the organization is suggested to take.

Such documents form the basis of review and discussion and ultimately serve as the nucleus for a corporate position. After such a position is ratified by management, a "sanitized" position paper may be made available for distribution to opinion leaders and the general public.

The Standby Statement

Organizations sometimes take actions or make announcements they know will lead to media inquiries or even public protests. In such cases, firms prepare concise statements to clarify their positions, should they be called to explain. Such standby statements generally are defensive—and certainly not meant to be volunteered.

They should be brief and unambiguous so as not to raise more questions than they answer. Such events as executive firings, layoffs, price increases, and extraordinary losses are all subject to subsequent scrutiny by the media and are, therefore, proper candidates for standby statements. At any one time, a public relations professional, doing his or her job right, will have several standby statements at the ready should the dreaded call come in.

Writing for the Ear

The Speech

In terms of writing for the ear, the most important public relations vehicle is the external or internal speech.

Speechwriting has become one of the most coveted public relations skills. Increasingly, speechwriters have used their access to management to move up the organizational ladder. The prominence they enjoy is due largely to the importance government and business executives place on making speeches. Today's executives are called on to defend their policies, justify their prices, and explain their practices to a much greater degree than ever before. In this environment, a good speechwriter becomes a valuable—and often highly paid—asset.

A speech possesses five main characteristics:

1. *It is designed to be heard, not read.*   The mistake of writing for the eye instead of the ear is the most common trap of bad speeches. Speeches needn't be literary gems, but they ought to sound good.
2. *It uses concrete language.*   The ear dislikes generalities. It responds to clear images. Ideas must be expressed sharply for the audience to get the point.
3. *It demands a positive response.*   Every word, every passage, every phrase should evoke a response from the audience. The speech should possess special vitality—and so, for that matter, should the speaker.
4. *It must have clear-cut objectives.*   The speech and the speaker must have a point—a thesis. If there's no point, then it's not worth the speaker's or the audience's time to be there.
5. *It must be tailored to a specific audience.*   An audience needs to feel that it is hearing something special. The most frequent complaint about organizational speeches is that they all seem interchangeable—they lack uniqueness. That's why speeches must be targeted to fit the needs of a specific audience. Beyond adhering to these five principles and before putting words on paper, a speechwriter must have a clear idea of the process—the route—to follow in developing the speech.

The Speechwriting Process

The speechwriting process breaks down into four components: (1) preparing, (2) interviewing, (3) researching, and (4) organizing and writing.

Preparing

One easy way to prepare for a speech is to follow a 4W checklist: Answer the questions who, what, where, and when.

- **Who.** The "who" represents two critical elements: the speaker and the audience. A writer should know all about the speaker—manner of speech, use of humor, reaction to an audience, background, and personality. It's almost impossible to write a speech for someone you don't know. The writer should also know something about the audience. What does this audience think about this subject?
- **What.** The "what" refers to two things: (1) the subject, the assigned topic of the talk and (2) the "object," the speaker's intent to convince the audience to take some specific action.
- **Where.** The "where" is the setting. A large hall requires a more formal talk than a roundtable forum. Often the location of the speech—the city, state, or even a particular hall—bears historic or symbolic significance that can enhance a message.
- **When.** The "when" is the time of the speech. People are more awake in the morning and get sleepier as the day progresses. The "when" also refers to the time of year. A speech can always be linked to an upcoming holiday or special celebration.

Interviewing

Interviewing speakers in advance is essential. A good interview with a speaker often means the difference between a strong speech and a poor one.

In the interview, the speechwriter gets some time—from as little as 15 minutes to more than an hour—to observe the speaker firsthand and probe for the keys to the speech. The interview must accomplish at least three specific goals for the speechwriter:

1. *Determine the object of the talk.*   Again, the object is the purpose of the speech—that is, what exactly the speaker wants the audience to do after he or she is finished speaking. The interviewer's essential question must be "What do you want to leave the audience with at the conclusion of your speech?" Once the speaker answers this question, the rest of the speech should fall into place.
2. *Determine the speaker's main points.*   Normally, an audience can grasp only a few points during a speech. These points, which should flow directly from the object, become touchstones around which the rest of the speech is woven.
3. *Capture the speaker's characteristics.*   Most of all, during the interview, the writer must observe the speaker. How comfortable is the speaker with humor? How informal or deliberate is he or she with words? What are the speaker's pet phrases and expressions? The writer must file these observations away, recall them during the writing process, and factor them into the speech.

Researching

Like any writer, a speechwriter sometimes develops writer's block, the inability to come up with anything on paper. One way around writer's block is to adopt a formalized research procedure.

1. *Dig into all literature, books, pamphlets, articles, speeches, and other writings on the speech subject.*   A stocked file cabinet is often the speechwriter's best friend.

2. *Think about the subject.*   Bring personal thoughts to bear on the topic. The writer should amplify the speaker's thoughts with his or her own.
3. *Seek out the opinions of others on the topic.*   Perhaps the speaker isn't the most knowledgeable source within the organization about this specific subject. Outside sources, particularly politicians and business leaders, are often willing to share their ideas when requested.

Organizing and Writing

Once preparation, interviewing, and research have been completed, the fun part begins. Writing a speech becomes easier if, again, the speech is organized into its four essential elements: introduction, thesis, body, and conclusion.

Introduction. An introduction must grab the audience and hold its interest. An audience is alert at the beginning of a talk and, the writer's job is to make sure the audience stays there. Audience members need time to settle in their seats, and the speaker needs time to get his or her bearings on the podium and win audience rapport.

Thesis. The thesis is the object of the speech—its purpose or central idea. A good thesis statement lets an audience know in a simple sentence where a speech is going and how it will get there.

Body. The speech body is just that—the general body of evidence that supports the three or four main points. Although facts, statistics, and figures are important elements, writers should always attempt to use comparisons or contrasts for easier audience understanding.

Conclusion. The best advice on wrapping up a speech is to do it quickly. As the old Texas bromide goes, "If you haven't struck oil in the first 20 minutes, stop boring." Put another way, the conclusion must be blunt, short, and to the point.

Making an Effective Presentation

A business presentation is different from a speech. A presentation generally is designed to sell a product, service, or idea. Everyone, somewhere along the line, must deliver a presentation. Like any other speaking device, an effective presentation depends on following established guidelines. Here are 10 points worth pursuing prior to presenting:

1. *Get organized.*   Before considering your presentation, consider the 4Ws of speechwriting. Who are you addressing? What are you trying to say? Where and when should something happen?
2. *Get to the point.*   Know your thesis. What are you trying to prove? What is the central purpose of your presentation?
3. *Be logical.*   Organize the presentation with some logic in mind. Don't skip randomly from one thought to another. Lead from your objective to your strategies to the tactics you will use to achieve your goal.
4. *Write it out.*   Don't wing it. If Jay Leno and David Letterman write out their ad-libs, so should you. Always have the words right in front of you.
5. *Anticipate the negatives.*   Keep carping critics at bay. Anticipate their objections and defuse them by examining and dismissing vulnerabilities in the presentation.

SIDEBAR

The Four Most Eloquent Words in History

At the end of the 20th century, a group of 137 communications professors from across the nation ranked the top speeches of the century.

Their list of the top 100 is a diverse mixture of race, gender, and philosophy, from women's suffragist Carrie Chapman Catt to Professor Anita Hill, from trial lawyer Clarence Darrow to novelist William Faulkner.

Three of the top 10 speeches were delivered by African Americans, reflecting the civil rights movement and also the rich oral tradition of African American culture. Seven speeches on the list were delivered in the 1990s, five by women. Topping the 1990s' list at number 35 was Hillary Clinton's address to the United Nations on "Women's Rights" in 1995.

Predictably, most speeches on the list are from politicians. A precious few are from business leaders. The Top 10:

1. "I Have a Dream," Martin Luther King, Jr., August 28, 1963
2. "Inaugural Address," John F. Kennedy, January 20, 1961
3. "Inaugural Address," Franklin D. Roosevelt, March 4, 1933
4. "War Message," Franklin D. Roosevelt, December 8, 1941
5. "Democratic National Convention Keynote," Barbara Jordan, July 12, 1976
6. "Checkers Speech," Richard M. Nixon, September 23, 1952
7. "The Ballot or the Bullet," Malcolm X, April 3, 1964
8. "The Challenger Address," Ronald Reagan, January 28, 1986
9. "Greater Houston Ministerial Association Speech," John F. Kennedy, September 12, 1960
10. "Voting Rights Speech," Lyndon B. Johnson, March 15, 1965

And the four most eloquent words in history? "I have a dream." *

*Dru Sefton, "I Have a Dream," *USA Today* (December 30, 1999): 8D.

6. *Speak, don't read.* Sound as if you know the information. Practice before the performance. Make the presentation part of you. Reading suggests uncertainty. Speaking asserts assurance.

7. *Be understandable.* Speak with clarity and concreteness so that people understand you. If you want to make the sale, you must be clear.

8. *Use graphics wisely.* Audiovisual supports should do just that—support the presentation. Graphics should be used more to tease than to provide full information. They shouldn't be crammed with too much information. This will detract from the overall impact of the presentation. Because many audiovisual channels are available to a presenter, from PowerPoint projection to overheads, it may be wise to seek professional help in devising compelling graphics for a presentation.

9. *Be convincing.* If you aren't enthusiastic about your presentation, no one else will be. Be animated. Be interesting. Be enthusiastic. Sound convinced that what you're presenting is an absolute necessity for the organization.

10. *STOP!* A short, buttoned-up presentation is much more effective than one that goes on and on. At his inaugural, U.S. President William Henry Harrison delivered a two-hour, 6,000-word address into a biting wind on Pennsylvania Avenue. A month later, he died of pneumonia. The lesson: When you've said it all, shut up!

L A S T   W O R D

Skillful writing lies at the heart of public relations practice. Basically, public relations professionals are professional communicators. Ergo, each person engaged in public relations work must be adept at writing.

In today's overcommunicated society, everyone from newspaper editors to corporate presidents complains about getting too much paper. So, before a professional even thinks of putting thoughts on paper, he or she must answer the following questions:

1. *Will writing serve a practical purpose?*   If you can't come up with a purpose, don't write.
2. *Is writing the most effective way to communicate?*   Face-to-face or telephone communication may be better and more direct than writing.
3. *What is the risk?*   Writing is always risky; just ask a lawyer. Once it's down in black and white, it's difficult or impossible to retract. And the risks have increased with the immediacy and pervasiveness of the Internet. So, think before you write.
4. *Are the timing and the person doing the writing right?*   Timing is extremely important in writing. A message, like a joke, can fall flat if the timing is off. The individual doing the writing must also be considered. A writer should always ask whether he or she is the most appropriate person to write.

The pen—or, more likely, the PC or laptop—is a powerful weapon. Like any other weapon, writing must be used prudently and properly to achieve the desired result.

Discussion Starters

1. What are the essential elements of a media kit?
2. What is the difference between a straight biography and a narrative biography?
3. What is a backgrounder?
4. What are the benefits of a roundup story?
5. When might an organization require a standby statement?
6. What are the essential characteristics of a speech?
7. What questions does one ask to begin the speechwriting process?
8. What are the elements that constitute an effective presentation?
9. What are the necessary four organizational components of a speech?
10. What are possible pitfalls that must be considered before writing anything?

Roger C. Parker

Roger C. Parker's Guide to Web Content and Design: Eight Steps to Web Site Success
New York: MIS Press, 1997

In the introduction to this lively, informed, and informative book, Jay Conrad Levinson (author of *Guerilla Marketing*) says, "One billion? Two billion? Five billion? I'm trying to figure how many dollars have been wasted by web site owners who lacked the information in this book."

Roger Parker, author of the all-time best-selling desktop publishing book, *Looking Good in Print,* now in its third edition, is a natural-born teacher. His style is engaging. As Levinson says, "What I personally like best about the book is that it asks you questions and when you have answered them, you have a roadmap to your own personal success."

For PR professionals increasingly involved in—even responsible for—company and client Web sites, *Guide to Web Content and Design* should be a welcome partner. Parker encourages readers to "let me know how things work out for you. Contact me through my web site located at www.rcparker.com."

C A S E   S T U D Y

Drafting the CEO's Speech

Congratulations.

You have been selected by your boss to draft the introduction to a speech your CEO will deliver before the 200 top officers of the organization.

You interview the CEO and find that she would like to address the general topic of "The Key Challenges for Us in the Year Ahead."

The object of her talk, according to the CEO, is to convince the officers that although this will be a difficult year, if everyone pulls together, it also can be a most successful one for our company.

Consequently, the CEO's thesis will be the following:

The year we face will be difficult. The environment, uncertain. The challenges, numerous. But if we all pull together in the several specific areas I'll describe, I'm confident that we will have a banner year.

This will form the basis of her remarks.

The CEO's views are based on the knowledge that the year just past was a mediocre one for the company, with profits down 7 percent year-to-year. To shore itself up, the organization has invested $2 million in new systems, adopted new bonus programs, and hired a dozen new executives from the outside.

With a 100-year heritage—the oldest firm in the industry—the company has always enjoyed a reputation for reliable products and quality service. It has traditionally ranked among *Fortune* magazine's "100 Top Places to Work." Indeed, in its 100 years, the company has never had to resort to any major layoff program.

The company's strong ethical streak emanates from a corporate mission that places integrity, product quality, and service as its three top values.

The setting of the CEO's speech is the annual officers' dinner of the corporation, held at the swankiest hotel in town.

The format calls for the chief operating officer to bang the gavel at around dessert time, say a few words of light spirited introduction, and bring on the CEO to deliver the "State of the Organization" speech.

The CEO desperately wants her important message to get across to all those in the room. So she hopes to begin strongly, soundly, and resoundingly.

Keep in mind the purposes of the introduction are to:

1. Ease the audience and the speaker into the speech.
2. Attract initial, favorable attention from the crowd.
3. Provide appropriate background to the audience on the subject.
4. Suit the occasion.

Question

1. What is the introduction you would write for your CEO?

TIPS FROM THE TOP

An Interview with Shaunee Lenise Wallace

Shaunee Lenise Wallace

Shaunee L. Wallace is an account executive with Chisholm-Mingo Plus, the public relations division of Chisholm-Mingo Group, Inc. (CMG), a multicultural advertising agency in New York City. Clients include Amtrak, Royal Caribbean International, and the United States Postal Service. She is also an adjunct professor at Iona College. She has done public relations work for the government of Hong Kong, Bravado Designs fashion company, and jazz vocalist June April.

What does it take to become an effective print writer?
A keen ability to interpret information answering the 5Ws—who, what, when, where, and why. Also being able to grab the reader's attention and describe events in which your audience feels as though they are actually present. Always reading other works to expand your vocabulary and writing not only journalistic and PR documents but also literary works—this, too, will contribute. In addition, attending wonderful writing seminars for professionals to stay ahead of the game is always beneficial.

What does it take to become an effective writer of the spoken word?
It takes a lot of creativity to be able to effectively create a spoken word document. Having a sense of who your target audience is and establishing a theme is always an added bonus. Possessing creative writing skills and keeping an ear to the latest trends will also help.

How important is it for a public relations student to hone his or her writing skills?
Writing skills are essential not only to our profession but also in life in general. Of course, within our discipline, one must be able to quickly assess the information and elucidate ideas. Writing could take up to 60 to 65 percent of your workload, depending on your

(Continued)

responsibilities. Learning the basic writing skills and constantly practicing should assist students in honing their craft.

What are the opportunities for speechwriters today?

Opportunities for speechwriters are endless. Corporations and government officials alike constantly have the need for speechwriters, whether in house or freelancers. A freelance speechwriter's salary can be quite lucrative. If not full time, it is definitely a career option for those who are interested in part-time work.

What kind of training does a writer require?

Most public relations professionals have some background of basic writing skills, whether from educational or past work experience. I strongly recommend students take an internship and request assignments to build their press-writing skills. Once in the workforce, I strongly encourage professionals to attend writing seminars given by a variety of public relations organizations.

What is the calibre of writing in public relations today?

Writing in PR is constantly changing from being very business formal to a little less formal in language. It is more suitable for the everyday person to be able to understand. This also makes the journalist's job easier. I have seen my exact press releases barely reworded in key publications.

How important will the ability to write be in the future for public relations professionals?

Extremely important! As public relations professionals, we must constantly read all types of publications, keeping our eyes and ears open to be able to adapt to different writing styles. This will benefit our clients in the long run. The writer must also remember his or her target audience and cater to them when writing press materials.

Suggested Readings

Bakshian, Aaron, Jr. *The American Speaker*. Washington, D.C.: Georgetown Publishing House, 1995. Written by a former Ronald Reagan speechwriter, this book receives more ingenious self-promotion than probably any work in the history of the world. But it does have its qualities, among them excellent anecdotes from a number of excellent public speakers.

Decker, Bert, and James Denney. *You've Got to Be Believed to Be Heard*. New York: St. Martin's Press, 1993. One of America's foremost speech coaches shares his secrets.

Detz, Joan. *How to Write and Give a Speech*. New York: St. Martin's Press, 2002.

Goldstein, Norm, ed. *The Associated Press Stylebook and Libel Manual*. New York: The Associated Press, revised and updated 2002. Appendices include "Copyright Guidelines," "Freedom of Information Act," "Photo Captions," and "Filing the Wire."

Hanson, Garth A. *Say It Right: A Guide to Effective Oral Business Presentations*. New York: McGraw-Hill, 1995.

Newson, Doug, and Bob Carrell. *Public Relations Writing, Form and Style*. Belmont, CA: Wadsworth, 2000.

New York Public Library Writer's Guide to Style and Usage. New York: HarperCollins Publishers, 1994.

O'Shaughnessy, William. *Airwaves: A Collection of Radio Editorials from the Golden Apple*. New York: Fordham University Press, 1999. Poignant, vividly portrayed, and emotion-laden stories written for the radio.

Smith, Terry C. *Making Successful Presentations,* 2nd ed. New York: John Wiley & Sons, 1991.

Speechwriter's Newsletter (Available from Ragan Communications, 407 S. Dearborn, Chicago, IL 60605).

Treadwell, Jill, and Donald Treadwell. *Public Relations Writing, Principles in Practice.* Boston, MA: Allyn & Bacon, 1999.

United Press International. *Broadcast Stylebook* (220 E. 42nd Street, New York, NY 10017). This is not a rule book, but it suggests methods and treatment for properly preparing news copy, with examples of wire copy and brief comments on correct and incorrect methods of news wire copy preparation. It's designed to help people write the kind of copy used by an announcer.

Variety (Available from 475 Park Avenue South, New York, NY 10016; published weekly on Wednesday). This paper publishes news, features, and commentary each week on every aspect of show business, with extensive reviews of productions around the world.

Wilcox, Dennis. *Public Relations Writing and Media Techniques*, 4th ed. New York: Longman, 2000.

Notes

1. George W. Bush, Address to the Joint Session of Congress, Washington, D.C. September 20, 2001.
2. G. A. Marken, "Public Relations Photos . . . Beyond the Written Word," *Public Relations Quarterly* (Summer 1993): 7–12.
3. Jeffrey D. Porro, Porro Associates, 1120 Connecticut Ave., Suite 270, Washington, D.C. 20036.
4. "Writing Irresistible Teaser Copy," *Communicator* (July 1998): 6.
5. "Farewell to the Pitch Letter," *Public Relations Journal* (July 1990): 13.

Chapter 19

Public Relations and the Internet

"If you're not online, you don't exist."

—*British Futurist Peter Cochrane*

Mr. Cochrane's bold 1998 prediction was almost right.

Sure, the Internet has changed communications forever, with its immediacy and pervasiveness. But, no, the Internet hasn't replaced human relationships as the essence of societal communications. Nor has it replaced human relationships as the essence of the practice of public relations.

Although some at the turn of the 21st century predicted that the Internet would one day dominate public relations work, that has not turned out to be the case. The Internet and communicating via the computer is but another tool in the public relations aresenal. An important tool, but a tool nonetheless (Figure 19-1).

Defining the Internet

What is the Internet?

It's a cooperatively run, globally distributed collection of computer networks that exchange information via a common set of rules. The Internet began as the ARPANET during the Cold War in 1969, developed by the Department of Defense and consultants who were interested in creating a communications network that could survive a nuclear attack.[1] It survived—even though there was, thankfully, no nuclear attack!—as a convenient way to communicate.

The World Wide Web, the most exciting and revolutionary part of the Internet, was developed in 1989 by physicist Tim Berners-Lee to enlarge the Internet for multiple uses. The Web is a collection of millions of computers on the Internet that contain information in a single format: HTML or hypertext markup language. By combining multimedia—sound, graphics, video, animation, and more—the Web has become the most powerful tool in cyberspace.

Without question, the Internet and the World Wide Web are playing an increasingly significant role in our everyday lives. They have transformed the way we work, the way we buy things, the way we entertain ourselves, the way business is conducted,

FIGURE 19-1 **Internet public relations source.** Odwyerpr.com is an up-to-the-minute Internet resource for public relations students and practitioners, conveying commentary and news about who is doing what to whom in the public relations business. (Courtesy of odwyerpr.com)

and, most important to public relations professionals, the way we communicate with each other. No question about it, the Internet phenomenon, pure and simple, has been a revolution.

In 1999, the Internet economy grew by 68 percent, topping one-half trillion dollars and far outpacing the growth of the overall U.S. economy.[2] Illustrative of how the Internet economy was replacing traditional economic names and values were the names of the new companies added that year to the Dow Jones industrial average: Microsoft, Intel, and SBC Communications. Who were the old-timers they replaced? Chevron, Goodyear, Sears Roebuck, and Union Carbide.

By 2000, Americans were spending nearly eight hours a week online, sending three times as much e-mail as regular mail, and spending $20 billion on online retail purchases. Internet traffic doubles every 95 days. Americans alone add 2 million pages to the World Wide Web daily.[3]

By 2001, the Internet seemed to know no bounds. But then reality struck.

The recession that gripped the United States and the world in late 2000 splashed cold water on the dreams of a burgeoning Internet economy.

- Internet-based companies, launched with great publicity fanfare and stratospheric stock market multiples—with names like Pets.com, Auto-trader.com, Britannica.com, Star Media, Dr. Koop.com, CMGI, and so on—crumbled to virtual worthlessness, losing millions of dollars for shareholders and shattering the Internet's promise as the "new economy" source of riches.
- The largest of the new high-tech leaders—Intel, Sun Microsystems, Cisco Systems, Hewlett-Packard, and so on—saw their pristine reputations and stellar stock prices battered.

- Companies, including those of the so-called "old economy," which counted on the Net becoming a primary method of commerce, were disappointed with results and significantly cut back Internet offerings.

Stated another way, by 2002, the promise of the Net as a vehicle of commerce and a mainstay of an expanding economy and stock market had fallen sadly short of its true believers' most optimistic expectations.

The Net as Communications Medium

On the other hand, although the Internet has not achieved its promise as a medium of commerce, its role as a medium of communications cannot be denied.

Every organization, from the largest corporation to the smallest nonprofit, today has a Web site. Often it is the Web site that serves as that organization's "first face" to the public. Public relations departments now have interactive specialists and groups responsible for communicating via the Net. Likewise, public relations agencies boast online departments that help clients access the Net. Although the expansive number of Net-oriented agencies that flourished in the late 1990s has been decimated, a handful of firms still specialize in Internet-related communications.

Journalists meanwhile—still the primary customers for most in public relations—have also embraced the Internet as their primary source for research and reporting. The vast majority of reporters today are online and prefer e-mail as their primary source of public relations correspondence. Nonetheless, personal contact with a journalist (i.e., building a relationship) is still the best way to ensure that your message will be heard.

For individual public relations practitioners then, although the Internet in many areas has fallen short of the full measure of its promise, familiarity with it, mastery of it, and knowledge of its effective use have become frontline requisites of the practice.

Public Relations Internet Challenge

Use of the Internet by public relations practitioners inevitably will grow in the future, for three reasons in particular.

- **The demand to be educated versus being sold.** Today's consumers are smarter, better educated, and more media savvy. They know when they are being hustled by self-promoters and con artists. So communications programs must be grounded in education-based information rather than blatant promotion. The Internet is perhaps the world's greatest potential repository of such information.
- **The need for real-time performance.** The world is moving quickly. Everything happens instantaneously in real time. As media visionary Marshall McLuhan predicted four decades ago, in the 21st century the world has become a "global village," wired for immediate communications. Public relations professionals can use this to their advantage to structure their information to respond instantly to emerging issues and market changes.
- **The need for customization.** There used to be three primary television networks. Today there are more than 500 television channels. Today's consumers expect more focused, targeted, one-on-one communications

relationships. More and more, organizations must broadcast their thoughts to narrower and narrower population segments. The Internet offers such narrowcasting to reporters, shareholders, analysts, opinion leaders, consumers, and myriad other publics.[4]

Such is the promise of the Internet to the practice of public relations. Beyond its role as an integral component in the Internet marketing mix, public relations has become prominent in several other cyber areas:

- **E-mail.** E-mail has become the most pervasive internal communications vehicle. In companies, schools, media institutions, and homes, e-mail, delivered online and immediately, has replaced traditional print and fax technology as a rapid-delivery information vehicle.
- **Web sites.** Another rapidly expanding use of the Internet by public relations professionals is the creation and maintenance of Web sites to profile companies, promote products, or position issues. A Web site gives an individual or institution the flexibility and freedom of getting "news out" without having it filtered by an intermediary. There are literally millions of Web sites sitting there, waiting for visitors. Many public relations agencies specialize in creating Web sites. Intranets, or internal Web sites, are another growing phenomenon.
- **Online media relations.** Beyond the creation of Web sites, public relations practitioners are using the Internet to communicate to the media. Journalists today use the Web as a primary source of organizational information. More journalists, too, are communicating with public relations sources via e-mail. Finally, the growth of online spinoffs of major print publications and the development of magazines on the Web—e-zines—like *Slate* and *Salon.com*, present a new, enlarged field of potential publicity play for public relations practitioners.
- **Online monitoring.** The Web's easy accessibility has also ushered in a whole new challenge to public relations professionals to monitor online media for negative comments and even threats against their organizations. The preponderance of rogue Web sites and antagonistic chat rooms that condemn organizations makes it a necessity that public relations professionals regularly monitor such Web sites, chat rooms, and discussion groups.
- **Product promotion.** The ability to reach customers and potential customers directly is another benefit created by the Web. In this area, public relations supports integrated marketing efforts on the Web.
- **Investor relations.** Speaking directly to investors and potential investors is yet another Web challenge to public relations people. The Web allows investors to check the activities of their holdings on a daily basis, enabling companies to increase their communications efforts relative to their shareholders. Investor chat rooms—or "threads"— also demand constant monitoring by public relations people to assess the latest shareholder undercurrent about the company.

In a general sense, what television and cable TV were to the advertising industry, the Internet is to public relations. Organizations, like never before, can "go direct" to build reputations with the public, investors, consumers, and the media. Using the Internet, organizations face no "interruption" of their message by some third-party filter, such as the press.

Directly delivering messages to key constituent publics is the true challenge and opportunity of the Internet to public relations.

E-Mail: The Dominator

E-mail has become far and away the most pervasive organizational communications vehicle. In most organizations, e-mail is the internal medium of choice for newsletters, bulletins, and internal announcements.

Although many managers are reluctant to confront employees face-to-face, e-mail tends to produce more honest and immediate feedback than traditionally had been the case. Because e-mail is quick and almost effortless, a manager can deliver praise or concern without leaving the office. Thus, e-mail has, by and large, improved organizational communications. That is not to say that face-to-face communication isn't always best. It is. But the ease and effectiveness of e-mail make it a viable alternative.

E-mail has also unseated the traditional employee print newsletter. Online newsletters are both more immediate and more interactive than print counterparts. Employees can "feed back" to what they've read or heard instantaneously. The organization, in turn, can apprise itself quickly of relevant employee attitudes and opinions. Such online vehicles also lend an element of timeliness that print magazines and newspapers often have a hard time offering.

E-mail newsletters for external use—to customers, investors, or the media—are equally popular and valuable. These differ from their print brethren in several important areas:

1. *No more than one page.*   People won't read lengthy newsletters on the computer. So e-mail newsletter writers must write short.
2. *Link content.*   Copy should be peppered with links to other material, such as teasers to full-length articles and product offers.
3. *Regular dissemination.*   It is also important to send e-mail newsletters at regular intervals, so that recipients expect them.
4. *Encourage feedback.*   Web site visitors should be required to provide full name, e-mail address, company name, and format preference (HTML or plain text).

E-mail newsletters and notices can be used to sell products and services. Advertising giant J. Walter Thompson marketed the Ford Taurus automobile with a comprehensive e-mail campaign, including online brochures, fliers, and chat room for prearranged cyber conferences. The chat room was set up much as a call-in radio show, with designers answering consumer questions about the new car.

Developing a Winning Web Site

In many ways, the organization's Web site is its most important interface with the public. Today, journalists and others turn to the Web site first for an introduction to the organization[5] (Figure 19-2).

So the Web site must sizzle. As the saying goes, "One never gets a second chance to make a first impression." Unfortunately, as powerful as Web sites can be as communications media, only a handful are realizing their potential.[6]

How should one create a winning Web site? By first asking and answering several strategic questions.

1. *What is our goal?*   To extend the business? Sell more products? Make more money? Win support for our position? Turn around public opinion? Introduce our company? Without the answers to these fundamental questions, the

Online Publication Planning Guide

E-mail has become the dominant internal communications medium. Here, according to Internet communications mastermind Shel Holtz, is the 10-step process to design a winning online publication.

1. *Establish the outcome.* Tie the publication's results to achieving business objectives. Answer the question: "Why are we launching this publication?" Is it to increase brand recognition, employee commitment, or product knowledge?
2. *Define the audience.* Because the Web allows narrowcasting, define the audience as rigorously as you can. Rarely is an Internet publication aimed at all Web surfers.
3. *Determine your strategy.* Strategies are specific milestones on the way toward achieving your goals. If you want to retain customers, for example, your strategy must be one of supplying the staff with ample product benefit arguments.
4. *Set objectives.* Each strategy consists of short-term, measurable goals. Setting such quantifiable objectives will enhance the effort in the eyes of management.
5. *Outline tactics.* What are the tactics you will implement to achieve your objectives? Will you include discussion groups, Q & As with employees, or some other interactive device that allows feedback?
6. *Assess technology.* Based on the profile of the audience, consider which technology would be best for you. Just as internal video producers must be sensitive to the sophistication of employee TV viewers, so, too, must internal e-mail publication editors understand the technology that is most familiar to employees.
7. *Set content guidelines.* Set standards for your publication. What will you include in e-mail? On your Web site? How long will articles be? (The shorter the better on the Web.) Will there be bite-sized news briefs, interviews, features, or a combination?
8. *Install interactivity elements.* This, after all, is the real benefit of the Web. It's interactive. So use it as such in your internal publication. Discussions, chats, polls, and reader idea submissions all should be included. The most successful Web publication is one designed to reach a subset of the entire group rather than "all employees."
9. *Develop templates.* This just means that every issue ought to look the same. Consistency, continuity, and uniformity are persuasive elements in communications.
10. *Measure.* The Web now is sophisticated enough so that one can evaluate whether the message has gotten through. It is incumbent, therefore, that internal Web-based communicators use online focus groups, online surveys, and telephone surveys to determine if Web-based messages are getting through to the rank and file.[*]

*Shell Holtz, "10 Step Online Publication Planning Guide," www.webinar.holtz.com.

"what" and "how" of a Web site are inconsequential. Just as in any other pursuit in public relations, the overriding goal must be established first.

2. *What content will we include?* The reason some Web sites are tedious and boring—and they are!—is because little forethought has gone into determining the content of a site. Simply cramming chronological news releases onto a Web site won't advance an organization's standing with its publics. Rather, content must be carefully considered, in substance and organization, before proceeding with a site.
3. *How often will we edit?* Often the answer to this question is: "Not often enough." Stale news and the lack of updating are common Web site problems.

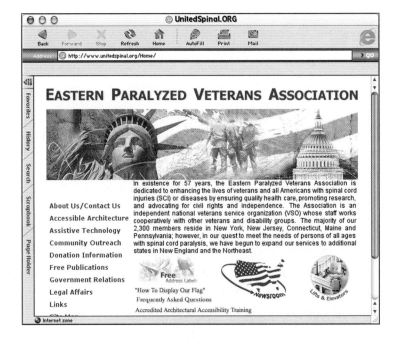

Sites must regularly be updated. Another problem is overwriting. People seem to feel that because the Web is "free," they can write endlessly. Of course, they can. But no one will read it. So an editorial process to cull information down to its most essential parts is a necessity for a good Web site.

4. *How will we enhance design?* Like it or not, the style of the site is most important. If an organization's homepage isn't attractive, it won't get many hits. Good design makes complicated things understandable, and this is essential in a Web site. The Web is a largely visual medium, so great care should be taken to professionally design a site.

5. *How interactive will it be?* Traditional communication is unidirectional, one way. You read or view it, and that's where the process stops. The great attraction of the Web, on the other hand, is that it can be bidirectional. Communication can be translated into an interactive vehicle, a game, an application, or an e-mail chat vehicle. This is what distinguishes good sites from mediocre ones.

6. *How will we track use?* As in any other communications project, the use of a Web site must be measured. The most basic form of cyberspace measurement is the very rough yardstick of hits to the site. But like measuring press clippings, this doesn't tell you whether your information is being appreciated, acted on, or even read. It is the site itself that allows direct "conversations" with customers and potential customers to find out what they really think. Measuring site performance, therefore, should be a multifaceted exercise that includes such analysis as volume during specific times of day, kind of access, specific locations on the site to which visitors are clicking first, and the sequencing through the site that visitors are following.

7. *Who will be responsible?* Managing a Web site, if it is done correctly, must be someone's full-time job. Companies may subordinate the responsibility to someone—occasionally in the public relations department—who has many other "more important" responsibilities. Wrong. Or, as noted, the function may be a shared one. Also, wrong.

Much better is to treat the Web site as a first line of communication to the public, which requires full-time attention.[7]

Making a Web Site "Sticky"

The aim of any Web site is to provide information that visitors are looking for. The more you achieve that objective, the more "sticky" your site becomes. Stickinesss is often measured by the amount of time visitors spend at a site and how many pages they view. For example, if visitors spend 10 minutes at the Web site and view five or more pages, you've achieved stickiness.[8]

How can one ensure that the site is sticky? The following six rules should be applied.

1. *No dead links.*   All links should work. Little is more annoying than to go to a site, click on a link, and—nothing. It's like reading a newspaper article that is supposed to continue on another page but doesn't. Links must do just that—link.
2. *Contact information.*   If the viewer needs more information, he or she should be told how to get it. Then the request must be answered. If not, the site and the company are stamped "unprofessional" in the mind of the prospect.
3. *Placement of information.*   Because we read from left to right, more important information should be placed on the left side of the screen to ensure the viewer reads it first.
4. *Use of color.*   Color schemes are important because they affect load time as well as represent the company. It is always best to use standard colors, which are handled best by most computers and browsers. Some exotic color combinations are difficult to read on the screen.
5. *Ease of use.*   Information also must be readily available and placed in logical order. Hyperlinks need to be accurate and clearly marked. Each level within the site should allow the user to get back to the previous level and go forward to the next. Also, the viewer must always be able to return to the homepage. Viewers are rightfully frustrated when they can't return to the homepage and start again.
6. *Purpose.*   The purpose of a Web site determines the quantity and type of information included. Web sites generally fall into three categories:
   * *Presence model:*   designed to establish a presence on the Web, used primarily as a promotional tool.
   * *Informational model:*   heavy with material, including press information, designed to provide a comprehensive organizational portrait.
   * *E-commerce model:*   designed to create and establish sales.[9]

Dealing with the Media Online

In the 21st century, the Internet has become the favored tool of reporters for discovering organizational information.[10]

When asked how they prefer to work with organizations in news gathering, journalists report the following:

* E-mail, 61 percent
* Telephone, 51 percent
* In person, 23 percent
* Fax, 4 percent

Research also indicates that journalists now overwhelmingly rank corporate Web sites as their most important source of financial information.

So reaching reporters online has become a frontline responsibility for public relations professionals.

The downside of the new technology is reminiscent of the downside of media relations generally. Specifically, many reporters complain that their e-mail has become as crowded as their voice mail, which became as crowded as the little pink telephone reminder slips on their desks.

The basics of online media relations include the following:

- **Web site newsroom.** The best organizations create extranets, devoted exclusively to serving the media, as derivatives of their Web sites. These corporate newsrooms include all the traditional press materials that the media require.

  News releases: Every Web site begins with news releases, most often organized chronologically. However, journalists complain that they don't know precisely when an organization raised its prices or announced its earnings or promoted its president. Therefore, the best Web newsrooms organize releases both chronologically and by subject, with a search engine capable of pointing readers toward specific subjects.

  Executive speeches: All major speeches delivered by management should be included at the corporate newsroom site. The best sites offer an interactive speech feature, through which speeches are automatically e-mailed to journalists or others who request them.

  Annual/quarterly reports: Every public company is obligated to report earnings to shareholders four times a year and typically issue three quarterly reports and one annual report. Quarterlies and annuals, too, should appear on the corporate newsroom site.

  Annual meetings: Companies in remote locations, in particular, have begun to videocast their annual gathering of shareholders over the Internet, so that those unable to attend in person may do so electronically.

  Interviews: Online press conferences and Webcasts have also become standard fare, with a company notifying journalists of the time and password necessary to access a particular executive presiding as an online interviewee (Figure 19-3).

  Digital press kits: All the material included in a corporate press kit—releases, photos, backgrounders—are duplicated on the Internet for downloading purposes to journalists.

  Photographs, profiles, ad copy, etc.: Online executive photographs and other relevant photographs are standard at corporate newsroom sites. So, too, are executive biographical profiles. Corporate newsrooms might even offer video versions of corporate advertising.

- **News release via newswires.** It has become essential for public companies to issue news releases over newswires. Why? Newswire copy gets picked up by online databases, such as AOL, Yahoo!, and LexisNexis. If a company wants its shareholders and potential investors to know of its activities, in order to notify them online, its releases must be included on newswires. Newswires are of three types:

  1. *General wires:* The Associated Press (AP) is the granddaddy of all general wire services, reporting on general news of interest to the broad society.

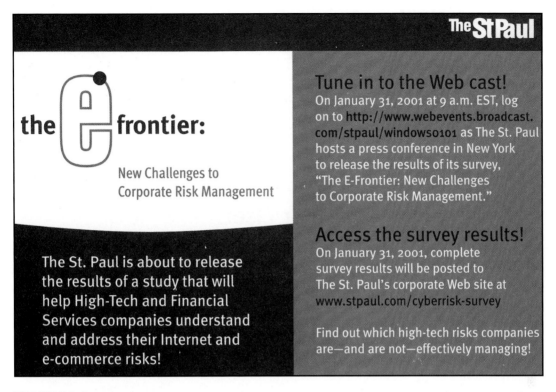

FIGURE 19-3   **Media Webcast.** When the St. Paul Companies hosted a news conference to announce the results of its study of Internet risks, it combined it with a live Webcast for reporters listening online. (Courtesy of the St. Paul Companies)

United Press International (UPI), which used to compete directly with AP, has fallen into financial ill health in recent years and has diminished as a news factor.

2. *Financial wires:*   Dow Jones, the wire service of the *Wall Street Journal*, the nation's business newspaper, is perhaps the most well-known financial wire. Reuters is known as the international financial wire. Bloomberg, the creation of a former Wall Street broker turned New York City mayor, has emerged as another powerful financial wire service force in both print and broadcast.

3. *Paid wires:*   As opposed to general and financial wires, other wire services—the most prominent being PR Newswire and Business Wire, as well as the newer Market Wire (formerly Internet Wire)—are paid services that reproduce organizational news announcements verbatim, for a fee.

   All of these wire services report online, which means that releases are automatically filed on online stock databases. This allows online users to track specific company announcements and is one reason why most publicly held companies today release via wire.

● **Online publicity.**   During the high-tech bubble of the 1990s, the proliferation of online versions of major periodicals, from the *New York Times* to *Business Week* to *U.S. News & World Report*, opened new publicity channels to public relations professionals. The puncturing of the bubble at the start of this century doused the ardor of media companies to invest in their online properties. Indeed some of the most venerable publications of the Internet era—from *The Industry Standard* to *Mutual Funds* magazine to *Upside* to *Forbes ASAP*—have all bitten the dust.

Nonetheless, online publications—e-zines—such as *Salon* and *Slate,* and online special-interest sites, such as oxygen.com and ivillage.com designed for women, netnoir for African Americans, seniornet for senior citizens, and so on, offer opportunities for publicity. Financial news services, such as fool.com, TheStreet.com, and CBSMarketWatch.com, are also ready outlets for online publicity.[11]

Monitor the Net . . . or Else!

Whether an organization uses the Internet for publicity, uses e-mail extensively, or even has a Web site, the one necessity for any organization today is to monitor the Internet.

In the 21st century, monitoring the Internet is another frontline public relations responsibility. The World Wide Web is riddled with unhappy consumers spilling their guts, disgruntled stockholders badmouthing management in chat rooms, and rogue Web sites condemning this or that organization.

Face it. The Internet is free, wide open, international, and anonymous—the perfect place to start a movement and ruin an organization's reputation. And so it is imperative that public relations people monitor the Net in consideration of the following.

- **Discussion groups and chat rooms are hotbeds for discontented shareholders, unscrupulous stock manipulators, and disgruntled consumers.** Any local or service provider message board, which solicits public input about an organization, is ripe for messaging contrary to the official position.[12] The Yahoo! finance boards, for example, are the source of continuing commentary about public companies from anonymous commentators, all using mysterious pseudonyms. One will start with a cryptic message. Then another will add to it. And a third will chime in. This continuous commentary—called "the thread" on Wall Street—is the bane of many a company. The thread has become such a source of corporate discontent that monitoring firms have emerged to keep track of what is being said about companies in chat rooms. One such firm, NewGate Internet, Inc., organizes "whisper campaigns." To wit:

    > Using our proprietary database as a starting point, we constantly monitor the public access areas of the Internet (newsgroups, listservs, and forums). Wherever we find such mentions, we use an extremely subtle approach to incorporate positive information about your business into the discussion. We never denigrate or criticize the competition; instead we add to the discussion by "whispering" useful reminders about your company or product. [13]

    Small companies, in particular, must be constantly vigilant of what is being said about them in online forums. That also means monitoring newsgroups, which can serve as rumor mills. Monitoring such groups can serve as public relations "radar" to help an organization anticipate problems.
- **Rogue Web sites must also be monitored by the organizations they attack.** Rogue Web sites seek to confront an organization by:
    - Presenting negative information

A QUESTION OF ETHICS

20/20 Foresight on the Internet

Ask most public relations people what you can do when you're caught in the crosshairs of a network television exposé, and they'll answer, "Not much."

Ask California public relations counselor Michael Sitrick, and he'll say, "Hit the Internet."

That's precisely what Mr. Sitrick and his client, weight control company Metabolife, did when they felt victimized by an interview on ABC's *20/20*. When the company's CEO didn't like the questions he was asked and worried about how the interview might be edited for air, Metabolife and its public relations agency took a bold step.

They preempted the ABC broadcast by offering an uncut videotape of the *20/20* interview on the Metabolife Web site—the first time the Internet had been used to issue an advance rebuttal to an upcoming broadcast. By displaying the entire interview, Metabolife hoped to blunt the impact of what, in its view, could have been a biased TV report. It supported the Web intervention with a $2 million nationwide advertising campaign.

Communications professionals were sharply divided over the ethics of Metabolife's bold move.

- One Internet author liked the idea. "Your comments can be taken out of context, or you can be misquoted. Through the Internet and cheap computing, you have the ability to set the record straight," he said.
- A journalism professor, on the other hand, disagreed. "In essence, it's an effort at intimidation. It's borderline prepublication censorship. I think it has a very chilling effect on journalism."

Metabolife wasn't phased by the criticism. In fact, the company was so confident, it purchased a 15-second ad that aired during the *20/20* broadcast itself, asking viewers to vist the site and vote on whether the Metabolife segment was balanced or not.*

Such public relations feistiness continued to distinguish Metabolife, as it faced added pressures in the new century (Figure 19-4).

*"Firm Uses Internet as Potent PR Tool," O'Dwyer's *PR Services Report* (November 1999): 20.

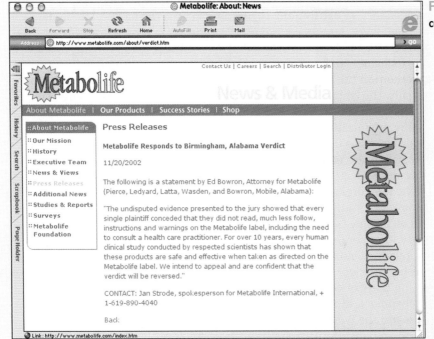

FIGURE 19-4 Feisty combatant Metabolife.

FIGURE 19-5 **Wal-Mart sucks.** This rogue Web site, designed to embarrass the mighty Wal-Mart company, is typical of anticorporate sites on the Internet, all of which must be monitored.

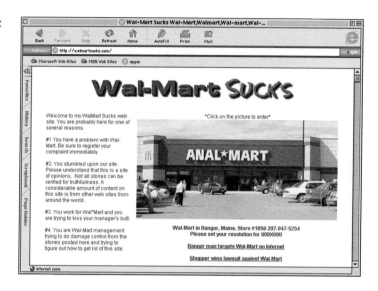

- Satirizing policy and management
- Soliciting employees, current and former, to vent publicly
- Serving as a gateway for complaints to regulators and media
- Confusing the public regarding which Web site represents the real organization[14]

  For instance:

www.untied.com	Target = United Airlines
www.walmartsucks.com	Target = Wal-Mart (Figure 19-5)
www.mcspotlight.org	Target = McDonald's

  A corporation's knee-jerk reaction—to call in the lawyers—hasn't resulted in great victory in battling the rogues. In perhaps the most celebrated case, Kmart sued www.kmartsucks.com, a Web site hosted by a disgruntled employee. The copyright infringement suit did succeed in forcing the site to change its name—to www.martsucks.com—but the considerable national media attention the suit received helped put the rogue Web site on the map.[15] Eventually, the embattled Kmart launched its own "good news only" site, called Kmartforever.com to combat the bashers.[16]

  Many organizations are now registering multiple URLs (domain names) to preclude access to them by others. Typically, what they register to preempt the troublemakers are names like:

  1. www.organizationsucks.com
  2. www.ihateorganization.com
  3. www.organisation.com (narrow spelling change)

  No technique is foolproof in the battle against rogue sites. The best response, therefore, is to keep such sites under close scrutiny as a regular public relations monitoring function (Figure 19-6).

- **Urban legends are yet another requisite for online monitoring.** There is a growing body of corporate horror stories that has emerged from bogus Internet rumors. Most are spread by e-mail at lightning speed across the country and the world. For example:
  - Upscale retailer Nordstrom was accused by an anonymous e-mailer of charging a $200 fee for its special cookie recipe. "Outrageous," cried the

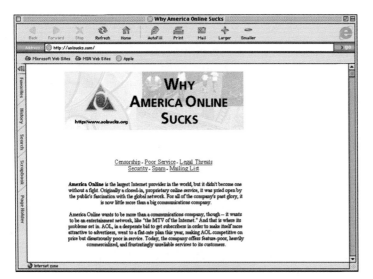

FIGURE 19-6 **Freedom of speech.** That's what the World Wide Web is all about, and that's why rogue Web sites such as this one are regularly monitored by companies like AOL.

thousands who received the e-mail. Also completely untrue. Nordstrom doesn't have a cookie recipe.

- Mrs. Fields also outraged the populace when an e-mail dispatch reported that she had sent a batch of her famous cookies to O. J. Simpson after he won his infamous murder trial. Also totally false.
- In perhaps the most pervasive and pernicious urban legend of all, retailer Tommy Hilfiger was, according to the official-sounding e-mail, evicted from *The Oprah Winfrey Show* by the lady herself, when the clothes manufacturer admitted his garments weren't made for "African Americans, Hispanics, and Asians" (Figure 19-7). The reality was that Tommy Hilfiger never met Oprah Winfrey, was never on her show, and certainly didn't design his clothing solely for white people.

The lesson: Public relations professionals must monitor the Web.

Subject: Tommy Hilfiger

MESSAGE:
I'm sure many of you watched the recent taping of the Oprah Winfrey Show where her guest was Tommy Hilfiger. On the show she asked him if the statements about race he was accused of saying were true. Statements like if he'd known African-Americans, Hispanics and Asians would buy his clothes he would not have made them so nice. He wished these people would *not* buy his clothes, as they are made for upper class white people. His answer to Oprah was a simple "yes". Where after she immediately asked him to leave her show.

FIGURE 19-7 **Stuff of legends.** Urban legends like this e-mail, discussing a bogus appearance by Tommy Hilfiger on *The Oprah Winfrey Show,* have become increasingly frequent as more people, some with questionable motives, access the Internet.

Product Promotion on the Internet

The Internet provides a virtual laboratory to mesh public relations, advertising, and marketing techniques to promote products. The shift from a "bricks" to a "clicks" economy was launched in full force during the nation's high-tech bubble economy of the last years of the 20th century.

On the positive side, buyers and potential buyers can access your information directly, without interference. On the negative side, you are competing with hundreds of thousands of other information providers for a visitor's attention. So promotional messages must be evocative, eye-catching, and brief.

One popular product promotion device is the "adlink." The adlink is a small display advertisement that promotes another site or page. The adlink may be less than a square inch or may stretch across the screen in a rectangular block. Usually, the adlink promotes another site with a tantalizing line of copy and bit of art. In addition, the adlink will automatically hyperlink, or connect you to the site referenced. Adlink hits are easily measured to determine their effectiveness. They can serve as excellent entry points for production promotional messages.

Online discussion groups provide another potential source of product promotion. As noted, the Internet is flooded with newsgroups. Smart organizations research newsgroups to see if their company's name, product's name, or specialty area is being mentioned. If it is, they respond by e-mailing participants with product information, thus increasing awareness and, hopefully, sales.

Web-based integrated marketing can create a new relationship with customers. Not only do good sites sell products, but they also offer information and education about those products. This is where public relations support comes in. At www.cdnow.com, for example, a potential record buyer can develop his or her taste in music. The site's "Album Advisor" recommends tune selections. By downloading an audio player, such as RealPlayer Plus, customers can play tracks from the albums they're interested in before they buy. Through another CDNow service, customers can create customized CDs, featuring only the tracks of the artists they want.[17]

All these product promotion opportunities introduced by a medium that communicates directly with the customer represent great potential for the practice of public relations.

Investor Relations on the Internet

The same is true with respect to investor relations, the public relations activity that deals with a company's stockholders and the communities—brokers and analysts—serving them.

Public companies increasingly use the Internet as a more controlled communications mechanism to reach potential investors. For the small investor, who has seen the flow of corporate information increasingly directed toward analysts, brokers, or larger institutions (thus forcing the SEC to impose Reg FD, discussed in Chapter 15), the Internet is an informational blessing. Investors can keep track of their investments and the markets in real time, without depending on intermediaries to inform them.

The government that watches over securities markets is less convinced that the Internet is such a blessing for investors. For one thing, securities regulators are worried about the anonymous nature of online information and the ability of short sellers and other people "whose interests stray far from fairness and transparency to misinform and corrupt the market for information."[18] For another, they cringe at the inadvertent Web-based mistakes that can send volatile markets into fits of apoplexy, such as the historic Emulex hoax of 2000 (see case study in chapter 15), which cost hapless investors millions and sent a 23-year-old college hoaxer to the slammer.

Despite government concerns, with the Internet now the number-one source of information for investors, the Web has opened up enormous new avenues of investor contact for public relations people.

Accordingly, companies have invested more heavily in the investor relations Internet space. Annual reports, earnings releases, and formal regulatory filings (called Edgar filings) all are included on corporate Web sites. Although the printed document remains the most prominent communications vehicle for most companies, online financial reporting, such as annual reports, are becoming more important for several reasons:

- Electronic versions are more easily integrated with other communications. Analysts can pull out financial data and spreadsheets in electronic reports, which don't depend on stapled pages. The electronic medium can reshape and update the report at the touch of a key, making analysis and study much easier.
- Electronic reports are less static than print reports. Electronic reports can help companies "come to life" before a stockholder or prospect. Graphics can be enhanced and sound and motion added. Not only might this provide a clearer portrait of a company but it also might help "sell" it to the viewer.
- Electronic versions are longer lasting. No longer are investors forced to keep dog-eared copies of printed reports in their files. Access to last year's report can be attained through the push of a button. Inevitably, in the 21st century, print annual reports will be subordinated to electronic versions.

In its purest form, using the Internet for investor relations can assure all stockholders, and not just large ones, an equal opportunity for access to corporate news and information.

Intranets, Extranets, CD-ROMs

Among the growing selection of additional cyberspace communications vehicles, three—intranets, extranets and CD-ROMs—deserve special reference.

- **Intranets,** discussed in Chapter 11, are a rapidly expanding internal communications phenomenon among U.S. companies. Generally defined, an intranet is an internal vehicle, which integrates communication with workflow, process management, infrastructure, and all other aspects of completing a job. Intranets allow communicators, management, and employees to exchange information quickly and effectively, much more quickly and effectively than any similar vehicle. Intranets, in other words, are Internets for specific organizations, designed to provide the necessary proprietary information to improve productivity.[19]
- **Extranets,** on the other hand, allow a company to use the Internet to communicate information to targeted external groups, such as the media, investors, vendors, key customers, Hispanic rap artists, left-handed female Good Morning America producers, or college soccer players with eye rings, for example. In segmenting the information in such a focused fashion—and protecting its dissemination through a complex series of firewalls—the targeted

audience is assured that the data will remain confidential. Only approved individuals can access the information by using an assigned ID and password, restricted to extranet users exclusively.

● **CD-ROMs** have become an important tool in public relations work. CD-ROM stands for Compact Disc Read Only Memory, which means you can read information from it but can't change that information. CD-ROMs boast great storage capacity, capable of holding 650 megabytes of information—the equivalent of 451 floppy discs. CD-ROMs can supply 72 minutes of sound and 20 minutes of video, not to mention text and graphics, to tell a full and rich story about a product, company, candidate, or issue. Public relations professionals have begun to dispatch CD-ROMs in place of print handouts—particularly releases, photos, and press kits—and videotapes. Indeed, whereas the VCR created the industry of bringing movies home and allowed greater access to information, the CD-ROM does the same thing but introduces one exciting extra element: interaction.

LAST WORD

In just a few short years, the Internet has evolved into an indispensable marketing tool for organizations and a favored weapon for angry customers, disaffected employees, and consumer activists bent on attacking those same organizations.[20]

As a consequence, mastering and monitoring the Internet have become a front-burner priority for public relations professionals.

The number of Americans over 16 years old who use the Internet has climbed to approximately 100 million, and the number of individuals making purchases online continues to rise dramatically.[21] Accordingly, American industry's 21st-century dash into cyberspace has sarcastically been compared to the gold rush of the 19th century, when prospectors panned for the elusive commodity that would make them rich.[22]

Not all the digital miners have found their fortune, and many in fact found "fool's gold" in their religious devotion to the Net. Indeed, the clear trend today is to pay for Internet content and, as opposed to the early days of the Net, to give little away for free.[23]

Despite the Net's fits and starts, the public relations profession must not take the new communications medium lightly. That means that knowing the new technology and becoming comfortable and competent with it is imperative for public relations practitioners.

Those who can blend the traditional skills of writing and media and communications knowledge with the online skills of the Internet will find a rewarding calling in the practice of public relations in the 21st century.

Discussion Starters

1. What is the status of the Internet and World Wide Web in public relations today?
2. How has the Internet impacted journalism? Commerce? Internal communications?
3. How has e-mail changed the ways people and organizations communicate?
4. What are the characteristics that make up a winning Web site?

5. How has the Internet influenced preferences of the media?
6. What elements might be included in a corporate newsroom site?
7. What is the impact of the "thread" on public companies?
8. What are the three types of newswires available to public relations people?
9. Why should public relations people monitor the Web?
10. What is the difference between an intranet and an extranet?

TOP OF THE SHELF

Shel Holtz

Public Relations on the Net
New York: AMACOM, 1999

This book's subtitle is about as direct, succinct, and thorough as public relations on the Internet should be: "Winning Strategies to Inform and Influence the Media, the Investment Community, the Government, the Public, and More!"

A five-time winner of the Gold Quill Award from the International Association of Business Communicators, Shel Holtz is not only a master of both subjects of his book—public relations and the Internet—but also of the synergistic relationship between the two.

At 322 pages, *Public Relations on the Net* is a veritable handbook, covering in detail such subjects as "The Principles of Influencing Audiences Online," "Monitoring Your Company or Client Online," "Media Relations," "Investor Relations," "Activism on the Internet," "Crisis Communication," "Going Directly to the Public," and "Measuring the Effectiveness of Your Online Efforts."

Appendices include "Working with IT Staff ("Who are these guys?")," "Writing for the Computer Screen," "Online Resources," and a seven-page "Recommended Reading."

CASE STUDY

Wassup at the Wassup Chat Room?

"Hip-hop geniuses."

That's what most people labeled the young founders of Wassup Jeans!, the nation's fastest-growing manufacturer of casual clothing.

Founded by young college graduates Serge "the Surger" Cornblatt and Hassan "Sheik" Jabuti, the idea for Wassup Jeans! was hatched in a West Islip, Long Island, garage. Friends since junior high school, Cornblatt and Jabuti envisioned a company built on being hip and edgy, in the Nike mold.

The two partners made an unlikely pair. Cornblatt, the son of a wealthy Long Island investment banker, and Jabuti, the son of Lebanese immigrants who ran a vegetable market, had big plans for their enterprise.

Using the contacts of Cornblatt's father, the pair raised start-up capital of $5 million and opened a retail store in Manhattan's hip Soho district. By importing inexpensive garments from India and Bangladesh, Cornblatt and Jabuti kept their costs down. Meanwhile, the sword and dagger Wassup Jeans! logo was advertised on billboards and busses all over town.

Within three years, Wassup Jeans! was the hottest, hippest company around.

1. New York celebrities, from Jay-Z to Robert DeNiro to David Letterman to P. Diddy Combs were all spotted in Wassup Jeans!.
2. Jennifer Lopez—JLo—sported Wassup Jeans! in her new movie, co-starring her latest love interest, Rob Schneider.
3. "Sheik" Jabuti was frequently mentioned in gossip columns as a denizen of all the hottest night spots.
4. The two founders were splashed on the front pages of leading business magazines, and the fame of the two "hip moguls" spread far and wide.

As a result of all this positive buzz, the company's initial public offering was oversubscribed, and Wassup Jeans! became a thriving public company, with thousands of shareholders and two very wealthy cofounders.

TROUBLE IN CHATVILLE

Upon becoming a public company, the scrutiny of Wassup Jeans! increased, particularly as consumers cut back spending and casual clothes companies began to do less well financially.

Not only did financial analysts and reporters begin to focus more closely on the company, but also nervous stockholders participated in greater numbers in online chats about the firm, its founders, and its fortunes in round-the-clock dialogue.

Although no one at Wassup Jeans! paid much attention to the chat rooms, the company began to receive some disturbing calls that rumors about it had begun to percolate online.

One morning Co-CEO Cornblatt paid a visit to the Yahoo! business chat room to gaze at the discussion surrounding Wassup Jeans! stock. He punched up the company's stock symbol, WSP, and his jaw dropped as he read the "thread."

From: Dissedman
Message-id: <20021216180717.26394. @gonzo1.aol.com>
I first bought WSP two years ago. The company is a dog, and the founders are crooks. Two spoiled brats, who've squandered their rich fathers' money. I think they're crooks.

-From: Tomtomakout
Message-id: <20021214215913.12567. @mbs.aol.com>
YOU'RE RIGHT. I WOULDN'T BUY THIS WITH YOUR SISTER'S DOWRY AND A HALF DEAD MULE. CORNBLATT IS A CROOK.

-From: GALPAL7348
Message-id: <20021212164502.01901.00003412@B08.aol.com>
Tom,
The real "crook" is Jabuti. His family has ties to Osama bin Laden and Al Queda. His parents hail from Riyadh. His father is still there, I believe as a biological chemist. If you catch my drift.

-From: AdGitOrangeman
Message-id: <20021130090617. @mbs-rdcey.aol.com>
I knew it. Jabuti traveled to Kenya, supposedly on "safari," just two years before the embassy bombings there. I had a feeling he and Cornblatt were shady characters. (Didn't Cornblatt hang around with the Goo Goo Dolls?!) I'm not buying those stinking jeans.

-From: carlabonhoff
Message-id: <200211271223453142. @mb-meroeol.com>

Even worse, they employ 11-year-old girls in sweatshops in Bangladesh to make their jeans, which they then sell here for 100 times the cost! They are sweatshop landords!

-From: GeeterMon3
Message-id: <20021127122142. @mb-meieaol.com>
Boycott the jeans. Sell the stock. These guys are terrorist sympathizers. They're anti-American and should be investigated.

-From: Schrambam
Message-id: <20021120225328. @mbs-m333333347.aol.com>
FBI is all over these guys. *60 Minutes* on CBS is doing an exposé on them. Company should be closed down within the year. They're fronts for Osama. Jabuti is a known Queda sympathizer, and Cornblatt is his money man. They'll be out of business soon, and if you hold the stock. . .

-From: Gezundheit8
Message-id:<20021129222057.00017924@df.aol.com>
. . . GOOD LUCK!

What Now?
Cornblatt was stunned.

The steady thread of accusations and innuendo was false.

1. "Sheik" Jabuti was American born. His parents came from Long Island, not Saudi Arabia.
2. Jabuti's father was a shop owner not a chemist. He despised Osama bin Laden and Al Queda as much as anyone else. And, certainly, the family had no "sympathy" for the terrorists.
3. The company didn't employ "sweatshop" laborers. True, the clothes were made overseas but by licensed, moderately paid employees.
4. He was unware that *60 Minutes* or any other TV program was doing an "exposé" on the company.
5. Finally, Cornblatt himself was no "crook." He and his partner had earned their money legitimately, through sweat equity. And he'd never even met the Goo Goo Dolls!

"We've got a real problem here," Cornblatt sadly explained to his partner. "If this spreads, it could kill Wassup Jeans!"

"What now?"

Questions

1. What's the first action the firm's founders should take in response to these online rumors?
2. How should they handle the discussion on the thread? Should they enter the online chat room? If your answer is "yes," should they do it anonymously or by name?
3. How should they handle the rumors of "sweatshop labor?"
4. How should they handle the rumors about a *60 Minutes* inquiry?
5. In general, what kind of public relations program would you recommend the company initiate?

An Interview with Deirdre Breakenridge

Deirdre Breakenridge

Deirdre K. Breakenridge is executive vice president of PFS Marketwyse, an integrated marketing communications firm headquartered in Totowa, New Jersey, that specializes in brand building. She is the author of *Cyberbranding: Brand Building in the Digital Economy*, published in 2001 by Prentice Hall PTR. Ms. Breakenridge's second book, *The New PR Toolkit*, will be published by Prentice Hall in 2003.

What is the role of the Internet in public relations today?

Although the word *revolutionize* was thrown around loosely during the heyday of the Internet, it does explain what has happened to the field of public relations. The Internet has freed the PR professional to be more of a strategic thinker and less of a paper shuffler. Technology allows PR professionals to work smarter, be more efficient, target audiences appropriately, access news 24/7, and be updated with media contacts and new PR resources at all times.

What is the best way for a company to use the Net for its communication?

In the past few years, the focus has centered on e-mail, opt-in or permission-based communication, and viral marketing. Of course, e-mail is the quickest and most efficient way to communicate a message, if and only if the recipient wants to receive the communication. With an opt-in strategy, companies ask their online visitors if they want to be a part of the regular communication on a daily, weekly, or monthly basis. Viral marketing is the "word of mouth" of the Internet. Viral marketing is as simple as including a button on a Web page that asks users if they would like to pass along information to a friend. Every time you see a button that says, "Send to a Friend" or "Tell a Colleague," you'll know viral marketing is at work.

How important is monitoring the Internet?

Monitoring the Internet is extremely important to a brand's reputation. With the ability for communication to spread like wildfire, monitoring may just be the key to tame the flames. Whether companies are using paid services such as CyberAlert, or eWatch, or they use choose to use their own legal department, searching the Net for positive and negative communication is invaluable. Companies need to know what their clients are thinking, what the media are reporting, what their competitors are doing, and who's speaking about them in less than favorable ways.

Should companies become involved in chat rooms that disparage them?

Opinions vary on whether or not companies should become involved in discussions in chat rooms. Sometimes it becomes extremely obvious to chat room participants when a representative of a company signs on and starts communicating. The best strategy might be to observe the communication to see how far it advances and then take the information back to the PR or marketing team to begin addressing the issues at hand. Making the wrong move or identifying yourself in a chat room as a member of the company that's being trashed may halt any further communication on the topic of interest.

What's the best way to craft a release for e-mail delivery to a reporter?

First, make sure that the reporters want to receive the e-mail. Have a subject line that catches their eye immediately and makes them believe that there is news in your release relevant to the subject matter they cover. The news release itself should never be sent as an attachment, unless you know the contact fairly well. Most reporters do not like to open attachments, which are often screened as junk mail. Many simply find it easier when the release is in the body of the e-mail. News releases should be developed the same way as off-line releases: treating every word as if it costs $50.

How important will the Internet be for the future of public relations practitioners?
The Internet will play a tremendous role in the future of the public relations practitioner. The Web keeps companies "in play" 24 hours a day, 7 days a week. Because information is available to reporters in any number of countries and individuals are always free to launch new message boards or Web sites, the PR practitioner's responsibilities will increase. The pace of technological change is not going to slow down. The Internet will cause PR people to listen more, learn more every day, and be open to new technological advances that affect their profession. PR professionals never stop and say, "I've learned enough today." On the contrary, the nature of the profession promotes continuous learning. Indeed, the Internet will add to the changes and challenges to prepare practitioners to be more proactive and responsive, the true definition of PR.

Suggested Readings

Bly, Robert, and Stephen Roberts. *Internet Direct Mail*. New York, NY: Contemporary Books, 2000.

Bonnett, Kendra. *An IBM Guide For Doing Business on the Internet*. New York: McGraw-Hill, 2000.

Chase, Larry. *Larry Chase's Need-to-Know Marketing Sites*, Web Digest for Marketers (www.wdfm.com), 2002. Carefully selected and annotated directory of 400 marketing Web sites divided into 33 categories.

Conner-Sax, Kierston, and Ed Krol. *The Whole Internet: The Next Generation*. Sebastopol, CA: O'Reilly & Associates, 1999.

Ellsworth, Jill M., and Matthew V. Ellsworth. *Marketing on the Internet*. New York: John Wiley & Sons, 1997.

Fidler, Roger. *Mediamorphosis: Understanding New Media*. Thousand Oaks, CA: Pine Forge Press, 1997.

Gralla, Preston. *How the Internet Works*, 6th ed. Indianapolis, IN: Que Corp., 2001.

Interactive Public Relations, biweekly published by Ragan Communications, 212 West Superior St., Chicago, IL 60610. Updates on public relations' progress on the Internet.

Janal, Daniel S. *The Online Marketing Handbook*. Crystal City, VA: Van Nostrand Reinhold, 1998.

Janal, Daniel S. *Risky Business*. New York: John Wiley & Sons, 1998. An eye-opening look at the numerous online threats that can wreak havoc with a business and about which public relations people should be aware.

Levinson, Jay Conrad, and Charles Rubin. *Guerilla Marketing Online*. Boston: Houghton Mifflin Co., 1996.

Marlow, Eugene. *Electronic Public Relations*. Belmont, CA: Wadsworth, 1996.

M. Booth & Associates. *Promoting Issues & Ideas: A Guide to Public Relations for Nonprofit Organizations*. New York: The Foundation Center, 1996. Excellent explanation of advantages of and requirements for designing a Web site for nonprofit organizations.

Negroponte, Nicholas. *Being Digital*. New York: Alfred A. Knopf, 1995.

O'Keefe, Steve. *Publicity on the Internet: Creating Successful Publicity Campaigns on the Internet and the Commercial Online Services*. New York: John Wiley & Sons, 1997.

SpinWARE. Miami, FL: SpinWARE Software Publishing, Inc., 1996. A computer software designed for public, media, and investor relations professionals. Assists in tracking media lists, distributing press releases and other messages by mail and fax, analyzing press clippings, and organizing schedules.

Thornburg, David D. <i>Putting the Web to Work</i>. San Carlos, CA: Starstrong Publications, 1996.

Vivian, John. <i>The Media of Mass Communications,</i> 4th ed. Boston: Allyn & Bacon, 2003.

Wong, Thomas. <i>101 Ways to Boost Your Web Traffic</i>. Intesync Web Professional Services, 2002.

Zyman, Sergio, and Scott Miller. <i>Building Brandwidth: Closing the Sale Online</i>. New York: HarperBusiness, 2000.

Notes

1. "Facts and Figures," www.internetindicators.com.
2. Sara Nathan, "Internet Economy Soars 68%," <i>USA Today</i> (October 27, 1999): 1.
3. Frank Rich, "The Future Will Resume in 15 Days," <i>New York Times</i> (December 18, 1999): A23.
4. Lawrence Weber, "Internet Rewrites Rules of Public Relations Game," <i>PR Tactics</i> (November 1996): 20.
5. Jerry Walker, "Middleberg/Ross Study Shows Internet Trends," <i>O'Dwyer's PR Services Report</i> (April 1999): 64.
6. "Corporate Websites Still Coming Up Short," <i>The Holmes Report</i> (February 18, 2002): 1–2.
7. Phaedra Hise, "Seven Common Mistakes in Developing Web Sites," @ <i>Issue</i> (Fall 1996): 26–31.
8. "Sticky Sites," Cybersavvy UK, www.webpr.co.uk/practical/sticky.asp.
9. Louis K. Falk, "Creating a Winning Web Site," <i>Public Relations Strategist</i> (Winter 2000): 39, 40.
10. Don Middleberg and Steven S. Ross, "The Middleberg/Ross Media Survey: Change and Its Impact on Communications," 2002.
11. Emily Benedek, "The Wealth of the Web," <i>Newsweek</i> (April 1, 2002): 70–72.
12. Charles Pizzo, "Shield Your Company's Reputation from the Dark Side of Cyberspace," P.R. PR, Inc., New Orleans, LA, cpizzo@compuserve.com.
13. newgate.com, NewGate Internet Web site.
14. Pizzo, "Shield your Company's Reputation."
15. "Control the Rogue," <i>Interactive Public Relations</i> (April 1998): 5.
16. "Where Do You Draw The line?" <i>Ragan Report</i> (September 30, 2002): 1.
17. Michael Krauss, "How the Web IS Changing the Customers," <i>Marketing News</i> (August 31, 1998): 10.
18. Bill Barnhart, "Nothing but Net: A Commentary on the Impact of the Internet on Investor Relations," <i>Journal of Corporate Public Relations–Northwestern University</i> (1996–1997): 16.
19. "What Do Intranets Look Like?" <i>Technology Workshop for Editors</i> (January 1997): 1.
20. Amelia Kassel, "Guide to Internet Monitoring and Clipping: Strategies for Public Relations, Marketing and Competitive Intelligence" in www.cyberalert.com/whitepaper.html.
21. "Surprise! Internet Use Increasing," <i>PR Tactics</i> (August 1999): 7.
22. Seth Schiesel, "Payoff Still Elusive in Internet Gold Rush," <i>New York Times</i> (January 2, 1997): C17.
23. Matt Richtel, "A Shift Registers in Willingness to Pay for Internet Content," <i>New York Times</i> (August 1, 2002): C4.

Chapter 20

Integrated Marketing Communications

It was "destiny."

Or, more specifically, "Destiny's Child." That's the pop singing group from which Pepsi-Cola chose its new spokeswoman in 2003—Beyonce Knowles, the group's frontwoman (Figure 20-1).

Knowles, who went "multimedia," with a film debut in Austin Powers in Goldmember and then in The Fighting Temptations, signed on to front for Pepsi in TV, radio, and Internet advertising. In addition, the cola company planned to sponsor a Knowles solo concert tour.

The good news for Knowles was less good for fellow pop idol, Britney Spears, whom Pepsi dropped in order to make room for Beyonce. (Perhaps the fact that Britney was caught on camera guzzling a rival can of Coca-Cola had something to do with her dismissal!) But with a net worth approximating $100 million, Britney seemed to take the Pepsi plunge with equanimity (Figure 20-1).

The Beyonce-Britney Pepsi sweepstakes was typical of organizations integrating show biz celebrities with their products to forge a unique promotional identity.

Pepsi, in fact, took the marketing integration platform to a new level in 2002, when it agreed to use the music from two alternative groups, Sev and Papa Roach, in its ads for Pepsi Blue. In return, the record companies involved timed new releases to the Pepsi commercials. And Pepsi got product placement in Sev and Papa Roach videos and piggybacked on radio airplay of the songs with Pepsi Blue promotions.[1]

Pepsi, of course, was not alone in using celebs.

- *Payless Shoe Source signed television personality Star Jones, who claimed to have 550 pairs of shoes, to be its "director of consumer style" and spokeswoman.[2]*
- *Wireless phone company T-Mobile International signed actress Catherine Zeta-Jones as its spokeswoman because of her "fiery character, hard work, and dedication."[3]*
- *Actor Michael J. Fox became a national spokesman for Parkinson's disease, with which he had been diagnosed.*

FIGURE 20-1 **In with the new, out with the old.** Pepsi-Cola named Destiny's Child singer Beyoncé Knowles (left) as its spokeswoman to replace Britney Spears, who after being caught on camera drinking Coke, was canned as Pepsi spokeswoman.

Using celebrities as spokespersons, inserting product placements in movies, sponsoring concerts, and a host of other publicity-seeking techniques are examples of integrated marketing communications—the intersection of public relations and publicity, advertising, sales promotion, and marketing to promote organizations, products, and services.

Those who decry "the fall of advertising and the rise of PR" are a bit overzealous.[4] Advertising ain't dead yet. Neither is marketing. But it is true that public relations and publicity integrated with these other disciplines are very much the rule in many organizations today.

Therefore, the need for "communications cross-training"—to learn the different skills of marketing, advertising, sales promotion, and public relations—becomes a requirement for all communicators.

The Customer's Perspective

Integrated marketing means approaching communications issues from the customer's perspective. Consumers don't separate promotional material or newspaper advertising or community responsiveness into separate compartments. They lump everything together to make judgments about services and organizations.

Integrated marketing expert Mitch Kozikowski lists six maxims that can guide public relations professionals through the communications cross-training process:

1. Integrated marketing communication is not about ads, direct-mail pieces, or public relations projects. It is about understanding the consumer and what the consumer actually responds to. In other words, behavioral change is the communicator's mission. If the customer doesn't act, the communicator—and the communication—have failed.
2. Organizations can't succeed without good relationships with their publics. Organizations need relationships with their customers that go beyond the pure selling of a product or service. They need to build relationships. As the world becomes more competitive in everything from health care to auto repair, from selling insurance to selling cereal, relationship building becomes more critical.

3. Integrated marketing communications require collaboration on strategy, not just on execution. This means that the entire communications function must be part of the launch of a product, service, campaign, or issue from its inception. In other words, communicators must participate in the planning of a campaign, not just in the implementation of communications vehicles.

4. Strategic plans must be clear on the role that each discipline is to play in solving the problem. The roles of advertising, marketing, and public relations are different; none of them can do everything by itself. Therefore, although advertising might control the message, and marketing and product promotion might provide support, it is public relations that should provide credibility for the product and, even more important, for the organization.

5. Public relations is about relationships. Public relations professionals can become proprietors of integrated marketing communications. Because the essence of public relations is building relationships between an institution and its publics, public relations professionals, perhaps more than any others, should lead the integrated marketing initiative. Public relations professionals have long understood the importance of the two-way communication that builds strong relationships with customers and others. Such an understanding is pivotal to the successful rendering of integrated marketing communications.

6. To be players in integrated marketing communications, public relations professionals need to practice more than the craft of public relations. Simply stated, public relations people must expand their horizons, increase their knowledge of other disciplines, and willingly seek out and participate in interdisciplinary skills building. In other words, public relations professionals must approach their task, in the broadest terms, to enhance customer relationships through a strategy of total communications.[5]

Elements of public relations—among them product publicity, special events, spokesmanship, and similar activities—can enhance a marketing effort. A new discipline—marketing communications—has emerged that uses many of the techniques of public relations. Although some may labor over the relative differences and merits of public relations versus advertising versus marketing versus sales promotion, the fact remains that a smart communicator must be knowledgeable about all of them.

Public Relations Versus Marketing

Marketing, literally defined, is the selling of a service or product through pricing, distribution, and promotion. Public relations, liberally defined, is the marketing of an organization. Most organizations now realize that public relations can play an expanded role in marketing. In some organizations, particularly service companies, hospitals, and nonprofit institutions, the selling of both individual products and the organization itself are inextricably intertwined.

Stated another way, although the practice of marketing creates and maintains a market for products and services and the practice of public relations creates and maintains a hospitable environment in which the organization may operate, marketing success can be nullified by the social and political forces public relations is designed to confront—and, thus, the interrelationship of the two disciplines.[6]

In the past, marketers treated public relations as an ancillary part of the marketing mix. They were concerned primarily with making sure that their products met the needs and desires of customers and were priced competitively, distributed widely, and promoted heavily through advertising and merchandising. Gradually, however, these traditional notions among marketers began to change for several reasons.

- Consumer protests about both product value and safety and government scrutiny of the truth behind product claims began to shake historical views of marketing.
- Product recalls—from automobiles to tuna fish—generated recurring headlines.
- Ingredient scares began to occur regularly.
- Advertisers were asked how their products answered social needs and civic responsibilities.
- Rumors about particular companies—from fast-food firms to pop-rock manufacturers—spread in brushfire manner.
- General image problems of certain companies and industries—from oil to banking—were fanned by a continuous blaze of media criticism.

The net impact of all this was that even though a company's products were still important, customers began to consider a firm's policies and practices on everything from air and water pollution to minority hiring. Beyond these social concerns, the effectiveness of advertising itself began to be questioned.

The increased number of advertisements in newspapers and on the airwaves caused clutter and placed a significant burden on advertisers who were trying to make the public aware of their products. In the 1980s, the trend toward shorter TV advertising spots contributed to three times as many products being advertised on TV as there were in the 1970s. In the 1990s, the spread of cable TV added yet another multichanneled outlet for product advertising. In the 2000s, the proliferation of Internet advertising intensified the "noise" and "clutter."

Against this backdrop, the potential of public relations as an added ingredient in the marketing mix has become an imperative.

Indeed, marketing guru Philip Kotler was among the first to suggest that to the traditional four Ps of marketing—product, price, place, and promotion—a fifth P, public relations, should be added. Kotler argued that a firm's success depends increasingly on carrying out effective marketing thinking in its relationships with 10 critical players: suppliers, distributors, end users, employees, financial firms, government, media, allies, competitors, and the general public. In other words, public relations.[7]

SIDEBAR

The Big 10

And the top 10 celebrity product endorsers for 2002 were all athletes, namely . . .

1. Tiger Woods—golf
2. Michael Jordan—basketball
3. Kobe Bryant—basketball
4. Anna Kournikova—tennis
5. Lance Armstrong—cycling
6. Shaquille O'Neal—basketball
7. Venus Williams—tennis
8. Serena Williams—tennis
9. Barry Bonds—baseball
10. Tony Hawk—skateboarding*

*"Tiger Woods on Top of List of Endorsers," *New York Times* (September 27, 2002): C6.

Product Publicity

To many, product publicity is the essence of the value of public relations.

In light of how difficult it now is to raise advertising awareness above the noise of so many competitive messages, marketers are turning increasingly to product publicity as an important adjunct to advertising. Although the public is generally unaware of it, a great deal of what it knows and believes about a wide variety of products comes through press coverage.

In certain circumstances, product publicity can be the most effective element in the marketing mix. For example:

- **Creating an identity.** Many organizations can't afford to blast out expensive advertising but must be "heard" above the din of thousands of competitors.
- **Introducing a revolutionary new product.** Product publicity can start introductory sales at a much higher level of demand by creating more awareness of the product.
- **Eliminating distribution problems with retail outlets.** Often the way to get shelf space is to have consumers demand the product. Product publicity can be extremely effective in creating consumer demand.
- **Small budgets and strong competition.** Advertising is expensive. Product publicity is cheap. Often publicity is the best way to tell the story. Sam Adams Boston Lager beer, for example, became a household word almost solely through publicity opportunities.
- **Explaining a complicated product.** The use and benefits of many products are difficult to explain to mass audiences in a brief ad. Product publicity, through extended news columns, can be invaluable.
- **Generating new consumer excitement for an old product.** Repackaging an old product for the media can serve as a primary marketing impetus.
- **Tying the product to a unique representative.** "Morris the Cat" was one answer to consumer uninterest in cat food. Ronald McDonald attended the Academy Awards ceremonies. On April Fool's Day, 1996, Taco Bell "bought" the Liberty Bell before announcing the ruse.[8] And then in 2001, the redoubtable Taco Bell raised the stakes even higher by aligning itself with a space station. (See accompanying Sidebar.)

Third-Party Endorsement

Perhaps more than anything else, the lure of third-party endorsement is the primary reason smart organizations value product publicity as much as they do advertising.

Third-party endorsement refers to the tacit support given a product by a newspaper, magazine, or broadcaster who mentions the product as news. Advertising often is perceived as self-serving. People know that the advertiser not only created the message but also paid for it. Publicity, on the other hand, which appears in news columns, carries no such stigma. Editors, after all, are considered objective, impartial, indifferent, neutral. Therefore, publicity appears to be "news" and is more trustworthy than advertising that is paid for by a clearly nonobjective sponsor.

Editors have become sensitive to mentioning product names in print. Some, in fact, have a policy of deleting brand or company identifications in news columns. Public relations counselors argue that discriminating against using product names

Taco Bell's Free Tacos Publicity Bull's-Eye

Few companies rival the creative Taco Bell when it comes to conjuring up ideas for product publicity.

The fast-food outlet, known for "thinking outside the bun," really outdid itself in the spring of 2001, when the Russian space station Mir was scheduled to land after 15 years in space.

Shortly before Mir was scheduled to touch down in the South Pacific, Taco Bell used a barge to tow a 40-foot-by-40-foot Taco Bell logo target out to sea off the eastern coast of Australia with the message, "Free Taco Here" (Figure 20-2).

FIGURE 20-2 **Inside the target, outside the bun.** Taco's Bell's South Pacific inducement for product publicity. (Courtesy of Taco Bell)

Contact:
Laurie Gannon or Carol Anawati
949-863-3915   FOR IMMEDIATE RELEASE

FREE TACOS FOR U.S. IF MIR HITS FLOATING *TACO BELL*® OCEAN TARGET

Taco Bell sets 40 by 40 foot target in South Pacific for Mir's Re-entry

IRVINE, CA, March 20, 2001 -- Taco Bell is offering a free taco to everyone in the U.S. if the core of the Mir space station hits a floating Taco Bell target placed in the South Pacific. Later this week, all eyes will be fixed on the sky in anticipation of the 150-ton space station's return to earth.

Taco Bell has created a 40 by 40-foot target, painted with a *Bell* bull's-eye and bold purple letters stating: "Free Taco Here." The floating target will be placed in the South Pacific Ocean off the coast of Australia in advance of Mir's descent.

"Taco Bell is capturing the imagination of millions of people as they eagerly await Mir's return to earth," said Chris Becker, vice president of brand communications, Taco Bell Corp. "If Mir rings our bell, we will offer a free taco to everyone in the U.S.," added Becker.

If the core of Mir hits the designated Taco Bell target upon its re-entry, every person in the U.S. will have an opportunity to obtain a coupon for a free taco, valid at participating Taco Bell restaurants. Coupon distribution, redemption and offer details will be made available to consumers on the Taco Bell website and in press materials should this event occur. Taco Bell has purchased an insurance policy to cover the anticipated cost of the free taco redemption should the core of Mir hit the target.

- more -

The company promised to give one free taco to each of America's 280 million citizens, if any section of the space station hit the target.

According to Laurie Gannon, Taco Bell's public relations director, "buzz marketing" (i.e., creating a "buzz" around a publicity event) was very much the objective of the Mir bull's-eye promotion.*

For any Buzz Marketing initiative to be successful, it must first be highly topical . . . for maximum exposure and impact," Gannon said. Tying a free taco to the Mir splashdown fit the bill perfectly, although Taco Bell took out an insurance policy worth "several million dollars" to cover itself in case Mir hit the target.

What immediately "hit the target" was the Taco Bell announcement of the potential payoff for every American—headlines, news reports, radio commentary—all "free" and all product publicity.

In the end, Taco Bell reported:

- Approximately 127,400,000 TV viewers
- 1,650 uses of Taco Bell video news releases by TV stations
- 188 U.S. markets
- 3 network news feeds

Also in the end (luckily for Taco Bell), the Mir came up thousands of miles short of its target (Figure 20-3).

So nobody won a free taco. But somebody got lots of free product publicity.

*Laurie Gannon, "Buzz Marketing," *Presentation at Ragan Communications Conference,* Chicago, IL, December 11, 2001.

FIGURE 20-3   The "bad" news.

Contact: FOR IMMEDIATE RELEASE
Laurie Gannon or Caroline Anawati
949-863-3915

SPACE STATION MIR-LY MISSES THE *TACO BELL®* TARGET

IRVINE, CA, March 23, 2001 – Even with millions of Americans chanting "TA-CO, TA-CO" as Mir plummeted to earth, it wasn't enough for the space station to hit the Taco Bell bull's-eye and deliver free tacos to America.

Since the Company announced the free taco offer on Monday, thousands of television, radio and print news reports have circled the globe. The Company's phone lines have rung off the hook and millions flocked to its Web site at www.tacobell.com to find more information.

"We captured the imagination and interest of millions of people around the globe and put a smile on their faces," said Chris Becker, vice president of brand communications, Taco Bell Corp. "We're disappointed that the space station Mir-ly missed our target, but we're happy people enjoyed the challenge and the fun personality that the Taco Bell brand is known for," added Becker.

Taco Bell Corp., a division of Tricon Global Restaurants Inc. (NYSE: YUM), is the nation's leading Mexican-style quick service restaurant chain serving tacos, burritos, signature Chalupas and Gorditas, nachos and other specialty items. Taco Bell serves nearly 40 million consumers each week in over 7,200 restaurants nationwide, generating $5.2 billion in system-wide sales.

# # #

FIGURE 20-4
Sticky subject. But also publicizable. When the Peanut Advisory Board wished to publicize its favorite product, it helped students at a high school in Peanut, Pennsylvania, create the world's largest peanut butter and jelly sandwich, measuring nearly 40 feet long.

does a disservice to readers, many of whom are influenced by what they read and may desire the particular products discussed. Counselors further argue that journalists who accept and print public relations material for its intrinsic value and then remove the source of the information give the reader or viewer the false impression that the journalist generated the facts, ideas, or photography.

Equally questionable are the public relations practitioners who try to place sponsored features without disclosing promotional origins. In other words, some companies will distribute cartoons or stories—either directly or through mail-order services—without identifying the sponsor of the material. Obviously, such a practice raises ethical questions. Understandably, editors do not soon forgive firms that sponsor such anonymous articles. One solution to achieve product recognition through the "endorsement" of objective editors is to create events that are certain to attract publicity (Figure 20-4).

Building a Brand

The watchword in business today is branding, creating a differentiable identity or position for a company or product.

In more traditional times, it took years for brands like Pepsi, Coke, McDonald's, Hertz, FedEx, and Wal-Mart to establish themselves. Today, with the advent of the World Wide Web, surviving Internet companies like Yahoo!, Amazon.com, eBay, and AOL have become household words in a historical nanosecond. Using integrated marketing communications to establish a unique brand requires adherence to the following principles.[9]

- **Be early.**   It is better to be first than to be best. This results from the "law of primacy," which posits that people are more likely to remember you if you were the first in their minds in a particular category. Whether yours is really

FIGURE 20-5 **Taking it to the streets.** Transportation displays to promote brands, such as this traveling Hershey's Kissmobile created by mobile marketing expert Marketing Werks, have become popular marketing devices for Web-based and non-Web companies alike. (Courtesy Marketing Werks)

the "first" brand is less important than establishing primacy in the minds of consumers.

- **Be memorable.** Equally important is to fight through the clutter by creating a memorable brand. There is no more competitive area in business today than the Internet. First, it's cheap. Second, it's accessible. Third, people use it. Hundreds of thousands of organizations, therefore, are fighting for recognition. So creating brand awareness requires boldness.

- **Be aggressive.** A successful brand also requires a constant drumbeat of publicity to keep the company's name before the public. Potential customers need to become familiar with the brand. Potential investors need to become confident that the brand is an active one. Indeed, more and more, marketers are "taking to the streets" to spread their message (Figure 20-5). The new competitive economy leaves little room for demure integrated marketing communications.

- **Use heritage.** Baby boomers are old. Gen Xers are getting older. And "heritage" is very much in vogue. This means citing the traditions and history of a product or organization, as part of building the brand. The hottest toys in the holiday season of 2002 were retreads from the 1980s—Care Bears, Teenage Mutant Ninja Turtles, and Cabbage Patch Kids (Figure 20-6). As society longs for nostalgia, heritage works.

- **Create a personality.** The best organizations are those that create "personalities" for themselves. Whose number one in rental cars? Hertz. What company stands for "overnight delivery?" FedEx. What's the East Coast

FIGURE 20-6 **Old faithfuls.** Chubby-faced Cabbage Patch Kids returned from oblivion to spark the craze for toy nostalgia. Post 9/11 Cabbage Patchers included a police officer and firefighter.

university that boasts the best and the brightest? Harvard. Or at least that's what most people think. The firm's "personality" should be reflected online and in all communications materials the organization produces.

As more and more companies each year attempt to bust through the advertising/marketing/Internet clutter by resorting to such marketing devices as banner ads, proprietary Web sites, free classified advertising, e-zines and e-mail marketing, the challenge to create a differentiable brand—either on or off-line—becomes that much more difficult.

Public Relations Integrated Marketing Activities

Beyond integrated marketing on the Web, a number of more traditional public relations activities are regularly used to help market products. These activities include article reprints, trade show participation, the use of spokespersons, and cause-related marketing.

Article Reprints

Once an organization has received product publicity in a newspaper or magazine, it should market the publicity further to achieve maximum sales punch. Marketing can be done through article reprints aimed at that part of a target audience—wholesalers, retailers, or consumers—that might not have seen the original article. Reprints also help reinforce the reactions of those who read the original article.

As in any other public relations activity, use of reprints should be approached systematically, with the following ground rules in mind:

1. Plan ahead, especially if an article has major significance to the organization. Ideally, reprints should be ordered before the periodical goes to press so that customers can receive them shortly after the article hits the newsstands.
2. Select target publics and address the recipients by name and title. This strategy will ensure that the reprint reaches the most important audience.
3. Pinpoint the reprint's significance. Accomplish this either by underlining pertinent information in the article, making marginal notes, or attaching a cover letter. In this way, the target audience will readily understand.
4. Integrate the reprint with other similar articles and information on the same or related subjects. Often several reprints can be combined into a single mailing piece. Also, reprints can be integrated into press kits and displays.

Trade Show Participation

Trade show participation enables an organization to display its products before important target audiences. The decision to participate should be considered with the following factors in mind:

1. *Analyze the show carefully.*   Make sure the audience is one that can't be reached effectively through other promotional materials, such as article reprints or local publicity. Also, be sure the audience is essential to the sale of the product. For example, how responsible are the attendees for the actual purchase?
2. *Select a common theme.*   Integrate public relations, publicity, advertising, and sales promotion. Unify all elements for the trade show and avoid, at all costs, any hint of interdepartmental rivalries.
3. *Make sure the products displayed are the right ones.*   Decide well in advance exactly which products are the ones to be shown.
4. *Consider the trade books.*   Often trade magazines run special features in conjunction with trade shows, and editors need photos and publicity material. Always know what special editions are coming up as well as their deadline schedules.
5. *Emphasize what's new.*   Talk about the new model that's being displayed. Discuss the additional features, new uses, or recent performance data of the products displayed. Trade show exhibitions should reveal innovation, breakthrough, and newness.
6. *Consider local promotional efforts.*   While in town during a trade show, an organization can enhance both the recognition of its product and the traffic at its booth by doing local promotions. This strategy involves visiting trade magazine editors and local media people to stir up publicity for the product during the show.[10]
7. *Evaluate the worth.*   Always evaluate whether the whole exercise was worth it. This involves counting, qualifying, and following up on leads generated as well as looking at other intangibles to see if marketing objectives were met.[11]

Use of Spokespersons

In recent years, the use of spokespersons to promote products has increased.

As pharmaceutical companies learned with embarrassment in 2001 (see "A Question of Ethics," this chapter), spokespersons shouldn't disguise the fact that they are advocates for a particular product. Their purpose is to air their sponsor's viewpoint, which often means going to bat for a controversial product.

Spokespersons must be articulate, fast on their feet, and thoroughly knowledgeable about the subject. When these criteria are met, the use of spokespersons as an integrated marketing tool can be most effective.

Lately, the use of spokespersons to promote products has become so crazed that in his rookie year professional basketball player Allen Iverson not only signed a $50 million multiyear contract for Reebok sportswear but also got stock on top of it. Then along came another rookie basketball phenom, Vince Carter, who walked away from a 10-year, $800,000 annual endorsement contract from Puma because the shoe company didn't quickly introduce a shoe line in the star's name.[12]

And the Nike-Adidas bidding for high school roundball pheenom Lebron James—the next "next Michael Jordan"—made the Iverson-Carter sweepstakes look like child's play. James signed with Nike in 2003 for $90 million (yeesh!).

FIGURE 20-7 **The champ.** George Foreman, celebrity spokesman without equal—for 137.5 million reasons!

Beyond question, however, the most lucrative spokesmanship contract in history belongs to former boxing champ George Foreman, who in 1999 sold his name and image to Salton, the maker of George Foreman's Lean Mean Fat-Reducing Grilling Machine (Figure 20-7). The price to Salton and payday for Mr. Foreman? $137.5 million.[13] Who says boxers are punchy?

Cause-Related Marketing

Public relations sponsorships tied to philanthropy are another effective integrated marketing device.

With the cost of print and broadcast advertising going up each year, companies increasingly are turning to sponsorship of the arts, education, music, festivals, anniversaries, sports, and charitable causes for promotional and public relations purposes.

Such cause-related marketing brings together the fund-raising needs of nonprofit groups with the business objectives of sponsoring companies. Toy company Zany Brainy sponsored contests to turn in "violent toys" and donated money to charity. Financial company Capital One's "Mascot of the Year" contest in 2003 was billed as a "scholarship competition," in which the best (good sportsmanship, community service, etc.) mascot—Penn State's Nittany Lion, Wisconsin's Bucky Badger, Georgia Tech's Yellow Jacket, and others—vied to see which mascot would emerge victorious at the Capital One Bowl.[14]

A QUESTION OF ETHICS

Heartfelt Advice or Hefty Fee?

Famed actress Lauren Bacall rarely is seen in public.

That's why it was big news in the spring of 2002, when she agreed to come on the NBC *Today* show to share the story of a friend who had gone blind because she hadn't been tested.

"It's frightening because it can happen very suddenly," Ms. Bacall lamented. She then mentioned a drug called Visudyne, a new treatment for the disease known as macular degeneration.

Only one thing was wrong with this picture.

Ms. Bacall never revealed that she was being paid to appear on the program by pharmaceutical giant Novartis, the maker of Visudyne.

"We realized people would accept what she was telling them," said the Novartis medical affairs director. "Our whole intent is to let people know they don't have to go blind."

Although few could argue with the purpose of the Novartis drug, many took issue with a third-party spokesperson failing to reveal who was paying her.

"It is highly problematic and may even be unethical," said one journalism professor.

After the Bacall appearance, actress Kathleen Turner appeared on CNN to discuss her battle with rheumatoid arthritis. She, too, failed to mention her appearance was paid for by Wyeth and Amgen, the marketers of the drug Embrel.

The Turner performance was the straw that broke the camel's back. Immediately, CNN announced a policy to disclose any financial tie between a celebrity and a company about whom the interviewee is speaking.

Although few journalists argued with the policy of using competent spokespersons to endorse products, they insisted on knowing whether such a spokesperson is getting paid to appear. Otherwise, said one consumer advocate, "It's basically lying and deceiving the public."*

*For further information, see "CNN Clamps Down on 'Stealth' Guests," *Jack O'Dwyer's Newsletter* (September 4, 2002): 3; Melody Petersen, "Heartfelt Advice, Hefty Fees," *New York Times on the Web* (August 11, 2002); and Melody Petersen, "CNN to Reveal When Guests Promote Drugs for Companies," *New York Times* (August 23, 2002): C1–2.

Such cause-related marketing will continue to grow in the 21st century. Middle-aged baby boomers, in particular, are more concerned about issues that affect their lives, like protecting the environment and aiding the less fortunate. This change in itself will drive the creation of events and decision-making by corporate sponsors.

In planning special events and cause-related marketing activities, public relations people should first determine what area will best suit their organization's particular marketing objectives—culture, sports, community sponsorship, entertainment, and so on. Once objectives are decided, cause-related marketing can significantly enhance the reception and overall sales of a product or institution.

In-Kind Promotions

When a service, product, or other consideration in exchange for publicity exposure is offered, it is called an "in-kind" promotion.

Examples of in-kind promotions include:

1. Providing services or products as prizes offered by a newspaper or charity in exchange for being listed as a cosponsor in promotional materials.
2. Providing services or products to a local business in exchange for having fliers inserted in shopping bags or as statement stuffers.
3. Providing services or products to doctors' offices, auto repair shops, or other businesses in exchange for having brochures prominently displayed.

4. Providing samples and gifts of products and services, along with sales literature.
5. Providing point-of-purchase displays, literature, events, demonstrations, and samples at the point where the customer decides on purchasing the product or service.
6. Providing posters of the product or service at well-trafficked locations.

The point of such in-kind promotions is to leverage the name and use of products and services, so that more potential buyers are exposed to the organization.

Public Relations Advertising

Traditionally, organizations used advertising to sell products. In 1936, though, a company named Warner & Swasey initiated an ad campaign that stressed the power of America as a nation and the importance of American business in the nation's future. Warner & Swasey continued its ads after World War II and thus was born a unique type of advertising—the marketing of an image rather than a product. This technique became known variously as institutional advertising, image advertising, public service advertising, issues advertising, and ultimately public relations—or nonproduct—advertising.

In the 1970s, opponents of American business began to flex their muscles, with ads critical of big business and its practices. Corporations responded with ads of their own that talked about social responsibility, equal employment hiring, minority assistance, and so on. This practice was labeled *image advertising*.

In the 1980s, the logical extension of image advertising was issues advertising, which advocated positions from the sponsor's viewpoint. Often these concerned matters of some controversy. Organizations, led by the outspoken Mobil Corporation—now, Exxon-Mobil—continued the practice of issue ads into the 2000s. Indeed, Mobil's practice of placing an issues ad on the Op-Ed page of the *New York Times* and other leading newspapers each Thursday, begun in the 1960s, is still going strong—although not every Thursday—in the new century.

In the 2000s, public interest groups have once again seized on the most pressing issues of the day and are running ads to characterize their opposition to government and business practices, often on controversial topics (Figure 20-8).

Purposes of Public Relations Advertising

Traditional public relations, or nonproduct, advertising—as opposed to image or issue positioning—is still widely used. Such advertising can be appropriate for a number of activities:

1. *Mergers and diversifications.*   When one company merges with another, the public needs to be told about the new business lines and divisions. Advertising provides a quick and effective way to convey this message.
2. *Personnel changes.*   A firm's greatest asset is usually its managers, its salespeople, and its employees. Presenting staff members in advertising not only impresses a reader with the firm's pride in its workers but also helps build confidence among employees themselves.
3. *Organizational resources.*   A firm's investment in research and development implies that the organization is concerned about meeting the future intelligently, an asset that should be advertised. The scope of a company's services also says something positive about the organization.

FIGURE 20-8 **Issues advertising.**
TomPaine.com, modeled in the best
traditions of pioneer public relations
pamphleteer Thomas Paine, wasn't afraid
to take on unpopular causes in its frequent
and prominent ads. (Courtesy
TomPaine.com)

4. *Manufacturing and service capabilities.*   The ability to deliver quality goods
   on time is something customers cherish. A firm that can deliver should
   advertise this capability. Likewise, a firm with a qualified and attentive
   servicing capability should let clients and potential clients know about it.
5. *Growth history.*   A growing firm, one that has developed steadily over time
   and has taken advantage of its environment, is the kind of company with
   which people want to deal. It is also the kind of firm for which people will
   want to work. Growth history, therefore, is a worthwhile subject for
   nonproduct advertising.

6. *Financial strength and stability.* A picture of economic strength and stability is one that all companies like to project. Advertisements that highlight the company's financial position earn confidence and attract customers and investors.

7. *Company customers.* Customers can serve as a marketing tool, too. Well-known personalities who use a certain product may be enough to win additional customers. This strategy may be especially viable in advertising for higher-priced products such as expensive automobiles or sports equipment.

8. *Organization name change.* With firms in industries from banking to consumer products to communications now either merging with each other or streamlining their operations, company names change—from AOL, Time, and Warner Brothers to AOLTime Warner; from Federal Express to FedEx; from Kentucky Fried Chicken to KFC. To burnish the new name in people's minds, a name change must be well promoted and well advertised. Only through constant repetition will people become familiar with the new identity.

9. *Trademark protection.* Companies such as Xerox, Kleenex, and Coca-Cola, whose products are household names, are legitimately concerned about the improper generic use of their trademarks in the public domain. Such companies run periodic ads to remind people of the proper status of their marks. In one such ad, a perplexed secretary reminds the boss, "If you had ordered 40 photocopies instead of 40 Xeroxes, we wouldn't have been stuck with all these machines!" (Figure 20-9). Ironically, Xerox, so worried about its name, lost its direction in the aftermath of the bubble economy and nearly lost its franchise.

XEROX

You can't Xerox a Xerox on a Xerox.

But we don't mind at all if you copy a copy on a Xerox copier.

In fact, we prefer it. Because the Xerox trademark should only identify products made by us. Like Xerox copiers and Xerox printing systems.

As a trademark, the term Xerox should always be used as an adjective, followed by a noun. And it's never used as a verb.

XEROX® is a trademark of XEROX Corporation.

Of course, helping us protect our trademark also helps you. Because you'll continue to get what you're actually asking for.

And not an inferior copy.

XEROX
The Document Company

FIGURE 20-9 **Too "household" a name.** Xerox was one company with the rare problem of a brand name that became so well known, it became a generic name for "copying."

10. *Corporate emergencies.*   Occasionally, an emergency situation erupts—a labor strike, plant disaster, or service interruption. One quick way to explain the firm's position and procedures without fear of distortion or misinterpretation by editors or reporters is to buy advertising space. This tactic permits a full explanation of the reasons behind the problem and the steps the company plans to take to resolve the dilemma.

21st-Century Integrated Marketing

Beyond advertising, marketing, and public relations techniques, integrated marketing, too, must keep pace with the ever-changing world of promotional innovations to help sell products and services. Selling products on the Internet, as noted, introduces a new spectrum of possibilities for public relations support. Communications professionals also must be familiar with such increasingly popular vehicles as infomercials, movie and TV product placements, as well as other promotional activities that stretch the bounds of ethics.

Infomercials

Infomercials were greeted with universal catcalls in the 1980s when they were introduced as program-length commercials, shamelessly hawking products.

Even today, the infomercial remains the Rodney Dangerfield of marketing, shunned and doubted for many reasons—state and federal investigations of infomercial producers, complaints about product performance, and, most important, the belief, still, that a lengthy commercial disguised as a conventional program—like a talk show, complete with theme song and studio audience—unfairly masks what has been described as "nothing more than a failed spiel."[15]

Nonetheless, infomercials remain strong for one reason: They work. Indeed, George Foreman's success with his grills is just one example. Between $1 billion and $2 billion worth of merchandise is sold each year—from dicing and slicing kitchen utensils to exercise paraphenalia to psychic hot lines—despite condemnation and even lawsuits. Celebrities from Cher to Martin Sheen to Suzanne Somers to Dionne Warwick have joined the growing parade of infomercial pitchmen.

TV-Movie Product Placements

Product placements in films and TV shows also are proliferating at a rapid rate.

The turning point in product plugs occurred three decades ago when M&M/Mars turned down filmmaker Steven Spielberg, when he offered to link M&Ms to the hero of his new movie; *E.T.* Reese's Pieces, however, took up the movie producer's offer, and the rest is history (Figure 20-10).

In the 21st century, product placements—also known as "embedded advertisements"—have become a more integral part of movies and TV shows.

1. In the 2002 Tom Cruise film *Minority Report,* 15 major brands, from Gap to Ben & Jerry's, paid a total of $25 million for the privilege of being featured.[16]
2. On CBS's *Survivor,* island-stranded contestants were offered Doritos and Mountain Dew as coveted "rewards."
3. Revlon paid the ABC soap opera *All My Children* to become a major plot line for three months' worth of episodes.

FIGURE 20-10 **The grandaddy.** This lovable alien professed his predilection for Reese's Pieces, and a new integrated marketing discipline was born.

4. And in perhaps the most unlikely product placement deal, Miller Beer traded 40 cases of Miller High Life with Johnny Knoxville, in exchange for being featured in Knoxville's movie *Jackass: The Movie.*

Such product placements have come a long way since Jerry Seinfeld did free "shout-outs" to Snapple and Junior Mints on his sitcom. Today, many companies consider product placements an integral part of their integrated marketing mix.

Questionable Integrated Marketing Tactics

In recent years, some companies' attempts to create publicity through integrated marketing techniques have gone too far.

In 2001, Columbia Pictures was discovered using fake movie reviews in its ads to hype upcoming pictures. The studio's advertising department created at least one bogus reviewer, "David Manning of The Ridgefield Press," and then plastered Manning's fictional reviews to movie ads. When the hoax was reported, parent Sony quickly labeled the deceit "an incredibly foolish decision" and immediately stopped the process.[17]

A week later, the studio further admitted that two employees had posed as fans in a TV testimonial for another Columbia Pictures movie. The two "fans" of the movie *The Patriot* were actually Columbia marketing employees.[18]

Such bogus practices are clearly unethical and wrong. But in a more fiercely competitive business environment, some companies may consider ethics "expendable" in order to enhance integrated marketing initiatives.

L A S T   W O R D

The key marketing question in the 21st century is, "How do we generate buzz?" How do we distinguish ourselves and get our voice heard in the midst of hundreds of thousands of competing voices?

To marketing expert Al Ries, who cut his teeth in the advertising industry, the answer is obvious. "In the past, it may have been true that a beefy advertising budget was the key ingredient in the brand-building process. . . . Today brands are born, not made. A new brand must be capable of generating favorable publicity in the media or it won't have a chance in the marketplace."[19]

In other words, says Ries, it is public relations and its attendant communications form—not advertising alone—that differentiate an organization, product, or issue. Ries makes this point also in his latest coauthored work, *The Fall of Advertising & The Rise of PR.*

Perhaps more precisely stated, what is needed now is an integrated approach to communications, combining the best of marketing, advertising, sales promotion, and public relations. Some public relations people feel threatened by such talk. The thought of working closely with marketing, advertising, direct mail, sales promotion, and database marketing specialists worries them.[20] They fear the subjugation of the practice of public relations to these other disciplines.

Such fears are baseless.

The clear marketing need now for organizations and those who serve them is to build lasting client relationships.

This means that a successful communications professional must be knowledgeable about all aspects of the communications mix. Integrated marketing communications, then, becomes paramount in preparing public relations professionals for the challenges of the 21st century.

Discussion Starters

1. What is meant by integrated marketing communications?
2. Describe the differences among advertising, marketing, and public relations.
3. What is meant by third-party endorsement?
4. In what situations is product publicity most effective?
5. Describe the pros and cons of using a well-known individual as a spokesperson.
6. What is cause-related marketing?
7. How can integrated marketing help build a brand?
8. What are the purposes of public relations advertising?
9. What stimulated the reemergence of public relations advertising in the 1990s?
10. What are infomercials? Product placements?

T O P   O F   T H E   SHELF

Al Ries and Laura Ries

The Fall of Advertising & The Rise of PR. *HarperBusiness, 2002*

The cover of this book features a deflated sock puppet, symbolic of the failure of Pet.com's sock puppet ads, which in turn is symbolic of the limitations of advertising, especially compared with the fact that skillful public relations is what sells.

The father-daughter writing team argues that public relations should be used instead of advertising to launch new brands. Once a brand is established, advertising may then be used to maintain the brand in the consumer's mind. They cite a number of brands—Palm, Starbucks, the Body Shop, Wal-Mart, Red Bull, and Zara—which have been built with virtually no advertising.

C A S E   S T U D Y

Giving George Some Teeth

On September 11, 2001, the terrorists hit the World Trade Center and the Pentagon. And in the process, they wounded George Washington.

Or, more specifically, they did severe psychic damage to Washington's home on the Potomac, just south of Washington, DC. Attendance at Washington's Mount Vernon home plummeted 50 percent after September 11 and stayed down for months.

Because most of Mount Vernon's visitors were school groups and because most school trips were canceled in the wake of September 11, Mount Vernon had to do something radical to restore its image as a historical tourist destination.

And so it added "teeth" to its program.

Or, more specifically, it exhibited for the first time George Washington's famous false teeth.

Exhibiting the famous wooden chompers was just part of Mount Vernon's ambitious integrated marketing campaign, initiated by Executive Director James C. Rees.

Among the marketing tools that Mr. Rees and his associates introduced to convert the image of the aloof "Father of Our Country" to a swashbuckling action hero:

1. Holograms
2. Computer imagery
3. Surround-sound audio programs
4. A live action film made by Steven Spielberg's production company in a theater equipped with rumbling seats and pipes that shoot battlefield smoke into the audience

The post–September 11 integrated marketing program followed a first foray that commemorated the 200th anniversary of President Washington's death. That, too, was an integrated marketing extravaganza that reinvigorated attendance. Here's what was done.

THE BACKGROUND

George Washington is the most familiar face in American history (Figure 20-11). If we're lucky, we see him every day when we open our wallets.

President George is a public relations professional's dream: a client with instant, universal name recognition. But getting people to focus on and appreciate Washington's importance is quite another matter.

Fifty years ago, George Washington's portrait hung in virtually every classroom in the nation. Thirty years ago, George Washington's birthday was an important national holiday, complete with a day off and commemorative parades. Today, alas, this is no longer the case. Indeed, some locales—New Orleans is a prominent one—have even taken to removing Washington's name from schools because he was a slave owner.

As the century ended, the problem of our first president's fading recognition was a particularly urgent one for the people responsible for managing and staffing historic Mount Vernon (Figure 20-12). Faced with shrinking attendance, due in part to an overall decline in America's interest in history museums, Mount Vernon officials contemplated steadily dwindling revenues from entrance fees.

Educational surveys provided the early warning signs:

FIGURE 20-11 **The big guy.**

- Half of America's children couldn't name the purpose of the Declaration of Independence
- Only 7 percent of fourth graders could identify "an important event" that took place in Philadelphia in 1776
- Only six of 10 children knew why the Pilgrims came to America
- Seven of 10 fourth-grade students believed that Illinois, California, or Texas were among the 13 original colonies

Clearly, Mount Vernon had a problem.

THE CHALLENGE

The "Big Guy" had lost his importance in the minds of many Americans.

To change perceptions about Mount Vernon and George Washington required the full panoply of communications tools: partners, programs, publications, exhibitions, special events, and lots of media attention. That, in essence, was the challenge.

FIGURE 20-12 **The homestead.**

THE HOOK

With society moving at warp speed, people needed a reason to slow down and learn more about George Washington.

They needed a "hook."

The hook became the 200th anniversary of Washington's death, December 14, 1999. Critics, upon hearing of the hook, warned that celebrating someone's death was not only morbid and depressing but, frankly, wouldn't work.

FIGURE 20-13   **The logo.**

FIGURE 20-14   **The death.**

FIGURE 20-15   **The death scene.**

THE LOOK

An early decision was to create a special logo for the bicentennial anniversary (Figure 20-13).

This approach was so innovative that it attracted a front-page story in the *New York Times,* "Calling Up the P.R. Troops for the Father of His Country." The story talked about how $3 million would be spent on the public relations face-lift. Mount Vernon's celebration was off and running. (Three years later, Mount Vernon generated another *Times'* lead story, "George Washington: Mr. Excitement?")

THE PARTNERS

Part of Mount Vernon's strategy was to enlist respected partners to help share the burden of mounting a major bicentennial celebration (Figure 20-14). (Mount Vernon officials learned early not to "celebrate" Washington's death but rather to celebrate his life and "commemorate" his death.)

Other patriotic groups were recruited to participate, and the Ford Motor Company, which had been a long-standing supporter of Mount Vernon, agreed to become a major partner.

THE PROGRAM

Armed with a hook, a look, money, and committed partners, Mount Vernon officials now needed "substance"—a program to celebrate, uh, commemorate.

They began, fittingly, with research, polling historians, surveying their publics, and relying on historical facts. They met with numerous experts to ensure historical accuracy of the programs contemplated. They discussed the delicate balancing act between morbid and educational, even including a facsimile of the room where Washington was bled four times with crude instruments and ultimately died (Figure 20-15).

Most of all, they set out to design events that would overcome the "George Washington boring" image and the Mount Vernon "been there, done that" syndrome.

THE PREPARATION

To mount a national exhibition, historic Mount Vernon had to literally be transformed. Buildings were painted, rooms restored, and acquisitions made. Enthusiasm among staff members was contagious.

THE PROMISE

Visitors were promised that, if they came to Mount Vernon, they would view an all-new property, including 100 different, original objects in Washington's home. To do this, Mount Vernon had to borrow most of the valuable artifacts from sister institutions.

In the process, the Mount Vernon board had to install a state-of-the art climate control, which angered some who believed authenticity would be ruined with such a system.

With the system in place, however, the museum was able to borrow and display rare items, such as Washington's last will and testament and his presidential desk (Figure 20-16).

THE PLAN

The first-ever traveling exhibition, "Treasures from Mount Vernon," was launched. It pictured Washington as a friend, father, and statesman.

Smaller exhibitions also were staged, and objects were loaned to other institutions. A 16-page bicentennial community celebration planner was mailed to 50,000 communities to help them stage their own celebrations. Nearly 1,000 did just that.

The U.S. Postal Service designed a special stamp and postcard. The U.S. Mint designed a commemorative coin. The governors of 38 states sponsored special Washington bicentennial proclamations. Three pieces of original music and nine new Washington statues were commissioned around the celebration.

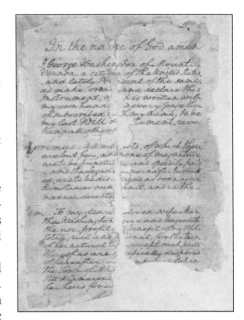

FIGURE 20-16 **The will.**

THE RESULTS

Mount Vernon closed the year with more than 1 million visitors, its highest attendance in two decades. Mount Vernon was featured in 10 articles in the *New York Times*, 25 in the *Washington Post*, five in *USA Today*, two in the *Wall Street Journal*, and at least one in the top 10 newspapers in the nation. Major features were run on *CBS Sunday Morning*, ABC's *Good Morning America, The CBS Evening News*, CNN, and C-Span. Major articles appeared in magazines such as *New Yorker, Modern Maturity, Colonial Homes,* and *Virginia Cavalcade*, which devoted an entire issue to the "Father of Our Country."

When the celebration ended with the reenactment of Washington's funeral (Figure 20-17), attended by the president's descendants and relatives of the original pallbearers—all dressed in 18th-century

FIGURE 20-17 **The tomb.**

mourning attire—the words of one of Washington's greatest admirers were recalled. Abraham Lincoln once said:

> Washington is the mightiest name of earth . . . To add brightness to the sun or glory to the name of Washington is alike impossible. Let none attempt it. In solemn awe pronounce the name, and in its naked deathless splendor leave it shining on.

The integrated marketing success of 1999 gave Mount Vernon's elders high hopes that a similar initiative in the 21st century will put new teeth in George Washington's popularity.

Questions

1. What was the public relations downside of launching such a massive integrated marketing program for Mount Vernon?
2. What other integrated marketing communications elements might the organizers have considered to reinforce the bicentennial?
3. How important was publicity in the program to restore Washington's image?
4. What follow-up programs to continue the bicentennial momentum might Mount Vernon consider?
5. Mount Vernon is using the Internet as part of its integrated marketing communications strategy (www.mountvernon.org.). What special events are being prominently promoted on the homepage? What is the purpose of the guest book on this site?

For further information see Stephen Kinzer, "George Washington: Mr. Excitement?" *New York Times* (July 29, 2002): E1-3; and Craig Wilson, "It's Like Pulling Teeth to get Visitors to Mount Vernon," *USA Today* (November 9, 2001): D-1.

TIPS FROM THE TOP

An Interview with Patrice Tanaka

Patrice Tanaka

Patrice Tanaka cofounded PT&Co. in 1990, upon completing a successful management buyback of her public relations firm from former parent company, Chiat/Day, Inc. Advertising. Over more than a decade, Ms. Tanaka has led PT&Co. to become one of the nation's leading independent public relations firms. The agency was rated the "#1 hot creative shop" in the country by *Inside PR* magazine and saluted by *Working Mother* magazine as one of "15 family-friendly workplaces in America."

What part does public relations play in the marketing mix?

It's not just another "good-to-have-if-you-can-afford-it" element of an integrated marketing program. The rightful role of public relations is as the key driver in establishing a brand's credentials and credibility through the objective, third-party endorsement of the media and other opinion leaders.

What is the role of other elements of the marketing mix, including advertising and direct marketing?

The role of the non-PR elements of the marketing mix is to more broadly disseminate to target audiences the credibility and "distinctions" conferred upon the brand by the media and other opinion leaders.

Because the non-PR elements of the marketing mix involve "paid for" media space/time, they can deliver "frequency" of message delivery that PR often cannot. In doing so, the non-PR elements of the marketing mix can provide valuable ongoing support for a brand.

What is the best way to integrate public relations into the marketing mix?

Public relations representatives must be at the table from the beginning. It is not good enough to bring PR into the discussion *after* the rest of the brand team has been convened and has already decided upon the marketing strategy. Brand marketers who operate in this fashion are not unleashing the full potential of what an integrated marketing approach can yield.

An example of the multiplier effect of a largely PR-driven program versus an integrated marketing program was a sales promotion that we created for

Godiva Chocolatier to generate awareness and trial of the brand's Valentine's collection. The "Chocolates & Diamonds" promotion was simple: seeding boxes of Godiva's Valentine's collection with certificates for diamond jewelry. By publicizing Godiva chocolates, diamond jewelry, and Valentine gift giving, we generated tremendous media coverage, totaling nearly 150 million consumer impressions in the month leading up to Valentine's Day, Godiva's single busiest selling occasion. The publicity our agency generated was responsible for producing a 15 percent increase in sales for Godiva compared to the previous Valentine's Day period.

Is public relations necessary in every marketing campaign?

It is critical for marketing campaigns involving new product launches and assignments involving repositioning and revitalizing brands—all of which have inherent "news" or the opportunity to create news.

Public relations is probably less effective for promoting product line extensions, especially if there's not much inherent news value, if it's a product category that is not covered extensively by the media, if it's a "me too" product, or if the budget is very modest.

What's the value of public relations in integrated marketing?

I often like to say that "PR is the Hamburger Helper of the marketing mix." What PR can do is s-t-r-e-t-c-h marketing dollars. A marketer may not be able to advertise in every media outlet that might reach a brand's target audience, but public relations programs can generate editorial coverage in media outlets that a brand can't afford to advertise in.

The ultimate goal of brand PR is to generate ringing endorsements from the media and other influentials that can really help clients to move the needle on awareness and trial.

Suggested Readings

Aaker, David A. *Building Strong Brands*. New York: The Free Press, 1995. Predicts over the next three decades there will be an unmitigated "battle of the brands."

Albrecht, Karl. *The Only Thing That Matters: Bring the Power of the Customers into the Center of Your Business*. New York: Harper Business, 1993.

Belch, George, and Michael Belch. *Advertising and Promotion, An Integrated Marketing and Communications Perspective*, 5th ed. New York: McGraw-Hill, 2000.

Caywood, Clarke L., ed. *The Handbook of Strategic Public Relations and Integrated Communications*. New York: McGraw-Hill, 1997.

Corporate Advertising Practices. New York: Association of National Advertisers, 1991.

Fowles, Jib. *Advertising and Popular Culture*. Thousand Oaks, CA: Sage, 1996.

Frank, Robert H., and Philip J. Cook. *The Winner Take All Society*. New York: The Free Press, 1996. A critical look at a marketing society that encourages economic waste, growing economic inequality, and senseless consumption.

Gregory, James R., and Jack G. Wiechmann. *Marketing Corporate Image*. New York: NTC Business Books, 1998.

Harris, Thomas L. *The Marketer's Guide to Public Relations*. New York: John Wiley & Sons, 1993.

Harris, Thomas L. *Value-Added Public Relations: The Secret Weapon of Integrated Marketing*. Lincolnwood, IL: NTC Business Books, 1998.

Hartman, Jason. *Become the Brand of Choice: How to Earn Millions Through Relationship Marketing*. Greensboro, NC: Lifestyles Press, 1999.

Janal, Daniel S. *Online Marketing Handbook*. New York: Von Nostrand Reinhold, 1998. How to sell, advertise, publicize, and promote products on the Internet.

Janal, Daniel S. *The Online Marketing Handbook: How to Promote, Advertise and Sell Your Products and Services on the Internet*. New York: John Wiley & Sons, 1996.

Marconi, Joe. *Reputation Marketing.* New York: NTC Business Books, 2001.

Mingo, Jack. *How the Cadillac Got Its Fins.* New York: Harper Business, 1995, out of print. Case histories behind the invention and marketing of famous products.

Ogilvy, David. *Confessions of an Advertising Man.* New York: Macmillan, 1963.

Parmerlee, David. *Preparing the Marketing Plan.* New York: AMA Management Services, 2000.

Ogden, James. *Developing a Creative and Innovative Integrated Marketing Communications Plan: A Working Model.* Upper Saddle River, NJ: Prentice-Hall, 1998.

Percy, Larry. *Strategies for Implementing Integrated Marketing Communications.* Lincolnwood, IL: NTC Business Books, 1997.

Ries, Al, and Laura Ries. *The 22 Immutable Laws of Branding: How to Build a Product or Service into a World-Class Brand.* New York: HarperCollins, 1998.

Ritchie, Karen. *Marketing to Generation X.* New York: Lexington Books, 1995. Foreshadowing the interactive, integrated marketing communications in the 21st century.

Schmitt, Bernd, and Alex Simpson. *Marketing Aesthetics: The Strategic Management of Brands, Identity and Image.* New York: The Free Press, 1997.

Schultz, Don E., Stanley I. Tannenbaum, and Robert F. Lauterborn. *Integrated Marketing Communications: Putting It Together and Making It Work.* Lincolnwood, IL: NTC Business Books, 1998.

Spataro, Mike. "Net Relations: A Fusion of Direct Marketing and Public Relations." *Direct Marketing* (August 1998): 16ff. Companies must use the Internet as an essential part of their marketing mix.

Notes

1. Theresa Howard, "Beat Is on for Pepsi," *USA Today* (August 28, 2002): 3B.
2. Stuart Elliott, "New Kind of Celebrity Promotoer Says the Words and Has Her Say," *New York Times* (November 25, 2002): C1–11.
3. A Good Fit," *Ragan's PR Intelligence Report* (September 2002): 1–4.
4. Al Ries and Laura Ries, *The Fall of Advertising & The Rise of PR* (New York: Harper Business, 2002): 251.
5. Mitchell Kozikowski, "The Role of Public Relations in Integrated Marketing Public Relations," address presented to the National Conference of the Public Relations Society of America, November 15, 1993, Orlando, FL.
6. Colloquium of Marketing and PR Spokespersons Agrees Organizations Suffer When Turf Wars Occur," *Public Relations Reporter* (February 13, 1989): 1.
7. Tom Harris, "Kotler's Total Marketing Embraces MPR," *MPR Update* (December 1992): 4.
8. Judann Pollack, "New Marketing Spin: The PR 'Experience,' " *Advertising Age* (August 5, 1996): 33.
9. Julie McHenry, "Building Brands on the Web," *Tactics* (November 1999): 15, 16.
10. Susan Friedman, "Tips for Internal and External Trade Show Visitors," *Business Marketing* (June 1995).
11. Kathy Burnham, "Trade Shows: Make Them Worth the Investment," *Tactics* (September 1999): 11.
12. Sam Walker, "NBA Star Cries Foul, Walks Away from Puma Shoe Deal," *Wall Street Journal* (December 1, 1999): B2.
13. Richard Sandomir, "A Pitchman with Punch," *New York Times* (January 21, 2000): C1, 4.

14. Mascots Is Lion King?" *Newsweek* (November 25, 2002): 11.

15. Stuart Elliot, "Some Big Marketers Join Audience for Infomercials," *New York Times* (June 5, 1992): D9.

16. Megan Turner, "Ads Nauseum," *New York Post* (June 24, 2002): 33.

17. John Horn, "The Reviewer Who Wasn't There," *Newsweek* (June 11, 2001): 8.

18. Sarah Tippit, "Studio: Workers Posed as 'Patriot' Fans," Reuters (June 15, 2001).

19. Al Ries and Laura Ries, "The Power of Publicity," *Public Relations Strategist* (Winter 1998): 19.

20. Integrated Marketing: Is It PR's Nemesis or Salvation?" *O'Dwyer's PR Services Report* (January 1995): 1.

Chapter 21

Crisis Management

On December 18, 2002, Trent Lott, Republican of Mississippi, the most powerful man in the U.S. Congress, reaffirmed that he intended to serve out his term as Senate majority leader, despite making a well-publicized racially insensitive comment.

Two days later, Senator Lott, through a spokesperson, resigned his Senate leadership position, the victim of one of the most sudden and dramatic falls from grace in recent political history. (See the case study at the conclusion of this chapter.)

Crisis, which public relations counselor James Lukaszewski once described as "unplanned visibility," can strike anyone at any time.[1] Trent Lott's 2002 blues were but the most recent example of sudden, unexpected, yet fatal crisis.

Indeed, in the new century, among the most well-regarded and highest-paid professionals in public relations are those who have achieved this status through their efforts in attempting to "manage" crises.

In a world of instantaneous communications, round-the-clock cable news commentary, tabloid news journalism, and exploding communications challenges, the number and depth of crises affecting business, government, labor, nonprofits, and even private individuals have expanded exponentially.

- *The September 11, 2001 attacks on America opened the door to a whole new level of violence aimed at defenseless civilians, putting government officials at all levels on constant alert.*
- *The business scandals of 2002, affecting some of the most prominent corporate names from Enron to Worldcom to Martha Stewart, from Solomon Smith Barney to Merril Lynch to George Soros, introduced the notion that every corporation must be crisis ready.*
- *In the nonprofit area, the American Red Cross was rocked by crisis after a special fund established for September 11 victims went instead for other purposes (see "A Question of Ethics" in this chapter). The 2002 Salt Lake City Olympic Games were marred by the biggest "fixing" scandal in history, when Russian organized crime figures bribed judges to vote for the Russian ice skating pairs contestants.[2]*
- *In the area of religion, the pedophile priest scandals of 2002 brought shame and suspicion to the Catholic Church.*

- *Political crises—from former Senate Majority Leader Lott's errant remark flameout to former SEC Chairman Harvey Pitt's forced resignation to former Congressman Gary Condit's demonization—seem like weekly occurrences.*
- *Even in public relations itself, when a car driven by New York publicist Lizzy Grubman mowed down Long Island nightclub goers in 2002, the crisis was page-one news for weeks.*

And these are but the tip of the iceberg—a very few of the hundreds of small and large crises that afflict elements of society today in ever-expanding magnitude (Figure 21-1).

No wonder when public relations professionals are asked what subject they want covered in midcareer seminars, "crisis communications" invariably heads the list. Helping to manage crisis is the ultimate assignment for a public relations professional. Smart managements value public relations advice in developing an organization's response not only to crises but also to public relations issues in general. Companies have created executive posts for "issues managers," whose task is to help the organization define and deal with the political, economic, and social issues that affect it.

The list of such issues—and of the crises they often evoke—is unending. In the 21st century, society is flooded with front-burner issues that affect individuals and organizations. From war to peace, poverty to abortion, discrimination to downsizing, environmentalism to energy conservation, the domain of issues management has become increasingly important for public relations professionals.

Issues Management

The term *issues management* was coined in 1976 by public relations counselor W. Howard Chase, who defined it this way:

> Issues management is the capacity to understand, mobilize, coordinate, and direct all strategic and policy planning functions, and all public affairs/public relations skills, toward achievement of one objective: meaningful participation in creation of public policy that affects personal and institutional destiny.[3]

Issues management is a five-step process that:

1. Identifies issues with which the organization must be concerned
2. Analyzes and delimits each issue with respect to its impact on constituent publics
3. Displays the various strategic options available to the organization
4. Implements an action program to communicate the organization's views and to influence perception on the issue
5. Evaluates its program in terms of reaching organizational goals

Many suggest that the term *issues management* is another way of saying that the most important public relations skill is "counseling management." Others suggest that issues management is another way of saying "reputation management"—orchestrating the process whose goal is to help preserve markets, reduce risk, create opportunities, and manage image as an organizational asset for the benefit of both an organization and its primary shareholders.[4]

If you can't do a thing about the way you look, call us.

Beauty is only skin deep. But if you're a battered woman, your bruises go straight to the heart. And you can make up, but it never lasts. You're not alone. One out of every two women in America will be abused by a man who says he loves her. You deserve our help. So do your kids. Call Rose Brooks' 24-hour crisis line at **861-6100**. Because you can't keep turning the other cheek.

 Rose Brooks
For Battered Women and Their Children

FIGURE 21-1 **Societal issues.** In a day of managed care and more competitive hospitals, health care institutions have accelerated communications appeals to the public to deal with individual crises.

In specific terms, issues management encompasses the following elements:

● **Anticipate emerging issues.** Normally, the issues management process anticipates issues 18 months to three years away. Therefore, it is neither crisis planning nor postcrisis planning but rather precrisis planning. In other words, issues management deals with an issue that will hit the organization a year later, thus distinguishing the practice from the normal crisis planning aspects of public relations.

● **Identify issues selectively.** An organization can influence only a few issues at a time. Therefore, a good issues management process will select several—perhaps 5 to 10—specific priority issues with which to deal. In this way, issues management can focus on the most important issues affecting the organization.

● **Deal with opportunities and vulnerabilities.** Most issues, anticipated well in advance, offer both opportunities and vulnerabilities for organizations. For example, in assessing promised federal budget cuts, an insurance company might anticipate that less money will mean fewer people driving and, therefore, fewer accident claims. This would mark an opportunity. On the other hand, those cuts might mean that more people are unable to pay their premiums. This, clearly, is a vulnerability that a sharp company should anticipate well in advance.

● **Plan from the outside in.** The external environment—not internal strategies—dictates the selection of priority issues. This differs from the normal strategic planning approach, which, to a large degree, is driven by internal strengths and objectives. Issues management is very much driven by external factors.

● **Bottom-line orientation.** Although many people tend to look at issues management as anticipating crises, its real purpose should be to defend the organization in light of external factors as well as to enhance the firm's business by seizing imminent opportunities.

● **Action timetable.** Just as the issues management process must identify emerging issues and set them in order, it must propose policy, programs, and an implementation timetable to deal with those issues. Action is the key to an effective issues management process.

● **Dealing from the top.** Just as a public relations department is powerless without the confidence and respect of top management, the issues management process must operate with the support of the chief executive. The chief executive's personal sanction is critical to the acceptance and conduct of issues management within a firm.

Implementing Issues Management

In a typical organization, the tactical implementation of issues management tends to consist of four specific job tasks:

1. *Identifying issues and trends.* Issue identification can be accomplished through traditional research techniques as well as through more informal methods. Organizations are most concerned about issues that affect their own residential area. One way to keep informed about what is being said about a company, industry, or issue is to be aware of issues from all perspectives— including those in print and on the Web that vehemently disagree with the view of the organization you represent. Such awareness of the "enemy" prevents you from being blindsided.

2. *Evaluating issue impact and setting priorities.* Evaluation and analysis may be handled by issues committees within an organization. Committees can set priorities for issues management action. At the Pharmacia & Upjohn Company,

which was acquired by Pfizer in 2003, for example, a senior policy committee—composed of managers in each of the firm's major divisions, as well as public affairs and legal staff members—meets quarterly to set issues priorities.

3. *Establishing a company position.* Establishing a position can be a formal process. After the Upjohn senior policy committee has met and decided on issues, Upjohn's public affairs staff prepares policy statements on each topic. At PPG Industries, individual issues managers prepare position papers for executive review on topics of direct concern.

4. *Designing company action and response to achieve results.* The best-organized companies for issues management orchestrate integrated responses to achieve results. Typically, organizations may coordinate those responses with their Washington offices, state lobbying operations, management speeches, advertising messages, and employee communications.

Emergence of Risk Communication

The 1990s saw the emergence of "risk communication" as an outgrowth of issues management. Risk communication began as a process of taking scientific data related to health and environmental hazards and presenting them to a lay audience in a manner that is both understandable and meaningful.[5]

Models of risk communication have been developed based on the position that "perception is reality"—a concept that has been part of public relations for years. Indeed, the disciplines of risk communication and public relations have much in common. Risk communication deals with a high level of emotion. Fear, confusion, frustration, and anger are common feelings in dealing with crises.

Occasionally—even often—intense emotion flows from a lack of knowledge and understanding about the science that underlies societal risk. Therefore, frequent and forceful communication is necessary to inform, educate, and even dampen emotion. The first rule in responding to a perceived public risk is to take the matter seriously. After this, seven steps are helpful in planning a risk communication program:

1. Recognize risk communication as part of a larger risk management program and understand that the whole program is based on politics, power, and controversial issues.

2. Encourage management to join the "communications loop" and help train them to deal effectively with the news media.

3. Develop credible outside experts to act as news sources for journalists.

4. Become an in-house expert in your own area of risk to enhance your credibility with journalists.

5. Approach the news media with solid facts and figures before they approach you. Verify the veracity of your data.

6. Research perceptions of your organization by the media and other publics to gauge credibility and help determine if your messages will be believable.

7. Understand your target audiences and how the news media can help you communicate effectively.[6]

Like any other area of public relations, risk communication depends basically on an organization's actions. In the long run, deeds, not words, are what count in communicating risk.

S I D E B A R

Managing a Pregnant Issue at Wal-Mart

As the world's largest and most visible retailer, Wal-Mart must be vigilant in its awareness of and ability to react quickly to impending crises.

This was clearly the case with some rapid issues management in the holiday season of 2002, when Wal-Mart acted with lightning speed to head off a firestorm involving Barbie's oldest friend.

Midge, who joined the Barbie doll collection in 1963, married boy-doll Alan in 1991, and had a 3-year-old son, Ryan. In 2002, Midge showed up on Wal-Mart shelves pregnant once again (Figure 21-2).

And that's when the "fun" started.

Wal-Mart customers complained of a pregnant doll with a detachable magnetic stomach to allow easy "delivery" of the baby. Some argued that the doll promoted teenage pregnancy.

The doll's creater, Mattel Inc., countered that the doll was designed to satisfy the desire for nurturing play by girls ages 5 to 8 and can be "a wonderful prop for parents to use with their children to role-play family situations—especially in families anticipating the arrival of a new sibling."

Wal-Mart wasn't convinced.

The world's largest retailer pulled its entire "Happy Family" set of dolls—Midge, Alan, and Ryan—from its shelves as soon as the crisis began.

Said Wal-Mart's spokeswoman, "What we try to do is listen to what our customers want. In this case, we decided to remove the product."

FIGURE 21-2   **Midge, pregnant but not "happy."**

Managing in a Crisis

The most significant test for any organization comes when it is hit by a major accident or disaster—that is; a *crisis.*

What is a crisis? According to the *Harvard Business Review,* "A crisis is a situation that has reached a critical phase for which dramatic and extraordinary intervention is necessary to avoid or repair major damage." [7]

How an organization handles itself in the midst of a crisis may influence how it is perceived for years to come. Poor handling of events with the magnitude of Exxon's *Valdez* oil spill, PepsiCo's syringe scare, Dow Corning's silicone breast implant controversy, Denny's racial bias accusations, or Tylenol's capsule poisoning not only can cripple an organization's reputation but also can cause it enormous monetary loss. In some cases, such as ValuJet's Everglades airline crash cited in the interview at the end of this chapter, it can cause the demise of an organization. It is essential, therefore, that such emergencies be managed intelligently and forthrightly with the news media, employees, and the community at large.

As any organization unfortunate enough to experience a crisis recognizes, when the crisis strikes, seven instant warning signs invariably appear:

1. *Surprise.* When a crisis breaks out, it's usually unexpected. Often it's a natural disaster—a tornado or hurricane, for example. Sometimes, it's a human-made disaster—robbery, embezzlement, or large loss. Frequently, a public relations professional first learns of such an event when the media calls and demands to know what immediate action will be taken.

2. *Insufficient information.* Many things happen at once. Rumors fly. Chat rooms come alive with wild stories. Wire services want to know why the company's stock is falling. It's difficult to get a grip on everything that's happening.

3. *Escalating events.* The crisis expands. The stock exchange wants to know what's going on. Will the organization issue a statement? Are the rumors true? While rumors run rampant, truthful information is difficult to obtain. You want to respond in an orderly manner, but events are unfolding too quickly.

4. *Loss of control.* The unfortunate natural outgrowth of escalating events is that too many things are happening simultaneously. Erroneous stories hit the wires, then the newsstands, and then the airwaves. As in the case of the mouse in the Coors can, rampant rumors can't easily be controlled.

5. *Increased outside scrutiny.* The media, stockbrokers, talk-show hosts, and the public in general feed on rumors. "Helpful" politicians and observers of all stripes comment to cable TV on what's going on. The media want responses. Investors demand answers. Customers must know what's going on.

6. *Siege mentality.* The organization understandably feels surrounded. Lawyers counsel, "Anything we say will be held against us." The easiest thing to do is to say nothing. But does that make sense?

7. *Panic.* With the walls caving in and with leaks too numerous to plug, a sense of panic pervades. In such an environment, it is difficult to convince management to take immediate action and to communicate what's going on.[8]

Planning in a Crisis

One irrefutable key in crisis management is being prepared. If there is one certainty in dealing with crisis, it is that all manner of accidents or disruptions make for spectacular headlines and sensational reporting. Reporters, as noted, march to a different drummer. They consider themselves the "guardians of the public trust" and, therefore, may be quick to point fingers and ascribe blame in a crisis.

Thus, heightened preparedness is always in order, with four planning issues paramount.

● **First, for each potentially impacted audience, define the risk.** "The poison in the pill will make you sick." "The plant shutdown will keep you out of work." "The recall will cost the stockholders $100 million." The risk must be understood—or at least contemplated—before framing crisis communications.

● **Second, for each risk defined, describe the actions that mitigate the risk.** "Don't take the pill." "We are recalling the product." "We are studying the possibility of closing the plant." If you do a credible job in defining the risk, the public will more closely believe in your solutions.

A QUESTION OF ETHICS

Red Cross Cross-Up

The American Red Cross has always "been there" for Americans when tragedy strikes.

That's why Americans poured out their hearts—and their contributions—in the aftermath of the 2001 terrorist attacks. The Red Cross September 11 Liberty Fund collected $1 billion, all of it ostensibly to benefit victims of the attacks.

By mid-October, however, Red Cross President Bernadine Healy, a distinguished physician and health care expert, was called on the carpet when it was disclosed that only 20 percent of Liberty Fund proceeds had gone to September 11 victims. The rest of the money had been placed in a reserve for "future needs."

At a Congressional hearing, President Healy explained, "The Liberty Fund is a war fund. We must have blood readiness. We must have the ability to help our troops if we go into a ground war. We must have the ability to help the victims of tomorrow."

Healy pointed out that Red Cross ads specified that unless Liberty Fund donations were specifically marked as "intended for the victims," the money could be used for other causes related to tragic events.

But to the Congress and the public, the Red Cross logic smacked of a classic "bait and switch." Adding to the crisis were claims of victims' families that the Red Cross would not honor their request for funds.

Within weeks, Healy resigned her Red Cross presidency (Figure 21-3). Her replacement, Harold Decker, quickly reiterated the organization's apology and stipulated a new Red Cross policy.

> We deeply regret that our activities over the past eight weeks have not been as sharply focused as America wants, nor as focused as the victims of this tragedy deserve. The people affected by this terrible tragedy have been our first priority, and beginning today, they will be the only priority of the Liberty Fund.

Although many felt the use of the Liberty Fund for other purposes was unethical, others felt it was

FIGURE 21-3   **Former Red Cross President Bernadine Healy.**

equally unethical to single out the outgoing president as a scapegoat.

What was not in doubt, however, was that as a result of its Liberty Fund crisis, the Red Cross would have its hands full for some time, winning back its lost credibility.*

*Impetus for this case was the public relations class of Prof. Bonnie Grossman at the College of Charleston, with particular contributions from Brian Finn, Ryland Hudnall, Mindy Murray, Nina Ita, and Kaitlin Rohan.

- **Third, identify the cause of the risk.**   If the public believes you know what went wrong, they are more likely to accept that you will quickly remedy the problem. That's why people get back on airplanes after crashes. Moreover, if the organization helps identify the cause of the problem, the coverage of the crisis is likely to be more balanced.
- **Fourth, demonstrate responsible management action.**[9]   Essential to the planning phase is to appear to be in control of the situation. Certainly early on in a crisis, control is lost. The best firms are those that seize command early and don't acquiesce it to outside so-called experts. Letting people know that the organization has a plan and is implementing it helps convince them that you are in control. Defining the issues means both having a clear sense internally of what the focus of communications should be and effectively moving that focus out into the marketplace to reach key constituents.[10]

Simple but appropriate watchwords for any crisis plan are the following:

- Be prepared.
- Be available.
- Be credible.

All of this implies that you must be willing to communicate in a crisis.

Communicating in a Crisis

The key communications principle in dealing with a crisis is not to clam up when disaster strikes.

Lawyers invariably advise clients to (1) say nothing, (2) say as little as possible and release it as quietly as possible, (3) say as little as possible, citing privacy laws, company policy, or sensitivity, (4) deny guilt and/or act indignant that such charges could possibly have been made, or (5) shift or, if necessary, share the blame with others.

Public relations advice, by contrast, takes a different tack. The most effective crisis communicators are those who provide prompt, frank, and full information to the media in the eye of the storm. Invariably, the first inclination of executives is to say, "Let's wait until all the facts are in." But as President Carter's press secretary, Jody Powell, used to say, "Bad news is a lot like fish. It doesn't get better with age."

In saying nothing, an organization is perceived as already having made a decision. Indeed, research sponsored by public relations agency Porter Novelli suggests that when most people—upwards of 65 percent—hear the words "no comment," they perceive the no-commenter as guilty. Silence angers the media and compounds the problem. On the other hand, inexperienced spokespersons, speculating nervously or using emotionally charged language, are even worse.

Most public relations professionals consider the cardinal rule for communications during a crisis to be: **Tell it all and tell it fast!**

As a general rule, when information gets out quickly, rumors are stopped and nerves are calmed. There is nothing complicated about the goals of crisis management. They are (1) terminate the crisis quickly, (2) limit the damage, and (3) restore credibility.[11]

The quickest way to end the agony and begin to build back credibility is to communicate through the media.

The Lessons of Valdez

Remember the Exxon *Valdez* case discussed in Chapter 3?

Because you've probably already dissected it thoroughly, it won't matter if we divulge here, courtesy of crisis expert Tim Wallace, how Exxon should have handled the situation.

1. *Develop a clear, straightforward position.*   In a crisis, you can't appear to waffle. You must remain flexible enough to respond to changing developments, but you must also stick to your underlying position. Exxon's position seemed to waver.

2. *Involve top management.*   Management must not only be involved, but it must also appear to be involved. In Exxon's case, from all reports, Chairman Lawrence Rawl was involved with the Gulf of Valdez solutions every step of the way. But that's not how it appeared in public. Rather, he was perceived as distant from the crisis. And Exxon suffered.

3. *Activate third-party support.*   This support may come from Wall Street analysts, independent engineers, technology experts, or legal authorities. Any objective party with credentials can help your case.

4. *Establish an on-site presence.*   The chairman of Union Carbide flew to Bhopal, India, in 1984, when a Carbide plant explosion killed thousands. His trip at least showed corporate concern. When Chairman Rawl explained that he "had better things to do" than fly to Valdez, Exxon effectively lost the public relations battle.

5. *Centralize communications.*   In any crisis, a communications point person should be appointed and a support team established. It is the point person's job—and his or hers alone—to state the organization's position.

6. *Cooperate with the media.*   In a crisis, journalists are repugnant; they're obnoxious; they'll stoop to any level to get the story. But don't take it personally. Treat the media as friendly adversaries and explain your side of the crisis. Making them enemies will only exacerbate tensions.

7. *Don't ignore employees.*   Keeping employees informed helps ensure that the organization's business proceeds as normally as possible. Employees are your greatest ally. Don't keep them in the dark.

8. *Keep the crisis in perspective.*   Often management underreacts at the start of a crisis and overreacts when it builds. The prevailing wisdom seems to be, "Just because we're paranoid doesn't mean they're not out to get us!" Avoid hunkering down. Exxon executives made this mistake, and it cost them dearly.

9. *Begin positioning the organization for the time when the crisis is over.*   Concentrate on communicating the steps that the organization will take to deal with the crisis. Admit blame if it's due. Then quickly focus on what you are doing now rather than on what went wrong.

10. *Continuously monitor and evaluate the process.*   Survey, survey, survey. Take the pulse of your employees, customers, suppliers, distributors, investors, and, if appropriate, the general public. Determine whether your messages are getting through. Constantly check to see which aspects of the program are working and which are not. Adjust accordingly.[*]

[*]Tim Wallace, "Crisis Management: Practical Tips on Restoring Trust," *The Journal of Private Sector Policy* (November 1991): 14.

Engaging the Media in Crisis

Handling the media is the most critical element in crisis.

Normally, treating the press as "friendly adversaries" makes great sense. But when crisis strikes, media attention quickly turns to "feeding frenzy." So dealing with the media in crisis demands certain "battlefield rules," among them:

● **Set up media headquarters.** In a crisis, the media will seek out the organizational "soft spots" where the firm is most vulnerable to being penetrated. To try to prevent this: Organizations in crisis must immediately establish a media headquarters through which all authorized communication must flow.

● **Establish media rules.** In a crisis, the media are sneaky. Their goal is to unearth any salient or salacious element that will advance the story line of the crisis. In this respect, they are operating very much at cross-purposes with the organization, which is desperately trying to put the crisis behind it.

It is imperative, therefore, that the organization in the crucible set firm rules—which parts of the operation are off limits, which executives won't be available, and so on—for the media to follow.

● **Media live for the "box score."** Crisis specifics make news. The grislier the better.

- How many were fired?
- How many were displaced?
- What was the cost of the damage?
- How much was extorted?
- How many perished?

Stated another way, crisis is about numbers. And an organization in crisis must be ready to provide enough numbers to "feed the beast."

● **Don't speculate.** If you don't know the numbers or the reasons or the extent of the damage, don't pretend you do. Speculation is suicidal in crisis.

● **Feed the beast.** The media in crisis are insatiable. The Internet, cable news, the wire services all must be fed 24/7. In the 21st century, the media never sleep. "Nature abhors a vacuum," goes the old saying. And in crisis, any "vacuum" will be filled by your enemies.

So a smart organization in crisis will strive to keep the media occupied—even "distracted"—with new information that advances the story.

● **Speed triumphs.** In crisis, the media mantra is speed first, accuracy second. This sad but true fact holds major implications for public relations people, who must monitor what is being wrongly reported, so that it can be nipped quickly before others run with the same misinformation.

● **Cable Rules.** Cable TV is a 21st century phenomenon—CNN, MSNBC, Fox News Channel, CNBC, CNNfn, and others.

They compete viciously with each other all the time—one of the last bastions of American reportorial competition. Which is good. What's not so good is that in a crisis the drumbeat of incessant hammering is relentless.

Once a crisis "victim" gets caught in the cable spotlight, it is close to impossible to be extricated. Round the clock the skewering continues, on talk show after talk show, "expert" after "expert."

So cable TV, like radio, like the Internet, must be monitored scrupulously in crisis.[12]

As to what is said to the media, the following 10 general principles apply:

1. Speak first and often.
2. Don't speculate.
3. Go off the record at your own peril.
4. Stay with the facts.
5. Be open and concerned, not defensive.

Last Rites for Opie & Dopey

It may have signaled the end for "anything goes" radio.

Two New York shock jocks, Opie & Anthony, found that out in the fall of 2002, when their Infinity Corporation station offered cash prizes, sponsored by Samuel Adams Lager, for couples willing to have sex in public places during the broadcast.

Where there's a will—not to mention, money!—there's a way. And the lovebirds pictured here were more than willing to bare not only their souls in the midst of St. Patrick's Cathedral for the payoff that the disc jockeys offered (Figure 21-4).

The couple was quickly arrested after attempting to copulate among the parishioners.

And although there were those who claimed that Opie and Anthony were merely exercising their rights of free speech and, therefore, shouldn't be reprimanded, the reaction was equally swift from the two companies cornered in the crisis.

- First, Samuel Adams denounced the contest and the dj's, and pulled back its prize money.
- Second, Infinity Broadcasting summarily fired the shock jocks.

The primary lesson: In crisis, when the organization's reputation is at stake, individuals are expendable.

The subordinate lesson: Careful, Howard Stern, you could be next.

FIGURE 21-4 **Collared lovebirds.** The "winning" listeners.

6. Make your point and repeat it.
7. Don't wage war with the media.
8. Establish yourself as the most authoritative source.
9. Stay calm and be truthful and cooperative.
10. Never lie.

LAST WORD

Although prevention remains the best insurance for any organization, crisis management has become one of the most revered skills in the practice of public relations. Organizations of every variety are faced, sooner or later, with a crisis. The issues that confront society—from energy and the environment, to health and nutrition, to corporate accountability and minority rights—will not soon abate.

All of this suggests that experienced and knowledgeable crisis managers who can skillfully navigate and effectively communicate, turning crisis into opportunity, will be valuable resources for organizations in the 21st century.

In the final analysis, communicating in a crisis depends on a rigorous analysis of the risks versus the benefits of going public. Communicating effectively also depends on the judgment and experience of the public relations professional. Every call is a close one, and there is no guarantee that the organization will benefit, no matter what course is chosen. One thing is clear: Helping to navigate the organization through the shoals of a crisis is the ultimate test of a public relations professional.

In the years ahead, few challenges will be more significant for public relations professionals than helping to manage crisis.

Discussion Starters

1. What is meant by the term *issues management*?
2. How can an organization influence the development of an issue in society?
3. What are the general steps in implementing an issues management program?
4. What is meant by the term *risk communciations*?
5. What are the usual stages that an organization experiences in a crisis?
6. What are the principles in planning for crisis?
7. What are important rules in dealing with the media in crisis?
8. What is the cardinal rule for communicating in a crisis?
9. What are the keys to successful crisis communication?
10. What are likely to be the flashpoint crisis issues in the new century?

 TOP OF THE SHELF

Clarence Jones

Winning with the News Media: A Self-Defense Manual When You're the Story, *7th ed.*
Tampa, FL Video Consultants, 2001

Now in its seventh edition has to say something about the popularity and usefulness of *Winning with the News Media*.

The author, Clarence Jones, speaks from experience. Before he wrote this book, he was one of the nation's most honored investigative reporters in both print and television. He explains the inner workings of the news business and offers cogent advice on how to build positive relations with the news media, get your organization's activities covered, and manage the inevitable "bad news" situation that can befall any of us.

C A S E   S T U D Y

A Slip of the Lott Lip

No one needs to remind Trent Lott that crisis frequently strikes without warning.

In December 2002, the Republican Senator from Mississippi had but one month to go before becoming majority leader, the most powerful position in the U.S. Congress. The Republicans had just won the majority in both houses of Congress, and Lott was on tap to lead the Congress as President Bush's point man in 2003.

Then he attended a birthday party for 100-year-old Mississippi Senate colleague Strom Thurmond. And disaster struck.

In toasting Thurmond, Lott said Mississippians were proud to have supported Thurmond for president when he ran in 1948 on a "segregationist forever" campaign platform.

"And if the rest of the country had followed our lead, we wouldn't have had all these problems over all these years either," Lott added.

Oooooooooooops.

CALLOUS RACISM

It took several days before Lott's comments got reported. But when they did, the response was immediate and unrelenting.

- Kweisi Mfume, president of the National Association for the Advancement of Colored People, called Lott's comment the "kind of callous, calculated, hateful bigotry that has no place in the halls of Congress."
- Rep. Elijah Cummings, chair of the Congressional Black Caucus, said, "Those are the kind of words that tear this nation apart."
- Other African American Democratic leaders called for Lott to resign immediately.

In response to the sudden but intense criticism, Lott described the comments, through a spokesperson, as part of a "lighthearted celebration."

Oooooooooooops.

"I'M SORRY"

The Lott crisis only intensified over the next several days.

The cable networks, with little else to talk about over the holiday season, focused on the Lott affair and wouldn't relent.

- Jeb Bush, the governor of Florida and the president's brother, offered that Lott's comments "weren't helpful" to Republicans after finally winning a majority.
- Secretary of State Colin Powell condemned the Lott remarks.
- And in perhaps the most telling noncommentary of the furor, President Bush refused to categorically endorse Lott continuing as majority leader.

Now, Trent Lott had a *problem*.

No longer could he hide behind statements or spokespersons. He had to go public.

And he did, saying, "A poor choice of words conveyed to some the impression that I embrace the discarded policies of the past. Nothing could be further from the truth."

Lott then reached out for black Democratic Congressman John Lewis, a legendary civil rights leader, to work with him to restore race relations. Lewis said he supported Lott and would assist him.

Yet the crisis refused to die. It was time to take one last desperate measure to save his political skin.

ONE LAST DESPERATE MEASURE

And so in the most unlikely of interviews, Senator Trent Lott agreed to sit for a 30-minute interivew on Black Entertainment Television (BET).

It was a most remarkable appearance, in which Senator Lott literally begged for forgiveness.

- He said, "I made a terrible mistake, used horrible words, caused hurt."
- In response to what he meant by supporting Thurmond's platform, Lott said, "I was talking about the problems of defense, of communism, and budget, of a government that sometimes didn't do its job."
- He said he was mistaken about earlier voting against making Martin Luther King, Jr's birthday a federal holiday.
- And he announced that despite popular wisdom, "I'm for affirmative action, and I've practiced it."

It was a stunning performance, drawing a record 830,000 BET viewers.

But did it work?

SAYONARA

After the BET performance, Lott's Republican support in the Senate began to dry up.

"I would like to see him leave," said Rhode Island Republican Lincoln Chafee. Oklahoma Senator Don Nickles and Virginia Senator John Warner seconded that emotion.

And Tennessee Senator Bill Frist announced he would oppose Lott for Senate majority leader.

Still Lott was defiant.

- On December 18, at home in Mississippi, Lott vowed to an interviewer, "I am the son of a shipyard worker from Pascagoula, Mississippi. I have had to fight all my life. And I am not stopping now."
- On December 19, a Lott spokesperson reiterated that the senator "had no intention of stepping down."
- But . . . on December 20, the office of Senator Trent Lott issued a written statement in behalf of the senator:

In the interest of pursuing the best possible agenda for the future of our country, I will not seek to remain as majority leader of the United States Senate for the 108th Congress, effective January 6, 2003.

In so doing, Trent Lott became the first Senate leader to ever step down because of crisis (Figure 21-5).

Questions

1. How would you assess Trent Lott's crisis communications strategy to save his job?
2. How would you assess Lott's strategy and tactics relative to his BET appearance?
3. Had you been Lott's public relations counselor, what would you have advised him to do to save his position as majority leader?

For further information, see Deborah Bayfield Berry, "Black Leaders Blast Lott," *Community-Black Voices* (December 12, 2002); Elisabeth Bumiller and Carl Hulse, "Lott Stands Firm as Colleague Urges Leadership Change," *New York Times* (December 18, 2002): A1-13; Alan Fram, "Sen. Trent Lott Resigns as Senate Majority Leader," Associated Press (December 20, 2002); Jesse J. Holland, "Lott Says He Has Enough Support to Stay," Associated Press (December 18, 2002); Jeffrey McMurray, "Lott Reaches Out to Civil Rights Leader," Associated Press (December 17, 2002); and Craig Offman, "Lott Boosts BET's Ratings," *Variety* (December 17, 2002): 1.

FIGURE 21-5 **Fallen leader.** Trent Lott in Mississippi a day after the announcement.

TIPS FROM THE TOP

An Interview with Lewis Jordan

Lewis Jordan

Lewis H. Jordan was president and CEO of ValuJet Airlines in 1996, when one of its airplanes went down in the alligator-infested waters of Florida's Everglades. The company's CEO responded with remarkable candor, honesty, and human concern in the face of unspeakable horror—the deaths of all 110 on board. CEO Jordan weathered the crisis by accepting virtually every interview request about the crash. Ultimately, the company was renamed AirTran, and Mr. Jordan succeeded in keeping it alive long enough to emerge with a new identity.

When you first got word of the crash, did you suspect the worst?
I knew that this was something very serious. You hope that a number of people survived and, even if there's been an accident, that maybe many people survived and it's all on a very serious but relative scale. I think human nature is such that you remain hopeful as long as you can.

What was going through your mind?
Extreme emotions of just the horror of losing the airplane with 110 people and a crew of five. We were recognizing names of people that we had known, like Captain Kubick, a woman I had personally participated in hiring.

(Continued)

Did you have a crisis plan?

Yes. There are responsibilities that go to each officer within the airline who is in touch with the National Transportation Safety Board. There is a "Go Team" that is immediately activated. An 800 number is set up for family members. And, of course, when we arrived at our office, the media were already sitting in the parking lot trying to get into the building. We knew we had to communicate whatever information we had as quickly as possible.

Were you concerned about saying something at the press conference that could cause legal problems?

I thought about many of the pitfalls that were possible in going public early and talking openly to the press, in dealing with the toughest questions. I decided not to screen out any questions, not to refuse to take any questions, and not to cut anybody short. I've been in the airline business long enough that I certainly had an appreciation that legal liability is a concern, that there were financial implications and insurance issues. But I can tell you that beyond any of those thoughts—far and above any of the other concerns—the human side of this issue was the most important. And it was my honest belief that in setting the tone for what kind of a company ValuJet Airlines is in the face of a crisis, it was a certainty to me to put human compassion above everything else.

How would you characterize the coverage the crash received and the treatment ValuJet was accorded?

The single, biggest factor that continues to stand out was what I call the "rush to judgment." I don't know how many times I urged the press to withhold their thoughts about what might have caused the accident. In the first 48 hours, reports aired all over the United States speculating what may have caused the accident—without any foundation. "These are 26-year-old airplanes; this must be an aging aircraft issue." People began to question the Pratt & Whitney engine, which had features in other airplanes. All of this was unfair, especially to family members who deserved to have the facts.

Did you feel it was your personal responsibility to interact with the families who lost people on the plane?

I knew it would be the toughest thing I had ever done in my life to walk into a large room full of families who had just lost loved ones on our airplane—recognizing that I would be allowing myself to be the most identifiable human being associated with ValuJet Airlines in a leadership role. But I remained very much involved with the families.

What was your overriding objective in managing the crisis?

We made a commitment not to give up. We had a company of 4,000 wonderful people who stood up and said they were proud of their company. I never had a doubt that we would make it back, because of the dedication of our people.

Suggested Readings

Antin, Angel. "Dealing with Deadly Bacteria." *Public Relations Tactics* (March 1998): 1–3.

Budd, John F., Jr. "The Downside of Crisis Management." *Public Relations Strategist* (Fall 1998): 36.

Caponigro, Jeffrey R. *A Step-by-Step Guide to Managing a Business Crisis*, New York: McGraw Hill, 2000.

Center, Allen H., and Patrick Jackson. *Public Relations Practices: Managerial Case Studies and Problems*, 6th ed. Upper Saddle River, NJ: Prentice Hall, 2000.

Cohn, Robin. *The PR Crisis Bible: How to Take Charge of the Media When All Hell Breaks Loose*. New York: St. Martin's Press, 2000.

Coombs, Timothy W. "An Analytic Framework for Crisis Situations: Better Responses from a Better Understanding of the Situation." *Journal of Public Relations Research* 10, no. 3 (1998): 177.

Davidson, D. Kirk. *Selling Sin: The Marketing of Socially Unacceptable Products.* Westport, CT: Quorum Books, 1996. Discusses the way crisis-oriented products, such as cigarettes, alcohol, gambling, and firearms, are marketed and the problems they present.

Dosier, Dow. "Employee Communications at Kerr-McGee in the Aftermath of the Oklahoma City Bombing." *Public Relations Quarterly* (Summer 1998): 13.

Fallows, James. *Breaking the News: How the Media Undermine American Democracy.* New York: Pantheon, 1996. *U.S. News & World Report's* editor-in-chief goes at the journalistic jugular vein, exposing the media as a collection of pompous pretenders who delight in creating crisis out of any insignificant issue. (And that's the good part!)

Fearn-Banks, Kathleen. *Crisis Communications: A Casebook Approach.* 2nd ed. Mahwah, NJ: Lawrence Erlbaum Associates, 2002. Recommends a plan for preventing and dealing with crises based on communication theories.

Ferguson, Mary Ann, Joann M. Valenti, and G. Melwani. "Communicating with Risk Takers: A Public Relations Perspective." *Public Relations Research Annual*, vol. 3. Hillsdale, NJ: Lawrence Erlbaum Associates, 1993.

Fink, Steven. *Planning for the Inevitable.* Place: iUniverse.com, 2000.

Frazier, Douglas. "Crisis Planning for Digital Disasters." *Public Relations Tactics* (July 1998): 16.

Gantz, Stanton A., John Slade, Lisa A. Bero, Peter Hanauer, and Deborah E. Barnes. *The Cigarette Papers.* Berkeley: University of California Press, 1996. The authors analyze some 10,000 pages of documents from Brown and Williamson Tobacco Corporation on the company's research into the addictive aspects of cigarettes and smoking. A fascinating dissection.

Gjelten, Tom. *Sarajevo Daily: A City and Its Newspaper Under Siege.* New York: HarperCollins Publishers, 1995. A story from the heart of the Bosnian crisis, written by the National Public Radio correspondent in the region during the vicious Bosnian war.

Gonzalez, Hernando, and William C. Adams. "A Life-Saving Public-Private Partnership: Amoco and Florida International University's Hurricane Preparedness Program." *Public Relations Quarterly* (Winter 1997–98): 28.

Harvard Business Review on Crisis Management. Cambridge, MA: Harvard Business School Press, 2000.

Hendrix, Jerry A. *Public Relations Cases*, 3rd ed. Belmont, CA: Wadsworth, 2000.

Howard, Elizabeth. "Swooshed! What Activists Are Teaching Nike." *Public Relations Strategist* (Fall 1998): 38.

Lerbinger, Otto. *The Crisis Manager.* Mahwah, NJ: Lawrence Erlbaum Associates, 1997. Focuses on organizations that have no choice but to accept crises as the price of doing business.

Logan, Dever. "Swissair Flight 111 Crash Tests PR Crisis Plans." *Public Relations Tactics* (December 1998): 4.

Marconi, Joe. *Crisis Marketing: When Bad Things Happen to Good Companies,* 2nd ed. Lincolnwood, IL: NTC Business Books, 1997.

Mickey, Thomas J. *Public Relations Criticism.* Mahwah, NJ: Lawrence Erlbaum Associates, 2002.

Mitroff, Ian I., et al. *The Essential Guide to Managing Corporate Crises: A Step-by-Step Handbook for Surviving Major Catastrophes.* New York: Oxford University Press, 1996.

O'Dwyer, Jack, ed. *Jack O'Dwyer's Newsletter.* Weekly newsletter. (271 Madison Ave., New York, NY 10016).

Pocket Guide to Preventing Sexual Harassment. Madison, CT: Business & Legal Reports, Inc., 1996. Thorough analysis of what constitutes sexual harassment and what to do about it.

Poe, Randall. "Where to Turn When Your Reputation Is at Stake." *Across the Board* (February 1998): 16.

PR Reporter. Weekly newsletter. (Box 600, Exeer, NH 03833).

Public Relations Review. Quarterly. (Available from the Foundation for Public Relations Research and Education, University of Maryland College of Journalism, College Park, MD 20742.)

Shrader-Frechette, K. S. *Risk and Rationality: Philosophical Foundations for Populist Reforms.* Berkeley: University of California Press, 1991.

Simon, Raymond, and Frank W. Wylie. *Cases in Public Relations Management.* Lincolnwood, IL: NTC Publishing Group, 2001. Two eminent professionals discuss some of the most famous crisis management cases, including Hill & Knowlton and Kuwait, and Procter & Gamble and news leaks.

Stanton, Peter V. "Ten Communications Mistakes You Can Avoid When Managing a Crisis." *Public Relations Quarterly* (Summer 2002): 19–24.

Suskind, Lawrence E. *Dealing with an Angry Public, The Mutual Gains Approach to Resolving Disputes.* New York: The Free Press, 1996. Recommends strategies for dealing with crises, issues, and major public policies.

Young, Davis. *Building Your Company's Good Name: How to Create the Reputation Your Organization Wants and Deserves.* New York: AMACOM, 1996. A how-to-book on reputation for business managers in organizations of all types.

Notes

1. Helio Fred Garcia, *Crisis Communications,* vol. 1 (New York: American Association of Advertising Agencies, 1999): 9.
2. Andrew Dampf, "Skating Scandals Details Emerge," Associated Press (August 2, 2002).
3. "Issues Management Conference—A Special Report," *Corporate Public Issues* 7, no. 23 (December 1, 1982): 1–2.
4. Kerry Tucker and Glen Broom, "Managing Issues Acts as Bridge to Strategic Planning," *Public Relations Journal* (November 1993): 38.
5. Jeffrey P. Julin, "Is 'PR' a Risk to Effective Risk Communication?" *IABC Communication World* (October 1993): 14–15.
6. William C. Adams, "Strategic Advice in Handling Risk," presented during the Business, Environmental Issues, and Risk Conference, Washington, DC, November 12, 1992.
7. Richard K. Long, "Seven Needless Sins of Crisis (Mis)management," *PR Tactics* (August 2001): 14.
8. Fraser P. Seitel, "Spotting a Crisis," odwyerpr.com (March 20, 2001).
9. Sam Ostrow, "Managing Terrorist Acts in the Age of Sound Byte Journalism," *Reputation Management* (November–December 1996): 75–76.
10. Garcia, *Crisis Communications*: 42.
11. Kathy R. Fitzpatrick and Maureen Shubow Rubin, "Public Relations vs. Legal Strategies in Organizational Crisis Decisions," *Public Relations Review* (Spring 1995): 22.
12. Fraser P. Seitel, "Crisis Media Battlefield Principles," odwyerpr.com (December 16, 2002).

PART V The Future

Chapter 22

The Golden Age

In the wake of war, recession, and the dot-com explosion, the practice of public relations, just like everything else, has had its ups and downs.

Nonetheless, with the communications revolution in full bloom, with convergence of communications technologies upon us, and with the world an eminently smaller sphere than ever before, the 21st century will most certainly be the "golden age of public relations."

Communicating with each other to resolve differences and reach common ground will be that important.

The first years of the new century have been mixed ones for public relations. On the one hand, worldwide revenues for public relations firms total well over $4 billion annually. On the other hand, those revenues are down from earlier periods.[1]

- *On the one hand, research indicates that communications within companies are more strategically important than ever before.[2] On the other hand, other research suggests that only four employees in 10 "trust" senior management.[3]*
- *On the one hand, salaries in public relations work have continued to increase as the field has enhanced its stature.[4] On the other hand, corporate communicators have faced unprecedented layoffs, declining morale, and job dissatisfaction.[5]*
- *On the one hand, public relations practice has never been more highly thought of, particularly in light of such high-profile counselors as Karen Hughes to President George W. Bush and Mary Matalin to Vice President Richard Cheney. On the other hand, public relations charlatans abound, such as the former wrestler turned cosmetic surgeon, who thrived on publicity about his buttock implant business.[6]*

The booming bubble economy of the late 1990s created a huge demand for public relations services, particularly to promote budding dot-com companies hopeful of quickly cashing in. With reality now returned to society, a more rational view of the practice has emerged.

- *Today, with competition fierce for scarce resources in virtually every area, the need to differentiate oneself from others is paramount. That means that effectively communicating differentiation is critical.*

- *Furthermore, the communications media around the world have truly converted the globe into one large "village," united by satellite and Internet technology. What happens in one corner of the globe is instantly transmitted to another. Organizations, therefore, need professional communicators to navigate through this "brave new world" of instantaneous communication.*
- *As organizations internationally have merged and affiliated and combined forces, the need to accurately interpret management's philosophies, policies, and programs to its customers, employees, the government, and other key constituent groups has intensified.*
- *As society has gotten more technologically savvy and automated, the human factor has diminished. The less appealing facet of voice mail and e-mail and the World Wide Web is their impersonal nature. Employee distrust has been exacerbated by corporate executive scandals.*

Again, organizations need communications specialists today, just as John D. Rockefeller needed Ivy Lee at the start of the last century, to help them humanize their approach to their markets and their publics.

All of these factors signal one clear conclusion: The 21st century promises to be the golden age of public relations.

Issues of the Millennium

Undeniably, the people who practice public relations today must be better at it than those who came before them. Institutions operate in a pressure-cooker environment and must keep several steps ahead of the rapid pace of social, economic, and political change. The environment is being shaped by many factors:

- **Economic globalization.**   This is affecting all organizations, even nonmultinational companies. The world is getting smaller. Communism is dead or dying. Democracy and free enterprise are dominant. Competition will intensify, and so will communications, making it easier to communicate around the world but much more difficult to be heard. Public relations has become a growth industry around the world.
- **Shifting public opinion.**   Sudden shifts in public opinion are being ignited by instantaneous communications, challenging the ability of communicators to respond to fast-moving events. Interest groups of every stripe are jockeying for position on the public stage.
- **Global jealousies.**   One such shift in public opinion is disdain among many in the world of the lifestyle enjoyed by people in the West, particularly the United States. Global jealousies, fueling terrorism and anti-Western feelings, are important and disturbing trends.
- **Aging of society.**   Baby boomers are nearing 60 and dominate society. Households headed by people over 55 are the fastest-growing segment of the consumer market in America, and this group controls an increasing percentage of all personal income. Meanwhile, Generation Xers are getting older, and those right behind are becoming more prominent and powerful.
- **Leanness and meanness.**   The new reality of employment is that "nothing lasts forever." Lifetime employment is no longer possible in most organizations. With downsizing, companies are continuing to pare overhead and trim staff to become

more competitive. Incoming employees understand that job hopping is much more a reality today than in years past. The effect on business and employee morale is profound, and the need for good internal communications is critical.

- **Corporate responsibility.** This buzzword of the 1960s and 1970s has become critical in the 2000s. The corporate scandals of 2002 have had a profound impact on how people assess corporations, their leaders, and their securities. Companies today must give back to society to begin to regain public trust.
- **Technology.** Knowledge of the Internet is imperative, not only in the practice of public relations but also in virtually every field of endeavor.
- **Bigness is back.** The trend toward linkages and mergers among huge industrial corporations, hospitals, banks, telecommunications firms, media companies, and others is unstoppable. In many cases, the only way to survive is to merge with others.
- **Accountability.** Again, with companies and CEOs suspect and with larger and larger companies delivering products, consumers, investors, regulators, and legislators are all demanding more accountability from all institutions, as well as higher standards of ethical conduct.

In the face of all these changes, it is understandable that management today is giving greater attention than ever before to the public's opinions of its organization and to public relations professionals who can help deal with these opinions.

21st Century Public Relations Challenges

As the significance of the practice of public relations intensifies, so will the challenges confronting the public relations profession. The challenges will be worldwide, just as the field itself has become worldwide. The power of communication, especially global communication, will no longer be an American domain. Among the significant challenges confronting public relations professionals are the following:

- **Need for tailored approaches.** Demographic changes will affect the way professionals communicate. Public relations practitioners will have to target messages across cultural lines to special groups within the population. This will involve narrowcasting as opposed to broadcasting. The mass media will play a less important role, and public relations professionals will have to deal with increased media fragmentation.[7]
- **Creativity.** As technology continues to advance, new and exotic forms of information dissemination will evolve. These media will capture public attention in the most creative ways—interactive video, talking billboards, blimps, in-flight headsets, and myriad others. Public relations will have to be equally creative to keep up with the new media and harness them for persuasive purposes.
- **Increased specialization.** Public relations professionals will have to be much more than a conduit between an organization and the public. They will have to be much more fully informed about company policy and activities. They will have to be specialists—experts in dealing with, for example, the media, consumers, and investors—possessing the sophisticated writing ability that management demands. At the same time, public relations will have to avoid what some have called the "balkanization" of the practice into discrete functions and away from management counseling.[8]

A QUESTION OF ETHICS

The Fall of Two Icons

2002 wasn't a good year for icons.

Not only did accounting and insider trading scandals rock the corporate world and shelve the credibility of some of the nation's most well-known CEO celebrities, but also even those unaffected by such charges also saw their credibility crushed.

Two such icons, both as it turned out inextricably intertwined, were the revered management publication, *Harvard Business Review (HBR)*, and the revered, retired CEO Jack Welch (Figure 22-1).

The editor of *HBR* sought to interview Welch, upon the publication of the best-selling *Jack from the Gut*, a memoir of the historic Welch years at the helm of General Electric.

But in learning about her subject, *HBR* Editor Suzy Wetlaufer got a bit too "close" as it turned out.

A splashy story in the *Wall Street Journal* revealed that Editor Wetlaufer and CEO Welch had become a lot more than interviewer and interviewee. They had become lovers.

The fallout from the Wetlaufer-Welch romance ravaged the reputations of one respected publication and one respected CEO.

1. Wetlaufer resigned, and *HBR* was criticized for not acting quickly enough to contain the crisis. Indeed, Ms. Wetlaufer's boss refused to kill the Welch interivew, even after she told him about their extracurricular activities. And even after she resigned, she was allowed to keep her office and hold a new position as editor at large.
2. Welch was sued for divorce, and his wife publicized the outrageous perks that GE

FIGURE 22-1 **CEO Welch.** Jack into the gutter.

shareholders were still paying him—an apartment, a chef, Knicks tickets, and more. Welch immediately said he would henceforth pay out of his own pocket for all the perks.

The Wetlaufer-Welch affair was a lose-lose for everybody. *HBR* was criticized by some for allowing things to go too far and by others for judging an editor too harshly because of her gender.

As for Welch, hailed as one of the all-time great CEOs, he learned the hard way that it takes years to build a reputation, but in the 21st century, credibility can be lost in a nanosecond.

For further information, see Carol Hymowitz, "An HBR Case Study: How the Magazine Failed to Respond to a Crisis," *Wall Street Journal* (May 14, 2002): B1.

- ● **Globalization.** As companies expand internationally, media coverage transcends national borders, and the practice of public relations becomes more accepted and coveted across national borders, the globalization of public relations will accelerate.
- ● **Technology.** Public relations professionals, as noted, will be blessed with an expanding array of technological tools to cope with the speed and impact of rapid, more global communications. Professionals must not only understand but stay current with and even ahead of the new technology if the field is to continue to develop.

- **Research/results orientation.** The growth of research to measure and evaluate public relations results will continue. Public relations professionals must find ways to improve their measurement capability and justify their performance—that is, the results of their actions—to management.
- **Decreased sexism.** Women are becoming more dominant in public relations and, in fact, outnumber their male counterparts. Indeed, in the years between 1970 and 1997, the proportion of women in public relations increased from 27 percent to 66 percent. The salary gap with men is narrowing. But as the field shifts to female majority, it "faces the realities of dwindling salary, status and influence."[9] This marks another challenge for the field in the new century.
- **Minority recruitment.** Although women continue to move in and up in public relations, the strides for minorities in the field have been slower. The emergence of groups like the National Black Public Relations Society (see "Tips from the Top" in Chapter 12) have helped, but the promotion of minorities in public relations remains a challenge in the 21st century.
- **Education.** The importance of public relations education, so vital if the field is to fulfill the jobs and promise of the new millennium, will also become more important. As management consultants, accountants, and lawyers all move to invade the influential turf that public relations has occupied, it will become more vital to train public relations leaders of the future.[10]
- **Ethics and reputation.** If public relations is truly to distinguish itself in the 21st century, it must represent the very highest values. Reputation matters, and public relations professionals are often "the keepers of the reputation." Most corporate CEOs look to their public relations professionals to oversee the firm's reputation.[11] In the 21st century, no challenge will be more important or critical to the field.

Counseling Top Management

In the new century, no challenge for public relations professionals is more important than counseling senior management.

Top managers in companies, hospitals, associations, governments, educational institutions, and most other organizations need counsel. Most CEOs think in terms of "tangibles"—revenue, income, costs per thousands, and so on. Public relations professionals think in terms of "intangibles"—attitudes, opinions, motivation, tomorrow morning's headline, and the like. Top management needs advice in these areas, and public relations practitioners must provide it.

Public relations people in the years ahead must be willing and eager to provide a counseling role to management. Accomplishing such a task will depend on the following 10 characteristics:

1. *Intimate knowledge of the institution.* A public relations professional may be an excellent communicator, but without knowledge of the industry or institution represented, his or her ultimate value will be limited.
2. *Access to and respect of management.* The public relations professional who acquires the respect of top management is a powerful force in an organization. Respect comes only from exposure. Thus, it is essential that the public relations professional have ready access to the most senior managers in an organization.

3. *Access to an intelligence network.* Public relations professionals need their own intelligence network to give them the unvarnished truth about programs and projects. If the executive vice president is an idiot, if the employee incentive program isn't working, or if the chairman's speech was terrible, the public relations professional must be able to tap a team of candid employees who will tell the truth so that the practitioner can tell the unvarnished truth to top management—unexpurgated, uncensored, between the eyes.

4. *Familiarity with the reporter on the beat.* A public relations professional, no matter how high up in an organization, should keep in touch with the reporters and analysts who follow the organization. Valuable information can be gleaned from such observers and can be most helpful to top management.

5. *Solid skills base.* The most competent public relations counselors don't just give orders, they demonstrate skills. They are generally good writers who don't mind pitching in to complete a job competently. In public relations, communications competence is a prerequisite for counseling competence.

6. *Propensity toward action.* In working for top management, results and performance are all that count. Certainly, planning and setting strategies are critical aspects of public relations. But practitioners, especially those who counsel management, must be inclined toward action. They must be doers. That's what management demands.

7. *Knowledge of the law.* Public relations work today confronts legal issues: privacy, copyright, lobbying, securities laws, broadcasting regulations, and so on. Although public relations professionals need not be trained lawyers, they must at least be conversant in the general concepts of the law in order to counsel management effectively and to deal with legal counselors.

8. *Knowledge of technological change.* The Internet, the World Wide Web, cyberspace—all must be part of the purview of the savvy public relations counselor. Harnessing the new technology is imperative for communications in this new century.

9. *Strong sense of integrity and confidence.* As noted throughout these pages, public relations professionals must be the ethical conscience of organizations. Their motives and methods must be above reproach. It's also important that public relations counselors demonstrate confidence in their own positions and abilities. They must surround themselves with the highest-caliber performers to enhance the status of the public relations function within the organization.

10. *Acceptance of anonymity.* Public relations counselors must understand that they are exactly that—counselors to top management. It is the chief who delivers the speeches, charts the strategies, and makes the decisions. Public relations counselors must remain in the background and should try to stay anonymous.

In the old days (when some of us, who shall remain nameless, started in this field), public relations people were *always* anonymous. Today, with newspapers demanding the names of spokespersons, with some public relations practitioners appearing on TV, and others attaining national celebrity status, and with the field itself becoming more and more prominent, the challenge of anonymity becomes increasingly more difficult.[12]

Nonetheless, it is the chief who should always derive the credit.

Skin Sells. . . . .

FIGURE 22-2 **Buzz on.** The publicity question for the 21st century is, "How does one create 'buzz' around a product?" Marina Maher Communications did it with a fashion show launching Airwonder by Wonderbra. (Courtesy of Marina Maher Communications)

Implications for Beginners

The reality of a more respected and, therefore, more competitive public relations profession has numerous implications for people just starting out in the field.

Although public relations professionals are highly sought today, competition for good jobs remains stiff. Experience is the great equalizer, and smart beginners can optimize their potential for employment by getting a jump on the competition through early experience. How?

. . . . .*Or Does It?*

FIGURE 22-3   **Buzz off.**
Portland Trail Blazer Rasheed Wallace reportedly was considering "renting out" his heavily tattooed body for a candy company to promote its product. At this writing, there were no takers for the body space "buzz." But don't hold your breath.

- By becoming involved with and active in student public relations organizations
- By securing—through faculty or others—part-time employment that uses the skills important in public relations work
- By attending professional meetings in the community, learning about public relations activities, and meeting public relations practitioners who might prove to be valuable contacts later on
- By seizing every opportunity—informal internships, voluntary work for nonprofit associations or political candidates, service on the school newspaper, merchandising in-class projects to local merchants

The key to finding and securing a good job in public relations is experience (Figure 22-4). So, rather than bemoan the catch-22 reality of a field in which you must have worked first in order to land a job, full-time students should use their college days to begin to acquire working knowledge in public relations. That way, when you look for that first job, you already have experience.

AGENCY OVERVIEW

TEHAMA GROUP
C O M M U N I C A T I O N S
Department of Journalism-CSU, Chico 95929-0600

Staff & Resources	About 15 public relations students participate each semester.
Clients	Seven to ten accounts are selected each semester.
Services Provided	Media Writing/Relations Special Event Planning/Assistance Strategic Planning Graphic Design Publications
Availability	Projects and services must be completed within the academic semester: August-December for the fall semester; January-May in the spring.
Client Selection	Clients are selected in August for the fall semester, and in January for the spring semester. Requests are accepted at any time.
Location	Tehama Hall, room 310 on the California State University, Chico campus.
Rates	Fees generally run between $500 and $4,000. There is no flat rate.

Tehama Group is a not-for-profit, educationally motivated organization. All revenues are used for operation and improvement of the agency.

Tehama Group Communications Staff, Fall 2002. Back row: Cheryl Taylor, Nikki Flynn, D'Anna Lee, Sarah Whorley, Kearsten Shepherd, Laura Langerwerf, Gennifer Horowitz, Erica Jostedt and adviser Keith Sheldon. Front row: Andrew Lemos, Leticia Lucero, Susan Olson and Alexis Dias.

FIGURE 22-4 **PR O.J.T.** The creation of Tehama Group Communications by students and faculty at California State University, Chico, was an example of for-pay, on-the-job public relations training. (Courtesy Tehama Group Communications)

LAST WORD

Most professions undergo constant change, but few experience more critical or frequent change than public relations.

In the 21st century, practitioners have been introduced to a tidal wave of primary concerns, among them distrust of institutions and their leaders, challenge to Western values, consumerism, environmentalism, government relations, and public policy. Areas of public relations opportunity expanded from marketing publicity to financial relations to employee communications to public issues management. Steadily, the field has expanded its horizons and increased its influence.

As such, the practice of public relations stands at the threshold of its *golden age*. To get there, however, public relations professionals must exemplify themselves and counsel to others the following indisputable values.

1. *Honesty*. Above all else, public relations people must tell the truth—always.

   This means being frank and candid with employees and shareholders. It means occasionally fessing up to business problems and performance shortfalls. It means not pulling punches or sugarcoating reality.

   All a CEO or a public relations adviser has to fall back on is his or her credibility. And if you lie—even once—you lose the public trust upon which your credibility depends.

2. *Professionalism*. Being professional means standing for something. At base, public relations people are professional communicators. Communications standards, therefore, must remain high, and practitioners must take pride in the communications products for which they are responsible.

3. *Ethics*. Public relations people must always do the right thing and CEOs counseled accordingly.

   The hardest admission for any CEO is, "We made a mistake."

   In the 2002 corporate scandals, it wasn't so much that executives took home outrageous compensation packages; it was that they acted deceitfully. Integrity, reputation, credibility and ethics are what public relations must stand for.

4. *Humanity*. Few in our society will any longer tolerate an unfeeling CEO, particularly in the current climate of CEO loathing.

   Public relations people must always act humanely, recognizing that, at base, all decisions involve people. As to advising CEOs, they, too, are human beings (in most cases, at least!). They should be counseled to act like it.

5. *Leadership*. Public relations people also must be leaders. They must advise their CEOs to act like leaders. Most, alas, don't.

   Leadership requires guts and risk and sticking out one's neck. That's what President Bush did, on the advice of Karen Hughes, to declare the war on terrorism.[13]

   Practicing these values will improve the image of public relations practice in the mind of the public (Table 22-1).

   To accomplish such leadership, public relations professionals must have the vision, courage, and character to lead themselves, their organizations, and their profession into the golden age.

   This is the 21st century challenge that awaits the new and future leaders entering the exciting, expanding, and ever-changing practice of public relations.

TABLE 22-1

The National Credibility Index

Measuring the Public's View of Credible Sources of Information in General.
Sample size 1,000; survey September 1998

Rank	Information Source	Mean Rating	Caucasian	African-American	Other
1	Supreme Court Justice	81.3	82.6	74.5	78.3
2	Teacher	80.7	80.7	81.7	77.4
3	National Expert	78.6	79.3	77.8	75.7
4	Member of the Armed Forces	73.0	73.9	70.4	71.1
5	Local Business Owner	72.2	73.5	70.1	67.0
6	Ordinary Citizen	71.8	71.2	76.3	70.2
7	Local Religious Leader	71.8	72.7	72.9	67.4
8	Local Ranking Military Officer	71.7	71.8	71.1	69.8
9	School Official	71.3	71.5	72.7	64.8
10	National Leader of People with Shared Traits	71.1	68.6	79.9	70.7
11	National Religious Leader	69.2	69.1	75.0	68.1
12	Network TV News Anchor	66.8	67.0	66.5	61.5
13	Governor	66.8	66.6	68.6	64.8
14	Representative of a Local Business/Trade Asso.	66.6	67.6	66.2	61.1
15	Reporter for a Local Newspaper/TV Station	65.8	66.5	67.0	59.1
16	National Civil Rights Leader	65.6	62.4	77.3	71.7
17	Locally Elected Council Member/Supervisor	65.2	65.1	67.8	63.1
18	U.S. Senator	64.2	63.7	65.7	63.1
19	Nationally Syndicated News Columnist	64.0	63.4	63.4	64.6
20	Mayor of a Large City	63.5	62.8	66.0	62.2
21	Head of a State Department or Agency	63.1	62.5	68.0	60.7
22	Head of a Local Agency or Department	62.9	62.8	64.4	59.8
23	Reporter for a Major Newspaper/Magazine	62.4	62.2	61.6	60.4
24	U.S. Congressman	62.2	61.7	58.5	63.5
25	President of a Large Corporation	61.6	61.7	58.5	63.5
26	Local Civil Rights Leader	60.3	57.2	74.2	64.8
27	U.S. Vice President	60.2	57.8	70.9	58.5
28	Head of a National Business/Industry Association	59.6	58.9	61.3	59.6
29	Community Activist	59.2	55.7	71.9	63.9
30	Wall Street Executive	57.9	58.0	58.5	57.4
31	Head of a Presidential Advisory Board	57.6	55.8	64.2	57.4
32	U.S. President	56.9	53.9	73.2	57.2
33	Member of a President's Cabinet	56.1	54.0	66.5	54.3
34	Pollster	55.9	55.4	62.9	53.1
35	Student Activist	53.3	50.8	68.0	55.7
36	Local Labor Union Leader	53.3	51.0	65.2	54.1
37	Candidate for Local Office	53.1	51.8	58.8	53.3
38	Head of a National Labor Union	53.0	49.5	68.0	53.3
39	Famous Athlete	52.1	50.3	60.3	54.1
40	Head of a National Interest Group	51.3	48.5	64.2	54.4
41	Political Party Leader	48.6	47.2	56.4	49.8
42	Public Relations Specialist	47.6	44.5	60.6	50.7
43	Famous Entertainer	46.8	44.6	58.0	48.0
44	TV or Radio Talk Show Host	46.6	44.8	55.7	47.6

The challenge. In terms of "whom the public believes," the public relations profession—ranking just ahead of famous entertainers and talk show hosts—still has a way to go. (Courtesy of "The National Credibility Index" study of the Public Relations Society of America Foundation)

Discussion Starters

1. What evidence can you point to that indicates the increased stature of public relations practice?
2. What factors are shaping the new environment in which public relations must operate?
3. What are the primary challenges for public relations into the 21st century?
4. What are the skills requisite for counseling management?
5. How should a public relations professional regard anonymity?
6. What are the status and outlook for women in public relations?
7. What are the status and outlook for minorities in public relations?
8. How important is technological knowledge for public relations practitioners?
9. How can entry-level public relations students get ahead in the 21st century?
10. What is the outlook for public relations practice?

TOP OF THE SHELF

Leonard Mogel

Making It in Public Relations: An Insider's Guide to Career Opportunities, *2nd ed.*
Mahwah, NJ: Lawrence Erlbaum Associates Inc., 2002

"Twenty-first-century public relations is on a roll," Leonard Mogel writes. "It is replacing advertising as corporation's primary source for getting its message across because it is often more cost-effective than advertising in building brands and reaching customers and constituents."

In this book, public relations enthusiast and career expert Mogel guides students and recent grads through the profession. He offers an overview of the various roles and responsibilities involved in PR work, the different types of PR functions and activities, and its application in a variety of settings and scenarios.

Mogel also profiles the 10 largest public relations firms, life on the fast track at a small PR firm, how corporate communications are carried on at a large financial institution, and public relations for diverse organizations.

CASE STUDY

NASA Rises to a Sad PR Challenge

On January 28, 1986, the space shuttle *Challenger* exploded before a national television audience 73 seconds after liftoff.

In its wake, the public relations reputation of the National Aeronautics and Space Administration (NASA)—with a public information budget of $5 million—exploded as well.

NASA's PR handling of the tragedy was an unmitigated disaster—an organizational primer on how "not to handle" a crisis.

1. When TV screens clearly showed a fireball less than two minutes into launch, NASA's mission control commentator would only acknowledge an "apparent explosion" and a "major malfunction."

2. Although NASA's own PR emergency plan emphasized the necessity of issuing rapid public statements after an accident, noting that "rumors and speculation creating further problems will result if release is delayed," the agency waited five full hours to hold its first news conference.

3. In the days following the disaster, NASA impounded all documents pertaining to the launch, including weather reports and temperature readings. Reporters were forced to search elsewhere for information, and speculation—from a failure of the solid-fuel booster rocket to sabotage—ran rampant.

4. NASA even tried to bamboozle the media by keeping the ships collecting *Challenger* debris offshore till nightfall, when pictures were harder to get, and by sending empty, decoy ambulances to a nearby Air Force hospital to divert the media when astronaut remains were recovered and returned.

NASA's *Challenger* PR meltdown—its tendency, as one official put it, "to circle the wagons and fight off attacks on the shuttle program"—helped ruin the agency's reputation and led to a two-and-a-half-year suspension of the shuttle program.

RETURN TO TRAGEDY

Seventeen years later, on Saturday, February 1, 2003, NASA proved that it had learned much about the practice of public relations since the *Challenger* disaster.

Early that morning, the space shuttle *Columbia*, plummeting toward reentry over Dallas, Texas, suddenly, horribly, broke into parts over the Texas sky (Figure 22-5).

But this time, NASA was ready to communicate, despite the unspeakable crisis it confronted.

Within hours, NASA Administrator Sean O'Keefe and Associate Administrator Bill Readdy appeared at a news briefing (Figure 22-6) to underscore the gravity of the situation and to express the agency's profound sorrow for "a tragic day for the NASA family, for the families of the astronauts who flew on STS-107 and, likewise, tragic for the nation."

The two administrators then meticulously traced the events of the day, including communication with astronaut families, President Bush, and other federal officials, so that reporters had at least some information to "hold" them until a more extensive news conference later in the day.

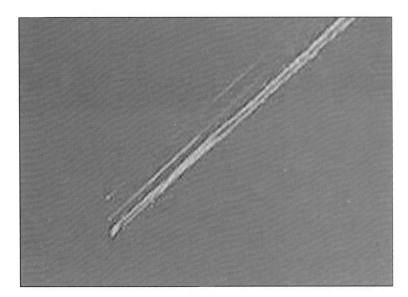

FIGURE 22-5
Reentry horror.
The space shuttle *Columbia* breaks apart over the skies of Texas.

FIGURE 22-6 **Sad announcement.** NASA Administrator Sean O'Keefe (left) and Associate Administrator Bill Readdy, both shocked and saddened, quickly advised the nation that the shuttle was gone and the astronauts dead.

Where NASA's response to the *Challenger* crash was slow and guarded, this time the agency responded in a timely and appropriate manner.

A few hours later, after President Bush confirmed to the nation that, "The *Columbia* is lost, and there are no survivors," NASA staged a satellite news conference from Houston, with links to reporters at its other U.S. facilities.

Shuttle Program Manager Ron Dittemore, obviously distraught and emotional, nonetheless frankly and straightforwardly answered a full hour and a half's worth of pointed yet respectful journalist questions.

Patiently Dittemore and a colleague answered every question as best as they could in the immediate hours after the tragedy. The NASA news conference was so riveting that the entire Q&A session was carried live by all the cable and broadcast networks.

Dittemore didn't duck, even when asked pointed questions about whether the *Columbia*'s thermal tiles, damaged at liftoff, might have been the cause of the tragedy.

"As we look at that now in hindsight . . . we can't discount that there might be a connection," he answered sadly.

When asked if he was now focused on what might have been done if the liftoff damage was to blame, Dittemore responded, "My thoughts are on seven families, children, spouses, extended family. My thoughts are on their grief. My thoughts are on what we missed—what I missed—to allow this to happen."

The NASA official's remarks were breathtaking in their candor.

NASA also quickly responded to dispel irresponsible speculation about the cause of the explosion.

With America on edge over terrorism and an imminent war in the Middle East, speculation immediately gathered about whether the *Columbia* was "attacked" from the ground. This was exacerbated by the presence on board of the first Israeli astronaut, Col. Ilan Ramon, a decorated hero who had been one of the pilots responsible for bombing a dangerous nuclear reactor in Iraq years earlier.

NASA and others acted quickly to cut off such rumors.

At Cape Canaveral, NASA Chief O'Keefe told an early news conference, "At this time, we have no indication that the mishap was caused by anything or anyone on the ground."

Later, NASA pointed out that at an altitude of about 203,000 feet over north-central Texas when it lost contact, the shuttle was out of range of surface-to-air missiles.

FIGURE 22-7   **Fallen heroes.** The seven brave crew members of space shuttle *Columbia*.

Whereas 17 years earlier, NASA fumbled with the report of sabotage bringing down *Challenger*, this time the agency successfully squelched the rumors about terrorism bringing down *Columbia*.

DEATHS IN THE "FAMILY"

What happened with the *Columbia* and the *Challenger* were, above all else, human tragedies.

Whereas NASA's public response to the *Challenger* had been detached—even clinical—there was nothing "detached" about the agency's response to *Columbia*.

Throughout the first awful weekend—beginning with the immediate NASA news conferences and following through on all the major interview programs—the overwhelming impression communicated by agency officials was that of a "grieving family."

Said O'Keefe, "The loss of this valiant crew is something we will never be able to get over. And certainly the families of all of them we have assured we will do everything, everything we can possibly do to guarantee that they work their way through this horrific tragedy."

Every NASA speaker who came forward at daily news conferences to update the world on investigation progress emphasized the "NASA family." So, too, did the NASA administrators, who made themselves available to a multitude of interviewers.

Even the NASA Web site, which, ironically, had been upgraded just nine hours before *Columbia*'s fall, emphasized information about the shuttle's mission and the seven crew members who gave their lives "in the service to all humanity," as President Bush put it (Figure 22-7).

Over the next several months, NASA officials were grilled on what happened and why. But the agency held up well. Mourning the human toll of *Columbia* remained foremost in the public posture of NASA—indicating that the agency had learned much about the practice of public relations in the nearly two decades between its two great tragedies.

Questions

1. Compare and contrast NASA's public relations responses in the *Challenger* and *Columbia* disasters.
2. What were the public relations lessons the agency learned by the time of the *Columbia* tragedy in 2003?

TIPS FROM THE TOP

An Interview with Peter Drucker

The great professor. The eminent Dr. Drucker and a less eminent friend.

Peter Drucker has been called "the greatest thinker management theory has produced" by the *London Economist*. He has written 29 books, which have been translated into nearly every language in the world; counseled presidents, bishops, baseball managers, CEOs, and symphony conductors on the finer points of management success; and, in his eighth decade, continued to write, lecture, and teach regularly at Claremont College in California.

What would you say have been your greatest contributions to business and society?

One, I made management visible. People say I've discovered management—that's nonsense. I made it into a discipline.

Second, I was also the first one who said that people are a resource and not just a cost, and they have to be placed where they can make a contribution. The only ones who took me up on it were the Japanese for a long time.

The third one is knowledge—that knowledge work would be preeminent.

Four, I was the first to say that the purpose of business is to create the customer and to innovate. That I think is a major contribution. That took a long time to sink in—that management is not this mad dog of internal rules and regulations, that it's a discipline that can be learned and taught and practiced.

I think those four. The rest are secondary.

What is your view of today's public relations practice?

There is no public relations.

There's publicity, promotion, advertising, but "relations" by definition is a two-way street. And the more important job and the more difficult is not to bring business and the executives to the outside but to bring the outside to these terribly insulated people. And this will be far more important in the next 20 years, when the outside is going to change beyond all recognition. I'm not only talking business CEOs but also university presidents and even bishops—several of my charity patients are bishops—all need to know what's going on outside.

Can you elaborate?

With an example. Have you ever heard of Paul Garrett?

Paul Garrett came out of journalism. He wanted to build a proper public relations department, to bring to General Motors what the outside was like. He would have been very effective. But GM didn't let him. Alfred Sloan (GM's CEO) brought Garrett in 1930 to keep GM out of *Fortune*. *Fortune* was founded as a muckraking magazine with investigative journalism.

Why didn't Sloan, supposedly one of the greatest managers of all time, want to listen to Garrett?
Neither Sloan nor anybody else in top management of General Motors wanted to hear what Garrett would have told them. And this was still the case much later.

Paul Garrett was a professional, who would have told them things they didn't want to hear and wouldn't believe. Killing the messenger is never the right policy.

And in GM's case, the employee relations people totally failed to warn the company of the horrible sit-down strike they would suffer. And then when investor relations became important, it wasn't assigned to the public relations people.

And to this day, most institutions still look upon public relations as their "trumpet" and not as their "hearing aid." It's got to be both.

What do you see as the future of the practice of public relations?
I think there is a need.

It is a very complicated and complex function. The media are no longer homogenous and are much more critical. But there is a need for an intermediary to tell the truth to management. Public relations people today don't do that because they're scared, because the people they work for don't like to hear what they don't want to hear.

Let's face it. There's an old saying, "If I have you for a friend, I don't need an enemy."

Suggested Readings

A Port of Entry: Public Relations Education for the 21st Century. New York: Public Relations Society of America. The Report of the Commission of Public Relations Education.

Careers in Public Relations. (Available from the Public Relations Society of America, 33 Irving Place, New York, NY 10003.)

Celente, Gerald. *Trends 2000: How to Prepare for and Profit from the Changes of the 21st Century.* New York, NY: Warner Books, 1998.

Design for Public Relations Education. (Available from the Public Relations Society of America, 33 Irving Place, New York, NY 10003.)

Drucker, Peter F. *Managing for the Future: The 1990s and Beyond.* New York: Plume, 1993.

Futurist. (Available from World Future Society, 4916 St. Elmo Avenue, Washington, D.C. 20014.) This bimonthly journal includes forecasts, trends, and ideas about the future on all topics.

Grates, Gary F. "Seeing Through New Eyes . . . A View on Optimizing the Future." *Public Relations Quarterly* (Summer 1998): 5ff.

International Directory of Business Information Sources and Services, 2nd ed. Chicago: Europa Press, 1996.

Kruckeberg, Dean. "The Future of PR Education: Some Recommendations." *Public Relations Review* (Summer 1998): 235ff.

Naisbitt, John, and Patricia Aburdene. *Megatrends 2000.* New York: William Morrow, 1990.

Pyle, Jack. "Strategy for the Millennium: Communicating Face-to-Face." *Public Relations Strategist* (Fall 1998): 47–48.

Taylor, Jim, and Watts Wacker. *The 500-Year Delta.* New York: HarperBusiness, 1998. The language of the millennium, say the authors, will begin with *re*—reengineering, reclamation, reintermediation—rather than the *dis* that characterized the 1990s.

Toth, Elizabeth L. *Public Relations Values in the New Millennium*, Special Issue of the *Journal of Public Relations Research*, 2000.

Notes

1. 2001 Public Relations Industry Revenue Documentation and Rankings," Council of Public Relations Firms, New York, NY.
2. Corporate Communication Practices & Trends 2001," Corporate Communications Institute at Fairleigh Dickinson University, www.corporatecomm.org, January 9, 2002.
3. The Five Traits of 21st Century Leadership," *The Mount Vernon Report* (Fall 2002): 1.
4. Corporate Communication Practices & Trends 2001."
5. Communicators Face Tough Times," *The Ragan Report* (December 2, 2002): 8.
6. Lisa Bannon, "Bottom Line on Fad: A Surgeon Thrives on Dubious Publicity," *Wall Street Journal* (April 16, 2002): A1–8.
7. PR Heads into a Golden Age as Advertising's Pitch Falters," *Business Wire Newsletter* (July 1999): 2.
8. Philip Lesly, "The Balkanizing of Public Relations," *Public Relations Strategist* (Fall 1996): 41.
9. Larissa A. Grunig, Elizabeth Lance Toth, and Linda Childers Hon, *Women in Public Relations: How Gender Inflences Practice* (New York: The Guilford Press, 2001).
10. Consultants, Accounting Firms Take 'Dead Aim' at PR Biz," *O'Dwyer's PR Services Report* (November 1999): 1, 62.
11. Ten Predictions for PR in the New Millennium," *PR Week* (January 10, 2000): 29.
12. Fraser P. Seitel, "Convincing Management of PR's Value," odwyerpr.com (April 3, 2001).
13. Fraser P. Seitel, "Becoming the CEO's Communications Consigliere," odwyerpr.com (July 30, 2002).

APPENDIX A

**PRSA Member Code of Ethics
2000**

Approved by the PRSA Assembly
October, 2000

Letter from the PRSA Board of Directors

It is with enormous professional pleasure and personal pride that we, the Public Relations Society of America Board of Directors put before you a new Public Relations Member Code of Ethics for our Society. It is the result of two years of concentrated effort led by the Board of Ethics and Professional Standards. Comments of literally hundreds and hundreds of members were considered. There were focus groups at our 1999 national meeting in Anaheim, California. We sought and received intensive advice and counsel from the Ethics Resource Center, our outside consultants on the project. Additional recommendations were received from your Board of Directors, PRSA staff, outside reviewers, as well as District and Section officers. Extensive research involving analysis of numerous codes of conduct, ethics statements, and standards and practices approaches was also carried out.

In fact, this Member Code of Ethics has been developed to serve as a foundation for discussion of an emerging global Code of Ethics and Conduct for the practice of Public Relations.

This approach is dramatically different from that which we have relied upon in the past. You'll find it different in three powerfully important ways:
1. Emphasis on enforcement of the Code has been eliminated. But,the PRSA Board of Directors retains the right to bar from membership or expel from the Society any individual who has been or is sanctioned by a government agency or convicted in a court of law of an action that is in violation of this Code.
2. The new focus is on universal values that inspire ethical behavior and performance.
3. Desired behavior is clearly illustrated by providing language, experience, and examples to help the individual practitioner better achieve important ethical and principled business objectives. This approach should help everyone better understand what the expected standards of conduct truly are.

Perhaps most important of all, the mission of the Board of Ethics and Professional Standards has now been substantially altered to focus primarily on education and training, on collaboration with similar efforts in other major professional societies, and to serve an advisory role to the Board on ethical matters of major importance.

The foundation of our value to our companies, clients and those we serve is their ability to rely on our ethical and morally acceptable behavior. Please review this new Member Code of Ethics in this context:

- Its Values are designed to inspire and motivate each of us every day to the highest levels of ethical practice.
- Its Code Provisions are designed to help each of us clearly understand the limits and specific performance required to be an ethical practitioner.
- Its Commitment mechanism is designed to ensure that every Society member understands fully the obligations of membership and the expectation of ethical behavior that are an integral part of membership in the PRSA.

This approach is stronger than anything we have ever had because:

- It will have a daily impact on the practice of Public Relations.
- There are far fewer gray areas and issues that require interpretation.
- It will grow stronger and be more successful than what we have had in the past through education, through training, and through analysis of behaviors.

The strength of the Code will grow because of the addition of precedent and the ethical experiences of other major professional organizations around the world.

Our new Code elevates our ethics, our values, and our commitment to the level they belong, at the very top of our daily practice of Public Relations.

PRSA Board of Directors

A Message from the PRSA Board of Ethics and Professional Standards

Our Primary Obligation

The primary obligation of membership in the Public Relations Society of America is the ethical practice of Public Relations.

The PRSA Member Code of Ethics is the way each member of our Society can daily reaffirm a commitment to ethical professional activities and decisions.
- The Code sets forth the principles and standards that guide our decisions and actions.
- The Code solidly connects our values and our ideals to the work each of us does every day.
- The Code is about what we should do, and why we should do it.

The Code is also meant to be a living, growing body of knowledge, precedent, and experience. It should stimulate our thinking and encourage us to seek guidance and clarification when we have questions about principles, practices, and standards of conduct.

Every member's involvement in preserving and enhancing ethical standards is essential to building and maintaining the respect and credibility of our profession. Using our values, principles, standards of conduct, and commitment as a foundation, and continuing to work together on ethical issues, we ensure that the Public Relations Society of America fulfills its obligation to build and maintain the framework for public dialogue that deserves the public's trust and support.

The Members of the 2000 Board of Ethics and Professional Standards

Robert D. Frause, APR, Fellow PRSA Chairman BEPS Seattle, Washington	Kathy R. Fitzpatrick, APR Gainesville, Florida	Linda Welter Cohen, APR Tucson, Arizona
James R. Frankowiak, APR Tampa, Florida	James E. Lukaszewski, APR, Fellow PRSA White Plains, New York	Roger D. Buehrer, APR Fellow PRSA Las Vegas, Nevada
Jeffrey P. Julin, APR Denver, Colorado	David M. Bicofsky, APR, Fellow PRSA Teaneck, New Jersey	James W. Wyckoff, APR New York, New York

Preamble

Public Relations Society of America
Member Code of Ethics 2000

- Professional Values
- Principles of Conduct
- Commitment and Compliance

This Code applies to PRSA members. The Code is designed to be a useful guide for PRSA members as they carry out their ethical responsibilities. This document is designed to anticipate and accommodate, by precedent, ethical challenges that may arise. The scenarios outlined in the Code provision are actual examples of misconduct. More will be added as experience with the Code occurs.

The Public Relations Society of America (PRSA) is committed to ethical practices. The level of public trust PRSA members seek, as we serve the public good, means we have taken on a special obligation to operate ethically.

The value of member reputation depends upon the ethical conduct of everyone affiliated with the Public Relations Society of America. Each of us sets an example for each other—as well as other professionals—by our pursuit of excellence with powerful standards of performance, professionalism, and ethical conduct.

Emphasis on enforcement of the Code has been eliminated. But, the PRSA Board of Directors retains the right to bar from membership or expel from the Society any individual who has been or is sanctioned by a government agency or convicted in a court of law of an action that is in violation of this Code.

Ethical practice is the most important obligation of a PRSA member. We view the Member Code of Ethics as a model for other professions, organizations, and professionals.

PRSA Member Statement
of Professional Values

This statement presents the core values of PRSA members and, more broadly, of the public relations profession. These values provide the foundation for the Member Code of Ethics and set the industry standard for the professional practice of public relations. These values are the fundamental beliefs that guide our behaviors and decision-making process. We believe our professional values are vital to the integrity of the profession as a whole.

Advocacy
- We serve the public interest by acting as responsible advocates for those we represent.
- We provide a voice in the marketplace of ideas, facts, and view-points to aid informed public debate.

Honesty
- We adhere to the highest standards of accuracy and truth in advancing the interests of those we represent and in communicating with the public.

Expertise
- We acquire and responsibly use specialized knowledge and experience.
- We advance the profession through continued professional development, research, and education.
- We build mutual understanding, credibility, and relationships among a wide array of institutions and audiences.

Independence
- We provide objective counsel to those we represent.
- We are accountable for our actions.

Loyalty
- We are faithful to those we represent, while honoring our obligation to serve the public interest.

Fairness
- We deal fairly with clients, employers, competitors, peers, vendors, the media, and the general public.
- We respect all opinions and support the right of free expression.

PRSA Code Provisions

FREE FLOW OF INFORMATION

Core Principle
Protecting and advancing the free flow of accurate and truthful information is essential to serving the public interest and contributing to informed decision making in a democratic society.

Intent
- To maintain the integrity of relationships with the media, government officials, and the public.
- To aid informed decision-making.

Guidelines
A member shall:
- Preserve the integrity of the process of communication.
- Be honest and accurate in all communications.
- Act promptly to correct erroneous communications for which the practitioner is responsible.
- Preserve the free flow of unprejudiced information when giving or receiving gifts by ensuring that gifts are nominal, legal, and infrequent.

Examples of Improper Conduct Under this Provision
- A member representing a ski manufacturer gives a pair of expensive racing skis to a sports magazine columnist, to influence the columnist to write favorable articles about the product.
- A member entertains a government official beyond legal limits and/or in violation of government reporting requirements.

COMPETITION

Core Principle
Promoting healthy and fair competition among professionals preserves an ethical climate while fostering a robust business environment.

Intent
- To promote respect and fair competition among public relations professionals.
- To serve the public interest by providing the widest choice of practitioner options.

Guidelines
A member shall:
- Follow ethical hiring practices designed to respect free and open competition without deliberately undermining a competitor.
- Preserve intellectual property rights in the marketplace.

Examples of Improper Conduct Under This Provision
- A member employed by a "client organization" shares helpful information with a counseling firm that is competing with others for the organization's business.
- A member spreads malicious and unfounded rumors about a competitor in order to alienate the competitor's clients and employees in a ploy to recruit people and business.

DISCLOSURE OF INFORMATION

Core Principle
Open communication fosters informed decision making in a democratic society.

Intent
- To build trust with the public by revealing all information needed for responsible decision making.

Guidelines
A member shall:
- Be honest and accurate in all communications.
- Act promptly to correct erroneous communications for which the member is responsible.
- Investigate the truthfulness and accuracy of information released on behalf of those represented.
- Reveal the sponsors for causes and interests represented.
- Disclose financial interest (such as stock ownership) in a client's organization.
- Avoid deceptive practices.

Examples of Improper Conduct Under this Provision
- Front groups: A member implements "grass roots" campaigns or letter-writing campaigns to legislators on behalf of undisclosed interest groups.
- Lying by omission: A practitioner for a corporation knowingly fails to release financial information, giving a misleading impression of the corporation's performance.
- A member discovers inaccurate information disseminated via a Web site or media kit and does not correct the information.
- A member deceives the public by employing people to pose as volunteers to speak at public hearings and participate in "grass roots" campaigns.

SAFEGUARDING CONFIDENCES

Core Principle
Client trust requires appropriate protection of confidential and private information.

Intent
- To protect the privacy rights of clients, organizations, and individuals by safeguarding confidential information.

Guidelines
A member shall:
- Safeguard the confidences and privacy rights of present, former, and prospective clients and employees.
- Protect privileged, confidential, or insider information gained from a client or organization.
- Immediately advise an appropriate authority if a member discovers that confidential information is being divulged by an employee of a client company or organization.

Examples of Improper Conduct Under This Provision
- A member changes jobs, takes confidential information, and uses that information in the new position to the detriment of the former employer.

- A member intentionally leaks proprietary information to the detriment of some other party.

CONFLICTS OF INTEREST

Core Principle
Avoiding real, potential or perceived conflicts of interest builds the trust of clients, employers, and the publics.

Intent
- To earn trust and mutual respect with clients or employers.
- To build trust with the public by avoiding or ending situations that put one's personal or professional interests in conflict with society's interests.

Guidelines
A member shall:
- Act in the best interests of the client or employer, even subordinating the member's personal interests.
- Avoid actions and circumstances that may appear to compromise good business judgment or create a conflict between personal and professional interests.
- Disclose promptly any existing or potential conflict of interest to affected clients or organizations.
- Encourage clients and customers to determine if a conflict exists after notifying all affected parties.

Examples of Improper Conduct Under This Provision
- The member fails to disclose that he or she has a strong financial interest in a client's chief competitor.
- The member represents a "competitor company" or a "conflicting interest" without informing a prospective client.

ENHANCING THE PROFESSION

Core Principle
Public relations professionals work constantly to strengthen the public's trust in the profession.

Intent
- To build respect and credibility with the public for the profession of public relations.
- To improve, adapt and expand professional practices.

Guidelines
A member shall:
- Acknowledge that there is an obligation to protect and enhance the profession.
- Keep informed and educated about practices in the profession to ensure ethical conduct.
- Actively pursue personal professional development.
- Decline representation of clients or organizations that urge or require actions contrary to this Code.
- Accurately define what public relations activities can accomplish.
- Counsel subordinates in proper ethical decision making.

- Require that subordinates adhere to the ethical requirements of the Code.
- Report ethical violations, whether committed by PRSA members or not, to the appropriate authority.

Examples of Improper Conduct Under This Provision
- A PRSA member declares publicly that a product the client sells is safe, without disclosing evidence to the contrary.
- A member initially assigns some questionable client work to a non-member practitioner to avoid the ethical obligation of PRSA membership.

RESOURCES

Rules and Guidelines
The following PRSA documents, available in The Blue Book, provide detailed rules and guidelines to help guide your professional behavior:
- PRSA Bylaws
- PRSA Administrative Rules
- Member Code of Ethics

If, after reviewing them, you still have a question or issue, contact PRSA headquarters as noted below.

QUESTIONS

The PRSA is here to help. Whether you have a serious concern or simply need clarification, contact Judy Voss at judy.voss@prsa.org.

PRSA Member Code of Ethics
Pledge

I pledge:

To conduct myself professionally, with truth, accuracy,
fairness, and responsibility to the public;
to improve my individual competence and advance the
knowledge and proficiency of the profession through
continuing research and education;
and to adhere to the articles of the Member Code
of Ethics 2000 for the practice of public relations as adopted
by the governing Assembly of the
Public Relations Society of America.

I understand and accept that there is a consequence for
misconduct, up to and including membership revocation.

And, I understand that those who have been or are sanctioned by
a government agency or convicted in a court of law of an action that
is in violation of this Code may be barred from membership or
expelled from the Society.

_____
Signature

_____
Date

Public Relations Society of America
33 Irving Place
New York, NY 10003
www.prsa.org

APPENDIX B

PRIA Code of Ethics

The Public Relations Institute of Australia is a professional body serving the interests of its members. In doing so, the Institute is mindful of the responsibility which public relations professionals owe to the community as well as to their clients and employers. The Institute requires members to adhere to the highest standards of ethical practice and professional competence. All members are duty-bound to act responsibly and to be accountable for their actions.

The following Code of Ethics binds all members of the Public Relations Institute of Australia.

1. Members shall deal fairly and honestly with their employers, clients and prospective clients, with their fellow workers including superiors and subordinates, with public officials, the communications media, the general public and with fellow members of PRIA.
2. Members shall avoid conduct or practices likely to bring discredit upon themselves, the Institute, their employers or clients.
3. Members shall not knowingly disseminate false or misleading information and shall take care to avoid doing so inadvertently.
4. Members shall safeguard the confidences of both present and former employers and clients, including confidential information about employers' or clients' business affairs, technical methods or processes, except upon the order of a court of competent jurisdiction.
5. No member shall represent conflicting interests nor, without the consent of the parties concerned, represent competing interests.
6. Members shall refrain from proposing or agreeing that their consultancy fees or other remuneration be contingent entirely on the achievement of specified results.
7. Members shall inform their employers or clients if circumstances arise in which their judgment or the disinterested character of their services may be questioned by reason of personal relationships or business or financial interests.
8. Members practising as consultants shall seek payment only for services specifically commissioned.
9. Members shall be prepared to identify the source of funding of any public communication they initiate or for which they act as a conduit.
10. Members shall, in advertising and marketing their skills and services and in soliciting professional assignments, avoid false, misleading or exaggerated claims and shall refrain from comment or action that may injure the professional reputation, practice or services of a fellow member.
11. Members shall inform the Board of the Institute and/or the relevant State/Territory Council(s) of the Institute of evidence purporting to show that a member has been guilty of, or could be charged with, conduct constituting a breach of this Code.
12. No member shall intentionally injure the professional reputation or practice of another member.

13. Members shall help to improve the general body of knowledge of the profession by exchanging information and experience with fellow members.
14. Members shall act in accord with the aims of the institute, its regulations and policies.
15. Members shall not misrepresent their status through misuse of title, grading, or the designation FPRIA, MPRIA or APRIA.

Adopted by the Board of the Institute on November 5, 2001, this Code of Ethics supersedes all previous versions.

APPENDIX C

Corporate Reporting Requirements

Periodically, the Hill & Knowlton public relations firm updates this compilation of "Disclosure and Filing Requirements for Public Companies." It details the specific requirements of the various exchanges as well as the Securities and Exchange Commission.

DISCLOSURE REQUIREMENTS

Reporting Required for:	Securities and Exchange Commission	New York Stock Exchange	American Stock Exchange	National Association of Securities Dealers	Generally Recommended Publicity Practice, All Companies
Accounting: Change in Auditors	Form 8-K; if principal accountant (or accountants for a subsidiary) resigns, declines to be reelected, or is dismissed or if another is engaged. Disclose date of resignation, details of disagreement (any adverse opinions, disclaimers of opinion, or qualifications of opinion occurring during the audits of the two most recent fiscal years), comment letters to SEC for former accountant on whether he agrees with the company's statements in the 8-K. See also Regulations S-K, Item 304.	Prompt notice to Exchange, 8-K when filed.	Prompt notification of Listing Representative, prior to filing of 8-K, *and* must state reason for change (Listing Form SD-1, Item 1a).	Prompt notification concurrently with press disclosure (company must file 8-K with SEC, and information may be material enough to warrant trading halt, see NASD Schedule D). Contact NASD's Market Surveillance Section at (202) 728-8187, preferably before public release and when in doubt about "material information."(NASD Schedule D.) Promptly confirm in writing all oral communications to NASD. If public release made after 5:30 P.M. Eastern Standard Time, notify NASD by 9:30 A.M. the following trading day. (NASD Schedule D.)	Press release desirable at time of filing 8-K if differences are major. Consider clear statement in annual report or elsewhere on independence of auditors, including their reporting relationship to Board's audit committee; state company policy on rotation/nonrotation of auditors periodically.
Annual (or Special) Meeting of Stockholders	10-Q following meeting, including date of meeting, name of each director elected, summary of other matters voted on.	Five copies of all proxy material sent to shareholders filed with Exchange not later than date material sent to any shareholder. Ten days' advance notice of record date or closing transfer books to Exchange. The notice should	Six copies of all material sent to shareholders should be sent to the Securities Division as soon as mailed to shareholders (Listing Form SD-1, Item 13). Other requirements same as for NYSE (Listing Form SD-1. Item 1H for notice regarding record date).	File 10-Q concurrently with SEC filing.	Press release at time of meeting. Competition for news space minimizes public coverage except on actively contested issues. Check NYSE schedules for competing meetings. Recommended wide distribution of post-meeting report to shareholders.

Reporting Required for:	Securities and Exchange Commission	New York Stock Exchange	American Stock Exchange	National Association of Securities Dealers	Generally Recommended Publicity Practice, All Companies
		state the purpose(s) for which the record date has been fixed. Preferably, notice should be given by TWX (TWX No. 710-581-2801); or, if by telephone, promptly confirmed by TWX, telegram, or letter.			
Annual Report to Shareholders: Contents	Requirements listed under Rule 14a-3 of the 1934 Act. They include audited balance sheets for two most recent fiscal years; audited income statements and changes in financial position for each of three most recent fiscal years; management's discussion and analysis of financial condition and results of financial operations; brief description of general nature and scope of the business; industry segment information; company directors and officers; stock price and dividends. SEC encourages "freedom of management expression."	Include in annual report principal office's address; directors' and officers' names; audit committee and other committee members; trustees, transfer agents, and registrars; numbers of employees and shareholders (*NYSE Company Manual* Section 203.01). Also include the number of shares of stock issuable under outstanding options at the beginning of the year; separate totals of changes in the number of shares of its stock under option resulting from issuance. exercise, expiration, or cancellation of options; and the number of shares issuable under outstanding options at the close of the year, the number of unoptioned shares available at the beginning and at the close of the year for the granting of options under an option plan, and any changes in the price of outstanding options, through cancellation and reissuance or otherwise, except price changes resulting from the normal operation of antidilution provisions of the options (NYSE Listing Agreement, Section 901.01).	Annual report must contain: balance sheets, income statements, and statements of changes in financial position. Financial statements should be prepared in accordance with generally accepted accounting principles, and SEC Regulation S-X.	No specific requirements, but NASD receives 10-K.	Check printed annual report and appropriate news release to ensure that they conform to information reported on Form 10-K. News releases necessary if annual report contains previously undisclosed material information. Trend is to consider report a marketing tool.

Reporting Required for:	Securities and Exchange Commission	New York Stock Exchange	American Stock Exchange	National Association of Securities Dealers	Generally Recommended Publicity Practice, All Companies
Annual Report to Shareholders: Time and Distribution	Annual report to shareholders must precede or accompany delivery of proxy material. State law notice requirements govern the timing of proxy material mailing prior to annual meeting. Form 10-K must be filed within 90 days of close of year.	Published and submitted to shareholders at least 15 days before annual meeting but no later than three months after close of fiscal year. Four copies to Exchange together with advice as to the date of mailing to shareholders. PROMPTEST POSSIBLE ISSUANCE URGED. Recommended release of audited figures as soon as available.	Published and submitted to shareholders at least 15 days before annual meeting but no later than four months after close of fiscal year. PROMPTEST POSSIBLE ISSUANCE URGED. Recommend release of audited figures as soon as available. Six copies of the report to be filed with the Securities Division of the Exchange (Listing Form SD-1, Item 17).	File 10-K concurrently with SEC filing.	Financial information should be released as soon as available; second release at time printed report is issued if report contains other material information. NYSE and AMEX urge broad distribution of report—including distribution to statistical services—so that company information is available for "ready public reference."
Annual Report: Form 10-K	Required by Section 13 or 15(d) of Securities Exchange Act of 1934 on Form 10-K. To be filed with SEC no later than 90 days after close of fiscal year. (Some schedules may be filed 120 days thereafter.) Extensive incorporation by reference from annual report to shareholders and from proxy statement now make integration of Form 10-K and report to shareholders more practical (see general instructions G and H of Form 10-K).	Four copies must be filed with Exchange concurrently with SEC filing; also provide notice to Exchange as to date mailed to shareholders. (*NYSE Company Manual* Sections 203.01 and 204.04.)	Three copies must be filed with Exchange concurrently with SEC filing. (See *Company Guide*, p. 12–2.)	File 10-K concurrently with SEC filing.	Publicity usually not necessary unless 10-K contains previously unreported material information.
Cash Dividends (see Stock Split)	All issuers of publicly traded securities are required to give notice of dividend declarations pursuant to Rule 10B-17. Over-the-counter companies must provide the NASD with advance notice of record date for subsequent dissemination to investors, extending comparable stock exchange requirements to OT market. Failure to comply places issuer in violation of	Prompt notice to Exchange and immediate publicity required for *any* action related to dividend, including omission or postponement of dividend at customary time. The NYSE prefers that it be given notice by TWX (TWX No. 710-581-2801) or by telephone promptly confirmed by TWX, telegram, or letter.	Same as NYSE. Notification to Exchange by telephone or telegram, with confirmation by letter (Listing Form SD-1, Item 1g).	Prompt notification 10 days before record date. File one copy of 10b-17 Report (included in "Reporting Requirements for NASDAQ Companies") with officer's signature.	Prepare publicity in advance and release immediately by a designated officer on word of declaration. Publicity especially important when dividend rate changes. Statement of dividend policy now common in annual reports. Statements of "intention" to take dividend policy now common in annual reports. Statements of "intention" to take

Reporting Required for:	Securities and Exchange Commission	New York Stock Exchange	American Stock Exchange	National Association of Securities Dealers	Generally Recommended Publicity Practice, All Companies
	Section 10(b) of the Securities Exchange Act of 1934.	Ten days' advance notice of record date. NYSE manual implies announcement of management intention prior to formal board action may be required in case of a "leak" or rumor. *Notice regarding declaration of a cash dividend should include* declaration date; record date(s) for closing or reopening transfer books (or any other meaningful dates); per share amount of tax to be withheld with respect to the dividend, description of tax, net after-tax fee share dividend; any conditions upon which payment of dividend hinges.			dividend action also becoming common.
Earnings	Form 10-Q required within 45 days of close of each of first three fiscal quarters. Include information outlined in 10-Q plus a narrative management analysis in form outlined in Form S-K, Item 303. Summary of quarterly results for two years in "unaudited" annual report footnote. Form 10-K required to report full year's earnings.	Quarterly. Publicity required. No fourth quarter statement is required, though items of unusual or nonrecurring nature should be reflected in the company's interim earnings statements.	Quarterly. Should be published within 45 days after end of the first, second, and third fiscal quarters. (No statement is required for the fourth quarter, since that period is covered by the annual report.) Five copies of release should be sent to the Exchange. Press release must be sent to one or more New York City newspapers regularly publishing financial news and to one or more of the national newswires.	Prompt notification and press disclosure if earnings are unusual. File 10-Q and 10-K concurrently with SEC filings.	Immediate publicity; do not hold data until printed quarterly report is published and mailed. Release no later than 10-Q filing; annual results as soon as available. Information in news release must be consistent with 10-Q. Breakout of current quarter results together with year-to-date totals desirable in second, third, and fourth quarter releases.
Legal Proceedings	Form 10-Q at start or termination of proceedings and in any quarter when material development occurs (generally damage claims in excess of	No notice to NYSE required unless proceeding bears on ownership, dividends, interest, or principal of listed securities, or start	"Significant litigation." Public disclosure if material. Prompt notice to Exchange.	Prompt notification and public disclosure if material or if company must file report with SEC.	Public disclosure recommended if outcome of legal proceeding could have material effect on company and news of proceeding has

Reporting Required for:	Securities and Exchange Commission	New York Stock Exchange	American Stock Exchange	National Association of Securities Dealers	Generally Recommended Publicity Practice, All Companies
	10% of current assets); also any suit against company by an officer, director, or major stockholder. See Regulation S-K, Item 103. See also appendix entry entitled "environmental matters."	of receivership bankruptcy, or reorganization proceedings.			not already become public. Court filings now commonly distributed to key business media with or without press release.
Merger: Acquisition or Disposition of Assets	Form 8-K if company acquires or disposes of a significant (10% of total assets or whole subsidiary) amount of assets or business other than in normal course of business. Proxy soliciting material or registration statement may also be required. Check application of Rule 145 (b) of Securities Act of 1933, to any such transaction involving exchange of stock (see also Tender Offers).	Form 8-K filed (where assets acquired). Immediate public disclosure. Prompt notice to Exchange where assets disposed of.	Form 8-K if filed, for acquisition or disposition of assets. Immediate public disclosure.	Prompt notification and public disclosure (8-K filed with SEC).	Exchange policy requires immediate announcement as soon as confidential disclosures relating to such important matters are made to "outsiders" (i.e., other than "top management" and their individual confidential "advisers"). Immediate publicity, especially when assets consist of an entire product line, division, operating unit, or a "substantial" part of the business.
Merger: Commenting on Unusual Market Activity	After SEC ruling in *In re Carnation*, and appeals court decision in *Levinson, et al., v. Basic Industries*, company can state "no comment" about merger discussions when stock shows unusual market activity. However, if company comments in response to Exchange or regulatory inquiry, it must do so truthfully and acknowledge that merger discussions are taking place.	Prepare to make immediate public announcement concerning unusual market activity from merger negotiations. Immediate, candid public statement concerning state of negotiations or development of corporate plans, if rumors are correct or there are developments. Make statements as soon as disclosure made to outsiders (from business appraisals, financing arrangements, market surveys, etc.). Public statements should be definite regarding price, ratio, timing, and any other pertinent information	Promptly and publicly disseminate previously undisclosed information contained in any "leak" that resulted in market action. If company unable to determine cause of market action, exchange may suggest that company issue "no news" release stating that there have been no undisclosed recent developments affecting the company that would account for unusual market activity. Company need not issue public announcement at each stage of merger negotiations, but may await agreement in principle	Prompt notification and public disclosure if material or if company must file report with SEC.	Either issue "no comment" statement or explain reason for market activity known to company. Comment asserting that company is "unaware of any reason" to explain market activity is a comment. If company knows the reason for market activity but denies its awareness, it has made a false comment and is probably liable.

Reporting Required for:	Securities and Exchange Commission	New York Stock Exchange	American Stock Exchange	National Association of Securities Dealers	Generally Recommended Publicity Practice, All Companies
		necessary to evaluation. Should include disclosures made to outsiders (*NYSE Company Manual*, Sections 202.01 and .03).	on specific terms or point at which negotiations stabilize. However, publicly release announcement setting forth facts to clarify rumor or report material information. (See *Company Guide*, pp. 4-7 to 4-8.)		
Projection: Forecast or Estimate of Earnings	See Reg. S-K General Policy (b). SEC policy encourages use of projections of future economic performance that have "a reasonable basis" and are presented in an appropriate format. Obligation to correct promptly when facts change. Should not discontinue or resume projections without clear explanation of action.	Immediate public disclosure when news goes beyond insiders and their confidential advisers.	Exchange warns against "unwarranted promotional disclosure," including premature announcements of products, and interviews with analysts and financial writers that would unduly influence market activity.	Prompt notification and public disclosure if material (NASD Schedule D).	Projections should be either avoided altogether or widely circulated, with all assumptions stated. Projections by others may require correction by company if wrong but widely believed. Once having made projection, issuer has obligation to update it promptly if assumptions prove wrong. Press releases and other communications should include all information necessary to an understanding of the projection. Legal counsel should be consulted.
Stock Split, Stock Dividend, or Other Change in Capitalization	10-Q required for increase or decrease if exceeds 5% of amount of securities of the class previously outstanding. Notice to NASD or exchange 10 days before record date under Securities Exchange Act's antifraud provisions.	Exchange suggests preliminary discussion, Immediate public disclosure and Exchange notification. Issuance of new shares requires prior listing approval. Either "telephone alert" procedure should be followed or, preferably, wire by TWX. Separate confirmation letter to Exchange. Company's notice to Exchange should indicate brokers' and nominees' requirements and date by which they	Immediate public disclosure and Exchange notification. Issuance of new shares requires prior listing approval. Treatment of fractional shares must be announced.	Prompt notification and public disclosure 10 days before record date. File one copy of 10b-17 Report (included in "Reporting Requirements for NASDAQ Companies") with officer's signature. File 10-Q concurrently with SEC filing.	Immediate publicity as soon as proposal becomes known to outsiders, whether formally voted or not. Discuss early whether to describe transaction as a split, dividend, or both and use terminology consistently.

Reporting Required for:	Securities and Exchange Commission	New York Stock Exchange	American Stock Exchange	National Association of Securities Dealers	Generally Recommended Publicity Practice, All Companies
		must notify disbursing agent of full and fractional share requirements. Exchange will publicize this in its *Weekly Bulletin* or special circulars. *Notice regarding stock dividend, split, or distribution should include* ratio of stock dividend or split; record date for holders entitled to receive distribution; conditions upon which transaction hinges; date for mailing of certificates for additional shares.			
Tender Offer	Conduct and published remarks of all parties governed by Sections 13(d), 13(e), 14(d), 14(e) of the 1934 act and regulations thereunder. Schedule 14D-1 disclosure required of raider. Target required to file Schedule 14D-9 for any solicitation or recommendations to security holders. (See also *Hart-Scott-Rodino* requirements.)	Consult Exchange Stock List Department in advance. Immediate publicity and notice to Exchange. Deliver offering material to Exchange no later than distribution date to shareholders. Consult Exchange when terms of tender are at variance with Exchange principles regarding tender offers.	Consult Exchange Securities Division in advance. Immediate publicity and notice to Exchange.	Prompt notification and public disclosure (NASD Schedule D).	Massive publicity effort required: should not be attempted without thorough familiarity with current rules and constant consultation with counsel. Neither raider nor target should comment publicly until necessary SEC filings have been made. "Stop, look, listen" letter permitted under Rule 14D-9(e).

Advertising Effectiveness Tracking Study

Contemporary Marketing Research Inc.
1270 Broadway
New York, NY 10001

6-1-107
February 1999

ADVERTISING EFFECTIVENESS TRACKING STUDY
MAIN QUESTIONNAIRE

CARD 1
(11-17Z)

RESPONDENT'S NAME: _____

1a. Today I am interested in obtaining your opinions of financial institutions. To begin with, I'd like you to tell me the names of all the financial institutions you have heard of. (DO NOT READ LIST. RECORD FIRST INSTITUTION MENTIONED SEPARATELY FROM ALL OTHERS UNDER "FIRST MENTION.") (PROBE:) Any others? (RECORD BELOW UNDER "OTHERS.")

1b. Now, thinking only of <u>banks</u> in the New York area, what (other) banks have you heard of? (RECORD BELOW UNDER "OTHERS.")

2. And what financial institutions, including banks, have you seen or heard advertised within the past 3 months? (DO NOT READ LIST. RECORD BELOW UNDER Q.2.)

3. FOR EACH ASTERISKED INSTITUTION LISTED BELOW AND NOT MENTIONED IN Q.1a/1b OR Q.2, ASK:

Have you ever heard of (<u>NAME</u>)? (RECORD BELOW UNDER Q.3.)

4. FOR EACH ASTERISKED INSTITUTION CIRCLED IN Q.1a/1b OR Q.3 AND NOT CIRCLED IN Q.2, ASK:

Have you seen or heard advertising for (<u>NAME</u>) within the past 3 months? (RECORD BELOW UNDER Q.4.)

	Q. 1a/1b AWARE OF FIRST MENTION (18)	AWARE OTHERS (21) (24)	Q.2 OF ADVTG.	Q.3 AWARE ADVTG. (AIDED)	Q.4 AWARE (AIDED)
Anchor Savings Bank	1	1	1		
Apple Savings Bank	2	2	2		
Astoria Federal Savings	3	3	3		
Bank of Commerce	4	4	4		
Bank of New York	5	5	5		
Bankers Trust	6	6	6		
Barclays Bank	7	7	7		
Bowery Savings Bank	8	8	8		
*Chase Manhattan Bank	9	9	9	9 (27)	9 (29)
*Chemical Bank	0	0	0	0	0
*Citibank	X	X	X	X	X
Crossland Savings Bank	Y	Y	Y		
*Dean Witter	1 (19)	1 (22)	1 (25)	1 (28)	1 (30)
Dime Savings Bank	2	2	2		

	Q. 1a/1b AWARE OF			Q.2	Q.3 AWARE	Q.4 AWARE
	FIRST MENTION (18)	(21)	AWARE OTHERS (24)	OF ADVTG.	ADVTG. (AIDED)	(AIDED)
Dollar Dry Dock Savings Bank	3		3	3		
*Dreyfus	4		4	4	4	4
Emigrant Savings Bank	5		5	5		
European American Bank	6		6	6		
Fidelity	7		7	7		
Goldome Savings Bank	8		8	8		
*Manufacturer's Hanover Trust	9		9	9	9	9
*Marine Midland Bank	0		0	0	0	0
*Merrill Lynch	X		X	X	X	X
*National Westminster Bank	Y		Y	Y	Y	Y
Prudential Bache	1 (20)		1 (23)	1 (26)		
Shearson-Lehman	2		2	2		
Other (SPECIFY):						
_____	X		X	X		
_____						
_____						

REFER BACK TO Q.2 AND Q.4. IF RESPONDENT IS AWARE OF ADVERTISING FOR CHASE MANHATTAN BANK IN Q.2 OR Q.4, ASK Q.5a. OTHERWISE, SKIP TO Q.6.

5a. Today we are asking different people about different banks. In your case, we'd like to talk about Chase Manhattan Bank. You just mentioned that you remember seeing or hearing advertising for Chase Manhattan Bank. Please tell me everything you remember seeing or hearing in the advertising. (PROBE FOR SPECIFICS) What else?

_____ (31)

_____ (32)

_____ (33)

_____ (34)

_____ (35)

5b. And where did you see or hear advertising for Chase Manhattan Bank? (Do <u>NOT</u> READ LIST) (MORE THAN ONE ANSWER MAY BE GIVEN)

	(36)
Television	1
Radio	2
Newspaper	3
Magazine	4
Billboard	5
Other (SPECIFY): _____	X

6. Different banks use different slogans. (START WITH THE X'D QUESTION BELOW AND CONTINUE UNTIL ALL FOUR QUESTIONS (Q.6a–6d) HAVE BEEN ASKED.)

START:

✓ 6a. What slogan or statement do you associate with Chase Manhattan Bank? (DO <u>NOT</u> READ LIST)

	(37)
Chase. The Experience Shows	1
You Have a Friend at Chase	2
Ideas You Can Bank On	3
The Chase Is On	4
Other (SPECIFY) _____	X

( ) 6b. What slogan does Chemical Bank use? (DO <u>NOT</u> READ LIST)

	(38)
The Chemistry's Just Right at Chemical	1
Other (SPECIFY) _____X	

✓ 6c. What slogan or statement do you associate with Citibank? (DO <u>NOT</u> READ LIST)

	(39)
It's Your Citi	1
The Citi Never Sleeps	2
Other (SPECIFY)_____X	

( ) 6d. What slogan does Manufacturer's Hanover Trust use? (DO <u>NOT</u> READ LIST)

	(40)
The Financial Source. Worldwide	1
We Realize Your Potential	2
Other (SPECIFY)_____	X

7. Now, I'd like to know how likely you yourself are to consider banking at several different banks in the future. For each bank I read, please tell me whether you would definitely consider banking there, probably consider banking there, might or might not consider banking there, probably not consider banking there, or definitely not consider banking there in the future. Now, how likely are you to consider banking at (READ X'D BANK) in the future? (REPEAT SCALE IF NECESSARY. OBTAIN A RATING FOR EACH BANK.)

START:	( ) CHASE MAN-HATTAN BANK	( ) CHEMICAL BANK	( ) CITIBANK	✓ MANU-FACTURER'S HANOVER TRUST
Definitely Consider Banking There	5 (41)	5 (42)	5 (43)	5 (44)
Probably Consider Banking There	4	4	4	4
Might Or Might Not Consider Banking There	3	3	3	3
Probably Not Consider Banking There	2	2	2	2
Definitely Not Consider Banking There	1	1	1	1
(DO <u>NOT</u> READ) l (Currently Bank There)	X	X	X	X

(45-1)

8a. Now, I'd like you to rate one bank on a series of statements—<u>Chase Manhattan Bank</u>. If you have never banked there, please base your answers on what you know about this bank and your perceptions of it. After I read each statement, please tell me whether you agree completely, agree somewhat, neither agree nor disagree, disagree somewhat, or disagree completely that this statement describes <u>Chase Manhattan Bank</u>. (START WITH X'D STATEMENT AND CONTINUE UNTIL ALL ARE RATED.)

START HERE:	AGREE COM- PLETELY	AGREE SOME- WHAT	NEITHER AGREE NOR DIS- AGREE	DIS- AGREE SOME- WHAT	DIS- AGREE COM- PLETELY
[ ] Is Responsive to Your Needs	5	4	3	2	1 (46)
[ ] Offers High-Quality Accounts and Services	5	4	3	2	1 (47)
[ ] Deals with Its Customers on a Personalized Level	5	4	3	2	1 (48)
[ ] Helps Make Banking Easier	5	4	3	2	1 (49)
[ ] Has Bank Personnel Who Are Concerned About You	5	4	3	2	1 (50)
[ ] Designs Accounts to Meet Your Special Needs	5	4	3	2	1 (51)
[ ] Is Responsive to Community Needs	5	4	3	2	1 (52)
[ ] Makes It Easy to Open an IRA Account	5	4	3	2	1 (53)
[ ] Has a Full Range of Banking and Investment Services	5	4	3	2	1 (54)
[ ] Is a Bank Where You Want to Have Most of Your Accounts	5	4	3	2	1 (55)

START HERE:	AGREE COM- PLETELY	AGREE SOME- WHAT	NEITHER AGREE NOR DIS- AGREE	DIS- AGREE SOME- WHAT	DIS- AGREE COM- PLETELY
[ ] Has Bank Personnel Who Are Experienced	5	4	3	2	1 (56)
[ ] Has Innovative Accounts and Services	5	4	3	2	1 (57)
[ ] Understands Your Banking Needs	5	4	3	2	1 (58)
[ ] Has Branches Who Are Pleasant to Bank In	5	4	3	2	1 (59)
[ ] Has Accounts to Help People Just Starting Out	5	4	3	2	1 (60)
[ ] Continuously Develops Services to Meet Your Needs	5	4	3	2	1 (61)
[ ] Has Bank Personnel Who Are Friendly and Courteous	5	4	3	2	1 (62)
[ ] Has Accounts and Services That Are Right for You	5	4	3	2	1 (63)
[✓] Puts Customers' Needs First	5	4	3	2	1 (64)
[ ] Is a Modern, Up-to-Date Bank	5	4	3	2	1 (65)

END CARD 1

Annual Meeting Checklist

By Frank Widder

The following annual shareholder's meeting checklist can be adapted to serve as a "pre-flight" plan for almost any major meeting.

I. Meeting announcement
   A. Shareholder's proxy statement and general notice
   B. Investment houses', major brokers', and institutional investors' notice and invitation
   C. Financial media invitations
   D. Employee notice of meeting
   E. Guests

   Follow-up (by phone or in person)
   A. Investor relations contacts with major shareholders to determine participation, major areas of interest, potential problems
   B. Major investment houses involved with company
   C. Local financial press
   D. Guest relations

II. Management announcement
   A. Notify all key management personnel to make sure they will be there and arrange alternates for those who cannot make it
   B. Notify all members of the board to determine their ability to make the meeting
   C. Arrange flight times and book hotel in advance; guarantee arrival if necessary

III. Management coaching
   A. Draft basic list of shareholders' problems and questions
   B. Arrange meeting with CEO and chairman to prepare answers, with key staff and legal department to run down answers, and practice those answers
   C. Review and practice management speeches

IV. Presentation materials
   A. Review orders for graphs and slides, compare with financial review speech
   B. Screen any films
   C. Review displays

V. Agenda: order of presentations with approximate running times (in minutes)
   A. Introduction—chairman calls meeting to order and introduces board and management (4:00)
   B. Opening comments by chairman and review of overall activities of company (6:00)
   C. President's message (with visuals) (15:00)
   D. Financial report by vice president, finance (with slide highlights) (5:00)

E. Film (20:00)

F. Present proposals in proxy (limit each shareholder to one statement per issue; hand out ballots to shareholders at beginning) (20:00)

G. Volting, collect ballots (3:00)

H. General discussion (limit shareholders to one question each) (30:00)

I. Announce voting results (3:00)

J. Present company awards of appreciation (2:00)

K. Adjournment (1:00)—total: 1 hour, 49 minutes

Agenda allows 20 additional minutes for discussion or for more questions during presentation of proposals. Final agenda will be printed and passed out by ushers at meeting.

VI. Site preparation

A. Staff
1. Electrician, lighting, and sound equipment specialists on hand from 8 A.M. to 5 P.M.
2. Supervisor of custodial, security, and equipment staffs
3. Walkie-talkie communications network with equipment staff
4. Waiters for lounge
5. Caterers for lounge

B. Parking
1. Traffic direction displays at parking lot entrances
2. Parking attendants directing traffic to proper area
3. Signs pointing to meeting entrance in parking lot

C. Entrance/reception
1. Reception tables with pencils and guest roster
2. Receptionists to staff tables and answer questions about facilities (need to be briefed beforehand)
3. Well-marked rest areas and signs indicating meeting area
4. Unarmed security guards to control crowd and provide protection
5. Armed security guards located in discrete areas of meeting room
6. Name tags for all representatives of company

D. Display area
1. Displays set up along walls, to avoid impeding foot traffic, and checked for operation 24 hours in advance
2. Representatives to staff each booth and be prepared for questions about display
3. Tables to display necessary financial information—annual report, 10-K, proxy statement, quarterlies

E. Lounge area
1. Adequate seating for participants and guests
2. Breakfast/luncheon tables

F. Meeting areas
1. Sound, lighting, and video checks
2. Sound mikes for all stage participants
3. Additional speakers for amplification
4. Alternate hookup in case of failures—sound, lighting, and video; alternate film in case of breakage
5. Large screen for slide and film
6. Slide and film projectors for presentation

       7. Audio and lighting mixers

       8. Portable, remote mikes with long cords for audience questions

       9. Tape-recorder hookup to record proceedings

    G. Construction

       1. Podium constructed high enough for everyone to have direct view of all participants

       2. Area blocked off for board and management to view film

       3. Area blocked off for lighting and sound equipment

       4. Exits properly marked

       5. Access to podium and all chairs necessary for seating board and management

       6. Logo prominently displayed and lighted above podium

    H. Staff

       1. Ushers with flashlights at all entrances for seating

       2. Security at far corners of room

       3. Backstage technicians for sound emergencies

       4. Remote mike monitors on both aisles or in front and back of room

       5. Photographer to shoot proceedings, displays, and key presentations

    I. Stage seating arrangements

       1. Podium in middle, chairs to either side

       2. Arrange board members in tenure order

       3. Management in hierarchy order

       4. Chairman sits on board side

       5. President on management side

       6. Nameplates for all participants on podium

       7. Glasses, water, and ashtrays

    J. Shareholder seating

       1. First-come basis

       2. Areas roped off for invited shareholders and guests

       3. Areas roped off for film viewing by participants

       4. Special area for members not represented on stage—public accountants, special staff, and guests

VII. Final run-through

    A. Day prior to meeting, complete mock session of annual report, with key principals and timing of presentation—including possible questions and responses.

    B. Review slide show and cues for hours before meeting.

    C. Check screening room communications to begin film; make sure time is allowed to clear stage.

    D. Make sure award is ready for presentation.

    E. Hand out scripts to key participants and technical people.

VIII. Day of meeting

    A. Review with supervisor to ensure that all technical checks are okay.

    B. See that all displays are up and working.

    C. Contact board and management people to check for emergencies in transportation; arrange backup accommodations if necessary.

    D. Sit-down breakfast with key participants to go over agenda and cover any last-minute questions.

E. Go to convention center, check in with supervisor, security head, parking attendant; ensure that copies of scripts are placed at podium.
F. Greet participants and guide to lounge.
G. Wait for shareholders and investors, media; be available for questions and arrange interviews.
H. Sit down and wait.
I. Guide participants and guests to luncheon in lounge; make sure bar is set up.
J. Have a drink—and good night.

credits

(p. 357) Courtesy of The National Center for Tobacco-Free Kids.

(p. 358) Courtesy of The National Center for Tobacco-Free Kids.

(p. 359) Courtesy of The National Center for Tobacco-Free Kids.

(p. 360) Courtesy of Tobacco Free Kids.

(p. 361) Courtesy of Murray Bring

(p. 362) Courtesy of Laura Ries

Chapter 15
(p. 366) AP / Wide World Photos

(p. 375) Courtesy of Andrew S. Edson

Chapter 16
(p. 381) Courtesy of Salo Productions

(p. 384) Courtesy of O'Dwyer's PR Service Report.

(p. 388, top) Greg Wietig

(p. 388, bottom) Courtesy of True Majority

(p. 391) AP / Wide World Photos

(p. 392) AP / Wide World Photos

(p. 393) Courtesy of Shashi Tharoor

Chapter 17
(p. 403) Courtesy of US Postal Services.

(p. 404) Courtesy of US Postal Services.

(p. 417) Courtesy of Bill Adams

Chapter 18
(p. 423) Courtesy of Levy Resturants

(p. 424) Courtesy of Sea World

(p. 425) Courtesy of Russell Stover and Vorhaus Public Relations.

(p. 428) Courtesy of the National Breast Cancer Coalition

(p. 437) Courtesy of Shaunee Lenise Wallace

Chapter 19
(p. 441) Courtesy of O'Dwyer.com

(p. 446) Courtesy of the Eastern Paralyzed Veterans Association.

(p. 449) Courtesy of The St. Paul

(p. 452) Courtesy of www.aolsucks.com.

(p. 453) Courtesy of www.walmartsucks.com.

(p. 460) Courtesy of Dierdre Breakenridge

Chapter 20
(p. 464, both) Courtesy of PepsiCo.

(p. 468-469) Courtesy of Taco Bell Corp.

(p. 470) Courtesy of Peanut Advisory Board.

(p. 471) Courtesy of Marketing Works, Chicago, Illinois.

(p. 474) AP / Wide World Photos

(p. 477) Courtesy of TomPaine.com, a project of the nonprofit Florence Fund.

(p. 478) Courtesy of Xerox.

(p. 480) Courtesy of Hershey Foods

(p. 483, all) Courtesy of George Washington's Mount Vernon Estate & Gardens, Mount Vernon, VA 22121.

(p. 484, all) Courtesy of George Washington's Mount Vernon Estate & Gardens, Mount Vernon, VA 22121.

(p. 485, all) Courtesy of George Washington's Mount Vernon Estate & Gardens, Mount Vernon, VA 22121.

(p. 486) Courtesy of Patrice Tanaka

Chapter 21
(p. 492) Courtesy of Rose Brooks for Battered Women and Their Children.

(p. 495) AP / Wide World Photos

(p. 497) AP / Wide World Photos

(p. 501) AP / Wide World Photos

(p. 505, top) AP / Wide World Photos

(p. 505, bottom) Courtesy of PR Strategist

(p. 505) Courtesy of Lewis Jordan

Chapter 22
(p. 512) AP / Wide World Photos

(p. 515) Courtesy of Marina Maher Communications

(p. 516) AP / Wide World Photos

(p. 517) Courtesy of Tehama Group Communications

(p. 521) AP / Wide World Photos

(p. 522) AP / Wide World Photos

(p. 523) AP / Wide World Photos

(p. 524) Courtesy of Peter Drucker

Index